Comrade Kerensky

New Russian Thought

The publication of this series was made possible with the support of the Zimin Foundation.

Boris Kolonitskii, *Comrade Kerensky*
Sergei Medvedev, *The Return of the Russian Leviathan*
Maxim Trudolyubov, *The Tragedy of Property*

Comrade Kerensky

The Revolution against the Monarchy and the Formation of the Cult of 'The Leader of the People' (March–June 1917)

Boris Kolonitskii

Translated by
Arch Tait

polity

The translation of this work was funded by the Zimin Foundation.

James Manteith's translation of Leonid Kannegiesser's 'On Review' originally appeared in *Cardinal Points*, vol. 7 (2017), edited by Boris Dralyuk and Irina Mashinski.

Polity Press
65 Bridge Street
Cambridge CB2 1UR, UK

Polity Press
101 Station Landing
Suite 300
Medford, MA 02155, USA

ISBN-13: 978-1-5095-3364-0

A catalogue record for this book is available from the British Library.

Typeset in 10 on 11 pt Times New Roman MT by
Servis Filmsetting Ltd, Stockport, Cheshire
Printed and bound in Great Britain by TJ Books Limited

For further information on Polity, visit our website: politybooks.com

Contents

In memory of Rafail Sholomovich Ganelin

Acknowledgements

The writing of this book has been a long and tortuous process, and my enthusiasm for it was not shared by all my colleagues. One distinguished scholar suggested that, if I was going to write a biography, Tsereteli was a more interesting and thoughtful personality. But it was not Kerensky's life I wanted to study. I have never seen myself as someone else's biographer. What interested me was what had been written and said, what words had been used, about Kerensky and other political leaders during the 1917 revolution, because I believe that brings out important aspects of how the revolution proceeded.

The topic captured my imagination in the mid-1980s, the historical sources themselves propelling me in that direction. I was astonished by how the rapturous language used to describe the revolutionary leaders in 1917 anticipated the extolling of the Soviet leaders in the 1930s, and I thought it could not simply be written off as evidence of coercion. Zinaïda Gippius's *Blue Book* made a powerful impression. It is based largely on the author's diary and illustrates the changing attitude of a section of the intelligentsia towards Kerensky. People who in spring 1917 were busily and creatively contributing to the cult of a Leader and saviour were, by the autumn, reviling the very leader they had set up: Kerensky was now the main, if not, indeed, the sole, culprit for the political crisis. They appeared quite unaware of any responsibility on their part for the actions of their anointed.

I had a similar reaction when I heard the recrimination in the late perestroika period. 'I so loved Gorbachev,' one good lady in Moscow told me with a sigh. She sounded like a young girl disenchanted with the object of her infatuation. She sounded like those people who see their way out of a crisis by bestowing on some new messianic Leader all manner of powers and authority, only later to berate him as they absolve themselves of all blame. I have been publishing since 1991 on Kerensky's various public images and have been gratified that some of my research has struck readers as having a bearing on the present.

Many people have taken an interest in my work, and there are many I need to thank for their help.

Alexey Miller and Vladimir Chernyaev were the benign, interested and critical readers of this book, and their comments and advice were exceptionally important for me.

Different versions of chapters, and subsequently the book in its entirety, have been discussed at meetings of the History Faculty of the European University at St Petersburg and the Department of the History of Revolutions and Social Movements of the St Petersburg History Institute of the Russian Academy of Sciences. I am grateful to Tamara Abrosimova, Alfrid Bustanov, Boris Dubentsov, Mikhail Krom, Vladimir Lapin, Nikolai Mikhailov, Anatoly Pinsky, Natalia Potapova, Pavel Rogoznyi, Yuliya Safronova, Nikolai Smirnov, Konstantin Tarasov, Igal Halfin and Samuel Hirst, who made valuable contributions in these discussions.

Dietrich Beyrau, I. F. Danilova, Victor Kelner, Louise McReynolds, Jan Plamper and Valeriy Sazhin all read chapters of the book, and their advice and comments have been a great help. Collaborating with Murray Frame, Melissa Stockdale and Steven Marks on editing a volume in an international project on the history of the First World War and revolution in Russia taught me a great deal. The advice of the other project participants, notably Anthony Heywood, David McDonald, John Steinberg and Christopher Read, was very helpful.

At various stages in my research I have presented my results at conferences and colloquia. The comments of Vladislav Aksyonov, Jörg Baberowski, Vladimir Buldakov, Ziva Galili, Klaus Gestwa, Katharina Kucher, Daniel Orlovsky, Mark Steinberg, Tanja Penter, Orlando Figes, Jutta Scherrer, Ingrid Schierle and Laura Engelstein were very important. I discussed many aspects of my research with William Rosenberg and was constantly aware of his support.

My consultations with Alla Lapidus, Irina Lukka and Olga Novikova were extremely useful. Dmitry Aziatsev, Vladislav Aksyonov, Alexander Astashov, Mikhail Bezrodny, Marina Vitukhnovskaya, Alexey Gnoevykh, Konstantin Godunov, Alexander Danilevsky, Ilia Doronchenkov, Boris Kotov, Alexander Medyakov, Andrey Nikolaev, Margarita Pavlova, Pavel Rogozny, Nikolai Rodin, Alexander Sokolov, Konstantin Tarasov, Yana Guzey, Yelizaveta Zhdankova, Ella Saginadze and Alexander Reznik all helped me to assemble materials.

Topics which subsequently morphed into paragraphs of the book were discussed in seminars attended by Felix Yakubson, Viktor Voronkov, Vladimir Gelman, Yelena Zdravomyslova, Maria Matskevich, Andrey Stolyarov, Dmitry Travin and Sergey Shelin. Remarks by sociologists, political scientists, journalists, writers and directors gave me a different perspective on my research.

My administrative experience as a provost of the European University at St Petersburg gave me new insights into political history, and my conversations with the university's rector, Professor Oleg Kharkhordin, constantly stimulated me to reflect on the practical application of political philosophy.

I am grateful to Victor Pleshkov, Nikolai Smirnov and other members of the administrative staff of the St Petersburg Institute of History of the Russian Academy of Sciences for their unfailing support.

I thank the senior staff of the European University at St Petersburg for granting me sabbatical leave, which gave me the opportunity to concentrate on this research project.

The support of the Kone Foundation and the Helsinki Collegium for Advanced Studies at the University of Helsinki enabled me to work in Finnish libraries and archives in 2013.

A grant from the German Research Foundation (Deutsche Forschungsgemeinschaft) and the support of the Institute for Eastern European History at the University of Tübingen gave me the opportunity to work for three months in German libraries in 2016.

I thank Irina Zhdanova and Anna Abashina, who edited this book, for their advice and comments.

I am constantly conscious of the support of my wife. 'If my husband is looking out of the window, that does not mean he is not working,' Katya will sometimes tell people. I am proud that, after some entirely understandable doubts, she has come to this view. Moreover, she has sought, if not always successfully, to defend my card indexes from the onslaught of our granddaughters, Faina and Taisia. I am, of course, gratified that the youngest members of my family are showing so much interest at such an early age in my old-fashioned research laboratory.

As my work on this book was nearing completion, my thoughts were constantly turning to Rafail Ganelin, who died in 2014. He was a most remarkable researcher and a wise person who did a great deal for generations of historians of Leningrad/St Petersburg. I am one of those he helped, and without his support my academic career would have been different. His advice saved me from many errors and blunders. I dedicate this book to the memory of Rafail Sholomovich Ganelin.

Introduction

George Buchanan, the British ambassador, heard a Russian soldier remark during the revolution, 'Oh, yes, we must have a Republic, but we must have a good Tsar at the head.' Buchanan regarded this pronouncement as an oxymoron and saw it as confirmation of the view he had formed of his host country's curious political culture: 'Russia is not ripe for a purely democratic form of government . . .'[1]

Analogous statements by simple people are quoted in the diaries of other foreigners.[2] They are eager to present Russia as even more exotic than it was, and evidently the desire of its inhabitants for a democratic republic with a good tsar bolstered their case. Military censorship reports also quote soldiers' letters along the same lines: 'We want a democratic republic and a father-tsar for three years'; 'It would be good if we were given a republic with a practical tsar'; 'The tsar has been toppled from his throne, now there's a new government, that's all right, fine, no bother, and when they choose a new tsar, a good one, it will be even better.' One censor concluded, 'Almost all the letters of peasants express a desire to see a tsar leading Russia. Monarchy is evidently the only mode of governance they can imagine.'[3]

It is hardly likely that all these peasants and soldiers were staunch monarchists. They had said they wanted to limit the tsar's term in office. They were anticipating he would have to seek re-election. Rather, we may suppose they saw the concepts of 'state' and 'tsardom' as synonymous. They struggled to picture a sovereign state without a sovereign, a strong head of state. Not a few soldiers refused to swear allegiance to the Provisional Government, because the very mention of 'the state' in the wording of the oath was regarded as endorsing monarchism. They shouted, 'We don't have a sovereign state, we have a republic.'[4]

We may, however, surmise that the soldiers aspiring to a democratic republic with a good tsar did in fact want to see a presidential republic established whose head of state would be endowed with extensive powers.

They could not give a precise formulation of their ideal system of government, for the simple reason that they lacked the necessary technical language. They did not know how to describe their 'authoritarian republicanism'. It was not only poorly educated people who experienced difficulty in translating their ideals into the language of contemporary politics: the same was true of such groups as professional army officers who had cultivated an apolitical stance before the revolution. Indeed, even those who concerned themselves with politics could not always find the right vocabulary to characterize an unfamiliar and rapidly changing reality.[5]

These examples give a sense of just how complex was the situation in which the former subjects of the tsar, now citizens of a new Russia, found themselves. The political messages being targeted at them needed to be translated, and this led to the appearance of a host of 'political dictionaries', which were greatly in demand.

People might have had different emotions about the monarchy, but it had been familiar and had seemed comprehensible. The language for describing the tsarist regime, the standard attitudes towards the tsar himself, even the range of emotions he was expected to evoke were traditional and had been passed on down the generations.

The overthrow of the monarchy necessitated new vocabulary, new rituals, new prescribed political emotions. How were the legitimacy and the sacrosanct nature of the new government to be conveyed? How should the political leaders be addressed? To what extent was it permissible to view the new bearers of political power ironically? These were urgent questions. Different parties and organizations tried to take on the role of devising the new political language. This process of creating new words, rituals and symbols was taking place in the midst of an intense power struggle, with competing forces trying to establish their right to develop the authoritative, 'correct' political terminology and determine how it was interpreted.

All this has a direct bearing on the key issues involved in studying revolutions. Few people would seek to deny that power is an important issue in any revolution, and yet that is not quite enough. Power is an important issue in any political process, so what is of more interest is what it is about power that is specific to revolutionary, as opposed to non-revolutionary, eras.

Max Weber, in his 'Politics as Vocation', a lecture delivered in 1918 under the influence of the revolutionary upheavals of the time, quoted Leon Trotsky's remark that 'Every state is founded on force.' Weber himself describes the state as a 'human community that (successfully) claims the monopoly of the legitimate use of physical force within a given territory.' He continues, 'The state is considered the sole source of the "right" to use violence.'[6]

If we adopt Weber's formulations, a revolution is a particular political situation when the state's 'monopoly of the legitimate use of physical force' is under constant challenge. The demonopolization and monopolization of the right to use force is paralleled by a delegitimation and legitimation of that right. One of the most important issues in a revolution is the legitimizing of force. Accordingly, what historians of revolution should be studying is the political tactics and cultural forms of that legitimation.

Weber identifies three basic 'legitimations of domination', while noting that 'the pure types are rarely found in reality.' There is the authority of tradition, of the 'eternal yesterday', based, for example, on religion. Then there is the 'authority of the extraordinary and personal gift of grace (charisma)'. Finally, there is domination by virtue of 'legality' based on rationally created rules.[7]

Different revolutions have had different attitudes to tradition. The leaders of the civil war in seventeenth-century England formulated their political ideas using the language of religion and talked about returning to an 'interrupted', 'perverted' tradition which needed to be revived after removing later accretions. This is an early meaning of the word 'revolution', taken from the language of astronomy and astrology: a return to an original state.[8] Other revolutions were insistent on their absolute newness, declaring they were creating a new world completely different from the old order. In the Russian Revolution the dominant trend demanded a radical break with the epoch of the old regime. A resolute overcoming of the past was a source of legitimation for the revolutionaries.

The authority of 'rationally based legality' is open to challenge during revolutions: the state's monopoly on lawmaking and how the law is applied is called into question, and multiple competing legal systems can appear. This occurred during the Russian Revolution: the Provisional Government, the Petrograd Soviet, the Ukrainian Central Rada and other political bodies set up their own jurisdictions, and sundry other associations initiated or supported 'lawmaking by the people' from below and based their own legitimacy on that.[9]

In order to research the phenomenon of revolutionary power, we need comprehensively to examine the authority of leaders, helmsmen, and individuals who underpin their charisma with prophecies which come true or by acts of heroism or extraordinary successes. Charisma is conferred not only by the real or imagined qualities of a leader but also by the extent to which he symbolizes the community recognizing the charisma which legitimizes his actions. The historian needs accordingly to take an interest in the words and deeds of people who, in various ways, contribute to making the Leader authoritative. Studying the tactics and techniques by which leaders are legitimized, and analysing the associated political conflicts, is important if we are to understand the social and political processes which form the background to the building up of the images of leaders.

The leader cults, without which it is impossible to imagine Soviet history, have long been a recognized research topic. Most attention has been devoted to studying the Lenin cult (see the work of Nina Tumarkin, Benno Ennker, Olga Velikanova and others).[10] Nevertheless, historians studying the key stages of the formation of the Lenin cult – the assassination attempt in 1918, Lenin's fiftieth birthday in 1920, his death, his embalming – deal cursorily with the events of 1917, despite the fact that this was an extremely important period in terms of evolving cultural forms for the glorification of charismatic leaders. Benno Ennker's approach is germane to this study's objectives. Examining the transformation of the Leader's charisma into the Lenin cult, Ennker correlates the process with the contemporary political aims of various groups of Bolshevik leaders.

Jan Plamper examines the personality cult of Stalin through images of the Leader.[11] I repeat, nevertheless, that those researching Soviet leader cults seem to me to underestimate the significance of changes during 1917 which favoured development of the political culture of the Soviet period.

This study will consider the tactics used both for bolstering and for destroying Kerensky's authority, together with the representation of his image, and how all these were perceived. I examine the texts and visual imagery, the symbolic gestures and rituals which were used to create, sometimes incompatible, images of the Leader.

This particular politician was chosen because of the authority he initially possessed. The connection between the extraordinary deference shown to Kerensky and the cults of Soviet leaders was noted by Vasiliy Maklakov, a prominent member of the Constitutional Democratic Party, who asserted that, after the monarchy was overthrown, ordinary Russians had 'a preference for individualized power, a boss'. 'This feeling provided the foundation for the adulation, first of Kerensky, then of Lenin, and ultimately for the deification of Stalin. I have no wish to compare people so dissimilar in spirit, but in all the regimes which succeeded each other after 1917 there was a latent craving for an authoritarian personality and a lack of trust in institutions.'[12]

For many contemporaries, Alexander Kerensky was the central figure of the February Revolution. For them he was the personification of that successful *coup d'état*. By the end of 1917 his opponents were speaking of the eight months of his 'reign', meaning from March to October, although Kerensky became prime minister only in July.[13]

In this book I examine images of Kerensky created by the man himself, by his supporters and allies, and by his opponents and enemies. By 'image' is meant a semantically coherent set of characteristics of the Leader, attributed to him in texts and illustrations.

The present book is about the political culture of the revolution and makes no claim to be a new biography of Kerensky. We cannot, of course, differentiate crisply between the biography of a politician and the cultural forms in which he was praised or damned. Our approach will enable us to see Kerensky in a new light, and his future biographers will have our observations and conclusions to draw on. It is not, then, my main purpose to augment the facts of Kerensky's biography. I attempt, through exploring the different images of the Leader, how they were created and the use that was made of them, to examine the organizations and the people who produced them. Through them I seek insight into the political, cultural and social processes of the revolutionary era.

Kerensky has been unlucky with his historians. Few have portrayed the 'revolutionary minister' sympathetically, or even without bias, and that is hardly a surprise. Historians quite commonly side with particular protagonists of the revolution and set themselves against others. The historiography of 1917, for the most part, also continues to settle for *parti pris*. Often researchers and, to an even greater extent, readers genuinely believe historiography cannot and should not be otherwise. To this day there are different versions of the history of the revolution, liberal and conservative, socialist and communist, nationalist and imperial, 'red' and 'white'. To this day there is a demand for historical narratives derived from the memoirs of participants in the events. It is not absurd to talk of an 'anti-party line', with anti-communist historians faithfully reproducing the bias of the Soviet historical narrative, only with the plus signs turned into minus signs and vice versa.

Few people identify with Kerensky now. As we shall see, although officially a Socialist Revolutionary, he did not bind himself to any one party and tried to be someone who brought together, acted as a bridge between, the moderate socialists and the liberals. His manoeuvring initially brought success, but by October the disagreements between the coalition partners had intensified. Kerensky's support base narrowed and weakened, and the room for manoeuvre became increasingly constricted. None of the leading political forces was giving him wholehearted support. Indeed, virtually all of them, to differing degrees and in different ways, were criticizing him. This coloured the attitude of several generations of partisan historians, the heirs of Kerensky's political opponents. In their view he was not 'with us', and those caught up in today's political tussles do not identify with him either.

Kerensky fared little better with his autobiographies, which, of course, influenced later biographies. In 1918, already the former head of the Provisional Government, Kerensky published a pamphlet titled *The Kornilov Affair*. Later he published several versions of his autobiography, rewriting his understanding of the history of the revolution.[14] One constant in these writings of different eras is Kerensky's desire to glorify the February Revolution and immortalize his role in it. Over time he changed his lines of argument and adjusted the narrative. Compared to the leader he actually was in 1917, Kerensky wanted to present himself as having been more modern, more Western, more judicious, far-sighted and confident. And, it has to be said, as a result – less interesting. These official self-portraits, idealizing and romanticizing their painter, overlay like palimpsests the more vivid image of a unique, tough-minded politician whose rise to become the leader of a revolutionary government was by no means a matter of chance, whatever the opinion of many of his contemporaries and of a certain number of historians.

The distortion of history in Kerensky's autobiographies, which it is tempting to call 'autohagiographies', came back to haunt their author. Researchers negatively inclined towards him used his memoirs as a punchbag but, in their polemics with him, tended to follow the outline of his narrative. They caricatured his self-portraits but perpetuated their approach. Kerensky's memoir campaigning certainly had an impact on the historiography of the revolution, but hardly as he might have intended.

Many historians of the revolution touched on aspects of Kerensky's career. Censorship during the Soviet period was an obstacle to publication of unbiased research, but Vitaliy Startsev managed to publish a worthwhile book on the autumn crisis of 1917.[15] In an innovative project, Gennadiy Sobolev studied the revolutionary consciousness of workers and soldiers.[16] In this connection he also examined aspects of Kerensky's popularity, as well as some features of the socio-psychological climate in which the leader cult appeared and flourished.

The most thorough account of Kerensky's life was written by Richard Abraham, a British historian.[17] He was unable to work in Russian archives at that time, but he carefully studied the press of the era, worked in the archives of several countries, and interviewed people who had known Kerensky.

Perestroika made it possible to study Kerensky's biography in depth in Russia. New sources became available and censorship taboos were lifted. By the end of the Soviet period, readers were taking an interest in work by Genrikh Ioffe. Glasnost made possible a different kind of research, and Ioffe devoted one of his publications to three leaders: Kerensky, Kornilov and Lenin.[18] This book invites us to give thought to the topic of personification of politics. Historians have a tendency to describe a period's conflicts by studying opposed leaders. Sometimes this is a literary device. Some readers perceive history as an interweaving of biographies, and this is what they demand. Historians often follow the example of contemporaries who contrasted Lenin, Kornilov and Kerensky not only as individuals but also as alternative approaches to social and political progress. This raises the issue of whether we need to study the techniques of personalization in use at the time.

Several biographies of Kerensky have appeared in the last few decades, some focusing on particular aspects of his life.[19] Stanislav Tyutyukin, for example, carefully examines Kerensky in action in the State Duma. Interesting sources have been brought into circulation and important observations have been made, but Kerensky's actions in 1917 merit further consideration.

For the current study, an article by Andrey Golikov on the public representation of the 'Kerensky phenomenon' and how it was received has been particularly helpful.[20] Golikov does view the period from March to October as a single unit, paying no attention to modification of images as the political situation changed. In writing about the life he draws on Kerensky's file in the State Archive of the Russian Federation and, when examining the Kerensky phenomenon, turns mainly to the periodical press in 1917.

On the basis of Kerensky's biography, having at our disposal the extensive research on the history of the revolution, we can embark on a study of the leader cult. This approach will enable us to examine aspects of the struggle for power which are not readily to be understood using more traditional methods of studying politics.

In examining images of the Leader, I have adopted approaches used by historians of public consciousness. Gennadiy Sobolev expanded historians' ideas particularly about the political aspect of the revolution. He drew attention to the political dimension of the way mass culture functions and to the political significance of changes in the Church. His close analysis of resolutions showed a significant dichotomy between the ideas of activists at various levels and the principles of parties' policy-makers. Historians had previously studied the environment in which the parties functioned and had focused primarily on socio-economic aspects. Sobolev raised the question of whether there was a need also to study issues of language and culture.[21]

I have also relied on Richard Wortman's approach to studying the representation of imperial power,[22] having previously adapted some of his research techniques for use in my work on the image of members of the tsar's family during the First World War.[23]

In *Tragic Erotica: Images of the Imperial Family during the First World War*, I attempted to describe not only the representation of the tsar but also the image of other members of the dynasty, which impacted on the monarch's public relations and gave a better understanding of the matter. My interest was not only in how an image was created but also in how it was used, and I studied not only positive but also negative images. Of course, whether an image is positive or negative can be a moot point, and in different contexts they could be perceived and used by players in different ways.

I have adopted a similar approach in this study, although the specifics of the cultural and political situation of the time, in particular the dynamism of the revolutionary era, have necessitated bringing in further research methods. More attention has had to be paid to the volatile politics which directly influenced the design of images of power. I compare the Kerensky cult with representation of other leaders of the time.

My aim, on the basis of the resources available, has been to construct a narrative about representation of the Great Revolutionary Leader. I have tried to bring order to the disparate sources of images of Kerensky, giving priority to images which became particularly important and were widely disseminated. At the same time, the frequent occurrence or absence of any such image in a particular category of sources has often raised issues to consider. In order to understand the creation, distribution and use made of images of Kerensky, I try to reconstruct the cultural and political context, paying particular attention to the political struggle. This 'multi-faceted contextualization' enables us to tie in study of the Kerensky cult with the overall political history of the revolution.

Studying the rumours about a leader is no less important than factual reconstruction of events.[24] A rumour passed on by an acknowledged expert has the status of an authoritative pronouncement and influences political decision-making, while rumours believed by masses of the population have a huge direct impact on the course of history. Contrasting rumours with 'what really happened' is methodologically naive: the researcher needs to take account of all the factors influencing the processes under study.

Clearly, Kerensky's own writings, and in particular his speeches and orders, are important for studying the cultural means of strengthening a leader's authority. Many party leaders exercised their leadership by publishing articles and pamphlets and devoted a good deal of time to correspondence. During the revolution many 'leaders' remained desk-bound. Lenin's *Collected Works* include several volumes of articles, pamphlets and letters written in 1917. In this he was not alone: the liberal politician Milyukov and the Socialist Revolutionary leader Chernov, the 'grandfather of Russian Marxism' Plekhanov and the Socialist Internationalist Martov, the conservative Shulgin and the revolutionary Trotsky wrote a lot at that time, and read even more.[25] In Russia political authority was often built on a foundation of writing: the Leader was a sage. The Soviet leaders who came after Lenin aspired to intellectual leadership. Styling themselves his 'faithful disciples', they sought the status of great teachers.

Kerensky asserted his leadership status by issuing orders and making speeches. His public speeches were widely disseminated in the press, and in 1917 several collections of his speeches and orders appeared as separate publications. This testifies to popular demand. The speeches of other politicians were of far less interest to publishers. At times, what Kerensky said in a particular speech is reported variously in different publications, and here the historian faces the task of evaluating one version against another. It is impossible to reconstruct exactly what was said, but studying the orator's rhetorical tactics provides a basis on which to generalize about how the Leader is presenting himself. An important question is the impact speeches had, and here the history of how and when they are quoted needs to be reviewed. Reports can also give a sense of audience reaction by mentioning applause or exclamations made by those listening. Different sources can also report variously on audience reaction.

Propaganda and news handouts are important. It might seem a simple matter to study them, but the researcher cannot always be sure of accurately understanding the meaning given to terms which appear straightforward to the modern reader – words such as 'democracy', 'tsar' and 'state'. The historian needs to bear in mind the different meaning their authors might have put into them and how readers and listeners might have interpreted them. There is a need to act as a translator from the language of revolution.

Another source is political resolutions, petitions, congratulations and collective letters. Historians differ as to their value as evidence, but the very fact that a letter is sent to a particular publication or institution signals a certain stance. They are usually sent to a body the writer deems authoritative. The views of people writing to *Izvestiya* ('News of the Petrograd Soviet') are probably going to be close to that newspaper's position. Those overtly opposed to its position are predictably underrepresented.[26]

Sometimes resolutions and collective letters are seen as having no value as historical evidence. The argument is that, to be valid, a source must illustrate the mood of those directly participating in events. Vladimir Fedyuk quotes a resolution published in a Yaroslavl newspaper after Kerensky's appointment as minister of war: 'The team of the Yaroslavl military hospital, meeting on 9 May to elect members of the disciplinary court, have unanimously resolved to send greetings to you, the first socialist minister, who command the love and respect of all Great Rus. We gladly place all our strength at your disposal.'

Professor Fedyuk is perplexed. 'A team in a hospital (how many people were in it? Twenty? Thirty?), meeting to resolve a very specific matter, for no reason at all send a telegram to the minister expressing their love and devotion. If you think about it, is that not just very odd?'[27] The same might be said of the many telegrams of greetings sent to Kerensky, which really did fill the newspapers at this time.

There are, however, other questions a historian might ask. Why, for example, would the newspaper deem it appropriate to print the hospital workers' telegram, which might, after all, appear comical? We may reasonably assume that it was not from whom the letter came that mattered but the substance of the resolution. This was exactly how it was hoped the newspaper's target reader might respond to Kerensky's appointment. Other periodicals, which had not hitherto been publishing resolutions or collective letters, began doing so in 1917. A signal was being sent to the newspaper's readers that exemplary citizens should do the same. If the newspaper had authority with them, then such a letter might provoke further such resolutions. The language of the resolution is also interesting: those who passed it are appreciative of the fact that Kerensky is a socialist. They express their confidence that 'all Rus' not only respects the minister but also loves him. Appropriate political emotion is being prescribed.

To answer Professor Fedyuk's question, no doubt whoever drafted the resolution on behalf of the hospital team would claim it was an expression of their opinion, using words he, as an activist, had authority to choose. Such resolutions did not always reflect the precise opinion of the collectives adopting them, but they enable us to judge the language of the populous 'committee class' – members of all manner of committees and soviets – who drafted them. That is important for understanding the attitude towards national leaders, and also for studying the influence of activists within collectives. No few *komitetchiki* ['committee devotees'] claimed their authority was based on the Leader's authority and did their utmost to enhance it.

Many of the sources mentioned above are mediated by newspapers. For no other period in Russian history does the periodical press prove such a valuable source of information. Abolition of censorship and interest in printed news led to numerous publications springing up: they reflect the entire spectrum of political views, down to its finer gradations. The historian sometimes enjoys a welcome boost from press surveys, thematic collections of newspaper clippings compiled by various government departments or individuals at the time.[28]

The diaries and correspondence of those involved in events can be of interest in the studying of leader cults, but caution may need to be exercised. Firstly, historians cannot always be sure they are dealing with an authentic source. The writers themselves, or scholars, may have distorted the text for various reasons, and later memoirs are sometimes misrepresented as diaries. Secondly, researchers may find that, rather than a balanced cross-section of social and cultural groups, there is a preponderance of letters and diaries kept by members of particular professions. For writers their diary is often a working tool, the raw material for creating new works (which are sometimes written in the form of a diary). Many diaries and letters of generals and officers are also of interest to historians. These are educated people, cut off from their families in wartime conditions, writing about the life they are living. There seems to be a dearth of diaries and letters written by entrepreneurs. Also, despite decades of interest in worker history, we know of few personal sources from them. Workers rarely kept diaries and did not usually retain their correspondence. The educational level and literary facility of individuals, of members of their families, and the ways they thought proper of communicating with each other, influenced the writing as well as the publication of letters and diaries. Political repression during the Soviet period also discouraged people at every level of society from preserving them. Here the surveys of correspondence prepared by military censors can be an asset for the historian, who can use excerpts from letters they found typical and/or interesting. Use can also be made of the censors' professional judgements in analyses summarizing the materials they have surveyed.

The greater knowledgeability of superiors can help us reconstruct the thinking of their illiterate or semi-literate subordinates. This applies particularly to soldiers, where the reports of commanding officers, political commissars and committee delegates of various ranks can be compared with assessments by individuals of diverse political views.

Memoirs are of limited use for the present study. It is impossible to judge the political mindset of participants in the events from writings created later. Their principal use is rather for reconstructing the historical mindset of the era in which they were actually written. Memoirs do, however, have a place in the present study because their writers have wielded, and continue to wield, vast influence on historiography. It is no easy matter to know in the writings of Leon Trotsky and Pavel Milyukov, of Anton Denikin and Fyodor Stepun, where the memoirs end and their analytical theorizing about history begins. This will be based not only on knowledge of what they remember of the past but also on their study of other sources. Conversely, the 'history' reconstructed by participants in the events includes fragments of autobiography. This is applicable to some extent to Kerensky's memoirs.[29]

Study of Kerensky's image obviously requires recourse to portraits, posters and postcards and to depictions of him in cartoons and caricatures, on badges and tokens. A consideration of such visual resources sometimes enables us to judge how popular Kerensky was at a particular time. The desire of consumers to acquire images of him provides a measure of this.[30]

The present work focuses on images of the Leader produced and distributed in March–June 1917, although, when necessary, I go beyond that chronological limitation. Many historians see this as a special time, the 'peaceful period of the revolution', the 'period of dual power'. This period has been chosen, however, not only to accord with historiographical tradition. I have studied all the categories of sources listed above – Kerensky's speeches, propaganda publications, political resolutions, personal documents, memoirs and visual sources – for the entire duration of the 1917 revolution.[31] Having worked on them, however, I am able to say that it is the period from March to June which is most relevant to the formation of the Kerensky cult. The head of the Provisional Government still had no few admirers in the summer, and even autumn, of 1917 and many supportive newspaper comments and political resolutions from this period could be adduced. But Kerensky's supporters were merely reusing positive images created in the initial stage of the revolution, and the principal armoury of means for glorifying the Leader was stocked in May and June. New images of the man at the helm of the Provisional Government which appeared after that already aimed to delegitimize him.

How, using which techniques, was Kerensky's authority enhanced (or weakened) in March–June 1917? What cultural forms did his authority assume and what were the tactics employed? What stages were there in the process? How did features of the political struggle in March–June 1917 affect these various projects of legitimation or delegitimation, and what forces and interests lay behind them?

These are the questions I will attempt to answer in this book.

I

Revolutionary Biography and Political Authority

In May 1917 Kerensky, having just been appointed minister of the army and navy, issued an order reminiscent in style of one of the tsar's manifestos. It contained a vivid autobiographical element. 'My new burden is immensely heavy, but as an old soldier of the revolution I have submitted myself unquestioningly to the severe discipline of duty and accepted responsibility before the people and the revolution for the army and navy.'[1]

The 36-year-old minister accounted himself a veteran of the liberation movement well accustomed to revolutionary discipline, which accorded him the right to demand iron discipline from all in the armed forces. It was an approach Kerensky was to use repeatedly when addressing the troops. These statements enhanced his authority as a revolutionary-turned-statesman, and the claim needed to be substantiated by the events of his biography. In 1917 both Kerensky and his supporters constantly recalled episodes from his life which could be put to political use.

We need both to examine that biographical contribution to establishing the authority of this revolutionary leader and to show the role he and his supporters played in disseminating information about his past career. We need to establish which episodes in Kerensky's life were most frequently exploited, which were 'edited', and which were quietly forgotten. Of interest too are the efforts of Kerensky's opponents, who had their own spin to put on his past.

1 Biography and biographers

In 1917 information about Kerensky's past life was obtainable from the minister's own testimony and reminiscences of his contemporaries. Mention of his career was made by politicians, journalists and those drafting resolutions. From these tesserae of the mosaic, people in Russia were able to piece together a reasonably convincing picture of the man. Of particular importance was writing undertaken specifically to familiarize society with Kerensky's biography.

There were quite a few reasons why writers and journalists, members of committees and generals might choose to bring up details of Kerensky's life, to quote his speeches and to recall his actions in the past. Some wanted to bolster the new leader's authority; others were responding to public demand (there was great curiosity about this suddenly popular politician). Nor can we overlook more mercenary considerations: publishers were prepared to commission writing on a hot topic, and Kerensky was selling like hot cakes. The minister could not directly control every project relating to his biography, but, as we shall see, he and his inner circle did often themselves initiate such writing, helped it on its way, and facilitated its distribution.

Kerensky was good with the press, and his staff knew when and how to release information to influential journalists hungry for news. Despite being overworked, he would find time to converse with publishers and journalists, writers and editors, to brief them on how he saw the changing situation and make recommendations. He periodically declared that he did not read items about himself in the newspapers, but without letting slip that he did study the reviews of the periodical press which his staff constantly provided.

Kerensky set up press and propaganda sections in the departments he oversaw: first in the Ministry of Justice and later in the Ministry of War. These had many shortcomings, and Russian wartime propaganda was overall inferior to that of the Germans and British, but, compared to others, Kerensky and his staff acted energetically and proactively to influence the press and get feedback about the state of public opinion.[2]

After the revolution, as minister of justice, Kerensky found himself in possession of a major asset. Order No. 1, signed by the new minister in February 1917, delegated Academician Nestor Kotlyarevsky to remove from the Police Department all papers and documents he might deem necessary and deliver them to the Academy of Sciences.[3] The Okhrana security department had secret files with sensitive information about many contemporary figures, and it was important that they should be stored securely. Actually, they were not all removed to the Academy of Sciences: the file on Kerensky, which went back to 1905, was delivered to the Ministry of Justice.[4]

Journalists were shown the documents and allowed to quote from them. There were also fairly extensive publications in the newspapers which drew on Okhrana materials about Kerensky.[5] The press likewise reported on researches undertaken by local activists in provincial police archives.[6]

The Central Committee of the Trud [Labour] Group in the Duma, to which Kerensky belonged, published a pamphlet containing excerpts from his file and two police circulars dating from 1915. The print run of 50,000 copies was large for the time[7] and indicates that the project received substantial funding. The publishers claimed that this collection of documents, prepared by political surveillance professionals, made possible an objective estimate of the scale of Kerensky's revolutionary activities: 'The reports of

Okhrana agents and the police were written before the revolution and come from the enemy camp, so they tell the story more objectively than we could.' The preface stated: 'He did not come to the revolution as something already accomplished but spent days and months preparing the coup whose protagonist he was destined to become.'[8] The documents showed informers and analysts of the Security Department detailing Kerensky's pre-revolutionary activities. They attributed acts to him which he had not committed, but now, in the circumstances of the revolution, even these exaggerations, 'confirmed' by the intelligence agents of his political opponents, contributed to boosting the authority of the minister formerly at the centre of their attention. It seems clear that this publication appeared with the assistance of the minister or his staff.

Several collections of Kerensky's speeches and orders were published, including the texts of pre-revolutionary speeches. Attention focused particularly on those previously banned, and here too we may assume Kerensky was personally involved in preparing them for publication. There were sometimes acknowledgements that he had provided the publishers with authentic transcripts of his speeches to replace the edited versions which had appeared in official publications. Supporters of Kerensky would now preface the text with a brief biography, placing him in the historical pantheon of famed 'champions of freedom'. In the preface to a collection issued by the Socialist Revolutionaries, his name was placed alongside such predecessors and heroes of the party as the Narodnaya volya [People's Will] volunteers and members of the SRs' Combat Organization, and his career was presented as an important part of the history of the revolutionary movement.[9] Other publications brought together facts about Kerensky's life with excerpts from his most famous speeches.[10]

In 1917 the life of politicians in general became a matter of public interest, but no other leader found himself on the receiving end of as much biographical writing as Kerensky. This resulted from the public demand for information about him personally, from the considerable financial resources invested in building him up, and also from the political needs of the forces supporting him. Finally, this famous politician had many supporters among writers and features writers, and they willingly and creatively extolled him, receiving commissions and possibly soliciting them.

Kerensky's first biographer was Vasiliy Kiriakov (1868–1923), who had known him for many years. His articles in 1917 were prepared and published with Kerensky's assistance. A rural teacher, active in teachers' associations and well known as a literary commentator in radical circles, Kiriakov came to prominence at the All-Russia Peasant Union in 1905 and was elected to the Second State Duma.[11] When the leaders of the Peasant Union were arrested and put on trial, Kerensky, as a lawyer, defended Kiriakov. They stayed in touch. In 1917 Kiriakov wrote for the Trudoviks' publications, and in the autumn he edited the Petrograd newspaper *Narodnaya pravda* [the People's Truth], which was published by supporters of Kerensky with American funding.[12]

In May 1917, Kiriakov wrote a feature on Kerensky for the popular illustrated magazine *Niva*.[13] The story in the magazine stopped short of the present, and readers were informed that Kiriakov was preparing a booklet about the life story of the champion of freedom for the publishing house Narodnaya vlast' [Power of the People], which had been set up by the right wing of the Socialist Revolutionary Party. This was to detail also the doings of the minister 'in these radiant days of the revolution, as the genius of Russia's freedom'.[14] Kiriakov duly published the pamphlet, whose first chapters were a revised and abridged version of the *Niva* feature. In it he included his reminiscences of meetings with Kerensky and newspaper articles and documents from the police archives (evidently provided by the minister's staff). Kiriakov quotes some of Kerensky's speeches, and indeed at times this stylistically heterogeneous biography turns into a dense assemblage of quotations.

As Kiriakov describes him, Kerensky is 'the first citizen of free Russia, the first people's socialist tribune, the first people's minister of justice, the minister of truth and fairness'. For Kiriakov, Kerensky is not only the principal leader but also an important symbol of the revolution – 'a noble symbol of the noble Great Russian Revolution'.[15]

Compared with other 1917 biographies of Kerensky, Kiriakov's is the most *Narodnik* [Populist] and moralizing. In it we find the theme of 'a debt for which there can be no recompense' which the intelligentsia owes the common people, romanticization of the long-suffering people, the *narod*, and the cult of champions of freedom. Kerensky's life is described as part of the history of the revolutionary movement as seen from a right-wing Socialist Revolutionary perspective. Kiriakov criticizes not only the Bolsheviks but also some moderate socialists, including fellow party members. He describes Kerensky as a Narodnik with a rare gift of leadership which enables him to establish a special connection with the people. 'A. F. Kerensky has the ability to see into the very soul of the people and to quicken with his speeches all the latent greatness and holiness there, to merge himself with it creatively, and thereby draw it to himself forever.'[16]

Kiriakov particularly notes Kerensky's energy and devotion to the revolution. 'Tempestuous and impulsive in his movements and his speech, he is fired by revolutionary emotion. His close friends say of him, "He does not walk, but runs; he does not speak, but bombards you."'[17] The hero in Kiriakov's narrative is even endowed with the gift of prophecy, which is what has made him the Leader of the revolution. 'A feature of A. F. Kerensky's psychology is a nervous sensibility for political events which often extends to foreseeing them.'[18]

Kiriakov was also the author of popular biographies of other veterans of the Narodnik movement who supported Kerensky in 1917.[19] In these sketches he makes use of the same techniques: through idealized biographies of the heroic Yekaterina Breshko-Breshkovskaya and Nikolai Chaikovsky, the author traces the history of the revolutionary organizations. He lays particular emphasis both on the special emotional connection between his heroes as they fulfil their moral duty and on the Russian people they are seeking to liberate. This theme of the reciprocated love of the revolutionary liberators and the people was prominent in the well-developed genre of Narodnik political hagiography within which Kiriakov was working. It is the same theme he develops in his description of the life of Kerensky.

Another pamphlet about Kerensky comes from the pen of Oleg Leonidov (Shimansky, 1893–1951), a prose writer, poet, dramatist, translator, critic and essayist who later became famous as the scriptwriter of renowned Soviet films.[20] During the revolution Leonidov was serving in the army, apparently mainly as a propagandist. His military service did not prevent him from frequently appearing in print. Leonidov bases his pamphlet principally on police documents but writes also about his meetings with Kerensky, so it is more than likely that the latter assisted with publication of the biography. *The Leader of Freedom, A. F. Kerensky* was brought out by a Moscow publishing house in an edition of 24,000 copies. This was evidently well received, because a second edition appeared shortly afterwards with additional paragraphs reflecting Kerensky's latest actions, by now as the minister of war.

This is the most literary of the Kerensky biographies published in 1917. Leonidov made an effort to write in a vivid, lively manner. He stays with Kiriakov's theme of a special connection between the Leader and the people but adopts a different style from the canonical Narodnik extolling of the champion of freedom. Kerensky is not a heroic martyr but a heroic victor. Leonidov hybridizes the genre of Narodnik hagiography with mass-media techniques of the early twentieth century for writing up celebrities, creating memorable portraits of Kerensky and graphically evoking his manner as an orator. The description of him as Leader in his title is significant and was obviously of significance also for both author and publisher. If the Socialist Revolutionary Kiriakov depicts Kerensky as a faithful member of the SR Party and a successor of the Narodnik tradition, Leonidov characterizes him as a national Leader, a Leader of the whole of the Russian people. This pamphlet is perhaps the most 'leaderish' of all Kerensky's biographies, and in this respect it departs from the canonical Narodnik description of a hero. For Leonidov, Kerensky is not only the 'finest son of the people', the 'true tribune of the people', but also, 'by the will of God, the Elect of the people'.[21] It is probably going too far to see in this the direct influence of monarchist tradition, but Leonidov's biography is hardly the product of a fully fledged democrat. In the additions made in the second edition, the themes of trust and devotion to the Leader, even of becoming identified with him, are yet more pronounced. 'Kerensky is as one with the Russian people and the Russian people is as one with him'; 'But for as long as we have Kerensky we have, and should have, faith in our future'; 'Our future is in the hands of the people for as long as it remains with Kerensky, the universally acknowledged Leader of freedom.'[22]

Like Kiriakov, Leonidov describes Kerensky as a hugely important political symbol, but he goes even further in developing that image, employing rhetorical devices to glorify the Leader which were later to be applied to Soviet leaders. 'The name of Kerensky has already become a legend among men. Kerensky is a symbol of truth and the guarantor of success. Kerensky is a lighthouse, a beacon to which the arms of swimmers who are exhausted are outstretched, and from his fire, from his words and appeals they receive an ever renewed infusion of strength to continue the great struggle.'[23]

In characterizing the personality of the Leader, Leonidov particularly emphasizes the amazing sincerity of this ardent enthusiast of the revolution. It is noticeable that the word 'enthusiast' constantly recurs in the text.[24] Describing Kerensky's appearance, Leonidov devotes special attention to his gaze, returning again and again to the Leader's 'steely, unwavering eyes', his 'steely gaze', his 'stern, fixed stare'. The Leader may be physically weak, even ill (Leonidov writes about a frail, puny, tired man), but in his eyes there is willpower, insight and masterfulness. 'Kerensky glowers, projecting a dark, masterful look of indignation.' The political leader gives the person opposite him an 'incisive, authoritative gaze it is difficult to withstand.'[25] With this kind of pen portrait Leonidov builds up the image of a strong-willed politician.

An individual in early twentieth-century Russia reading the pamphlet might have recalled a number of writings prophesying the appearance of a 'new kind of person'. Leonidov was not the only author to present Kerensky in this light, as we shall see.

In Odessa, Vlast' naroda published a pamphlet titled *A. F. Kerensky, the People's Minister*.[26] Kerensky's Odessan biographer was a sympathizer of the Socialist Revolutionary Party. We may speculate that he drew on Kiriakov's writings. At all events, here too the biography is tied in with the history of the Socialist Revolutionaries, and both pamphlets are similar in style and in their choice of material. Like Kiriakov, the author quotes Kerensky's speeches at length. He makes use of both documentary publications of 1917 and family photographs. In this biography too there are pen portraits made by someone who has been present when Kerensky was giving speeches. The final paragraph is devoted to Kerensky's personality. His Odessan biographer is confident that the people's minister will go down in history as the creator of a new social system and as the personification of the revolution.

> When the peaceful life of the nations in obedience to the unseen operation of the laws of history bursts in full flood, people appear on the crest of the foaming waves of a turbulent sea whose names are later preserved with love and pride in the memory of the people. The great Russian Revolution has already brought forth a man so intimately identified with it that at times you are hard pressed to tell whether he is directing events or events are directing him That man is Alexander Fyodorovich Kerensky, the first love of free Russia.[27]

In this text, too, the author, writing about a unique Leader and saviour, brings in the themes of love, first love, and the merging of the Leader with the people.

Spring 1917 saw the appearance in Petrograd of a weekly magazine titled *Heroes of the Day: Biographical Essays*. It was intended that it would include articles on the lives of prominent contemporaries. The names mentioned were the Swedish politician Karl Branting; the 'Grandmother of the Russian Revolution' Yekaterina Breshko-Breshkovskaya; General Alexey Brusilov; the revolutionary publisher Vladimir Burtsev; the Belgian socialist Emile Vandervelde; US President Woodrow Wilson; the writer Maxim Gorky; Kerensky's predecessor as minister of war, Alexander Guchkov; the radical German Social Democrat Karl Liebknecht; the anarchist Peter Kropotkin; the Bolshevik leader Vladimir Lenin; the British prime minister David Lloyd George; and other Russian and foreign political and public figures.[28] The first issue of this publication, *A. F. Kerensky: the Love of the Russian Revolution*, was devoted to the revolutionary minister.[29] This is clear testimony to Kerensky's popularity. The author, 'Tan' (Vladimir Bogoraz, 1865–1936), had been a member of the People's Will circles and became famous as an ethnographer, linguist and writer. Tan, like Kiriakov, was active in the All-Russia Peasant Union and the organization of the Trud (Labour) Group, so was acquainted with and politically close to Kerensky.

The theme of political love for Kerensky, which Tan featured in his title, is found in other popular biographies but is particularly stressed by Tan. 'I would call him "the Revolution's love", that first virginal love.' He returns to the theme at the end of his study. 'The Russian Revolution will have many favourites and special intimates, but that first, virginal love of the young revolution will never fade, never be forgotten.'[30] Like other biographers, Tan reminded the reader of Kerensky's Socialist Revolutionary allegiance and pointed out the special place he had in the party: 'Kerensky is the highest type of SR. He is a dazzling member of that heroic generation of heroes who threw at the struggle their personal fearlessness, their indomitable spirit and their sublime heroism.'[31] This endorsement from a veteran of the revolutionary movement would have carried special weight with readers, although it is unlikely that all the Socialist Revolutionary leaders would have gone along with it. Like other biographers, Tan writes of his subject's 'prophetic insights' and calls him 'the Leader' and even 'the spiritual focus of Russia'. He too writes about Kerensky's singular hard gaze: 'There is something leonine in the depths of those wide-open eyes.'[32]

After the July Crisis,[33] when Kerensky became prime minister of the Provisional Government, the Moscow Educational Commission of the Provisional Committee of the State Duma brought out another biography of him. Its author, a certain Lieutenant Vysotsky, hailed the achievements of the 'tamer of the unquiet spirits of the rank-and-file soldiers'. 'The army obeyed him. It obeyed him as its Leader.'[34]

However, this is the only biography published in 1917 which contains some cautious criticism of Kerensky. Vysotsky felt that some of the reforms in the armed forces were unrealistic and that Kerensky, as the minister of war, had been too slow to recognize the need to fight Bolshevism. It was, nevertheless, on Kerensky that Vysotsky pinned his hopes for stabilization of the situation in the country. Even while criticizing him, Vysotsky laid the blame for the army's collapse on 'leading circles of Russia's democratic forces' – that is, the leaders of the moderate socialists.[35] This could be read as a call for Kerensky to distance himself from the leaders of the Mensheviks and Socialist Revolutionaries.

Vysotsky notes both the extreme fatigue of an 'ill and exhausted' Kerensky and the inspired vitality of 'the great enthusiast' and 'romantic', which exercises an almost hypnotic effect on the masses. This writer too points out the special relationship between the Leader and the people, the emotional connection between the minister and his audiences. 'Outbursts of that same inspiration and delight thunder towards him, reciprocation of the enthusiasm by which the speaker is himself possessed.' 'The people "feel" Kerensky, and Kerensky feels the people.' 'The people itself creates Kerensky, itself creates around him an atmosphere of boundless trust and love, in which his every word can assume almost biblical power.'[36] Like some of Kerensky's other biographers, Vysotsky sees the source of Kerensky's influence not only in his ability to mesmerize his listeners but also in the need of the people for a strong ruler. 'Additionally there is alive in [the people] a longing for Kerenskys, for someone to believe in, to whom it can surrender its soul, whom it would want to follow, into whose hands it could surrender its power in order then to submit to him.'[37] This interpretation of the relationship between the Leader and the people may be in line with Leonidov's writing, but it is far from the Narodnik canon of praise of famous heroes as practised by Kiriakov.

In the autumn of 1917, Lidiya Armand (née Tumpovskaya, 1887–1931) wrote a pamphlet titled *Kerensky*. She more usually wrote on pedagogy and popularization of culture, and also fiction. The main focus of her writing, however, was the organization of cooperatives and the cultural and educational work they did. In 1917 Armand was on the right of the Socialist Revolutionary Party, and in May the Left Socialist Revolutionaries had labelled her articles 'social chauvinism' and 'social patriotism'.[38] In other words, politically she was close to Kerensky. It seems safe to assume this item was published with the support of some grouping of the Right Socialist Revolutionaries.

Like other biographers of Kerensky, Armand includes reminiscences of occasions when she met him: 'I knew him while he was still a lion cub. In 1906 in Petrograd I met him only in connection with party matters.'[39] Armand finished work on the text on 15 September, and it bears the impress of that time. Her main aim is to defend the Leader from increasingly threatening attacks from both the left and the right. 'The lion is wounded. He has been wounded by slander and demagogy and just about everyone seems to be trying to kick him when he is down.' The image of

Kerensky sacrificing himself for the revolution is sanctified, Armand even comparing him to Christ. 'Perhaps he is already at the top of his crimson Golgotha. The time will come when the crowds will demand that monuments be erected to Kerensky. They will compose legends and sing songs about him. For the present, however, they are under the spell of the high priests and are yelling, "Crucify him!" '[40]

Armand stoutly defends her political Chosen One from the attacks of his opponents, including some in the ranks of the Socialist Revolutionary Party, who, in her opinion, have delivered 'the unkindest cut'. If the aim of earlier biographers had been to enhance Kerensky's influence, Armand's priority is to put down those questioning the Leader's authority. She does not deny he has made mistakes but insists on his right to have made them: 'How could a great man not make great mistakes when he is so in love, with a passion born of despair, with his doomed homeland, and who is so infinitely alone?'[41]

The portrait Armand sketches of Kerensky affirms his reputation as an ardent revolutionary. 'He was tireless in his work, appearing everywhere there was a need for conciliation, soothing, pacifying. Pale, joyfully intense, he was often totally overcome by fatigue and passionate emotion. On more than one occasion he blacked out at the end of a speech. He is ablaze, incandescent.'[42]

As we see, some of Kerensky's first biographers were very talented. The names of several are familiar to literary and academic historians. Armand and Kiriakov, Leonidov and Tan knew Kerensky personally and included fragments of reminiscence in their biographical essays. In writing their accounts of the life of the Leader they sometimes quote from published and unpublished documents, including (Kiriakov and Leonidov) materials from the police archives. They make use of the press of the revolutionary period and publish photographs from the Kerensky family archive. Some of them clearly enjoyed Kerensky's confidence.

Most of these biographies were written in May–June 1917 when Kerensky, after being appointed minister of war, was preparing a military offensive. As we shall see, this was when the major elements of the political cult of the revolutionary Leader took shape. The popular biographies of Kerensky reflected that process.

Those primarily involved in creating these biographies of the Leader were neo-Narodniks, the Labourites [Trudoviks] and, above all, the Right Socialist Revolutionaries. The texts of Kiriakov and Armand reflect intraparty conflicts. They contain criticism of the Left Socialist Revolutionaries and even of some of the 'centrists' who had criticized Kerensky. Leonidov and Vysotsky depict their protagonist as a national Leader above party politics, and this is evident in their writing style.

The Kerensky biographies which appeared in 1917 are highly emotional. Their authors were not only seeking to provide the Leader with political support by using his past career as an instrument of legitimation; they also wanted to communicate a needful political emotion to their readers. The theme of love, of the strong, reciprocated love between the people and its Leader, is very much to the fore. Some of Kerensky's biographers seem, indeed, to have been under his spell themselves.

We should not exaggerate the influence of these popular biographies on public opinion, but they are of interest in helping us to understand how Kerensky's supporters set about building his image. The biographies reflect certain features of the political culture of the revolutionary period. They are a valuable source for studying efforts both to create the image of a new Leader of a new country and to develop a new rhetoric of political legitimation.

2 The youth of the Leader

Kiriakov saw the date of Kerensky's birth as portentous. The history of the political struggle against the tsarist regime provided the background for his description of the childhood of the future champion of freedom.

> Alexander Kerensky's first breath (he was born on 22 April 1881) came just a week after some of the great champions of freedom for Russia – Sofiya Perovskaya, Andrey Zhelyabov, Timofey Mikhailov, Kibalchich and Rysakov – breathed their last, hanged by order of Alexander III on Semyonovskaya Square.
>
> His first movements as a little child, his first babbled words, almost coincided with the last movement, the last mumbling of a cowed Russia.[43]

Kiriakov also found significance in the place where Kerensky was born – Simbirsk – which played a role in how the hero chose his path in life. 'The Volga brought this child not only "songs that sound like moaning" but also freedom-loving songs about the much admired folk hero Stenka Razin, whose famous cliff was near Simbirsk.'[44]

Readers have it explained to them that, from childhood, Kerensky was in the force field of memories of the people's sufferings, of great uprisings that were rooted in his haunts, and that these memories were already influencing his outlook on the world.

Such a biography fitted into the canon of Narodnik description of the life of a hero. Kiriakov gives the backstory of the mutual love between Kerensky and Russia, emphasizing the place and time of the Leader's birth. Other authors, however, did not write about Kerensky's childhood and youth. 'A. F. Kerensky's personal life, like that of many giants of thinking and action, reveals a paucity of external events. He seemed to be saving himself for an immense task, in order to burn up all his energy and powers later, in the flames of the All-Russia conflagration. His biography is that of a typical Russian intellectual,' declares the Odessan biographer.[45] The very ordinariness of Kerensky's early life, however, is turned to account in the propaganda and serves as a further foundation of the Leader's authority. The 'giant of thinking and action' is initially indistinguishable from others, thereby stressing his democratic beginnings, his rootedness in the rank-and-file intelligentsia. It is only in the days of great tribulation that there becomes manifest the greatness of a Leader who has been building up his strength by spending his childhood in an ordinary milieu.

Kiriakov, quoting the testimony of the minister himself, tells the reader, 'The first childhood memories of A. F. Kerensky, then a six-year-old child, are, in his own words, a vague memory of the unspoken horror that engulfed Simbirsk when people there learned of the execution of the son of the local supervisor of people's schools, the student Alexander Ilyich Ulianov (brother of our 'sealed carriage' N. Lenin), for his involvement in a plot by the last members of People's Will to assassinate Tsar Alexander III.'[46] (One cannot help recalling the Soviet biographies of Lenin which never failed to mention the fate of his brother as a decisive factor in the career of that leader.)

Not all his biographers made mention of Kerensky's parents. Some reported that at the time of Alexander's birth his father was the headmaster of the grammar school in Simbirsk.[47] Bogoraz-Tan wrote, not entirely accurately: 'His father . . . taught Russian language in Simbirsk and was later headmaster of a grammar school in Kazan.'[48]

Not one of Kerensky's biographers during the revolution mentioned that, in 1887, his father, Fyodor Mikhailovich Kerensky, had been promoted to the status of full state councillor (the Civil Service equivalent of a general in the army), or that two years later he was further promoted to the post of chief inspector of schools in the territory of Turkestan. The father of the future minister had enjoyed a successful administrative career in the Ministry of Public Education, which was an inconvenience for anyone writing about the revolutionary biography of his son.[49] (This too is reminiscent of the canonical Soviet biographies of Lenin, which kept quiet about the award to his father of the rank of full state councillor.)

Kerensky's 1917 biographers did not write about his paternal forebears either. Like many intellectuals he came from a family of priests, a detail in his pedigree which would not have enhanced a politician's standing during the revolution.

Nor did they mention Nadezhda, Kerensky's mother, née Adler, whose father had been an officer in the Russian army and in charge of the land survey service of the Kazan Military District.[50] Her origins were nevertheless frequently discussed: some supposed she was German, others that she was Jewish.[51] (Speculation about Kerensky's supposed Jewish antecedents did find its way into the Russian periodical press in 1917.)[52] His mother's foreign maiden name and the position occupied by his maternal grandfather would have done nothing for Kerensky's authority as the Leader of the Russian Revolution, and this is doubtless why his first biographers kept quiet about them.

Some biographical sketches had photographs of Kerensky as a grammar-school student, which must have been given to the publishers by the minister himself or by his family.[53] Tan, clearly in contact with Kerensky or his relatives, emphasized the future Leader's successes at school. 'A. F. Kerensky showed exceptional ability from childhood. He went to school in Tashkent and graduated from the grammar school as the top student, with a gold medal.' (One is ineluctably reminded of Soviet biographies of Lenin.) Success at school pointed to the Leader's giftedness, manifest already in his childhood and early youth and a useful indicator of his worthiness to be a Leader. Tan noted also the future Leader's artistic temperament. 'From early youth he showed evidence of great spiritual energy. He was attracted to art and music and excelled in the title role of Gogol's *The Government Inspector*.'[54] A histrionic bent, as we shall see, did stand him in good stead in the first months of the revolution. Nevertheless, his biographers as a rule wisely remained silent about Kerensky's performance of the role of Khlestakov. The well-known traits of the character in the play, an air-headed impostor, could only too easily be attributed to the schoolboy who had performed the role so well. When things were going wrong for Kerensky as head of the Provisional Government, and later in emigration, he was openly compared to Gogol's character. In mid-July 1917, the right-wing popular newspaper *Narodnaya gazeta* [the People's Newspaper] reprinted a report in the German *Vossische Zeitung* in a manifest attempt to discredit Kerensky. The author was Friedrich Dukmeyer, who had been a teacher at the grammar school in Tashkent. Among his students had been Sasha Kerensky, about whom Dukmeyer reminisced in 1917. The article reported Nadezhda Adler's German antecedents and that Kerensky's grandfather had held the rank of general. The ex-schoolmaster recalled that his pupil 'dressed somewhat foppishly', was fond of dancing and theatrical performances, and that the role of Khlestakov 'seemed to have been written specially for him'. He observed that, 'even then', Kerensky was pale.[55] The frailty of the minister's health, which was, as we shall see, much discussed in 1917, seems from Dukmeyer's account to have been with him almost from birth.

Kiriakov tells us that Kerensky chose his political destiny while still at school. It is said to have been then that he decided to dedicate his life to the liberation of the Russian people.

> From all that he read, heard and saw, the lively imagination of Sasha Kerensky re-created in his mind the age-old picture of the slavish life of the entire Russian people – toiling, slow to anger, all-enduring, all-forgiving and long-suffering. He fell in love with this toiling Russian people with all the ardour of his boyish heart. He was filled with profound respect for the first champions of the freedom and happiness of the people. We can hardly doubt that the first heroes Sasha Kerensky wanted to imitate were the heroic fighters of the People's Will.

Even the city where the future leader went to school is seen as a factor revolutionizing the young schoolboy: 'Tashkent is the gateway to Siberia. The groans of Russia's political fighters in the cause of freedom, languishing in penal servitude and exile at that time, were closer and more keenly felt there.'[56] Kiriakov is manifestly exaggerating the revolutionariness of his hero. Kerensky himself makes no mention in his memoirs of having held radical views then, or of having read pamphlets about the People's Will. 'Neither I nor my classmates were aware of the problems that were exciting young people of our age in other parts of Russia, leading many of them to join clandestine societies while still at school.'[57] Kiriakov was clearly exaggerating, but that, in the view of this Narodnik, was how the childhood of a true champion of freedom should have passed. That was the canon for writing the biography of a Leader of the people, and the traditions of the revolutionary underground moved Kerensky's supporters to come up with a biography to bolster his authority.

Kerensky's years as a student at St Petersburg University (1899–1904), first in the faculty of history and philology then in the law faculty, were important for the Leader's biography because it was then that he 'developed his world view, a robust system of thought which set him on the path to honour, glory and the salvation of Russia,' as the Odessan biographer puts it.[58] The mention of the conscious education and self-education of the future politician is not fortuitous: a 'robust' world view, consciously elaborated as the result of independent assimilation of knowledge, was an important qualification for a radical Leader.

Some of Kerensky's biographers mention his marital status. In 1904 he married Olga Baranovskaya.[59] Sometimes a piece of writing would be accompanied by photographs showing Kerensky's wife and sons, or sometimes just the minister himself with his children.[60] It was accepted that the Leader's family life was of public interest. No doubt on these occasions his family had assisted the writers.

Some of his biographers were given to exaggerating Kerensky's radicalism in his student days, too, and his involvement with the Socialist Revolutionary Party. 'His love for the people, the dispossessed toiling people, grew ever strong and expanded in Kerensky's honest breast. It was this love which impelled him towards the party closest to the people, the peasants and workers, to a party which had inscribed on its banner, "Land and Freedom for all the toiling people. Through struggle justice shall be yours", the party of Socialist Revolutionaries.' So wrote Kiriakov, bringing the biography of his hero ever closer into line with the programme of the Socialist Revolutionary Party.[61] In reality, the young student's oppositional leanings did not move him towards adopting the platform of any party.

After Kerensky graduated from university, his aspiration was to join a group of 'political barristers' who defended people accused of committing political crimes. Becoming a member of this association was not straightforward: only lawyers who were particularly trusted in radical circles were accepted. To a scion of the 'bureaucracy', the son of an official prominent in the Ministry of Public Education with connections in the capital, the initial attitude was one of wariness. He even experienced difficulties being admitted to the legal profession at all, which was dominated by people with liberal or radical views. Kerensky's biographers omitted to mention these difficulties when writing in 1917.

Kerensky became an assistant attorney-at-law. Eager to become a 'political' defence lawyer, he gave free legal advice to the poor of the capital. Like many of his contemporaries he was greatly shocked by the events of Bloody Sunday, 9 January 1905, which he witnessed at first hand. Kerensky visited the families of demonstrators who had been killed by the troops, giving them legal advice. He signed a protest against the arrest of prominent intellectuals who had tried to avert the tragedy. In this connection he first came to the notice of the secret police, and a file was opened on him. The 1917 pamphlets reported this, and the attention paid to the young lawyer by the tsar's Okhrana, confirmed by the publication of documents, further bolstered his revolutionary credentials.[62]

His Odessan biographer wrote: 'Supporting the Socialist Revolutionary Party, Kerensky suffered all the adversities of 1905 with it. Despite the strict secrecy, despite the fact that the party was doing its best to protect Alexander, aware of his extraordinary strength, he was arrested and put in prison.'[63] In reality, the party leaders are unlikely to have been acquainted with the young assistant attorney.

In May 1917 Kerensky described his position at the time: 'After 1905, in the midst of general exhaustion, I was one of those who demanded an attack on the old regime.'[64] Reminding the public of a time when he had demanded new, more radical action against the regime served to legitimize his right to curb the excessive demands of the soldiers. For Kerensky, who had by then become minister of war, that was a high priority.

On 23 December 1905, the young lawyer was arrested, accused both of preparing armed insurrection and of belonging to an organization seeking to overthrow the existing order. On 5 April 1906, however, he was released under special police supervision but prohibited from residing in the capitals. Kerensky went back to Tashkent, where his father still worked. With the aid of his family and influential family friends he managed to have that restriction lifted, and he returned to St Petersburg in September.[65]

Kerensky's biographers did not report that it was connections in bureaucratic circles that helped him to escape exile. They found different explanations: 'There was no hard evidence, however, and the future minister of justice was released from a Russian prison,' the Odessan biographer ad-libbed.[66] Neither did they write in 1917 about Kerensky's return to St Petersburg. Mitigation of his sentence did nothing for his revolutionary reputation. Mentioning his arrest, on the other hand, was very much to the point. After Kerensky was appointed minister of war, the ministry's main newspaper wrote: 'A. F. Kerensky was arrested several times by the old government for belonging to far-left movements before commencing his political work as a member of the State Duma.'[67] In the circumstances of the revolution, having been in prison under the old regime was a source of authority, even an important qualification for holding such a position. His biographers (Kiriakov and the Odessan biographer) also wrote about his arrest, and Leonidov, implying he had spent a considerable time in prison, claimed that, 'If Kerensky ever did rest, it was only while in prison.'[68]

The arrest was important for his political career, but returning to St Petersburg was no less important: in the provinces Kerensky's future would have developed quite differently. Once back in the capital, the young lawyer again became active politically, although again the scope of his activities is exaggerated by some biographers. Here, for example, is the Odessan biographer describing his role in organizing elections to the Second State Duma: 'To prepare for the elections, a special organization of Socialist Revolutionaries was set up in St Petersburg, with A. F. Kerensky as its soul. For tactical reasons the party did not nominate him personally as a deputy.'[69] The truth of the matter was evidently that the Socialist Revolutionary leaders did not consider this junior lawyer a suitable candidate.

Kiriakov recalls the episode, but frames it differently:

> This was all taking place in Zemlya i volya, the Land and Freedom movement, a group of Petersburg intellectuals organizing preparations for the elections to the Second State Duma, in the late summer of 1906. He immediately won everybody's hearts and several times surprised them with his practical understanding of how the state worked, something in short supply among the old party workers, who had been obliged before 1905 either to keep their heads down in the underground or to live most of the time abroad.[70]

As described by Kiriakov, Kerensky is seen not as a prominent Socialist Revolutionary – which, at that time, he was not – but as belonging to a radical non-partisan association of intellectuals. It is interesting to find the young lawyer being portrayed as the representative of a new generation, more practical and attuned to affairs of state, coming up to replace the veterans of the revolutionary movement. The pragmatism of a statesman, already evident in the young man, further qualifies him for leadership in the revolutionary era, when the new politicians assuming power need skills and knowledge which the radical figureheads of the previous generation simply do not possess. Kiriakov, on the right wing of the Socialist Revolutionary Party, was clearly contrasting Kerensky with Victor Chernov and other party leaders who favoured more centrist positions.

Kerensky's arrest and subsequent political activity enhanced his reputation in radical intelligentsia circles. In October 1906, Nikolai Sokolov, a Social Democrat and prominent 'political lawyer', asked Kerensky to go as a matter of urgency to Revel to defend Estonian peasants who had participated in rioting on the estates of the Ostsee barons. Kerensky immediately travelled to the capital of Estland and conducted a successful defence: most of the defendants were released, unpunished, in the courtroom.[71]

One biographer describes this development in Kerensky's career: 'Into the dark, dreary night of reaction, A. F. Kerensky brought these persecuted brothers his love and professional skill. He abandoned his practice as a talented young lawyer to devote himself wholly to political trials. Few took place without Kerensky acting for the defence.'[72]

The reader is being offered the image of a successful, highly paid Petersburg lawyer who, for the sake of an ideal, was renouncing a career which promised to provide him with a substantial income. This was not the case, although idealistic motives did influence the assistant attorney's decision. Tan too wrote of Kerensky's hardships, apparently exaggerating them somewhat. 'He received 25 rubles a month from his patron, for a long time suffered want, and lived with his family in an attic.'[73] As we shall see, the image of an ascetic devoting himself entirely to the struggle for freedom was an important part of how he was represented as the Leader of the revolution.

After the trial in Revel, Kerensky was accepted as a fully fledged political defence lawyer. Almost all his biographers mention this occupation, and the minister of war himself, working on his credibility, reminisced both about his time in prison and his defence of people accused of crimes against the state. In the course of an important speech on 26 March 1917 in front of the soldiers' deputies in the Petrograd Soviet, he stated: 'I have spent much time in the dungeons of Russian justice, and many champions of freedom passed through my hands.'[74]

3 'Tribune of the people'

The specialization of 'political defence lawyer' was not lucrative, but it did bring renown in radical circles. It was a career which required observance of an unwritten but strict code of conduct well understood by both lawyers and defendants. Political defence lawyers confronted a number of ethical and professional issues. They were expected to have the accused acquitted while at the same time defending their client's political views. To do both things simultaneously was difficult, and at times impossible. For the Constitutional Democrat Vasiliy Maklakov, one of the most prominent lawyers of the time, the first priority was legal defence of the client. 'If he [the lawyer] should not offend or denigrate the political views of his client, if he could not, without humiliating himself, hypocritically dissociate himself from them because he agreed with them, he must nevertheless respect the duty of judges to observe and uphold the existing law. It was not permissible to conflate the obligations of political campaigner and defence lawyer,' he reminisced.[75]

Many lawyers, however, were perceived by society as politicians and behaved as such. This role of 'tribune of the people', denouncing the regime and its 'servants', was one Kerensky assumed. For him, every trial was a battle with a hateful government personified by the state prosecution. Here is how his role is described by Leonidov: 'A. F. Kerensky was least of all a professional lawyer, selling his time and powers to individuals to protect their selfish interests and rights. He has always been drawn to defend the interests of the disenfranchised social classes, has always battled for their right to life, and invariably tried to bring them to that wonderful day when they would enjoy their rights in full measure.'[76]

This description harmonizes with the tenor of Kerensky's speeches in 1917, denouncing the failings of the judicial system of the old regime. It is, nevertheless, an unfair representation of the reality of the pre-revolutionary judicial system, where many of the empire's judges and prosecutors were highly professional lawyers conscientiously performing their duties. When he became minister of justice, Kerensky effectively recognized the good faith of some of his former opponents in court and appointed them to positions of power.

As counsel for the defence, the future minister of justice had found himself involved in high-profile trials. The case of the so-called Tukum Republic, in which he defended Latvian insurgents, attracted much publicity. Kerensky also conducted the defence of Labourites (Trudoviks) who signed the Vyborg Appeal. He participated in the trials of the leaders of the All-Russia Peasant Union, of the St Petersburg Military Organization of the Social Democrats, of St Petersburg province's Union of Teachers, of Tver province's Peasant Brotherhood, and of the Northern Flying Squad of the Combat Organization of the Socialist Revolutionary Party. Kerensky's clients included Bolsheviks: he defended the fighters who participated in the raid on the Miass treasurer's office. These trials were duly recalled by his biographers in 1917. Even this partial list of cases demonstrates how much the young defence lawyer was in demand. He was admitted as a full member of the Corporation of Lawyers, and the Council of the St Petersburg Circuit of Courts of Justice called him to the bar in 1909.

Of particular importance for Kerensky's career was the trial of the Armenian socialist Dashnaktsutyun Party in 1912, when the elite of the Armenian intelligentsia found themselves in the dock. Kerensky was able to prove the falsehood of witness statements presented by the prosecution. It was a resounding victory for the defence, and one of the investigators was even formally charged with perjury and falsification. (The authorities declared him mentally unfit in order to save him from being prosecuted.) Of the 145 accused, 95 were acquitted.[77]

This trial was a favourite of Kerensky's biographers. Leonidov wrote of a political victory for the defence, Kerensky having supposedly proven that it was not the investigator who was sick and unfit but the court system created by Minister of Justice Ivan Shcheglovitov, who, for oppositionists, and particularly for the radical lawyers, was the personification of the regime they detested.[78] Kerensky's Odessan biographer represents the trial as a tragic duel between an honest, idealistic lawyer and an all-powerful system, a duel whose outcome was predetermined.

> Kerensky had again to contend with that stone wall. The court chairman did not let him speak, cutting him off in mid-sentence when his accusations were becoming too near the mark. He kept threatening to have him removed from the court and made vitriolic remarks during the course of the trial. The shocked courtroom witnessed the heroic struggle of a man unarmed with one who was armed, a battle between lawfulness and brute force, a struggle whose outcome was – alas! – a foregone conclusion.[79]

This style of writing about Kerensky's legal career was at odds with the actual history of the trial but in tune with the general climate of denouncing the old regime, which was a major component of Kerensky's own speeches. The image of a valorous, uncompromising champion fighting a pitiless system was grist to the mill of those aiming to promote him.

There were occasions when Kerensky's success in the role of tribune of the people had an adverse effect on the fate of those he was defending. His colleagues warned: 'If you want him to defend the revolution, he will do so brilliantly, but if it is the defendant you want defended, go to someone else because the revoutionary always takes precedence over the lawyer in Kerensky. The military judges hate him!'[80] This testimony has the ring of truth, although, as we have seen, Kerensky did have his successes in court. What is perhaps more to the point here, however, is that his biographers believed their readers would be more taken by the description of a lawyer who gave priority to the revolution rather than to defending his client. In 1917 it was the image of the fiery revolutionary lawyer which was effective in underpinning his authority.

Some defendants, indeed, wanted just such a defence lawyer who shared their radical beliefs, and Kerensky's reputation had revolutionary activists seeking him out. Yevgenia Bosh, a Bolshevik arrested in 1912, was eager to be defended by such a lawyer. Her mother wrote to Kerensky, 'She does not want to be defended by a lawyer in whom she could not have total confidence and respect for his previous work and very much wishes to ask you to defend her.'[81] She was not the only revolutionary to appeal for support to the radical barrister.

Sensational trials were widely reported in the press, and Kerensky's reputation and influence in radical circles grew. Even in August 1917, such an opponent of the head of the Provisional Government as Sergo Ordzhonikidze recalled the Kerensky 'who at one time, acting as a defence lawyer, forced all Russia to heed his ardent speeches.' The prominent Bolshevik was contrasting Kerensky the earlier radical lawyer with Kerensky the minister.[82] The political lawyer had been respected by left-wing Social Democrats too, and it is striking that, when later they were attacking Kerensky as head of the Provisional Government, they respectfully recalled this earlier period in his life.

A further contribution to spreading Kerensky's fame across the nation was made by the events at the Lena goldfields, on which nearly all his biographers dwell. In April 1912 police and troops opened fire on strikers there and 250 people were killed. There was a public outcry and a government commission was sent to investigate. The opposition in the Duma insisted, however, that a special commission, independent of all government departments, should be established, and the money to pay for it was raised by public subscription. The commission, consisting of a number of lawyers from Moscow and Petersburg, was headed by Kerensky. The lawyers helped the workers conclude a new agreement with the company. Armand asserts that his colleagues on the commission described Kerensky as 'a wonderful young man, but hotheaded. It is difficult to conduct an investigation if you are burning with indignation.'[83] Leonidov does not see this as negative, and many readers in the revolutionary era also viewed it positively. Society's radically inclined members endorsed Kerensky's strident denunciation of the perpetrators, even if their guilt had not been legally established. His image as a fiery tribune of the people unmasking the regime helped to establish his reputation as a politician, both before the revolution and, to an even greater extent, after it.

The investigation contributed to his reputation, even if his achievement is sometimes plainly overstated. 'Kerensky forced the government to admit its responsibility for the atrocity, and before the truth proclaimed by Kerensky even the most dedicated servants of the fallen regime had to bow their heads,' Leonidov declares.[84]

His public speeches made the young lawyer a true celebrity, as the leaders of the Trud group noted. Some had been clients of Kerensky when he made the case for the defence in the trial of the All-Russia Peasant Union. In the autumn of 1910 prominent Trudoviks suggested he should run for election to the State Duma. Despite his links with the Socialist Revolutionaries, Kerensky accepted their suggestion and was elected as a deputy from the second municipal curia of Volsk in Saratov province, which had a reputation as a radical town.[85] Kiriakov, who is keen to emphasize the Leader's links with the Socialist Revolutionaries, stresses that his election to the Duma was forced on him. 'He had to go underground, to camouflage himself.'[86] His biographers try hard to demonstrate that, even as a deputy, Kerensky remained a radical. 'In his speeches on agrarian issues, as well as those concerning workers, budgets and other matters, he was always vigilant in the interests of democracy and openly declared himself a socialist.'[87]

Kerensky's status as a member of the Duma strengthened his authority in radical circles and opened up new opportunities for political action. The young politician could never have played such a role in the February Revolution had he not been a deputy, but, within a few months of the overthrow of the monarchy, the Duma, elected on a 'qualified' franchise, was losing popularity with the masses, who were moving to the left. Some of Kerensky's biographers prefer to describe his 'parliamentary' period as forced upon him, and even as an ordeal: 'He felt fettered by his work in the Duma, and the need for constant interaction with the bourgeois parties was burdensome and irritating.' They emphasize that his speeches, which sounded 'trenchant and bold' within the walls of the Tauride Palace, met with 'hostility from the vast majority of those elected to the restricted-franchise Duma' but elicited 'a fervent response from the ranks of democracy'.[88] Kerensky's Odessan biographer highlights his unique situation in the Duma, contrasting the radical politician with the other deputies.

> He became the conscience of the Fourth Duma, one of its few bright spots. At moments when Russia's prematurely born parliament was crushed by contempt and arrogance from the ministerial box, when the tsar's lackeys from the podium of the State Duma derided the people's representatives with such maxims as the notorious 'that is how it was, and that is how it will be!', only one voice rang out invariably firm, invariably bold and confident. That was the voice of A. F. Kerensky. . . .
>
> The five years of Kerensky's battle for freedom and truth are all that can redeem the five years of lassitude and impotence of the Fourth State Duma.[89]

The members of the Provisional Government, the Executive Committee of the Petrograd Soviet, and the former deputies of the State Duma – Mensheviks, Trudoviks, progressives and Constitutional Democrats – would hardly have concurred with that judgement. Nor would anyone who read the Duma reports attentively. Nevertheless, some readers of the era of revolution who were only just beginning to take an interest in politics might well have believed that Kerensky was the only real representative of the people in the restricted-franchise and 'bourgeois' Duma.

During the revolution, Kerensky himself described his work in the State Duma as a constant struggle against the enemies of the people. 'For five years from this rostrum I battled with and denounced the old government. I recognize enemies of the people and I know how to deal with them,' he declared in his speech of 26 March to the soldier's section of the Petrograd Soviet.[90]

The young lawyer very soon became the Trudoviks' principal speaker. His meteoric rise caused alarm to some of the old guard of the Trudovnik group. Armand mentions that they periodically discussed plans to mount resistance to 'Socialist Revolutionary domination', but Kerensky's authoritativeness, she claims, frustrated this. 'His forcefulness won naturally, without tension.'[91]

Kerensky's Duma speeches were quite dissimilar to the businesslike addresses of parliamentarians discussing budget and legislative bills. From the rostrum of the Duma, just as in court, he passionately denounced the regime and its servants. Kerensky was addressing his speeches not to the deputies and ministers but to the whole of Russia. The speeches were brilliant, emotive, sometimes defiant. Nor was his behaviour in the Duma chamber always in accord with standards of parliamentary decorum. An official observing the sessions noted, 'The Duma chairman did not react to a whistle, directed at the representative of the government, which echoed round the chamber, although everybody had seen that it was Member of the Duma Kerensky who was responsible.'[92] Unsurprisingly, he was regarded as the left-wing *enfant terrible* of the Duma.[93]

The right-wingers reacted angrily to Kerensky's impassioned speeches. There were scenes. Those chairing the sessions interrupted the speaker, deprived him of the right to speak or debarred him for several sessions. His reputation as a troublemaker could mean that quite unforeseen meanings could be read into the most innocent expressions. There was even a joke that the official preamble, 'Honourable members of the State Duma . . .', had caused the chairman to react with, 'Member of the Duma Kerensky, I am issuing you with a first warning.' Armand writes proudly about his insubordinate behaviour and the reaction it evoked.[94] His aggressive manner only increased respect for Kerensky in radical circles.

It is hardly surprising that his speeches provoked conflict and attracted the attention of the press. Journalists in the Duma who were hungry for sensations often reported them. Kerensky became popular and was much quoted. His influence grew, and he began chairing meetings of the Trudoviks. From 1915 he was officially their leader.[95]

There were times when Kerensky was perceived as the most prominent and best known of all the left-wing deputies. Nikolai Chkheidze, the leader of the Menshevik group, was a lacklustre orator, incapable of firing up his colleagues or attracting the attention of journalists. His adherence to Marxist orthodoxy prevented him from engaging in tactical negotiations with 'bourgeois' groups, and, as a result, the more dynamic Kerensky sometimes conducted negotiations on behalf of both the left-wing groups – a further boost to his standing.

Not everyone was taken by the histrionic style of Kerensky's speeches, which ran counter to traditional expectations of parliamentary oratory. Senator Nikolai Tagantsev remembered them as 'demagogic', and, while not denying that he had a gift for it, considered that his rhetoric was fit only for making speeches at protest rallies.[96] In 1917, of course, that kind of rhetoric was just what was needed to enthuse huge rallies. Leonidov lavishes praise on Kerensky's oratorical style. 'You will not find exquisite honing in the speeches the present minister made in the Duma, nor will you find oratorical flourishes. Everything is improvised. These are not speeches in the narrow, commonly understood sense: they are the howls of a rebellious, bleeding heart, the great, ardent heart of a true tribune of the people.'[97]

Popular in radical circles, the Duma deputy found himself invited to all manner of meetings, assemblies and conferences. In 1913 he was elected chairman of the Fourth All-Russia Congress of Trade and Industry Workers,[98] which elicited derisive comment from right-wingers. In the Duma, Nikolai Markov characteristically declared, 'Deputy Kerensky is, to the best of my knowledge, and to yours too, a lawyer. At all events, not just a ledger clerk. Unless a ledger clerk of a Jewish Qahal. But only in a figurative sense . . . Can we really allow the propaganda of the likes of Mr Kerensky in the whole society [*sic*] of poorly educated people?'[99] In radical circles, such speeches by the hated far-right supporters of the Black Hundreds only burnished the halo of the Trudoviks' leader. Many people living in Russia saw Kerensky as their own defence lawyer. He received many letters from 'unimportant people' exposing abuses and injustices and hoping he would intercede.

Kerensky continued to involve himself in illegal and semi-legal undertakings. He had a fat dossier in the Police Department, where a close eye was kept on him, with informers being infiltrated among those close to him. In 1913 Kerensky worked with the Petersburg Collective of the Socialist Revolutionaries. Okhrana agents based in Paris even reported that he had become a member of the party's Central Committee. The information was false but indicative of the Interior Ministry's suspicions about him. In reality, Kerensky declined an invitation from the Socialist Revolutionaries to become their representative in the Duma, aiming instead to unify all the Narodnik groups politically. These police reports were nevertheless published by supporters of Kerensky in 1917, which may have given readers an exaggerated impression of the scale of his illegal activities. This was all to the good as far as his status was concerned.[100]

On 23 July 1914, on the eve of the First World War, Kerensky was detained in Yekaterinburg at a gathering of teachers which had not been officially sanctioned. He was saved from actual arrest by his immunity as a Duma deputy.[101]

In 1911 or 1912, the young politician had been invited to join the Great Orient of the Peoples of Russia, a secret society established in 1910 on a basis of Masonic lodges.[102] Kerensky played a major role in the organization and became both a member of the Supreme Council of Lodges and, in 1916, its secretary (a position he may still have been holding in early 1917). A historian of Freemasonry even writes of this as Kerensky's organization, seeing the Great Orient of the Peoples of Russia as distinct from Russian Freemasonry in the preceding period.[103]

To what extent did the Freemasons contribute to Kerensky's advancement? The lawyer Alexander Galpern, who replaced him as secretary of the Supreme Council and became the Provisional Government's principal civil servant, recalled: 'It was, after all, we ourselves who put him forward and indeed created him, so it is we who bear responsibility for him.'[104] If the Masons advanced Kerensky's career, the popular politician for his part was exceptionally important for the brothers, who were seeking to enrol influential people in their ranks. He was an important figure in the public eye before joining the lodge.

Kerensky's biographers had nothing to say in 1917 about his being a Mason. There was almost no discussion of Freemasonry at the time, although a febrile public was susceptible to suggestions of conspiracy. All manner of conspiracy theories were, in fact, used by both the left and right wings for political mobilization. The sympathy of foreign Masonic organizations for the anti-monarchist revolution in Russia was well known, and it was even possible to read about ties between the Masons and Kerensky in the newspapers. On 24 May a newspaper of the Ministry of War, which Kerensky by this time headed, published greetings from Italian members of the International Mixed Scottish Masonic Rite to 'renewed Russia'. The addressee was the Russian minister of war. The Italian Freemasons congratulated the Russian people 'on their deliverance from traitors to their homeland who had sought to compel Russia to conclude a shameful peace.' They expressed the hope that the Russian army 'will make every effort to bring the war to a victorious conclusion' and invited 'all our Russian colleagues to join with the Italian Masons for the joint dissemination of our shared ideals.'[105]

One can only speculate as to why this address from the Italian Freemasons to their 'Russian colleagues' was not exploited by Kerensky's opponents (among whom were 'brothers' who were to become the minister's foes after February and right-wingers who had been furiously decrying 'Yid Freemason plots' before the revolution). At all events, the revolutionary minister's Freemasonry had no obvious impact on his public image in 1917.

Of no small importance to Kerensky's reputation were some trials in which he was not personally engaged. In 1911–13 Russia was greatly exercised by the case of Menahem Beilis, a Kievan Jew accused of ritual murder. Senior officials in the Interior Ministry and the Ministry of Justice exerted pressure on the investigation, and right-wingers unleashed anti-Semitic propaganda in the Black Hundred press and the State Duma. In such a situation the code of conduct of a radical intellectual called for resolute action.

Leftists, liberals and even some conservatives launched a campaign in defence of Beilis, and Kerensky made a speech in the Duma about the trial on 23 October 1913. That same day a meeting was held of barristers of the St Petersburg Circuit of the Courts of Justice. Radical lawyers turned a routine meeting into a political rally. Having mobilized their supporters, who came to the meeting in large numbers, Kerensky and Nikolai Sokolov insisted on a discussion of the Beilis case. A resolution was adopted condemning 'violations of the foundations of justice' by the government.

Those who had organized the protest were accused both of contempt of court and the Russian government and of attempting to influence the outcome of an ongoing trial. The government attempted to deprive Kerensky of his immunity from prosecution as a Duma deputy, and the minister of justice, Ivan Shcheglovitov, informed the chairman of the Duma that Kerensky was required in court to face criminal charges. The

Duma Commission on Personnel Matters decided by a majority vote that Kerensky could not be expelled from the Duma.[106] In June 1914 the court reached its verdict in the case of the Petersburg lawyers, and Kerensky was sentenced to eight months' imprisonment. He continued, however, to be protected by his immunity as a deputy. Banquets were organized in his honour, telegrams of greetings were sent to him, and like-minded deputies gave the leader of the Trudoviks a standing ovation in the Duma.[107] Kerensky's biographers write about this episode but do not always mention his parliamentary privilege, which might have given readers the impression that he had actually been in prison for that length of time.

Kerensky's attitude to the First World War was of great importance for his career, but some biographers simply omit to mention it. In 1917 Russian society was completely split over this issue, so, for any statesman seeking to create a broad political coalition, being pinned down on the matter could only have adverse consequences. In his memoirs, Kerensky describes his position as simultaneously defencist and revolutionary. These apparently contradictory positions he reconciled on the basis that it was essential to overthrow the tsarist government because it was not competent to win the war.[108]

It was impossible for him to adopt that position publicly. Nevertheless, as leader of the Trudovik group, he had no option but to state his position on the war at an emergency meeting of the State Duma on 26 July 1914. In his speech Kerensky declared:

> Citizens of Russia, remember that you have no enemies among the working classes of the belligerent countries. Defending to the utmost everything you hold dear from attempts to seize it, remember that this terrible war would not have come about if liberty, equality and fraternity were guiding the actions of the governments of all countries. All you who desire the happiness and prosperity of Russia, heighten your resolve, summon up all your strength and, having successfully defended your country, liberate it. To you, our brothers, shedding your blood for your own motherland, we bow low and send fraternal greetings!

It was a skilfully constructed speech, acceptable to the radical intelligentsia because its call to defend the country could be read as a signal to liberate it politically. The patriotic pathos of the speech earned Kerensky applause from all sides of the Duma. Indeed, his speech was interrupted by applause, in which even right-wing deputies joined.[109]

In the course of devising autobiographical sources of legitimation in 1917, Kerensky could not avoid the topic of the war, and when it was tactically to his advantage he could even present himself as an internationalist. Addressing the First All-Russia Congress of Soviets on 4 June, he declared, 'From the very beginning of the war, at the first session of the State Duma on 20 July 1914, we and the Social Democrats in Russia were the first – remember this – the only parties in Europe to vote publicly against military appropriations.' This claim was greeted with applause.[110] Remembering the past in this manner was what that particular audience at that particular moment wanted to hear.

Kerensky publicly condemned chauvinism and criticized all the governments of Europe for unleashing war, but, most importantly, he never omitted to harshly attack the Russian government. He did not exclude the possibility of a civil truce within the country but made it conditional on the introduction of a whole raft of reforms. At other times he was more radical. His Trudovik colleague Vladimir Stankevich, who was close to him, described Kerensky's position as 'contributing to the war effort by criticizing the government.' Kerensky was influenced by the decisions of the Zimmerwald International Socialist Conference held in September 1915, and he would often use the phraseology of the internationalists, even while remaining a defencist who never stopped opposing the government. When it was to his advantage Kerensky would even describe himself as 'a left-wing Zimmerwaldian'. This was untrue, although some of his contemporaries did believe he was opposed to the war.[111] Depending on the situation, seeking to create the widest possible coalition against the government, Kerensky could express different views, adapting what he said to his audience.

At illegal meetings Kerensky found himself under pressure from radically minded Socialist Revolutionaries who were conducting anti-war propaganda, and would use words they would find persuasive. With time, however, his differences with the internationalist wing of the Socialist Revolutionaries became more marked.[112] He wanted to create a 'red' or 'left' bloc uniting all socialists, whatever their attitude to the war.[113] In his public speeches he took every opportunity to denounce the government – common ground for all the forces he was trying to bring together.

Together with Nikolai Sokolov, Kerensky organized the legal defence of five Bolshevik deputies of the Duma who had been arrested in November 1914. From the tribune of the Duma he protested against the arrest of 'our comrades' and headed a group of radical lawyers who defended these Social Democrats in court. He continued subsequently to demand the release of 'the five'.[114] The celebrated memoirist Nikolai Sukhanov, a Menshevik internationalist, recalled that Kerensky behaved like a professional revolutionary. He used his trips around the country as a Duma deputy for illegal work, delivering public lectures, helping to organize opposition, supporting it with funds provided by his liberal friends. This was not something which could remain unnoticed. The right-wing politician Nikolai Tikhmenev wrote: 'The revolutionaries' leaders, the likes of Kerensky, are busily travelling round Russia delivering talks and lectures, and in the meantime evidently arranging a bit of this and a bit of that. Financed by murky sources, new social-democratic newspapers are popping up like bubbles out of the mud in provincial towns. The insolence of the "progressive" press is on the increase.'[115] Kerensky's opponents in the Duma may have exaggerated the scope and results of his activities, but his renown was increasing all the time. His connections with those in the underground, and his reputation as someone with those links, were of importance to him during the events of February 1917.

Kerensky, as we have noted, did not confine his illegal activity only to supporting Socialist Revolutionaries. Meetings aimed at bringing about unity among the left-wing organizations took place in his own apartment. On 16–17 July 1915 a conference of representatives of the Narodnik groups of Petrograd (as St Petersburg had been renamed at the outbreak of war), Moscow and the provinces was held there. The police considered Kerensky to be the prime mover of this meeting, at which a central bureau was established to coordinate the activities of the Trudoviks, the People's Socialists and the Socialist Revolutionaries. Disagreements on the issue of the war, together with police harassment, prevented the union from becoming a reality. Meetings of the capital's Socialist Revolutionaries also took place in Kerensky's apartment, as the secret police were well aware. In July 1915, police posts on the Russo-Finnish border received a secret order advising them that Kerensky was travelling around the empire, 'engaging in anti-government activity'. They were instructed to keep him under observation. After the revolution this document was put up at Beloostrov railway station at the Finnish border for the public to see, as publications supportive of Kerensky duly reported.[116]

The police exaggerated the role of the Trudovik leader in organizing protest. A report from the director of the Police Department linked the strikes of summer 1915 to Kerensky's propaganda activity, claiming he had called for the establishment of factory collectives to form soviets along the lines of those which had appeared in 1905. In the report Kerensky was named as 'the principal leader of the current revolutionary movement'. In reality, Kerensky and Chkheidze had urged the workers not to waste their energy on individual strikes but to prepare for future decisive action against the regime. After February 1917, police assessments of this kind, even if factually erroneous, were all to the good of the reputation of the champion of freedom. Newspapers published such documents, provided by Kerensky's supporters who had the archives under their control. His biographers readily quoted from them.[117]

Kerensky's wartime experience was important training for the politician. He tried persistently, if not always successfully, to reconcile fundamentally different political forces in order to enable them the better to fight their common enemy, the existing regime. He kept his position on the most controversial issue – his attitude towards the war – unclear, and at times in front of different audiences described it in different ways or with different emphases. It would, nevertheless, be a mistake to classify Kerensky as a centrist. His behaviour was more a matter of pragmatic ideological flexibility, sincere if bordering on opportunism. This ambiguity prevented him from becoming the leader of any one party, but it also meant he was welcome in very diverse circles, which was crucial for someone attempting to broker interparty agreements and who saw his mission as being to build a broad coalition of oppositionists.

It is not easy to assess Kerensky's actual contribution to organizing the underground. Michael Melancon, a historian of the Socialist Revolutionary Party, believes the clandestine revolutionaries used Kerensky and the resources he controlled but rejected him as a leader.[118]

Other illegals also discussed relations with Kerensky, whose influence was on the increase. Revolutionaries were no doubt also attracted by the money at his disposal. Alexander Shlyapnikov seems to have raised the question of possibly making use of these resources with Vladimir Lenin. In his reply in September 1915, the Bolshevik leader characterized Kerensky as a 'revolutionary chauvinist' with whom it was impossible to enter into any alliance but with whom there could be cooperation in technical matters. Lenin's letter can be interpreted both as a recommendation to make use of Kerensky's resources and as a call for joint action to achieve the destruction of the regime. 'Our relations should be direct and clear: you want to overthrow tsarism to gain a victory over Germany, while we are working for the international revolution of the proletariat.'[119] As we see, the possibilities for a broad front of the forces of the opposition which Kerensky was trying to create could have included the Bolsheviks. The experience of negotiations during the war, even those which were unsuccessful, did influence the behaviour of its members during the February Days and what they had to say about each other. The initial restraint shown by some of the Bolsheviks in their criticism of Kerensky may have gone back to joint initiatives in the years before the revolution.

During 1917, other Bolsheviks recalled their contacts with Kerensky. For example, at the end of August, Ivan Skvortsov-Stepanov published an article in which he touched on the career of Kerensky, who by then was already the head of the Provisional Government. The Bolshevik recalled a meeting with him in November 1916, by which time Stepanov believed the Trudovik leader had moved to the left. Nevertheless, he claims, Kerensky believed the hand of the Okhrana and imperial court, which he considered Germanophile, was behind workers' unrest.[120] We might take this as an attempt by a prominent Bolshevik to discredit the head of the Provisional Government by suggesting Kerensky had failed to understand the real mood of the workers, and hence was questioning the democratic credentials of the leader of the February Revolution. The article can, however, be read in a different way, with even Kerensky's political opponents, the Bolsheviks, acknowledging his involvement in the activities of the illegals. This could only be to the benefit of his standing.

Other actions during the war redounded to Kerensky's credit. Well informed about the mood among the illegals, he urged the liberals to give no quarter in the fight against the regime and insisted that the country was on the brink of revolution. Most of them thought he was being overly optimistic,[121] but after the downfall of the tsar the Trudovik leader's surmises were sometimes treated as infallible predictions.

During the war years Kerensky's popularity grew steadily, aided by his speeches in the Duma. Banning them from publication only drew attention to them, and they were distributed in handwritten copies or as typewritten texts. Illegal organizations issued leaflets quoting them. After February 1917 the speeches were printed, and boosted his reputation as an opponent of the old regime, endowed moreover with the gift of prophecy.

In 1915 a former police officer, Sergey Myasoyedov, was executed. He had been falsely accused by the General Headquarters of the Supreme Commander-in-Chief of spying for Germany. It was intended that the spy-mania campaign, instigated by the High Command, would divert public opinion from the bungling of the military leadership.[122] The Myasoyedov Affair – and people from all parts of the political spectrum were convinced of his guilt – unleashed a deluge of conspiracy theories which proved a helpful propaganda asset. Right-wingers emphasized that Myasoyedov was married to a Jewish woman and had business connections with Jewish entrepreneurs, while left-wingers pointed to the officer's past in the police. Kerensky successfully exploited the Myasoyedov Affair to denounce 'treason at the highest levels'. As a deputy, he wrote to the chairman of the Duma, Mikhail Rodzyanko, demanding the immediate reconvening of the Duma. Without providing any evidence, Kerensky wrote that 'treason has built its nest' in the Interior Ministry, where, he alleged, 'a robust organization of full-blown traitors were calmly and confidently at work.' These forces, he declared, were attempting to 'stymie a successful conclusion of the conflict abroad in the interests of the enemy.' Kerensky was not making the accusation against a particular group of top officials in the ministry but denouncing this extremely powerful ministry as a whole. 'The leading circles of the Interior Ministry are in very close touch with a highly influential political tendency in Russia which considers it a matter of the utmost urgency to restore swiftly a close unity with the government in Berlin.' To save the country was the duty of those elected by the people. 'The State Duma must do everything to defend the nation from a shameful stab in the back.'[123] Kerensky's letter gained widespread distribution, with some people writing it out in full in their diaries. According to the police, the letter was the subject of lively debate in politically engaged student circles, leaflets with the text were distributed at Petrograd University, and left-wing student groups – social democrats and internationalist Socialist Revolutionaries – tried to use it as anti-war propaganda.[124] Even the Bolsheviks published it.[125] It was distributed in Moscow, Kharkov, Kiev, Kronshtadt and at the front, and it was also translated into Estonian.[126]

The climate of increasing spymania and xenophobia during the war caused competing conspiracy theories to spring up. Almost all the political parties made use of Germanophobia for their own purposes, although right-wing theories were tinged with anti-Semitism and Anglophobia. The opposition talked ever more insistently about a 'German party' at court who were angling for a separate peace, and rumours spread about the 'empress's plot'.[127] After the revolution, the most far-out conspiracy theories had conferred on them the status of proven fact, and those who had come up with them and spread them assumed the reputation of courageous patriots who had exposed the treacheries of the old regime. Hatred of the police force, which was abolished after the February Revolution, contributed, in the light of Kerensky's 'exposure' of the would-be conspiracy at the Interior Ministry, to further increasing the popularity of the revolutionary minister.

Creating his own version of a 'stab in the back of the Russian army', Kerensky discredited the conspiracy theories of his adversaries. During the war, right-wing politicians and high-ranking military officers spread rumours that, at the front line, practically the entire Jewish population was spying for the enemy and, in the Jewish shtetl of Kuzhi, Jews allegedly even opened fire on Russian troops. Kerensky travelled to Kuzhi and conducted an investigation, on the basis of which in the Duma he called the accusation a vile slander.[128] One of his 1917 biographers also writes about the Kuzhi investigation.[129] A reputation as a defender of national minorities was a considerable asset after February 1917.

During the revolution, journalists supportive of Kerensky recalled another earlier episode. In 1916 many residents of Kazakhstan and Central Asia were conscripted to work in the rear, following which there was an uprising accompanied by bloody ethnic conflicts. It was brutally suppressed by Russian troops. Kerensky, having lived in Tashkent in his youth, and feeling himself a 'Turkestani', took these events very much to heart and, together with Duma deputies representing the empire's Muslim population, travelled to Turkestan.[130] On his return to the capital, he talked about his trip at a closed session of Duma deputies. Giving his interpretation of this complex conflict, he ascribed all the region's ills to the foolish actions of the tsarist administration. There was, in fact, no denying the incompetence of the government, and after February 1917 Kerensky's version of events was just what people wanted to hear. The old regime got the blame for everything that had gone wrong. His expedition to Turkestan enhanced Kerensky's standing with the Muslim intelligentsia, and this was manifested in 1917 when the Central Bureau of Russian Muslims and the Muslim Committee in Moscow gave him a rousing welcome.[131]

Leonidov, in his biographical sketch, even insists that it was thanks to Kerensky's decisive actions that the situation in the region had not deteriorated further in 1916. 'When these regrettable events were playing out, Kerensky had yet to recover from a serious operation. Straight out of bed, still unwell, in defiance of all the prohibitions of his doctors, he set off to try to persuade General Kuropatkin that he should not turn the formerly loyal peoples of Turkestan into rebels and not allow Russia, which was engaged in fighting a foreign enemy, to trample this peaceful outlying region underfoot.'[132]

The mention of illness needs elaboration. Doctors discovered Kerensky was suffering from renal tuberculosis, and he had a kidney removed on 16

March 1916 in a clinic in the Finnish resort of Bad Grankulla. For several months his ability to work was severely impaired, and even in early 1917 many people noticed he was looking very unwell. He received numerous letters and telegrams wishing him a speedy recovery.[133] Journalists and writers did their best to give him support. These included the economist Ber Brutskus, the publisher and political activist Yakov Sakker, the poet Sergey Yesenin, the writer Alexey Chapygin and the essayist Dmitry Filosofov. Among those urging him to get well soon was his biographer Lidiya Armand. Collective letters from groups of students give a sense of the reputation Kerensky enjoyed among radically inclined young people. An open meeting of students at Moscow University sent greetings to their 'greatly esteemed comrade' and expressed the hope that they would soon be able to hear the 'ardent words of a true representative of Russian democracy'. Participants in an open meeting of students of the Psychoneurological Institute sent congratulations on the occasion of his recovery to the 'courageous tribune of the people' and also hoped they would soon again hear the 'strong, ardent words of the deputy who defends the cherished aspirations of Russian democracy.' Kerensky was sent good wishes also by the Social Democratic bloc in the Duma, the Jewish Democratic group, and the Trudovik fraction.[134] Many of those who sent good wishes after his operation went on to support Kerensky politically in 1917 after he had become a minister. It was testimony not only to Kerensky's authority but also to the emotional ties between the Leader and his supporters. This sympathy for Kerensky when he was ill, as we shall see, also influenced the formation of images of the Leader during the revolution.

Returning to the matter of how well informed Kerensky was, we should mention that he also knew of plans for a *coup d'état* which were being made in political and military circles. He later recalled: 'We too, the leaders of the Masonic organization, knew of the conspiracy and, although unaware of all the details, also prepared for the decisive moment.' Kerensky was himself present at some of the conspirators' meetings. On one occasion he had a visit from officers intent on arresting the tsar who wanted to enlist his support.[135] The fact that various groups involved in complicated political intrigues wanted to involve Kerensky is testimony to his reputation and influence. Later Kerensky himself admitted he had been hoping for a coup as early as 1915.[136] These episodes, however, did not feature prominently in efforts to boost his reputation in 1917.

We find Kerensky under consideration for possible inclusion in a new government in the event of a change of regime.[137] Rumours to that effect circulated widely, and it is noteworthy that even Lenin in Switzerland was writing in early 1917 about the possibility of a government being established in Russia by Milyukov and Guchkov or by Milyukov and Kerensky.[138] Kerensky's growing authority was even more evident to the political elite of Petrograd.

By the beginning of 1917 Kerensky was in a unique situation. His social position, his personal qualities and the resources he had at his disposal made him welcome in highly diverse political circles whose representatives rarely had any contact with each other. Kerensky was both a parliamentarian and a lawyer; he associated with Freemasons and the political underground. His status as a member of the Duma, his parliamentary immunity, his knowledgeability and his fame enabled him to render effective assistance, without undue personal risk, to those in the underground. His position as someone with access to the world of the illegals made him interesting and respected by politicians who confined themselves to legal activities. In different ways and for different groups he was the mouthpiece of public opinion, a source of influence, a moral authority and a well-informed expert. The peculiarities of the political system which had developed in 1905–7 and during the war made it possible for Kerensky to act in such diverse roles at the same time, but only someone endowed with exceptional personal and professional qualities could have taken advantage of these opportunities.

Kerensky was at the centre of diverse political coalitions which united some who supported preservation of the empire and federalists; opponents of the war and defencists; and various kinds of monarchists and republicans of many hues. It is tempting to explain this as having been achieved through Masonic connections, but it needs to be said that such an 'explanation' is no more than an intellectual skeleton key. Conspiracy theories can be used to explain any social occurrence, but their cognitive value is minimal. It is more useful to observe here that Kerensky was greatly assisted simply by his non-partisan, non-factional status. He was not signed up to any party programme, and his non-partisanship was most dramatically evident in his attitude to the war. At different times and in different companies he expressed different views, and this cannot always be explained away as political mimicry. As a politician, he was striving – sometimes perhaps instinctively – to create a broad, flexible ideological framework conducive to achieving his unwavering goal of a revolution during the war. For some of Kerensky's negotiating partners this was revolution in order to continue successful prosecution of the war; for others it was in order to bring the war to an end. It was not only Kerensky who engaged in forming such associations, but his role was highly noticeable. This practice at creating coalitions out of such ill-assorted constituents was of great value to Kerensky during the revolution in his negotiations with representatives of very diverse elites.

Kerensky's experience as a defence barrister in political trials and as a radical deputy in the State Duma was important for creating his public persona and for consolidating his authority as a tribune of the people and fighter for workers' rights, as well as for his position as a champion of the law, a defender of national minorities, and a representative of the radical intelligentsia in the realm of big politics. All these facets of Kerensky's image came into play at the time of the February Revolution.

4 'Hero of the revolution'

In the first issues of the Petrograd newspapers produced after the overthrow of the monarchy, a greeting to Kerensky was published from the Socialist Revolutionaries: 'The Conference of Petrograd Socialist Revolutionaries sends greetings to you, Alexander Fyodorovich, as a steadfast, tireless fighter for a government of the people, a Leader of the revolutionary people who has joined the Provisional Government to defend the rights and freedom of the toiling masses.'[139]

The authors of the address approved of Kerensky's becoming a member of the government and, unlike most of the leaders of the Petrograd Soviet, gave him a mandate to join it. Such trust stemmed from his personal prestige based on his reputation as a steadfast and tireless fighter, and he was singled out from other fighters as a 'Leader of the revolutionary people'. The awarding of such a title was a considerable rarity at that time and resulted from the great appreciation of Kerensky's role in the February Revolution. The first legally convened forum of a party which was to play a major role in subsequent events proclaimed him a revolutionary Leader, substantially enhancing his status in the eyes of all the Socialist Revolutionaries' supporters.

The speeches Kerensky delivered on the eve of the revolution were of great importance for his image as a steadfast fighter and leader, and were much quoted. In retrospect the speeches were perceived as bold and accurate prophecies. Journalists favourably inclined towards him wrote of the Leader's inspired and accurate predictions and of the sense of the impending revolutionary storm which his speeches had conveyed.

Different writers used similar words.[140] The gift of 'foresight', even of 'clairvoyance', which journalists attributed to Kerensky marked him out as a unique Leader. One speech, banned by the tsarist censorship, was published during the revolution under the title 'The prophetic words of A. F. Kerensky, pronounced on 19 July 1915 in the State Duma'.[141] The foreword to another edition of his speeches declared: 'We can see that his last speeches in the Duma were prophetic, and that the first socialist minister of free Russia showed himself to be one of our most far-sighted statesmen.' His prophetic speeches were evidence that the minister was endowed with the 'ardent heart of a revolutionary patriot and the sage foresight of a statesman' – small wonder that Kerensky's political allies published them after the February Revolution. His allies drew the attention of readers to the exclamations and remarks of the Duma's chairman, Mikhail Rodzyanko, and of other liberal deputies who formed the Provisional Government, in which these moderate politicians interrupted the speeches of the 'revolutionary deputy' as he foretold the destruction of tsarism.[142] Readers were given to understand that, in the Duma, Kerensky alone had possessed the gift of political foresight and the fortitude of a revolutionary. Accordingly, his was a special place in the government.

The selection of texts for publication is also instructive, with Kerensky's speeches of late 1916 and early 1917 much republished and talked about. The opposition's attack on the regime had intensified in the autumn. On 1 November a famous speech by the leader of the Constitutional Democrats, Milyukov, with its refrain of 'stupidity or treason?', had resounded in the State Duma. This sensational speech eclipsed an even more radical speech by Kerensky, who that same day attacked the government so vehemently that the chairman deprived him of the floor. Not, however, before he had managed to brand the tsar's ministers 'traitors to the country's interests' and effectively called for overthrow of the government.

Three days later Kerensky went even further, declaring that the state had been taken over 'by an enemy power' and a regime of occupation installed. This time it was the head of state himself who was accused of treason: 'Ties of family and kinship take priority over the interests of the state. . . . The interests of the old regime are closer to people living abroad than to those inside Russia.' Kerensky called for destruction of the regime, 'this dreadful ulcer of the state'. On 16 December he repeated that compromise with the government was impossible and called on liberals to take decisive action; a professional lawyer, he argued that, under the circumstances, the duty of a citizen was not to obey the law. For that he was deprived of the floor. A speech he made on 15 February became particularly famous: Kerensky denounced 'state anarchy' and demanded 'surgical methods', calling for the physical removal of 'violators of the law'. The orator declared that he shared the views of the party 'which has openly inscribed on its banner the possibility of terror, the possibility of armed struggle with those representing the government, the party which has openly acknowledged the necessity of tyrannicides.' In the forum of the Duma he acknowledged his support of the terrorist tactics of the illegal Socialist Revolutionary Party. He excoriated a 'system of unaccountable despotism' and demanded the destruction of a 'medieval regime'. Responding to the chairman's remark that such language was inadmissible, Kerensky went even further and made absolutely clear that he was 'talking about what the citizen Brutus did in classical times.' This was perceived as a public call for regicide. Kerensky's friends were sure that after such statements he would be arrested, and they expressed their sympathy in advance. He himself did not believe that parliamentary immunity would save him and told friends that, if the Duma was dissolved, he would be arrested.[143] It was a mood which may have influenced how Kerensky behaved in February 1917: he had burned his bridges, and only a swift replacement of the regime could keep him out of prison.

Kiriakov called his speech on 15 February 'his first historic and by now manifestly revolutionary speech'.[144] He was referring to the exceptional role Kerensky was to play in the coup. On the very eve of the February Revolution, Kerensky was receiving letters asking him for the text of his speeches which had been banned by the censorship, but of which thousands of typewritten and handwritten copies were disseminated throughout Russia. The speeches were distributed also in the form of leaflets, with many copies reaching the army. The Duma's right-wingers expostulated that Kerensky was 'Wilhelm's aide'. Kerensky's speeches did not go unnoticed in the imperial residence either: in a letter from the empress to the tsar, dated 24 February, she expresses a characteristic wish: 'I hope that Duma man Kedrinsky [she means Kerensky] will be hung for his horrible speeches – it is necessary (wartime law) and it will be an example.'[145] However, some members of even the highest levels of society were not unappreciative of the speech: 'Today ... Kerensky said much that was true, and we all think as he does about many things,' Rodzyanko's wife remarked in a letter to – Princess Zinaida Yusupova.[146]

Kerensky was the best-known and most gifted orator of the left, constantly transgressing the limits of what was permissible. For the radical intelligentsia, he was 'their man in the Duma'. To many people in Petrograd his face would have been familiar because his portraits were printed in a variety of publications. In a time of crisis, to be recognizable is a political asset. The banning of his Duma speeches only added to his renown, and he found himself hailed as 'the most popular person' in town.[147] Many people had no doubt that, in the coming crisis, Kerensky was destined to be centre stage. Indeed, at that time of unrest a number of deputations came to see him and demand that he 'seize power'. The same demand was made in letters to him.[148] There is nothing surprising about the fact that delegates from the Putilov factory came to Kerensky on 22 February (another group went to Nikolai Chkheidze, the leader of the Social Democratic group). They warned the 'citizen deputy' that the strike and lockout at their huge factory might have serious political consequences.[149]

The following day Kerensky made the statement of the Putilov workers known in the State Duma, stressing how moderate their demands were. A Duma resolution was amended to include the demand 'that all dismissed workers of the Putilov factory should be reinstated and operation of the plant immediately resumed.'[150] The resolution had no practical impact because the revolution had already begun that day, but the strikers may have felt heartened that the Duma's demands and the speeches of the opposition deputies showed support for their actions. More and more enterprises went on strike, and the strikers headed for the city centre. Mobs ransacked food stores and political rallies began.

Kerensky's speeches now stood him in good stead. His supporters wrote that, 'long before the revolution, he had said in the Duma that a revolution was the only way of saving Russia from a state of anarchy which was being fomented from the throne. It was Kerensky who prompted the Russian Revolution to take the final step.'[151]

Kerensky's subsequent influence was to be due largely to the decisive and effective action he took during the February Revolution. Already on 25 February, at what was to prove the last meeting of the State Duma, he called upon it to lead the movement and create a new government. In the evening, he made a speech at the Petrograd City Duma, protesting at the shooting of demonstrators and demanding establishment of 'a responsible ministry'. He rejected compromise with the government. During these days Kerensky was present at a number of meetings with clandestine groups. One such was held on the evening of 26 February in his own apartment, to which he had invited activists of the socialist groups. Kerensky was to recall that he participated in setting up an information bureau to coordinate the actions of the socialist groups: the Trudoviks, Mensheviks, Bolsheviks, Interdistrict activists, Socialist Revolutionaries and People's Socialists. Those assembled were unable, however, to come to any agreement because the rifts between them were just too great, but at least the exchange of views and the move to coordinate the protest movement was a big step forward.[152] Even on that day Kerensky seems himself to have been unaware that the revolution had begun.[153]

Kerensky tried unsuccessfully to persuade Rodzyanko to convene an official session of the Duma on 27 February. He and his allies wanted the Duma to take a tougher line, but the chairman was not to be persuaded: the official meeting was scheduled for 28 February. At an informal meeting of the Council of Elders in Rodzyanko's office, however, it was agreed to hold a closed meeting of the Duma on 27 February at two in the afternoon.[154]

Maintaining contact with the revolutionary underground, Kerensky was receiving information from illegal circles, and this bolstered his status in the eyes of his Duma colleagues who were desperate for up-to-the-minute intelligence on the popular movement. (He went out of his way on 27 February to show them how well informed he was, and may even have exaggerated.)

Kerensky's role in those days at the end of February became a topic for the rumour mill. It was said that he and Chkheidze, hearing of unrest in the Reserve Battalion of the Volhynia Guards Regiment, had gone there on 26 February and fired up the soldiers, and that this had brought about the regiment's mutiny the following day.[155] In reality, Kerensky learned of the rebellion of the Volhynians early on 27 February.[156] At about eight o'clock that morning Duma deputy Nikolai Nekrasov, a left-wing Constitutional Democrat and prominent Freemason, phoned him at home to say the Volhynians had mutinied and that the State Duma had been prorogued by royal decree. Kerensky hastened round to Nikolai Sokolov, who also lived near the Duma. After a brief conference with him and Alexander Galpern, he made for the Duma.[157] Kerensky and other radical deputies tried to have the Duma continue in official session in defiance of the tsar's decree and also urged that contact should be established between the Duma and the insurgents filling the streets of Petrograd.[158]

At the Tauride Palace, Kerensky found himself the centre of attention. He was both the best known of the left-wing deputies and the most left-wing of the deputies who were well known. His name was familiar to anyone who took an interest in politics, and the sociable and energetic Kerensky had already met a good number of the capital's citizens.

Accordingly, it is unsurprising that many activists who made for the Tauride Palace wanted to see Kerensky and were expecting him to tell them what to do next. Spontaneously arising groups of insurgents, breakaway groups from units of the armed forces and individual activists battled their way through to him from all over the city. Already in the morning many people who knew Kerensky had been coming to the Duma bringing him information, and they conveyed the mood of the revolutionary crowds in the streets. Kerensky's position straddling the boundary between legal and illegal politics was crucially important in those days, not least because illegals, members of the underground opposition, were not individually known to the masses (and some were in no hurry to take the risk of coming out into the open). The position he came to occupy, however, was very much dependent on Kerensky himself and the feverish activity on which he now embarked. He phoned round political friends, demanding they should go to the barracks and get insurgent troops sent to the Duma. Other politicians were doing the same, but Kerensky was outstanding. Every ten or fifteen minutes he was receiving up-to-the-moment information on the situation in different parts of the city by telephone. Duma deputies approached Kerensky to hear the latest news about action on the streets from the leader of the left. Rather anticipating developments, he assured them that the insurgents were on their way to the Tauride Palace. Many deputies were alarmed by this, but Kerensky insisted that the revolution was already in progress and that the Duma should welcome the mutineers and support and lead the popular movement. Time passed, however, and the troops Kerensky had 'promised' were nowhere to be seen. Anxious deputies asked him, 'Where are your troops?' He was already being seen not only as the best-informed member of the Duma but also as the representative of an illegal centre of insurgents, if not their leader.[159]

Kerensky and the radical members of the Duma were demanding that a meeting of the Council of Elders, scheduled for twelve noon, should be brought forward, but Rodzyanko refused. At this a group of deputies arbitrarily convened a closed session of the council. Kerensky and several others demanded that the Duma should take power into its own hands, but not all those in attendance could support this. Rodzyanko protested against this meeting which he had not sanctioned but then convened an official meeting of leaders of the Duma groups in his office. Speaking on behalf of the Trudoviks, Social Democrats and Progressists, Kerensky again called for the tsar's decree proroguing the Duma to be disregarded. This proposal openly to defy the monarch was rejected, opposed not only by Rodzyanko but also by Milyukov. The liberals were not prepared for this level of confrontation with the government. It was decided, nevertheless, that the Duma would not disperse, and the deputies were urged to remain where they were and, as planned, convene in the Semi-Circular Hall for an 'unofficial' meeting of such members of the chamber as were present. The choice of venue indicated that the Duma was not formally violating the tsar's decree that it should dissolve, because official meetings were traditionally held in the Great Hall.[160]

Kerensky's Odessan biographer exaggerates the importance of his speech. 'After Kerensky's fiery speech, the deputies decided not to disperse, but to remain where they were.'[161] The journalist Vasiliy Vodovozov, who was on friendly terms with Kerensky, even claimed that to him belonged 'the merit of the initiative for a session of the State Duma, in defiance of the tsar's command that it should be prorogued.'[162] Kerensky later wrote the same thing himself, but in fact, as we have said, the private meeting had already been scheduled and was not a reaction to the tsar's subsequent decree.[163]

By one in the afternoon, groups of excited soldiers finally began to arrive at the Tauride Palace. One group introduced itself as representing the rebels, who wanted to know what the Duma's position was.[164] The appearance of insurgents at the parliament building had a considerable impact on wavering deputies and strengthened the hand of Kerensky, who demanded decisive action from the Duma deputies.

At 2:30 pm the closed meeting of Duma members began. Vladimir Zenzinov recalled that Kerensky 'technically' convened it himself, wantonly pressing the bell to summon the deputies. There may have been nothing technical about it: the bell was an invitation to the deputies to convene in the Great Hall, and Kerensky was attempting to call the deputies for an official rather than a closed meeting. Certainly that was how some of the deputies interpreted his act. Rodzyanko ordered the bell to be switched off, and a closed meeting assembled, as scheduled, in the Semi-Circular Hall. At 2:57 Kerensky appeared in the hall and expressed a desire to go out to the rebels and announce the Duma's support for the movement of the people. He asked the meeting to grant him the necessary authority. His proposal did not meet with enthusiasm from a majority of the deputies, who were wary of revolutionaries. Some of the liberals suspected the uprising had been instigated by pro-German interests. Under the pressure of events, however, the Duma had little option but to shift to the left. No doubt the spread of the uprising would have forced the Duma deputies to become more radical, but the impact of Kerensky's decisiveness cannot be disregarded. He harassed his Duma colleagues, encouraged them to adopt a radical stance, and was not averse to confronting them with a fait accompli. Kerensky and other left-wing deputies went out to the crowd, gave speeches, issued instructions, and returned to the meeting, urging their colleagues now to undertake positive action.[165] This course of action accorded both with Kerensky's views and with his temperament, given as he was to romanticizing and idealizing the revolutionary movement. It is also a fact that Kerensky reacted to the emotions of a crowd. He was infected by the elation of the rebellious people constantly arriving at the Duma.

A detachment of mutinous troops approached the Tauride Palace, there was a clash with the Duma sentries and the commander of the guard was wounded.[166] This greatly agitated the deputies. Kerensky rushed out and welcomed the mutineers, thereby setting a precedent for speeches by Duma deputies to newly arriving soldiers becoming something of a ritual. The Social Democratic deputies Skobelev and Chkheidze also addressed the rebels, but it was the leader of the Trudoviks who was unquestionably the more lively and trenchant. 'The Social Democrats were very reserved: Kerensky had a more authoritative tone,' recalled Alexander Polyakov, a journalist. It is no surprise that contemporaries often remembered only speeches by Kerensky.[167]

Even conservative publications wrote enthusiastically about Kerensky's doings in the early days of the revolution. *Novoye vremya* [New Time] reported:

> In the Tauride Palace the deputies were in a state of shock. The Council of Elders had a meeting, not knowing what to do. The order proroguing the Duma was read out. They decided not to disperse, but had not the courage to declare themselves the new government immediately. Even the left-wingers were perplexed, and it was only when someone shouted, 'A crowd! Soldiers!', that Kerensky, not stopping to get a coat or hat, ran out to Shpalernaya Street to greet them.
>
> 'We are with you. We thank you for coming, and promise to go forward with the people.'
>
> The crowd raised Kerensky shoulder-high and tossed him up and down.[168]

The report is not wholly accurate, but it is noteworthy that the reporter made Kerensky the main protagonist. Nearly all Kerensky's biographers write about his speech to the insurgent soldiers,[169] and it became a central plank of his claim to be regarded as the Leader of the revolution.

Kerensky urged the rebels to enter the Tauride Palace, replace the old guards and protect the Duma. He gave orders on where to place sentries. The Duma telegraph and entrances to the palace were occupied by soldiers. The invasion of the palace by an armed crowd changed the deputies' mood, strengthening the position of the left wing and demoralizing the conservatively minded. The new atmosphere was something of which Kerensky was better placed to take advantage than others. These were bold and dangerous acts: by placing himself at the head of mutinous soldiers he was openly declaring himself the leader of an armed uprising. From the point of view of law-abiding subjects of the tsar, he was a rebel, but by his decisive actions he acquired, in the eyes of the insurgents, the status of a revolutionary leader. In particular, his authority with the soldiers was greatly enhanced. In March an influential journalist was entirely justified in calling Kerensky 'one of the most prominent leaders of the mutinous army'.[170]

Kerensky himself subsequently made use of the episode. 'I led the first contingent of revolutionary troops into the Tauride Palace and set up a token guard,' he told a meeting of the soldiers' section of the Petrograd Soviet on 26 March, when his actions were criticized by leaders of the Soviet.[171] This line of argument enabled Kerensky to maintain his standing with the main body of deputies. The entry of troops into the building of the State Duma was one of the most important moments in the history of the February Revolution. In 1917 there were differing accounts of what exactly happened, but all the authors agreed that Kerensky had played a major role, which they often exaggerated. For example, a Nizhny Novgorod newspaper wrote:

> A company of some regiment or other with an officer happened to be passing the Tauride Palace. . . . Suddenly Kerensky appears in the driveway and shouts, 'Soldiers, the State Duma is with you!'
>
> With a fiery speech he gains the support of the company and its officer, and a minute later Kerensky utters in the parliamentary chamber the call everyone has so desperately been waiting for in those hours of indecision: 'Members of the State Duma, the soldiers are with us! Here they are!'
>
> A moment later Kerensky delegated a squad of soldiers to arrest Minister Shcheglovitov and bring him to the Tauride Palace, and a moment after that the Volhynia Regiment knew what it had to do and where it needed to go.
>
> That was the beginning of everything.
>
> Whether it is fact or legend, there is good reason why this formula of a fusion of the democratic 'idea' (the Duma) with the democratic 'matter' (the soldiers) was arrived at by Kerensky. It is the formula which resolved the whole 'problem' of the revolution.[172]

According to other accounts, Kerensky was entirely ready to win the army over to the revolution. His Odessan biographer writes: 'Twenty-five thousand armed soldiers were marching towards the Tauride Palace. To what end? Was it in order, at the command of the tsar, to raze to the ground this hotbed of sedition? Or was it to bring tidings of the liberation of the people and emancipation of the army? It seemed there was no one to give an answer. It was approaching, with the tramp of soldiers' boots and of horse-drawn artillery.' It was at this critical moment, when, according to the author, 'chilling doubt' assailed the deputies' hearts, that 'a thin little man, as pale as death and without a hat in the bitter cold', leaped forth to greet the troops. The revolution was about to win. 'That little lawyer from Saratov had no way of knowing what he would face on the porch: a red flag or the bayonets of tsarist soldiers. With heroic self-sacrifice he detonated the revolution, and to this day bears that heavy cross.'[173] This factually inaccurate version of events is of interest because Kerensky is presented as the saviour of the revolution, heading off a planned punitive campaign.

Kerensky's leading of the mutinous soldiers into the Duma was exploited by his supporters also to back his claim to the post of minister of war in May 1917. 'Kerensky was the first to take command of the revolutionary army when its regiments arrived at the Tauride Palace.'[174]

For many contemporaries, this was the act which accorded Kerensky the status of Leader of the revolution. An address from the sailors on the Baltic cruiser *Rossiya*, adopted after the April Crisis[175] but before 5 May 1917, read:

> Did anyone see even a single *burzhui* [bourgeois] on the revolutionary streets? The whole lot of them, Milyukov, Guchkov, except Comrade Kerensky, all hid themselves away. When, arising, the revolutionary people came to the Tauride Palace and asked to be given a leader, only Comrade Kerensky agreed to be it and lead them who were asking for bread and freedom, but all the rest of the ministers of the present Provisional Government could do was take their portfolios in their hands stained with the blood of our brothers, champions of freedom.[176]

It tells us something about those times that this text, composed by grassroots activists, was sent to *Soldatskaya pravda* and that this newspaper of the Military Organization of the Bolsheviks published it, even though by that time Bolshevik propaganda was already attacking Kerensky, the new minister of war. Even to some Bolshevik supporters Kerensky was still a hero of the revolution, whom they contrasted with the 'bourgeois' ministers.

On 27–8 February Kerensky several times made speeches to soldiers. His biographers have latched on to these events to sculpt an image of him as the leader of an armed uprising. 'When revolutionary regiments began appearing at the State Duma, it was invariably Kerensky who met them. His speeches were brief and powerful and kept up the morale of the revolutionary troops, guiding them towards the only path which could lead them to freedom.'[177]

In those days there were, of course, other Duma deputies delivering speeches to the rebels, but we note that it is Kerensky whom his biographers depict as the Leader with the gift of defining the truly correct path to freedom.

Shortly after the troops entered the Tauride Palace, Kerensky addressed a crowd gathered in the Catherine Hall. His audience was demanding that the leaders of the old regime should be punished. It was the struggle with the internal enemy they saw as the most urgent task. Kerensky called for arrests but demanded that there should be no extrajudicial executions. The crowd wanted names and was thirsting for immediate action. Kerensky ordered that the hated 'public enemy' Ivan Shcheglovitov, formerly the minister of justice and later chairman of the State Council, should be brought to him.[178] It is interesting that the chairman of the upper chamber rather than any representative of the executive branch was named as the first candidate for arrest. That choice by their new Leader was approved by his listeners, although, from a tactical point of view, it would have seemed more logical in the struggle for power to capture the leaders of the army and police force. This testifies to the role of snap decisions in how the revolution developed.

At this time Kerensky and his comrades were busy organizing the insurgent forces. Present-day researchers write about the creation of a Kerensky General Headquarters, a body which tried to secure the Duma, to draw troops over to the side of the uprising, to arm the rebels and to occupy strategic institutions. That evening a military commission was created, with Kerensky's group at its core. The Trudovik leader was himself on the commission, and several of its orders are over his signature.[179]

At about 3:00 pm on 27 February, the socialists came to Rodzyanko and Kerensky, seeking accommodation in the Tauride Palace for the emergent Soviet of Workers' Deputies. With Rodzyanko's permission they were allocated the hall of the budget commission and the adjacent office of its chairman. A provisional executive committee was created, which took the initiative of convening the Soviet, and at about the same time Kerensky and Chkheidze authorized the issue of *Izvestiya Komiteta zhurnalistov* [News of the Journalists' Committee]; this newspaper became a crucial source of information for the residents of Petrograd.[180]

When students with drawn swords delivered Shcheglovitov to the Duma, Kerensky arrested him 'in the name of the people', brushing aside Rodzyanko's attempt to treat the chairman of the upper chamber as a 'guest'.[181] This outcome reflected a shift in the balance of power in the Tauride Palace: the authority of the Trudovik leader had greatly increased, and the chairman of the Duma had no option but to acknowledge the fact. Rumours that Kerensky had arrested Shcheglovitov and personally locked him up spread throughout the city. The arrest was a key moment in the myth of the revolution and influenced perception of Kerensky as the real Leader of the coup.

Vladimir Zenzinov, a prominent Socialist Revolutionary, wrote in the first issue of the party's newspaper: 'A. F. Kerensky refused to release Shcheglovitov from the Duma, locked him up in the ministerial pavilion, and obliged those present to take the path of revolution. This moment was one of the turning points of the movement.' Zenzinov returned to this episode in his memoirs, noting that it had been one of the important 'gestures' which determined the course of the revolution.[182] Kerensky's supporters often made mention of the arrest of Shcheglovitov after the February Days, sometimes presenting it not as a spur-of-the-moment act but as a prudently and meticulously prepared blow devised by the Leader of the revolution to crush the old regime. It was claimed that Kerensky had had a list of people to be arrested.[183] Some of his biographers see the arrests he ordered as enabling him to uncover conspiracies against the people's revolution on the part of servants of the old regime. It is said that his skilful questioning of them helped him win the battle against 'enemies of Russia' and carry the coup forward to a successful conclusion.

Kerensky also managed, however, to prevent summary justice being meted out to those who had been arrested and brought to the Tauride Palace. This also strengthened his authority. Some contemporaries saw it as a demonstration of the power he wielded, while others saw it as proving, more importantly, that the young Duma deputy was humane and opposed to rough justice.

Meanwhile, a closed meeting of State Duma deputies elected from its midst a Provisional Committee of the State Duma to restore order in the capital and communicate with individuals and institutions. The committee was charged with monitoring how the situation was developing and with taking appropriate measures, up to and including assuming full executive power. Rodzyanko was appointed chairman and Kerensky was included as a member. The committee tacitly endorsed Kerensky's action in arresting the tsar's top officials and confirmed his authority.[184]

On the evening of 27 February, at the first meeting of the Petrograd Soviet of Workers' Deputies, Kerensky was nominated by the Socialist Revolutionaries and elected to the Executive Committee of the Soviet, then appointed vice chairman of the Soviet. He was absent from the meeting and learned of his appointments only later.[185] He was also absent from the first meeting of the Executive Committee.

A majority of those setting up the Soviet, activists of the socialist parties, were wary of this dynamic politician but, in appointing an influential Duma deputy to the post of vice chairman, evidently felt they were consolidating their own positions. (The setting up of the Soviet itself had come about with Kerensky's help.)[186]

His bold speeches to the mutinous soldiers, his personal contact with the centres of the protest movement and, finally, his arresting of the tsar's ministers all gave Kerensky exceptional popularity. Of the protagonists known to the general public, only he had acted so decisively and brilliantly. 'He was the only person who flung himself with total abandon and confidence into the chaos of the popular movement. Only he had every right to talk to the soldiers as "we" and believed that the masses wanted exactly what was historically necessary at that moment,' recalled the Trudovik Vladimir Stankevich. The unique role played by Kerensky was acknowledged by the Social Democrat Nikolai Sukhanov, who was later to become a harsh critic. 'The indispensable Kerensky of the last gasp of tsarism; Kerensky the monopolist of those days of February and March'. Some conservative members of the Duma perceived him, indeed, as a revolutionary dictator.[187]

Kerensky's wife had her own perspective on the feverish pace of his actions during the February Days. 'Those first days he never left the Duma, working day and night, and only when they had worked themselves to a standstill did he and other deputies force themselves to take a short nap, collapsing where they were, on the sofas and chairs in the offices of the Duma.' At times those close to him literally forced him to drink a cup of coffee or a glass of brandy. The journalist Alexander Polyakov recalled, 'On the steps of a small staircase leading to the journalists' box, A. F. Kerensky was sprawled, completely exhausted, and his wife was spooning egg yolks she had brought in a tumbler from home into his mouth.' At times the deputy seemed only semi-conscious, which mesmerized the agitated crowd. Kerensky was to recall rather nostalgically that state of extreme stress. For him, the February Days remained the most important and 'real' period in his life. 'It's worth living to have felt such ecstasy,' he explained.[188]

He was sometimes depicted later as a bloodthirsty mutineer, but those assertions appeared in the press only in the autumn. For example, Vladimir Purishkevich's newspaper claimed in October that Kerensky had done nothing during the uprising to prevent officers from being beaten and humiliated.[189] In the first months of the revolution, however, Kerensky's role was described only in positive terms and confirmed his status as Leader. It is perhaps only to be expected that his biographers saw the success of the coup as being due to Kerensky's actions, but his contribution was rated highly in political resolutions adopted at the time. If journalists supportive of him exaggerated his role, so did many rank-and-file participants in the events. For example, Nikolai Kishkin, the Provisional Government's commissar in Moscow, declared in early March, 'I can testify that, but for Kerensky, we could never have achieved as much as we have. His name will be inscribed in letters of gold in the annals of history.'[190]

Kerensky's reputation as the revolution's champion was central to creating his image of 'the Leader of the people'. When Kerensky was seeking to bolster his authority, he frequently harked back in his speeches to those days. His supporters, defending their Leader's decisions and deflecting attacks on him, also referred back to the exceptional role he had played in 'the February Days'.

Kerensky's 1917 biographies dwell particularly on that period, usually bringing in his 'prophetic' speeches and his arresting of representatives of the old regime, while his actions leading to the entry of the mutinous troops into the Duma are seen as uniquely endorsing him as the best politician to stand at the head of the revolution.

5 'Champion of freedom' and the cult of champions of freedom

In 1917 many people were calling Kerensky a champion of freedom. For example, on 26 July 1917, representatives of the Kuzhenkino garrison passed a resolution that

> . . . all elements of the country who love their motherland must rally round the Provisional Government, giving it their full support and

> confidence, in the hope that the coalition government, under the leadership of such a proven champion of freedom for working people as everybody's favourite politician, our comrade KERENSKY, will devote all its energy to defending the motherland and revolution from the insolent attempts to encroach of both the foreign enemy and enemies of the revolution both on the right and the left.[191]

Those drafting the resolution adopted a tactic of legitimation which can be found in other texts of the time: a political Leader deserves support because he has been tested by years of fighting for the freedom of the people; his irreproachable revolutionary reputation is a guarantee that he will faithfully implement the political programme of the government he heads.

Kerensky's actions in earlier years, and especially during the coup, contributed to establishing just such a reputation, and it comes as no surprise that in many of these greetings he is described as a 'champion of freedom'. The conference of the Petrograd Socialist Revolutionaries in early March had described him as a 'steadfast, tireless champion of a government of the people'.[192] 'We send heartfelt greetings to a champion of freedom. May heaven bless your future great achievements,' political exiles encouraged him.[193] It mattered that veterans of the revolutionary struggle were using such language about him, particularly impressing the masses who were now in the process of becoming politicized.

National organizations called Kerensky 'a magnificent champion of freedom for Russia and its nationalities'. Those composing other resolutions hailed him as 'a champion of social liberation'. Kerensky was called 'a champion of the freedom of the working people', 'a proven champion of the happiness and freedom of working people', 'a tireless champion and defender of the dispossessed people and its freedom', and 'a champion of freedom for the insulted and humiliated'.[194] In many other resolutions the revolutionary minister was called a 'champion of freedom', 'a champion of freedom for the people', 'a champion for the liberation of the motherland', and 'our dear and tireless champion of freedom and rights'.[195] Particular significance was seen in the length of his political service and faithfulness to his chosen political path. Kerensky was regularly described as a 'proven', 'indefatigable', 'tireless', 'steadfast' champion.

As we have seen, Kerensky's 1917 biographers created and affirmed his revolutionary reputation, thereby asserting his right to political leadership at a time of revolution. Actually, in this he was not alone. The status of adversary of the old regime became an important source of political legitimation, so not a few leaders of the time were celebrated by their supporters as 'champions of freedom'.

In March many people in Russia thought it appropriate to congratulate Rodzyanko, the chairman of the State Duma and of its Provisional Committee, on the success of the revolution.[196] Those congratulating him were not always entirely clear about his status. He was referred to as 'the

Head of the Free Russian State', 'the Head of Free Russia', 'the President-Minister', 'the Chairman of the Provisional Government'. Rodzyanko was also called 'a champion of freedom', 'the liberator of Russia'[197] and sometimes even 'the Leader of freedom'.[198] Some of these titles awarded to him were later used to characterize other leaders, including Kerensky: Rodzyanko, chairman of the State Duma, was called, for example, 'the genius of Free Russia'.[199] More commonly, however, he was called the 'first citizen', 'the first free citizen of this free country', 'the best citizen' and 'the first citizen of free Russia'. The barrister Iosif Balinsky greeted Rodzyanko as follows: 'Long live the State Duma . . . Long life to its splendid chairman, the first and most worthy citizen among equal citizens of free Russia.'[200]

Some projects of memory politics were associated with Rodzyanko's name. The Yekaterinoslav City Council hastened to perpetuate the memory of their august major local landowner: resolving to instal a marble statue of him in the hall of their duma, naming the town square after him and, in addition, planning to erect a monument to Liberation in the city centre with a statue of Rodzyanko in the middle of the composition.[201]

The political parties glorified their leaders, recalling their revolutionary past. This method of enhancing authority was deployed with particular energy when the party leaders were under fire from opponents. The Socialist Revolutionaries, for example, fought back against attacks in the conservative and liberal press on Chernov, whom they dubbed a 'highly prominent champion of the freedom and happiness of working people'.[202]

When Lenin and the 'Leninists' found themselves furiously attacked, the Bolsheviks felt the time had come to publish several biographical sketches of their own, making known their Leader's contribution to the revolutionary struggle.[203] They declared: 'It is not right to refer to false, sordid accusations against Comrade Lenin because Lenin is an old party Leader, not just one since March.'[204] This form of words could be seen as concealed criticism of politicians who had come to prominence only during the February Days – a reproach that veteran revolutionaries might have been inclined to level at Kerensky.

After the overthrow of the monarchy, constructing revolutionary biographies was a common method of consolidating authority, and people of quite different views described their leaders as 'true' and 'proven' champions of freedom, even as they cast doubt and sought to refute similar claims on the part of their political opponents.

For Kerensky, his claim to the image of a champion of freedom was particularly important, and we have seen that both he and his supporters went to great lengths to build it up. No other political leader was on the receiving end of quite so many biographical essays in 1917.

Kerensky's supporters sometimes went further and sought to place him in a higher league than other champions of freedom. Some time before 23 March the chairman of the students of Kharkov University who were from Borisoglebsk greeted him as 'foremost among the great champions of freedom'.[205] In the months that followed, other citizens pointed out how special was his place in the pantheon. On 10 July a telegram was sent to the minister declaring that the Socialist Revolutionaries of the Molitovka factory in Nizhny Novgorod 'greet you, the foremost champion of free, revolutionary Russia, and express to you, and through you to the Provisional Government, our complete confidence.' A representative of the Mogilyov Soviet of Peasant Deputies called him nothing less than 'the apostle of revolution and liberator of the peasantry'.[206]

In some writing of the time, this still youthful politician was seen as a unique, and even single-handed, liberator of Russia. The attitude is found in letters and resolutions addressed to Kerensky even in the autumn of 1917. 'You are the person to whom all Russia is indebted for liberation from the oppression of tsarism.'[207] In another instance, he is described as Russia's principal liberator and Leader of the champions of freedom. A non-commissioned officer called Romanov, who wanted permission to change his name, which had become an unwelcome reminder of the old regime, wrote, 'I beg you, great champion!!! For all the Russian people who endured this yoke and bridle, you, Mr Kerensky, leading all the others, were the great liberator from this oppression and lifted this yoke.'[208]

The image of Kerensky as the great liberator was even (negatively) exploited by propagandists of the Austro-Hungarian army in an Austrian leaflet targeted at Russian soldiers on the front line. The minister, it was claimed, had earlier stated he was seeking to end hostilities. 'Your trustworthy Comrade Kerensky took, as the liberator of the people, all power into his hands and promised the people the war would soon end.'[209]

Kerensky himself regularly referred in his public speeches to his service to the revolution, and he used that approach more frequently than other politicians in the spotlight. He also took an active role in promoting the cult of champions of freedom, sometimes at the prompting of public opinion. A general meeting of the trading officials of Tyumen, held on 5 March, sent him the following message: '. . . on this momentous day of elections to the city's Soviet of Workers' Deputies, [this assembly] asks you, dear Alexander Fyodorovich, to convey our greetings to the holy martyrs and champions of freedom Yekaterina Breshkovskaya, Vera Figner, Nikolai Morozov and other veterans of the liberation movement and to tell them we will give our lives for the ideals for which they fought.'[210] In this address Kerensky is mentioned as the worthiest representative of the new generation of revolutionaries, authorized to intercede with his legendary predecessors who symbolize the fraternity of champions of freedom. In other messages he is even mentioned as ranking with the 'holy martyrs'. The All-Russia Congress of Teachers, for example, passed a resolution sending greetings to Kerensky, Breshko-Breshkovskaya, Figner, Plekhanov 'and other great revolutionaries'.[211]

The young politician occupied an honourable place in the ranks of the acknowledged veterans of the revolutionary movement, which meant all efforts to promote the cult of champions of freedom redounded, particularly, to his credit. Moreover, consolidation of the cult was in harmony with the vector of the new politics of memory after February 1917.

Revolutionary Russia needed to rewrite its history to create a portrait of the past suitable for political use in the new situation. Some events needed to be forgotten, others to be radically rethought. All political organizations found themselves drawn inescapably into implementing projects of the politics of memory, and sometimes initiated them. There were occasions when party leaders at various levels had no option but to respond to spontaneous crowd action, when monuments of the old regime were destroyed or there were demands to change names reflecting the tsarist era. Streets, institutions and villages had to be renamed, new monuments created, and thought given to the old burial sites of revolutionaries. Proper tribute had to be paid to fallen champions of freedom and proper recognition given to living veterans of the revolutionary struggle.[212]

The clash of rival cultural memory projects was not at the forefront of political battles, but aspects of the struggle for power were evident in numerous conflicts regarding memorable sites and sites of remembrance. Having the right to initiate such projects could be important in confirming authority and was sought by politicians and administrators, military commanders and members of all sorts of committees. In elaborating the politics of memory there was great reliance on the already advanced political culture of the revolutionary underground, with its long tradition of sanctifying its heroes and martyrs. During the revolution, earlier propaganda texts were republished. Later there were new biographies.[213] The Socialist Revolutionaries were particularly busy in this respect, glorifying their party comrades and famous terrorists.[214] The status of champion of freedom was retrospectively bestowed on figures from Russian history: Alexander Radishchev had already been named as the first Russian champion of freedom,[215] although others awarded that accolade to the Decembrists.[216]

The promotion of the cult of champions of freedom was in line with the public mood, and this had an impact on how mass culture developed. Impressive numbers of new cinematographic films were made: *The Grandmother of the Russian Revolution (Martyr for Freedom)* about Yekaterina Breshko-Breshkovskaya; *Champions of Freedom*; *The Sun of Freedom (Hail to the Champions of Freedom)*; *The Death of Lieutenant Schmidt*, and others.[217] There was demand from cinema-goers, readers and consumers for the memorialization of champions of freedom, and that was fertile ground for implementing projects of the politics of memory.

The need for funerals of participants in the revolution brought forth new symbols and rituals based on the revolutionary tradition. As a result of burials and reburials of opponents of the old regime, as well as of other symbolic acts, the cultural and political topography of towns and villages changed, and that reflected back on the ritual of revolutionary celebrations and the scenarios of political rallies. Urban political spaces were recodified and new politically sanctified locations appeared. The emergence of local cults of champions of freedom was exploited by diverse political forces, and the revolutionary past became an important asset in the struggle for power. A number of local rallies assumed national significance. The revolutionary authorities in Sevastopol sent an expedition to recover the remains of Lieutenant Pyotr Schmidt and other participants in the 1905 uprising. These champions of freedom were reburied with due ceremony in Sevastopol, with Admiral Alexander Kolchak, the commander of the Black Sea Fleet, playing a prominent role. He headed those following the revolutionary hero's coffin. The event was an impressive demonstration by those in favour of continuing the war against Germany. It seems unlikely that Schmidt's actions in 1905 were consonant with the admiral's understanding of the naval code of honour, but he recognized the political necessity of a solemn reburial of the revolutionaries. In the aftermath of February 1917, Kolchak succeeded in maintaining discipline in the fleet for some time, helped by his authority as a respected naval commander, his ability to find common ground with the local committees, and his pragmatic ability to employ rhetoric, symbolism and revolutionary ritual to achieve his goals.

It seemed that, under his leadership, the relatively 'healthy' Black Sea Fleet could become a focus for patriotic mobilization, and the politics of memory had a contribution to make to this. The admiral and his officers reminded the country of the outstanding role played by the Black Sea Fleet in Russia's history. The defence of the city of Sevastopol during the Crimean War and the mutinies at the time of the First Russian Revolution bolstered the view that the officers and committees of the navy had a right to act as a nationwide focus of patriotic mobilization. Some of Admiral Kolchak's supporters went even further, representing him as the heir of Lieutenant Schmidt.[218]

Modern biographers of the Black Sea Fleet commander tend to omit mention of his role in advancing the cult of champions of freedom, and Kolchak himself can hardly have been at ease glorifying the mutineers. However, both he and his supporters understood the practical necessity of behaving as if they did, and they lent their authority to the movement.

The cult of fighters fallen in the cause of freedom was exploited pragmatically by others who supported continuing the war. On 25 March, at the opening of the Seventh Congress of the Constitutional Democratic Party, the deputies honoured the memory of those fighters who had 'laid down their lives for the freedom of our people and opened up the way for developing our work.' Prince P. D. Dolgorukov, a prominent representative of the party, included members of the armed forces among the champions of freedom, declaring: 'I suggest you unite the sacred memory of the champions of freedom from the foreign threat, from the external foe, with the sacred memory of the champions of Russia's freedom from the enemy within, and honour their sacred memory by rising and standing in solemn silence.' The deputies, naturally, responded to his call.[219] If the socialists, when glorifying their champions of freedom, had in mind principally their participation in the struggle for social liberation ('champions of freedom for working people'), the liberals sought to combine the rhetoric of the liberation movement with the language of patriotic wartime propaganda. The simultaneous existence of projects of diverse, and sometimes rival, cults of champions of freedom is evidence both of just how prevalent the tendency was and of its potential for political application. The fact that representatives of literally every political movement, from the supporters of Lenin to those who venerated Kolchak, were busily promoting this cult testifies to a short-lived consensus on the memorialization project of sanctifying fallen revolutionaries.

Kerensky's involvement in promoting the cult of champions of freedom did not, of itself, stand out as anything exceptional, but his biography, his political position and authority, and the resources he controlled imbued his actions with a special significance and importance. Compared with Kolchak and others active in the political process, the 'revolutionary minister' venerated the champions of freedom more enthusiastically and more sincerely. From early youth he had been a bearer of the radical intelligentsia's political culture; the cult of champions of freedom was extremely important for him personally, for his friends and family, and he kept in his apartment a relic of the mutiny led by Lieutenant Schmidt.[220] The rhetoric and rituals of sanctification of the champions of freedom were well familiar to Kerensky and emotionally important to him.

The version of history the revolutionary minister proposed to the new Russia did also have a place in it for certain tsars. On 5 March 1917 he ceremonially presented to the First Department of the Senate the acts of abdication of the throne of Nicholas II and Grand Duke Mikhail Alexandrovich. In the process, Kerensky had words of appreciation for this 'institution created by the genius of Peter the Great to protect the laws and the rule of law.' That is unlikely to have gone down well with all who were opposed to the monarchy, but it is significant that Tan, a veteran of the revolutionary movement, quoted him, remarking only: 'It is instructive to note this tribute from a man of culture to the genius of Peter the Great, who had been such a fierce and mighty revolutionary on the throne. Unlike others, Kerensky could see clearly the difference between Peter the Great and Nikolai Romanov, his pathetic successor.'[221]

Kerensky's respect for Peter the Great was manifested in other ways. A number of warships which bore the names of monarchs began to be renamed. The Central Committee of the Baltic Fleet suggested changing the name of the *Peter the Great*, a training vessel, to *The Republic*. Kerensky thought, however, that it should retain its historical name. Many sailors evidently also thought it appropriate to let the 'crowned revolutionary' keep his place in the pantheon of great predecessors of the new Russia. There were three ships in the navy named in honour of Peter I, and they all kept their original names despite the revolution.[222]

It was, however, the cult of heroes of the revolutionary movement which had a special role in the version of the past which Kerensky was proposing to Russia. There was a clear link between the sources of his own power and his practical involvement in the revolution's politics of memory: in the process of promoting a sacrosanct cult of champions of freedom, he was simultaneously reinforcing his own authority.

The Decembrists had an important place in Kerensky's version of Russian history. In the stressful climate of the revolution, he found time to discuss the project of a memorial to the first generation of champions of freedom. He discussed the idea of erecting a monument to the Decembrists with Grand Duke Nikolai Mikhailovich, a Freemason with specialist knowledge of the era of Alexander I. This scion of the Romanov dynasty declared himself willing to donate a substantial sum of money to the project.[223] About a month later Kerensky sent a letter to the main newspaper of the Socialist Revolutionary Party, offering his opinion on where the monument might best be sited.[224]

Kerensky's veneration of the memory of the Decembrists was evidently sincere, but, at the same time, commemorating officers who had challenged the autocracy was an important political gesture in 1917. Reminding rank-and-file soldiers of this particular cohort of champions of freedom could help to ease tensions between them and their officers, and this was a particularly sensitive issue in the early days of the February Revolution. On 14 March, during a meeting with the writers Dmitry Merezhkovsky and Zinaida Gippius, Kerensky asked Merezhkovsky, who was working on his novel *The Decembrists*, to write a pamphlet reminding soldiers of the feat of those first revolutionary officers, with the aim of reducing friction in the army. Merezhkovsky's pamphlet, *The Firstborn of Freedom*, was published in short order. (It was actually written by Gippius: in the earlier version of her diary she writes that she is working on *The Decembrists* 'for Kerensky'.) The first version of the text, published in the journal *Niva*, was dedicated to 'A. F. Kerensky, who continues the Decembrists' cause.'[225] Kerensky's revolutionary work was presented as the culmination of the struggle begun by the 'firstborn of freedom', of whose memory he was the guardian. The revolutionary minister took to recalling the firstborn of freedom in speeches addressed to soldiers.[226]

The Decembrist theme figures in Kerensky's speeches particularly often after he was appointed head of the Ministry of War. To some of the guards' regiments he pointed out their historical legacy and 'drew especial attention to the guards' regiments from which the Decembrists had emerged.'[227]

The minister of war returned to this topic at the All-Russia Congress of Officers' Deputies in Petrograd. He urged the deputies to think of themselves as the heirs of the Decembrists' cause and to apply the memory of them to strengthen the morale of the revolution's armed forces. 'I am fully confident that a tradition of the Russian army which dates from the times of the Decembrists will be raised by the officer corps to the level required.' His speech was enthusiastically received.[228]

Speaking shortly afterwards, on 17 May in Sevastopol, Kerensky reminded his listeners of the 'fighting and revolutionary traditions' of the Black Sea Fleet: 'The cherished memory of Lieutenant Schmidt is closest of all to you, and I am certain, comrades, that you will fulfil your duty to your country to the end.' In Sevastopol, Kerensky was trying to resolve conflicts which had flared up between Kolchak and the fleet's elected organizations, between the naval command and the ordinary sailors. Referring to the memory of a revolutionary officer was intended to contribute to resolving urgent political problems. Kerensky was seeking to reinforce Kolchak's authority, mentioning the role of the navy's commander in stabilizing the new order. He reminded the sailors of their historic responsibility, of their duty to remain true to the memory of the champions of freedom and carry their mission forward. 'We cannot recklessly fritter away the great legacy won by the blood and toil of many generations of the Russian intelligentsia from the Decembrists onwards. By good fortune we have become the first to enjoy great freedom, and we must protect it and pass it on to our descendants.'[229]

The cult of champions of freedom, promoted by different political players in 1917, would have been unimaginable without glorifying the surviving veterans of the movement. Members of the various groups celebrated the old revolutionaries who were ideologically closest to them, 'living monuments' to the struggle who, by their support, could legitimize the current leaders.[230] Of particular importance was the celebrating of Yekaterina Breshko-Breshkovskaya, who had joined the revolutionary ranks in the 1870s and had spent more than three decades in prison and exile. The Socialist Revolutionary Party of which she was a member established a personal cult of the 'Grandmother of the Russian Revolution'. Portraits and biographies were printed, numerous resolutions were addressed to her, and when she spoke in public she was invariably the centre of attention.

Breshkovskaya was not celebrated as a leader of the party, but her authority as a heroine and martyr who had lived her life by the precepts of the party's saints was assiduously promoted by the Socialist Revolutionaries. It served to strengthen the party's influence and was a tool in the power struggle between sundry factions of the party. Breshkovskaya was one of the most popular figures of the February Revolution. As we have seen, a film was made about her life, and groups of soldiers and students declared themselves the respectful grandchildren of the beloved grandmother. Socialist Revolutionary propaganda urged their supporters to continue the legacy of the aged revolutionary.[231]

Kerensky never tired of showing his respect for the veterans of the revolutionary movement, provided they were supportive of his policies. Their authority was a valuable asset which bolstered his influence. At the Congress of the Socialist Revolutionaries he referred with demonstrative piety to the party's 'teachers', 'guides' and 'doughty champions'. Kerensky modestly referred to himself as one of the disciples and rank-and-file workers, one of the Socialist Revolutionary Party's younger generation which, in the period of reaction, feeling its way in the dark, had, as best it could, carried forward the 'spark of our party's faith and way of life'. Concluding his speech, Kerensky told the delegates that, having gained so much from rubbing shoulders with the 'best champions, he nevertheless always strove to feel, if for only a moment, that he was once again their ordinary, insignificant fellow party member and comrade.'[232] Speaking earlier, at the All-Russia Congress of Soviets of Peasants' Deputies, he had said much the same thing: 'Old teachers came to my aid whose names we have known since childhood.'[233]

In the first weeks of the revolution Kerensky appeared several times at public ceremonies in the company of the veteran revolutionary Vera Figner. She gave her support to a number of his initiatives – for example, heading a fund he created as minister of justice to support former political prisoners. In a single week, 17–24 March, 340,000 rubles were donated for their needs. The donations were addressed to Vera Figner and Olga Kerenskaya. Including money previously sent to Olga Kerenskaya, the final total of donations amounted to 2,135,000 rubles.[234] Such a huge response testifies to the respect enjoyed by Kerensky, and the participation of Figner gave the venture even greater reach. The ability to extend support to former prisoners and exiles, many of whom were joining the political elite of revolutionary Russia, was a valuable political lever for the minister.

Of particular importance for Kerensky was his friendship with Yekaterina Breshko-Breshkovskaya, which underlay their later political cooperation. They met in 1912 when he had travelled to Siberia. One of Kerensky's first actions when he became minister of justice was to order her immediate release. He demanded, moreover, that the local authorities should convey her with due pomp and ceremony to the capital. On 29 March, when, after a triumphal progress, she finally arrived in Petrograd, Kerensky was there to meet and spend the day with her. Sharp tongues scoffed that he was playing the role of page-boy to a grandmother. Breshkovskaya was naturally flattered by the attention paid to her by the popular hero of the February Revolution.

At Kerensky's suggestion, the old revolutionary lady lived in his residences: first in the Ministry of Justice building and later in the Winter Palace. During working lunches attended by politicians and diplomats she acted as hostess. Breshko-Breshkovskaya reminisced later, 'I went with him to the headquarters of the minister of justice, and he put me up there. I kept asking how I could find a place to stay, but he was having none of it. "Don't you find it comfortable here?" And so we remained good, true friends all that time. In fact, I will say, forever.'[235] The former revolutionary did not always feel at ease in the tsar's old quarters but acceded to Kerensky's request. 'I wanted to be set free again, but could not bring myself to leave. I could not deny Alexander Fyodorovich's wish to have me as his neighbour,' she recalled.[236]

In 1917 Breshkovskaya spoke about her special ties with Kerensky. Her speech in April in Revel, where she had gone with the minister of justice, is illustrative: 'The strength of the Provisional Government is that it includes Kerensky, a socialist, a devoted friend of the people. You have a loyal friend, and that friend is Kerensky. He and I are kith and kin, related not by family ties, but in spirit.'[237]

The friendship between the grandmother of the Russian Revolution and her 'grandson' was of considerable political importance for both of them. Breshko-Breshkovskaya was a living legend for the Socialist Revolutionaries. For decades she had been praised by the party. Her biography was presented as the life of a martyr who had dedicated herself to service of the people. The moral and political backing of such an illustrious champion of freedom reinforced Kerensky's standing and sanctified his actions. For Breshko-Breshkovskaya too, however, the alliance was important: her young ally was proof that she had been right, and justified the battle she had waged against the regime for the whole of her life. Kerensky was the personification of a new generation of revolutionaries who were successfully carrying forward the mission she had begun so long ago. At the same time, the revolutionary minister was a guide for the old Narodnik warrior in the complicated and sometimes confusing world of modern politics.

The relationship between Kerensky and Breshko-Breshkovskaya was warm and relaxed, and it remained so in later years when both were in exile. In her memoirs she refers to him as the most outstanding member of the Socialist Revolutionary Party.[238] (Other Socialist Revolutionary leaders might not have agreed.) In a different version of her memoirs there is an even more ecstatic description of Kerensky: 'He has always lived, and probably always will, with the most positive imaginable belief in the future of mankind in general and of the Russian people in particular. This quality of his soul, this great talent of selfless love and an unbounded willingness to serve his people are probably what provided the foundation of the mutual understanding which formed between him and me. I have the greatest respect for this man. I admire his personality as among the best things our land has ever produced.'[239]

In 1917 Breshkovskaya spoke publicly of her admiration for what Kerensky was doing. After visiting Taurida province, she had this to say about the morale of the inhabitants of Crimea (believing that everyone who came to her speeches or with whom she spoke shared her attitude towards the revolutionary minister).

> Nor is there any mistrust of the new composition of the Provisional Government, although those who comprise it are not particularly well known.
>
> This drawback is satisfactorily dealt with by confidence that, as long as Alexander Fyodorovich Kerensky is one of the ministers, nothing bad will be allowed to happen. In the five years that the

> repute of Kerensky has stood untarnished in the arena of Russia's politics, the population, even in remote corners of our far-flung land, has come to revere his name and to see it as a guarantee of truth, lawfulness and justice. They have come to see him as a knight, always resolute, always prepared to occupy the most dangerous positions in pursuing his ideal of selfless service to his motherland. To his people.[240]

In the autumn of 1917, Breshko-Breshkovskaya tried to shield the head of the Provisional Government from attacks from the left and right, reminding people of the biography of a hero who was sacrificing his health, and perhaps even his life, to the cause of the revolution. 'He has given a full decade of his young life to Russia, sparing neither his strength, his health, nor his very life.'[241]

Whenever Kerensky's authority was under threat, he and his supporters sought to shore it up by recalling his biography as a champion of freedom and authenticating his reputation with the aid of authoritative endorsement from veterans of the revolutionary movement.

* * *

All manner of conflicts of the time are reflected in the controversies around the accounts of Kerensky's life, and these conflicts are, in many ways, of interest. Particular aspects of Kerensky's life – his social antecedents, his family ties with the bureaucratic elite, and a number of scenes caused by his actions in the State Duma – were omitted or hushed up. Others recur in the various biographies and biographical articles, in resolutions and newspaper reports, and, indeed, in autobiographies, in Kerensky's speeches and even in the orders he issued. The biographical elements of particular importance for establishing his revolutionary credentials were occasions when he was persecuted by the old regime, his clandestine activities, his legal defence of political cases in court, and his bold and 'prophetic' speeches in the State Duma. Then there were his actions in late February, of which the most spectacular was bringing the mutinous soldiers into the Tauride Palace. The references back to his biography served to substantiate the status of a 'tried and tested', tireless champion of freedom, a prerequisite for the image of a revolutionary Leader. Much was made also by some biographers of the gift of foresight they believed he possessed. To have been able to 'prophesy' the revolution was surely also grounds for qualifying as a charismatic leader.

For decades before the revolution, Russian revolutionaries had developed the genre of glorification of their martyrs, heroes and teachers. Their techniques of political hagiography were exploited by Kerensky, his supporters and his adversaries. The cult of champions of freedom became the official political religion of the new Russia, and initiatives to establish it enhanced politicians' authority. Simultaneously, Kerensky's political collaboration and friendship with authoritative veterans of the liberation movement enabled him to turn their sacralization to his own account.

Even as he actively participated in building up the cult of champions of freedom, Kerensky was a part of the cult, enhancing his own reputation within it by being a contender for the role of true Leader of the people. His heroic biography as an ardent revolutionary fitted well into the sanctified history of the revolutionary movement, which became core to the politics of memory of the new Russia.

The controversy surrounding the biography of Kerensky, who was claiming the status of Leader of the revolution, was rooted in the affirmation of the clandestine political subculture as the basis of new Russia's political culture. The discussions in effect led to the establishment of a canon of texts and images, symbols and rituals deemed appropriate to inform the cult of the revolutionary leader. In the process some came to acknowledge Kerensky as an authentic Leader. Others did not. As far as the set of qualities the ideal revolutionary Leader needed to possess, both sides were in agreement. The existing cult of fallen or still living champions of freedom provided the requisite discursive framework for forming the cult of the Leader.

The creativity manifest in the cultural politics of the first months of the revolution, in which Kerensky himself played an active role, exerted no little influence on Soviet political culture. The latter was also to include a cult of 'champions of freedom', a canon for describing the life of the Leader, and a combining of the patriotic military and revolutionary traditions. The texts, symbols, ceremonies and rituals, created on a foundation of revolutionary tradition to resolve current political tasks at the time of the February Revolution, were to prove applicable to the tasks of later years.

II

'Revolutionary Minister'

In the Provisional Government, established on 2 March 1917, Kerensky was appointed minister of justice. It might have seemed that the sole socialist minister in a cabinet dominated by liberals would have only a secondary role to play. In fact, however, it was Kerensky who was perceived as the strongman in the government and as Russia's foremost politician. The leader of the Socialist Revolutionary Party, Victor Chernov, declared on 3 May: 'We have seen that A. F. Kerensky, having joined this government on his own initiative and at his own risk, was at one time awarded the title of "the most powerful man in Russia" by the newspapers, even though in the Provisional Government he was alone. The weight a minister carries depends not purely on personal qualities but, to a much greater extent, on whom he has behind him.'[1]

We cannot tell how sincere the leader of the Socialist Revolutionaries was: Victor Chernov was addressing socialists who were wary of participating in a coalition government where representatives of the 'bourgeoisie' were in the majority. It is noteworthy, however, that there were no public objections to his judgement, so clearly he was not alone in considering Kerensky 'the most powerful man in Russia'.

How did the young minister come to wield so much influence? There are many ways to answer that question, and Chernov offered an entirely rational, if insufficient, explanation. In accordance with the objectives of our present study, this chapter will examine how Kerensky was characterized in March–April 1917 and also the techniques he employed to boost his authority. This will make it possible to understand how, within two months, he gained the reputation as the strongman of the Provisional Government. It was an image, a reputation he was going to need when a new coalition government was formed in May.

1 The great conciliator

Already in 1917 Leon Trotsky was sarcastically describing Kerensky as 'the great conciliator, mediator, arbitrator', commenting that, 'When history declared a vacancy for an arbitrator, it was unable to find anyone better suited to the post than Kerensky.'[2] Behind these remarks we detect not only contempt for a loser, a defeated adversary, but also rejection of his policy of reconciliation, his 'compromise-mongering'.

For many, however, it was precisely Kerensky's ability to broker important agreements and reach compromises that they found most valuable. On 6 March, the Constituent Assembly of the Union of Engineers, held in Petrograd, sent greetings to the minister over the signature of a well-known engineer and public figure, Professor Dmitry Zernov. The address stated that the meeting 'acknowledges your service to the motherland in achieving unity between the Provisional Committee and the Soviet of Workers' Deputies on major matters of state. It has confidence that you, as a member of the Provisional Government, will continue to achieve similar successes, consolidating the authority of the Provisional Government which is essential for victory over the foreign enemy and to deliver well-earned freedom.'[3]

Different people had differing assessments of Kerensky's role in the February events. Some singled out his speeches in the State Duma, others the fact that it was he who invited the mutinous soldiers to enter the Tauride Palace. Others pointed to his arrest of the leaders of the old regime. The address of the Union of Engineers, which evidently reflected the opinion of other members of the Petrograd intelligentsia, focuses on his role in unifying the forces which had carried out the coup. Kerensky's political involvement had been crucial in achieving cooperation and coordination of the actions of the Provisional Committee of the State Duma and the Petrograd Soviet.

We find similar appreciation of Kerensky's work in other sources. *Petrogradskaya gazeta* dubbed him 'the good fairy of the Russian Revolution', and went on: 'He was the first of the deputies to welcome the revolutionary troops. He it was who sanctioned the arrest of the mastermind of the old regime, Ivan Shcheglovitov, and locked him up in the ministerial pavilion at the Tauride Palace. It is to A. F. Kerensky too that we owe the highly important establishing of contact between the Provisional Government and the Soviet of Workers' Deputies.'[4]

We note that the Union of Engineers expressed confidence that Kerensky would continue to consolidate the authority of the Provisional Government, which was recognition of his political power. It was power based both on the authority he had gained through his active participation in the coup and on the respect that, as a minister of justice who was simultaneously the deputy chairman of the Executive Committee of the Petrograd Soviet, he enjoyed among the deputies of the Soviet.

The same thing is noted by an unknown 1917 biographer of the minister, who described him as 'the mortar binding together the democratic forces and the government'. 'Kerensky's role in binding them together is so great we can safely say that without his involvement it would have been impossible to achieve the immensely difficult task facing the Provisional

Government of realigning free Russia. In spite of all the friction between the Soviet and the government, and there was no shortage of that, Kerensky managed to overcome it from the very outset.'[5]

From then on, the role of unifier, establishing, consolidating and restoring agreement between the soviets and the liberal politicians, between the 'democratic forces' and the 'bourgeoisie', was exceptionally important. Kerensky was directly involved in all negotiations over reorganizing the Provisional Government, and his political role seemed only to increase. From May, all the offices of government were a coalition which included socialists and 'bourgeois' ministers. Even before the coalition was established, however, the minister of justice himself embodied, if not a coalition of the 'live forces of the country' (he was not officially delegated to the government on behalf of any political party), then a personal coalition of the two power structures created by the revolution.

'Dual power' is a term applied to this era. It was used in 1917 by politicians with differing views and went on to become an analytical concept used by researchers, although there was never agreement about the chronological period of dual power.[6] Sometimes the term was applied only to the relationship between the Provisional Government and the Petrograd Soviet. At other times it was applied to the highly complex relationship between institutions which acknowledged only the unconditional legitimacy of the Provisional Government and other bodies which laid claim to the right to govern.

A crucial component of the system of dual power was a network of committees in the armed forces which sprang up after February and which restricted the authority of the higher institutions of command. The powers of these committees and the way they were organized differed widely between the various units and groupings. The initial impetus for 'democratization' of the army and navy was given by Order No. 1, adopted by the Petrograd Soviet on 1 March even before the Provisional Government had been established. That order set in train a process of establishing committees among the troops, and the impossibility of resisting 'democratization' was soon evident. The best that could be hoped for was to control it. The government, the High Command and the soviets had accordingly no option but to recognize the committees' existence and discuss how far their authority extended. The question of who governed Russia centred on this issue of dual power and, primarily, of authority in the armed forces.

Their attitude to the dual power situation divided the main political forces in Russia, and the problem was closely related to another acute issue: the question of their attitude to the ongoing war. The left-wing socialists – Bolsheviks, the Interdistrict Group, Menshevik internationalists and Left Socialist Revolutionaries – all demanded an early end to it and criticized the Provisional Government for failing to take meaningful measures to bring the global conflict to an end. The most radical position was that of Lenin, who returned from emigration in early April. He firmly linked the problem of the war with the problem of political power, stating that only the transference of power to the soviets could bring an end to it. Lenin did not at first find support even in the ranks of the Bolsheviks, but he did manage to articulate inchoate radical feelings to be found among lower- and middle-ranking party activists. These sentiments were strengthened by the April Crisis, and the Bolsheviks' conference in April supported Lenin, although, as we shall see below, by no means all the Bolsheviks could have been described as loyal 'Leninists' at that time.

If Lenin's aim was to end the dual power situation and see all power transferred to the soviets, in effect to the socialists, then the aim of liberal and conservative groups was to see all power in the hands of the Provisional Government. After the February events, parties to the right of the Constitutional Democrats, the 'Cadets', all but ceased to exist. Conservative political groups were in disarray for a while, with the result that many entrepreneurs and bureaucrats, officers and generals, journalists and publishers lent their support to the Cadets. Pavel Milyukov, the leader of the Cadets, was appointed minister of foreign affairs, which made the party's approach to foreign policy particularly prominent. The Constitutional Democrats were insistent that the war must be prosecuted to a victorious conclusion, which they saw as including the annexation by Russia of a number of Austro-Hungarian, German and Ottoman territories.

After the February Days, the moderate socialists – primarily the Mensheviks and Socialist Revolutionaries – began to play a significant role. However, they consisted of warring factions. Thus, if on the issue of the war the position of right-wing Mensheviks and Socialist Revolutionaries was at times close to that of the Cadets, the Left Socialist Revolutionaries and Menshevik internationalists often made common cause with the Bolsheviks. The leadership positions of the moderate socialists were held predominantly by centrists, who did their best to maintain party unity (although, measured against socialists in Western Europe, Russia's centrists looked a left-wing lot).

Before the revolution, several influential Socialist Revolutionaries and Mensheviks were opposed to the war and supported the resolutions of the Zimmerwald International Socialist Conference. After the overthrow of the monarchy, however, they had second thoughts. Now it was a matter not of defending the hated autocracy but of preserving the 'most democratic nation', and a number of socialists did a U-turn and became 'revolutionary defencists'. At the same time, however, their notion of defence was formulated in terms of the anti-imperialist and anti-bourgeois rhetoric of Zimmerwaldism. The moderate socialists proposed to end the 'imperialist war' by having all the belligerent parties conclude a democratic, just peace 'without annexations and idemnities'. Such was the programme in the manifesto adopted by the Petrograd Soviet on 14 March. Until that peace was concluded, of course, the revolutionary defencists took the view that Russia had no option but to continue to participate in the war. They would not countenance the idea of a separate peace. If for Milyukov and his supporters the war could not be allowed to end in a draw – Russia should take territories from the enemy nations – then for the revolutionary defencists such a programme was 'imperialist'.

The attitude towards the war was bound up with the question of the attitude towards the Provisional Government. Although the leaders of the Petrograd Soviet had participated in the negotiations for establishing the government and elaborating its programme, that did not mean the Soviet fully supported it. The cooperation of moderate socialists with the Provisional Government was conditional on how well ministers actually implemented the programme agreed with the Soviet. This conditional support, 'payment by results', significantly limited the government's authority. A coordinating commission was set up to align the actions of the two power structures, but it could not eliminate the possibility of conflicts. The leaders of the Soviet sought to control the Provisional Government, while not wishing to take responsibility for its actions. Some influential socialists certainly did perceive Kerensky as an inspector who had joined the government in order to keep an eye on his 'bourgeois' colleagues. A resolution, adopted on 2 March by the Petrograd Conference of Socialist Revolutionaries, read: 'Considering it essential that the toiling masses should monitor the activities of the Provisional Government, the conference welcomes the entry of A. F. Kerensky into the Provisional Government as minister of justice in order to defend the interests of the people and its freedom, and expresses its full endorsement of his conduct during the days of the revolution, which proceeded from a correct understanding of the circumstances of the moment.'[7]

The minister of justice was sometimes perceived as the Petrograd Soviet's representative in the government. It was claimed he had been included in it on the insistence of the Soviet, which was untrue, but is how the situation was described by, for example, the US naval attaché.[8] Nevertheless, support from the soviets and committees, whose influence was growing, undoubtedly bolstered Kerensky's position.

This tricky situation, with Kerensky in office in two power structures, one of which was seeking to control the other, presented him with many difficulties but also offered many opportunities. On the one hand, he could be seen as sitting between two stools, both of which were constantly being moved, because an already complex alignment of forces changed rapidly. On the other hand, there were advantages to being a skilled and responsible unifying presence in both the Soviet and the government. Kerensky showed himself to be adept at tactical improvisation. He did not confine himself to negotiating with the elites but addressed himself over the heads of their leaders to those sections of the population and organizations which formed the power base of the politicians. He gave imaginative expression to, and ably articulated and strengthened, a grassroots longing for unity which existed at the time, and exploited those aspirations as an important way of putting pressure on party leaders.

Kerensky emphasized his special position in power. He called himself a 'hostage for the forces of democracy'. Welcoming the delegation of the Black Sea Fleet, which visited the Provisional Government, he stated:

> I beg you not to believe rumours spread by the enemies of the people and of freedom who are seeking to undermine the bond between the Provisional Government and the people. I vouch with my life, and I am your hostage among the members of the Provisional Government, that you and the people have nothing to fear. If there was even the slightest suggestion that the Provisional Government was incapable of fulfilling the obligations it has taken upon itself, I myself would come out of it to you.[9]

The lack of clarity about the exact role of a 'hostage for the forces of democracy' did not stop that memorable formulation from catching on. When Kerensky visited Helsingfors in May, the head of the local soviet greeted him by saying, 'Minister, Comrade Citizen, or just comrade and friend of our people, Kerensky, . . . we were all confident and knew that you were our hostage, the hostage for the socialists.'[10] The minister defined himself as a hostage for maintaining unity between 'the people' and the government. It was a sobriquet which indicated his unique and privileged status in the world of Russian politics, and underlined his special role in comparison with other ministers.

Among friends Kerensky criticized the leaders of the Soviet, considering their Order No. 1, their manifesto of 14 March and other decisions to have been overly radical. He was also critical of the moderate socialists' aspiration to control the Provisional Government.[11] Such comments, however, were confined to private conversation, although they did sometimes become known to other players in the political process.

In any case, his relations with the leaders of the Executive Committee of the Soviet were soured after he joined the government in defiance of their opinion. The new minister also rarely turned up to meetings of the Soviet. Kerensky himself recalled trying in vain to artificially create a counterbalance to the Soviet by provoking a more vigorous right wing. He is said to have urged Rodzyanko to put pressure on the Provisional Government, on behalf of the Provisional Committee of the State Duma, to maintain a balance within the cabinet.[12] We can probably trust his memory on this: for a politician trying to maintain a balance that development would have been all to the good.

However, Kerensky wisely refrained from publicly criticizing the Soviet, and the Mensheviks and Socialist Revolutionaries refrained from criticizing an influential politician who was, at least technically, the deputy chairman of the Executive Committee of the Soviet. The moderate socialists tried to use Kerensky as a tool for 'correcting' the course of the government. A prominent Socialist Revolutionary, Nikolai Rusanov, declared at the Petrograd Party Conference that Kerensky's actions had compelled the government to move towards the aspirations of the socialists. 'Only one person, with a very high specific gravity within it as a result of his ties with socialism and democracy, deflects its resultant force significantly to the left,' and it 'is obliged to develop, and in part already to implement, a programme of democratic reforms which, taken together, now puts Russia ahead of the Western European democracies, where war has terribly constrained human and civic rights.'[13]

To some extent Kerensky justified the hopes of the moderate socialists. While refraining from open criticism of the leaders of the Soviet, the minister of justice publicly attacked his cabinet colleague Milyukov and denounced his foreign policy. The disputes between the ministers spilled out on to the pages of the newspapers. Kerensky had conversations with ambassadors of the Allied powers, although that was clearly outside his brief.

Simultaneously conducting several complicated plots, Kerensky made use of the power of public opinion. He cooperated more effectively with the press than any other minister and devoted much attention to his public speaking. The minister developed his own image. Both his political stance and the role of unifier to which he laid claim figured in his representation of himself.

The minister of justice, then, occupied a position on the frontier between the 'bourgeois' and socialist parties. In the Duma, Kerensky was the leader of the Trudovnik (Labour) Group, and after the February Days he declared his allegiance to the Socialist Revolutionary Party. The Trudoviks continued, nevertheless, to consider him their representative and voiced their support for him as a minister and for his policies. Their political influence was not, however, very great and they could offer him little significant support.

After the overthrow of the monarchy, the Socialist Revolutionaries became the most numerous political party. In reality, the influx of 'March' Socialist Revolutionaries was a mixed blessing in terms of effective party work. The Socialist Revolutionaries subsequently won convincingly in local authority elections and then, after the fall of the Provisional Government, in elections to the Constituent Assembly. One might imagine that collaboration of the revolution's most popular leader with the leaders of the largest political party could only have been to the benefit of both. In fact, however, only the 'Right' Socialist Revolutionaries gave Kerensky unconditional support. They were not entirely happy with the actions of those in the centre of the party. The rightists had substantial financial resources, and on 29 April they began publishing the *Volya naroda* [People's Will] newspaper in Petrograd. It was particularly supportive of Kerensky and appears to have been financed with assistance from the influential minister. However, the faction lacked mass support.

When it was tactically advantageous, Kerensky would sometimes talk with pride about his membership of the Socialist Revolutionary Party. He would talk of its heroic history, its wise teachers, its respected and authoritative leaders. In reality, however, Kerensky was not particularly enamoured of it: his real political territory was the middle ground between the two camps which were now in a temporary alliance: the 'democrats' (the socialists influential in the soviets and military committees) and the 'bourgeoisie'. Kerensky's home territory was the space where these major vectors interacted. He personified their compromise agreement and was both the major protagonist and the symbol of a broad 'coalition of all the live forces in Russia' which united the moderate socialists and liberals.

Kerensky, an idiosyncratic political soloist, had little connection with the Socialist Revolutionaries' work among the masses or with their party's administrative apparatus. By his own admission he had no interest in party programmes.[14] He viewed with scepticism, perhaps even disdain, theorizing socialists who claimed to have a scientific understanding of social processes and believed they could manage history by following a textbook. In his memoirs he writes disparagingly of 'scribes' who tried to force the extraordinary and unpredictable situation of the revolution into a narrow framework of party dogma. In unpublished writing he was even more uncharitable towards them.[15]

Kerensky had no settled, principled views about many issues – social, agrarian, relating to industrial regulation – and this was to haunt him later when the need was for major, swift and painful decisions. In the initial stage of the revolution, however, his individual brand of theoretical fuzziness afforded tactical advantages, giving considerably more room for political manoeuvring and manipulation and for bringing divergent forces together. Later his lack of a party apparatus for exerting systematic influence on the masses, weak contacts with the political parties, and a lack of tried and tested supporters who could be promoted to major positions fatally undermined his position. In the initial stages of the revolution, however, not being encumbered with party allegiances was a political trump card. 'Unity is power' was a popular slogan in February.[16] Partisanship, on the other hand, was perceived by neophytes of political involvement as synonymous with factionalism and schism and was considered a threat to the unity of the revolution's forces. The masses, newly interested in politics, irritably brushed aside disputes and debates between the parties, seeing no point in them. The euphoric 'Eastertide' mood of the first months of the revolution was fuelled by the ideal of universal brotherhood and national unity. Kerensky, the 'people's minister', was its very embodiment.

Sukhanov had some justification for calling Kerensky an 'undemocratic democrat'. The minister's very individual democratic beliefs were grounded neither in experience of involvement in mass democratic organizations nor in knowledge of the Western European democratic model. 'I am not much given to partisanship,' Kerensky admitted at a meeting of the Executive Committee of the Petrograd Soviet. 'I belong today to no party. All working, all honest citizens are in my party and I am in theirs,' he declared in a speech in Kiev.[17] Perhaps unsurprisingly, many old-timers in 'his' Socialist Revolutionary Party saw him as a greenhorn, even as a bit weird. Milyukov later wrote that Kerensky was 'alien' to the Socialist Revolutionaries.[18]

It is odd that Kerensky, talking of 'his' party which united all patriots, was almost quoting a famous 1914 speech by Wilhelm II. The democratic minister was following in the footsteps of the emperor of an enemy nation, who had declared at the outbreak of war: 'For me, there are no more parties – there are only Germans.' In another, even more important speech, Kerensky reduced the range of the forces he claimed to represent. On 22 May, at a meeting of the Petrograd Soviet, the minister said, 'There are no parties for me now, because I am a Russian minister. There is only the people and one sacred law: to submit to the will of the majority of the people.'[19]

His position of non-partisan politician was reflected in cartoons. In July he was portrayed as a benign, sensible teacher trying to calm a fight between schoolboys representing the different parties.[20]

Even a political ally of Kerensky, the Menshevik Irakliy Tsereteli, later called him 'an individualist with no party allegiance' and claimed the minister's closest ties were not with the socialist milieu but with the democratic intelligentsia, which wavered between the socialist, soviet, and purely bourgeois democratic alternatives. Tsereteli noted that Kerensky was trying to play the role of national statesman and that his ideal was power not tied to any party but above them all. According to this prominent Menshevik, Kerensky valued his nominal link with the Soviet because of the influence that body wielded; yet he consciously avoided becoming too closely tied to the Executive Committee of the Soviet because he believed that, by remaining on the margins of the Soviet and bourgeois parties, he could speak for the national, inclusive character of the revolution.[21]

Commentators well disposed towards Kerensky also saw him not as a party leader but as above partisanship. Oleg Leonidov wrote of his pre-revolutionary speeches, 'Not in a single word, not in any of the slogans Kerensky proposed was there ever any sense of narrow partisanship, of political group clichés or petty-mindedness. It was truth itself which spoke through Kerensky, a truth which knew neither party nor faction. What was heard in his speeches was the frenzied, hysterical cry of the trampled conscience of the Russian people, desperate to find a way out of the mire of stagnation and dungeons.'[22]

The right-wing Menshevik Alexander Potresov tells us that this personal element, 'embodied in Kerensky, met a need of the Russian Revolution, represented, for good or ill, a temporary resolution of its tangled contradictions. It was an evil needed to ward off an even greater evil. . . . Russia, on the verge of being torn asunder, clutched at Kerensky, this puny little individual bridge which spanned the gulf between the two sides.'[23]

In different words, but in the same vein, Victor Chernov wrote in his memoirs:

> But, the more events developed, the more his [Kerensky's] personality was reassessed in its [the revolution's] ranks. In the end his role began to come down to no more than keeping a balance between the

> right-wing, nationalist, liberal and the left-wing, socialist parts of the government. Neutralizing the former with the latter, neutralizing the latter with the former, seemed to be how Kerensky saw his mission in a role above party, with himself cast as the super-arbitrator, making himself 'indispensable' as the central axis of power. It seemed that keeping the government in that state was what he most wanted, and that he even tried to aggravate it by systematically removing from the cabinet, one after another, all the major, colourful party personalities and replacing them with increasingly second-rate, indecisive and characterless individuals. This created the danger of a personality-centred regime, at the mercy of chance events and even of an individual's mood swings.[24]

Chernov singles out the personal qualities of Kerensky which affected the nature of the coalitions he devised. So do many other memoirists. Without disputing their judgements, which are in many respects justified, we ought to recognize that the politician embodying this 'personality-centred regime' was himself a hostage to the political situation. With time, his opponents on the right began complaining about Kerensky's balancing act, always hesitant, failing to make the 'necessary choice' to use force to crush the Bolsheviks and their allies. Others at this time, however, were demanding that there should be a strike at the centre of the Mensheviks and Socialist Revolutionaries, with Chernov himself being a particular hate figure. The moderate socialists had their own 'necessary choice' for Kerensky to make – necessary, that is, for them. Their fear was that the influence of the right would increase.

Any such definitive choice would, of course, have been political suicide for Kerensky. Other than in a grand coalition uniting the democratic elements and the 'bourgeoisie', he had no part to play in national politics. He did not have the support of a mass political party; he had no organization behind him; he controlled no party machine. None of the parties considered this minister to be wholly on their side, and in any new political configuration which did not include cooperation between moderate socialists and liberals he would be elbowed to the sidelines of public life. It is worth emphasizing again that Kerensky was not the leader of a political party: he was a unique conciliator, an irreplaceable inspiration, organizer and guardian of a compromise embodied in agreements and coalitions.

We should acknowledge that the compromise between even a part of the bourgeoisie and a part of the democratic forces saved the country from sliding into civil war. By October 1917 the basis for such agreement had been eroded, which meant that Kerensky was doomed. The philosopher Fyodor Stepun is a thoughtful memoirist and researcher of the revolution and worked for Kerensky in 1917. Fairly critical of him, he recalls:

> It was really only Kerensky who doggedly held on to his old stance. Conscious that with every passing day the united, freedom-loving

revolution the entire nation had embraced and which was so dear to him was ever more hopelessly degenerating into two extremist, partisan counter-revolutions, he continued to insist that the only way out of this tragic situation remained consolidation of all the nation's live forces in a strong coalition government which placed the interests of the revolution above those of party.[25]

In the spring of 1917, however, society's desire for a conciliator capable of constructing and maintaining just such a compromise was palpable, and Kerensky possessed the unique qualities and necessary resources to enable him to square the circle.

Leon Trotsky explained the 'Kerensky phenomenon' as having been due not to the politician's personality but to his historical function. On 13 May he described Kerensky in the Petrograd Soviet as the 'mathematical focal point of Russian Bonapartism'. We will see that characterizing Kerensky as Bonapartist, and even as a Bonaparte, was to become fairly common.[26]

Many people remembered Trotsky's formulation. Kerensky himself used that exact expression, while, of course, denying the accusation of Bonapartism. Describing his position at the Moscow National Conference held in August, he subsequently claimed that the Provisional Government was the only centre uniting these two Russias. In that centre he had been the 'mathematical focal point' of unity.[27]

Kerensky was reproached both by the left and by the right for sitting between two stools. Trotsky called him 'vacillation incarnate'. Pavel Milyukov later described him as cowed by 'danger from two directions, struggling to keep his balance at the mathematical point where those dangers converged.'[28] Both Milyukov and Trotsky use mathematical metaphors, and behind their disparagement of the dilettante who had broken through to the highest position of state power, elbowing aside more experienced politicians, we detect their envy and animosity towards this first, unworthy 'Elect of the revolution'.

We should stress once again that, in spring 1917, someone able to play the part of conciliator and unifier was exactly what was needed, and that is why the theme figures so prominently among the propaganda clichés favoured by Kerensky's supporters. They even called him (harking back to Ivan III) 'the gatherer of the people', 'the tireless gatherer of the Russian land'.[29]

Lenin subsequently asserted that the Provisional Government had 'wanted to reconcile the interests of the landowners and peasants, of the workers and factory owners, of labour and capital.'[30] If we ignore his pejorative charge of 'compromise-mongering', we can accept that as a fair judgement, especially in respect of Kerensky, who played the role of conciliator between the 'compromise-mongering' socialists and the 'bourgeoisie'.

Trotsky's assertion that Kerensky was the mathematical focal point of Russian Bonapartism is inaccurate. The minister did not just passively occupy an enviable position. Maintaining that balance called for skill and unflagging efforts, new political initiatives and propaganda campaigns. What enabled Kerensky to fulfil his unifying role was having one foot in two rival power structures, his position on the spectrum of the political parties, his tactical flexibility, and firm orientation towards creating and re-creating compromise. The people's minister possessed the qualities essential to renewing a political compromise again and again in extremely difficult situations. He was a master of politicking, well able to plot, bargain, blackmail and exploit his authority to compel cantankerous and ambitious party leaders to reach agreement. Additionally, he knew how to bring the power of public opinion to bear on the partners in a negotiation.

The young minister's influence in government institutions was primarily the result of his immense popularity in the country, 'in the streets'. 'From the very first Kerensky had been the central figure of the revolutionary drama and had, alone among his colleagues, acquired a sensible hold on the masses,' the British ambassador recalled.[31]

The ambassador noted the special position of the minister of justice in the first Provisional Government and associated it with his influence on public opinion. The value of such retrospective judgements of his contemporaries needs to be taken with a pinch of salt, but there is no doubt that Kerensky's public speeches did attract huge attention and that he was a great favourite with the press. That strengthened his position in the government and in negotiating with the Soviet. It also helped him perform the politically crucial role of unifier.

Kerensky's 'compromise-mongering' and his 'vacillation' were not a matter of political tactics: they were fundamental to his principles. They corresponded to his ideals and his personality. He was still trying to resuscitate a spirit of national common purpose on the eve of the fall of the Provisional Government, when this was long gone and disillusionment with the idea of coalition was all but universal. In the spring of 1917 there had been many factors contributing to the popularity and demand for a unifier.

Kerensky was perceived as a special kind of politician, and in the section of the political spectrum which he occupied no other leader could equal him. No other figurehead had anything like his influence down in the streets, and that was an influence which made him a force to be reckoned with in reaching agreements at the top. His status as an irreplaceable political figure was fundamental to establishing his image as the unique Leader-cum-saviour which was to emerge in June. The authority necessary to function as a conciliator also stemmed from the fact that Kerensky very soon earned the reputation of a businesslike, effective, democratic and, indeed, revolutionary minister.

2 The omnipresent 'minister of the people's truth'

In 1917 a series of postcards was printed depicting prominent figures of the February Days: ministers of the Provisional Government; the chairman of the State Duma, Mikhail Rodzyanko; and the chairman of the Executive Committee of the Petrograd Soviet of Workers and Soldiers' Deputies, Nikolai Chkheidze.[32]

The artist Sergey Kushchenko placed a portrait of a politician in the upper part of each postcard, and in the lower part an illustration representing his area of responsibility. Typically, the illustration depicted people representative of recognizable professional or cultural groups against the background of a landscape designating the occupation of the politician. For Rodzyanko there is a mixed crowd in front of the Tauride Palace, home of the State Duma, which is flying a huge red flag; for Chkheidze, a worker and a soldier shake hands against a background of a barracks and factories. Beneath the portrait of the procurator general of the Holy Synod, Prince Vladimir Lvov, are pilgrims in front of a church; under the image of the state comptroller Ivan Godnev are members of different social classes and estates, studying a ledger of revenues and expenditure of the state budget.

The area of responsibility of the new minister of justice and prosecutor general is shown as a prison building in flames. Kushchenko evidently envisaged Kerensky's principal occupation as being the revolutionary destruction of places of detention. There are no grounds to believe that Kerensky himself had any plans to burn down all the prisons, but Kushchenko was not alone in seeing that as the primary task of the new minister of justice.

In 1991 the present author had the privilege of a conversation with Anna Markovna Maiskaya, who very emotionally recalled the first days of the revolution. Her parents were convinced members of the Jewish Social Democratic organization the Bund, and she described her mother as an 'ardent believer in socialism'. The members of her family were delighted when the monarchy was overthrown, but, when they discovered that the prisons had not yet been destroyed in the new Russia, the ardent believer exclaimed, 'This is not my revolution!'

This testimony is in line with that from other sources. Many people living in Russia believed that the great revolution would bring about not only political, economic and social transformation: they were expecting radical and immediate moral changes. They sincerely believed that the benign effect of the revolution would lead to complete eradication of crime, so that prisons would no longer be necessary. These high expectations might, indeed, have been prompted by the exuberance of those at the helm during the February Revolution: 'We must create a realm of truth and justice,' Kerensky himself had said.[33] The destruction of prisons and guardhouses did take place in the course of the revolutionary assault on the government authorities in many cities. In the early days of the revolution the rebels not only strove to free the prisoners of tsarism (not excluding common criminals or enemy agents), they sought to destroy the very prisons, to smash the shackles and to burn down every bastille. There was no place for prisons in the new realm of eternal freedom. The flames rising from places of imprisonment in Petrograd (the Lithuanian Castle, the police stations), Shlisselburg, Revel and other cities were vivid symbols of the revolution. They were photographed as local sights and depicted on postcards. For some, the total elimination of prisons was seen as a precondition for the coming of a new world.[34]

Such euphoric, utopian 'Eastertide' sentiments testify to the unrealistic hopes many rapturous contemporaries pinned on the minister of justice. Interestingly, months later not a few naive revolutionary enthusiasts were still his fervent admirers. This was because of Kerensky's actions as minister, the way he presented them, and the way they were perceived.

This section will examine the images of the minister of justice created by Kerensky himself, by his supporters and his opponents, by people of different persuasions and different classes who sent messages to the minister.

Kerensky's candidacy for the position of minister of justice is recorded in various lists of possible members of a replacement government which circulated in liberal and radical circles on the eve of the revolution. According to Iosif Gessen, a prominent Cadet, what clinched the decision to bring Kerensky into the Provisional Government was the fact that he was already playing a prominent role in the Petrograd Soviet. His name figures in a draft list of members of the new government dated 1 March, although a rival candidate being discussed was the Cadet Vasiliy Maklakov, who was one of the commissars of the Provisional Committee of the State Duma in the Ministry of Justice.[35] Kerensky's authority, which had increased spectacularly during the February Days, was also needed to give the Provisional Government greater legitimacy.

An example of how this popular politician's reputation could be used was demonstrated no later than 2 March, when Milyukov, the leader of the Constitutional Democrats, was announcing the composition of the newly created Provisional Government in the Catherine Hall of the Tauride Palace to a diverse and radically minded public.[36] His listeners were expressing dissatisfaction that he was naming only representatives of a 'qualified' [property-owning] electorate. At just that moment Milyukov read out the name of Kerensky, evidently calculating that mention of a radical renowned for his challenging speeches in the Duma and his resolute actions in earlier days would go down well with his restive audience and change their attitude to the nascent government. 'But, gentlemen, I am glad to tell you that the non-property owning members of our society also have a representative in our cabinet. I have just received the agreement of my comrade, A. F. Kerensky, to occupy a post in Russia's first democratic cabinet.'

The announcement was greeted with enthusiastic applause. Relations between the two politicians were less than straightforward and were subsequently to become even more strained, but in a tricky situation Milyukov was pleased to call Kerensky his 'comrade', which helped to win over a restless crowd. Milyukov, an experienced orator, went on to spin out his success, eloquently describing the main avenues the new minister of justice would be pursuing.

> We were immensely pleased to place in the safe hands of this prominent individual a ministry which will enable him to visit the retribution they deserve on the sycophantic servants of the old regime, all these Shtyurmers and Sukhomlinovs. (Applause.) The cowardly heroes of days which will never return will now, as fortune has decreed, find themselves facing the justice not of Shcheglovitov but of Minister of Justice A. F. Kerensky.

The righteous verdict of revolutionary justice will be pronounced, a formal decision will confirm the sentence that public opinion has already passed on the servants of the old regime, and Kerensky's reputation will guarantee that they do not escape the retribution they deserve. This was just what those assembled wanted to hear: Milyukov's words were met with prolonged, tumultuous applause and loud exclamations of approval – no doubt, just as the experienced orator had hoped.[37] There were other instances where politicians of various ranks sought to resolve the issues facing them by reference to the authority of this currently most popular politician. It was a technique which further boosted Kerensky's standing.

Milyukov continued to point out that Kerensky's joining the government had been of great political importance. On 27 March, speaking at the Seventh Congress of the Constitutional Democratic Party, he said, 'I well remember the decisive moment when I congratulated myself on final victory. It was the moment when, over the telephone, A. F. Kerensky agreed to our request to become minister of justice.' It is difficult to judge how sincere this was, but, significantly, his audience agreed with his assessment: there was clapping and shouts of 'Bravo!'[38]

If Milyukov, in his 2 March speech, was currying favour with the public by referring to a minister who would prosecute the servants of tsarism, Kerensky was himself soliciting support several times that same day by promising popular action. In the Catherine Hall, addressing 'soldiers and citizens', some of whom had probably already heard Milyukov's speech, Kerensky announced he had agreed to become minister of justice. There was loud applause and cries of 'Hurrah!' Kerensky then listed several actions the government had taken, which he knew were bound to please his audience. Unlike Milyukov, however, he began with the swift freeing of imprisoned and exiled 'champions of freedom'. 'Our comrades, deputies of the Second and Fourth Dumas, who were illegally exiled to the Siberian tundra, will be immediately released and brought back with full honours.' Only after that did he come to the fate of the servants of tsarism. 'Comrades! I have under my control all the former chairmen of the Council of Ministers and all the ministers of the old regime. In accordance with the law, they will answer to the people for all their crimes.' At this there were cries from the crowd, 'Without mercy!' Kerensky continued, 'Comrades! Free Russia will not resort to the shameful means of repression used by the old regime. No one will be punished without a fair trial.'[39] He outlined his priorities: speedy liberation of the 'captives of tsarism', the firm prosecution through the courts of the servants of tsarism, and the establishment of genuine justice.

This speech was a rehearsal for a more important one he delivered later the same day. Having become minister of justice, Kerensky was keen to retain his politically important position as deputy chairman of the Executive Committee of the Petrograd Soviet. Getting no support for this from the Executive Committee, he appealed over the heads of the socialist leaders directly to the ordinary deputies in the plenum of the Soviet. In this speech too he spoke about what he had already done as minister, choosing this time to start with a guaranteed winner: retribution against the servants of tsarism. Kerensky reminded his audience that it was he who initiated those first arrests and put the prisoners under lock and key. 'Comrades, I had in my hands the members of the old government, and I had no intention of letting them give me the slip.' There was a storm of applause. Kerensky then moved on to another popular measure, announcing his orders for the release of all political prisoners. There was more enthusiastic applause, which turned into a standing ovation. The decision that Kerensky should join the government was approved by the Soviet's plenary session, and he retained his job as deputy chairman of the Executive Committee. The deputies were greeting him as already the minister of justice.[40] Kerensky not only efficiently resolved a political dilemma but at the same time enhanced his authority with the deputies, although his ploy did nothing for his relations with the Soviet's leaders. This important speech was quoted at length in Kerensky's 1917 biographies.[41]

Some of the conservatives and liberals who put Kerensky forward for minister of justice were under the misapprehension that he would have little political influence in that position. They were very much mistaken. Kerensky paid no attention to the official limits of his portfolio, barging, for instance, into the sphere of the Duma's commissar in charge of the Ministry of the Imperial Court.[42] He placed the Winter Palace under the jurisdiction and protection of the Provisional Government and arranged for the fact to be formally minuted. It was said in the city that he had declared the palace to be the property of the nation.[43] This was hugely symbolic. Sometimes the dynamic minister acted on his own initiative, presenting his colleagues with a fait accompli, but on other occasions individuals and organizations, including members of the government, sought to invoke his help in coping with various emergencies.

In addition, the post of minister of justice turned out to be exceptionally important, and Kerensky made full use of the opportunities it afforded. All decisions of the Provisional Government passed through his ministry. It was Kerensky who confirmed the order of the Duma's commissars in the Ministry of Justice to release imprisoned members of the Duma who were Social Democrats and, as we have seen, who ceremoniously made the announcement. Public opinion attributed this important and popular decision to Kerensky personally. The minister of justice sent a telegram to all prosecutors for the immediate release of all political prisoners and instructed them to congratulate the prisoners on behalf of the revolutionary government. The receipt of this telegram was often an important moment for the revolution in the provinces, emboldening opponents of the old regime to act decisively. Not infrequently the prisoners were released immediately after the minister's instructions were received, and in some places this was staged as a ceremony. Public reading of the telegram became part of the 'festival of freedom' in various cities and also contributed to Kerensky's growing popularity.[44] An army doctor with responsibility for the health of an army corps wrote, 'I am very touched to read that, by order of "Minister of Justice Citizen Kerensky", those who fought for freedom are now being released from all the jails and from the "dark depths of Siberian mines".'[45]

One of Kerensky's first acts had been to order the seizure of the files of the secret police and transfer them to the safekeeping of the Academy of Sciences. Commenting on this act, an American in Petrograd remarked that Kerensky was a skilled practitioner of public relations.[46]

Finally, Kerensky continued to be in charge of the conditions for high-ranking prisoners and, after their arrest, for the royal couple too. (Originally the guards of the former tsar were subordinate to General Lavr Kornilov, who, after the February Days, became commander of the Petrograd Military District.) The press supportive of the minister of justice reported that he had the conditions in which his royal prisoners were kept under his personal constant, strict supervision. 'Even the dismissal of cooks and scullery maids has to be sanctioned by A. F. Kerensky,' a Menshevik newspaper reported.[47] The taking prisoner of the royal family had great symbolic importance, and it too augmented the minister's power. While some saw Kerensky as the guarantor of revolutionary retribution, others believed that only he stood between his captives and a vengeful rabble. That opinion was shared by some of the aristocrats close to the royal couple, and at this time Nicholas II himself viewed Kerensky positively.

The commandant of the Peter and Paul Fortress, where the top officials who had been arrested were confined, did not at first know whose orders to obey, but in the end decided it was 'Kerensky's ministry'. Also under the jurisdiction of the minister of justice was the Extraordinary Investigative Commission, established by the Provisional Government to investigate the crimes of the old regime.[48]

Kerensky had additionally chosen energetic deputies for himself from among the political defence lawyers he knew, entrusting them with the day-to-day running of the ministry, leaving him to concentrate on matters of general political importance. The officials in the Ministry of Justice operated competently and efficiently, which distinguished them to their advantage from a number of other ministries.

His status as the liberator of political prisoners was also important: those who had returned from penal servitude and exile sent all manner of requests to the minister of justice. Many of them now joined the political elite of revolutionary Russia, highly respected as champions of freedom, which meant that establishing political and personal relationships with them also became an important source of strength. Funds were sent to Kerensky to help 'those who had suffered for their political beliefs'. On 4 March the Committee of Congresses of Representatives of Private Commercial Banks resolved unanimously to donate over 500,000 rubles to the minister of justice for that purpose. The Board of the Russo-Asian Bank also directed Alexey Putilov to transfer 500,000 rubles to Kerensky for the welfare of the 'former politicals'.[49] News of these donations was printed in the newspapers, inviting readers to aid, through the good offices of the minister of justice, those who had languished in captivity under the old regime. Kerensky's central role was confirmed by the entrepreneurs' donations.

Public opinion credited Kerensky with many popular measures which were in fact taken by the Provisional Government as a whole. Contributing to this was the fact that government decisions were often given legal form and signed by the minister of justice. Some statutes were initially elaborated in the Ministry of Justice, which also added to the prestige of the man at its head. Many people believed the minister had personally declared an amnesty and abolished the death penalty, when in fact these were collective policy decisions of the government. Rapturous congratulations on these measures were sent to Kerensky, and his supporters did nothing in their propaganda to correct the mistake. His biographer Oleg Leonidov wrote that, 'In his short tenure at the Ministry of Justice, Kerensky introduced legislation of exceptional historical importance. He abolished the death penalty in Russia for all time, raising Russia's legal conscience to a level which was a shining beacon in the midst of a churning sea of passions.'[50]

The matters dealt with by the minister of justice were relatively uncontroversial, which was certainly not the case with issues relating to the war and political power, which even then were causing heated debate. In the euphoric atmosphere, many hearts melted as criminals were released from jail, often perceived as also being 'prisoners of the regime' and 'victims of the social system'. The expectation was that they would be reborn as virtuous citizens in the beneficent new conditions of the revolution. Some former criminals did volunteer for the front, and others became political activists. Many of these 'victims of the old regime', however, returned to their old ways, agreeably surprised by the easy pickings in the social disorder of the period. After a time these hardened criminals came to be known sarcastically as 'Kerensky's hatchlings'.[51] In the euphoric climate of that spring, however, faith that the miraculous healing power of the revolution would transform inveterate criminals into responsible citizens was very strong.

Kerensky has gone down unjustly in the memory of history as a politician who offered fine words in place of serious action. Within a few months of the February Revolution he was being called a phrasemonger, a windbag, all talk, someone too fond of the sound of his own voice. Initially, however, it was the minister of justice who was seen as exceptionally hardworking, a statesman, an efficient administrator, a man of deeds who did not waste words.

Petrograd's *Malen'kaya gazeta* [Little Newspaper] lavished praise on what he was doing. Shortly after the formation of the Provisional Government, it described him in these terms:

> From his speeches he would not have been judged an outstanding deputy: there was little vivid language or imagery in them. On the other hand, he was always there in the thick of a skirmish. His is evidently a decidedly active personality rather than a verbose one.
>
> His first steps as minister show that in him we have lost a run-of-the-mill State Duma deputy but found something a hundred times rarer and more precious – a statesman of honesty and integrity! His first steps have been bold and energetic. . . .
>
> And Kerensky, enthusiastically undertaking this creative work, this bold replacement of the old with the boldly new which brings such joy to everyone, is doing precisely what the people passionately want from the new government. That is the very definition of an excellent minister.[52]

The newspapers' journalists were, moreover, highly critical of other ministers of the Provisional Government and considered some in charge of ministries to be simply unfit for their positions. In that context, such an enthusiastic assessment of the minister of justice carries added weight. Significantly, the French ambassador, who can hardly have been familiar with the contents of this local newspaper, contrasted the young politician with his colleagues: 'They have one man of action among them, the young Minister of Justice, Kerensky.'[53]

Newspaper reports chronicled Kerensky's feverish workload: receiving delegations and individual visitors, preparing important documents, meetings which went on day and night, speeches in different parts of the city, travels round the country. A correspondent received by the minister wrote, 'As he himself confirms, the day has been filled with countless delegations, hundreds of documents and quick-fire trips around the city.'[54] An author in an Odessa magazine reported that the 'ubiquitous and ever-vigilant' Kerensky possessed unique abilities and 'does the work of ten men', performing miracles of revolutionary creativity, organizing the new order and drumming up revolutionary enthusiasm. 'He is a magician, but one who works not by sleight of hand and verbal facility but with iron fortitude and vision. . . . Kerensky is everywhere. With his fiery eyes intoxicated by overwork and sleepless nights and his gaunt, sallow face, he suddenly pops up, bringing order, calm and even jubilation.' The gushing journalist concluded, 'All hail the Omnipresent Kerensky!'[55]

A cartoon by Nikolai Radlov depicts Kerensky in a clock shop asking for clock with a 30-hour dial: 'In these times and in my ministry, 24 hours is simply not enough!'[56]

Kerensky's supporters emphasized that, with his arrival, the way the department operated changed completely. A Saratov lawyer representing 'young barristers', who was also a deputy of the local soviet, reported on his trip to Petrograd. This was minuted as follows.

> In the Ministry of Justice everything has changed drastically. The morals and way of doing things are something that could never have been dreamed of before the revolution. Comrade Kerensky is overburdened with work, and his role is extremely difficult and demanding. He is the lynchpin of, on the one hand, the revolutionary government and, on the other, the mass of the people, and for as long as Comrade Kerensky is in the ministry we can rest assured that the interests of all the workers will be fully protected.[57]

Very diverse social groups submitted their demands to the new minister. The greetings and appeals sent to him in March give a sense of their expectations. Several forms of salutation contained the implication that this minister would act in a fundamentally different manner from his predecessors. He was addressed, for example, as 'the first minister of the people's conscience',[58] 'the minister of fairness',[59] the 'minister of fairness and the new justice'.[60]

Prisoners wrote from jail to ask, even demand, their early release. The prisoners of the prison in Astrakhan, for example, wrote:

> We send greetings to the new government and, in the person of Your Most High Excellency, welcome the dawn of truth and impartiality in court. In tears we repent our past transgressions and, as victims of arbitrariness now, in these days of hope in Russia, we beg you to liberate us and give us the opportunity of joining the ranks of our troops to defend the fatherland.[61]

Sometimes the inmates did not directly ask to be released, but the general tone of their letters implied that the revolution would now bring freedom for everyone. Whoever wrote the letter on behalf of the criminal inmates of Saratov province's prison had a good command of the idiom for conveying a sense of revolutionary enthusiasm.

> Bright the dawn! Russia is free! The Russian soul which has for centuries been suffering, now overflowing with joy, is still. Tears of joy are flowing. We kiss the hands of the workers, soldiers and members of the State Duma who fought for the freedom, honour and greatness of our beloved homeland. . . . We welcome the joining of the Provisional Government by our beloved Alexander Fyodorovich Kerensky from Saratov, tireless champion and defender of the dispossessed Russian people and their freedom.[62]

'Minister of Justice A. F. Kerensky.' Artist S. Kushchenko. Postcard, 1917. © Russian National Library/Prints Collection.

‘State Comptroller I. V. Godnev.’ Artist S. Kushchenko. Postcard, 1917. © Russian National Library/Prints Collection.

‘[Profiteers] Leaving the Kerensky Concert.’ Artist A. Khvostov, *Budil’nik* [The Alarm Clock], no. 21, June 1917, p. 12. © Russian National Library/Prints Collection.

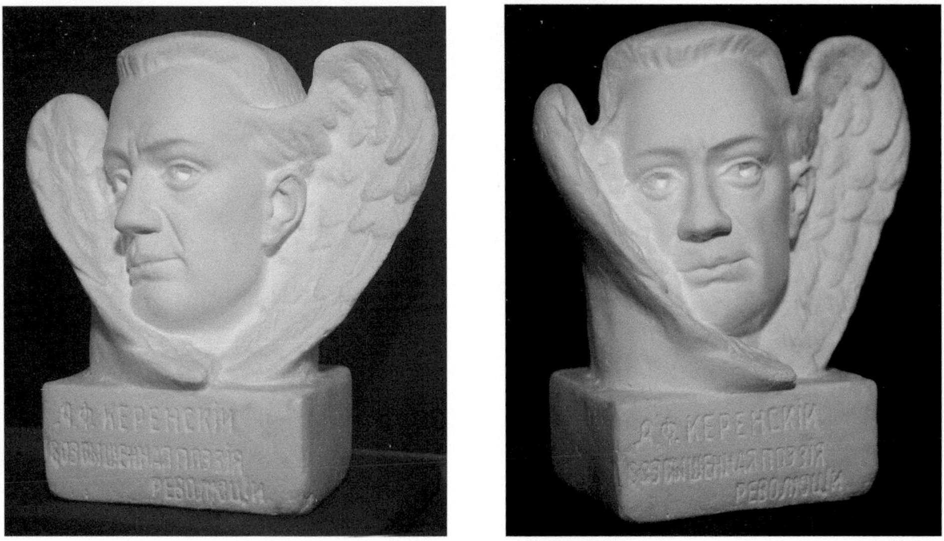

Plaster busts, inscribed ‘A. F. Kerensky, sublime poetry of the revolution.’
© The State Central Museum of Contemporary History of Russia.

Cover of *Bich* [The Scourge], no. 20, May 1917.
© Russian National Library/Prints Collection.

'A truly comradely favour from one socialist minister to another.' Artist M. Aza, *Bich* [The Scourge], no. 22, 1917, p. 8. © Russian National Library/Prints Collection.

'Kerensky as Bonaparte, or What Comrade Trotsky dreams when he has a 40-degree temperature.' *Bich* [The Scourge], no. 23. © Russian National Library/Prints Collection.

'"Sensation!" "Brink of Disaster".' Cover of *Budil'nik*, no. 24, 1917. © Russian National Library/Prints Collection.

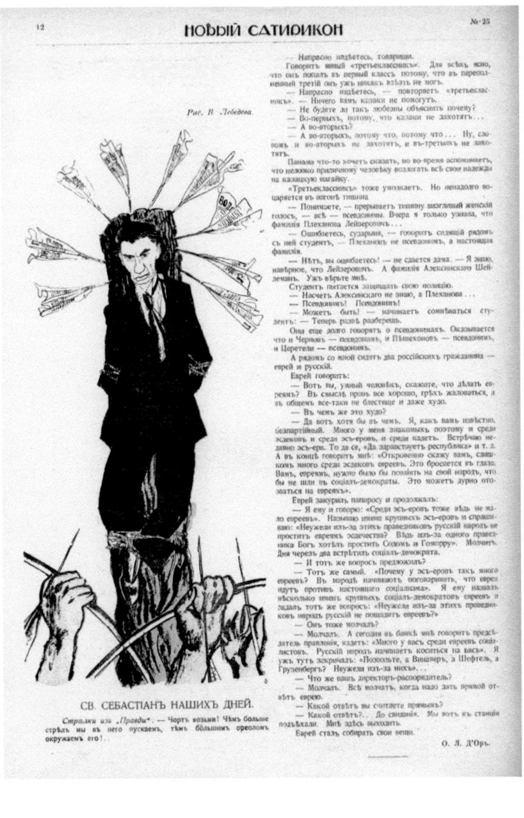

12 НОВЫЙ САТИРИКОН №·25

Рис. В. Лебедева.

СВ. СЕБАСТІАНЪ НАШИХЪ ДНЕЙ.

Стрѣлки изъ „Правды". — Чортъ возьми! Чѣмъ больше стрѣлъ мы въ него пускаемъ, тѣмъ бо́льшимъ ореоломъ окружаемъ его!..

— Напрасно надѣетесь, товарищи.

Говоритъ явный «третьеклассникъ». Для всѣхъ ясно, что онъ попалъ въ первый классъ потому, что въ переполненный третій онъ ужъ никакъ влѣзть не могъ.

— Напрасно надѣетесь, — повторяетъ «третьеклассникъ». — Ничего вамъ казаки не помогутъ.

— Не будете ли такъ любезны объяснить почему?

— Во-первыхъ, потому, что казаки не захотятъ...

— А во-вторыхъ?

— А во-вторыхъ, потому что, потому что... Ну, словомъ и во-вторыхъ не захотятъ, и въ-третьихъ не захотятъ.

Панама что-то хочетъ сказать, но во-время вспоминаетъ, что неловко приличному человѣку возлагать всѣ свои надежды на казацкую нагайку.

«Третьеклассникъ» тоже умолкаетъ. Но ненадолго воцаряется въ вагонѣ тишина

— Понимаете, — прерываетъ тишину визгливый женскій голосъ, — всѣ — псевдонимы. Вчера я только узнала, что фамилія Плеханова Лейзеровичъ...

— Ошибаетесь, сударыня, — говоритъ сидящій рядомъ съ ней студентъ, — Плехановъ не псевдонимъ, а настоящая фамилія.

— Нѣтъ, вы ошибаетесь! — не сдается дама. — Я знаю, навѣрное, что Лейзеровичъ. А фамилія Алексинскаго Шейдеманъ. Ужъ вѣрьте мнѣ.

Студентъ пытается защищать свою позицію.

— Насчетъ Алексинскаго не знаю, а Плеханова...

— Псевдонимъ! Псевдонимъ!

— Можетъ быть! — начинаетъ сомнѣваться студентъ: — Теперь развѣ разберешь.

Они еще долго говорятъ о псевдонимахъ. Оказывается что и Черновъ — псевдонимъ, и Пѣшехоновъ — псевдонимъ, и Церетели — псевдонимъ.

А рядомъ со мной сидятъ два россійскихъ гражданина — еврей и русскій.

Еврей говоритъ:

— Вотъ вы, умный человѣкъ, скажите, что дѣлать евреямъ? Въ смыслѣ правъ все хорошо, грѣхъ жаловаться, а въ общемъ все-таки не блестяще и даже худо.

— Въ чемъ же это худо?

— Да вотъ хотя бы въ чемъ. Я, какъ вамъ извѣстно, безпартійный. Много у меня знакомыхъ поэтому и среди эсдековъ и среди эсъ-еровъ, и среди кадетъ. Встрѣчаю недавно эсъ-ера. То да се, «Да здравствуетъ республика» и т. д. А въ концѣ говоритъ мнѣ: «Откровенно скажу вамъ, слишкомъ много среди эсдековъ евреевъ. Это бросается въ глаза. Вамъ, евреямъ, нужно было бы повліять на свой народъ, что бы не шли въ соціалъ-демократы. Это можетъ дурно отозваться на евреяхъ».

Еврей закурилъ папиросу и продолжалъ:

— Я ему и говорю: «Среди эсъ-еровъ тоже вѣдь не мало евреевъ». Называю имена крупныхъ эсъ-еровъ и спрашиваю: «Неужели изъ-за этихъ праведниковъ русскій народъ не проститъ евреямъ эсдечества? Вѣдь изъ-за одного праведника Богъ хотѣлъ простить Содомъ и Гоморру». Молчитъ. Дня черезъ два встрѣтилъ соціалъ-демократа.

— И тотъ же вопросъ предложилъ?

— Тотъ же самый. «Почему у эсъ-еровъ такъ много евреевъ? Въ народѣ начинаютъ поговаривать, что евреи идутъ противъ настоящаго соціализма». Я ему назвалъ нѣсколько именъ крупныхъ соціалъ-демократовъ евреевъ и задалъ тотъ же вопросъ: «Неужели изъ-за этихъ праведниковъ народъ русскій не пощадитъ евреевъ?»

— Онъ тоже молчалъ?

— Молчалъ. А сегодня въ банкѣ мнѣ говоритъ предсѣдатель правленія, кадетъ: «Много у васъ среди евреевъ соціалистовъ. Русскій народъ начинаетъ коситься на васъ». Я ужъ тутъ закричалъ: «Позвольте, а Винаверъ, а Шефтель, а Грузенбергъ? Неужели изъ-за нихъ»...

— Что же вашъ директоръ-распорядитель?

— Молчалъ. Всѣ молчатъ, когда надо дать прямой отвѣтъ еврею.

— Какой отвѣтъ вы считаете прямымъ?

— Какой отвѣтъ?.. До свиданія. Мы вотъ къ станціи подъѣхали. Мнѣ здѣсь выходить.

Еврей сталъ собирать свои вещи.

О. Л. Д'Оръ.

'The St Sebastian of our days.' Artist V. Lebedev, *Novy Satirikon* [New Satirikon], no. 25, 1917, p. 12. © Russian National Library/Prints Collection.

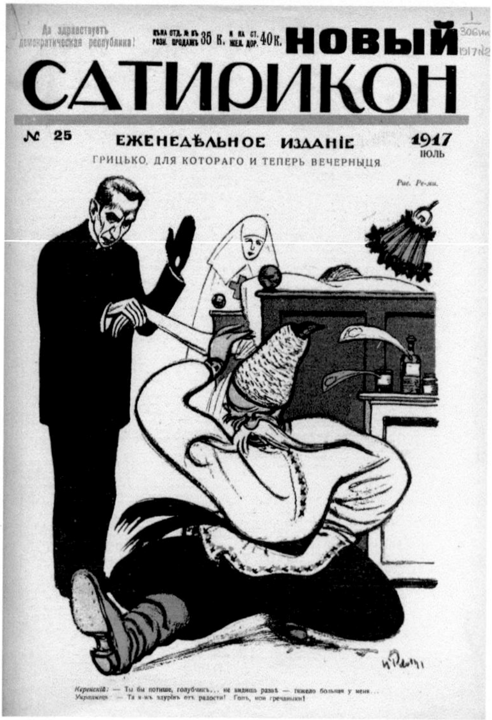

'Hryts'ko, for whom this is party time.' Artist Re-mi (N.V. Remizov), cover of *Novy Satirikon*, no. 25, July 1917. © Russian National Library/Prints Collection.

'A living barrier.' Artist N. Nikolaevsky, cover of *Bich* [The Scourge], no. 30, 1917. © Russian National Library/Prints Collection.

A token depicting Kerensky.
© State Museum of Russian Political History, St Petersburg (GMPIR).

'Kerensky, the Russian Moses.' Artist V. Lebedev, *Novy Satirikon*, no. 41, 1917.
© Russian National Library/Prints Collection.

Portrait of A. F. Kerensky by Isaak Brodsky.
© State Museum of Russian Political History, St Petersburg (GMPIR).

In several messages, Kerensky was described as the 'guardian of law and the rule of law'. That was the form of address chosen by the Omsk Women's Union.[63] Sometimes the salutations differed little from official ways of addressing pre-revolutionary officials. Judges and prosecutors congratulated the new minister in the style of the old regime, adhering strictly to the traditional form of words appropriate to such a communication. Kerensky was at first regularly called by the tsarist title of 'Your Most High Excellency'. Sometimes the old titles found their way into the resolutions of even radical organizations, combining different modes of address.

Peasants of Stavropol province, who were members of the Trudovik group, addressed Kerensky as follows: 'We greet in the person of Your Most High Excellency a true champion of truth and the rule of law.' Sometimes revolutionary twists were included in traditional greetings. A missive from the prosecutor's office of the Samara Circuit Court read: '[The Chancery] greets Your Excellency as a dedicated champion of the honour of the motherland and the freedom of the Russian people. We take pride in the first people's minister of justice.'[64] Those drafting congratulations and petitions were reaching for new ways to address a statesman respectfully, drawing on old patterns and new forms. As we see, this could generate eclectic combinations.

Simultaneously, however, fundamentally new imagery was being devised for the revolutionary minister. In some addresses Kerensky was represented as a man restoring the abused virtue of the law, and the guarantee of this was his reputation as a champion of law. The barristers of Tsaritsyn expressed their confidence that the minister would restore the rule of law. 'We are confident that your appointment signals the end of Shcheglovitov justice and that, in your new high post, you will defend the ideals of democracy.' The Odessa Committee of Assistant Barristers declared: 'The junior barristers, proudly aware that the first truly democratic minister in Russia has emerged from the members of the bar, hail you as the first minister of justice reborn, the first prosecutor general appointed by the people and, in your person, the new government.'

Representatives of the justice department of Graivoron district sent greetings to 'a champion fighting for freedom for the people, for the good of the motherland and the glorious return of justice, swift, merciful, and equal for all.' The barristers of Velikiye Luki praised Kerensky as a steadfast defender of the law: 'Your name at the head of the Ministry of Justice is fearful for traitors but a symbol of the courageous struggle for rights and truth and a guarantee of the victory of light over darkness in the courts.'[65] Significantly, these greetings demanding restoration of the impartiality of the law came from lawyers.

This image of a minister of state taking on the heavy burden of asserting the rule of law was promoted by Kerensky himself. On arriving in the Ministry of Justice on 4 March, he described his mission to the ministry's officials.

> Gentlemen, from the Executive Committee of the State Duma I have accepted the post of minister of justice, the post of the guardian of law and the rule of law in this country. Hitherto, this lofty obligation has been turned by those who served the old regime into a travesty of law. These lofty concepts existed only on paper. Now they will be realized in full measure in action. I give my word that, when I leave the post of minister of justice, not one of the most malicious enemies of free Russia will dare to say that, during Kerensky's tenure of the post the law, the rule of law and the exercise of justice continued in this ministry to be mere words. That is my mission. It is brief in formulation but will be titanic in implementation.[66]

In some of the resolutions and addresses sent to him, Kerensky is portrayed not only as someone who will restore the rule of law, but as someone who will, for the first time, introduce legality into institutions which, it is claimed, had constantly repudiated it. In a resolution from the Kronshtadt Soviet of Deputies of 15 March, the minister is praised 'for selfless, valiant service to Russian democracy in a post which, until now, has been used only to legalize outrageous arbitrariness and lawlessness.'[67]

Some lawyers demanded that Kerensky should not only restore legal propriety but also radically transform the entire Russian judicial system. His first reforms elicited enthusiastic approval from some of them.

In messages to Kerensky he is described as 'the Elect of the people', who has been made minister 'by the will of the people'.[68] In other messages, the 'minister of the people's truth' is perceived as the incarnation of revolutionary retribution. Some who had returned from exile demanded that he should 'take decisive measures against all the minions of the old order.' 'Strangle mercilessly the hydra of reaction throughout the land so that it never rises again,' demanded another resolution. One peasant assembly called for Nicholas and his spouse to be brought before 'the impartial court of Kerensky'.[69]

Although, as we have said, there was a general public consensus about the issues falling within the purview of the minister of justice, already the fault lines of possible future conflicts were detectable. First and foremost, this was the issue highlighted by Kerensky, Milyukov, journalists and those writing to the minister: the question of punishment of the enemy within. This need was seen by many as especially important and urgent. 'A very great deal depends on Kerensky. All the pillars of the old regime are now in his hands. He is promising strict but fair justice in accordance with the will of the people of such traitors as Sukhomlinov and Shtyurmer,' noted one contemporary in his diary on 3 March.[70]

The actions and speeches of the minister of justice sent different signals to different sections of the public. On some occasions he stated that there would be no escape from severe punishment, while on others he emphasized that clemency was preferable. To members of the soviets and committees he promised to prosecute enemies of the revolution rigorously. To the deputies of the Helsingfors Soviet he pointed out, 'I am not only the minister, but also the prosecutor general, and all the power to punish is in my hands. None of the enemies of the new Russia will elude me.' He spoke in the same vein in Mogilyov, addressing the officers and soldiers of General Headquarters: 'As prosecutor general I watch vigilantly for the slightest activity on the part of the defeated reactionaries and take all necessary measures to consolidate freedom.'[71] In the Petrograd Soviet he declared on 26 March, 'I know who the enemies of the people are, and I know how to deal with them.'[72] Many of the revolution's most fervent supporters expected just such declarations from Kerensky.

It is not surprising certain public bodies were concerned when the minister of justice ordered alleviation of the conditions of detention of leading figures of the old regime. Kerensky tried to reassure revolutionary activists.[73]

These were disturbed when Kerensky ordered the release of the frail and elderly General Nikolai Ivanov on 24 March. (The general signed a pledge of loyalty to the Provisional Government and gave an undertaking not to leave Petrograd.)[74] Kerensky was reproached for freeing this enemy of the people without consulting the Executive Committee of the Soviet. On 26 March the minister explained himself to a meeting of the soldiers' section of the Petrograd Soviet. In the speech he made frequent reference to his struggle against the old regime before the revolution and during the coup. Kerensky's explanations were accepted, the chairman confirmed his status as revolutionary Leader, and the enthused deputies bore him shoulder-high out of the hall.[75] The minister had again used the method he had tried and tested in the days of the revolution of speaking over the heads of their leaders to the ordinary deputies of the Soviet. And, again, it worked. Kerensky's relations with the leaders of the Executive Committee became even more fraught, but they could not go against the mood of the soldiers who were bearing the popular minister aloft.

Many people were certain that the tsar, and especially the tsaritsa, were traitors and accomplices of the enemy, and their view seemed to have expert backing. Prominent politicians, military leaders, members of the tsar's court, and even some members of the imperial family were saying much the same thing.[76] Such was the climate in which the Socialist Revolutionaries' newspaper reported: 'The Tsar . . . was close to an organization of spies working in the cause of Wilhelm II. Not only that, he actually appointed people known to be traitors, enemies of the motherland, to be his top ministers.'[77]

It was hardly surprising, then, that there were widespread calls for retribution against the tsar, the tsaritsa and servants of the old regime. These were reflected in collective letters and resolutions. There were demands that they should be be locked up in 'the Shlisselburg fortress, as it is the most reliable, on soldiers' rations.' (Those drafting the resolution were evidently unaware that the notorious 'Russian Bastille' had been burned down during the February Days.) Other resolutions demanded the former tsar should be incarcerated in the Peter and Paul Fortress or a prison in Kronshtadt, where the garrison was known for its radicalism. (The newspapers wrote about the travails of officers who had been held in Kronshtadt prisons since the revolution.) Some of these resolutions were passed in May, when Kerensky had already ceased to be minister of justice but remained in charge of the person of the tsar. Earlier in the revolution, however, there had been collective demands for harsh punishment. In the second half of April a peasant congress in Yenisey province demanded 'confiscation of the property and capital of the former tsar . . . [and] appointment of a strict court for capital punishment'.[78] Public opinion in this, as in many other cases, favoured passing a severe sentence without the formality of a trial.

At the same time, many others were demanding that the minister should show clemency. At the Congress of the Constitutional Democratic Party, Prince Yevgeny Trubetskoy, a noted philosopher, declared on 27 March: 'The death penalty was abolished the day after the revolution by our profoundly congenial neighbour on the left, A. F. Kerensky, who uttered a historic phrase destined for immortality, a phrase which will for all time proclaim the superiority of the Russian Revolution to all which have hitherto occurred: "The Russian Revolution must astound the world by its magnanimity." '[79]

As we see, some were demanding strict application of the law by Kerensky, others expected him to show leniency, while yet others insisted on harsh retribution. Fully satisfying all these expectations would have been tricky, but the minister displayed exceptional tactical skill and retained the broadest possible base of political support. Here too a balancing act was called for to prevent, or at least postpone, possible conflict. Kerensky managed to find a solution to the situation. Assuredly, some of the arrested dignitaries and their friends and relatives were critical of Kerensky, but in these first months of the revolution no one criticized him publicly. Indeed, some dyed-in-the-wool monarchists acknowledged the correct manner in which the minister of justice behaved towards the last of the tsars.[80]

Kerensky did incur criticism for being too soft on the leaders of the old regime, and those were accusations he must have seen as potentially undermining his reputation as a resolute revolutionary. In March and April, however, his authority was so great that not one organized political force – not even the Bolsheviks – tried to take advantage of these occasional manifestations of discontent to campaign against him.

In April, Kerensky's relations with some of the deputies of the Kronshtadt Soviet soured. During the February events quite a few officers in the fortress were arrested and kept in bad conditions. Kerensky tried to intervene – something being demanded by conservative and liberal publications – and sent a commission to Kronshtadt to investigate. The Soviet's Executive Committee refused, however, to cooperate with the commission, and the lawyers appointed by Kerensky resigned. Some deputies of the Kronshtadt

Soviet felt they had put the minister in his place, but others, making clear their respect for Kerensky, denied it. Nevertheless, the newspapers reported that hostile remarks had been heard. Possibly conservative journalists were trying to fuel a conflict between the popular minister and the Kronshtadt radicals.[81] At all events, criticism of the Ministry of Justice did not necessarily imply disregard for the authority of its minister.

When Kerensky became a minister he assumed an important political position, and he exploited very skilfully the opportunities that offered. We should not, however, underestimate the challenges facing the minister of the people's truth. These emanated from unrealistic expectations on the part of the citizens of the new Russia. Kerensky's supporters were demanding that he carry out mutually contradictory reforms. At one and the same time he was being called on to show clemency, to enforce the law, and to be the agent of retribution. Convicts wanted to be freed, many lawyers wanted restoration of the rule of law, while supporters of the socialists wanted root-and-branch transformation of the legal system. Finally, many idealists with utopian revolutionary notions expected all prisons to be destroyed, all punishment to be abolished, and compulsion by the state to be ruled out completely. The statements Kerensky made during speeches to different audiences had the potential to arouse such, arguably incompatible, expectations.

Under these difficult conditions, Kerensky managed not only to retain but even to extend his political power base. He successfully managed the department entrusted to him, swiftly introducing reforms for which there was a consensus in society. His reputation as an outstanding minister was due also to the fact that he was not only the minister of justice. There was good reason why he was called the 'minister of the revolution'. He used his prestige as a champion of freedom and a hero of the revolution to resolve political problems which confronted not only his own department but the government as a whole, and other ministers quite often encouraged him to do just that. In the process Kerensky strengthened his authority by creating new images of himself as the 'democratic minister' and 'the poet of the revolution'.

3 'Democratic minister'

In early March Kerensky was sent a telegram, on behalf of the workers of the Shifman plant in Odessa, informing him that, 'associating themselves with the national rejoicing at the liberation of our beloved fatherland from the old despotic regime, they send warm greetings to the leader of democracy in all of Russia and express their willingness to devote all their strength to defending the freedom which has been won from efforts to destroy it by adherents of the old government.'[82]

Now what Kerensky and his supporters needed to do was reinforce that reputation as the 'Leader of democracy in all of Russia'.

Something that contributed to the image of the 'Leader of democracy', which Kerensky was cultivating, was his reputation as the 'democratic minister', the 'socialist minister', and the 'first minister of the people'. It was supported by his actions as minister, his political tactical manoeuvring, and the specifics of the 'democratic' self-presentation he manifested in gestures and rituals. Kerensky himself constantly emphasized his special connection with the working people, with the 'democratic forces'. He signalled this connection both with his politics and with his rhetoric, trying to demonstrate a style of administration new to Russia. Kerensky was eager to show that, even after becoming a minister, he was not turning into a bureaucrat cut off from the people but, on the contrary, remained a democrat and an exemplary citizen. Many of the supporters who sent him resolutions expected democratic politics, defence of democracy (in several senses of the word) and 'democratic' behaviour.[83]

The democratic minister's very personality made him stand out among his cabinet colleagues, the liberal ministers, who were increasingly being called representatives of the 'bourgeoisie' (and not only by socialists). Kerensky constantly emphasized and used his special position as the 'hostage for the forces of democracy' for political purposes. In his memoirs, too, he pointed out: 'Because of my position in the Revolution and in the Provisional Government I happened to be in closer touch with the people and felt more keenly the beating of the nation's pulse than the other members of the government.'[84] Although in his memoirs Kerensky rarely misses an opportunity for showing himself in a good light, here he is accurately conveying the mood in spring 1917. Even those opposed to him considered the minister a democrat and contrasted him with the other members of the Provisional Government. The Moscow Bolshevik newspaper *Sotsial-demokrat* wrote in late April: 'We have already seen an example of this in the person of the democrat Kerensky, who has constantly had to be taking responsibility for the behaviour of Guchkov and Milyukov.'[85]

Kerensky himself contributed to creating that image. As a number of contemporaries noted approvingly, he signed his appeals, instructions and orders: 'Citizen Minister'.[86]

Kerensky stressed his democratic credentials with calculated gestures. When, for example, he first arrived at the Ministry of Justice as the new minister, he shook hands with the senior porter and then spoke to the lowest-ranking staff to urge them to organize themselves in order to promote their political and professional interests. Kerensky even declared that lower-ranking officials should influence the ministry's policy, and he promised to support them.

All ranks of the ministry were asked to remove their decorations, medals, ribbons and other marks of distinction. News of this instruction was swiftly communicated to the press. It was hardly by chance that there were journalists present to witness the arrival of the new minister; they had evidently been given a tip-off that the minister would be making some newsworthy statements of interest to their readers.[87]

Kerensky was to repeat his call for democratization of the appearance of civil servants later. He made a point of shaking hands with doormen, lackeys and couriers in ministries and embassies 'in accordance with his custom of greeting everybody in the same way'. Many people felt this was just the right way a truly democratic minister ought to behave. The newspapers initially delighted in reporting this emphatic demonstration of an untraditional political style.

There were subsequent occasions when Kerensky took the opportunity to show respect to the maintenance staff. On 1 May, upon learning that the ministry's couriers were gathering to celebrate the twenty-five years of service of A. P. Tarasov, a senior courier, the minister attended the celebration, congratulated him and made a short speech.[88] It is notable that, at the height of a government crisis, Kerensky should have found time to do that. Interestingly, the episode came to the attention of the press, and the senior courier's celebration was considered an important news item. We may safely assume that Kerensky's staff responsible for press relations had realized it would be useful during the crisis to remind everyone of their chief's democratic reputation. It is even possible that the minister himself had that in mind.

Sometimes the respect the minister so pointedly showed to lower officials of the Ministry of Justice upset other officials.[89] It can safely be assumed that Kerensky's preference arose not from any desire to demean the role of judges and prosecutors but purely from political calculation: shaking hands with them would yield no political dividends, whereas his unusual democratic greeting of couriers went down well with journalists and their readers and served to enhance the authority of the citizen minister.

In other situations, too, the minister made a point of fraternizing with the 'lower ranks' and shook hands with a great many people. The process could be protracted. When visiting Revel, Kerensky shook hands with sailors for a full three hours.[90] These encounters with the hearty and enthusiastic sailors seriously tested his health. His right hand was very painful and for a time he had it in a sling, later tucking it behind the lapel of his tunic. Even after that, Kerensky did not give up shaking hands, although sometimes he used his left hand. In Moscow in late May he commissioned 500 cadets as officers, shaking hands with each of them.[91] Handshakes became the fashion, and some generals, trying to win over the revolutionary masses, followed the democratic minister's example, even shaking hands with soldiers in a guard of honour.[92]

To maintain the image of a democrat, Kerensky needed constantly to be mixing with the common people, as his supporters pointed out. 'He is all the time absorbed in an energetic mixing with the people. Without this daily refreshing "plunge", the fibres of his brain and the vigorous circulation of his will might slow down. Looking at him, you feel he is well aware of that.' The distinguishing features of a democratic leader should be 'exceptional simplicity and approachability'. The minister displayed them tirelessly. The correspondent of a provincial newspaper reported approvingly: 'People do not stand on ceremony with him, and he, in turn, is at ease with everybody. Kerensky receives everybody. Often at two in the morning a rally of some description expresses a desperate need to hear Kerensky. A phone call, and the minister, impelled by his destiny, appears on stage and gives a speech. He is responding to his destiny, because there is something predestined about this mutual attraction between the common people and their citizen minister.'[93]

With his common touch, his demonstrative approachability and his straightforwardness, Kerensky won the hearts of many front-line soldiers and provincial people who made pilgrimages to the revolutionary capital. Their rapturous response is reminiscent of the textbook Soviet descriptions of peasant representatives who came to visit Lenin. One soldier wrote, 'I, a simple village teacher, was visiting the minister. He came to see me. "Sit down, comrade," he says. Has ever any minister called a simple soldier his comrade before? That minister was Kerensky. He has done something splendid, not only for Russians. It will go out beyond the borders of our land and have something to teach the rest of the world.'[94]

Further evidence of the Leader's democratic nature was his asceticism, real and imagined.[95] The requisite 'anti-bourgeois' style was revealed in how he behaved and in how he dressed. Pre-revolutionary photographic portraits of Kerensky show an elegant, successful young man who takes care over his appearance: a neat haircut, a jacket or even a frock coat, a tie, a soft or stand-up collar. That was the way a deputy of the State Duma wanted to appear, and such photographs were used in the biographical directories of members of the Duma and supplied to journalists. That was how many people living in Russia saw Kerensky in 1917: these were the photographs used by manufacturers of postcards and posters, the writers for illustrated journals. Large photographic portraits were held aloft at demonstrations. Now, however, the minister decided he wanted the revolutionary country to see him in a different light.

Kerensky once informed Milyukov that the masses could never accept a government that wore jackets and ordinary civilian dress.[96] This testimony is confirmed by Kerensky himself, who gave this characterization of the Provisional Government's dress sense: taken as a whole, it 'did not capture the imagination of the crowd (educated or uncultured), was not attractive, did not make people want to follow it. Its speeches, everything about it was dowdy, too modest, too common, too accessible – a government of jacket-wearers.'[97]

It was true. The age-old tradition of seeing a military-style imperial government, dressed in authoritative military uniforms, conditioned the expectations of contemporaries, who had their own idea of what the leaders personifying a powerful nation ought to look like. 'The president was a pathetic civilian wearing a short jacket with dandruff on the collar and pin-striped trousers,' was how one military cadet recalled his perception of a head of government in the republics.[98]

There was another aspect to the rejection of a government of 'jacket-wearers'. In 1905–6, tsarist officials, their hair streaked with grey, were horrified at the sight of State Duma deputies who appeared not to know how to dress. They were wearing jackets! Contemporaries recall being struck by the contrast between the 'dazzling crowd of courtiers' and the deputies, 'people who looked very common indeed'. Their fears proved premature, because many Duma deputies soon took to frock coats, and some even affected morning dress. Over time, however, jacket and trousers did become increasingly popular.[99] Kerensky's refusal to wear a jacket, although that had become common within the walls of the Tauride Palace in previous years, marked a break with the traditional image of a public politician which had evolved before the revolution. The jacket was too 'democratic' for the old regime, but during the revolution it could be perceived as a 'bourgeois' symbol.

In the first post-revolutionary photographs, the minister of justice is captured still wearing a jacket or frock coat, but he then resolutely democratized his appearance, removed his tie, renounced the starched collar, and instead donned a dark, buttoned-up military-style tunic. Vladimir D. Nabokov, who also took great care over what he wore, describes Kerensky's marked change of image as a spontaneous act which he performed on 2 March: 'I remember a strange gesture he made. He was dressed as usual (that is, before he adopted the role of a "hostage for the forces of democracy" in the Provisional Government): he was wearing a jacket, and a shirt with a starched collar bent down at the corners. He took it by the corners and tore it off so that, instead of looking smart, he now had a kind of emphatically proletarian look.'[100] It is by no means certain that Nabokov has pinpointed the exact moment of Kerensky's transformation: in some post-revolutionary photographs the minister is shown still wearing a tie. However, in a diary entry dated 5 March, the artist Alexander Benois describes the young minister's unusual attire: 'He is wearing a black tunic buttoned right up to the collar, which gives it a somewhat ascetic but also very businesslike look.'[101] At the solemn ceremony of swearing in of the Provisional Government in the Governing Senate building on 15 March, Kerensky stood out among his colleagues. It appeared to the correspondent that he was wearing a 'homely windcheater'.[102]

Be that as it may, after the overthrow of the monarchy, Kerensky wore a military-style jacket. His choice of clothing was far from random. The minister thought carefully about his image. His contemporaries could not fail to notice such a dramatic change, and many mention his new look in their diaries and memoirs. Kerensky's jacket reminded foreigners of ski wear worn over the 'black shirt of a Russian artisan'; other contemporaries recall a 'black workman's jacket, buttoned to the collar, with no sight of a shirt'. To a reporter from *Petrogradskaya gazeta*, the minister's 'workman's jacket' made him look like a young student. If to his contemporaries Kerensky resembled a worker, a student or a soldier, one French diplomat believed the look implied a special classless status: 'He was dressed in a jacket buttoned to the neck, without a hard collar or a tie: not a bourgeois, not a worker, not a soldier.'[103]

Zinaida Gippius wrote about her meeting with Kerensky on 14 March. 'He is in a black military jacket (comrade minister) the like of which he never wore before. Previously he was downright elegant, with no outward trappings of "democracy".' It is interesting that Gippius saw wearing a military jacket as signalling his democratic affiliation. She is reading the style as proclaiming his role as the comrade minister, the democratic minister, the socialist minister. In her diary she is writing almost word for word what Dmitry Filosofov, describing the same meeting, wrote in his diary. 'Kerensky has just been here. In his jacket. He used not to look so democratic. Rather elegant, even.'[104] This comment makes the contrast between the new revolutionary, democratic look and Kerensky's elegance even more stark. The appearance of the minister of justice in his military jacket is more down-to-earth, more republican. Next to him, the other ministers, who continue to wear ties, look overly respectable, 'bourgeois'. That was just the effect the 'democratic' Kerensky was striving for.

The humble military jacket, together with the other calculated gestures, suggested modesty and asceticism and pointed to constant engagement with matters of state which left no time for being elegant. The democratic way Kerensky behaved and his democratic appearance were, in the eyes of some of his supporters, part and parcel of the wise and timely political decisions he was taking in the interests of the people and democracy. One adherent wrote in 1917:

> This is the source of the astonishingly 'common man' touch in his masterfulness, which does not derive from any kind of decorum (where is the decorum when he is perpetually wearing that jacket which looks in need of a good clean!). It does not come from a sense of awe at the extent of the power he wields, but is rooted in the emotion with which any peasant, intellectual, soldier or (surreptitiously) Bolshevik, looking at him, murmurs to himself, 'This man is one of us.'
>
> Kerensky is one of those people whose inborn democratic nature can propel them in an auspicious moment to unimaginable feats of heroism, of dazzling insight, of astounding demonstrations of willpower.[105]

The new image of a politician in a grimy jacket, notable for his authentically democratic aura, was important for the minister of justice. He said of himself, 'The head of government, in a jacket and unarmed.'[106] His contemporaries noted the militarization of Kerensky's appearance and dismissed it as a necessary 'tribute to the revolutionary era and his role in it'. A further militarization of his appearance was manifest in his now being accompanied by young officer adjutants who doubled as bodyguards. Kerensky evidently saw this as contributing to his new militarized image, because in a photograph taken in his office he is shown wearing the dark jacket, sitting at his desk, and flanked by two young officers in modish and not entirely regulation military tunics. Later, in August, the presence of this escort elicited not a few sarcastic remarks from regular officers, but in spring 1917 no one was criticizing him. The prosecutor general gazes out sternly at the viewer, and the photographer has clearly intended to convey the image of a dynamic and decisive statesman.

Another official photograph, taken the same day, depicts Kerensky wearing the same jacket, sitting at his desk, with a pen in his right hand and documents in front of him. The impression is that the minister has been obliged for the moment to break off his constant labour of governing the country.

Another photograph taken during this session was extensively distributed. Kerensky is depicted from the waist up, in Napoleonic pose, his right hand tucked in behind the edge of his jacket, his left, clenched, on his desk. A pen lies on an as yet unsigned document, and a stack of books serves as the backdrop. The image could certainly be taken to depict a democratic minister ready to use force to uphold the law. This was the image published in the illustrated magazines.[107]

It might be thought that the democratic minister's image-manipulation tactics, manifested in his hand-shaking, his changing the style of his clothing, and his new ritual meetings 'with the people', are hardly deserving of so much attention. Many researchers of political history, if they mention such matters at all, see them merely as exotic decorative detail peripheral to the serious narrative. There was, however, political significance behind all these actions. The historian should not regard the symbolism of power as something divorced from the practice of governing. Kerensky gave considerable thought to the decorative details. He evidently decided they were worth spending time on, despite his extraordinary workload. This cannot be explained away as a mere weakness on Kerensky's part for play-acting and posturing, as some memoirists and historians suggest. In the periodical press, in letters and diaries of the time, these symbolic actions are often mentioned and often admired. Contemporaries considered the rituals, gestures and words to be socially important.

This kind of behaviour, this kind of rhetoric, was exactly what was needed. Words and deeds of this sort were judged by the press to be significant news stories in March and April. By making a show of his democratic ways, Kerensky was strengthening his political reputation at minimal risk. If some of the practical measures the minister of justice took were already being perceived by some as too harsh and by others as unjustifiably lenient, the democratic minister's image management created and reinforced the reputation he needed. It served to ward off attacks from the left and contained the criticism of the right. In this regard, Kerensky differed little from modern politicians in many countries who spend a lot of time shaking hands, ostentatiously 'listening' to the people, and democratizing their appearance. What is different about the minister of the revolution's behaviour is that the political culture of the new Russia was being created on the basis of the traditions of the revolutionary underground. Its rituals, texts and symbols needed, however, to be adapted to national and governmental purposes, adjusted to the needs of a new openly public politics, and used to solve actual problems. Kerensky was acting as the setter of revolutionary fashion, and that, alongside other factors, was a major source of his authority. He was setting an example of political behaviour and political presentation, performing the role of an exemplary democratic politician.

In a situation where millions of people had just woken up to the demands of participating in political life, such an example was much needed. Tens, hundreds of thousands of young, energetic people had suddenly come to power as members of all sorts of committees and soviets. They were receiving their training in how to 'do' politics when already in power and exercising it. Members of the 'committee class' were getting to grips with previously unknown political texts, adopting political gestures and participating in political rituals. Kerensky's democratic style was copied by committee members at all levels, who were influenced by his rhetoric and presentational tactics. They industriously shook hands, showed off their asceticism, and wore ostentatiously modest jackets.

Kerensky, unlike other politicians aspiring to leadership status, was not called a 'teacher', and his supporters did not call themselves 'disciples'. He influenced his supporters, allies and even opponents not by offering a doctrine but by giving an example to members of the new committee class of how to behave.

Here we should pause and give Kerensky credit for the creativity and artistry he displayed. He deserved his reputation as a politician creating something new. It was a reputation which contributed in no small part to legitimizing him as a democratic Leader.

4 'Minister of revolutionary theatricality' and 'poet of the revolution'

In June 1917, the front cover of the Moscow theatre magazine *Rampa i zhizn'* [Footlights and Life] carried a portrait of Kerensky. The caption read, 'The great enthusiast and inspired romantic of the Russian Revolution'.[108] The minister of war was depicted as a famous actor, the artist having taken a well-known pre-revolutionary photograph of Kerensky (who by this time had taken to wearing a khaki-coloured military tunic) and represented him in an elegant suit with a light-coloured tie propping up a stand-up collar. The minister appears to be wearing make-up, complete with eye-liner and lipstick. The reason for Kerensky's appearing on the cover of a theatre magazine was a speech he had given at the Bolshoy Theatre (discussed below in chapter III, § 6). Evidently, professional theatre people had regarded the minister's performance as a dazzling display of the art of the theatre, hence his being awarded the cover portrait.

The portrait could serve as an illustration for descriptions which were coming Kerensky's way. Many people were calling him an actor, and not in any flattering sense. Even in 1917, many contemporaries, quite independently of each other, were referring to him in their letters and diary entries as an actor, and this was building up into a negative attitude towards the minister. Other considerably less flattering versions are encountered: 'a buffoon', 'a circus turn', 'a juggler', 'a tightrope walker'. Kerensky was even likened to an overly histrionic actress. From May onwards this theme of the minister's histrionics recurs on the pages of certain newspapers.[109]

The soubriquet of 'actor' implied a politician who was too much given to producing too many extravagant speeches and not taking enough action, who was paying too much attention to superficial theatricality and vacuous displays of power, to decorative frippery aimed at concealing the reality of his political performance. In June 1917 Lenin called Kerensky 'the minister of revolutionary theatricality', claiming that his eloquent speechifying was designed to disguise the class nature of the Provisional Government, while such 'bourgeois' ministers as Shingaryov, Tereshchenko and Lvov got on with organizing things their way.[110] Kerensky's acting the role of a dynamic political strongman in reality served, according to Lenin, only to mask the real policies of the government being sneaked through behind the scenes by other ministers who were cynically, artfully, surreptitiously implementing the policies required by the ruling class.

Lenin's characterization points to another aspect of Kerensky which he found objectionable: his style of politics. It was an attitude shared by many contemporaries across the political spectrum. His 'theatrical' rhetorical techniques and gestures, the hysterical Kerensky-mania of his admirers (especially his female admirers), irritated even some of his supporters. This was not how they expected a serious and level-headed statesman to behave.

Another implication was that the minister was insincere. Kerensky, it was felt, was prepared to play very different roles, easily donning one mask after another, pretending to be someone who, in reality, he was not, adapting himself to suit the changing tastes of his public. Opponents accused the minister of acting, with variable success, whichever role was called for at a particular moment: the democrat, the socialist, the hero, the revolutionary, the authoritative politician, the internationalist, the man of action, the true patriot, the non-partisan politician, the party member . . . It seemed impossible to get behind all these political masks to see what the politician's real personality and true beliefs were.

The minister's thespian artifice was pondered by actors, who analysed his performance technique with professional insight. Alisa Koonen later recalled:

> I ended up on one occasion at the Assembly of the Nobility where, it was said, Kerensky was going to speak. The hall was packed. It was such a crush that I was all for making my escape without waiting

> for it to start, but I found it impossible to reach the exit. The crowd was made up predominantly of ladies, elegantly dressed, waiting for the start of the rally in a fever of anticipation. Both Kerensky's performance and the atmosphere in the hall resembled some hysterical theatre performance. Kerensky struck me as the type of the neurasthenic actor (a métier which had not yet gone out of fashion). He threw himself into acting the role of a Leader, drawing the crowd in his wake. The ladies as they listened to him clutched their heads, sobbed, plucked rings and bracelets from their hands and flung them on to the stage. I could make no sense of their shrieking and for some reason found my attention focused on the question of what Kerensky would do with all these jewels which had been thrown at his feet.[111]

Koonen's memoirs date from the Soviet period, so it is hard to judge her own sincerity when she speaks of Kerensky's insincerity. In 1917, though, she was not alone in seeing him as a politician diligently, and not unsuccessfully, acting the part of a Leader.

And yet it might be premature to consider the portrait on the cover of *Rampa i zhizn'* as a wilful caricature of Kerensky, because at just that time many people liked his theatrical style. On 6 September two schoolgirls sent him a letter, enclosing postcards with his portrait. The friends wrote:

> We are writing to you, greatly respected Alexander Fyodorovich, to ask a big, special favour! We would really, really like to have you write something for us on these two postcards. Please do not be surprised or cross at what is perhaps not a wholly appropriate request, but we know you are a sensitive, responsive person, so you will understand us and not judge us too strictly.
>
> We would like to find superhuman words to convince you of our sincere wish to have a souvenir of the great man to whom all of Russia is looking with hope and boundless trust, before whose intelligence and brilliant talent as a speaker the entire Russian people bow down and will bow down. With our respect, Anya Solomatova, Ira Fadeyeva.

There is an accompanying postscript: 'What a joy it would be to have real photographs of you.'[112]

Can this letter of schoolgirl admirers eager for a handwritten inscription from Kerensky really be of any interest to historians? The girls still retain their enthusiasm for the politician in September 1917 when, after the Kornilov Affair, Kerensky's popularity was rapidly declining.[113] In the spring, of course, this kind of attitude had been commonplace. The letter resembles messages sent by lady theatregoers to their idol, a famous opera singer, perhaps, or an adored actor. Some admirers of Kerensky, like the fans of theatre celebrities, referred to the minister as 'my angel', but this immediately led to ironic put-downs. We can take it that Anya Solomatova and Ira Fadeyeva were dreaming of portraits of Kerensky hanging in their rooms, sanctified by his autograph, and this too is suggestive of the cult of popular actors. This letter, however, is being sent to a 'great man', whose deeds have ensured him a place in history. He is remarkable for his 'brilliant talent as a speaker', his gift of eloquence which brings him closer again to actors and authors and delights readers, spectators and listeners. In their letter, alongside their political and aesthetic assessment of Kerensky, there is also a moral evaluation: he is described as a 'sensitive and responsive' person, somebody able to understand others, and this is also reminiscent of the letters of rapturous theatregoers to their idols. The schoolgirls' letter seems fairly typical, but it is worth remembering that the 'minister of revolutionary theatricality' strongly appealed not only to schoolgirls but also to grim-faced soldiers on the front line.

Kerensky gave a lot of speeches in 1917. He delivered them in famous theatres: the Mariinsky, the Alexandrinsky and Mikhailovsky in Petrograd, the Bolshoy in Moscow, and the Opera in Odessa. People in other cities also witnessed his speeches, crowding the auditoriums of theatres, circuses and picture houses. Kerensky spoke in city squares and on regimental parade grounds, at workers' rallies and to troops preparing for battle. Most of the speeches remembered by his contemporaries were, nevertheless, those delivered in theatres.

As a young man the future minister dreamed of a career as an opera singer, for which he had the necessary natural attributes.[114] The young Alexander Kerensky took singing lessons, and his well-modulated voice proved useful later when speaking in public as a barrister and as a deputy of the State Duma, but especially in 1917 when he had to speak before crowds of thousands. In March and April alone, Kerensky visited Moscow, Mogilyov, Kronshtadt, Revel and Finland (twice). The geographical reach of his expeditions expanded in May and June after he became minister of war. Everywhere he gave speeches, and everywhere he met with an enthusiastic welcome. 'Compared to the royal progresses, this meeting was remarkable for its unfeigned sincerity. It bore the hallmark of a truly popular festival,' recalled Eduard Pantzerzhansky, a naval officer who observed the minister's speeches in Revel.[115] This testimony in the memoirs of a famous Soviet naval commander inspires confidence, especially if we remember that he wrote them at a time when the USSR was trying not to allow Kerensky any positive assessments.

Politics in different eras has lent itself to many very different forms of theatricality, and many rulers and politicians have been good actors. Parliamentary politics, of course, substantially increased the number of participants in 'government performances'. The revolutionary period, however, had its own specific features. One of the most popular theatrical genres of the time was the concert rally, at which speeches by veterans of the revolutionary movement and by current politicians were interspersed with dramatic readings and the performance of songs and tunes appropriate to the occasion by professional singers and musicians. Kerensky, an influential politician and creative orator who plainly enjoyed giving speeches, and who could improvise adroitly before an appreciative audience, was a recognized star practitioner at concert rallies.

The demand for performances in this genre reflected the holiday mood felt by many people in Russia. People were happy to spend their leisure time and money on 'politics'. The politicization of leisure spilled over into the politicization of the theatre, and that in turn left its imprint on a certain dramatization of politics. In a climate of what seemed like universal enthusiasm there was a demand for a synthesis of artistic creativity and politics. At the same time the revolution involved large numbers of people in politics who had hitherto been apolitical, and that also served to increase interest in all sorts of festivities. For political neophytes, the holiday aspect of the revolution was particularly attractive and even took pride of place, answering as it did their euphoric expectations. In this context, the theatricality of Kerensky's performances did not seem peculiar or vulgar. It was what people wanted. It fitted the mood of the time.

There were also certain features of early twentieth-century culture which influenced the way the image of the revolutionary minister was perceived. The greater public participation in politics favoured dramatization, but there was also an eager expectation that art and life were destined to merge. From the moment broad representative political institutions appeared and captured the public's imagination, parliamentarians began exploiting techniques of dramatization. The era of mass political movements, however, called for the creation of new genres of political theatre. This was manifest in popular demand for a new type of politician, appealing directly to the masses and offering a hybrid of politics and art. We have only to think of the public personas of d'Annunzio, Mussolini and Hitler. A theatrical, artistic reputation, the introduction of aesthetics into politics and the politicization of art all played a part in determining the tactics to be used to construct political authority – the more so in revolutionary times. It is no surprise that Kerensky and his supporters employed such methods for glorifying the Leader, who, moreover, attracted the label of 'poet of the revolution'.[116]

This attitude towards the Leader was probably intensified by some of the peculiarities of the traditions of Russian culture. The use of police methods to restrict public participation in politics meant that, for several generations of intellectuals, art and literature became a surrogate for politics and ideology. This hypertrophied introduction of politics into art and of ideology into aesthetics brought in its train a specific introduction of aesthetics into politics. The radical political changes of 1905–7 altered that situation, and after the establishment of the State Duma a category of professional politicians appeared (one of whom was Kerensky). Large numbers of people, however, remained estranged from politics, and the deputies of the Duma, while acting as the public face of governmental power, had no responsibility for what the government actually did. Accordingly, the 'theatre' of the State Duma was quite different from the theatricality typical of parliaments of fully-fledged constitutional states.

Some of Kerensky's supporters described themselves as his followers or admirers: he found himself the beneficiary of attitudes more traditional towards an adored actor, painter or author, or other 'intellectual lawgiver'. The tradition which emerged in the late nineteenth and early twentieth centuries of adulation of theatre celebrities established a pattern for attitudes towards Kerensky. Famous actors, and particularly opera singers, were deified and worshipped by their fans. Some fans tried to imitate their idols in their manners and how they dressed; others attempted to establish a direct personal relationship, which brought about the appearance of the genre of fan letters, mostly written by women. The behaviour became so widespread it was the butt of satire. Writers referred to the obtrusive and hysterical fans of opera singers as 'psychopathic ladies'.[117]

Kerensky was quite unabashed about using theatrical gesture to punctuate his speeches, singing *The Marseillaise*, leading the singing of an ecstatic auditorium or professional choirs, or conducting an orchestra. An announcement that Kerensky would be participating in a concert rally guaranteed a crowd. In late April one Petrograd newspaper noted (during the April Crisis!) that ticket sales were down in the theatres and that even celebrity guest appearances were no longer pulling in the public. Only concert rallies, especially if the minister of justice would be speaking, could be sure of selling out.[118]

Kerensky's popularity was exploited by dishonest businessmen, which at least testifies to his box-office appeal. Speculators resold tickets at thrice the price, and some organizers shamelessly announced he would be taking part in a concert rally even though they had conducted no preliminary negotiations with him. When the minister's saturated and rapidly changing schedule really did make it impossible for him to give a promised speech, the disappointed audience was likely to suspect the organizers of being up to no good. The Petrograd correspondent of a Helsingfors newspaper reported:

> This name has lately become so popular that there is not a poster in the city which it does not adorn. It has only to be announced that Kerensky will be at a rally for all the tickets to be sold out in a single day. The popular minister does not by any means participate in all the meetings where that is announced, and this can give rise to major misunderstandings. At a rally held at the House of the People, the public, disappointed when Kerensky did not appear, almost rioted, despite the fact that the organizers had announced he could not come owing to the burden of urgent business. It is notable that some 10,000 people were waiting in the square outside the House of the People for Kerensky to arrive. Another incident occurred a couple of days ago at the Conservatory. The organizers offered the audience a refund but they refused it.[119]

The crowds waiting outside theatres for their idol to arrive included people who did not have tickets for the concert. Some were hoping only for a glimpse of the celebrity, while others, in the expectation of an impromptu speech, hoped to sample his renowned rhetorical skills for free. What is striking, though, is the patriotism displayed by the audience at the Conservatory who declined to have their money returned. It was to be used for political purposes. We can only hope those organizing the event were equally patriotic.

Even ordinary performances turned spontaneously into political demonstrations if Kerensky was present. On 13 March the minister entered the auditorium of the Mariinsky Theatre when a performance had already begun. The public demanded that he should give a speech, and the performance was temporarily suspended while he did so.[120] Kerensky had only to appear at congresses and meetings for an outbreak of celebrations and ceremonies to ensue. On 7 April he arrived at the Congress of the All-Russia Teachers' Union. The delegates elected him an honorary member of the union and a choir of teachers sang *The Marseillaise*. On 1 May, at the height of the government crisis, Kerensky appeared after difficult negotiations at the Alexandrinsky Theatre, where a crowded rally was being held. In his speech he announced that the crisis had been resolved, the government was secure, and it would be consolidated by including members from the ranks of the forces of democracy. This reassuring statement was rapturously received.[121]

An important ritual for greeting Kerensky was presenting him with flowers, predominantly red (the minister's working apartment was full of bouquets).[122] He milked this for all it was worth, which again brings to mind the way a celebrated actor might behave. The newspapers reported that, when the minister returned on 8 March from Moscow to Petrograd, he was holding a bunch of carnations presented by girl students in Moscow (a piece of information which must have been passed on to the journalists either by Kerensky himself or by those accompanying him). After giving speeches, the minister would be showered with red roses. His biographer wrote in 1917, 'Kerensky's path may be thorny, but his motor car is entwined with roses. Women throw him lily of the valley and sprigs of lilac; others take flowers from his hands and share them among themselves like talismans and amulets.'[123]

We get a sense of the atmosphere at Kerensky's speeches from the description of a regional convention of front-line soldiers in Odessa which took place on 15 May in the city's renowned opera house. The audience was waiting for Kerensky to arrive. The atmosphere was one of intense anticipation, and an outlet for the emotion was found when the chairman suggested the audience should donate their awards and medals to Kerensky for the needs of the army. (Donating medals to the minister had become a common ritual.)[124] The response to his challenge was a positive hail of medals on to the stage from the tiers of the theatre and from the boxes. Delegates who had neither orders nor medals brought up money.

Someone called out, 'Women – donate your jewels!' Young women rushed to the chairman's table, tearing off their jewellery; soldiers took off their wedding rings. At this moment the minister of war appeared, to be greeted with a roar of enthusiasm. All those present got to their feet cheering and gave Kerensky a tumultuous ovation. The theatre choir sang the sailors' anthem and the minister was presented with a bouquet of red roses.

In his speech, Kerensky described the atmosphere at the meeting. 'In the way you have greeted me I see the tremendous enthusiasm which has gripped the whole country. Rare indeed is a miracle like the Russian Revolution which turn slaves into free people.' He was given a standing ovation, the choir sang *The Marseillaise*, and all present joined in singing the anthem of the revolution. Someone exclaimed, 'Comrade brothers! Let us swear an oath that we will advance, only advance!' 'We do!' the hall responded. Kerensky began to scatter the red roses that had been given to him earlier: he threw them to the stalls and then went up to the boxes, where the consuls of the allied nations were sitting, and greeted them. There were exclamations: 'Lead us true to your conscience, and we will follow you.' 'We will follow you!' thousands of voices responded.[125]

It is a safe bet that the reports in many newspapers of this very theatrical meeting influenced the atmosphere a few days later in Moscow's Bolshoy Theatre. This was just how Kerensky's press relations staff wanted him presented, and many newspaper readers looked forward to this kind of news item. The sense of euphoria called for constant psychological reaffirmation, and this was provided by spectacular celebrations. Kerensky, the emissary from revolutionary Petrograd, brought this inspirational atmosphere to the front line and the provinces. His lightning trips around the country were ever new celebrations of freedom. The waves of enthusiasm generated by the famed minister's expeditions played an important role, creating an atmosphere in which it was easier for him to defer, smooth over, and sometimes resolve the numerous local conflicts which were often the reason for his making the trips in the first place. At the same time, the local organizers of his visits – members of soldiers' committees and generals, local government leaders and activists of the Socialist Revolutionary Party – could use the political kudos bestowed on them by the arrival of the popular minister to raise money, conduct election campaigns, and generally enhance their local standing. Kerensky's detractors did have some justification for comparing his visits to the touring of a matinee idol, but his behaviour was also a response to what his audience wanted and expected. The minister's style of oratory was in tune with the tastes and expectations of the political theatre of the revolution.

Something that contributed to Kerensky's success was his rhetorical manner and his own sense of the revolution. Even in autumn 1917, when his popularity as the head of the Provisional Government was waning, an activist of the Socialist Revolutionary Party, who had publicly criticized the minister in the spring, wrote, 'I do not like Kerensky as an orator: he is too lyrical for a statesman. But in him the romance of those first days of the revolution has not yet died. He has a manner that can engage and kindle the masses.'[126]

Both Nikolai Sukhanov and Victor Chernov called Kerensky a 'political impressionist'.[127] That is an apt description of a politician who showed tactical 'flexibility' in different situations, adjusting his views to his audience. This was seen sometimes as a lack of responsibility and sometimes as a lack of principle. Something similar can be said of Kerensky's oratory. He was sensitive to the mood of his audience and, improvising skilfully, mirrored their mood back to his appreciative listeners, making it more vivid, enhancing it, and receiving back new impulses from the public for further rhetorical improvisation. The technique was not always successful. Left Socialist Revolutionary Sergey Mstislavsky (Maslovsky) wrote of Kerensky: 'His peculiarity as an orator was his exceptional ability to perceive the mood of the audience he was addressing. It was not he who possessed the audience, but the audience who possessed him. This made him powerless if confronted by a hostile crowd. He was not strong enough to face down the mood and thinking of the masses by the force of his own words, and will, and power.'[128]

This judgement is only partly fair. Assuredly, Kerensky did suffer defeats as a propagandist, but he was well able to fight to engage his listeners and to overcome apathy and even hostility. While sensitive to his audience, he could in fact galvanize them with his own mood. One journalist who was well disposed towards him commented that his eloquence was not ideally suited to an audience of ordinary Russian people and soldiers: he used too many foreign words; he expressed his thoughts too abstractly. Nevertheless, his speeches did work for a less educated audience because his physical expressiveness conveyed emotion to the listener which was close to what he himself was feeling. If what he was saying remained a mystery, he could still move an audience from the phlegmatic curiosity with which it had come to take a look at this visiting celebrity to heartfelt enthusiasm. 'Kerensky is a great master of communicating emotion to a mass of people who have come to hear him.'[129] Mstislavsky's remark gives insight into the seemingly self-contradictory judgements made about Kerensky: we often find one and the same person speaking of his 'histrionics' while simultaneously acknowledging his sincerity.

Here the testimony of theatre people is of particular interest. In the Soviet period, Mikhail Narokov, a professional actor whose métier was heroic roles, recalled Kerensky's 'laboured theatrical pathos', which bowled over those who were 'politically unschooled'. Even so, Narokov gave him credit for his 'acting'.

> Kerensky gave a speech at the Bolshoy Theatre. His appearance was greeted with loud applause. Two young officers in adjutant's uniform lifted Kerensky and with great care placed him on the presidium table. He raised his arms in a practised manner, like a bishop (for some reason he was wearing gloves), and stood there on his tribune

> looking like a statue. The dramatic pose of a Bonaparte, brow rumpled, face pale, registering sombre determination.
>
> From the outset his voice was a high-pitched, blood-curdling shriek, and so he continued until the end of the speech. His voice was clearly strained from addressing endless rallies. His speech exploded in short volleys and had an unnerving, hysterical tone which kept the audience in a state of extreme tension. . . .
>
> The pathos of an actor, skilful, calculated use of rhetorical effects and flowing gestures achieved their aim. The actor played his role, well attuned to the audience he was addressing and well versed in all the ways and techniques of having an emotional impact on it.[130]

This analysis by a professional actor is interesting, despite the obvious bias. Narokov's description is similar to Koonen's judgement: Kerensky is an actor playing the role of a leader and hero, a Bonaparte. Of course, Narokov could hardly have got a more sympathetic assessment of the oratory of a minister in the Provisional Government published in Soviet times. He does mention that Kerensky enjoyed the public's rapt attention and acted the 'role' well, and that avid theatregoers who had seen many celebrities in their time were genuinely enthused by the performance. After the rally, Narokov found himself in a group of 'bourgeois intellectuals' around Vasiliy Nemirovich-Danchenko, a popular writer and journalist. Profoundly excited, Nemirovich-Danchenko exclaimed, and his listeners agreed, 'I'm sure I don't know. I don't even want to think through what is right here and what is wrong, but I am terribly moved. This was the speech of a great statesman.'[131]

A few days later, Nemirovich-Danchenko published an article reflecting on Kerensky's style.

> Kerensky is not only himself ablaze but sets light to everything around him with the sacred flame of his enthusiasm. As you listen you feel your nerves reaching out and becoming bound with his in a single knot. You have a sense that you yourself are the orator, that in this hall, this theatre, on this square, it is not Kerensky but you who stand before the crowd, holding sway over their thoughts and emotions. Their hearts and yours are one, and right now that heart is as big as the world and, like the world, it is wonderful. Kerensky has delivered his speech. Now he is gone, and you wonder how long he had been speaking. Was it an hour? Was it three minutes? Try as you may, you cannot answer because time and space were suspended, halted, and it is only now that they are back with you.
>
> Is he eloquent? No. Often his sentences do not manage to hold hands across his erratic, unexpected pauses. He is in the grip of something that impels him to leap from one idea to another, and like a dazzling kaleidoscope they are forming and reforming at fearful speed in his imagination. He does not always have the time to grasp

> these magnesium flashes and is himself left blinking before them. Thoughts may be left unfinished, abandoned because he has no time to continue them. Others, which he cannot afford to miss, are already crowding in, but you have seen what he means and it is not his aim to give a smooth performance. He may repeat himself when the thread suddenly breaks and the next beacon is not yet lighting up the darkness. A complete lack of affectation and calculation, but in every sound there is a strong, racing pulse . . . sometimes painful, reflected by a spasm in his face. What affectation, what ploy could control the explosion of this raging conflagration, because what opens up before us is a volcano, and with apparent irregularity, without measure or system, it hurls out bundles of all-incinerating fire. His face, so ordinary, so grey, often tormented, fatigued, becomes beautiful and overpowering, because suddenly, through the crimson flickering of deadly anathemas, we glimpse a child-like smile, a touching expression in his all-forgiving eyes.[132]

It is entirely possible that, as Narokov was working on his memoirs, he recalled or even re-read this article, because he mentions the selfsame moments in Kerensky's speech which Nemirovich-Danchenko describes in a completely different way. He too, for example, notes the moment the Leader gets up on to the presidium table (and uses the word 'Leader' in his article). The nervous tic, however, Nemirovich-Danchenko treats not as the amusing technique of a play-acting hack politician but as the magnificent and inspiring symptom of a sincere leader confidently establishing unseen contact with his audience.

> He finds intolerable any obstacle between him and the person listening to him. He wants to be wholly present, in front of you, from head to toe, so that all that separates him from his audience is air permeated by the powerful invisible currents flowing between him and you. That is why he wants to know nothing of chairs or rostrums or tables. He will come out from behind the lectern, jump up on to a table, and when he stretches out his arms to you – volatile, yielding, fervent – trembling in an access of rapturous prayer – you seem to feel him touch you, take you in these arms and irresistably draw you to him.[133]

In his assessment of Kerensky, Vasiliy Nemirovich-Danchenko might well have been showing bias: he had long ago become a member of a Masonic lodge and may have been seeking to support his fellow Mason in these very important speeches. However, his description of the minister's oratory chimes with those of other contemporaries. Even Narokov admitted that Nemirovich-Danchenko's praise was endorsed by those other 'bourgeois intellectuals'. There is something predictable about how a Soviet-era memoirist writes about the same occasion. Kerensky's 'gushing, verbose lava' overwhelmed many 'politically immature minds, perverting their healthy sense of patriotism'. The success of the minister, whom Narokov denounces as a 'rabid enemy of the people', is due to the naivety and political inexperience of his audience. Narokov dismisses the bourgeois intellectuals who share the opinion of Nemirovich-Danchenko as 'political oafs'.[134]

Kerensky's contemporaries, from different political perspectives, largely agree on the secret of his popularity: the style of his speeches was consonant with the mood of his audiences. A variety of reviewers, with no conferring, wrote of a 'merging' of the speaker with his listeners. The latter were greatly taken by his theatrical style, his euphoria, and the great political optimism of the revolutionary minister as he enthused about the 'fairy tale' of the revolution. In describing the Kerensky phenomenon, his contemporaries use words such as 'hysterical rapture, 'mass psychosis' and 'hypnosis'. These sometimes ironic and at times pejorative judgements by writers who were influenced by specialists on crowd psychology, such as Gustave Le Bon, or on social psychology, such as Gabriel Tarde, only confirm the extraordinary impact of his speeches. Kerensky's supporters, too, describe his success as an orator and point to the coincidence of the emotional state of audience and orator. 'When Kerensky came on stage the crowd became one with him, a man personifying the power of the people.'[135] Kerensky designed the style his audience was demanding; he intensified the emotion and confirmed with his personal authority the faith his listeners had in the miracle of revolution. He was perceived as a sincere politician – which, in a way, he was.

Leaders of other parties wrote of the merging with the revolutionary minister of an audience in the process of becoming politicized. Where Koonen and Narokov focused on Kerensky's technique as an actor, party leaders paid more attention to how the political context favoured the way his speeches were received. Not without a twinge of professional jealousy, Leon Trotsky, himself a renowned orator, in 1917 explained why he thought Kerensky's speeches went down so well. 'The unthinking man in the street, by now half-awake, delighted in these speeches. He seemed to hear himself speaking from the rostrum.' This suggests why Kerensky's speeches were so successful: both as a politician and as an orator he was what the Russian masses, 'wakening' to political involvement, needed. He expressed, reflected and, at the same time, moulded their consciousness. The Socialist Revolutionary leader Victor Chernov also wrote about the political and psychological merging of orator and audience.

> In contrast to the deliberative political pulsation of Milyukov, Kerensky's political pulse was feverish. Revolutionary eras are eras of mass hysteria and psychological epidemics, and their tub-thumpers need psychologically to be of one flesh with the crowd. They need to become affected, readily and completely, and to be able to affect others, with the unbridled but blinkered power of passionate emotion set loose. Such tub-thumpers are often born actors, consciously or

> unconsciously looking for a way to the hearts of those around them through theatricality, prepared to vulgarize their own words and gestures. There was a lot of that kind of histrionics with Kerensky, but it did not prevent him from pouring out his soul, his deepest, private, spiritual self in the visible forms of artifice and ham acting.[136]

It is notable that Chernov, while referring disdainfully to Kerensky's ham acting, does not deny his sincerity, or that he expressed it vividly.

Kerensky was a tough and calculating politician, and yet his audiences were not wholly mistaken in believing him to be sincere. Many leading political figures expressed optimism after the February events, but not all of them believed what they were saying. For the liberals, to say nothing of the conservatives, the revolution had, in its earliest stages, already gone too far. For most socialists, however, even the moderate ones, it was, on the contrary, so far only 'bourgeois'. It did not measure up to their ideals, and they argued for it to go further and 'deeper'. Unlike them, Kerensky identified himself totally with the revolution as it was, and that was an attitude shared by many people entering political life for the first time after the overthrow of the monarchy.

The words 'miracle', 'enthusiasm' and 'delight' recur regularly in Kerensky's speeches. He meant them. They corresponded both to his personal feelings about the coup and to the emotional state of his audiences: they too believed in the miracle of the revolution. Their politician genuinely shared the enthusiastic mood of the masses, and, with great talent, he gave it expression and heightened it.

Every revolution raises unrealistic expectations; enthusiasm and optimism are endemic. There was, however, an additional source in 1917 of belief that a miracle had happened. The political revolution was bound up with a religious revolution, and to a significant extent political thinking was influenced by religious thinking. Many people perceived the revolution as a profoundly religious experience vested in secular form. The revolution was seen as Easter, a festival of a great resurrection of Russia. Conversely, the celebration of Easter assumed a political character, with revolutionary symbolism evident during the Easter ceremonies.[137]

Several interests, including conservatives, tried to bend the Easter mood to their own advantage. A commentator who proclaimed the ideal of a new imperialism of a new Great Russia wrote: 'At this radiant Christian festival of Easter, as the church bells ring out, one longs to believe that the colour of the flag raised in Russia is not that of blood, dark and repugnant . . . One longs to see it expand to embrace the blue of the sky and the whiteness of God's world. Beneath that tricoloured banner one longs to imagine the destiny not of the Russian people alone but of all nations, of all mankind.'[138] It is difficult to believe this writer's optimism was sincere, but any manifestation of pessimism, or even of caution, was not going to be well received by a public carried away by the revolution. Many politicians, whatever they may have thought personally, felt obliged to go along with all these highly optimistic aspirations. Kerensky, however, did so readily and sincerely. He was a convinced and skilled believer in the power of optimism.

It would be a mistake to dismiss the description of revolutionary enthusiasm in its varied manifestations as merely a colourful and exotic adornment of historical narratives. Strong emotion shared by large numbers of people is a major political resource. In a time of revolution, when the scope for 'normal' ways of governing becomes increasingly limited, exploiting the potential of strong, widespread emotions assumes even greater importance. Kerensky readily and skilfully set about arousing enthusiasm and then making use of it. Speaking in Helsingfors, he called on his audience to turn revolutionary enthusiasm into 'organized steel machinery of governmental creativity'.[139]

Other ministers saw arousing enthusiasm as a high political priority, and many agreed. General Andrey Snesarev, who was at the front, approvingly quoted Andrey Shingaryov, a Constitutional Democrat, in his diary: 'Some 300 years ago Russia was saved by the enthusiasm ignited by Minin and Pozharsky, and today we again need to light the fire of popular enthusiasm. If Kerensky can fire up the army and Peshekhonov can do the same for food suppliers, Russia will be saved.' To this the general added, 'If we are to depend on the enthusiasm which Shingaryov, for example, sees as so important, we must use it to the full, to instil resolve even to make the supreme sacrifice.'[140]

Despite his love of public speaking, Kerensky sometimes absented himself from major ceremonial occasions. He was noticeably absent from the funeral for victims of the revolution on 23 March. This was one of the largest rallies in the history of Russia, attended by ministers of the Provisional Government and the leaders of the Petrograd Soviet. The newspapers reported that illness had prevented Kerensky from attending.[141] This seems implausible because he was working that day. In conversation he said he had been too busy and needed to get through his work without the distraction of ceremonies. 'This is a time for working, not for playing with toys.'[142]

We do not need to believe this. Kerensky took ceremonies and festivities very seriously when they served his purposes. His absence from the funeral ceremony may have been because he did not wish to play second fiddle: the ceremony had been organized by the Petrograd Soviet, with whom his relations were strained. Attending it would have obliged him to choose symbolically between his roles of government minister and of deputy chairman of the Soviet's Executive Committee, which he was keen to avoid. He could not have been simultaneously in the group of members of the Provisional Government and in the group of leaders of the Soviet. Retaining his position in both these power structures was a high political priority, and the best way to do that was to stay away from the rally.

The mix of theatricality and sincerity in Kerensky's political style called for gestures and rituals calculated to enhance the impact of his speeches.

If the innumerable handshakes underlined his reputation as a democrat and the donation of military medals to the minister of war reinforced his authority as Leader of the revolutionary army, hugs and kisses bore witness to the special, emotional relationship Kerensky had with ordinary citizens. Sometimes this intimate, symbolic political connection could be established with a whole category of citizens, as when the minister embraced and kissed their authorized representatives. On other occasions he obliged other people to kiss as a sign of reconciliation. This predilection of Kerensky and his audiences for hugging and kissing was the cause of much ironic comment. A Muscovite who followed politics closely described in his diary the atmosphere at these festivals of the revolution. 'Tumultuous applause, happy faces, kisses. (Kerensky, for example, kissed Tsereteli.) A. F. Kerensky is quite some kisser. He has bestowed his kisses on both Breshko-Breshkovskaya and General Alexeyev!'[143]

The ritual hugging and kissing was indicative of the political emotions citizens of the new Russia were intended to feel towards their Leader. Your author has in the past pointed out the special place of love in the political culture of the monarchy: the tsar's subjects were expected not only to venerate him but also to love him, and there were some monarchists who, on the eve of the February Revolution, were genuinely upset to find they had lost the ability to continue to love their 'beloved Sovereign'.[144]

The search for the appropriate emotional attitude towards republican leaders is a problem for countries which have rejected monarchy but remain under the sway of monarchist political culture. Not infrequently the political emotions required under the old regime (and sometimes also monarchist rhetoric) are transferred wholesale to the leaders of the new system to reinforce their authority. Whole collectives at a time declared their political love of Kerensky. How they showed it took a variety of forms, some of them decidedly theatrical. The language of love implies at least a modicum of sincerity, and we conclude again that sincerity and theatricality in the relationship between the Leader and his supporters were not incompatible.

The historian Natan Eidelman was fond of saying that only a few handshakes separated Pushkin from Pasternak.[145] He was pointing out the physical dimension of cultural continuity: Pasternak knew people who had met Pushkin's contemporaries. His memory of the age of Pushkin was not only cultural, based on book knowledge, but also alive, warm, continuous. The same was true of Kerensky and his physical reality for many people in Russia: just a few handshakes (hugs, kisses) separated some woman who lived in a remote Siberian village from the revolutionary minister. Her husband (a soldier in a rifle regiment on the front line) would almost certainly have shaken hands with a member of the regimental committee, and the latter had quite likely shaken hands with Kerensky, or even hugged and kissed him. What mattered was not only the numerousness of the handshakes, kisses and hugs, but the desire for them, which came from the psychological 'infectiousness' contemporaries wrote about. 'Everybody loves Kerensky. . . . Everybody idolizes him and their eyes glaze over when they talk about him,' one provincial journalist claimed.[146] This love for the 'poet of the revolution' made possible the combination of theatricality and sincerity. Their fusion was an important element of the Kerensky phenomenon and a prerequisite for creating his image of Leader.

If hugging and kissing testified to love, the ritual of carrying Kerensky shoulder-high was a demonstration of enthusiastic veneration. When the minister appeared on 26 March in the soldiers' section of the Soviet to respond to accusations made against him, confirmation that his speech had been a success came when the deputies carried him out shoulder-high. It was a demonstration of support that even those members of the Executive Committee of the Soviet, who privately spurned the speech as 'demagogic', could not ignore.[147]

While at that time it was not only Kerensky who enjoyed this form of approval, it was nevertheless something his contemporaries very much associated with him, and it was to his acclamation that the press paid most attention. When on 5 May Kerensky came to the end of an important speech to the All-Russia Congress of Peasant Deputies, a holder of the order of St George brought a chair on to the stage and asked the permission of 'our Leader' to carry him on his way.[148] The following day Kerensky was carried shoulder-high at the Ministry of the Navy, and, a day after that, participants of the All-Russia Congress of Officers' Deputies bore him aloft in a chair. Next he was carried shoulder-high to his car by enthusiastic soldiers of the 1st Reserve Infantry Regiment, and later by delighted naval cadets who had just been commissioned as officers.[149] Even then the newspapers were no longer bothering to record every instance of a ritual that was becoming no longer newsworthy. A jaundiced view of one of Kerensky's send-offs is given in his memoirs by Victor Shklovsky, who in May became a front-line commissar of the Provisional Government. 'I saw Kerensky another time after I had been appointed as a commissar. I wanted to consult him about something and caught up with him outside the Ministry of the Navy. I spotted his grey Locomobile and talked to the chauffeur while I was waiting. "They'll be bringing him out any minute," the driver told me. Sure enough, a few minutes later Kerensky was carried out of the building. He was sitting in his usual, weary pose in a chair and being held high above the crowd.'[150]

By the time Shklovsky was writing his memoirs, many memoirists were doing their utmost to discredit Kerensky: the memory of the earlier naive 'veneration' was now sneered at. Nevertheless, his memoirs do convey a significant feature of that time: a gesture which had initially been the expression of a spontaneous emotional reaction degenerated into a routine ritual of power. It is, of course, not every government representative who is commonly carried shoulder-high. It can come about that successful politicians, even Leaders who very much want to be loved, ensure that their relationship with their supporters is on a different level. They make it clear there is to be more distance, political and physical, and less spontaneity in manifestations of the political emotion they insist on.

There was great scorn from some of Kerensky's contemporaries for the theatrical style, the claim to the role of a sincere politician, the ostentatious manifestations of love expressed by all those hugs and kisses, the euphoria over the coup, which Kerensky with his leadership ambitions did his best to intensify. All this is, nevertheless, extremely important for an understanding of the nature of power in the era of revolution when Kerensky, a talented orator, proved an invaluable asset both to the Petrograd Soviet and to the Provisional Government. Foreigners called Russia at this time 'the land of 180 million orators', and Kerensky was the most famous, the most popular, the most successful of them all. In the peevish assessments of Kerensky's theatrical style by other famous orators – Chernov, Lunacharsky, Trotsky – we sense jealousy, outright envy even.

Kerensky's images as 'the minister of revolutionary theatricality', the 'poet of the revolution', 'the sincere politician', were just what was needed for the political, aesthetic and ethical sensibility in the initial stage of the revolution, when masses of people found themselves unceremoniously inducted into the world of contemporary politics. These images were important for creating his reputation as 'the Leader of the people', and Kerensky by virtue of his abilities became the political Leader of a people which was becoming politicized. His simultaneously theatrical and sincere style was copied by many activists, for whom Kerensky's way of representing himself was a model. Dmitry Furmanov, who went on to become the personification of a Bolshevik commissar, was no exception. He noted in his diary on 29 May that he had given a speech 'Kerensky-style'.[151] Many of Kerensky's theatrical techniques were subsequently exploited by the very politicians who referred disparagingly to the style of 'the people's minister'. The technique of whipping up enthusiasm the better subsequently to exploit it was employed by those of Kerensky's opponents who subsequently came to power.

5 'Great martyr of the revolution'

In 1938 Mikhail Zoshchenko published a novella, *Inglorious End*, in which he described Kerensky as follows:

> In his physical appearance he was a son of his time, a typical representative of the pre-revolutionary intelligentsia: pigeon-chested, burdened by illness, weak nerves and an unbalanced mentality.
>
> He was the son and brother of the pre-revolutionary petty-bourgeois intelligentsia who created decadence in art and brought skittishness, scepticism and ambiguity into politics.
>
> He was a weak person with no willpower.[152]

In this pen portrait we can sense the circumstances of time and place. Derogatory assessments of Kerensky were obligatory in the years of the Great Purges. Despite that, we detect echoes in the writing of the real attitude of former front-line officer Zoshchenko to the head of the Provisional Government. Back in 1918 Mikhail Zoshchenko wrote a Nietzsche-tinged article, 'Marvellous Audacity', in which he gave the savage determination of the Bolsheviks its due, contrasting them with the 'impotent potentate' Kerensky.[153]

In his writing of 1938, Kerensky's 'weakness and lack of willpower', noted by Zoshchenko twenty years previously, is attributed to his ill health. The poor health of the weakling minister is an indicator of how misguided and inept his politics are. This was to become a stereotype. Numerous memoirists and historians wrote about Kerensky's hysteria, his unhealthy, grey, ashen face. Some even recalled the 'diseased skin' of his 'unhealthy face'.[154] The image of a politician sick in body and soul served as an illustration in recurrent disquisitions on the weakness of the head of the Provisional Government and the perversity of his policies.

Kerensky really did have serious health problems. As already noted, in March 1916 he had a tuberculous kidney removed. The young politician himself admitted that his strength was being stretched to the limit. Just before the revolution he was using a walking stick and looked seriously ill. The February Days put a terrible strain on his body. It was not only biased memoirists but also diarists, including those sympathetic to him, who described his 'terribly pale', worn-out face, haggard yet at the same time swollen, with signs of constant sleep deprivation, his sallow, 'almost corpse-like' pallor and bloodless lips.[155] However, unlike the descriptions in memoirs, contemporary private sources, while they refer to Kerensky looking ill, often do so without negative connotations. They frequently express sympathy (which sometimes transitions into solidarity). The mention of his infirmity was sometimes read as confirming that he had the qualities of a real Leader. This attitude towards an ill politician who, precisely because of his illness, is perceived as a strong Leader calls for further comment.

That Kerensky was in poor health was no secret. The newspapers reported how pale and tired his face was, how weary and cracked his voice seemed.[156] A friendly journalist wrote: 'They say Kerensky is very ill. He has renal tuberculosis. One kidney has already been excised. What keeps him going is only his state of constant nervous exhilaration. When, for natural, physiological reasons, that exhilaration ends, the political career of this tribune of the people will also come to an end.'[157]

The newspapers reported to their readers the fainting fits which accompanied the minister's speeches. Later this fainting would be described as a manifestation of his weakness, his sickliness, his hysteria and effeminacy, but in March and April his infirmity made a quite different impression. While giving a speech in Moscow, the minister collapsed. When he came to, he told his anxious audience he had not slept for a week.[158] The audience appreciated his selfless dedication. A prominent Socialist Revolutionary recalled: 'Pale, haggard, worshipped not only by girl students, Kerensky made a huge impression on the audience just by his appearance, quite independently of what he had to say. In the end he was repeating himself, but his intensity and drive were transmitted to his listeners, and they experienced his own ecstasy. At the end of his speech at the Polytechnic Museum, Kerensky collapsed, which only added to the effect of his speech.'[159]

On other occasions Kerensky did not collapse, but his listeners could tell that his strength was almost at an end, and the minister stepped down from the podium 'almost staggering with fatigue'. This made his speeches all the more impressive and memorable. Viktor Shklovsky, a memoirist not at all favourably inclined to Kerensky, recalled, 'With the haggard face of a man whose days are already numbered, he was shouting and finally, completely exhausted, fell back into a chair. It left a terrifying impression.'[160]

Kerensky made no secret of his extreme tiredness. Speaking to the Helsingfors Soviet, he announced, 'All these days, since the 27th, I have hardly slept and have done what I could.' A different record of the speech is more dramatic: 'I will not be able to speak for long. I must ask you to believe that I have not slept since 27 February. That is how great the tension is in the atmosphere surrounding the leading circles of young Russia.'[161] Influential journalists wrote to the same effect. 'Those first days he was working round the clock.'[162] His poor state of health was attributed to someone who was devoting himself totally to the revolution and overstretching his powers.

This image made a great impression. A deputy of the All-Russia Assembly of Soviets said, 'I want to say that we should not incinerate with our attacks a heart which is already aflame with the people's cause, for the cause of our revolution. Anyone who has seen him speak from this rostrum will tell you that he is already burning in full view of all of us, and it is a crime to offend him, comrades.' This statement was greeted with applause.[163] Such reminders of the revolutionary minister's self-sacrifice aimed to restrict criticism directed at him.

Seen in this light, Kerensky's poor health did not rule out his acquiring the status of a strong Leader: on the contrary, it confirmed that status. Infirmity was seen as a sign of asceticism: here was a politician knowingly sacrificing his health, even his life, for the sake of the revolution. His contemporaries believed that Kerensky's willingness to endure constant pain and overcome his illness was evidence not only of dedication but also of an iron will and unconquerable spirit.[164] The minister's admirers saw these qualities in the Leader's eyes. Leonidov wrote that what revealed the true measure of Kerensky – a 'frail, puny' person, a youth more than a man – was his steely, indomitable gaze. His eyes, truly mirroring his soul, told of the extraordinary willpower enabling him to subjugate his physical ailments. His ability constantly to surmount serious illness testified to the amazing fortitude of a stricken leader who had been tempered in the battle for freedom:

> We are told that Kerensky lacks one kidney, that his lungs are in a parlous state, that there is something wrong with his right arm, which keeps swelling up. And yet, despite all this physical infirmity, which would have left another man bedridden, Kerensky, unquenchable, burns with the fire of his ardent spirit, his unconquerable love for his country's people. He is himself aflame and sets others on fire, literally performing miracles. He is sublime, as if under hypnosis, like a prophet sent by Providence who, 'passing over land and sea, with words of fire sets all men free!'[165]

Another biographer wrote in much the same vein. 'He inhabits a physically frail body, has to live with only one kidney, yet manages a way of life in which a mere sixteen-hour working day must seem an unattainable ideal.' The writer sees in this a feat of revolutionary patriotism. 'Truly the revolution does not spare its loves: it consumes its blazing torches from both ends. But this is not what concerns A. F. Kerensky. If he were less modest, he could say of himself, as did Peter the Great, "As for ourself, know that we set little store on our life but that Russia should prosper." '[166]

Sometimes, in supportive descriptions, Kerensky miraculously overcomes his ailments and is young again, in striking contrast to the decrepit old dignitaries of the old regime. Leonidov, having just reported all the minister's illnesses, describes his arrival. 'The door burst open and Kerensky ran in with lilacs in his arms, so young, so sunlit, in spite of all the fatigue and all the speeches he had just delivered.'[167] The rejuvenating effect of the revolution brings healing to its Leader; communing with the masses restores his strength. Thus does Kerensky's biographer write in his praise in 1917. Such is the evidence he finds to confirm the unique qualities of a born Leader.

His superhuman qualities enable the Leader, in spite of everything, to fulfil his mission. His admiring supporters are amazed by his capacity for work. A provincial journalist wrote, 'As I looked at this exhausted man, I often asked myself where it was all coming from. Where did he get the strength and energy to work day and night without collapsing on the floor?'[168]

If, for Zoshchenko, Kerensky's infirmity was a sign of insufficient manliness, for many others at the time of the revolution it was a sign of his true courage that every day the Leader overcame his illness, and this miraculous triumph over physical infirmity was a portent that the body politic of the state would in time also recover.

Another of Kerensky's supporters went so far as to compare him to Hercules liberating that 'homespun Prometheus', the Russian people. The politician's physical weakness was contrasted with his miraculous doings and set off their grandeur.

> You follow him because you do not doubt for a moment that, if he is summoning you to some act of heroism, you can be sure that he

> will be in the forefront, bearing with that sunken chest on his weak, narrow shoulders everything the still breathing monster of the old, evil world can throw at him. . . . You are baffled as to where this frail, exhausted man, as physically vulnerable as a reed, draws such inexhaustible strength for labours no athlete could survive![169]

Sympathy for the ailing Leader, sympathy for the ascetic revolutionary, admiration for his 'superhuman' acts, called for immediate expressions of solidarity. These feelings of anxiety, compassion and sympathy found an outlet in emotional displays of concern for their Leader by his supporters. One of the first documents of this kind was a letter from a group of 'working women of the city of Tver', dated 10 March. Those who wrote it called for care to be taken of their beloved Leader: 'We, grandmothers, mothers, sisters and daughters, "cumbered Marthas", beg you, brothers, you who are close to him, guard his life, guard his time, make sure he gets at least a minimum of sleep and proper food, so that the strength of New Russia's Sun is not overtaxed.'[170] A meeting of citizens of Krasny Kholm in Tver province sent a message. 'We thank A. F. Kerensky for his dedication to strengthening and extending the achievements of the revolution and urge him to take care of his health in the interests of the Russian people. He does not have the right to squander his life, which belongs to the people, and let those around him take care he gets rest and peace, let only those who really need to take away his time and health.'[171]

The Leader's health belonged to the nation, and the need to protect it was an urgent political priority. The country's future depended on it. It is significant that the appeal was published in the main Socialist Revolutionary newspaper: authoritative party members considered it appropriate for their leaders to be written about in this manner.

It was not only the political situation but the Leader's health which were seen as indicative of the state of the country. The delegates at a meeting of the Black Sea Fleet, the garrison and workers of Sevastopol sent an address to Kerensky in early May. 'It is clear to everyone that the decline in your health is a sign of bloody anarchy, and that, if you perish, Russia's freedom will perish with you.'[172] A provincial newspaper also wrote of the importance of preserving the health of such a unique leader. 'Kerensky is ridiculously overtired. They say he is staggering on his feet, that he falls asleep while standing, while walking. He has undergone a medical operation. Oh, how important it is to take care of him – this love of our revolution! Otherwise, according to people who have seen him and kept an eye on him, "he won't last long."'[173]

The Leader's self-sacrifice was suggestive of a religious ascetic whose self-mortification endows him with the power to perform miracles.[174] Someone writing a month later in the same newspaper likened Kerensky to a mythical hero.

A gatherer of the people.

That is the title *Russkaia volia* has bestowed on A. F. Kerensky, who is currently engaging in the labours of Hercules.

It is astonishing that these labours are being performed by someone who is ill, physically weak, and strong only in spirit.

But this spirit is performing miracles, moving upon the face of crumbling Russia, as in the Bible the Spirit of God moved upon the face of the waters.

Let there be light![175]

Such a comparison was not seen as sacrilegious, or even as over the top. Two months later the newspaper of supporters of reformation in the Orthodox Church wrote of the mysterious energy of the self-sacrificing Leader which enabled him to fulfil the mission of redeeming the Fatherland. 'What a powerful hidden force there is in this sick, tormented man who has almost no blood left! How is he not to stumble under the burden of the Cross he has taken upon his shoulders? How is it possible that this voice is not faltering, but summoning and annihilating like the voice of conscience? Is there not something ineffable about the secret of his omnipresent and inextinguishable energy?'[176]

It was not only the minister's health which gave his supporters cause for concern. The press reported attempts on his life. It was asserted that Staff Captain G. A. Leving, who had intended to assassinate Kerensky, had committed suicide in the Tauride Palace on 6 March. A commission of inquiry found, however, that he had had no such intention.[177] But the news did prompt several organizations hastily to pass resolutions in support of the minister. The officers and men of the 2nd Baltic Fleet crew expressed their sympathy to a politician whose merits they especially valued and for whose life, 'so precious at this time to our dear homeland', they were especially concerned.[178]

Rumours of danger threatening Kerensky circulated constantly, and sometimes were fully justified. On 27 April, when a ceremonial meeting was being held in the Tauride Palace of members of the four State Dumas, past and present, a person acting suspiciously was detained. He was found to have an explosive and admitted he had been plotting to kill Kerensky.[179] There were also rumours subsequently that Kerensky was dead, and these provoked outbreaks of panic. No other politician came close to figuring in so many rumours, and there is no doubt they reflected widespread serious anxiety over the life of the Leader.

After Kerensky became minister of war, concern for his welfare changed somewhat. It was a theme developed particularly by the newspaper *Svobodnaya Rossiya* [Free Russia], which was edited by the writer Alexander Kuprin. He wrote: 'We must all covenant to protect the life so dear to us of Alexander Fyodorovich, to cherish it as the apple of our eye, as a pearl of great price, because it is through him that the salvation of Russia will come.'[180] On the same day, in another edition of the newspaper, the journalist B. Filatovich urged: 'Citizens, protect Kerensky!' He shared his concerns about the state of the Leader's health.

> I saw him the other day and stopped, shocked by his appearance. It is plain that this man has been overburdened, but that he is capable of superhuman feats.
>
> If he cannot be relieved of this burden, if it is so necessary for the motherland, then other measures must be taken. We must protect him. It is essential.
>
> Kerensky is threatened from two directions: externally and internally. Externally he is threatened with assassination by a traitor, because the citizen minister shuns protection and is accessible to everyone, which might easily include agents of the Germans and of reactionaries who could take that precious life.
>
> The internal danger is Kerensky himself, his body. The nerves and heart of this precious person are subjected to excessively great and, I would say, over-frequent demands. He does not even get to eat regular meals because of people who need to see the minister, and some who do not particularly need to. . . .
>
> For Russia's sake, protect Kerensky.[181]

Soon, however, journalists and orators were joyfully, almost like family members, recording an improvement in the Leader's health. By visiting the front line he was spending a lot of time in the fresh air. Sergey Tretyakov, an entrepreneur and public figure, greeted Kerensky with satisfaction: 'The minister has become more robust lately, has grown and become stronger!' It is curious that these were the words he chose when publicly addressing the statesman.[182]

Nevertheless, the image of a politician sacrificing himself for the sake of his country and the revolution does not disappear from political discourse. A further cause for concern appears: fear for the life of a Leader who is putting his personal safety at risk when visiting the front line. The resolution of one military committee makes the point.

> Upon hearing that, when visiting the Riga Front, disregarding the obvious danger, you sat with General Radko-Dmitriev on the parapet in the forward trenches, our regimental commander said, 'Kerensky has no right to risk his life, because at present there is no one who could replace him.' The Regimental Committee of the 389th Nizhnedneprovsky Regiment wholly supports the opinion of the commander, and requests and insists that Comrade Kerensky must take care of his life for the good of free Russia, in order that the army and people of free Russia should not lose in the person of the comrade minister the hope of retaining the freedom so dear to us.[183]

The resolution makes explicit what particularly contributed to the spread of anxiety about the life and health of the Leader: his irreplaceability. The Leader's uniqueness makes his physical existence and well-being politically important.

The health of the self-sacrificing Leader became an important argument in combating opponents of the June Offensive.[184] An anti-Bolshevik resolution was adopted at a general meeting of the Yelisavetgrad Hussar Regiment on 2 June.

> Straining his damaged lungs, selflessly burning up his precious life, Minister of War Kerensky shouts, warns, implores, abjures the troops not to surrender Russia to disgrace and slavery but instead, uniting into a single, mighty army, to send the enemy packing! . . . Let all those of you who put the interests of your party above the interests of our homeland, and let all those looters in the rear, all those who are dodging conscription, all who hinder Kerensky in his work, know that the revolutionary army will find you guilty.[185]

This regimental meeting was evidently under the control of the commanding officers, and their resolution was published by the Constitutional Democrats and in the newspaper of the Russian nationalists. The newspaper of the Right Socialist Revolutionaries, however, was writing along precisely the same lines. 'Kerensky is using the last of his strength at the front to inspire the army with the spirit of revolutionary defence,' while irresponsible internationalists 'cold-bloodedly sink a knife into his back.'[186] For a time Kerensky becomes the Leader of a broad front of those who support continuing the war, from 'revolutionary defencists' to nationalists, and all the participants in that ill-assorted coalition use the image of the self-sacrificing Leader who is burning up his life to save the fatherland.

In some respects this image of the suffering yet heroic and strong-willed politician is reminiscent of that of Marat, the ailing 'friend of the people' who was prepared to immolate himself on the altar of the nation, and who by his suffering gained the status of a symbol of the revolution even while alive.[187] Speaking on 7 March to the Moscow Soviet of Workers' Deputies, Kerensky publicly declared his unwillingness to follow in his footsteps. 'I will never be the Marat of the Russian Revolution.'[188] The minister of justice was making it clear that he would not pursue a policy of revolutionary retribution. That same day he announced that he had drafted a law abolishing the death penalty in Russia 'forever', and the next day he signed it. But, by repudiating the image of the French revolutionary leader, Kerensky perhaps revealed that, in cultivating a reputation as the friend of the people, he had indeed been modelling himself on Marat.

Kerensky's infirmity was an important component of his positive representation in 1917, and, tellingly, it features in several of his biographies published then. This hardly suggests collusion or an explicit commission.

It seems more reasonable to speculate that all the biographers were in the force field of the tradition of glorifying ascetic heroes who overcome all difficulties to achieve a great goal and are prepared to lay down their lives in the process.

We encounter manifestations of that tradition during the revolution. As we have seen, a meeting of trading officials in Tyumen sent Kerensky a request to convey their 'greetings to the holy martyrs and champions of freedom Yekaterina Breshkovskaya, Vera Figner, Nikolai Morozov and other veterans of the liberation movement and to tell them we will give our lives for the ideals for which they fought.'[189] The holy martyrs were envisaged as a sacred community of champions of freedom, and Kerensky's aura as another of their number raised him to a new level.

The feat of martyrdom on behalf of the people, of victory over one's body, served as proof that Kerensky possessed exceptional spiritual and political qualities, confirmed his charisma, and suggested he had a unique gift which differentiated him from the other leaders of the revolution. This manifestation of concern for the Leader's well-being from many participants in the political process was an important asset for establishing the cult of the Leader.

6 Kerensky as Louis Blanc: features of the Bolsheviks' political propaganda

Kerensky had no shortage of opponents both on the left and on the right, but in the spring of 1917 his opponents were in no hurry openly to criticize the popular and influential minister of the people's truth. Up until the April Crisis not a single article appearing in *Pravda*, the centrally controlled newspaper of the Bolshevik Party, criticized Kerensky openly. To the best of its ability, the newspaper avoided making any mention at all of the popular minister, although there were plenty of news leads they could have followed. During this time thirty-six issues of the paper appeared, yet only eight neutral news items mentioned Kerensky.

At closed meetings, the Bolsheviks damned him. At a meeting of the Petersburg Committee on 4 March, for example, there was reference to 'Kerensky's demagogic speech'.[190] Such comments did not, however, make it on to the pages of the Bolshevik press. The opinions of party activists were not used in their printed propaganda.

It is instructive to observe the attitude towards Kerensky of Vladimir Lenin, an émigré living in Switzerland, with the use made of his comments by Bolsheviks who were actually in Russia. As early as 6 March, in a 'telegram to the Bolsheviks leaving for Russia', Lenin instructed: 'Our tactics: no trust in and no support of the new government; Kerensky is especially suspect.' That text, however, was first published in Russian only in 1930.[191] Even many party activists were unaware of his view. In March both the Russian Bureau of the Central Committee and the Petersburg Committee of Bolsheviks considered Lenin's position excessively radical, and his views were not widely disseminated.[192]

Lenin several times mentions Kerensky in his 'Letters from Afar'. On 7 March 1917, in a letter entitled 'The First Stage of the First Revolution', he criticized Kerensky as one of the 'principal representatives' of the 'petty bourgeoisie' who, in the Provisional Government, 'is a balalaika on which they play to deceive the workers and peasants'. Lenin even accused him of latent monarchism. 'The *whole* of the new government is monarchist, for Kerensky's *verbal* republicanism simply cannot be taken seriously, is not worthy of a statesman and, *objectively*, is political chicanery.'[193]

This letter from Lenin, frequently quoted by Kerensky's biographers, was published in *Pravda* on 21 and 22 March, but the excerpts quoted were omitted. It seems reasonable to assume that Lev Kamenev and other prominent Bolsheviks in Petrograd recognized that absurdly accusing Kerensky of monarchism would arouse indignation even among many supporters of the Bolshevik Party. Publication would undermine the party's credibility, and they accordingly firmly redacted the letter.

In his second letter (dated no later than 9 March) Lenin used historical analogies to describe the Russian Revolution. 'The appointment of the Russian Louis Blanc, Kerensky, and the appeal to support the new government is, one may say, a classical example of betrayal of the cause of the revolution and the cause of the proletariat, a betrayal which doomed a number of nineteenth-century revolutions, irrespective of how sincere and devoted to socialism the leaders and supporters of such a policy may have been.'[194] Lenin, conceding that Kerensky was personally honest in defending his views, accuses him of in reality betraying the revolution. However, this stern judgement too remained unknown to many Bolsheviks: the article was first published only in 1924. The Bolshevik leader, still living abroad, saw the Provisional Government as a single unit. Lenin either failed to notice the internal contradictions in the cabinet or decided to ignore them. He characterized Kerensky as a secondary, decorative figure, which was simply wrong. It was precisely at this moment that the minister of justice was gaining the reputation of the strongman in the cabinet.

Louis Blanc, to whom Lenin compared Kerensky, was a utopian socialist and a prominent figure in the 1848 revolution, a member of the Provisional Government of France, and known to Marxists principally from a famous work by Karl Marx titled 'The Class Struggle in France from 1848 to 1850'. Marx later reinforced the negative assessment of Blanc he had given there. 'Louis Blanc, representative of sentimental phrase-socialism, joined this clique of second-rate pretenders in an *intrigue* against another traitor of the people, *Ledru-Rollin*.'[195] Lenin could readily apply that description to Kerensky.

Finally, any Marxist was sure to remember the beginning of Marx's 'The Eighteenth Brumaire of Louis Bonaparte'. 'Hegel remarks somewhere that all great world-historic facts and personages appear, so to speak, twice. He forgot to add: the first time as tragedy, the second time as farce. Caussidière for Danton, Louis Blanc for Robespierre. . . .'[196] Louis Blanc in this interpretation is a character out of farce, aping the actions of a great revolutionary while not in fact being one. This was indeed how people from a variety of viewpoints later assessed Kerensky.

Lenin, who viewed the French Revolution of 1848 primarily through the writings of Marx, often applied the experience of that conflict when analysing the situation in 1917. In this he and other Marxists differ from most politicians and commentators, who drew analogies between the Russian Revolution and the eighteenth-century French Revolution. (Russian conservative writers tended to favour images from the seventeenth-century Russian Time of Troubles.)

In mid-March, Lenin wrote a declaration addressed to Russian prisoners of war, in which he described the minister of justice as follows: 'The "democrat" Kerensky has been brought in only to create the semblance of a "people's" government and to have a "democratic" stump speaker to feed the people high falutin but empty *phrases*, while the Guchkovs and Lvovs *work against* the people.'[197] This was calling Kerensky's democratic credentials and his authority into question: the eloquent minister of justice was only there to disguise government by the bourgeoisie. Lenin's letter was published in leaflet form but, as far as one can tell, distributed only outside Russia, so that it had no impact on the current controversy.

On 12 March, Lenin began working on an article, 'The Revolution in Russia and the Tasks of the Workers of All Countries', where he repeated some of the same comments about Kerensky. 'One quite insignificant post, that of Minister of Justice, has gone to the glib-tongued Trudovik Kerensky, whom the capitalists need – to pacify the people with empty promises, fool them with high-sounding phrases, reconcile them to the government of landlords and capitalists who, in union with the capitalists of England and France, want to continue the predatory war.'[198] This view was wide of the mark. The post of minister of justice was, as we have said, very important, and, thanks to his political weight, Kerensky was able also to influence the resolution of many issues not within the purview of his department. Lenin's article was not, in any case, completed and was published only later.

In his lecture 'The Tasks of the Russian Social-Democratic Labour Party in the Russian Revolution', Lenin noted a tendency in the Soviet to put its trust 'in Kerensky, that hero of the empty phrase, that pawn in the hands of Guchkov and Milyukov, that representative of the worst type of "Louis Blanc politics", past master of the empty promise and of the sonorous phrase in the spirit of the European social-patriots and social-pacifists *à la* Kautsky and Co. In reality, however, he "reconciles" the workers to the continuation of the predatory war.'[199] Lenin's summary appeared on the pages of *Volksrecht*, a Swiss newspaper, but it too remained unknown to Russian newspaper readers of the time.

So in March, still in emigration, Lenin was harshly criticizing Kerensky, but even many of his supporters in Russia knew nothing about it because the local Bolshevik leaders abridged the published texts or suppressed them altogether.

The Bolshevik leader might have been expected, upon returning to Russia, to make his view of Kerensky public, but that did not happen. Lenin, who, as usual, subjected his political opponents to outspoken criticism in April, refrained from directly attacking Kerensky. In a number of critical articles he clearly had the minister of justice in mind but did not name him. Thus, on 8 April, he published 'Blancism', which quite clearly was also about Kerensky.[200] Only readers familiar with Marx's views on Louis Blanc, however, would have been able to understand the allusion. Such allegorical references were not going to irritate readers for whom Kerensky remained the popular leader of an anti-monarchist revolution. The article made public Lenin's criticism of Kerensky as a 'petty-bourgeois' politician, but only initiates would have known at whom the criticism was directed.

> Louis Blanc, the French socialist, won unenviable notoriety during the revolution of 1848 by changing his stand from that of the class struggle to that of petty-bourgeois illusions, illusions adorned with would-be 'socialist' phraseology, but in reality tending to strengthen the influence of the bourgeoisie over the proletariat. Louis Blanc looked to the bourgeoisie for assistance, hoped, and inspired hopes in others, that the bourgeoisie *could* help the workers in the matter of 'labour organisation' – this vague term purporting to express 'socialist' tendencies.[201]

In the same article, Lenin directly criticizes Nikolai Chkheidze, Irakliy Tsereteli and Yury Steklov, moderate socialists heading the Petrograd Soviet. He calls them 'Louis Blancs' and uses the term 'Blancism' to characterize the entire political trend favouring agreement between the socialists and the 'bourgeoisie'.[202] The article is not only about Chkheidze, Tsereteli and Steklov, however, and reference is made to other leaders of the Soviet who have adopted the position of Louis Blanc. Clearly Kerensky, who combined the post of deputy chairman of the Soviet's executive committee, is also implied, but on this occasion too Lenin refrains from criticizing him directly.

Lenin nevertheless remained critical of Kerensky's political role. On 10 April he finished writing a pamphlet, *The Tasks of the Proletariat in our Revolution*, in which Kerensky gets the same treatment: 'A. Kerensky, a Trudovik and "would-be socialist", has no function whatsoever, except to lull the vigilance and attention of the people with sonorous phrases.'[203] However, the pamphlet was published only in September 1917, when Kerensky was already being openly and harshly criticized not only by the Bolsheviks but by many other politicians.

On 14 April, Lenin spoke at the Petrograd City Conference of the Bolsheviks, not without contempt, of Kerensky's analytical skills, criticizing him from a Marxist standpoint. 'A Bolshevik must differentiate between the proletariat and the petty bourgeoisie, and leave such words as "revolutionary democracy" and "revolutionary people" to Kerensky.' Such judgements were known to the party's activists, but not to the readers of Bolshevik newspapers: the text was first published in 1925.[204]

In some situations the Bolsheviks even tried to make use of Kerensky's authority. Defending themselves from accusations following Lenin's return through Germany, they were only too willing to quote excerpts from the publications of their authoritative opponents that were beneficial to them. On 15 April an appeal by Lenin, 'Against the Riot-Mongers', was published. This item, about an anti-Bolshevik propaganda campaign, contained a reference to the main newspaper of the Socialist Revolutionaries: 'The paper *Dyelo naroda*, to which Minister A. F. Kerensky is an active contributor, has already pointed out that the methods used by these newspapers are helping the riot-mongers.' Lenin also appealed to Kerensky's authority in other publications in April.[205]

The Bolshevik leader's circumspection in refraining from publicly criticizing the minister of justice was understandable. Even the most radical soviets and committees were expressing support for Kerensky at that time. During debates in the Kronshtadt Soviet, people with very different viewpoints, including extreme radicals, deferred to the authority of Kerensky.[206] Even supporters of the Bolsheviks and deputies close to them spoke of the first people's minister with the greatest respect.

Some readers of Bolshevik publications had a lot of trust in this popular politician, and the editors of party newspapers had no option but to bear that in mind. On 20 April, the day the April Crisis began, a general meeting of the clerks of the Officers' Electrotechnical School and the Reserve Electrotechnical Battalion gave the following mandate to their delegate to the Soviet: 'Insist in the Soviet of Workers' and Soldiers' Deputies on dismissal of all the bourgeois ministers, except Citizen Minister Kerensky.' Although the clerks included the minister of justice among the bourgeois ministers, he was also addressed as 'citizen' and they expressed confidence in him. This position was typical of a proportion of grassroots supporters of the Bolsheviks, despite being in clear contradiction of the view of Lenin and other party leaders. A few days later, during the April Crisis, this item was published in *Pravda*.[207] The editors of the party's main newspaper evidently felt the view of some of its readers could not just be ignored.

Some who were later held up as exemplary Leninists viewed Kerensky positively. Sergey Kirov contributed at that time to *Terek*, a newspaper published in Vladikavkaz. In May he hailed the establishment of a coalition government as 'a brilliant end to the first act of the Russian Revolution, which opens up a vast field for consolidation of the positions which have been won.' He saw the work of Kerensky as a guarantee of future success. Kirov was a member of a united Social Democratic organization which included both supporters of the Bolsheviks and others inclined to support various shades of Menshevism.[208] The Vladikavkaz organization was nothing out of the ordinary: many Social Democratic groups in the provinces and at the front remained united even in autumn 1917.[209] Their members did not have one standard attitude towards Kerensky and Lenin. Even in Petrograd, where the lines of political differentiation were starker, the Bolsheviks were divided over how they thought of the minister.

There were personal reasons for this. Kerensky had defended some of the Bolsheviks in court, and it took time for political differences to erode the relationship of trust between a 'political defence lawyer' and his clients. In addition, the minister was in a position to help former prisoners, exiles and political émigrés. As mentioned, he had funds at his disposal to support those who had championed freedom or were otherwise victims of the old regime. It is hardly surprising that a variety of socialists, including some prominent Bolsheviks, appealed to him for help.[210] This made difficult, or at least deferred, Bolshevik criticism of the minister. At the same time, in March and April, Kerensky did in fact give left-wing socialists grounds for dissatisfaction, and they made that known in public speeches and resolutions. Nevertheless, Lenin and other Bolsheviks did not exploit these tactical opportunities to attack him.

In early March many contemporaries criticized Kerensky's announcement that the Provisional Government was intending to send the royal family abroad. As we have seen, activists were displeased that servants of the old regime were being held in relatively comfortable conditions. The Bolsheviks, like other members of the Executive Committee of the Petrograd Soviet, were indignant that Kerensky had scant regard for its authority, and even urged the committee to rebuke the minister publicly, but undertook no action on their own account.

The Bolsheviks began criticizing Kerensky in the press, for being overly lenient towards servants of the old regime, only in the latter half of May. The first such article was published not in the Petrograd but in the Moscow party newspaper.[211] It is significant that Lenin and other Bolsheviks, who usually seized on any excuse or sign of public discontent to launch bruising propaganda attacks on their political opponents, on this occasion held off. There could be several explanations for this unwonted restraint. For the Bolsheviks, other politicians personified the enemy, primarily Guchkov, the minister of war, and Milyukov, the minister of foreign affairs. To proliferate their main targets would not have been in the Bolsheviks' interests. Lenin did, though, as we have seen, publicly criticize Chkheidze, Steklov and Tsereteli, but for some reason made an exception for Kerensky.

It would be more plausible, however, to explain the absence of criticism as being due to Kerensky's immense authority. The most innocent critical remark about him could cause a storm of protest. The Bolsheviks were already under propaganda attack because of Lenin's return to Russia through Germany. Even in Petrograd 'anti-Leninist' feeling was widespread among the soldiers, and criticizing the popular minister might have provoked a violent and unpredictable reaction from those in the services;

they were more amenable to accusations directed at Steklov, Chkheidze and even Tsereteli.

Among the few items in the press that did contain criticism of Kerensky was an 'Open Letter to the Minister of Justice, Citizen Kerensky', written by Fyodorov, a gunner, and published on 18 April in the Bolshevik *Soldatskaya pravda*. The author was writing to the minister to protest at reserve companies being sent to the front from Petrograd. 'You, guardian of justice, tell me this, a rank-and-file fighter for freedom, why don't you say anything or do anything?' Perhaps the letter was edited by the newspaper, because in places the style does not seem that of an ordinary soldier. 'Or do you think a few fancy theatrical phrases and poses are enough to save the gains of the revolution?'[212]

The writer was, of course, criticizing Kerensky for government decisions outside his competence as minister of justice, in effect demanding he should intervene in matters which were the responsibility of the minister of war. The letter also takes a sideswipe at the theatrical style of Kerensky's speeches. Even so, the criticism is fairly cautious. The criticism of Kerensky's action, or, more precisely, inaction, was coming from a 'rank-and-file soldier', so could not be construed as expressing the view of the Bolsheviks. It was also raising an issue of importance to many in the forces who, for whatever reason, did not want to be sent to the front. In this instance there was little likelihood of its leading to an outburst of 'anti-Leninist' anger, because many soldiers shared the writer's opinion.

It was only after Kerensky became minister of war in May, and particularly after 11 May when he signed the order 'On the Rights of Members of the Armed Forces', that the Bolsheviks took advantage of the situation to launch a massive propaganda attack on him. By then they no longer feared that criticizing Kerensky might provoke an angry reaction among the soldiers which might be dangerous for them.

Studying how Kerensky was portrayed in Bolshevik propaganda enables us to clarify details of the history of that party. Alexander Rabinowitch has shown that it was not a highly disciplined steel cohort unquestioningly acting in accordance with the will of its Leader. He has demonstrated that different party bodies, even in Petrograd, were not all following the same line but formed a range of alliances.[213] Khanan Astrakhan has also shown just how complicated the internal alignment of forces was among the Bolsheviks.[214]

Studying the language of the revolution enables us to approach the issue from a different angle. Ordinary supporters of the Bolsheviks, the grassroots activists, were a diverse collection of people. In spring 1917 they included admirers of the minister of justice, and some radical soldiers thought it should be possible to create a united front from Lenin to Kerensky. In early May, one front-line soldier wrote, 'We need to distance ourselves from Milyukov, but Kerensky and Lenin should shake hands.'[215] It seems unlikely that point of view was widespread, but there were among the Bolsheviks' supporters some who had doubts about Lenin and some who were favourably inclined towards Kerensky. The party leaders, aware of these sentiments, proceeded cautiously when articulating their attitude to the most popular leader of the February Revolution. Accordingly, Lenin's criticism of Kerensky was encrypted, and only the educated party elite familiar with the texts of Marxism would have been able decipher the coded message in his writings about the 'Russian Louis Blanc'. It was only after Kerensky had taken decisions widely unpopular with the soldiers that the Bolshevik leaders, sensing a change in their supporters' mood, spoke out openly against the 'revolutionary minister'.

The Bolsheviks' reluctance to attack Kerensky openly in March and April helps us to assess more precisely the extent of the authority he possessed. His immense popularity made him unassailable even for those who opposed his policies. It was only after the April Crisis transformed the situation that the politics changed.

7 'Rebellious slaves' and the 'great citizen'

It was at the height of the April Crisis that Kerensky delivered his most famous speech. His contemporaries particularly remembered his remarking: 'Is the free state of Russia really a state of rebellious slaves? I lack my previous confidence that what we see before us is not rebellious slaves but intelligent citizens creating a new state.' That expression – 'rebellious slaves' – has gone down in history and been widely used.[216] It is extraordinary that Kerensky, whose memoirs are not notable for their modesty, makes no mention of this speech in his best-known memoirs.[217] His resounding speech is, nevertheless, of great interest.[218]

On 18 April, Russia celebrated 1 May by the new, Gregorian calendar for the first time. Memoirists with diverse viewpoints recall the festive atmosphere in the streets of Petrograd. It was shared by A. F. Kerensky. Speaking at a concert rally, he urged his audience to observe 'iron discipline', before conducting a regimental band playing *The Marseillaise*. In the electric atmosphere, a soldier called out, 'Citizens, let us swear to answer at the first call from the citizen minister, A. F. Kerensky.' There were answering cries: 'We do!' A musician from the band addressed the audience. 'A. F. Kerensky hasn't made a bad job of conducting the band (general laughter), but he conducts the Russian Revolution even better. Allow me to wish him strength to occupy his important post for a long time yet.' More applause, then Kerensky sang *The Internationale* and the whole hall joined in.[219]

The minister had grounds to be pleased: that very day the Provisional Government had approved a note laying out Russia's war aims for the Allies. This came at the end of protracted and difficult negotiations, behind-the-scenes plotting and propaganda campaigns. The foreign minister, Pavel Milyukov, had wanted to keep open the possibility for Russia to enjoy the spoils of a victory which seemed inevitable: the annexation of certain territories of its enemies. The Petrograd Soviet, however, under the control of moderate socialists, was demanding peace without annexations and idemnities. Kerensky was under constant pressure from the Mensheviks and Socialist Revolutionaries, who, in turn, were being criticized for their half-heartedness by left-wing socialists, particularly the Bolsheviks. Kerensky and Milyukov fought it out at government meetings and in the press. These conflicts were no secret from foreign diplomats. The British ambassador wrote on 17 (30) April: 'A battle royal is being fought between Kerensky and Miliukoff on the famous formula "Peace without annexations", and as the majority of the Ministers are on Kerensky's side, I should not be surprised if Miliukoff has to go.'[220]

The government meeting on 18 April too was fairly contentious, but a compromise was found, the ministers approved an agreed version, and the text of the note was released to reporters. The document did, however, contain elements which were perceived as concessions to Milyukov. The sentence that the Provisional Government, 'protecting the rights of our homeland, will fully comply with the obligations assumed in respect of our Allies' was interpreted as support for the pre-revolutionary war aims, and hence in violation of the principle of rejection of a policy of annexations and idemnities. Mention of fighting the war 'to a victorious conclusion' ruled out the possibility of collaboration between the socialists of the belligerent countries in achieving peace, which was one of the aims of the leaders of the Soviet. When the note was received in the newspaper offices it caused outrage even among moderate socialists, and it was clear that publishing it would precipitate a political crisis.

Kerensky cannot have been unaware of that. On 19 April he again spoke at a concert rally, and this time his speech was unusually pessimistic. The French ambassador forwarded his words: 'If you will not believe in me and follow me, I shall give up power. I will never use force to secure the acceptance of my opinions . . . When a country means to cast itself into the gulf, no human power can prevent it, and those who conduct its government have only one course open to them – to retire.'[221] The diplomat's testimony appears entirely plausible: Kerensky was preparing his audience for publication of the 'Milyukov Note'. In his speech there were the themes of trust or distrust of a leader, the threat to step down from power, the refusal to use violence when resolving a crisis. There was mention of irrational, self-destructive forces in the revolution. These were all to become relevant in the course of the April Crisis and to be reflected in Kerensky's speeches.

On the night of 19 April the Executive Committee of the Petrograd Soviet condemned the note, whose text appeared in the newspapers the following morning. The news of the Milyukov Note was a spark which caused a serious fire. The protest spilled out on to the streets, and several regiments drew up in front of the seat of government demanding Milyukov's resignation. Some called the crisis the Milyukov Days, although the ministers, including Kerensky, bore collective responsibility for the note. The agitated soldiers were persuaded to return to barracks, but by this time both supporters of Milyukov and radically minded workers coming to protest about the note were heading to the city centre. Demonstrations continued the following day, clashes occurred, and there were fatalities and injuries. The Soviet demanded a halt to all demonstrations, and its decision was respected.[222]

Kerensky, who usually needed no prompting to make a crowd-pleasing speech, refrained from making any public statement for several days. On 20 April a crowd gathered in front of the Ministry of Justice, eager to hear the opinion of their popular minister, and, when he arrived, Kerensky was given a loud ovation. The minister, 'tired and ill', passed through, indicating by gestures that he was unable to speak. People were reluctant to disperse, and the minister's adjutant announced to the crowd, which overflowed into the adjacent streets, that Kerensky was ill and the doctors had forbidden him to speak. The public shouted 'Long live the Provisional Government!' and dispersed.[223] The crowd were probably hoping to hear a slogan along those lines from Kerensky, but that would obviously have caused ructions with the Soviet.

The purportedly ill minister did find the strength to take part in government meetings that day, receive foreign diplomats, and meet delegates of the peasantry, and even representatives of socialist Esperantists and anarchists. Meanwhile, however, many people were puzzled as to how he, the deputy chairman of the Executive Committee of the Soviet, could have supported the note when it was in contravention of the political line of the Soviet.[224]

Some supporters of Milyukov, on the other hand, tried to make use of Kerensky's authority. A portrait of the minister of justice was seen to be carried in their demonstration, and there were shouts of 'Support the government of the Russian Revolution! Support Milyukov and Kerensky!'[225] The demonstrators believed the two ministers were acting in unison, and this only deepened suspicions among the socialists about the minister of justice's conduct. The disillusionment among left-wingers was particularly strong: they had been pinning their hopes on Kerensky standing up to the 'bourgeois' foreign minister. There were rumours that the minister of justice had voted against approving the note, possibly circulated deliberately by his supporters.[226]

Kerensky's popularity was shored up by news of attempts on his life which became known at this time. The minister commented, 'I regard the attempt to assassinate me as an inevitable part of my job. It will probably not be the last.' To another interviewer, Kerensky said: 'This is already the second time there has been an attempt on my life. . . . Of course, when all is said and done, it is difficult to stay safe. There is no escaping your destiny.'[227] His reputation as the friend of the people, who constantly put his life at risk for the ideals of the revolution, was strengthened.

Various plans to overcome the crisis were mooted: creating a government headed by Kerensky was discussed, and he considered that option himself.[228] An increasing number of politicians wanted to bring moderate socialists delegated by their parties into the government, and Kerensky felt that would strengthen his own position.[229] The leaders of the Soviet, however, were not in a hurry to join the government. They preferred to keep the government as it was and not burden themselves with responsibility. Milyukov, on the other hand, wanted to retain as much influence in the Provisional Government as possible and increase its independence from the Soviet.

Given this situation, on 26 April Kerensky published a statement he had sent to the Central Committee of the Socialist Revolutionary Party, the Petrograd Soviet, the Duma fraction of the Trudovik (Labour) party and the Provisional Committee of the State Duma. Appealing to the organizations to which he was answerable, Kerensky proposed filling government posts on the recommendation of the parties and said he would be unable to remain in the government unless its composition was changed. In effect, the most popular politician presented the political elite with an ultimatum to create a coalition of liberals and socialists. Thereby, according to Milyukov, Kerensky caused a ministerial crisis.[230]

On the same day, an invitation was issued by the Provisional Government inviting representatives of the socialists to join it. Kerensky urged the leaders of the Soviet to accept the offer, but on 28 April the Executive Committee of the Petrograd Soviet declared itself against coalition.[231]

At the same time, the politicians opposing the socialists were seeking to limit the shift of the focus of political cooperation to the left. In order to influence public opinion, they made use of an event which aroused considerable interest: on 27 April, the anniversary of the initiation of the First State Duma, a joint meeting of deputies of the four successive Dumas was held. This reunion, which attracted considerable press attention, would, it was hoped, act as a counterbalance to the influence of the Soviet.

The ministers sat in the front row, while Kerensky occupied his usual seat as a deputy in the left section of the hall of the Tauride Palace. Those present later recalled how pale his face was – 'a mask of tragedy with folds of suffering' – and his arm was in a black sling.[232]

The gathering was not a prim meeting of members of the political elite. In the boxes and balcony, and even in the aisles, there were many front-line soldiers delegated to the revolutionary capital by their formations. They reacted vociferously to the speeches, acclaiming those of their favourites and heckling those of their opponents. Holding the attention of such an assembly was no easy matter.

Kerensky did not speak at the meeting, but his popularity was unmistakable even when he said nothing. Maxim Vinaver, a prominent figure in the Constitutional Democratic Party, spoke about the history of the Duma, his recalling of its glorious past intended to reinforce the authority of the 'Cadets'. 'The first act of the new government created by the people was to declare the amnesty which back then we sought in vain.' Loud applause interrupted his speech, and a Trudovnik deputy in the second

Duma, Mikhail Berezin, shouted from his seat, 'Kerensky did that!' The minister of justice received an ovation. (One can only imagine how the other ministers felt about that, knowing that the amnesty had been backed by the entire government.) Vinaver continued: 'Our present people's government heeded this voice of the people's representatives and, as one of its first acts, abolished the death penalty.' Again there were shouts of 'Kerensky!', followed by another ovation.[233] In the context of the ongoing political crisis, the liberals sought to reinforce their authority by referring to the history of popular representation, while their audience attributed the adoption of popular laws solely to Kerensky.

There was particular interest in a verbal duel between the nationalist Vasiliy Shulgin, who asserted that the Provisional Government was being held under house arrest, 'under the supervision of the Soviet', and the Menshevik Irakliy Tsereteli, who spoke against him. At the end of the meeting, Fyodor Rodichev, the old figurehead of the Constitutional Democratic Party, with unprecedented élan, delivered a 'thunderous' speech:

> Only a slave can live in a monarchy, under autocracy; a slave whose nature it is to know how to rebel but not how to live in freedom; a slave who can commit an act of violence against someone he hates, who can threaten him with violence, but who does not know how to stop short before the law and to respect the line that justice places between people. (Loud applause.) A republic is infinitely more difficult than monarchy, because in a republic what is essential is obedience to the law of one and all, freely, not through compulsion, not under duress, but through free will. In order to live in a republic, you need to work harder than in a monarchy. (Exclamations of 'Quite right'.) To live in a republic, you need citizens to exercise self-restraint.[234]

Guchkov's speech was particularly well received. He had been due to speak at the beginning of the meeting but appeared in the hall much later. Nobody had actually been expecting him to come: the minister of war was ill and the newspapers had been printing bulletins about the state of his health. Guchkov clambered heavily up on to the stage and took a seat at the presidium table. After the speech in progress ended he was immediately given the floor. His speech, the journalists reported, was 'a voice of sorrow and despair'. He called for the establishment of 'a strong government', expressed his 'mortal anxiety', and concluded, 'Gentlemen, the whole country at one point acknowledged that our fatherland was in danger. Gentlemen, we have taken a step forward, there is no time to lose: our fatherland is on the brink of disaster!' There was applause from all the benches, except those of the 'extreme left'.[235]

Guchkov's speech caused a sensation. Politicians of his rank never made such pessimistic statements. The 'serious' newspapers treated his speech sympathetically. The commentator of one, with which the defencist Mensheviks collaborated, wrote (possibly still under the impact of Rodichev's speech), 'The minister who stands at the head of the army felt compelled to utter the following words: "Our fatherland is on the brink of disaster." . . . For centuries tsarism fostered a sense of servility in the population; for centuries it kept the population in a state of slavery. Now the moment of truth is at hand when the new, revolutionary Russia comes before the tribunal of history and must answer the fateful question: are you slaves or citizens?'[236]

Guchkov decided to retire: he no longer saw the government as the centre of real power. The experience of earlier weeks had shown that politicians acting outside the government could exercise considerable power if they skilfully built up their authority by delivering vibrant and topical public speeches which were then propagated in the press. The departure from the government of such a senior figure in Russian politics inevitably had an impact on public opinion and could be read as a move to rally and consolidate conservative forces, and that was certainly how it was seen by the Executive Committee of the Petrograd Soviet. 'In the present circumstances Guchkov's withdrawal is not just a resignation but an appeal to the country and the army to oppose the Soviet of Workers' and Soldiers' Deputies. Guchkov is not alone. He has the backing of certain strata of the bourgeoisie.'[237] Guchkov's resignation also caused indignation among the members of the Provisional Government.[238]

Before the resignation of a politician warning of disaster could be used to mobilize the non-socialist forces of Russia, there was work to be done on public opinion. As a suitable platform, Guchkov chose a meeting of delegates from the front line which had been working in the Tauride Palace since the April Crisis was at its height. The delegates had already invited Guchkov and were eager to meet the minister of war, but the prospect of becoming a butt for criticism from seasoned soldiers of the army in the field, who were rapidly becoming politicized, did not appeal to him.

Owing to his ill health, the speech was postponed to 28 April, but Guchkov did not appear that day either, although he had spoken at the Duma meeting the day before. The minister said he would come on 29 April, but warned he would only deliver a speech and not answer questions.[239] The meeting looked to be interesting and the hall was full, everyone now expecting something sensational. They were not to be disappointed.

Kerensky was to recall that on the day of that speech he had tried to change Guchkov's mind about resigning.[240] Be that as it may, the minister of justice was aware of the proposed departure of the minister of war and decided that he too would address the meeting. The make-up of the audience was important to Kerensky, because he was anticipating that he would be appointed the next minister of war.[241] The popular Kerensky entered the hall as Guchkov was speaking. The historic speech broke off in mid-sentence as the soldiers' delegates gave Kerensky an ovation. When their applause died down, somebody shouted, 'Long live the son of the

Russian Revolution!', which evoked more applause. The enthusiasm in the hall may have been partly an expression of sympathy, because that day the newspapers had carried reports of the foiled attempt to assassinate Kerensky.

The applause came to an end and Guchkov was able to resume his speech, but the attention of the audience was already elsewhere. Kerensky was invited to speak next, but then a soldier appeared next to him who had been awarded all the classes of the prestigious St George's Cross. He welcomed the minister, and a 'tumultuous and prolonged' ovation followed.[242] This may have been demonstrating not only the audience's wish to welcome a popular politician but perhaps, too, the negative feelings of front-line soldiers towards Guchkov.

Kerensky was guaranteed a warm reception. His friendly audience was looking forward to another of the renowned speeches of the inspirational minister of the revolution, but this time he did not live up to expectations. This was nothing like his previous speeches. He touched on the very sensitive issues already raised by Guchkov, and even went further. Enumerating the threats facing the country, he said: 'At this time the situation of the Russian state is complex and difficult. The transition from slavery to freedom cannot, of course, take the form of a ceremonial parade the way things were done in the past. It is hard, painful work, impeded by a whole succession of misunderstandings and breakdowns of communication which provide fertile ground for the weeds of faintheartedness and mistrust to sprout luxuriantly and turn the freedom of our citizens into sheer misery.'[243]

He elaborated this theme of slaves and slavery and of the bearers of a political culture of servility. 'If we, like unworthy slaves, cannot form a strong, well-organized state, a dark and bloody period will come of clashes between ourselves, and our ideals will be flung under the heel of that principle of governance for which power is all the law, and the law is without power.'[244] Then this unsettling sense of disquiet was suddenly flung at his audience: 'Comrades! For ten years we were able to suffer in silence. You were able to carry out the orders imposed on you by the old, hated regime. You were able to shoot into crowds when that was demanded of you! Is it really now that our patience has come to an end? Is the state of free Russia no more than a state of rebellious slaves?'[245]

After these words, the journalists report 'great agitation on all the benches'.[246] We can imagine the shock felt by the army's finest, the proud, battle-hardened soldiers whose loyalty the foremost representatives of the political Olympus had been courting for several days. Kerensky, sensing his audience's reaction, continued: 'Comrades, I have not the guile, I simply do not know how to lie to the people or hide the truth from them.' A soldier in a state of great agitation exclaimed, 'Long live the pride of Russia!', which provoked 'stormy, prolonged applause'.[247]

Kerensky's speech now was becoming confessional, but the theme of rebellious slaves was still there. 'I have come to you because my strength is running low, because I no longer feel the old boldness I had . . . I am no longer so confident that we see before us not rebellious slaves but intelligent citizens creating a new state with a passion worthy of the Russian people.'[248]

Having presented himself as an exhausted leader disillusioned by the reckless behaviour of compatriots not yet ready to become free citizens, Kerensky called on his listeners to turn their thoughts to the country's future. He mentioned the danger of fraternizing with the enemy, before returning to the tragedy of the Leader of a revolution whose expectations have been disappointed. 'I regret not having died then, two months ago. I would have gone to another world in the firm belief that once and for all a new life for Russia had been born, that we were capable of mutual respect one for the other without the whip and the rod, that we were capable of governing our state in a way much different from how it had been ruled by the former despots.' The journalists again registered great agitation in the hall.[249]

Sensing he had discomfited his audience, Kerensky justified his right to speak the bitter truth by referring to his past merits. 'I came here because I reserve the right to speak the truth exactly as I see it. People who walked tall under the old regime cannot be intimidated!' This statement too evoked stormy applause.[250]

Kerensky did, nevertheless, remain hopeful that events would develop favourably, providing self-discipline was universally accepted. 'Our country's fate is in your hands, and our country is in great danger. We have tasted freedom and become a little drunk. But what we now need is not intoxication but the utmost sobriety and discipline. We want to go down in history with our heads held high, and may the inscription on our graves read, "They died, but they were never slaves."' Again there was stormy, prolonged applause.[251]

Kerensky stepped down, barely able to stand. There was more applause, and further expressions of sympathy and trust were heard. Irakliy Tsereteli, however, recalled that, 'At the meeting, despite the newspapers reporting that Kerensky's speech was met with tumultuous approval by those attending, most of the delegates reacted to it very coldly. The trouble was that the orator, despite his highly visible emotion, was speaking obscurely and avoided making clear who exactly he was criticizing.'[252]

Newspaper readers, however, seeing the reports in the press, were given to understand that the speech had been received with 'loud applause' and 'tumultuous ovations', and the journalists reported it as a terrific success. The ambiguity of what he had said enabled readers to identify with Kerensky, and they did not demand greater clarity. They reacted sympathetically to the overall tenor of the speech. It is possible too that Tsereteli was projecting his impression of the speech on to the audience. He had grounds for concern that, given the propaganda offensive being mounted against the Soviet, Kerensky's speech could be used against it.

Some socialists were alarmed by elements in Kerensky's speech: a positive view of rebellious slaves was ingrained in European socialist culture, and during the war years this was perpetuated by the group of German internationalists who called themselves 'Spartacus'.

After Kerensky had answered questions, it was Tsereteli's turn to speak. He tried to play down the tragic picture of the situation presented by Guchkov and reinforced by Kerensky. 'The anxiety Kerensky talked about is certainly something we feel, but this is not anxiety about the future happiness of our homeland, which is already near at hand.' Tsereteli, while attempting to clarify, and even refute, what Kerensky had said, was at the same time trying to keep the popular politician onside.[253]

It is a fair assumption that, but for Kerensky's speech, which caused a political sensation, Guchkov's would have provoked a heated debate. The delegates had plenty of questions for him and would not have let slip the opportunity of criticizing the 'bourgeois' minister of war. A controversy of that kind could have affected the negotiations over reorganizing the government. Guchkov did not want to join the new cabinet and did not participate in the coalition negotiations, but the impact of his speech and the controversy around it would have ensured him the sympathetic attention of the conservative and liberal press. At a time when public opinion was playing a major role in the acquisition and exercise of political power, Guchkov, politically preparing the ground for his resignation from the government, could have strengthened his personal standing with his speeches on 27 and 29 April. Instead, it was not Guchkov who ultimately benefited from them but Kerensky, who was fighting for a coalition.

Contemporaries had differing recollections of Kerensky's famous speech, and that comes through in the different ways it was covered in the papers. For example, the passage where he regretted not having died during the revolution was excised by *Delo naroda*, the principal newspaper of the Socialist Revolutionary Party, of which Kerensky was nominally a member. That this was no accident is suggested by an article shortly afterwards by Nikolai Rusanov, a prominent Socialist Revolutionary, in which Kerensky's speech was cautiously criticized. Rusanov noted, 'Until now Kerensky has been unusually felicitous in his speeches.' From this it followed that his latest speech was considered less so. Like Tsereteli, Rusanov sought to distance himself from it while at the same time keeping the influential orator as an ally. He put the minister's pessimism down to fatigue and expressed the hope that he would soon be his old self again. 'We venture to hope that our comrade has only for a moment been under the influence of a gloomy spell, and that he will soon step forth again, bold and optimistic, on the path of the selfless actions which have so endeared his name to all the workers and people of revolutionary Russia.'[254]

In an article titled 'They Try to Frighten Us, But We're Not Scared', a writer for *Soldat-grazhdanin*, the newspaper of the Moscow Soviet of Soldiers' Deputies, described the situation similarly. 'Russia is on the brink of disaster, says newly resigned Minister Guchkov. And even Kerensky, a man above suspicion, the favourite of the revolution, is saying the same thing. Yet somehow we're not scared.'[255] Here too moderate socialists, highly appreciative of Kerensky, distanced themselves from what he had said in his speech.

> Kerensky's supporters used the speech to spread his image as a fearless tribune of the people. The socialist minister had the courage to tell the whole truth to the people, to speak out as only very few can. . . . What truth there is in [his words]! What courage! Such words can be spoken only by the great in spirit, genuine tribunes able to speak to the people on equal terms, without timorousness or ingratiating demagoguery. . . . For as long as we have such people, disaster has not befallen the country, no matter how menacing the thunderclouds surrounding it.

Kerensky's 'exceptional' speech and his 'formidable warnings' were also used later by the newspaper to mobilize his supporters. 'We would have been worse than rebellious slaves, would have been the lackeys of those slaves had we not risen up against the demagogy degrading our country. The fatherland is in danger. Let us show that we are not rebellious slaves but free citizens. Let us save Russia.'[256] *Russkoye slovo* [the Russian Word], the most widely read Russian newspaper, also praised the minister's speech. 'Never before, it seems to us, has A. F. Kerensky spoken with such boldness and inspiration.'[257]

The 29 April meeting was an important news story and well covered in the press. Even some newspapers supportive of the revolutionary minister substantially 'edited' the text. Some did not mention the speech to their readers at all; the silence of the Menshevik *Rabochaya gazeta* [Workers' Newspaper] is eloquent: perhaps those in charge of the party's principal newspaper shared Tsereteli's concerns. Kerensky's speech was hushed up by other titles of the moderate socialists, as the Liberal newspapers gleefully pointed out, as they used the minister's authority in polemics with their opponents. 'A. F. Kerensky's desperate plea is very weakly and vaguely reflected in the newspapers of the left-wing parties, which are busily pursuing their factional wrangling.'[258]

If the Mensheviks held back from expressing their opinion frankly and publicly, certain Bolsheviks did so raucously and vindictively. One of the leaders of the Military Organization, commenting on Kerensky's 'pathetic remarks about rebellious slaves', compared him to a pregnant woman 'carrying events he had not expected and was scared by.' 'The minister, squeezed from one side by the capitalists and landowners and from the other by the starving people, this minister, helpless, all at sea, has now admitted his impotence.' The author of an article titled 'The Tragedians' wrote, 'The retired Guchkov, just like Kerensky, has surprisingly agreed on one thing: "The situation is tragic!"' The writer declared the minister of justice was 'not strong enough' and 'chicken-hearted'.[259] It was after this speech that the Bolsheviks set to work on the image of Kerensky, which later became widespread, as weak and effeminate. The party leaders, however, still steered clear of direct attacks on him.[260]

If some of the socialists reacted with reserve, or even critically, to the speech, the liberal and conservative newspapers and publications of the right-wing socialists praised it warmly. They too noted that Guchkov and Kerensky were in agreement, but saw that as a good thing. 'Two leaders of our national policy, representing in the government two distinct currents of our public life, were at one in their assessment of the current state of affairs,' the newspaper of the Ministry of War observed.[261]

Late on 29 April, Guchkov resigned from the government, which gave added weight to his speech about the 'disaster' facing Russia. Nevsky Prospect was filled with people excitedly discussing the speech and resignation, and everyone was talking about 'disaster'.[262] The political impact of his resignation, however, was diminished, because it was Kerensky's speech that was the focus of public discussion.

Rusanov's wish came true: Kerensky was soon once more radiating revolutionary enthusiasm and infecting audiences with his optimism. It is possible that his sensational speech really was the result of a short-lived nervous breakdown, but it seems more likely that it was a calculated move. The choice of time and place for his speech, even the timing of his appearance in the conference room in the middle of Guchkov's speech – was hardly random. Kerensky consciously exploited the propaganda value of an important political moment, redirecting the attention of those present, and subsequently of newspaper readers, to his own speech. The delegates, journalists and other members of the audience had come to the meeting in the expectation of witnessing a political sensation, and their hope was realized twice over. Moreover, the second, unscheduled, sensation eclipsed the first. We have already seen Kerensky appealing over the heads of party leaders to grassroots activists. His dramatic address to front-line delegates was an anticipatory propaganda strike which established the preconditions for him to be effective as minister of war.

His remark about rebellious slaves was literally the next day on everyone's lips. It was an image used to characterize the Bolsheviks' tactics. There were others too who, like Kerensky, felt regret at having outlived the early days of the revolution. On 3 May, at a meeting of delegates from the front, Sergey Svatikov, a historian and assistant chief of the Central Militia Directorate, said: 'I would like to say, together with our great Citizen Kerensky, "How sad that I could not have died in the first three days of the revolution." I would not then have seen the motherland falling apart.' As evidence, Svatikov quoted the riots and unrest sweeping the country.[263] Commenting on this speech, the author of an article in the Socialist Revolutionary *Delo naroda* remarked caustically, 'Like Shakespeare, life puts comic characters on stage alongside tragic figures.'[264]

It might seem that this was an inappropriate reaction to what Svatikov had said, because he was someone with access to information about the state of public order in the country. Unsurprisingly, the jeering tone of the article in *Delo naroda* drew condemnation from the liberals.[265] The reaction of some of the socialists becomes more understandable, however, if we bear in mind the news climate of the political crisis. Liberal and conservative newspapers were full of reports of all manner of unrest, many of which were true. The authors and editors were not in fact motivated solely by a desire to write up a difficult situation. (On other occasions they turned a blind eye to tragic events which accompanied the revolution.) They were playing on the anxiety felt by a broad swathe of the population in the hope of curtailing the influence of the Soviet and the socialist parties and ensuring an outcome of the government crisis which would suit them. That public anxiety could be put to considerable political use. The most blatant writing in this genre was 'Disaster', an article by the famous writer Leonid Andreyev published in *Russkaya volya* on 30 April, after Guchkov had announced his resignation. The article was written under the impact of Guchkov's speech, and Andreyev used its final words as an epigraph.[266] The article caused a great stir, and readers demanded it should be republished as a pamphlet.[267]

The reaction of readers was, nevertheless, not quite what the publisher had anticipated. In other circumstances the article would have heightened the impact of Guchkov's resignation, but on the same day, 30 April, the text of Kerensky's speech appeared in the newspapers. Accordingly, Andreyev's article was more often seen in the context of the speech not by Guchkov but by Kerensky. Simultaneous publication of an article by a famous writer and a speech by the popular minister of justice reinforced the effect of Kerensky's speech.

Andreyev's article, and much writing from a similar viewpoint, elicited biting commentary from the left-wing press. 'There are certain temporarily fashionable words whose rise to prominence is completely baffling. . . . In recent days, the competition for fashionable word of the moment has been won hands down by "disaster". "Russia is facing disaster", "on the brink of disaster", "one step away from disaster", "disaster looms" . . . This catchy word runs the gamut of syntax,' wrote a journalist in *Novaya zhizn'*, the newspaper of the internationalists.[268] An alarmist campaign in liberal and conservative newspapers played an important part in intensifying and moulding the mood of disquiet which replaced the euphoria of March. The speeches of Shulgin and Guchkov articulated that new mood, and they had used their speeches to reinforce, spread and exploit it. This is behind Tsereteli's sharp reaction to the speeches. The Menshevik leader feared that feeling and sought to limit it. This also explains the adverse reaction of Tsereteli and Rusanov to Kerensky's speech. These moderate socialists were concerned that the revolutionary minister's speech would be grist to the mill of their adversaries, because he had very precisely and vividly given voice to a newly prevalent mood. In fact, however, Kerensky adroitly channelled the mood in a different direction, having on his side not only the major newspapers, replicating the most startling parts of his speech, but also the press of the Constitutional Democratic Party, as well as some of the newspapers of the moderate socialists. His speech moulded the fears and anxieties of the public to his advantage as he argued for a coalition government which would bring more socialists to power. Moulding the public opinion on which he relied, Kerensky compelled the vacillating leaders of the Soviet and the liberals to reach agreement and, unlike the authors of other disquieting communications, left his audience hope for the ultimate success of the revolution. He demanded firm action from 'citizens' as opposed to 'rebellious slaves'. Some contemporaries even saw Kerensky's speech as the sign of a breakthrough.[269]

The speech had an impact on the masses, particularly on moderate socialists. If talk of disaster and calls for discipline emanating from liberal and conservative circles could be dismissed as counter-revolutionary, Kerensky's declaration could neither be ignored nor classified in that manner: his established reputation as a revolutionary leader ruled that out. Kerensky redirected the patriotic anxiety expressed and articulated in Guchkov's speech, Andreyev's article, and other writing about the disaster facing Russia, repurposing it to support his own approach.

With the resignation of Guchkov, the government crisis entered a new phase. Kerensky was an active participant in negotiations to create a coalition, putting pressure on the leaders of the Soviet.[270] During the night of 5 May a new government was established which included Menshevik and Socialist Revolutionary leaders. Kerensky became head of the army and navy. Interestingly enough, some commentators saw his right to that post as having been earned by the civic courage he had shown by making the famous speech. 'Who can say to the many millions intoxicated by freedom, "Atten-shun!" "Attack!"? There is only one person. Only the person who resolved, and indeed did not even resolve but simply said to the whole country: "Slaves!" He will say, "Attack!" That is Kerensky.'[271]

In the new political situation, Kerensky's speech continued to be discussed. On 4 May, Vasiliy Maklakov suggested where that arresting image might have come from:

> No matter what form of words we choose, the main insight remains the same. Whether we talk like Kerensky – paraphrasing Ivan Aksakov's old anathema, who exclaimed in a moment of exasperation, 'You are not children of freedom, you are rebellious slaves!' – or whether we use the diplomatic language of the Provisional Government, which explained that the old social cohesion was breaking down faster than a new one could be formed, no matter what language we use, the major thought underlying our words is that Russia has proved unworthy of the freedom it won.

Kerensky would hardly have been pleased to see his speech used in this way, but the fact is that it lent itself to such an interpretation. Maklakov pointed out: 'The thought that Russia may be unworthy of the freedom it has obtained made Kerensky regret that he had not died earlier, but for others this thought may not come as a disappointment but, rather, as confirmation of doubts they were already reluctantly harbouring.'[272] Maklakov's remarks could also be taken as covert criticism of Kerensky, who had belatedly come to conclusions the liberals had reached long before him.[273]

Among the many varied responses to Kerensky's speech, one letter stands out. It was signed by Vladimir Nemirovich-Danchenko and Konstantin Stanislavsky, together with the actors, workers, staff and administration of the Moscow Art Theatre:

> The speech you delivered to delegates from the front on 29 April has profoundly moved the entire collective of the Moscow Art Theatre. We can find no words to express the deep emotion which gripped us as we read your speech. It raises from the very depths of the soul all that is most noble, humane, and civically responsible: tears of affection and sorrow, a surge of great joy and veneration at the mighty truth of your inspired heart, your insight and intelligence. . . .
>
> When your sorrowing soul cries out in extremis to unbridled passions to embrace the loftiest discipline of the spirit, to embrace that wonderful freedom which, simultaneously with the granting of extensive rights, makes heavy demands for responsibility, we see embodied in your person the ideal of the free citizen to which the soul of mankind has aspired over the centuries, and which the poets and artists of the world pass on from generation to generation. We experience that sublime happiness when the citizen and artist become as one.
>
> When in anguish you exclaim, 'I regret not having died two months ago,' we want to send you not only our tears, our affection, our greetings, but also our ardent faith that your noble, self-sacrificing ardour will not be swallowed up in the vortex of a destructive revolt but that the strength of the rulers and the wisdom of the Russian genius will vanquish the civil devastation, that wonderful aspirations will become reality and that the crowning achievement of your life will be the proud and marvellous grandeur of Russia.[274]

These theatre people appreciated professionally the sincerity and beauty, the emotional impact and didactic significance of Kerensky's speech. In their address he is represented as the personification of civil virtue, a role model. The unknown writer of this letter, signed by the foremost representatives of Russian culture, was seeking to lend the weight of their authority to support the Leader at a difficult time.

We find similar themes in responses to the speech. The artist Tatiana Gippius, for instance, was particularly taken by its sincerity. On 30 April she told her sister, Zinaida Gippius, 'Today Kerensky's speech in the newspapers is very good, although tragic: blood and sweat. Bloody sweat, "spiritual anguish". I so respect the "gnashing of teeth" in his speeches.'[275] His memorable metaphor was quoted by such well-known writers as Nikolai Breshko-Breshkovsky, Arkadiy Averchenko and Ivan Lukash.[276] References to rebellious slaves recur in the letters of army officers (and were duly recorded by the military censors).[277]

The theme of solidarity with the suffering Leader is also found in resolutions of the time. One sent to the Petrograd Soviet from the 1st Submarine Division reads, 'We sympathize with the deep sorrow in the soul of Comrade Kerensky, friend of working people.'[278]

There is no mention in the letter from the Moscow Art Theatre of rebellious slaves, but the expression recurs constantly in responses to the speech. The contrasting of politically aware, free citizens with ill-disciplined rebellious slaves did become an important propaganda theme and crops up repeatedly in other written responses. The soldiers and officers of the battery of the Caucasian Infantry Artillery Brigade declared, 'At this fateful time, let us not behave like a "mob of rebellious slaves".'[279] In other resolutions, soldiers declared themselves 'free citizens' as opposed to 'slaves'.

The image of 'rebellious slaves' became particularly significant in preparations for the June Offensive. Kerensky increasingly used the contrast between slaves and citizens for making optimistic statements, such as he expressed, for example, on 24 May at a meeting of the Soviet of the 12th Army: 'Russia's democratic forces are not slaves. They have no need of the lash and the cat o' nine tails to fulfil to the end their duty to the motherland.'[280]

The minister continued to contrast 'politically conscious citizens', the steadfast soldiers of the revolutionary army, with 'slaves', among whom he included deserters and conscientious objectors to the war. The image was much used by government commissars, members of military committees and journalists. For Boris Savinkov, a well-known terrorist who became a Provisional Government commissar at the front, members of assault battalions who were prepared to sacrifice their lives were the personification of the free citizen and the antithesis of a slave, while, for Leonid Andreyev, soldiers of the punitive anti-retreat units were the prototype for the New Man.

> And can you really not have noticed how, alongside the rebellious slaves, a new free Russian man is being born? . . . Those shameful ones who fled the front, who surrendered and betrayed, are the slaves of the black days of yesteryear. Those who held them back, who did not spare themselves and gave their lives, who, with a bleeding heart but with a hand that never wavered, shot the fleeing slaves, those are the people of today, the children of our young freedom which has enlightened minds and consciences.[281]

The impact of Kerensky's speech continued to be felt later. We find the image percolating into personal diaries.[282] His imagery was also used by supporters to glorify the Leader.

Kerensky's speech exerted an influence on the formation of several images of the Leader. The February leaders, primarily Mikhail Rodzyanko, were called 'leaders of freedom', and the appellation 'first citizen' was also in use. Over time, however, Kerensky acquired the status of a uniquely special Leader. It was not only Svatikov who dubbed him a 'great citizen'. On 4 May the defencist *Soldatskaya mysl'* [Soldier's Thought'] saluted the 'great citizen' and 'Leader of the democratic forces'. On 5 May the Central Committee of the Petrograd Union of Civilian Employees of All Main Departments, Institutions and Educational Institutions of the Ministry of the Army and Navy addressed him as 'Free Citizen of Great Free Russia'.[283] On 6 May the author of another defencist newspaper wrote, 'What matters now is for us to justify unconditionally the trust of this great citizen and martyr for the destiny of his people. We must demonstrate that we are not "rebellious slaves" but citizens worthy of our Great Leader.'[284]

The simultaneous use of such forms of address of Kerensky by different people in different writings testifies that both his status had been enhanced and his authority as Leader had been further consolidated by the crisis.

News of the attempted assassination of Kerensky, made public on the day of the famous speech, his general appearance of infirmity, the *cri de cœur* in his speech, all heightened concern for the Leader, which has already been mentioned as a component of a leader cult. We observe a certain 'patriotic sacrifice contest' in the speeches of the infirm Guchkov and the ailing Kerensky, the latter the victim of an assassination attempt and with his arm in a sling. We find calls to protect the Leader in the letters and resolutions quoted above and in newspaper articles.

As depicted by Alexander Solzhenitsyn, the minister of justice is speaking of rebellious slaves because he is an ambitious politician desperate for rhetorical success at any price. The newspaper reports allow that interpretation, and rivalry on 27 April between two of the Duma's best speakers could have prompted Kerensky to give the speech he did. If we look at its political context, however, that interpretation seems deficient. Kerensky's actions in late April and early May 1917 were a succession of rational steps aimed at bringing about a coalition government of liberals and moderate socialists, with himself in the post of minister of the army and navy. A study by Ziva Galili has shown that Guchkov's resignation and the public reaction to it compelled Tsereteli and some other Mensheviks to alter their strategy and agree to form a government.[285] Kerensky's speech influenced the state of public opinion and, to some extent, their taking of that decision.

Kerensky showed himself a stubborn, energetic and tough politician who used both persuasion and threats, both behind-the-scenes pressure and public speeches. His expertise at influencing public opinion through the press was very much needed. He skilfully isolated his political opponents, and obliged his allies to compromise, with the aim of creating a coalition that would be advantageous for him. His 'rebellious slaves' speech was a successful tactical move which contributed to achieving his political goals, a well-thought-through 'improvisation' which made a valuable contribution in his struggle for power. The speech was not without risk, and it certainly did nothing to improve his relations with the Menshevik and Socialist Revolutionary leaders. It was, however, a risk which paid off. The moderate socialists could not afford openly to criticize Kerensky too severely, because he remained a popular idol and an ally they very much needed.

Having given currency to the 'rebellious slaves' image, Kerensky armed activists at different levels with a rhetorical weapon they were able to use in many conflicts. At the same time, he further established his image as 'Leader of the revolution'. Building on his moniker of 'first citizen', he facilitated the shaping of his image as a 'great citizen' facing down both the old regime and the rebellious slaves. His numerous supporters, pursuing their own agendas, moulded that image and strengthened the authority of the revolutionary minister. Kerensky became a role model for Russians who wanted to cast off the shackles of slavery and become real citizens. By creating the image of a Leader educating the people in a spirit of civil pride, doing down rebellious slaves and presenting a model of civil responsibility, Kerensky added a powerful resource to his armoury.

Kerensky the memoirist, by 'forgetting' to mention his most famous speech, deliberately distorted the image of Kerensky the 1917 politician. We can only speculate about the reasons for his self-censorship. Perhaps the memoirist wanted to play down his negative image as a man of words, a mere windbag, which seemed to be gaining ground in memoir and research literature, and therefore preferred to concentrate less on what he said and more on what he actually did. Possibly too Kerensky had no wish to contribute to a full and accurate reconstruction of his own power struggle. He preferred to promote the romantic self-portrait of a noble, idealistic revolutionary far removed from the kind of calculation typical of lesser politicians pursuing narrowly party interests. Kerensky managed to mislead many memoirists, writers and historians, with the result that they underestimated his ability as a tough politician who manipulated his audiences, the press and his partners in negotiations, persistently moving society in the direction of agreement between liberals and moderate socialists, with himself playing a central role.

III

'Leader of the Revolutionary Army'

1 The iron discipline of duty

During the night of 29 April, Alexander Guchkov resigned as minister of the army and navy. The following day he publicly announced his decision to the front-line delegates who, the day before, had heard his and Kerensky's speeches on the subject of rebellious slaves. It was Kerensky who accepted Guchkov's resignation, because that day he was acting as chairman of the cabinet.[1] The government crisis entered a new phase. Negotiations over a coalition, which the Executive Committee of the Petrograd Soviet had rejected on 28 April, resumed. The Soviet found itself under pressure, and in that Kerensky played a central role, speaking at a meeting of the Soviet's Executive Committee.[2]

Kerensky participated in the negotiations and sought to sway public opinion. (During the April Crisis both the socialists and the liberals had grounds for accusing him of double-dealing.) Rumours circulated that he would be the new minister of war, which journalists reported on the afternoon of 30 April. They also named another candidate, Pyotr Palchinsky, an engineer who had been put forward in the February Days and had a reputation as a good organizer. The Menshevik Matvey Skobelev and Admiral Alexander Kolchak, commander of the Black Sea Fleet, were mentioned as possible candidates for the post of minister of the navy.[3] Mostly, however, the talk was of Kerensky.[4] Intense negotiations about creating the new government were continuing, but the newspapers were already reporting Kerensky's appointment as a fait accompli, which, 'it is expected, will greatly strengthen discipline among the troops and contribute to undermining disruption of our armed forces.'[5]

Kerensky and Palchinsky really were being considered as the candidates for the post of minister of war. They were the two candidates nominated by the supreme commander-in-chief, General Mikhail Alexeyev. By 2 May the newspapers were reporting that the General Headquarters of the commander-in-chief had declared Kerensky's candidacy for the post of minister of the army and navy 'highly germane at the present time'.[6]

On 3 May Kerensky took up his new duties, although he was still formally head of the Ministry of Justice. That day he met the generals, who came to Petrograd for a meeting with government ministers. They were Supreme Commander-in-Chief Mikhail Alexeyev and the commanders-in-chief of the fronts: the Southwest, Alexey Brusilov; the North, Abram Dragomirov; the West, Vasiliy Romeyko-Gurko; and the chief of staff of the Romanian front, Dmitry Shcherbachyov. (The King of Romania was considered commander-in-chief of the Romanian front.) The generals did not conceal the disturbing situation in the army, manifested by fraternization of soldiers with the enemy and desertion.[7] Publicly endorsing the appointment of Kerensky, the generals believed that only he would have the influence as minister to carry through the changes essential for the armed forces.

The opinions of the military leaders duly appeared in the press. General Alexeyev stated: 'The appointment of A. F. Kerensky to the post of minister of war will be received with much satisfaction in the army. Both officers and soldiers have great confidence in him. They know that he is a man of strong character, and that will be of great benefit to the army.' General Romeyko-Gurko commented: 'There is no need for me to talk about Kerensky's enormous popularity in the army. The soldiers most highly respect the signature of this member of the government.'[8] General Brusilov also waxed eloquent: 'A. F. Kerensky is just the person Russia needs at the present time in such a responsible post as minister of war.'[9] General Shcherbachyov spoke along the same lines: 'You have heard the voice of the Coalition Ministry, and particularly strong and authoritative has been the voice of the popular Minister Kerensky, who enjoys the respect of all of us.'[10] We should remember these endorsements: only too soon the generals would change their tune, but at this time they had high hopes of Kerensky's influence and sought to bolster his authority. It was popularity and trust among the soldiers that they saw as his essential qualifications for the post of minister of war, and the supreme commander-in-chief also commented on Kerensky's 'strong character'. Such was his reputation at that time.

The support of the generals was very important for Kerensky: a civilian with a reputation as an anti-militarist, he now headed the war department of a vast country in the middle of a major war. Building up the reputation of the new minister of war now became an important task for those favouring continuation of the war. Already on 7 May, *Soldatskoye slovo* [the Soldier's Word] published a soldier's letter: 'And now at the head of our Ministry of the Army and Navy there stands the people's hero and leader, that great champion of the rights of the Russian people, A. F. Kerensky.'[11] Was the letter authentic? This was, at all events, the way the newspaper believed real soldiers and true patriots should respond to the appointment of 'the people's Leader'. The news should be greeted with joy by people from across much of the political spectrum. *Krymsky vestnik* [the Crimean Herald] described the atmosphere at a rally of the Constitutional Democratic Party. '"Comrades! Comrades! Listen, our Comrade Kerensky has been appointed minister of war! Hurrah!" A fervent "Hurrah!" and thunderous applause! For several minutes, everyone stood, clapping and shouting "Hurrah!"'[12] Even before Kerensky had published his plan of action, people were welcoming his appointment on the strength of his popularity and reputation.

The crew of the dreadnought *Sevastopol'*, one of the most powerful ships of the fleet, sent greetings to Kerensky.

> We warmly congratulate you on assuming this new, very responsible and difficult post, and wish you strength and success with all our heart.
>
> We are proud that now we have at the wheel of our state such a helmsman, whom the eyes of the whole world are watching. You are our leader. We trust you wholeheartedly. Lead us forward in the battle for fraternity, equality and liberty not only in Russia but for all enslaved peoples.'[13]

The image of the revolutionary helmsman appears at this time also in a congratulatory telegram from the sailors of a battleship based in Odessa. They addressed it to 'the comrade helmsman of the ship of state of revolutionary Russia' who was 'steering the ship past the reefs of anarchy and the shoals of reaction, and who first sighted the coast of the democratic republic.'[14]

If one resolution highlighted the importance of reviving military action under an acknowledged leader, and another emphasized the need to maintain revolutionary order, the resolution from representatives of the Moscow garrison stressed the need for the minister to cooperate with elected organizations. 'The Moscow Soviet of Soldiers' Deputies greets socialist Minister of the Army and Navy Kerensky, firm in the belief that, with the coordinated support of soldiers' organizations, an effective and powerful revolutionary army will be created which will act in close and complete unity with the Soviet of Workers' and Peasants' Deputies to defend the motherland.'[15]

The Kiev Republican Military Union expressed its confidence that 'the creative forces of the revolution, uniting around the minister, will create a government capable of protecting free Russia from all its enemies, consolidating the gains of the revolution, and bringing the country forward to the Constituent Assembly.'[16] It was the new minister of war, not the head of the Provisional Government, who was perceived as the focus around which the creative forces of the revolution would unite. A group of Russian patriots who were not socialists (to judge by the text) believed that strengthening the minister's personal power was a prerequisite for political consolidation. According to a newspaper which particularly excelled in extolling Kerensky, a soviet deputy from the Rezhitsa in Latvia said that, to save the front from anarchy, 'we need strong government, and that has been found in the person of A. F. Kerensky.'[17] Here too the new minister of war is seen as a strong politician representing all the power of the government.

We observe nuances in the responses to Kerensky's appointment. Those drafting the resolutions took advantage of his appointment to high office to lobby for decisions important to them. The Leader was variously characterized in the different resolutions, but invariably their writers, and the editors publishing them, were eager to strengthen the minister's standing. The qualities they highlighted might differ, but they were always positive. Kerensky himself did his best not to disappoint the expectations of his supporters on both the right and the left wing. He needed the support of both generals and influential representatives of the soviets and committees. He also needed the assistance of a wide range of newspapers, representing not only moderate socialists and liberals but also a section of the conservatives. In this he succeeded: newspapers of various shades of opinion published the comments of professional soldiers, well-known politicians, businessmen and figures in the arts who supported his appointment.

Already on 3 May Kerensky spoke at a joint meeting of the commissions drafting provisions relating to life in the army and navy and revising military legal regulations. The way he formulated his speech took account of the sensitivities of the left wing. 'No other state in the world has a system as free and democratic as that which now exists in Russia.' The minister went out of his way to emphasize new principles for the exercise of power. 'We would rather die than lower ourselves to using physical force before it is needed and unless it is recognized as necessary by the people itself.' If in retrospect such statements seem naive, they were precisely what Kerensky's public wanted to hear from him. His statement was interrupted by exclamations of approval. Agreement on the principles of government had not yet been reached, and Kerensky needed to persuade the moderate socialist leaders to compromise. His speeches should be viewed in the context of the pressing political issues he faced. He was seeking to reassure his left-wing allies and to persuade them of the need for a coalition. At the same time, the minister found words to reassure the generals.

> At this present time Russia's refusal to attack has already had consequences, enabling Germany, while fraternizing on our front, to halt a major French offensive. We have achieved the opposite of the result we wanted. By seeking, entirely sincerely, to bring peace closer, we have set it back because we have given comfort in Germany not to the democratic elements of the population but to the strata of the reckless bureaucracy and the Junker class of the population.

Kerensky sought to ride the mood of anxiety expressed in Guchkov's speech about the imminent disaster facing Russia and in his own speech about rebellious slaves. 'The state', he said, 'is in danger in a very real sense.'[18]

These first actions of the new minister gave an idea of his plans for reorganizing the armed forces. The text of his order of 5 May read,

> Having taken upon myself the military power of the state, I announce:
> 1. The fatherland is in danger, and everyone must avert it to the utmost of their capacity and strength, at whatever cost. Accordingly, I will not accept any requests for resignation from senior ranks motivated by a desire to evade responsibility in these times.
> 2. Those who without authorization left the ranks of the army and naval crews must return by the time specified (15 May).
> 3. Those disobeying this order will be punished to the fullest extent of the law.[19]

The first target of the new minister's imposition of revolutionary discipline was the generals, which gained him the support of socialist members of the troop committees who viewed their commanders with suspicion. Newspapers of the moderate socialists expressed their hope that the new minister would purge the officer corps of 'unworthy elements'.[20] The next point of the order, however, demanded measures to combat desertion, which was just what the military leaders wanted from the minister.

Contemporaries commented not only on the substance of the order but also on the statesmanlike tone of the document, which was something new for Kerensky. As head of the Ministry of War, Kerensky was adjusting his image as an authoritative politician and changing his rhetoric.

Many people were enthusiastic about the order, as we gather from propaganda publications, resolutions, and private documents. Contemporaries who were less than enthusiastic about the revolution wrote positively about the order in their diaries. 'An order from Minister Kerensky. . . . About time too!' (Felix Rostkovsky); 'Kerensky has got off to a good start. Here is his first order . . .' (Nikita Okunev).[21] However, some considered that the minister was not sufficiently rigid in formulating his tasks. A corps military doctor noted in his diary, 'At the peasant congress Kerensky promised to introduce iron discipline in the army. God give him strength! This first order to the army and navy, though, seems to be coming down quite hard on the senior military commanders, but as regards the grey masses – all those skivers and deserters – he seems relatively soft and sentimental. Right now there is an urgent need for antidotes to the anarchy which is poisoning the people and the army.'[22]

Some army bodies promised to establish new discipline. The Committee of the 2nd Army reported that, 'having heard the first order of the first revolutionary minister of war in Russia with enthusiasm, we warmly welcome the strong will and authoritative call of our Leader to save the motherland and victory of the revolution. The Soviet is confident that the army will make every effort and, led by the people's hero, will not flinch in the hard struggle ahead.'[23]

This greeting has a number of important features. Kerensky is 'the first revolutionary minister of war', with the implication that his predecessor, General Guchkov, was not. The order is seen as demonstrating Kerensky's 'strong will'. Finally, Kerensky is called the people's hero. Clearly these plaudits are the result of his existing revolutionary reputation, because as yet he had had no time to demonstrate either heroism or a strong will as the minister of war.

In the congratulations from the Executive Committee of the Soviet of Soldiers' and Officers' Deputies of the Headquarters District of the Romanian Front (the title given in the publication of the document), the primary task identified is to establish 'proper order for the soldiers'. The Executive Committee resolved 'to salute you as the first socialist minister, expressing full confidence and our readiness to support you with all our strength as you take upon yourself the burden of power in the difficult times our fatherland is living through. We are confident that, relying on the democratic forces of Russia and our military power, you will not hesitate to take the most resolute measures against individuals violating proper order for the soldiers, no matter what post they occupy and no matter how great their numbers.'[24] In other words, the committee was calling upon the minister to rely on the soviets and the soldiers' committees and pledging to support him both in a possible confrontation with high-ranking commanders and in the struggle against deserters.

In another order, also issued on 5 May, Kerensky included the address from the front-line delegates' congress, the assembly to which he had delivered his speech referring to rebellious slaves.[25] The minister of war, the democratic minister, strengthened his position by referring to the authority of the forum of representatives of front-line activists.

As his closest aides Kerensky chose relatively junior officers from the General Staff with whom he had previously worked. (These energetic colonels had, for their part, been instrumental in ensuring it was Kerensky who became minister of war.) Some contemporaries took a wry view of their rapid career advancement.[26] However, we may surmise that, for the peers of these aides, their promotion gave rise to hopes of similarly rapid progress in the circumstances of the revolution. The first orders of the new minister of war gave further encouragement to brave and enterprising soldiers and officers. Thus, an order of 6 May provided for promoting non-commissioned officers who directly took part in combat to the rank of ensign. In a newspaper published by the Ministry of War, this innovation was described as 'democratization of the army'.[27]

Also on 6 May Kerensky had a meeting with Fedot Onipko, a deputy of the First State Duma and member of the Socialist Revolutionary Party, who, after the overthrow of the monarchy, had returned from emigration. Onipko became the government commissar of the Baltic Fleet. There were other appointments. A sensational one was that of Boris Savinkov, a well-known terrorist and writer, as commissar of the 7th Army. The appointment as commissars of revolutionaries who had authority with the Soviet and elected bodies in the army was an important political victory for Kerensky. The Petrograd Soviet had been keen to appoint its own supervisory commissars, but Kerensky persuaded the leaders of the Soviet that there should be only one commissar in each army, and he should be subordinate to the minister of war.[28]

Ensign Andrey Kozmin, a Socialist Revolutionary who in 1905 had been a leader of the 'Krasnoyarsk Republic', was appointed aide to the head of the Petrograd Military District. In 1912, Kozmin had returned from emigration and been convicted (Kerensky had been involved in defending him). The Socialist Revolutionary newspaper recommended him for a commission as an ensign by stating that 'he is well acquainted with the rules of revolutionary discipline, which he will be able to instil in the troops of the Petrograd District.'[29]

Kerensky's letter to Kozmin, published in the main newspapers, contained principles which were to be developed in the course of justifying his policies as minister.

> As a socialist minister of the army and navy I have a duty to create a democratic army, firm in discipline and united by revolutionary ideals, to lead humanity along the path to the shared goal of both our democracy and that of the Allies: to peace on earth and the establishment of a life built on the foundations of labour and justice. The democratic army must achieve these goals by the most resolute deeds, which alone can lead to the rapid achievement of the ideals of democracy and the aspirations of the people.
>
> In order to create such an army, it is particularly important to establish a correct relationship between those in command and the soldiers, a relationship of complete mutual trust and understanding which will form the basis of a new discipline, without which the existence of the army is inconceivable.[30]

The army must be transformed into a democratic armed force on the basis of this new discipline in order to extend Russia's revolutionary mission 'to all of humanity'. The foundation underlying this discipline must be a 'correct' relationship between commanders and their subordinates. This was the task of the socialist minister, and his ideal collaborator was a veteran of the revolutionary struggle, an 'old soldier' persecuted by the old regime. The democratic army would be capable of 'the most resolute deeds' – that is, of launching an offensive to achieve a democratic peace. Those in favour of continuing the war saw the letter as giving an undertaking to prepare an offensive, while socialists were attracted by its revolutionary rhetoric (and it was quoted in detail by the main socialist newspapers). The task of disciplining the army was to be achieved by exploiting the rhetoric of the revolution, by referring to the revolutionary reputation of Kozmin, and by making use of the unique status of the socialist who had just become minister of war.

Kerensky's letter, his orders and his speeches were open to a number of interpretations. In some cases emphasis was placed on the urgent need to achieve 'peace on earth'. A general meeting of representatives of the Petrograd 127th Cargo-Handling Battalion saluted the minister and expressed confidence that 'The acceptance by a socialist of a post which is so critical and difficult at the present time will bring closer the culmination and ending of the war.' 'Long live the unity of the army and the new comrade minister!' they exclaimed. Significantly, their address was published in *Delo naroda*, the main Socialist Revolutionary newspaper.[31] This made clear that the party's leaders supported this interpretation of Kerensky's speeches.

A series of public speeches by Kerensky was planned to provide a propaganda underpinning for his transformation of the army. On 5 May, the very day his first orders were made public, he declared at the All-Russia Congress of Soviets of Peasants' Deputies, 'I have never been in a zone of military conflict. I have never experienced the reality of discipline, but I intend nevertheless to establish iron discipline in the army.' Addressing this audience supportive of socialists, Kerensky made reference to the authority of the veterans of the liberation movement and the recognized leaders of the parties. Pointing to the members of the presidium, he declared, 'You must remember that we have on our side our venerable teachers.' The speech elicited an enthusiastic response from the deputies.[32] Kerensky needed the support of the congress, and the delegates duly adopted just the kind of resolution he was hoping for: 'We must go forward with Kerensky, our new minister of the army and navy, to whom we must fully entrust the fate and good fortune of Russia, and who will lead our army to glory and an honourable peace.'[33] The resolution did not refer directly to an offensive, but it could certainly be interpreted as a call for decisive military action.

The following day the minister spoke at the rally of a delegation of the Black Sea Fleet. Thanks to political manoeuvring by Admiral Kolchak, Sevastopol for a time became a centre for consolidating the defencists; the High Command and local organizations believed that defencists would aid recovery of the situation at both the front and the rear, and the delegation was given political and financial support in Petrograd. It will hardly have been a coincidence that an important political resolution from Sevastopol, addressed to Kerensky, was published in several Petrograd newspapers on the very day of the rally.

> A meeting of delegates of the Black Sea Fleet, the garrison and the workers raised a hearty and unanimous cheer on hearing the news that you have accepted the post of minister of the army and navy. . . .
>
> Serve the Motherland just as you have served it before and after the revolution.
>
> No dark forces will succeed in subverting the people's boundless trust in you.
>
> We believe and always will believe that what you have to do and

say will be to the benefit of our own democracy and that of the whole world, and we undertake to obey all your orders without question.[34]

Enthusiasm that a revolutionary who stood opposed to 'dark forces' had been appointed minister of war had unquestioning discipline as its corollary. Such were the sentiments the Petrograd rally of the sailors of the Black Sea Fleet was intended to awaken in the army and navy. At the rally Kerensky pointed to the iron discipline of tested champions of freedom as an example to the soldiers of the new Russia. 'We revolutionaries were able to achieve our mission only by submitting to iron discipline, by submitting fully and unconditionally to the bodies in charge of us.' From his listeners Kerensky demanded resolute support. 'All of you, on hearing my summons, must close your eyes and follow me to where I call you.' Many voices answered: 'We shall! We shall!' There was thunderous applause and cheering.[35]

Kerensky spoke about iron discipline in other speeches during this time.[36] If the reports are to be believed, his audiences responded to these calls enthusiastically. The message needed, however, to be conveyed to the soldiers of the Petrograd garrison, about whom the government was apprehensive. On 7 May Kerensky, accompanied by Kozmin, began visiting the troops. The press focused particularly on his inspection of the Reserve Battalion of the Volhynia Guards Regiment – the first military unit to support the revolution on 27 February. That same day Kerensky visited other reserve battalions. The inspections turned into rallies, and everywhere the minister gave speeches, everywhere he called for iron discipline based on mutual trust. In some regiments he referred to their heroic past, especially when visiting those units to which Decembrists had belonged.[37]

His whirlwind visiting of regiments continued into the following day, the minister's energy greatly impressing his supporters.[38] Already by eight in the morning, Kerensky, travelling by car, was visiting the Naval Life Guards; at 8:30 he was greeting the soldiers of the Kexholm Guards Regiment; at 9 o'clock he was with the Finland Guards Regiment, and fifteen minutes later he was giving a speech to the men of the 180th Reserve Infantry Regiment. The minister then left Vasilievsky Island and hastened to Vyborg District. By 9:40 it was the turn of a battalion of the Grenadier Regiment; at 10 o'clock Kerensky greeted the guardsmen of the Moscow Regiment; and fifteen minutes later was with the 1st Machine-Gun Regiment, the garrison's most radical military unit. He stayed a bit longer there, but at 10:40 was off again to visit the Bicycle Battalion, before departing for the 1st Reserve Infantry Regiment, where a particularly warm reception awaited him. There Kerensky promoted, to the rank of General, Colonel Konstantin Neslukhovsky, who in the February Days had been the first officer to march his unit to the State Duma. A number of other ranks were commissioned as officers, and the rapturous soldiers carried Kerensky shoulder-high back to his car. It tells us a lot that the regiment's representative addressed the minister of war not only as 'Leader of Russian democracy' but also as 'Leader of the Russian army'. As for Neslukhovsky, he declared, 'We are filled with profound faith in our Leader.'[39]

Still on the same day of 8 May, Kerensky received deputations, attended a meeting of the Provisional Government, gave a speech to the Congress of Officers' Deputies and congratulated cadets of the Naval College on their being commissioned as officers. The young midshipmen responded with thunderous cheers and a rendition of *The Marseillaise*, before they too carried Kerensky in their arms to his car.[40] In a politically important speech to the delegates of the officers' congress, the minister of war reworked the same themes of the need for iron discipline and a reminder of revolutionary traditions. He again talked of the discipline of the veteran revolutionaries as a model for a new discipline in the new army and spoke of his right to introduce iron discipline.

> I come from a milieu alien to you and have never worn a military uniform. I did, however, attend the school of iron discipline in a revolutionary party. There, just like you now, we swore an oath to be victorious or die in the name of free Russia. The army of professional revolutionaries had its officers and its soldiers. All were equal, and all equally respected each other. In the name of duty, and aware of the necessity for some to submit and for others to point the way, we obeyed our officers. And we understood the duty of officers to be a privilege, the honour of bearing a double burden of work and a double share of responsibility.

The ecstatic officers in their turn sat the minister in a chair and carried him to the exit. The chairman of the congress declared to the deputies' approval, 'We all, as one, say to the minister, let him take our will and direct it to where it is needed for the flourishing of Russia. Long live Alexander Fyodorovich Kerensky!'[41]

In its report on the officers' congress, the Socialist Revolutionary Party's newspaper included a declaration by Lieutenant Colonel Alexander Dutov that 'The Cossacks support the people's leaders, with the people's minister A. F. Kerensky at their head.'[42] In so doing, the future leader of the White movement implied a hierarchy of 'people's leaders' (the others did not get a mention), in which the minister of war was ahead of the rest.

What effect did Kerensky's review of the troops of the Petrograd garrison actually have? Of his review of the reserve battalions of the Preobrazhensky and Pavlovsky Regiments, Kozmin wrote,

> During the parade Kerensky's greetings either evinced no response at all, or just a few voices came back from the entire company. This rather took aback both Kerensky and his retinue, but it was explained that it was difficult to respond on the march, and they were reassured.

> It was nevertheless revealing. What we saw was not soldiers marching past their commander, when every word addressed to them causes a reflexive response from the whole live being, but a lot of armed people showing their comrade how they could march with rifles on their shoulders.[43]

Perhaps the imperfections of the reviews were due to the decline of discipline. Perhaps, too, it was down to the unusual style of the march pasts, which, at Kerensky's instigation, turned into political rallies during which the soldiers broke ranks and surrounded the minister as he gave his speeches.

For the citizens of Russia, however, the main source of information about Kerensky's reviewing of the regiments was newspaper reports, and these were often wildly enthusiastic (Kozmin himself writes that there was 'great enthusiasm'). The correspondents reported that the soldiers presented the minister with a bouquet of red roses and that his speech 'was met with the unanimous "Hurrah!" of a thousand voices and enthusiastic handclapping.' There were shouts of 'Long live the minister of war!'[44] That diverges from Kozmin's account. Nevertheless, Kerensky's speeches to the soldiers, even in regiments that were to be epicentres of agitation during the June and July crises, did not result in any untoward incidents, which the Bolsheviks and other opponents of the minister would certainly have seized on. (A month later visits to these regiments would hardly have been feasible.)

Some Petrograd reserve battalions did send reinforcements to the front at this time, and Kerensky's speeches did, apparently, play a part in that. One newspaper reporter asked soldiers of a reserve company heading for the railway station, 'What regiment do you belong to, comrade?' 'We are the Kerensky Guards,' came the reply. 'We are all his,' another chimed in. 'Marching from the fire of the revolution to the fire of the trenches.'[45]

Perhaps the reporter embellished this story, or simply made it up, but activists will certainly have used the prestigious name of the minister of war when organizing reinforcements for the army in the field. The reinforcement company of the Reserve Battalion of the Moscow Regiment, in which there had been strong opposition to being sent to the front, marched to the station behind a red flag bearing the legend 'Greetings and trust in Citizen Kerensky – the pride of revolutionary democracy'. The banner of the reinforcement company of the Petrograd Regiment bore the slogan 'Faith in Kerensky'.[46]

Representatives of military organizations reported that the minister's instructions were being implemented. The delegate of one army corps stated in Moscow, 'The army, faithful to the commands of our leader Kerensky, is instilling the requisite discipline.'[47] This claim did not correspond to reality. Did the speaker believe his own words? It was, at all events, what many of those listenening wanted to believe.

Kerensky became minister of the army and navy because of the support he enjoyed both from the top military leaders and from moderate socialists representing the military committees. His reputation as 'Leader of the people', 'the hero of free Russia', 'the great champion of rights of the Russian people', 'the steadfast and inspired champion of all Russia's democratic forces', 'the citizen minister' and 'the socialist minister' was what ensured his appointment had broad public support.

Kerensky's first speeches and orders contained a demand for iron discipline, discipline of a new kind, with reference back to the authority of the revolutionary tradition. The minister saw the top priorities as being to combat desertion and instigate the promotion of brave and enterprising officers and soldiers. He makes mention of the possibility of an offensive (as does the declaration of the Coalition Provisional Government). The generals and committee members put their authority behind the policy, the opinion of the former counting for a great deal with the officers, while the support of the committees was of great importance for influencing the soldiers. It is difficult to measure how strong the support actually was, but at the time no one publicly questioned the reports of manifestations of great enthusiasm. In the opinion of those who made up the thoroughly diverse coalition which welcomed the idea of establishing iron discipline and preparing for an offensive, that level of emotional commitment was essential. The views of the members of this coalition might differ, but all, in supporting Kerensky, were seeking to consolidate their own authority. They were pursuing different goals, had different political priorities, and interpreted the minister's speeches in whichever way best suited them. Some were trying to lay the groundwork for the offensive, others to strengthen the authority of the committees, and energetic careerists eager to take advantage of Kerensky's appointment were to be found in every camp.

Not every nuance of opinion among Kerensky's supporters was expressed in public. Private documents indicate that high-ranking military figures and politicians saw his appointment as the last chance to establish discipline in the armed forces. Diverse individuals used similar expressions quite independently of each other. On 12 May, Admiral Vasiliy Altfater wrote to a naval officer, Mikhail Cherkassky, 'My only rational hope lies with Kerensky's authority and talent and with the party of the Socialist Revolutionaries and Trudoviks – that is, with reasonable socialist organizations. If they succeed in getting a grip on this dark mass of humanity and inculcating a healthy, calm sense of national responsibility, the whole thing may fizzle out and everything get back to normal.'[48] Foreign Minister Mikhail Tereshchenko told General Alexey Kuropatkin that 'Kerensky and his trip to the front is their last throw of the dice.' Some people Kuropatkin talked to also pinned hopes on the new minister, but others were pessimistic. Former Minister of War Guchkov and his staff, who had lost their jobs, had no faith in Kerensky's transformations. Colonel Boris Engelgardt, influential in military and political circles, said, 'Kerensky is their last bet, and he thinks they will lose.'[49] The firm belief that Kerensky was the last chance of establishing discipline was reflected in the tone of public expressions of support for him and on how they were perceived. The minister was accorded the status of the saviour of Russia who, alone, could revive the army. That assessment, at first heard only in private, began to be expressed more publicly. Some were becoming impatient for Kerensky to restore full pre-revolutionary military discipline. Representatives of the Ochakov Fortress garrison, for example, sent a telegram in May to Prince Georgiy Lvov and Kerensky, reading: 'In order to save our dying homeland we need prompt restoration of iron discipline among the troops on a new foundation and a change of policy from the disastrous inaction at the front to active support of the Allies.'[50] In this text we find the theme of disaster, a demand for iron discipline, and support for the idea of an offensive. Appeals of this kind hardened suspicions, particularly among radically minded activists, that the minister of war was really trying to restore full pre-revolutionary military discipline. The Bolsheviks and other left-wing socialists and anarchists were soon accusing him of precisely that.

Kerensky, however, never did promise to restore the old discipline. He declared he would create a completely new, revolutionary 'discipline of duty' based on the sense of responsibility of the new 'citizen soldier'. In practice, this did not eliminate the dual power situation in the armed forces (which was what the left socialists suspected him of) but it did level out and rationalize the system which had evolved after the overthrow of the monarchy. At the First Congress of the Soviets of Workers' and Soldiers' Deputies in June, Kerensky again declared: 'My task is to create a truly revolutionary army and iron discipline, the discipline of duty.' He called for a 'discipline of reason and conscience'.[51]

In hindsight, the project of creating an effective army on that principle seems utopian, which is how some memoirists and many historians subsequently qualified it. However, in the circumstances of spring 1917 the plan was viewed differently, and the idea of the revolutionary education of the citizen soldier had many supporters. No fewer than three newspapers which appeared in 1917 bore the title of *Soldat-grazhdanin* [the Citizen Soldier]; the best known was the newspaper of the Moscow Soviet of Soldiers' Deputies.[52] Initially not even the professional army publicly criticized the notion of an 'iron discipline of duty'. It was the aspiration to restore military discipline along pre-revolutionary lines which looked unrealistic. One could hardly expect that the energetic young officers and soldiers who were now members of all manner of committees would give up their newly acquired power.

In any case, all the belligerent countries were now faced with the necessity of a 'remobilization', the patriotic mobilization along the lines of 1914 having run its course. Some modern researchers take the view that it was during the First World War that the character of the citizen-soldier of modern times was formed as the result of 'military experience gained'.[53]

New political challenges brought adjustments in the way the 'revolutionary minister of war' was represented, and the existing images of the democratic minister needed to be put to work to establish the iron discipline of duty. Kerensky's revolutionary biography confirmed his credentials for reforming the army. In those of his speeches we have mentioned there was no direct reference to rebellious slaves, but that speech had not been forgotten, and the model of the civically responsible citizen he proposed was contrasted with the rebellious slave who might push Russia over the brink into disaster. A role model for the responsible citizen was the people's hero himself.

The title 'Leader' acquired new meanings and was applied to Kerensky more frequently now than in March and April. At the beginning of May he had himself talked of assuming the 'heavy duties of a Leader of the Russian army and navy'.[54] This new status was not questioned by the heterogeneous forces that supported the policy of establishing iron discipline.

2 The visit to Helsingfors

If you mention the name of Kerensky when Finns are present, they are apt to recall a defiant ditty:

> Kerensky is kneading a dough not yet leavened,
> Finland as salt now he's adding with glee.
> Uh-oh, Kerensky, your hopes are ill-founded,
> Suomi from Russia already is free.
> Poland's the flour and the yeast is Estonia,
> Sugar's Ukraine and Livonia the spice,
> Caucasus, Vepsia, Ingria, Olonia,
> Don and Crimea comprise 'all things nice'.
> The dough rises archly, the pudding is swelling,
> Kerensky is furiously stirring his treat.
> Kneading a dough like you see all too rarely,
> Fragrant and textured, and so honey sweet.
> Enters a big German dog and it's over.
> Gone in a gulp are the salt and the yeast.
> Exit the cook, who hightails it to Paris.
> Uh-oh, Kerensky, goodbye to your feast.[55]

In the song, Kerensky is presented as a hapless politician, clumsily failing to prevent the collapse of the Russian Empire. It was a reputation he began to gain among the Finns already in May 1917.

On 9 May Kerensky arrived in Helsingfors, the capital of the Grand Duchy of Finland. This was his first trip outside Petrograd as minister of the army and navy. The government was becoming increasingly concerned about the main base of the Baltic Fleet. The overthrow of the monarchy had been accompanied by an uprising there, with dozens of officers murdered, including the fleet commander, Admiral Adrian Nepenin. The memory of these events continued to have repercussions on the discipline of soldiers and sailors, and the relations between sailors and officers of the fleet were particularly tense.

Another factor affecting the mood of the army and navy was the nationalist movement in Finland. The Provisional Government confirmed all the rights of the Grand Duchy which had been suppressed before the revolution. An amnesty was granted for Finns previously arrested on political grounds. On 7 March an act was passed confirming the Constitution of the Grand Duchy with an instruction that it was to be applied in full. As minister of justice Kerensky participated in elaborating these measures; acts were published over his signature, which contributed to his popularity in Finland. After the fall of the monarchy, however, some Finnish politicians demanded an extension of Finland's autonomy, while others even raised the issue of independence. If Finnish social democrats were minded to enlist Russian soldiers and sailors as allies in their confrontation with the forces of the 'bourgeoisie', many other residents of the Grand Duchy watched the crisis of discipline in the Russian armed forces with increasing apprehension, and as it worsened it became a further argument in favour of distancing Finland from the empire. These interrelated processes, a multifaceted radicalization, gave a particular character to the dual power situation in Finland. The power of military and civilian representatives of the Provisional Government weakened, the Finnish government did its utmost to strengthen its position, and the interaction of social, national and political rivalries exacerbated the situation.[56] Additionally, the soviets and committees of the Russian army and navy in Finland were better organized than analogous bodies in other parts of Russia. Admiral Andrey Maximov, who had been 'elected' commander of the Baltic Fleet during the uprising, tried to collaborate with the Soviet and committees, which made him popular with the sailors. He enjoyed diminishing authority among the officers, however, and was not regarded as a strong commander in the Ministry of the Navy. There was, accordingly, good reason why the minister chose Helsingfors for his first diplomatic foray outside the capital.

Finland held special memories for Kerensky. In 1916 he had had a kidney removed there, and he returned to a local sanatorium to convalesce.[57] After the revolution the minister several times visited the Grand Duchy. His first visit took place on 16 March. At the conclusion of a welcoming ceremony at Helsingfors railway station, in which Finnish students carrying banners participated, Kerensky laid red flowers at the statue of the poet Johan Ludvig Runeberg and delivered a speech. In the Sejm the minister of justice expressed his confidence in the firmness of the eternal union of Russia and Finland, before kissing Social Democrat Oskari Tokoi, who was leader of the Senate.[58] Addressing the deputies of the Soviet representing Russian servicemen and workers, Kerensky said he had come 'to bring the Finnish people the news of its freedom, which it has been given by the free Russian peasant, worker and soldier.' His rhetorical exclamations of goodwill towards Finland were jubilantly welcomed by audiences of Russians and Finns alike.[59]

In March, Russian and Finnish politicians regularly exchanged ardent greetings, but even in this context the euphoria surrounding Kerensky's visit was exceptional. In May, the socialist newspaper *Kansan Lehti* [the People's Newspaper] recalled those days in March: 'When the great Russian Revolution forced imperialism to release our country from its lion's claws and cast down the predatory eagle of tsarism, he, Kerensky, was the first officially to bring us the news of freedom. He flew here like the dove bearing an olive branch. He came, he saw, he conquered. He congratulated us on our liberation with words which deeply pierced our hearts, and kissed Tokoi.' *Uusi Päivä* [New Day] commented that Kerensky was the member of the Provisional Government 'on whom Finns . . . most pinned their hopes.'[60]

In late March and early April, Kerensky again visited Finland. He spoke in the Sejm and expressed the hope that 'the free Finnish people at this present difficult time, when a new democratic Russia is being created, will, for their part, help us in an open alliance and choose a common path for achieving equality and fraternity.' The deputies stood throughout the minister's speech and saluted it with loud, prolonged applause. Kerensky then went to rest in a sanatorium, but here too there was no respite from festivities. The guest was greeted by pupils from the local schools and expressed his admiration for Finnish teachers who were raising such conscientious citizens. He enjoined the pupils never to submit to slavery. When the minister returned to Petrograd, his carriage was full of flowers the Finns had presented to him.[61]

For people in Finland it was Kerensky who symbolized the new Russia.[62] The hopes they pinned on him related to plans the Finnish Social Democrats had to fundamentally change the relationship between Helsingfors and Petrograd. The party's leaders told Kerensky the Grand Duchy could no longer be satisfied with its current status. They later claimed that, at Kerensky's request, they had enumerated to him the rights they hoped Russia might offer the Grand Duchy. They proposed that Finland should be conceded the right to choose its form of government, elect its head of government, and conclude trade and economic treaties with other states. In peacetime Russia should not station more troops in Finland than was necessary for the defence of Petrograd. Finland should be granted independence in all areas with the exception of foreign policy. The Finnish Social Democrats claimed that these were the minimal requirements and proposed that the relevant act should be countersigned by other powers.

Through the deputy governor-general, Kerensky supposedly informed the Social Democrats that he approved all their proposals except for the final point regarding international guarantors. When, however, the Finnish Senate submitted a draft to Petrograd to extend its rights, the Provisional Government rejected the plan to divide the powers of the Grand Duke (the no longer existent Russian emperor) between the Senate and the Provisional Government. At this the Finnish newspapers pointed out that the minister of justice had gone even further in his promises. 'Kerensky promised us, in the name of the revolution and of the Provisional Government, as whose authorized representative he visited us in March, a special revised and amended version of internal self-government. He even promised he would grant us independence the moment we asked for it.'[63]

On the eve of his second visit to Finland, Kerensky read a translation of the Finnish Social Democrats' statements and was outraged by their 'ingratitude'. He was even going to refuse to speak at the Sejm, but changed his mind and, as mentioned, greeted the deputies in the name of the peoples of Russia.[64] We may suppose that the general atmosphere surrounding the minister's visits gave the Finnish Social Democrats unjustified hopes so that, when later they did not receive a positive response, they felt cheated.

For this study it is not a priority to reconstruct the history of Kerensky's intricate negotiations with Finnish politicians. There was much mutual misunderstanding, aggravated no doubt by exaggerated expectations on both sides dating from the euphoric atmosphere in March. We will note only that it hardly seems likely that the minister of justice personally 'approved' such radical changes, although his statements were not always carefully considered. No serious political force in Petrograd would support such a project, as Kerensky well knew. Be that as it may, the hopes the Finns pinned on Kerensky were not realized and their attitude towards the Provisional Government changed for the worse. Tokoi, so recently kissed, after the end of Kerensky's second visit to Finland explicitly stated it was essential that Finland should achieve independence. Although 'bourgeois' senators, unlike the Social Democrats, were more circumspect, the Sejm greeted his statement with tumultuous approval. Tokoi's speech raised concerns in Russia and among the Allied powers, who feared the influence of Germany in this strategically important area might be strengthened.[65]

Tensions in the relationship between the Finnish Senate and the Provisional Government increased. When Kerensky arrived in Helsingfors on 9 May there was no Finnish public figure waiting to meet him, and the general atmosphere was markedly different from his earlier visits. Nevertheless, Russian organizations welcomed him enthusiastically. A sailor who was a member of the Socialist Revolutionary Committee in Helsingfors described the atmosphere in their meeting. 'Immediately he became minister of the army and navy, A. F. Kerensky made it his first duty to visit the Baltic Fleet he had long loved . . . a crowd of several thousands . . . was eager to see their Great Leader and hear his practical, fervent words.'[66] The Bolsheviks commented sarcastically on the celebratory efforts of the Socialist Revolutionaries, but the minister's visit was an important boost which his party comrades exploited.[67]

Preparations for the meeting with Kerensky provoked a debate which reflected how tangled the political forces in Helsingfors were. The commander of the fleet ordered that a parade should be organized in his honour, but the Central Committee of the Baltic Fleet cancelled his order.[68] Despite this, Kerensky's visit proceeded with considerable pomp. Accompanied by Admiral Maximov, the minister visited the fleet's ships and land units. He started with the 1st Brigade of battleships, which included the dreadnoughts *Petropavlovsk*, *Gangut*, *Poltava* and *Sevastopol*. Kerensky spent no more than twenty minutes on each ship. Everywhere he made speeches and answered questions, before going on to other ships and units. It was reported that he 'was greeted by the soldiers and sailors with rare enthusiasm.'[69] This report, reprinted in several publications, was partly true. At his meetings with the crews of the battleships *Petropavlovsk* and *Respublika* and the cruiser *Rossiia*, sensitive topics were raised. His exchanges on *Respublika* (before the revolution, *Pavel I*), where the minister was presented with a list of disagreeable questions, were particularly hard going. The ship's committee wanted to know his reasons for signing the note that provoked the April Crisis. The members of the committee were also inquisitive as to Kerensky's position on the war before the revolution. The sailors stated afterwards that 'to all the questions submitted . . . to the minister . . . we received unsatisfactory answers.'[70] The sailors of *Respublika* did not conceal their dissatisfaction from Kerensky. (Their exceptional radicalism stemmed partly from the fact that the crew had been particularly active during the days of the February Revolution.) The majority of soldiers and sailors in Helsingfors did, however, give him an enthusiastic welcome.

There was a lunch at the Executive Committee of the Soviet, and the fact that this was organized by the Soviet rather than by the commander of the fleet or the governor-general of Finland tells us something about who was in charge. Kerensky gave a speech there in which he acknowledged that Helsingfors was the most problematical part of the fleet and called for a move from words to action. He returned to the topic of the new discipline, 'a discipline not of mechanical coercion, but of reason and conscience'. The local leader of the Left Socialist Revolutionaries raised the issue of putting pressure on the Allies who were refusing to accept the principles of the Russian Revolution's foreign policy, and Kerensky replied that, in order to accomplish that diplomatic task, Russia must first demonstrate strength. In other words, he was explaining the need for an offensive.[71]

In the evening, Kerensky spoke at the House of the People, where his audience numbered some 2,000 members of committees and deputies of the Soviet. The minister returned to topics he had already emphasized, glorifying the revolutionary armed forces and calling for the establishment of a discipline of duty. He said that the revolution was creating 'not some English or German system, but a democratic republic in the full sense of the word'. The transformation of the armed forces, he declared, was unparalleled. 'The Russian fleet is the most free of all fleets.' The minister demanded that the fleet should act 'with the precision, certainty and logical consistency of the best and most sophisticated machinery'. He called for revolutionary enthusiasm to be converted into 'a steely, systematic machine of national creativity'. He again held up the careers of the socialist ministers as an example for the soldiers and sailors now called upon to establish a new kind of discipline. The government had in it some of his own comrades-in-arms who had worked for the revolution, ready to sacrifice their lives for freedom. He included himself in their number. 'Our ranks marched forward serenely, going if necessary one after the other to our deaths.' It was an image to inspire his audience. 'Today the battle at the front is that same revolutionary struggle.' The minister spoke out against fraternization, which met with approval from his audience of Helsingfors soldiers and sailors, for whom fraternization was a considerably less problematical topic than it was on the front line.

The concluding section of Kerensky's speech attracted much attention from those living in the Grand Duchy. Raising his voice (as was particularly emphasized in some newspaper reports), Kerensky said: 'And here in Finland we need to be particularly careful, because our magnanimity, our love, can be misunderstood as weakness and impotence, and not only by Germans.' The pointed reference to excessive demands by Finnish politicians was understood by his Russian audience, evoking applause and cries from the floor of 'Absolutely!' Kerensky continued, 'Revolution is creative. Revolution is strength, and let none suppose that the revolutionary people of Russia are weaker than the old tsarist government and can be pushed around. Don't try it!' Here the transcript records 'tumultuous applause'. Kerensky's speech was particularly important as propaganda for the defencists. Unsurprisingly it was reprinted both by military publishers and the right-wing socialist publications.[72]

The speech was interrupted by clapping and cheering. There was particular approval of his assertion that the state system of the new Russia would be in advance of the political systems of other countries. His message was endorsed by local representatives, who emphasized his democratic spirit. The chairman of the Executive Committee of the Soviet declared: 'Mr Minister, citizen and comrade, and just plain comrade and friend of our people Kerensky, . . . we were all confident and knew that you were our "hostage", the hostage of socialists.' Admiral Maximov tried to turn the minister's authority to his own advantage. 'Soldiers and workers! Can you vow to this minister without epaulettes, this minister of the workers, that you will carry out his orders better than you did those of the ministers who were adjutants general of the tsar?' Kerensky then answered questions, and the left-wing socialists took the opportunity to make their position clear.[73] The question of publishing the secret treaties with the Allies was raised, and Kerensky said that international agreements should be published only if this was done simultaneously in all the belligerent countries. The sympathies of a majority of those attending were on Kerensky's side, and even a writer in the Bolshevik newspaper, when describing the event, held back on criticism, only commenting dryly that 'Mr Kerensky's reply at the meeting on 22 May confirms exactly what we have been saying.'[74]

The newspaper of the Socialist Revolutionaries, on the other hand, described the Leader's visit as a triumph which would contribute to strengthening discipline. 'At this time many warm words were heard from the comrade soldiers and sailors, and almost all of them had the same thing to say. "Now we have trust in our Leader and believe that our army will be united steadfastly as one, and that all attempts to disorganize the front will be crushed." '[75] The tone of the Petrograd Telegraph Agency was likewise optimistic as it reported that Kerensky's stay in Helsingfors had been 'a solid triumph for him. Wherever it was anticipated that the popular revolutionary Leader would appear, crowds of soldiers and sailors assembled with extraordinary speed, eager to see the socialist minister and hear his ardent revolutionary speech. . . . Those who were dismayed and sick at heart when they noticed a certain disharmony developing among the sailors were once more filled with hope.'[76]

The testimony of some who were present at the meetings is imbued with similar feelings. One gunner gave his impressions in a letter to the Socialist Revolutionary newspaper. 'We experienced a great day on 9 May with the arrival of our dear comrade, the comrade socialist Kerensky.' The soldier had done his utmost to get close to his idol. 'It is entirely understandable that all of us, comrade Socialist Revolutionaries, had just one ardent desire – to be as close as possible to our dear Leader, and I was standing beside him during his speech.' It made a big impression on the gunner when the dear Leader considerately gave him a glass of water, 'without any affectation, as straightforwardly as if he were giving it to a comrade in the barracks.' His listeners gave Kerensky various souvenirs, sailors passed him the ribbons from their caps. The writer of the letter took the crossed cannons insignia of the artillery troops from his epaulette and presented it to the minister, who kissed him in return. The gunner wrote in delight, 'Comrade socialists, behold how simple, how sincere and trusting is the bond between us and our people's Leaders.'[77] The gunner's attention is focused not on what the minister said but on his style: the closeness he had witnessed between the Leader and the people demonstrated a natural simplicity possible only for a minister who was also your comrade. We learn something also from the fact that this letter was published in the newspaper of the Socialist Revolutionaries, who evidently deemed this reaction to the minister's speech not just appropriate but exemplary.

Some newspapers were particularly taken by the part of his speech where Kerensky gave Finland a warning. The liberal *Birzhevye vedomosti* [Stock Exchange Gazette] commented that 'Finland's ambition to break away from Russia has had a sobering effect on the mood of the army and navy troops in Helsingfors.' The minister's riposte gained support from a number of moderate socialist publications. Needless to say, both his speech and the comments it elicited provoked a sharp reaction in the Finnish press. *Kansan Lehti* expressed regret at the words which, 'with the decisiveness of a true military commander', had been uttered by 'a friend Finland has just lost.' 'It is painful to see how a darling of the revolution such as Kerensky can so readily exchange the perspective of a socialist for that of an imperialist.'[78]

Subsequently a number of Russian socialists expressed solidarity with Finland. However, several days passed between Kerensky delivering his speech and these rejoinders, during which the Bolsheviks and their allies acquired further serious grounds for dissatisfaction with the minister and new opportunities for mounting propaganda attacks on him. In the changed circumstances they could also reproach Kerensky with his speech in Helsingfors. His criticism of the Finnish nationalist movement did not initially arouse protest among soldiers and sailors serving in Finland. Rather the reverse: they were in favour at that time of a call to preserve the unity of the empire. It is more than likely that Kerensky deliberately raised the topic in order to rally the armed forces and reinforce discipline by instigating a confrontation with Finnish separatism. At the very least he could be sure of having the support of the Russian liberals, the conservatives, and at least some of the socialists.

In public Kerensky took an optimistic view of the visit. He had, he said, been able to check personally that the Baltic Fleet was combat-ready, and that all the 'difficulties associated with the transition period' were close to being satisfactorily resolved.[79] The newspapers favourable to him described the visit as a propaganda success, while the Socialist Revolutionary newspaper even called it an 'unqualified triumph'.[80]

In later years Bolshevik memoirists and Soviet historians claimed that revolutionary sailors had rebuffed the minister, and that judgement would seem, in fact, to be confirmed by Kerensky's own memoirs. 'At the public gatherings I was subjected to thinly veiled attacks by Bolsheviks, and at private meetings I was sometimes forced to listen to very harsh criticism from spokesmen for the officers, whose lives under the watchful eye of the sailors' committees had become sheer misery. But the majority of my audiences, both officers and men, were friendly.'[81]

These unambiguous assessments by memoirists of diverse political outlooks must be considered overstated. In retrospect, eyewitnesses 'evened out' their assessment of the radicalization of servicemen in Finland. Kerensky's visit undoubtedly did have a certain propaganda success, and for some time the defencists strengthened their influence in the main base of the navy. The local Socialist Revolutionaries drew on Kerensky's authority to conduct political campaigns. Their call to tighten discipline was headed 'Support Kerensky!'[82] A number of companies were in favour of the resolution of the crew of the *Sevastopol*, whose sailors issued a demand 'to make clear to the army that only a vigorous offensive can bring about the fall of the Hohenzollerns' iron fist, liberation of the German proletariat, and an early end to this fratricidal war.'[83] For Kerensky, preparing an offensive, such support was important.

The Bolsheviks in Finland found themselves in a tricky situation. A prominent member of the party recalled, 'At the very beginning of May . . . in connection with Kerensky's arrival in Helsingfors and demagogic speeches against the Bolsheviks, the climate of opinion against us worsened dramatically.'[84] The Executive Committee of the Soviet adopted a declaration condemning 'underground agitation' and calls for violence, as well as 'unworthy persecution' directed 'against the left wing of the Social Democratic Party, and especially against Comrade Lenin and his followers'.[85] This confirms there was a significant amount of 'anti-Leninist' sentiment.

Even the radically inclined committee of the battleship *Respublika* felt obliged to explain itself.

> Recently an unfriendly attitude towards the sailors of our ship has been very noticeable. All sorts of ridiculous rumours are flying around in the city claiming that the *Respublika* does not wish to go to sea, that there is anarchy on her. To this there have been added rumours in the past few days which it would be shameful to believe. They allege we forced the minister of the navy off the ship, that we were 'insulting' towards him, and so on.[86]

Understanding that most sailors did not agree with criticizing Kerensky, the ship's activists had presented a list of their questions to the citizen minister. They portrayed their actions as a perfectly proper political polemic. The Bolshevik criticism of Kerensky in Helsingfors was very cautious at this time and refrained from personal attacks on him.

An explanation from the committee was published in the Bolshevik newspaper, and a representative of the battleship, speaking at a meeting of the Soviet the day after Kerensky's visit, was even more restrained. He asked to speak out of turn (which indicates the urgency of the issue) in order to deny rumours that the crew had spurned the minister. The speaker reported the 'ovations' with which their guest's speech had been greeted and described the questions put to him and his ensuing answers.[87] The efforts of *Respublika*'s committee paid off: the joint meeting of ships' committees of the 2nd Battleship Brigade dismissed the rumours about *Respublika* as being a 'provocation'.[88] It did not, however, endorse even moderate criticism of the minister, which testifies to the considerable difficulties facing any activists opposed to Kerensky.

To bolster their propaganda effort, the Bolsheviks summoned to Helsingfors Alexandra Kollontai, well known as a speaker for the Bolshevik Party. She delivered speeches at rallies to considerable effect, and by the end of May the local Bolshevik newspaper was openly voicing criticism of Kerensky.[89] That Kollontai's speeches were being well received is suggested by a letter from a worker in the port of Sveaborg to the Socialist Revolutionary newspaper. He condemned an overly trusting audience which could too easily have its mind changed for it. 'Yesterday we gave an ovation to Comrade Kerensky, but today the wind is blowing from another direction, and we welcome Comrade Kollontai and forget the oaths we swore to Kerensky.' He recalled the minister's speech. 'We heard his golden words. We understood that his policies were good for our long-suffering people. With his speeches Comrade Kerensky healed our wounds and infused our ailing hearts with healing balm so that now we can again say we are alive, that free Russia lives!' The writer spoke of the Leader's merits and declared, 'We will go through fire and water with this Leader and die for him. He is our genius.'[90] Publication of this ardent letter in defence of the Leader and genius of the revolution is testimony to the fact that Bolshevik propaganda criticizing him was having an effect. Not all Kollontai's listeners meekly agreed with her, however, and it was reported that the discussion at rallies where she participated became 'heated' and gave rise to very outspoken language.[91] The Bolsheviks' intensified campaigning encountered resistance in Helsingfors.

The success of renewed attacks on Kerensky, on grounds not only of solidarity with the Finns but also of criticism of the minister's orders, should probably be attributed less to the oratory of Kolontai than to a change in the political climate. Kerensky found himself in a radically different situation, as we shall see, in mid-May after signing the Declaration of Soldiers' Rights. Even so, the minister's authority was sufficient to bring about changes in the command structure of the Baltic Fleet. Admiral Maximov, who enjoyed the support of the committees, was replaced as head of the fleet by Admiral Dmitry Verderevsky, who was both respected by the officers and, at the same time, capable of negotiating with the committees. The crews of a number of ships protested against violation of the principle of 'democratic' appointment of the commander. The hotbed here was the dreadnought *Petropavlovsk*, whose sailors wanted to elect all senior officers. This was in itself evidence of the crisis in discipline. The new commander-in-chief did, nevertheless, take up his duties on 5 June, a part having been played by Kerensky's address to the crew of the *Petropavlovsk*.[92] In tandem with other measures, that appeal contributed to a temporary stabilizing of the situation.

The visit to Helsingfors was important for Kerensky also for the opportunity it afforded to sharpen up the tactics of how he presented himself. In the course of the visit a certain procedure was developed. It included administrative meetings with the civil and military authorities, political negotiations with members of soviets and committees, and rallying speeches to activists, as well as to entire sections and units of the army and navy. The press focused its attention on how Kerensky got on with the troop committees and rank-and-file soldiers and sailors. In this connection, one particularly dramatic speech would be singled out for detailed coverage. It would be wrong to imagine that this standard plan for visits was devised solely by Kerensky and his entourage. For local activists who considered themselves his allies, the arrival of the Leader was an important political asset, and they did their best to influence how the visit was organized and the coverage it received in the press. The High Command of the fleet also tried to make good use of the minister's authority to strengthen their own. Both the activists and the commanders emphasized their visitor's importance, which could help them resolve local problems. The visits contributed to the invention and spread of new ways of glorifying the Leader. It was during these visits he was referred to as 'the popular revolutionary Leader', 'our dear Leader', 'the Leader of the revolutionary army', and even 'our Great Leader and genius'.

The minister's visit to the main base of the Baltic Fleet could not on its own bring about a substantial improvement in the discipline of the military forces stationed in Finland. Nevertheless, the atmosphere of the visit and the political mobilization it involved helped both to create more favourable conditions for defencist propaganda and to wrong-foot the Bolsheviks and their allies, at least temporarily.

Finally, however, after the visit, the minister, who had seemed to enjoy almost universal support, found himself for the first time the butt of serious public criticism. For the Finnish nationalist movement he became the personification of Russian imperialism. Finnish politicians tried to gain allies among Russian politicians. In connection with the controversy surrounding the Declaration of Soldiers' Rights, voices were raised more markedly in solidarity with the Finnish Social Democrats, and on 20 May the Second Regional Congress of Soviets of the Army, Navy and Workers in Finland promised to support the demand for independence of the Grand Duchy if a majority of Finns expressed it.[93] Activists who had acclaimed Kerensky's threats against Finland, literally within ten days did a complete U-turn. The cause was new orders by the minister which received a very mixed reaction in the army and navy.

3 The 'Kerensky Declaration'

On 10 May, Kerensky returned to Petrograd. Directly from the railway station he went to the Naval Guards to report that there were no problems in the fleet. This was not true, but public opinion in Petrograd was not well informed about the situation in Helsingfors, and Kerensky, seeing his job as being to arouse enthusiasm, demonstrated optimism.

That same day the minister was on his way to the front by train. His departure had been turned into a rousing demonstration with a large crowd, consisting largely of soldiers and officers gathering at the station, and a band playing *The Marseillaise*. Kerensky was accompanied by his adjutants and other officers, representatives of the Russian press, and Claude Anet, a well-known French journalist.[94] The minister was intending in the course of the trip to assemble delegates of military units 'for the purpose of making very clear to them the necessity of introducing iron discipline in the army'.[95] Elected army organizations were seen as a vitally important tool for establishing the new discipline.

The train passed through Dno, Novosokolniki and Vitebsk. Everywhere

Kerensky was greeted by crowds of thousands of people with red flags and warmly welcomed. The speakers who addressed the minister 'expressed their profound faith that under his leadership the army's morale would be restored and it would go wherever the Leader of the people, now head of the army, would lead them.' So, at least, the official communiqué reported. Such announcements were published in the official gazette of the Ministry of War and in *Delo naroda*, the main newspaper of the Socialist Revolutionary Party. The rhetoric was accepted by a broad spectrum of political forces. Kerensky openly told his supporters of the impending offensive. 'We are advancing to gain land and freedom for the toiling peasantry and, with our strong discipline, we shall obtain those. We shall win the peace to which we aspire, with no wish to rob or oppress anyone.'[96]

In the evening the minister arrived in Kiev, where a guard of honour of the Cuirassier Guards Regiment, with a band, several delegations and thousands of citizens were waiting for him. Those welcoming him were enthused by the speech of their high-ranking visitor, in which he expressed his conviction that the Constituent Assembly would come out in favour of a federal structure for the country. This was just what many Ukrainians wanted to hear, and they carried him shoulder-high.[97] In Kiev he was joined by Albert Thomas, a French socialist minister, which gave even greater weight to his visit to the front.

On 12 May, Kerensky arrived in Kamenets-Podolsk, the headquarters of the Southwestern Front, whose armies were to play a crucial role in the offensive. There was a festive mood in the city and shouts of 'Hurrah for the Leader of Russian democracy!', 'Long live heroic Kerensky!', 'Hurrah for the people's minister!' At the Congress of the Front the chairman welcomed the 'foremost champion of freedom'. Kerensky's inspiring speech at the congress struck just the right propaganda note for preparing the offensive.[98] On 13 and 14 May the minister visited front-line units, and among the slogans on the red flags was 'Who is with Kerensky is with us'.[99] The press carried reports of these enthusiastic meetings. On 14 May newspaper readers could read about an important document Kerensky had signed on 11 May.[100] This was an order to the army and navy which became known as the Declaration of Soldiers' Rights.

The propaganda both of those supportive of the minister and of those hostile to him often referred to this order as the 'Kerensky Declaration'. Some publications of the order sported a portrait of the minister, and Kerensky was sometimes described as its author. He was evidently hoping the declaration would enhance his authority.

The document was a compromise between moderate members of the committees and those generals and officers who were prepared to accept some of the revolutionary changes in the army. Guchkov, Kerensky's predecessor as minister of war, had refused to endorse it because he considered the reform harmful. In this he had the support of General Alexeyev, the supreme commander-in-chief, and of the commanders of the fronts. The Coalition Government had promised to consolidate the radical 'democratic' changes in the army, but it was essential to give a legal definition of what 'iron discipline' meant. The resulting document was not something that could be ignored.

Researchers believe that by early May the struggle between the Provisional Government and the Petrograd Soviet for the soul of the army had ended in favour of the latter.[101] It became obvious that the government could restore discipline in the armed forces only with the agreement of the Soviets and military committees in concert with the moderate socialists, but also that without adoption of the declaration it would be impossible.

The declaration stated that military personnel enjoyed full civil rights, had the right to belong to public, political and professional organizations, and could not be subjected to corporal punishment (including even those serving time in military prisons). Mandatory saluting was abolished and replaced by 'voluntary mutual greeting'. Point 14 of the declaration read: 'In a combat situation, a commander has the right, on his personal responsibility, to apply all measures, up to and including the use of armed force, against subordinates who do not obey his orders.' This amended the ideal of complete abolition of capital punishment already proclaimed by the first Provisional Government. Point 18 reserved 'solely to commanders' the right to appoint or dismiss personnel from their posts, thus abolishing the principle of electing commanders proclaimed by Order No. 1 of the Petrograd Soviet and implemented in a number of units of the Petrograd garrison.[102] Points 14 and 18 were very soon the favourite targets of Bolshevik propaganda.[103]

Many generals believed that adopting the declaration would finally undermine all discipline. Liberal, conservative and right-wing forces were later to accuse Kerensky of having, by endorsing this document, given the go-ahead to the destructive processes initiated by Order No. 1 of the Soviet. In the autumn there were even rumours that Order No. 1 had been Kerensky's idea.[104] Back on 2 May there had been a meeting at General Headquarters when the commanders-in-chief of all the fronts spoke out categorically against adopting the declaration. General Mikhail Alexeyev was credited with saying that it would be 'the last nail in the coffin of the Russian army'.[105] At the 4 May meeting with ministers, the military leaders also spoke against the declaration. The generals hoped that Kerensky, whom they had just supported, would not be in too much of a hurry to approve it.

The minister of war did, nevertheless, sign it into law on 11 May, albeit after amending the text. He increased the power of the officers, which was reflected in the wording of paragraphs 14 and 18. Guchkov would never have won that concession from the socialists.[106] The declaration was published three days later. Simultaneously Kerensky's order of 12 May was published, announcing an impending military offensive against the enemy. In this document, addressed to the 'warriors of free Russia', Kerensky made reference to the reputation he had cultivated of a champion of freedom and called for the establishment of the discipline of duty in the world's freest army. Stylistically the order was a mishmash of the rhetoric of revolutionary speech-making and the imperious style of a tsarist manifesto:

> At this great and terrible moment in the life of our country I have been summoned by the will of the people to take my place as leader of all the armed forces of the Russian state. Immeasurably heavy as that burden is, as an old soldier of the revolution I have unquestioningly submitted to the stern discipline of duty and assumed before the people and the revolution responsibility for the army and navy.
>
> All of you, the warriors of free Russia, from the soldier to the general, are carrying out the hard but glorious duty of defending revolutionary Russia. That alone – remember this – is your duty. But in defending Russia you are fighting for the triumph of the great ideals of the revolution, for freedom, equality and fraternity! Not one drop of your blood will be spilled in the cause of iniquity.
>
> It is not to seize territory or for the sake of violence but in the name of saving free Russia that you will advance to wherever your leaders and the government lead you. We cannot drive out the enemy by standing still. You will bring on the tips of your bayonets peace, law, truth and justice. You will advance, free sons of Russia, in orderly ranks, bound by the discipline of duty and unconditional love of the revolution and your homeland.[107]

The biographer Vladimir Fedyuk has suggested that simultaneous publication of the declaration and the order for the offensive was timed to coincide with news of the success of Kerensky's propaganda trip to the front. The declaration, targeting the left wing, was designed to enlist their support for the offensive, while the order for the offensive was designed to reconcile the generals to the declaration.[108] This suggestion seems entirely plausible. The revolutionary rhetoric of the order was targeted at the left, while its substance was intended to win over the liberal and conservative press to Kerensky's side. These newspapers did indeed praise the order for the offensive.

Kerensky's allies regarded adoption of the declaration as 'a major victory for democracy', and the endorsement of the Executive Committee of the Petrograd Soviet was particularly important.[109] The declaration was also supported by a number of military committees: representatives of the 3rd Army Corps, for example, welcomed 'this historic document which lays a solid foundation for democratizing the armed forces.'[110] Nevertheless, among the many resolutions endorsing various aspects of Kerensky's policy, we rarely find explicit support of the declaration as a whole. The expectation that the order for the offensive would cancel out protests against the declaration which could be anticipated from the right did not prove wholly justified, although even in the ranks of the Constitutional Democratic Party it was met with cautious optimism. 'The declaration has the aim of enhancing discipline in the army, which took a knock during the days of the revolution, and of restructuring the army way of life on a new, democratic basis.'[111]

The reaction of the High Command was predictably negative: disapproval of the declaration was rarely shown publicly, but it could be felt. The dissatisfaction came into the open in July after the failure of the offensive, when abolition of the Declaration of Soldiers' Rights became one of the main demands of the generals, who no longer stopped short of direct criticism of Kerensky. Already in May, General Romeyko-Gurko, the commander-in-chief of the Western Front, resigned in protest against the signing of the declaration. Kerensky, acting in the spirit of his first order, refused to accept his resignation, and the general was deprived of the right to occupy posts above head of a division. Kerensky's decision caused resentment on the right but met with approval from the left. It came at the same time as an order from the minister, to disband several regiments which had refused to carry out orders, was welcomed on the right. For moderate socialists the demonstrative punishment of a 'reactionary general' made reprisals against undisciplined soldiers acceptable. Kerensky acknowledged in an interview with journalists that the simultaneous signing of the orders was not coincidental.[112] In this instance, too, even-handed action by the minister gained him support from opposed political forces. Most professional soldiers were in no hurry openly to criticize the declaration, evidently feeling that was inappropriate while an offensive was under preparation. The absence of any generals stepping forward publicly to endorse this very major act by the minister of war was, however, very noticeable.

It might have seemed that socialists should welcome the declaration. Captain Ignatiy Dzevaltovsky, the leader of the Bolsheviks in the Grenadier Guards Regiment, had been distributing the text before it was confirmed, claiming that the officers were concealing this important document from the soldiers.[113] Positive reactions to the declaration were to be found even in the Bolshevik press. On 12 May *Soldatskaya pravda* welcomed the order, which had not yet been published officially. 'This is a huge victory for us. It is a victory for the revolution,' wrote Alexander Zhilin, a leading Bolshevik in the 1st Machine-Gun Regiment, who had participated in drafting the provisions on soldiers's rights and knew how heated the discussion had been.[114]

Leon Trotsky was one of the first people to criticize Kerensky publicly, and he did so cautiously. The minister was described not as an enemy but as someone condoning actions by the enemy. At a meeting of the Petrograd Soviet, Trotsky said, 'Take due note of Kerensky's absence from the Soviet, and of all the publicity in the bourgeois press around the name of Kerensky. Is the press by any chance trying to use Kerensky in the interests of Russian Bonapartism?' Trotsky did not at this moment attack Kerensky's reforms in the Ministry of War, but even such comparatively mild criticism was regarded by the minister's supporters as unacceptable hostility.[115]

In fact, however, there is evidence of a negative attitude towards Kerensky even before publication of the declaration and the ordering of the offensive. Already on 8 May there were reports from the army in the field that at rallies and in conversation with soldiers claims were being heard that the minister of war had 'sold out to the bourgeoisie'.[116] Kerensky's call for iron discipline was of itself enough to set many against him, but it was undoubtedly the publication of the declaration that caused a sharp change of attitude in the armed forces towards the minister. Particular exception was taken to Points 14 and 18. Here was an opportunity for political agitation even among soldiers who were instinctively opposed to Lenin's approach, and the Bolsheviks did not let it slip. They immediately set about criticizing first the orders and then the minister himself. It would be a mistake, however, to suppose that a decision was taken at party headquarters and then executed by disciplined functionaries. Discontent over Kerensky's orders simultaneously became apparent in different places and in different ways.

The Congress of Representatives of the Baltic Fleet, for instance, did not accept the declaration and prevented its being implemented throughout the fleet. The congress's decree is notable for its radicalism. This was just the moment when many sailors were challenging the government's right to replace the commander of the fleet. Simultaneously, the congress primly sent greetings to 'citizen minister of the navy, Comrade Kerensky'. This odd combination, of rejection of the declaration and respect for the head of the ministry which approved it, may be explicable by how the genesis of the declaration had been represented to the deputies. Pavel Dybenko described a meeting of the members of the Central Committee of the Baltic Fleet with Kerensky. 'In the Declaration of Soldiers' Rights, the minister himself does not fully agree with Points 14 and 18, which need to be examined closely.' In short, Kerensky's own authority was being used by his opponents to undermine a document he had approved. Several military committees, in most of which the moderate socialists held control, also criticized the declaration. Although their discussions often ended with the victory of supporters of Kerensky, the discussion itself contributed to political mobilization of his opponents. Helsingfors Soviet, for example, after a heated debate, passed a Socialist Revolutionary resolution endorsing the declaration, but a meeting of representatives of ships' committees, including those of the battleship *Respublika* and the dreadnoughts *Petropavlovsk*, *Gangut* and *Sevastopol*, demanded the abolition of Point 18.[117] This shows us opposition to the Kerensky Declaration bringing together activists of *Respublika*, who had previously been critical of Kerensky, and members of the committee of *Sevastopol*, who had previously welcomed him.

The resolutions were condemning the substance of the order, but in the course of the debate discussion sometimes moved on to the minister of war himself. At a meeting of the Executive Committee of the Western Front on 17 May, the focus was on Point 14. One committee member said, 'It is not

Kerensky I am protesting against: I would have protested against Tsereteli or my own father. The problem is not the name, the problem is the paragraph.' Another speaker detected the negative influence of the generals on the minister of war. 'Kerensky finds himself in the worst position of any of the ministers because he has to rely on the staff officers. To summarize the declaration, it does away with the total lack of rights of the soldiers but without proclaiming his new rights.' Evidently the mood of rank-and-file soldiers was influencing the members of the executive committee. One of those who spoke mentioned that front-line soldiers, after studying paragraph 14, had called Kerensky a swindler.[118] On 17 May the committee of the Reserve Battalion of the Izmailovsky Regiment also came out against the declaration. So we can see that some radically inclined activists came out against Kerensky's order, even before the hostile newspapers of the Bolsheviks began to have an impact.[119]

For many soldiers the declaration seemed to be eliminating the gains of the revolution. The Bolsheviks used these sentiments to launch a propaganda attack on Kerensky. On 16 May *Pravda* published an article by Grigoriy Zinoviev, 'A Declaration of Rights or a Declaration of No Rights?' The next day, *Soldatskaya pravda* was also writing about a 'Declaration of No Rights'. Zinoviev's article set the tone for Bolshevik propaganda, and on 18 May Lev Kamenev joined the attack, claiming that 'the declaration of the new government and Kerensky's actions make it blindingly obvious that the leaders of the Mensheviks and Narodniks are traipsing along the path laid down for them by English, French and Russian imperialism.'[120] At rallies and meetings the Bolsheviks proposed resolutions condemning the declaration which, by their own admission, served as 'admirable propaganda material'.[121]

This Bolshevik activity did not go unremarked. A prominent Socialist Revolutionary who had participated in the drafting of the declaration wrote: 'These last few days an intensive propaganda campaign is being conducted in the Petrograd garrison against the order of Comrade Kerensky about the general rights of service personnel. . . . There is a great hullabaloo being raised around the name of Comrade Kerensky in connection with the order.'[122] The propaganda 'around the name of Comrade Kerensky' was bearing fruit, and the minister's supporters needed to react to it. Articles appeared in their newspapers in defence of the declaration and against the Bolsheviks' propaganda attacks. *Izvestiya*, the newspaper of the Petrograd Soviet, wrote: '*Pravda* has declared the Declaration of Soldier's Rights a Declaration of No Rights and turned it into a one long indictment of Kerensky.'[123] Their quoting of Zinoviev's slogan testifies to the fact that it was catching on.

The minister's supporters were right to be concerned. At a meeting of the Bolshevik Military Organization in Petrograd on 23 May it was observed that the soldiers wanted to take to the streets to protest against Kerensky's orders, and moreover the 'combative spirit' of some of the regiments was such that they might do so without bothering to consult the centre. At the same time, Vladimir Nevsky, one of the leaders of the Military Organization, stated, 'It is impossible in practice to organize a demonstration, because the majority of soldiers in the Soviet of Workers' and Soldiers' Deputies support Kerensky, the man who signed the declaration oppressing soldiers.'[124] The unpopularity of Kerensky's order did not necessarily mean there had been any decrease in his authority, which made it difficult to assess the chances of holding a successful demonstration against him.

Bolsheviks in other cities joined in the criticism of the declaration. On 24 May an article damning the minister was published in the Moscow *Sotsial demokrat*. 'Kerensky's order on the rights of military personnel is also plainly reactionary. It leads not forwards but back towards the orders there were under the tsar.' Criticism of the declaration continued in subsequent issues.[125] The Bolshevik newspaper *Volna* [The Wave] in Helsingfors also attacked Kerensky: 'If the representative of the socialists, Comrade Kerensky, is capable of issuing orders which cut back our freedom, of giving back all their old power to the military leaders and restoring executions, what can we expect from the class of our age-old oppressors?'[126] Even at the end of May, however, we find some Bolsheviks who criticize the deeds of the minister of war but still acknowledge him as a representative of the socialists, a 'comrade', and contrast him with the class of the age-old oppressors. This was despite the fact that their party comrades had already moved to harsher criticism of Kerensky, accusing him of practically restoring pre-revolutionary traditions.

The Bolsheviks had corresponding resolutions passed at rallies and printed in party newspapers. On 16 May, the very day the article was published, a rally of sailors and soldiers of Kronshtadt passed a resolution condemning the Declaration of Soldiers' Rights, and especially Points 14 and 18. On 18 May a meeting of soldiers of the 1st Infantry Reserve Regiment, which had only recently given the minister a warm welcome, resolved: 'We consider the Kerensky Declaration, and especially Point 18 [concerning] elections in the army, an attempt to curtail the gains of the revolution and a step in the bourgeoisie's campaign to turn the army into a blind tool of the bourgeoisie.'[127] At the same time, a group of soldiers in the 9th company of the same regiment condemned speakers 'who urge us not to trust Minister Kerensky, claiming he has sold out to the bourgeoisie.'[128] It was probably supporters of the moderate socialists who introduced a resolution warning against renewed armed clashes in Petrograd. Their attitude towards Kerensky was already beginning to divide soldiers serving in the same military unit, as we see in the formulations devised by activists fighting for the right to express the view of their fellow soldiers.

Some of the more radical regiments passed resolutions that not only rejected particular points in the declaration but went on to criticize the minister. A resolution of the soldiers of the Pavlovsky Regiment read: 'This assembly believes that Minister Kerensky has abandoned the idea of democratizing the army . . . The meeting believes that Minister Kerensky is thus not fulfilling the will of the democratic forces from which he emerged. He is taking a right away from the soldiers and giving this right to the military commanders.'[129] This resolution was used as a model for several others.[130]

Even so, not all Bolsheviks yet considered it appropriate to attack Kerensky. The Helsingfors Bolshevik newspaper, for example, reported the resolution of a meeting of the Social Democrats of the Tavastguss garrison. This rejected some points of the declaration and set out conditions essential if the army was to be reformed. 'We demand that, until new declarations are issued, account should be taken of the opinion of the soldiers. Only then, Citizen Kerensky, will you be able to create "iron discipline".'[131] Those who drafted the resolution were not themselves condemning the idea of iron discipline, but they were insisting on a 'democratic' approach to the issuing of orders.

Some resolutions rejected not individual points of the order but the document in its entirety.[132] The sailors of the minelayer *Msta* demanded a referendum. Protesting about an order which 'serves rather to disenfranchise the soldier', they insisted it should either be rescinded immediately or put to a vote 'in all military units'.[133]

On 9 June, Yelena Stasova, on behalf of the secretariat of the Bolshevik Central Committee, wrote to the party's Moscow regional bureau, 'The mood has become more fraught in the last 2–3 weeks on the basis of dissatisfaction with the coalition ministry, Kerensky's Declaration of Soldiers' Rights, and the disbandment of regiments.' Several grounds are listed for aggravation of the situation, but the initial impetus for the political mobilization is identified as the declaration. That same day an appeal from the central committee and the Petersburg committee of the Bolsheviks was adopted; in the thick of the June Crisis, criticism of the order was used to draw soldiers and sailors to the party. 'Far from delivering soldiers' rights, the Kerensky "Declaration" violates those rights on a number of very important points.'[134] This appeal from the Bolsheviks' central organizations criticized the minister but, unlike a number of Bolshevik resolutions, did not call for outright rejection of the declaration.

Neither did the All-Russia Conference of Bolshevik Military Organizations, held from 16 to 23 June, call for outright rejection. 'Although this declaration contains much that is appropriate and necessary for soldiers,' the resolution observes, 'there are at the same time in some of its main provisions important points which are in fact a declaration of deprivation of soldiers' rights.'[135] Thus, unlike certain radical activists, this forum of army Bolsheviks found 'much that is appropriate' in the declaration. We may speculate that those drafting the resolution were obliged to take account of the range of opinions in front-line Bolshevism, which could differ markedly from that of Petrograd, which was, of course, itself far from monolithic.[136]

At the same time, some who opposed the Bolsheviks also reacted negatively to the declaration. Such sentiments were evident in the army in the field. The Bolshevik newspaper wrote that the 'sadly notorious' declaration was being rebuffed not only by the far left but also by 'moderate to Menshevik' circles.[137] There really was no unity in the ranks of the moderate socialists: some Mensheviks and Socialist Revolutionaries also criticized the declaration. Even the Socialist Revolutionaries of Helsingfors, who actively defended Kerensky, demanded changes to the 14th and 18th points 'in order fully to comply with the principle of democratizing the army,' although they sought at the same time to defend the authority of the Leader. 'Bypassing General Headquarters, we need to submit amendments directly to Kerensky and to point out to him from the perspective of the grassroots the mistakes that have crept into the general provisions of the order, through no fault of his.'[138] The moderate socialists were doubtless taking account of the attitudes of those in the army and navy who were dissatsified with the order. The Bolsheviks jubilantly registered the splits in the ranks of their opponents. Zinoviev referred with considerable glee to the Socialist Revolutionaries' newspaper publication of a remark made by a Socialist Revolutionary sailor: 'We deeply respect A. F. Kerensky, but we do not find it possible to accept his instructions without criticism. . . . We have crossed these two points out and will not be enforcing them.'[139]

Those political groups which did support the declaration and lionized the Leader of Russian democracy had little success in mobilizing their supporters. Their newspapers published articles supporting the declaration. They printed soldiers' resolutions extolling the people's minister in connection with other issues, but resolutions in support of the declaration they did not publish. Evidently there were very few, unlike resolutions supporting the idea of an offensive.

At the same time it would be wrong to say that the declaration dealt a mortal blow to Kerensky's popularity, because in May and June, as we shall see, he scored a number of propaganda victories. Publication of the declaration and the order for the offensive put him squarely at the centre of political debate, with some fervently supporting and others furiously attacking him. Kerensky came to personify a growing conflict. Arguments over the minister as the embodiment of the burning issues of the day were on the lips of the politically awakening citizens of Russia. The correspondent of one newspaper testified after a visit to Kronshtadt that the minister was the main topic of conversation of all those travelling with him. 'Some sing Kerensky's praises, others disparage him.'[140]

The Bolsheviks and other radical socialists made use of the dissatisfaction many in the armed forces felt over declaration. We can see a difference between the Bolsheviks' verbal and printed propaganda. In the context of soldiers saying among themselves that Kerensky had 'sold out to the bourgeoisie', the left-wing press moved to overt criticism first of certain points, then of the declaration as a whole – and only then moved on to attack the minister himself. In some instances criticism of the declaration led on to very outspoken condemnation of the minister. Members of the Reserve Battalion Committee of the Petrograd Guards Regiment indicated that many soldiers were even likening Kerensky's policies to the doings of Nicholas II.[141]

Their attitude to the order, and to Kerensky personally, provoked a division between those who continued to build him up as the Leader of the people and those who began to distance themselves from him. The coalition supporting the declaration, a document of crucial importance for Kerensky, was quite limited, although the liberals, conservatives and right wing generally refrained from open criticism because they were pleased to see the preparations for the offensive. Sometimes they even openly supported the order in the press, but without making any effort to mobilize their supporters politically, and this was reflected in the very small number of resolutions supporting the declaration.

The controversy over the Kerensky Declaration did nothing to contribute new positive images of the minister of war. These did appear, but in connection with other political processes. On the contrary, it is at this time that negative images of Kerensky began to proliferate. It would be going too far, however, to say that these arguments amounted to a propaganda defeat for the Leader. His main goal was to prepare the ground politically for the offensive, and for that the adoption of the declaration was essential. The criticism coming from the 'Leninists' actually prompted many of the minister's allies from different parts of the political spectrum to rally round him, to search for arguments in support of him, and to make use of effective rhetorical constructs and memorable imagery.

The disputes over the declaration give us an insight into the state of the armed forces and the fraught atmosphere in which preparations were being made for the June Offensive. The political battle over the offensive escalated towards the end of May and ensured that criticism of the declaration and the minister of war became increasingly vehement.

4 'Tireless victor': Kerensky at the front

The main Russian newspapers reported on the incredible success of Kerensky's visits to the front. The reality was more complicated, but the visits themselves, and the way they were reported in the press, influenced the formation of Kerensky's images, so the visits, the press reporting, and how the news was perceived deserve our scrutiny.

The speech Kerensky gave at the Congress of Delegates of the Southwestern Front was to prove the most important of all those he delivered during his visit to the army in the field. Once more he called Russia's soldiers the freest in the world. Once more he denounced fraternization. Once again he looked back to the revolutionary tradition to inspire the soldiers. 'My comrade Socialist Revolutionaries died one after another in the battle against autocracy. If it be your lot to die an honourable death, witnessed by the whole world, call on me. I will advance with a rifle in my hands ahead of you!' He summoned the soldiers to acts of heroism and solemnly promised to set an example himself. 'Our stake is the fate of millions of people. Forward, in the battle for freedom. It is not to death but to a great celebration that I call you! We, the revolutionaries, have earned the right to die!' These words were greeted with thunderous applause and such exclamations as, 'We are right behind you, comrade. Forward, for freedom!' The minister promised General Brusilov, commander-in-chief of the front, that the soldiers would obey his order to attack.[142] These topics recurred in Kerensky's speeches in the following days. Shortly afterwards, Brusilov addressed the armies under his command. 'I am glad to attest before the troops of the front entrusted to me that, in all units and all committees, the minister of war was welcomed with exceptional elation, enthusiasm and spirit.'[143]

The renowned commander sought to exploit Kerensky's propaganda as a political asset. He asserted that his troops were prepared to forget old misunderstandings, restore iron discipline, and stop fraternizing with the enemy. He insisted that they were all ready to go on the offensive. Kerensky would probably have been unhappy about the reference to 'restoring' discipline (which was exactly what his left-wing opponents were accusing him of),[144] preferring instead to talk about establishing the fundamentally new discipline of duty.

In later years Brusilov recalled Kerensky's visit somewhat differently. 'The mass of soldiers greeted him enthusiastically and promised the earth, but nowhere did they fulfil any of their promises. Self-seeking conduct and a total lack of discipline took over, which was entirely understandable.'[145] General Brusilov's memoirs need to be viewed with caution: he does not choose to refer to his own speeches of that time, in which he extolled the minister of war. If Brusilov availed himself of Kerensky's authority in his efforts to strengthen discipline and raise the troops' morale, then by his speeches in this vein the commander contributed to boosting the minister's popularity.

Kerensky's trips to the front played a large role in preparing for the offensive, as well as reinforcing his image as the Leader of the revolutionary army. After visiting the Southwestern Front he held talks with the Command on the Romanian Front, took part in important meetings in Odessa and Sevastopol, and spoke at rallies. On the return journey he again stopped in Kiev, before going on to Mogilyov to the headquarters of the supreme commander-in-chief. On 21 May Kerensky was back in Petrograd, and on 22 May he was off again to the Northern Front.

Many newspapers reported on the enthusiastic welcomes Kerensky received. After a rally where the 3rd Caucasian Corps was stationed, thousands of soldiers ran after the minister's car, many crying. Some jumped into it, hugging and kissing Kerensky. The newspapers also reported that some regiments confronted the minister with anti-war slogans but, under the influence of his speeches, declared their willingness to attack. Special mention was made of the fact that the minister also visited trenches directly on the front line.[146]

These reports in the main newspapers of Kerensky's propaganda successes had a mixed reception, in which political views, social status, profession, and also location had a bearing on how the news was perceived. The opinion of soldiers on the front line was often sharply at variance with the views of readers in the rear.

General Andrey Snesarev never did hear Kerensky speak, but he recorded in his diary the impressions he garnered from officers and generals who had attended the rallies. On 14 May, while Kerensky's visit to the front was still in progress, Snesarev wrote,

> Yesterday Stanyukovich . . . attended a rally of the minister of war (dressed like an Englishman, with gaiters, peaked cap . . . very smart). He shouted and jumped about, shrieked hysterically, quite the rabble-rouser . . . He concludes particular sections with questions to which there is only the one answer he obviously requires. ('Yes, right!' 'Much better!' 'The army of the tsar or the one we have now?' and so on.) After him it's Brusilov, also shouting and waving a red banner about. ('I have been given this revolutionary banner by the minister of war . . .,' etc. Kerensky periodically grabs the banner off him and waves it about even faster and higher, standing on tiptoe.) He plays on the word 'tsar' and also does his impression of a rabble-rouser. . . . After Kerensky, Stanyukovich had the impression that Brusilov was speaking with too much artifice, did not believe what he was saying, and did not really believe they would go on the attack. . . . It was only for a moment, a short while, before Kerensky was carried shoulder-high, and then he was gone, not a trace, like sea foam. Already in our divisional wagon train and in the 17th Finnish Regiment they are saying 'What's he think he's got to tell us, Kerensky? We know the score.'[147]

Although critical of the content of Kerensky's speech and of his rhetorical style, the officer Snesarev was talking to was much taken by the minister's new look. He had replaced his dark jacket by this time with a khaki uniform.

When Kerensky initially visited the front he had the appearance of a private soldier of the revolutionary era: a cap without a cockade, baggy trousers, boots with leg windings and a tunic without epaulettes. It reminded enraptured foreigners of 'a simple Russian peasant shirt'.[148] He later adopted a field jacket, kepi, breeches and gaiters. The democratic minister in charge of the ministry of war made his image more military and more Western. Some contemporaries later likened his appearance to that of the quasi-military rustic volunteers ironically known as 'Zemstvo hussars'.[149] Nevertheless, as we have seen, even critically inclined professional officers saw nothing wrong with his new look.[150]

Nevertheless, negative assessments of Kerensky's propaganda speeches predominate in Snesarev's diary entries. Both his manner of speaking and what he had to say are criticized as ill-suited to the task in hand. Professional soldiers are suspicious of a rabble-rouser. They question Kerensky's sincerity and, while acknowledging the impact of his speech (he was carried shoulder-high), judge it short-lived.

Similar criticisms recur in subsequent entries in Snesarev's diary. He uses the same expression, 'a rabble-rouser', to characterize Kerensky's rhetorical style. Sometimes, referring to people who heard the minister, he even writes about speeches falling flat.

> What is clearly observed is that Kerensky makes an impression, perhaps even arousing enthusiasm, in large units of the front or the army, where there are no actual soldiers, only workers dressed up as soldiers. What they warm to in him, knowingly or unknowingly, is a socialist, a comrade, not the minister of war. Where he encounters a real large number of soldiers, there is no contact, he is alien, and he is met with a deathly silence. That is when Kerensky is at a loss, out of his element.

Other people to whom Snesarev talked did, however, describe the minister as 'a seasoned orator' who made an impression on the soldiers and junior officers.[151] The well-informed diarist, despite his critical attitude towards Kerensky, accepts that the speeches had a positive effect on certain unruly units.[152] This gives support to some reports in the newspapers.

In a number of cases the judgements noted by Snesarev coincide closely with the opinion of the military doctor Vasiliy Kravkov, who also served on the Southwestern Front. He notes, 'The impression Kerensky makes on me is not of a statesmanlike person but merely of a grandiloquent conjuror, an excellent rabble-rouser. In an interview with correspondents after his tour of the Southwestern Front and in a report to the Provisional Government, he claims with extraordinary naivety that he has victoriously raised the soldiers' morale and that now everything is going well in the army. He even says he has noticed "healthy growth" of some description. Stuff and nonsense!'[153]

This diarist too had not seen Kerensky personally but spoke to people who had heard him, and Kravkov and Snesarev were both mixing with staff officers at divisional and corps level. We may assume that these judgements were widespread in such circles (and they crop up frequently in later memoirs). In the mainline press of the day, however, these views are absent. The enthusiastic descriptions of the minister's visits are in accord both with public statements and with the private judgement of many of his contemporaries. People at the front looked forward eagerly to his visits. His prestige made people want to hear him speak. The rabble-rousing style may have alienated some officers, but the masses of politicized soldiers could not wait to hear this amazingly popular speaker who could hold spellbound rallies attended by thousands. Even before Kerensky arrived at the front he was guaranteed a good hearing from well-wishing representatives of the military committees who looked forward to meeting him. It was a mood the organizers of the front-line congress wanted to communicate and build on.

> The Congress of Delegates of the Southwestern Front has been delighted to hear the news of your imminent arrival and warmly welcomes you, the beloved Leader of Russia's revolutionary democratic forces. We express the boundless joy of all units of the front to see you at the head of the people's army. We are profoundly confident that, under your leadership, the Russian army will succeed in emerging cohesive and powerful from all the trials of the time of transition and will fulfil its duty to liberated Russia in full measure.[154]

Rank-and-file soldiers too looked forward eagerly to meeting Kerensky. One soldier in a telegraph unit had written, back in April,

> You have a rumour going round there in Moscow that our soldiers do not want to go on the offensive. No, it is not true. It is made up by the Black Hundred, and what our soldiers say is we need only to be ordered by the liberator of the human race, our minister of war, Comrade Kerensky, and we will always be ready to die for free Russia. We hope to see him here at the front with us. It would be so fine to see our saviour, this second Jesus Christ. They crucified the first one, of course, but this one I think that every soldier will pay with his life but will not let him be harmed.[155]

Its unusual style makes this text stand out, but the desire to see Kerensky is evident in other letters from soldiers. 'Today we waited all day for our dear guest, the sun of Russia, Minister of War A. F. Kerensky, but he did not come. He will probably be our guest tomorrow. Well, Misha, you have no idea what a great mood, what spirit there is in the army, how much everyone is looking forward to seeing this great genius. If I manage to take a picture of the minister I will send you it.'[156] Kerensky was quite frequently referred to in the press at this time as the genius and sun of Russia.

Kerensky literally was carried shoulder-high. We know it was something of a ritual after many of his speeches, but that is not to deny that it demonstrated a spontaneous outburst of emotion. Florence Farmborough, a British nurse who was present on the Southwestern Front, witnessed the minister give a speech to 12,000 soldiers. She noted in her diary, 'When he left, the soldiers carried him on their shoulders to the motor car. They kissed him, his uniform, his car, the ground on which he walked. Many went down on their knees and prayed, others wept. Some were shouting and others sang patriotic songs.' Miss Farmborough writes that there was a hysterical explosion of enthusiasm and passionate patriotism.[157] Thus, the official communiqués and reportage of correspondents were not always exaggerating the degree of enthusiasm of the soldiers who saw him. It is directly confirmed in private accounts.

If some contemporaries wrote about Kerensky's 'hysteria' (and the criticism was both to be repeated later in propaganda hostile to the minister and to find its way into many memoirs), others noted no less hysteria in his audience. This reverberation of emotional states between the orator and his listeners was something which contributed greatly to his rhetorical success. Florence Farmborough clearly found no exaggeration in the enthusiastic descriptions of Kerensky's speeches published in major Russian newspapers. It seems safe to guess that many of the soldiers who saw the minister found the reports satisfying and trustworthy.

There were, nevertheless, readers who were more sceptical of the press reports. Nikita Okunev, the Moscow agent of the Samolyot Shipping Company, who had expressed delight at the minister of war's first orders, was already writing in his diary on 12 May: 'Kerensky has begun touring all the fronts. Of course he gives fiery speeches which are greeted with "tumultuous applause", but whether that will be enough to revive military discipline is quite a different matter, and without that the revolutionary army is even weaker than the old tsarist one.' Even before reading any newspaper reports about how the minister's speeches had been received, Okunev was sceptical about their effectiveness. It is no surprise that later his judgements became increasingly pessimistic and sarcastic. 'In Kiev Kerensky again kissed Konstantin Oberuchev, his own appointee as commander-in-chief of the Kiev Military District.' 'Kerensky travels around the front, kissing people, talking like Minin and Pozharsky, getting himself tossed in the air. The soldiers clap, swear oaths to attack, but there's no actual sign of that. They crack sunflower seeds and issue sundry demands.'[158]

Felix Rostkovsky, a retired general living in Petrograd, was similarly inclined. 'The overall consensus is that he has achieved nothing. The Russian army will not go forward and is completely disorganized.' 'There is a lot being written about his trips, a lot of noise, but almost no visible result.'[159]

The topic of Kerensky's trips to the front constantly came up in conversations between General Alexey Kuropatkin and high-ranking military men and with politicians he spoke to in May. He recorded their opinions in his diary. Kuropatkin remained doggedly optimistic. He wished the minister success but, while recognizing the impact of propaganda in the army, he considered it insufficient. 'News from the south and southwest, from the armies and cities Kerensky is touring, is favourable. He is being welcomed with enthusiasm and met with promises to advance, but so far everyone is only talking, endlessly talking, while our allies, especially the French, are bleeding,' he wrote on 20 May.[160] None of the people Kuropatkin spoke to were optimistic about the situation, but not all of them considered it hopeless. Some called the offensive Kerensky was preparing 'our last hope'. This feeling influenced the nature of the assessments specialists gave outside their own circle: pessimistic judgements were kept quiet, while optimistic assessments were made public. That was true both of statements intended for the public at large and for confidential communications.

Foreign Minister Mikhail Tereshchenko wrote to the Russian ambassador in Paris on 14 May: 'Kerensky's visit to the front was triumphal and has already produced noticeable results. The senior military officers report that his arrival came at just the right moment and has changed the mood in the army dramatically. . . . In the rear, as a result of Kerensky's speeches and the measures he has introduced, there is an energetic campaign being waged against deserters, with the prominent participation of soldiers' committees.' Shortly afterwards Tereshchenko wrote in a similar vein to the ambassador in the United States.[161]

To people who saw the offensive as Russia's last chance, no amount of optimism seemed overdone. Unsurprisingly, any sign of an improvement in the situation, or even rumours that there were any, was described as a definite trend. It was difficult to distinguish genuine manifestations of enthusiasm from exaggerated descriptions of them. Nevertheless, Kerensky's propaganda successes, whether actual or only rumoured and promoted in the press, were of considerable importance. News items, whether true or not, were put to use by different political forces.

Newspaper readers believed what they wanted to believe, and at this moment Kerensky had many admirers who were expecting a miraculous regeneration of the army, accomplished by the beloved Leader.

The various nuances of pessimism and optimism in respect of Kerensky's actions were not always made publicly, but attentive newspaper readers could sometimes discern them. Contemporaries paid close attention to what Finance Minister Andrey Shingaryov, a prominent member of the Constitutional Democratic Party, had to say at a congress of organizations supplying the country with food. 'Three hundred years ago Russia was saved by enthusiasm fired by Minin and Pozharsky. It is necessary to fan the flames of national enthusiasm. If Minister Kerensky can ignite enthusiasm in the army, and Peshekhonov in the field of national food supply, they will save Russia.' Here was an ally of the minister of war declaring that firing enthusiasm was Kerensky's most important task, and that if he succeeded in doing that he would stand comparison with the two great heroes of the early seventeenth-century Time of Troubles who were enshrined in Russia's historical memory. It tells us a lot that the opponents of the Constitutional Democrats, the Socialist Revolutionaries, were also writing at that time: 'We must inspire creative enthusiasm in the revolutionary masses.'[162]

General Snesarev, despite his sceptical attitude towards Kerensky, did not consider these hopes unrealizable. 'If we are to rely on the ideal of enthusiasm to which Shingaryov, for example, attaches such importance, we must be prepared to give it our all, to the point of sacrificing ourselves. In any case, for the army, as for the country, the Coalition Ministry,

Kerensky and, for example, the ideal of a death battalion are the last wager. If it loses, all hope will be gone.' Both in the rear and at the front, quite different people, without conferring, were using similar expressions: 'the last hope', 'the last wager', 'enthusiasm'. Even the cautious optimism of Shingaryov raised doubts, however. An article was published on 13 May in *Birzhevye vedomosti* with the predictable title of 'The Last Wager'. The author, clearly referring to Shingaryov's speech, commented that the call for enthusiasm was 'essential' but doubted that it could help 'when it becomes a spell, when it is proposed as the last, desperate wager.' Snesarev found this convincing and quoted it in his diary, but he probably did not fully share the author's pessimism, because he made a note in the margin of the paper: 'Mood of the bourgeoisie'.[163] It is unlikely the general identified himself with the bourgeoisie.

News reports of Kerensky's rallies enable us to detect adjustment of the minister's image strategy. The generals and members of committees and soviets, vying with each other to demonstrate their hospitality, as well as ordinary members of the minister's audience, all influenced the way different sections of the public perceived his image.

During Kerensky's speech at the Congress of Delegates of the Southwestern Front, one enthusiastic delegate presented his St George's Cross to him. This proved contagious, and at subsequent meetings frontline soldiers often presented their combat awards to Kerensky. Previously, soldiers and sailors had donated their orders and medals to patriotic charities and political parties.[164] In this case, however, these were gifts not to an organization but to the Leader who personified preparation for the offensive. Sometimes the decision was made by entire military units. The soldiers and officers of the Semyonovsky Guards Regiment wrote to Kerensky, whom they addressed as their senior comrade. 'Having cast off the yoke of tsarism and tasted the blessings of freedom, we bow to the ground before the best of the best, the first democratic minister.' 'For the defence of free Russia', the guards donated 454 crosses of St George, 575 St George medals, and chain necklaces, rings, icons and crosses made of precious metals.[165]

It seems unlikely that all the Semyonovsky guardsmen regarded Kerensky as the best of the best, and even less likely that all the officers of that elite regiment were wholehearted supporters of democracy. It would be difficult, however, to argue that over a thousand military awards could have been donated by these veteran soldiers to the minister had he not enjoyed great authority among them. This cannot be written off as a stunt got up by zealous and ambitious committee men. What is certain is that the initiative of the oldest regiment in the Russian army served as an example to other soldiers and sailors, and the donating of awards became part of the ritual of Kerensky's visits.

The sheer scale of donations could not fail to impress. In all, during Kerensky's visit to the front he received donations of some 200,000 rubles to support 'champions of freedom' and for other purposes. A journalist reported that, in the minister's railway carriage, there were piles of crosses of St George and gold items donated to him by various individuals.[166] These donations could be seen as proof that Kerensky's propaganda was succeeding: the heroes of the Great War, by donating their military awards to the minister of war, also contributed to his authority.

Shortly after, the Leader of the army was offered a new mark of recognition from front-line soldiers. On 13 May, after Kerensky had visited the 3rd Caucasian Army Corps and been welcomed with egregious hospitality, a meeting of knights of the Order of St George in that illustrious grouping decided not merely to donate but to award him a St George's Cross, 'as an outstanding hero who has accomplished great deeds in the battle for the freedom of the Russian land, and as our Leader who . . . has fired the hearts of the fighting men of the 3rd Caucasian Corps with his ardent words and instilled in them a passionate urge to rush as one at the enemy to save the honour and glory of Russia and reinforce the freedom we have gained.'[167]

A special delegation was sent to present the Order. Battle-hardened veterans publicly acknowledged that the 'minister of the forces of the revolution' was a hero who had earned the award. Kerensky, however, evidently decided that it would be tactless to accept a decoration awarded for outstanding bravery in combat, and that might well have been the verdict of public opinion. It would have been difficult not to recall the parallel award of the St George's Cross to Nicholas II in 1915. A substantial number of socialists considered the entire award system an anachronism and a relic of the old regime. Several soldiers were nevertheless indignant about Kerensky's refusal. One colonel wrote from Revel, 'You must accept this decision, and reverently accept and wear the cross you have been awarded.'[168]

The knights of the Order of St George of the 3rd Caucasian Corps, the soldiers who gave Kerensky their awards and the colonel who demanded that the minister should accept the order all considered him a hero. Kerensky had been called a hero previously, but a hero of the revolution. On 17 March, for example, Zinaida Gippius, Dmitry Merezhkovsky and Dmitry Filosofov sent him a letter in which they called him 'the true hero of the people's uprising'.[169] In other messages the revolutionary minister was called 'the hero of Russia', 'a selfless champion, hero and citizen', 'the people's hero' and 'a valorous historic hero'. At the beginning of May the Committee of the 2nd Army had expressed its confidence that 'the army will do its utmost and will not flinch in the bitter struggle under the leadership of the people's hero.'[170] These accolades were based on Kerensky's reputation as a champion of freedom, a 'hero of the revolution' whose exploits were feats of self-sacrificing struggle against the old regime. In the second half of May, however, Kerensky was being proclaimed a hero also of the army, inspiring regiments to battle a foreign enemy. This reputation was endorsed by the authority of famous commanders and heroes of the most prestigious regiments. Now his image was being presented not only as the ideal model for free citizens but also as an example for future officers. In Odessa the minister was greeted by students of the cadet corps. He kissed them, and they, in accordance with an already established tradition, carried him shoulder-high to his motor car. The director of the corps issued an order on the occasion of this visit by 'the genius of Russian freedom, the beloved Leader of the people, great patriot and honest citizen'.[171]

If Kerensky was already being called a genius and Leader, his visit to the front made it possible to slot these epithets into the system of patriotic military education: the 'people's Leader', transfiguring the armed forces, became the focus around which all the country's citizens would unite. The eloquent instruction he was given by the Odessa colonel was not unique. The All-Russia Congress of Representatives of Cadet Corps welcomed the 'Leader of the army of the revolution' and expressed its profound gratitude 'for his heroic endeavours in reviving the free, mighty army of the revolution.'[172] It is just possible that military pedagogues were keen to gain Kerensky's support as the system of cadet corps was reformed. There was no shortage of critics of their 'old-regime' approach to bringing on the officers of the future. Those at all events were the expressions they chose to use in lobbying for their corporate interests.

The representation of the democratic minister was militarized and the images of the 'romantic of the revolution' made more heroic. After Kerensky's tour of the front they were perceived differently and took on a different meaning for his public. The dangers to which he had exposed himself with the army in the field gave new meaning to the Romantic style of the enthusiast of the revolution.

The atmosphere surrounding meetings with the Leader was an important element of how they were perceived. The military commanders, deputies of the Soviets, and members of committees brought initiative and ingenuity to their efforts to make a visit by Kerensky an important and memorable event. Celebratory salvoes and 'democratic lunches', ships decked with bunting, and fly-pasts by planes added to the excitement and gave the press something to write about. The minister himself was expert at attracting press attention. In Sevastopol he laid flowers at the grave of Lieutenant Schmidt (or, according to other sources, laid on the tombstone the St George's Cross which had been presented to him). Every visit to a town turned into another 'festival of revolution'. Kerensky's visit to Odessa was a particular highlight. The atmosphere of tumultuous enthusiasm is described in the diary of Yelena Lakier, a young woman studying at the Conservatory. Already in March she is clearly a fan of the minister. 'I absolutely adore Kerensky, the Leader of our revolution. What energy and ardour, what sincerity! Dear, wonderful Kerensky!' Small wonder then that she describes the day she sees her idol as 'one of the best and happiest' of her life. She has set eyes on 'the hope of all Russia'! She was not the only person eagerly waiting for him. 'Something indescribable was happening.' 'Everyone was in a kind of religious ecstasy and the crowd went wild. They were furiously yelling "Hurrah!"'

When the minister's car appeared, the crowd rushed towards it, breaking through the soldiers' cordon. In the crush Yelena almost fainted, but this did not lessen her enthusiasm: 'Everyone was so excited. How people love him, how they worship him! Many stood weeping tears of joy and affection.' Her idol fully lived up to the expectations of his young fan: 'I will never forget the expression on his energetic face: concerned and sorrowful and yet at the same time infinitely kind. And what an enchanting smile he has! And how much good he had to do in order to earn such universal adoration. Nobody can say anything bad about him, not even his enemies, not even the Leninists.'[173] It seemed everybody in Odessa, indeed in Russia, shared her adoration of the Leader.

> All the newspapers are full only of him and his visit and sing his praises rapturously. . . . Kerensky said at one of the rallies that he had not been welcomed anywhere as he had in Odessa. I can quite believe it! People in Odessa are expansive and emotional. Many kissed his hands, and even his feet, and touched his clothing . . . Our defenders were particularly moved, grey, bearded soldiers who stood there, overcome by emotion and wiping away tears with their callused fists. It was a really touching sight. God grant that his health remains good and that the homeland he loves so well should at last find at least a degree of calm. What an amazing, well-deserved respect he enjoys! He really has won the hearts of the Russian people. I read in a newspaper that portraits of Kerensky can be seen in the homes of every peasant family, where he is revered like a saint, and they even pray to him. It has got to the point where his portrait crowds out even that of Archpriest John of Kronshtadt, who is so revered by the common people.[174]

The atmosphere in Odessa apparently really was different from that in other cities, even though there, too, Kerensky was warmly welcomed. There was something special about his speech in the Odessa Opera House, a mood of optimism which harked back to the speeches he had delivered in March.

In assessing the impact of Kerensky's propaganda visits we need to bear in mind the divergent interests of players in the political process. The established reputation of the minister of war focused attention on his speeches and set the emotional climate in which they were perceived. Some contemporaries genuinely considered the trips a success, while others saw them as the last hope for Russia and spoke positively about their effect only because they felt it was the right thing to do. Finally, many pessimists did not believe in the spirit that was supposedly being awakened but felt it would be wrong to voice criticism of Kerensky publicly. It all contributed to euphoria and high expectations.

The 'battle for Kerensky' also warmed up. Diverse political forces not only defended the minister from attacks by the Bolsheviks and other opponents but used him as an authority when arguing with their rivals. An example is the ongoing controversy between *Rech'* and *Delo naroda*, the main newspapers of the Constitutional Democrats and Socialist Revolutionaries respectively.[175] Selective quotation of Kerensky with accompanying commentary to prove their points further indicates his authority. Such reverential quotation placed him above party differences and confirmed his status as a non-party Leader who acted as an arbitrator and had organized a broad coalition.

Kerensky was subsequently to agree with generals and officers who said the impact of his speeches was transitory. 'Of course, the change in mood after my visits was generally short-lived, but, in the units in which the commanders, commissars and military committee members were able to grasp the psychological importance of what I told them, morale was strengthened and the men regained faith in their officers.'[176]

The support of the military committees did legitimate the orders of commanders, and some officers and generals used that approach. Sometimes, though, even coordinated joint action by the commissars, commanders and committees was not enough to impose discipline. Nevertheless, the minister's trips were not fruitless: they led to a strengthening of influence of the military committees and of supporters of the offensive within the committees. Authoritative Bolsheviks within the army were forced to retreat. Ensign Nikolai Krylenko, chairman of the 11th Army's committee, publicly stated that he would himself obey the order to attack but would make no attempt to persuade the soldiers of the need for the offensive. He found himself obliged to resign as chairman, and some other Bolsheviks also left committees. At army congresses the mere mention of Kerensky's name met with applause. His influence was felt most strongly at the level of fronts and armies, while in divisional and regimental committees the position was sometimes less clearcut.[177]

Indirect evidence that the visits to the front were not without effect is the consternation Kerensky's popularity caused among left-wing politicians. Not only the Bolsheviks but also Menshevik and Socialist Revolutionary internationalists who opposed the impending offensive believed the minister's popularity in the army could resuscitate counter-revolutionary tendencies. Some began to see him as a possible dictator, while others saw him as a tool of opponents of the revolution. This too led to the emergence of new images of the Leader: in May his name was increasingly mentioned in the context of discussions about 'Bonapartism'.

5 'Wanted: a Napoleon': Kerensky and Bonapartism

Kerensky has often been described as a false Napoleon with pretensions to the role of commander of the army and head of state, only lacking the essential qualifications. Soviet artists and writers were later to recycle this image. A caricature by Dmitry Moore (1920) became widespread and was later reproduced in *The History of the Civil War*.[178] Vladimir Mayakovsky offered various satirical images of Kerensky. In the poem 'Good!' (1927) he directly likened him to Napoleon.

> Forgetting his class and his party,
> he's off to deliver a speech,
> his glittery eyes Bonaparty
> and practised the stuff that he'll preach.[179]

Sergey Eisenstein, in his film *October* (1927), depicted the head of the Provisional Government as a self-satisfied, boastful would-be Napoleon. The conflict between Kornilov and Kerensky was represented by two statuettes of Bonaparte facing each other, an analogy of the Kornilov Affair, which contemporaries experienced as a confrontation between two candidates for the role of Napoleon. In the film script there is a scene where Kerensky, 'wearing a bathrobe and with his invariable ironic smirk, signs a decree titled "Restoration of the Death Penalty". He adds the final full stop and rises proudly to his feet, considering "Everyone is shit, and I am Bonaparte." The effect is comical.'[180]

The image of Kerensky as a false Bonaparte is not exclusive to the Soviet politics of memory: we also find it in the memoirs of émigrés. 'He is no Napoleon, but certainly fancies himself as one,' wrote General Pyotr Krasnov.[181] Another general, Boris Gerua, recalled his meeting with the minister on the eve of the June Offensive: 'Where had I seen that exact face? Unhealthy pallor, gingery brush-cut hair, no beard or moustache, large wart? That expression in the eyes and mouth: enigmatic, redolent of vanity and weakness, envy and vengefulness, falsity and coldness? In short, where had I seen such a remarkably repellent mask? It suddenly came to me: Grishka Otrepiev! That was exactly the face looking at us now. No, this was no Bonaparte!'[182] That mask of a great commander and resolute statesman concealed a traitor to the nation. We can only assume that before the meeting Gerua had been expecting Kerensky to be a real Bonaparte.

We should not entirely trust memoirists, especially if they are reconstructing their impressions from times long past, but images of Napoleon, of a would-be Napoleon, and even of the False Dmitry were often used during the revolution. 'What that bastard Kerensky has reduced our Russia to! He fancied himself as Napoleon, but his dreams have not come true,' wrote a soldier from the front line in autumn 1917.[183] We find comparison of Kerensky to Napoleon even earlier. The atmosphere in May 1917 saw the image of a 'Russian Napoleon' emerging, and discussion of Bonapartism was rife.[184]

After the fall of the monarchy, educated people in Russia were bound to turn to France at the end of the eighteenth century as they tried to understand the complex new world around them.[185] Many also looked back to the Time of Troubles, which traditional Russian monarchist patriotism would have encouraged. For some of the socialists the parallel was with the revolution of 1848 and the Paris Commune. They used Marx's writings to describe what was happening in the Russian Revolution. These were analogies commonly used by Lenin, who talked of Louis Blanc and Lamartine, Cavaignac and Napoleon III. (In discussions of Bonapartism there was frequent reference to 'le petit Napoléon'.) Most often, however, those living through the Russian Revolution looked back to the French Revolution. Various forces were described as Girondists or Jacobins, while the role of a Marat or a Danton was ascribed to Russian politicians. Some awaited with hope, and others with horror, the coming Thermidor and the appearance of a Bonapartist 'grave-digger of the revolution'. Many were hoping that a general would come and put an end to the 'troubles'. 'The paths of revolution are the same until a Napoleon or a Gallifet appears,' General Snesarev noted in his diary as early as March.[186]

Ambitious young officers studied the biography of the French emperor, aspects of whom were thought to be detected in various contemporaries. During political crises the search for a Napoleon escalated. A contributor to the Constitutional Democrats' *Rech'* saw the future dynamic saviour of Russia as a supporter of Milyukov who would have stood firm against the 'Leninists' during the April Crisis. The author of the note confessed he often imagined this person.

> I tried to picture him. I looked for his face among people passing by in the street. I tried to divine his name in the long list of hitherto unknown names that turn up every day in the newspapers. . . .
>
> He must, I suppose, be fairly waspish, confident about what he is doing, outrageously self-absorbed (but able to hide it). His thinking will be completely unemotional, sober, free of illusions, and as sharp and flexible as a rapier.
>
> Words such as 'fatherland', 'freedom', 'the proletariat', 'equality', 'democratic forces', 'socialism' and 'universal happiness' will cut no ice with him. He will find other people's enthusiasm in the name of an ideal merely puzzling, but precisely for that reason he will know how to use other people's enthusiasm to his own ends. He will be prepared to exploit any words and all current ideas to his own advantage. . . .
>
> On 21 April, immediately after the first gunfire on Nevsky, I thought for a moment I had seen him.
>
> The agitated crowd was roaring like the sea, and suddenly there, like a swimmer on the crest of a wave, on the shoulders of a group of soldiers, I spotted an officer in a leather jacket with three stripes on his sleeve signifying three wounds. Over his shoulder was a rifle he had just confiscated from a Red Guard.
>
> He was not tall, but agile and graceful. A dark, bronzed face like that of an Italian. His shining black eyes had a keen, intent gaze.
>
> His profile was that of . . . well, yes, of course, only a spectre-like similarity – but he did remind me of the young Napoleon. General

> Bonaparte on the eve of his first Italian campaign, before he had put on weight, grown heavy and fat, and instead looked like this man . . .[187]

The article was among the first of many devoted to a new breed of men who wore leather jackets, and discourses on Bonapartes who would exploit any convenient ideology became commonplace. The text could be read as a dire warning: if the self-willed discipline of free citizens did not stand in opposition to the rebellious slaves, a dictator would come to establish iron discipline. That was something the newspaper had written about the previous day. The 'Napoleon' article in *Rech'* could, however, equally be read as a call to establish a military dictatorship, which the author clearly considered inevitable. 'Sooner or later he will come.' These articles drew the attention of other newspapers.[188] Soon Kerensky was being checked out for the role of Napoleon.[189]

At various stages of the revolution different images were used to characterize the popular minister. The memory of the heroes of the Time of Troubles was disinterred: in the spring Kerensky was being called the new Minin or, less commonly, Pozharsky. The Diocesan Congress in Simferopol addressed Kerensky as follows: 'The ideological Leader of toiling Russia and commander of the people's army and navy. Send out the call, Minin of the land of Russia . . .'[190]

Kerensky was regularly compared to such figures in the history of the world as Brutus, Gracchus, Joan of Arc and Garibaldi. One orator from America called him 'the Russian George Washington'. In late June, British newspapers wrote that Kerensky combined the fiery energy of Léon Gambetta with the organizational talent of the great Lazare Carnot, and the Russian press passed on these characterizations to its readers.[191] Kerensky was compared to other French revolutionaries, and he himself took his cue from images of that era. 'Kerensky undoubtedly felt like a hero of 1793,' recalled Nikolai Sukhanov. In the minister of war's speeches his contemporaries detected echoes of the era of the French revolutionary wars.[192]

We can find references to the events of the late eighteenth century in Kerensky's speeches and orders. Sometimes he spoke openly about the legacy of revolutions. 'We are destined to repeat, a hundred years later, the magical story of the Great French Revolution about building a new world on wonderful impulses and enthusiasm,' Kerensky told his audience in Odessa. He had weighed his words, and a day later, speaking now in Sevastopol, he again declared, 'The magical story of the French Revolution lives again!'[193] By May socialists were commenting that 'bourgeois' newspapers were using the minister's rhetoric in support of their own political programme. A journalist writing in the internationalist *Novaya zhizn'* commented about the conservative *Novoye vremya*, 'they are co-opting Citizen Kerensky, who in his speeches often resorts to the style of the heroes of the French revolution of 1789.'[194]

The minister's promises to punish the servants of the old regime were in the mould of Marat, the 'friend of the people', but Kerensky had contrasted himself with Marat, and this further analogy he rejected outright.[195] His rejection of the role of the Marat of the Russian Revolution cheered some contemporaries but caused consternation among the leaders of the Socialist Revolutionary Party, of which Kerensky was supposed to be a member.

> Is it really possible to become a steadfast 'friend of the people' just by wanting it? You may reject Marat's methods of fighting, but it is impossible to set ablaze your whole being with the fire of his hatred just because you want to. One can hate that much only if one can love that much, and where the heart has once and for all retained in memory the people's agony on the cross and will not forget what the source of its sufferings is.[196]

That is what the Socialist Revolutionaries were writing after the Kornilov Affair in August.[197] In September things were being said publicly which in March had been said only behind the scenes, in private in Socialist Revolutionary circles. Condemning Marat was hardly going to be acceptable to members of a party which glorified revolutionary terror and romanticized the Jacobin tradition.

Kerensky did not complain when he was compared to Danton. The Belgian socialist Emile Vandervelde wrote, 'Will Kerensky be the Danton of the Russian Revolution? Will he get the upper hand over reckless elements destroying order and discipline in the army?' Not everyone, however, considered this comparison was doing Kerensky any favours. Semyon Vengerov, a well-known literary critic, wrote, 'It always makes me angry when people call Kerensky the Russian Danton. He is Kerensky, and for immortality that is quite enough.'[198]

Increasingly, the minister of war was compared to Napoleon, which caused controversy. Once again it was provoked by *Rech'*, which quoted the letter of a front-line soldier published in the newspaper of supporters of Georgiy Plekhanov. The author, describing fraternization at the front, asked, 'Is this really not going to be stopped? Can we really not do without a Napoleon? Are we really going to be satisfied with just talking about iron discipline?'[199] This could be read as covert criticism of Kerensky, urging him to move from words to deeds in order to forestall the coming of a military dictatorship. It could, however, also be interpreted as a call to take a leaf out of Napoleon's book, and that is how Lenin chose to interpret it in order to use the article to mount an attack on his political opponents: 'Is it not obvious that this sentence is inciting Kerensky or the "appropriate" generals to take the role of Napoleon upon themselves? The role of the stifler of freedom? The organizer of firing squads against the workers?'[200]

Lenin's article in turn provoked protest from the Socialist Revolutionaries, who defended their party comrade: 'It is not difficult to guess why *Pravda* is trying to attribute the role of Napoleon even to A. F. Kerensky.'[201] The accusation struck the Socialist Revolutionaries as so absurd as not to merit refutation, and yet comparison of the minister of war to Bonaparte recurred again and again, for a number of reasons.

Kerensky's trips to the front prompted speculation about the possibility of a military dictatorship. The minister's opponents wrote about the 'triumphal procession' of a power-hungry conqueror, which his supporters did their best to negate.[202]

Some generals did Kerensky no favours by making speeches which merely showed up their political ineptitude. On 7 May, General Alexeyev declared at the opening of the officers' congress, 'Russia is dying. It stands on the brink of the disaster. . . . The enemy has occupied one-eighth of its territory, and he cannot be bribed with some utopian phrase about "a peace without annexations and idemnities". He bluntly replies, "With both annexations and idemnities".'[203] For no obvious reason, the supreme commander-in-chief threw down the gauntlet to both the moderate socialists and a government which had just officially repudiated annexations and idemnities. (There were not a few people with liberal and conservative views who broadly agreed with the disingenuous general, but most politicians considered this an inappropriate moment to be voicing criticism of the government.) To make matters worse, Kerensky's propaganda campaign to prepare the ground for the offensive was premised on the idea of a 'democratic peace'. Alexeyev succeeded only in making things more difficult for the minister of war.

No small part in promoting the image of a Bonapartian Kerensky was played by Leon Trotsky. The influential Moscow business newspaper *Utro Rossii* [Morning of Russia] pointed out that it was none other than Trotsky who was creating an 'aura of Bonapartism' around the minister.[204] On 13 May, at a meeting of the Petrograd Soviet, Trotsky declared that the socialist ministers were being kept away from exercising real power. 'In reality, the only person in charge now is Kerensky personally.' Moreover, the minister of war was acting without accountability, failing to inform the Soviet about his plans. Trotsky recalled Kerensky's speech in Helsingfors. 'He does not turn up and does not send anyone to explain even the speech he made in Finland.' The actions of the minister, who was good at making speeches, were establishing conditions for political rallying cries by the generals. 'In the meantime, Commander-in-Chief Alexeyev is organizing counter-revolutionary congresses and insulting the entire Provisional Government.' Trotsky declared that Kerensky was the 'the mathematical focus of Russian Bonapartism'. 'I see the Russian bourgeoisie and press bestowing a halo on Kerensky, and I will not be mistaken if I say that the property-owners are making him the mathematical focus of Russian Bonapartism.'[205]

Trotsky subsequently returned to this representation of Kerensky. In September, he stated at the Democratic Conference, 'Competing parties create a regime where the person in charge becomes the mathematical focus for Russian Bonapartism. Accordingly, responsibility for the regime cannot fall on the ill-will of a single individual. In the historical period of an interregnum, there arises a need to find an arbitrator, a dictator, a Bonaparte. That is why, before Kerensky occupied the place he now occupies, the weakness of Russian democratic forces created the vacancy for Kerensky to fill.'[206]

Trotsky used the widespread negative connotations of the image of Napoleon Bonaparte (the dictator, the 'grave-digger of the revolution') but denied Kerensky Napoleon's romantic aura: he was not a man of iron will creating history but the personification of a political function, a parody of Bonaparte. In this judgement we detect the arrogance of a Marxist armed with the laws for understanding history, looking down from a great height on politicians who do not understand the correlation of forces pushing them to the forefront of the political struggle. In Trotsky's assessment of Kerensky we detect also a belittling of the stature of the strongman of the Provisional Government: the minister is denied the qualities of genuine leadership. In August, Trotsky described the Kerensky government as 'a nursery class of Bonapartism', and in September he wrote an article titled 'The Bonapartlets'. Not bothering to disguise his disdain, Trotsky declared he found Napoleon preferable to Kerensky.[207]

Trotsky's speech on 13 May went down well with some of the Soviet's deputies. They were resentful that Kerensky was ignoring them and outraged by Alexeyev's speech to which Kerensky seemed not to have reacted. The moderate socialists opposed Trotsky, although even their speeches contained demands for a change of supreme commander-in-chief. Tsereteli acknowledged the danger of Bonapartism but put full responsibility for that on the Bolsheviks and other socialists who were challenging the government. The deputies gave their approval to the actions of the socialist ministers, with only a small group voting against the resolution. Some of the Bolsheviks had walked out of the meeting.[208] The deputies, however, were expressing support for Irakliy Tsereteli, Matvey Skobelev and Victor Chernov, ministers who had given them reports, rather than for the absent Kerensky.

Kerensky's supporters denied he had dictatorial leanings and claimed he was a greater man than the French emperor.[209] A supportive journalist wrote in July,

> Someone imagines they see elements of Napoleon in his personality.
>
> What an insult to this self-sacrificing tribune of freedom! The smug Corsican who used liberty as a stepping stone for his personal aggrandizement, this dumpy, cold little book-keeper of the coup, who calculated how to make things work out in his favour – and Kerensky! Napoleon appeared once on the Bridge of Arcole. It was a test for the future emperor which he passed brilliantly, but then never again did he take such a risk. Kerensky has been standing throughout his political life on the Bridge of Arcole, and if any such Napoleon fell

> into his hands he would most certainly lock up the dazzling predator in a dungeon of the Peter and Paul Fortress.
>
> Yes, the Kerenskys lay down their lives for freedom and do not shove it under their saddle. They are its standard-bearers, not its executioners.
>
> Kerensky is a tribune, not a condottiere leading a gang of mercenaries.
>
> Let those who imagine they see elements of Napoleon in him hang their heads in shame.[210]

The conservative newspapers, however, were effectively confirming the accusations against Kerensky of the left. A correspondent wrote in *Novoye vremya*:

> I have no idea whether Citizen Kerensky resembles Napoleon or, more to the point, whether he has ambitions to imitate the career of the great Corsican. Probably not: he is, after all, a socialist, and that says it all. But if he or someone else were to duplicate a part of Bonaparte's programme, namely, defeating the Germans and Austrians and forcing them to bow at the feet of his fatherland, the fatherland would be grateful to him. If subsequently, or at the same time, he could crush the lawless anarchy within the country, the fatherland would be doubly grateful to him.[211]

Given this situation, the newspaper, which was internationalist in its outlook, called on Kerensky to put a stop to efforts to push him towards playing the part of a Napoleon 'We are confident that the lascivious howling of bourgeois sirens represents no danger to A. F. Kerensky, but he unquestionably needs to take note of them and draw the necessary conclusions before it is too late.'[212]

In left-wing propaganda there were many variations on the Bonaparte theme. Lenin and Trotsky did not directly call Kerensky a Napoleon, merely commented that his actions were paving the way for 'Bonapartism'. Some activists, however, did directly compare him to the grave-digger of the revolution. The minister's supporters believed the Bolshevik press was having an effect on the soldiers and sailors in Finland. The newspaper *Golos soldata* [the Soldier's Voice] noted that, 'Thanks to the efforts of *Pravda* and the Helsingfors *Volna*, the poisonous slander has already been sown among the soldiers that Kerensky and the "Declaration of Deprivation of Rights" are bourgeois and Bonapartist.'[213]

At the same time, other contemporaries saw the likening of Kerensky to Napoleon as proof of his greatness. The accusations of Bonapartism served to confirm his reputation as a strong politician. Supporters of Kerensky bemoaned the fact that his 'enemies are aided, completely unawares, by his most rapturous admirers, this whole mass of common people as far as the eye can see who have not yet been reborn as citizens and who are desperately looking for stability, floundering without a "firm hand", without the town mayor and the local policeman.'[214]

Among Kerensky's 'rapturous admirers' was Marina Tsvetaeva, who wrote a poem about him on 21 May.

Someone is holding a winning card,
Not sleeping in his sleep.
A hint of Bonaparte
Is in my Russia.
For someone, thunder is pealing:
'Come hither, bridegroom!'
A young dictator is flying,
Like a blistering whirlwind.
His eyes above a mischievous smile
Are like a starless night!
There burns on a sunken uniform
A soldier's cross
He summons to calmness the peoples,
The fever is stilled.
He breathes, his hand still calming
The universe's brow.[215]

For Tsvetaeva, the French emperor is a great figure in history, towering above the uncountable ranks of inexpressive mediocrities. The hopes she pinned on the Russian Bonaparte, as which she saw Kerensky, reconciled her to the revolution. Tsvetaeva saw the Leader, decorated with a military order (which Kerensky had in fact declined), as a victorious dictator. She saw him as a symbolic Napoleon, made manifest by the introduction into the Prague Restaurant in Moscow of a bust of the minister of war. 'I remember a bust of Bonaparte during the war years, which the February Revolution replaced with Kerensky.'[216] Other contemporaries who compared Kerensky with Napoleon also expressed hopes that a leader would emerge, a saviour of the fatherland who would create a new state. Some of Kerensky's supporters turned to the cult of Bonapartism in the European romantic tradition.

It should not be supposed that it was only intellectuals who were hoping Kerensky would fulfil the mission of a Napoleon. At the end of June a front-line soldier wrote in a private letter, 'About Kerensky, what some people are saying is that Kerensky is a bloodthirsty man and another Napoleon. Actually I worship Napoleon; in my opinion he was the biggest genius of all time.'[217] Negative images of Kerensky as a would-be Napoleon were spread in the army but sometimes interpreted in ways favourable to him. Soon, however, people hoping a strong politician would emerge and stop the revolution became disillusioned with Kerensky. In July a military doctor at the front noted approvingly, '*Russkaya volya* is moaning that we have completely run out of people; we have no one, not even a Yuan Shikai like the Chinese. There is no dominant Napoleon, not even a sad, tiny little semblance of one.'[218] No doubt back in May the newspaper's staff, and readers, were still hoping for one.

In the second half of May, Kerensky faced steep challenges. He needed to reinforce his reputation as a strong politician, but that risked being accused of Bonapartism and losing the support of moderate socialists. At the same time he needed the support of the influential 'bourgeois' newspapers which were demanding strong government and an authoritative ruler. Some socialists rejected the idea of an offensive, while the conservative and liberal politicians saw preparations for active combat operations as the minister's main merit. Kerensky needed to remain mindful of these conflicting demands. He wanted to keep all his allies onside while, if possible, even extending his power base.

Meanwhile, in the Petrograd Soviet there was continuing criticism. At a session of the workers' section of the Soviet on 18 May, one deputy declared that the offensive could lead to 'Bonapartism'. Some speakers supported that view, others objected. Another deputy protested that such accusations, with Kerensky absent and unable to give explanations, would be a treacherous stab in the back. This was met with applause and the issue was dropped.[219]

It became clear to Kerensky's supporters that he really did need to speak in the Soviet if he was not to risk the independent deputies turning against him. On 22 May he appeared in the Petrograd Soviet to speak on an item in the agenda designated as 'Explanations from A. F. Kerensky'.[220]

The minister of war argued that the Declaration of Soldiers' Rights had been drafted in consultation with the Soviet and pointed out that his foreign policy statements were in accordance with the Soviet's line. Kerensky addressed the charge that he was usurping power by saying that those attacking him were only paving the way for a real dictatorship. In response to a question about Finland, the minister commented that only the All-Russia Constituent Assembly would have authority to decide the question of independence. To give his speech a resounding conclusion, Kerensky had saved up a sensational announcement. 'I have also been asked what measures I have taken in response to the speech of the supreme commander-in-chief. Which one?' The hall was suddenly listening intently as he continued, 'The previous one was General Alexeyev, but now the commander-in-chief is General Brusilov.' This unanticipated news detonated a great burst of applause. Soldiers leapt from their seats and shouted, 'Thank you! Thank you!' A newspaper correspondent reported, 'These concluding words aroused a degree of enthusiasm not seen since the first days of the revolution.' Kerensky had chosen just the right time and place to make a major government announcement. That same day the order was published of General Gurko's demotion. The news that General Alexeyev, unpopular with the deputies, had been replaced by Brusilov, who was at least outwardly optimistic and made use of revolutionary rhetoric, delighted the deputies and was well received by the leaders of the Mensheviks and Socialist Revolutionaries.

After greetings from a front-line soldier who declared that the soldiers 'worship Kerensky', it was the turn of the minister's opponents – the anarchist Iosif Bleikhman, internationalist Anatoly Lunacharsky and Bolshevik Lev Kamenev – to address the deputies. Bleikhman, whose speech was several times indignantly interrupted, linked the minister's actions to the danger of Bonapartism. 'The French revolution was destroyed not by an external enemy but by an internal enemy, Napoleon I. It is a Declaration not of Rights but of Deprivation of Rights that Kerensky has given the soldiers.' Criticism of the minister by the other speakers was less robust. Lunacharsky spoke of his respect for Kerensky and acknowledged the purity of his intentions. He added that criticism of him was cooperation of a sort. Kamenev expressed the hope that Kerensky would adjust his actions by heeding criticism from the left, spoke of his confidence in the minister and wished him success. The absence of any harsh attacks on Kerensky may have been a result not only of the relative moderation of Lunacharsky and Kamenev but also of the positive mood of the assembly. Even some Bolsheviks applauded the minister that day.

In a letter to his wife, Lunacharsky described Kerensky's speech in withering terms.

> Kerensky appears, young and slim, in khaki and high boots. An ovation. He speaks in short, hoarse sentences, sincerely, often skilfully, for the most part with a noble vacuousness. About us, his critics, he expresses that opinion that we fight him behind his back, with gossip, 'like cowards'! . . .
>
> . . . Kerensky concludes and has gone down well. . . .
>
> Poor man! Histrionic and hysterical, not a sincere democrat, he will probably come to grief over his half-hearted position. For the bourgeoisie he and his still immense popularity are a screen and their last line of defence. He is the last weapon of the imperialists.[221]

Lunacharsky does, nevertheless, concede that Kerensky won that skirmish. He was helped by speeches by soldiers: a delegate of the Semyonovsky Guards Regiment presented the minister with medals, which were poured out on to the table of the presidium, and Kerensky kissed front-line soldiers. Medals were also handed over to the minister by a representative of the reserve battalion of the same regiment, adding that four marching companies of the Semyonovsky were ready to go to the front. This announcement caused a new burst of applause. Kerensky was then greeted by a delegate from one of the divisions: more applause and cries of 'Long live Kerensky!' The minister of war evidently felt the necessary effect had been achieved and declared, 'Long live the Russian Revolution and the revolutionary army! Long live the impending brotherhood of the peoples!' This brought more applause, and Kerensky left the meeting. The Soviet gave him a standing ovation as he departed.

The minister's speech was skilfully engineered. The arrival in the

Tauride Palace at just the right moment of delegations with donations of medals will hardly have been coincidental, and news of the dismissal of Alexeyev produced the desired effect. That evening Kerensky departed for the Northern Front. The square in front of the station was crowded with people, and a guard of honour from the Semyonovsky Regiment was lined up for him on the platform, complete with band. The choice of regiment was probably not random either.

Kerensky had responded to the deputies' criticism and the Soviet had been persuaded. Its support was essential if measures were to be taken which were unpopular with the soldiers but necessary for preparing the offensive, such as disbanding regiments which were refusing to obey orders and the cancellation of leave.

Nevertheless, that was not the end of criticism of Kerensky from the left. He had had to respond, mentioning the 'Napoleonic' issue, which indicates it was a concern. The minister's supporters also sought to neutralize this unwelcome historical analogy. An ensign wrote in the newspaper of the right-wing Socialist Revolutionaries, 'Do not forget that at the head of the ministry of war we now have A. F. Kerensky, the only man who may be Russia's Garibaldi, but will never be Russia's Napoleon.' By a happy coincidence the same issue contained the text of Kerensky's speech to the Congress of the Socialist Revolutionaries, in which he again rebuffed accusations of Bonapartism.

At the same time, the minister himself contributed to creating and consolidating his reputation as a candidate for the role of Napoleon. This was not all because of his speeches and orders, but also on account of some aspects of his self-presentation. In many photographs he is caught in a Napoleonic pose, with his left hand behind his back and his right tucked inside his jacket. This was the Kerensky pose cartoonists and satirists such as Moore, Eisenstein and Mayakovsky pounced on. In part there was a simple medical explanation for it: Kerensky's right hand was painful because of the wear and tear caused by vast numbers of handshakes. For a time he wore his arm in a sling, and that is how he is depicted in some photographs.[222] Evidently, however, the dynamic politician did not want to make such a public demonstration of his human frailty and instead adopted the Napoleonic pose. Pavel Milyukov wrote, 'Hundreds of thousands of soldiers and citizens saw the slim figure of a young man in a crumpled jacket, without decorations or insignia of rank, with a sore arm bent at the elbow and tucked in his jacket.'[223]

We cannot, however, dismiss the Napoleonic pose as a result solely of Kerensky's ailment. He deliberately adopted the pose for the photographers, and the position of his arm was provocative. Why did Kerensky, who in his public speeches was denying any intention of becoming Russia's Napoleon, continue to provoke accusations with his Napoleonic pose?

We often find him described in memoirs and historical works as a vain actor who loved being popular in the moment. That offers a simple answer to the question. Did he just want to look good? If we examine more closely Kerensky's goals at that time, however, and the configuration of the political forces he had to take into account, we may prefer a different explanation.

Kerensky is rarely described as 'Napoleonic' in the letters and diaries of the time. It would seem that his educated contemporaries simply did not see him as a potential Russian Bonaparte. We have found no positive references to Napoleon or Bonaparte in the contemporary resolutions. Liberals and conservatives were unlikely, any more than those drafting petitions, resolutions or collective letters, to call openly for Kerensky to follow in the footsteps of the 'great Corsican'. Curiously, though, nor is that imagery used with negative connotations in the resolutions the Bolsheviks and left-wing socialists were getting adopted. In May and June they evidently did not find the topic likely to help with political mobilization.

Liberal and conservative newspapers, however, were demanding that the minister of war should adopt tough policies (which was interpreted as urging him in the direction of Bonapartism), and for many people there was nothing alarming about the idea. They were hoping he would prevent the revolution from developing any further, and that first and foremost he would reimpose discipline in the army. Even some veterans of the revolutionary movement saw little cause for alarm at the prospect of a Russian Napoleon. Nikolai Chaikovsky wrote, 'Russia is living through a moment when Bonapartes are born, and the Russian people should consider themselves infinitely blessed that a great man has emerged from their midst in whose hands even the role of Bonaparte represents no danger.'[224] That pronouncement appeared in a newspaper particularly given to lionizing Kerensky.

The arguments of the Bolsheviks and left-wing socialists, on the one hand, and of the conservatives and liberals, on the other, in fact gave impetus to the idea that Kerensky might/should become a Bonaparte. The moderate socialists tried to counter the alarmism of the left even as they denounced their opponents on the right for trying to push Kerensky into taking on this mantle. The leaders of the Mensheviks and Socialist Revolutionaries were demanding that this popular politician should state definitively that such a role was one he found unacceptable. In the discussion about Napoleons, the 'struggle for Kerensky' was showing itself to be a tussle between the members of an unstable coalition which supported an offensive. The moderate socialists, the liberals and the conservatives were proffering roles and images to the minister of war which were in accordance with their own interests.

In preparing for the offensive, the minister of war was seeking to create, consolidate and expand a political coalition to support active combat operations. The coalition included moderate socialists, as well as liberals and conservatives, but Kerensky was being required to meet self-contradictory public expectations. Given the situation, his tactics over how he presented himself had major political significance: he needed to be seen as a Napoleon even as he denounced Bonapartism. In his speeches he rejected the political role of Napoleon, while at the same time he struck the Napoleonic pose of a strong leader. This constant rejection of the image of Bonaparte, combined with repeated 'quotation' from it in Kerensky's words and deeds and in the actions of his supporters and opponents, played an important part in the emergence of the image.

6 The Bolshoy Theatre and the birth of the New Man

Nikolai Berdyaev recalls the attitude of Andrey Bely to the revolutionary Leader as follows: 'In the summer of 1917 he was a passionate admirer of A. F. Kerensky, almost in love with him, and communicated his feelings for him in our living room by a succession of dances. Later he was no less infatuated with Bolshevism and saw in it the birth of a new consciousness and the New Man.' We may suppose that, before his infatuation with Bolshevism, Bely associated the appearance of the New Man with the actions of Kerensky. In her notes to this passage in Berdyaev's memoirs, his sister-in-law Yevgenia Rapp offers this information.

> One time I was alone at home. The bell rang. Outside the door of our drawing room stood Andrey Bely. Without a word of greeting, his voice trembling, he asked, 'Do you know where I've just been?' Without waiting for an answer, he continued, 'I saw him, Kerensky . . . he was speaking . . . the crowd a thousand strong . . . he was speaking . . .' In a state of ecstasy Bely raised up his hands. 'And I saw', he went on, 'a ray of light fall on him, I saw the birth of the New Man . . . This is a Man.' N. A. [Berdyaev] had come into the room and, at these last words, burst out laughing. Bely cast a lightning-quick glance at him and, without saying goodbye, fled from the room. It was a long time before he came back to see us again.[225]

Bely's rapturous reaction was engraved in the memory of the participants in this scene. Berdyaev recalled it as having been on a summer's day, but most probably what Bely had witnessed was Kerensky's famous speech at the Bolshoy Theatre on 26 May, already mentioned.

Bely's attitude to Kerensky and his speech is registered in other sources. In a pamphlet he wrote in June–July 1917 we read, 'Even before the revolution, before the war, still far off the revolution nods audibly, wordlessly. And when Minister Kerensky says "We are going to be romantics," we poets and artists answer him: "We – are, we – are."'[226] The pamphlet explicitly states that Bely is quoting Kerensky's speech in the Bolshoy Theatre.

To understand better this obscure reference, we need to look at a preceding part of the text, also fairly obscure, which refers back to Bely's work interpreting Friedrich Nietzsche.

> The transitory image of a broken form is a symbol: the world of those arts which are given to us is not the world of art, of the art of creating life; he is still a symbol which, according to Nietzsche, merely nods wordlessly; the world of the arts which spoke to us once has long been silent and nods wordlessly; what has spoken is the distant rumbling of a word as yet imperceptible, of which the first letter is war, and the second a rising . . . from the dead.[227]

Bely described the revolution and the revolutionary minister in terms of his interpretation of Nietzsche. We learn this from several sources: the New Man (when describing the early works of Nietzsche, Bely did not write about the Superman but used this term), 'Ecce homo' in the memoirs of Berdyaev and Rapp, also 'nods wordlessly' in Bely's own article.[228] Several contemporaries, attempting to describe and interpret the phenomenon of Kerensky, turned to Nietzsche's writings, sometimes referring to him explicitly. Thus one article about the minister ends, 'People who know no better end in life than to perish, lavishing their great soul on something magnificent and impossible (Nietzsche), people who can shine only by burning up – such people are immortal.'[229] This was written some two weeks after Kerensky's speech in the Bolshoy, and perhaps made that writer, too, quote Nietzsche.

The idea of holding a grand concert rally in the Bolshoy Theatre came from Sergey Kusevitsky, an outstanding musician and conductor. The main star was to be Kerensky. The Moscow Union of Actor-Soldiers undertook to organize the event, which was given the rousing title of 'Songs and Speeches of Freedom'. Proceeds from the rally were to be donated to further cultural and educational work among the troops of the Moscow Military District. Kusevitsky got the leaders of the Moscow Soviet of Soldiers' Deputies to approach the minister and persuade him to speak. Kerensky replied that he could not be present on the proposed date but promised to come on 25–26 May. The organizers promptly changed the date: it was the participation of Kerensky that was going to make it special. Kusevitsky immediately set about making the preparations and in an incredibly short time assembled an orchestra of 200 musicians.[230]

On the morning of 26 May, Kerensky arrived in Moscow on a special train. The station square was filled with a crowd of several thousands, and the minister was welcomed on the platform with a huge guard of honour: every military college and regiment of the garrison had sent a squad. Kerensky was greeted by representatives of various organizations. The presidium of the Soviet of Soldiers' Deputies, in their capacity as the hosts, turned up in full force. A representative of the Soviet addressed the 'Leader of the Russian army': 'You are a mighty organizing power. Your words, like an electric current, strike every heart inspiring enthusiasm and faith in the victory of the revolution.' After an exchange of speeches and repeated playing of *The Marseillaise*, Kerensky took his place in a motor car covered with garlands of lily of the valley and red roses. The vehicle dispayed a poster reading 'Citizen Soldier', the name of the newspaper of the Soviet of Soldiers' Deputies, and a wording in accord with the spirit of the minister's policies.

A cadet from the Moscow College of Ensigns presented his combat medals to Kerensky, who kissed him. Then the car, buried under flowers, headed to the former residence of the governor-general, where the Moscow Soviets now sat. Crowds greeted the minister, threw flowers at his car, and ran after it so as not to miss Kerensky's speeches. He greeted the citizens and was answered with a roar of 'Hurrah!' and 'Long live Kerensky!' A correspondent describes the minister's progress through Moscow.

> This is a spectacle. This small, frail person, raised above the crowds and in command of the masses, personifying 'the powers that be', by the force of his ardent words alone. There is something classical in all this, something closely resembling not only the times of the revolution in France but also the age of Pericles, the first citizen, the 'spiritual dictator' of Hellas, or the days when the people of Rome allowed their beloved tribunes to speak to their hearts.[231]

The minister's triumphal entry was not marred by the fact that, owing to a yardsweepers' strike, the streets of Moscow were not looking their best. At a crossroads Kerensky's car was close to the strikers, who were demanding the abolition of night duty and an increase in their wages. Their slogans were a discord, given the tenor of Kerensky's speeches calling on those in the rear to make sacrifices and aid the army in the field. There could have been a scuffle between irate members of the rally welcoming the Leader of the army and the striking yardkeepers, but the minister managed to prevent trouble.[232]

Kerensky gave a speech to the deputies of the Soviet and from the balcony addressed a huge crowd, which greeted him with a rousing ovation. The minister then went on to the City Duma, where there were speeches by him and the city councillors. There followed a conversation with the prosecutor of the Moscow Court of Justice, an inspection of the staff of the Kremlin Armoury, a visit to the university and another to the headquarters of the military district. Again the crowds welcomed Kerensky and demanded speeches. It was five in the afternoon before the minister finally arrived at the Bolshoy Theatre.

There the audience, many of whom had come specifically to see him, was anxiously discussing why he had not appeared. The auditorium was packed; representatives of the Allied powers sat in one box while foreign officers were sitting in two others. Almost the entire stage was occupied by the extremely large orchestra.

It was impossible to postpone the performance, and the chairman of the Soviet of Soldiers' Deputies formally opened the concert. Kusevitsky ascended the conductor's podium. The orchestra played *The Marseillaise* three times. Next was the overture from Rossini's opera *William Tell.*

Konstantin Balmont read his poems and gave a speech, the choir sang Alexander Grechaninov's anthem *Long Live Russia, a Country Liberated*, repeating it three times. The choir then sang *The Song of the Volga Boatmen*, twice (in Alexander Glazunov's adaptation), and then Henry Litolff's Robespierre Overture was played.

Leonid Sobinov, a famous singer, appeared on stage in his capacity as the first elected representative of the Bolshoy Theatre. He called for support of the Provisional Government and wished good health and long life to the socialist ministers.

Abram Gots, a prominent figure in the Socialist Revolutionary Party, brought greetings from the Petrograd Soviet, but had a reproach for the members of the Moscow business community seated in the boxes and stalls. He declared there was a threat, because the response on the part of 'certain commercial and industrial circles' to the government's invitation to purchase Freedom Bonds had not been up to expectations. The country's financial situation had become even more difficult.

Victor Chernov, the leader of the Socialist Revolutionaries who had just become minister of agriculture, tried to lighten the atmosphere. The imposing 'minister for the peasantry' had a reputation as an excellent speaker. He stepped out on to the stage with a large red rose in the buttonhole of his frock coat and spoke energetically about successes in organizing the peasantry. His speech was eclipsed, however, by the arrival of the principal: at five in the afternoon Kerensky finally came on stage. He was welcomed with applause and flowers, and the orchestra obliged with a fanfare.

The journalists report that Kerensky spoke with great élan, his speech constantly interrupted by applause. He tried to keep his audience animated: 'A great enthusiasm has engulfed us, for we sense that Russian freedom will now never die.' He addressed the topic raised earlier by Gots. Just back from the army in the field, Kerensky spoke of the debt owed by the rear to the front and about the patriotic duty of the monied classes to actively support the troops.

> You live here, you come to these halls flooded with light, you sparkle with diamonds, while at the front people are eaten alive by insects, nobody knows what the next morning or evening will bring, what awaits them in the next hour . . . And think carefully: do you suppose that out there in the trenches the soldiers do not know how much jollity, warm fires and bright lights draw in great numbers of people out for a good time?

He called upon his listeners to make sacrifices. 'Let those who are rich give up their riches to their motherland.' Bringing his speech to a climax, the minister exclaimed, 'Let people laugh at us! We shall remain romantics and dream great dreams!' Another reporter recorded the words a little differently: 'Let the sceptics think what they will: we shall always remain romantics and dream great dreams!'[233] It was this part of the speech that Andrey Bely quoted.

Red roses showered down on Kerensky, who bowed at great length as the theatre applauded thunderously. Ecstatic ladies in the audience, responding to his call, flung their jewellery on to the stage. The British diplomat Bruce Lockhart later recalled:

> As he finished his peroration, he sank back exhausted into the arms of his aide-de-camp. In the limelight his face had the pallor of death. Soldiers assisted him off the stage, while in a frenzy of hysteria the whole audience rose and cheered itself hoarse. The man with one kidney – the man who had only six weeks to live – would save Russia yet. A millionaire's wife threw her pearl necklace on to the scene. Every woman present followed her example, and a hail of jewellery descended from every tier of the huge house. In the box next to me General Wogak, a man who had served the Tsar all his life and who hated the revolution as the pest, wept like a child. It was an epic performance – more impressive in its emotional reactions than any speech of Hitler or of any orator I have ever heard. The speech had lasted for two hours. Its effect on Moscow and on the rest of Russia lasted exactly two days.[234]

Kerensky and Chernov soon left the theatre. That day the minister of war managed to fit in several more speeches: to the soldiers' section of the Regional Congress of Workers' and Soldiers' Deputies and at the food congress, and towards the end of the day he hastened to the Congress of the Socialist Revolutionary Party. Kerensky's speeches to yet more audiences in Moscow continued on 27 May.

Let us return to the grand concert rally. After the ministers had left, the Bolshoy Theatre was noticeably emptier. To conclude the performance, two portraits of Kerensky, which he had found time to autograph, were auctioned. One went for 5,000 rubles, the other for 16,000.[235]

The organizers of the concert were well pleased. Ensign N. Lavrov, a representative of the Soviet of Soldiers' Deputies, wrote in an open letter of thanks to 'Citizen Kusevitsky': 'The people, Moscow saw their Leader, thousands of people heard Kerensky's titanic call to work, a great sense of festivity filled thousands of hearts, a festival which Moscow experienced, which the whole theatre and people experienced on 26 May. Word and sound joined in their strength and beauty on this day, an ideal fusion of human beauty was witnessed in the theatre, and lit a great fire in the soul and mind of everyone.'[236] Lavrov found particular significance in the solemn manifestation of the Leader to the people and judged the concert rally not only politically but also aesthetically: the merging of the music of the great orchestra with the speeches of famous orators, above all the speech of Kerensky himself, had the effect of demonstrating 'the fusion of human beauty'.

The notion of a gifted Leader able to combine politics and art is also found in Bely's pamphlet. He considered the synthesis an urgent task: 'the joining of the revolutionary and the artist in the ardent enthusiasm of both, in the romance of the attitude of both towards the events taking place.'[237] Bely approvingly quoted Kerensky and spoke warmly of the 'romantic' political style of a revolutionary minister who united the politician and the artist in a single being. In this way of perceiving the Leader of the revolution, Bely was by no means alone. It corresponded to a panaesthetic perception of reality which had developed in Russian culture of the Silver Age, largely under the influence of Nietzsche's ideas.

In the spring of 1917 the notion of a revolutionary Leader embodying a synthesis of politics and art appealed to many people. In this respect, Andrey Bely, Sergey Kusevitsky and Ensign Lavrov were no exception. Many of Kerensky's supporters expected that he would achieve this union of art and life. His speech in the Bolshoy Theatre was the high point of the evolution of his image as a politician-cum-artist, something so much desired in the initial stage of the revolution.

No doubt it was Kerensky's performance at the Bolshoy that set the tone for how leading cultural figures responded to the minister. We have already mentioned, while considering the theatricality of his technique, the reaction of professional actors and of Vasiliy Nemirovich-Danchenko to the Bolshoy speech. Characterizing the minister's speeches, the writer Alexander Kuprin called him 'the heart of the people': 'In every era and in every nation in their days of tribulation there has been that unfathomable and unmediated spiritual receiver of radio waves, that divinely appointed resonator, that oracle expressing the will of the people which I call the living, beating heart of the nation. Kerensky is guided by his heart, the heart of the people, its collective will.'[238] A charismatic leader, the saviour of a nation in its days of tribulation, exactly expressing the will of his fellow citizens in vivid, emotional speeches, is able to fulfil his vocation because of a special gift, because he is a divine resonator, without need of elections, referendums and plebiscites. It is unlikely that anyone who supported a democratic form of government, even if they supported Kerensky, could have regarded Kuprin as expressing their views. But their idol for many of the minister's admirers was an artistic and conquering Leader and saviour, arousing enthusiasm and bringing hope to those who had faith in him. There were other contemporaries who interpreted Kerensky's Moscow visit along similar lines.

> Suffering often engenders love, and the love of our suffering people was displayed yesterday in all its elemental power. Passionate, crazy, frenzied howls of ecstasy and veneration, rapturous ovations, young eyes fanatically ablaze; arms stretched out towards a car adorned, carpeted with flowers; and every eye riveted to that pale, almost boyish, face, wordlessly expressing so much . . . Comrade Kerensky? No, for the crowd yesterday this was no comrade, this was a god, an

idol, a sacrosanct fetish sent down by heaven for the redemption of Russia.[239]

The reaction to Kerensky's speech sends us back to the electric, emotional atmosphere of those days in March, the rapture that Russia had been raised from the dead, and the love for the people's Leader. Journalists wrote about the atmosphere of love that reigned in the streets of Moscow on 26 and 27 May 1917, and there are words of love in the speeches addressed to the minister. The provincial press, for such it was, approvingly quoted the writer Teffi when she declared that 'The Russian Revolution has fallen in love with Kerensky.' The minister was described by his supporters as a 'tireless conqueror' personifying at once faith, hope and charity.[240] The New Man of the revolutionary era was born in an atmosphere of requited love between the Leader and the people.

And yet we should not conclude that the reaction to Kerensky's speech in the Bolshoy Theatre was no more than a repeat of the paschal atmosphere of the March Days. The birth of the New Man is something Bely saw only in May. The success of the grand gala rally cannot be put down only to Kusevitsky's skill in the selection of music and the quality of the speakers. The reaction to Kerensky's performance cannot be explained without reference to his trips to the front and his triumphal progress through the streets of Moscow. At a time when the Bolsheviks and left-wing socialists were condemning Kerensky's supposed Bonapartism in preparing for an offensive, thousands of Muscovites enthusiastically welcomed a minister of war who inspired them with hope in the face of a growing economic, social and political crisis. That public support was important to him. It was the aura of the tireless conqueror and hero, risking his life to inspire grim-faced front-line soldiers, that aura combined with his already established image of an artist-politician, which created a new image of the Leader, the New Man, and aroused such enthusiasm.

Not all contemporaries, however, were so beguiled. The Moscow newspaper *Utro Rossii*, which expressed the views of business circles, described the mood in the street as follows: 'The car drives on, garlanded with flowers . . . "Hurr-rah! Thank you! We will all give our lives . . .!" the crowd roars. Then the crowd cools down a bit, does not quite complete the sentence, and runs off home to its hovels and its entrance gates.' 'God forbid that these raptures do not prove mere soap bubbles . . . In the crowd so passionately expressing its desire to die for Kerensky are faces which, in mid-March, were burning with an ardent desire to die for Guchkov. The same exclamations: "Lead! We will die for you! Thank you!" '[241] The newspaper was registering the mood of people who, no longer believing in the significance of words, were now demanding action. The reaction is similar, we will recall, to Lockhart's assessment of the impact of Kerensky's speech. If some saw his trip to the front line as a major symbolic act confirming his status as a strong politician, others now wanted to see effective action.

These sentiments were behind some of the criticism of the minister's political style.

This contrasting of fine words with actual deeds was particularly evident in the critical speeches of Kerensky's left-wing opponents. Thus *Pravda* in June 1917 was writing about 'theatrical' speeches.[242] 'Theatricality', it was implied, was something unworthy of a serious politician. Let us recall that, even before the April Crisis, the Bolshevik newspaper printed a sarcastic remark about Kerensky's 'spectacularly theatrical phrase-mongering and theatrical poses'.[243] At that time it was in a letter from a reader, but by May similar comments were being penned by writers expressing editorial opinion. The Bolsheviks intensified their criticism of the minister of war in connection with the publication of the Declaration of Soldiers' Rights, preparations for the offensive, and the disbandment of certain unruly regiments at the front. They ironically compared the propaganda trips of the 'people's minister' to the noisy operatic touring of some fashionable prima donna dear to the heart of stockbrokers. They used the same language to describe his visit to Moscow. Here is how a writer for the Moscow edition of *Sotsial-demokrat* portrayed the visit, which other newspapers were describing as a triumph: 'An enormous car, all trimmed with red roses. In it Kerensky reclines on soft cushions, drowning in an ocean of flowers. What is this? The arrival of a ballet dancer or the business trip of a minister?' The imagery the Bolsheviks came up with was sometimes replicated in newspapers of the Russian nationalists, who were supposed to be at daggers drawn with the 'Leninists' but seemed to quote them suspiciously often.[244] Even such caricatures convey a sense of the triumphal atmosphere and adoration which greeted the speeches of the tribune of the people.

Later Kerensky's histrionics and this feminization of his image were to be used in propaganda attacks on him, but even some of his supporters and allies, while endorsing his policies, cringed at his romantic and theatrical political style. According to Nikolai Valentinov, Georgiy Plekhanov commented, 'His gender is not male but, rather, female. His speech is what you might expect of some Sarah Bernhardt from Tsarevokokshaisk.'[245] Comparing the minister to a famous French actress, who by then was seventy-two, combines several negatives: Kerensky is being likened to an effeminate provincial actor living on past glory. It is worth noting that Plekhanov, who was politically very close to Kerensky, was here all but quoting the Bolshevik newspapers. We find similar assessments in the private correspondence of left-wingers. 'He spoke like Sarah Bernhardt, posturing and modulating his voice. Finally, after an hour of melodramatic speechifying, he barely managed to drag himself to a couch in the next room and collapsed in a swoon. Politically, his speech was dull and vacuous,' Lunacharsky wrote on 6 June.[246]

The theorists of several national and political movements of the early twentieth century believed their efforts would lead to the birth of a New Man. Some ideologies supposed he would be born as the result of social processes, others that the New Man was the prerequisite for social transformation. Sometimes both projects were considered much the same thing and synchronous. In this context, the Russian Revolution was not unusual, except that here the model New Man was not an outstanding action man but a Leader generated by the revolution.

The idea of the emergence of a Superman different from 'great people' of the past, a Superman defying the old morality and endowed with the Will to Power, was popular in Russian society at the beginning of the twentieth century. Numerous translators and interpreters, popularizers and epigones of Nietzsche went a long way towards ensuring that the words and images he had found took on new life on Russian soil. Nietzscheanism was assimilated and replicated by representatives of a variety of artistic and philosophical trends – Narodniks, Marxists and Symbolists. Andrey Bely was not the only person to view the revolution 'through the prism of Nietzsche'.[247]

Early twentieth-century culture proclaimed the ideal of complete individual self-expression. It was permeated by anticipation of the appearance of the New Man, whose life would truly be a masterpiece, and whose exceptionalness would be confirmed by the emotional acclaim of his followers. This was precisely the context in which the cult of Mussolini arose, the New Man, Man with a Capital Letter, as his supporters called him.[248] The same words could be used to describe the climate in which the cult of Kerensky arose: the Leader's image embodied the expectations of the Silver Age. Nietzschean words and images reflected an important dynamic in the mood of the age of revolution: a significant section of society was looking for a saviour-leader, a conqueror combining the qualities of military leader and creative politician, an artist-politician corresponding to the aspirations of the Silver Age. The theatricality of Kerensky quietly receded into the background and made way for his image as a military leader, the 'Leader of the revolutionary army', but this only heightened the impact of his theatrical speeches, compelling people to perceive them as something integral to the revolution.

In any case, some people were beginning to get tired of and annoyed by Kerensky's overly theatrical style of politics, and in May their sentiments began to be reflected in the newspapers. These sentiments were seized on and exploited by the minister of war's political opponents as they criticized his transformation of the army and preparations for the offensive. In the changing circumstances, the widespread image of the artist-politician began to take on negative connotations. Criticism of Kerensky intensified even in the ranks of the Socialist Revolutionary Party to which the minister of war belonged. Shortly after his speech in the Bolshoy Theatre, Kerensky was beginning to feel this.

7 Kerensky and the Socialist Revolutionary Party

On 10 March 1947, under the impact of a new volume of memoirs by Vasiliy Maklakov, Kerensky wrote to this prominent member of the Constitutional Democratic Party:

> In any case, one certainly does not have to belong to the conservative-liberal monarchist wing to see now, and indeed then, that after the Manifesto of 17 October and during the period of the First Duma the Cadets played a fateful role (as did the Socialist Revolutionaries in the February period. I wrote about the parallel in my review of your first book, but Rudnev excised it, to keep the party's vestments snowy white in the eyes of outsiders).[249] The so-called Leaders of both parties destroyed the power essential for them to work fruitfully for Russia, not because they did not love Russia, not because they were overly ambitious, but because they saw reality only through books or doctrine and lacked the faculty of 'direct vision' – i.e., of political intuition – and that is something without which you cannot be a politician, just as you cannot be a violinist if you do not have an ear for music but have only knowledge of the theory of how to play the violin. One formulated policies in accordance with book learning and/or historical precedent, another on the basis of the party's programme, dating from when it was still underground, completely blind to the fact that neither books nor the programme were applicable in the reality surrounding them. But in neither party did they have any rivals in the central party apparatus to challenge their power. You and I had one failing in common, despite all the differences in what we believed about the balance of power in Russia: we neglected the existing party apparatus and did not create one of our own. That is why your entirely correct intuitions remained examples of inconsequential intra-party criticism, and the fatal blow to my own work after February was dealt not by Lenin, or by Milyukov and Kornilov, but from within: by the Central Committee of the Socialist Revolutionary Party.[250]

Kerensky considered himself and Maklakov to have been hostages, if not, indeed, victims of the dogmatic, unrealistic, bookish policies of Pavel Milyukov and Victor Chernov, the overambitious leaders of the respective parties to which they belonged. In writing not intended for the eyes of others, Kerensky judged the situation more harshly than in any of the versions of his published memoirs: he named the leaders of the Socialist Revolutionary Party, and in particular Chernov, as the main culprits for his own political defeat. By describing his opponents as dogmatists capable only of following bookish theory, Kerensky was seeking to persuade his readers that he himself had the qualities of a gifted improviser who could make the music of the revolution, and that not having the requisite musical instrument, a political organization, had prevented him from performing successfully.

For their part, prominent Socialist Revolutionary leaders pondered the degree of Kerensky's culpability for the crisis in the ranks of the Socialist Revolutionaries. In testimony given to Soviet NKVD (political police) investigators in 1937, Abram Gots commented:

> The leaders of the Socialist Revolutionary Party always regarded Kerensky as a chance member of the party, not organically integrated with its main nucleus of leaders – to some extent, a fellow traveller who did not participate in the party's illegal work in the pre-revolutionary period. For broad swathes of the population, Kerensky and the Socialist Revolutionary Party were a single, indivisible whole. In the eyes of the nation, Kerensky was the party. That cost the party a heavy price in the first months of the February Revolution, when Kerensky's extraordinary popularity attracted into the party huge numbers of sympathizers from the intelligentsia, the petty bourgeoisie and the cooperative movement. These socially alien elements rapidly diluted the main party cadres forged during the years of struggle with the tsarist government and moved the party to the right. The party suffered even more, however, when Kerensky's popularity went into a steep decline, especially after the June Offensive, and the working class and the peasant part of the army transferred their disillusionment with Kerensky to the Socialist Revolutionary Party in general. At the same time, because of Kerensky's participation in the government from the very first days of the revolution, the party had no period when it was in open opposition to the government, and for any political party a period of opposition is a time for building up forces and shaping and organizing them, a time of political consolidation and building ideological solidarity.[251]

It would be absurd to overlook the dramatic situation in which this testimony was produced.[252] It seems safe to assume that, during his interrogation by the NKVD, Gots deliberately exaggerated the differences between the party's tried and trusted leaders and the minister who had been so popular in 1917, but from whom twenty years later it was only politic to distance himself as much as possible. It is telling, however, that both in Kerensky's very frank letter and in Gots's testimony the conflict between Kerensky and the leaders of the party is considered a factor of the greatest political importance. They are also close in their assessment of the bonds of party loyalty, if from different directions. The head of the Provisional Government admits that he was entirely willing to sacrifice 'party dogma', while Gots indicates that the most popular leader of the February Revolution remained an outsider as far as the leaders of the Socialist Revolutionaries were concerned.

No doubt the opinions of both Kerensky and Gots were influenced by the hugely important fact that, in the revolution and the Civil War, the Bolsheviks were victorious and the Socialist Revolutionaries defeated. Nevertheless, tensions between the party elite and Kerensky became apparent in May 1917 and soon ceased to be any secret from the public. At the Third Congress of the Socialist Revolutionaries, held in Moscow from 25 May to 4 June, Kerensky failed to obtain sufficient votes to be elected to the Central Committee. The result of the vote caused a political sensation: the popular minister who for many people was the best-known leader of the Socialist Revolutionaries did not have the backing of the party's elite.

In March few would have foreseen the possibility of such a development. Many Socialist Revolutionary organizations and newspapers sent enthusiastic greetings to the minister of justice and called on their members to support him. In *Delo naroda*, the main newspaper of the Socialist Revolutionary Party, which first appeared on 15 March, no fewer than twenty resolutions adopted in March and April in support of Kerensky were published. *Zemlya i volya*, the newspaper of the Socialist Revolutionaries' Petrograd Regional Party Committee, first appeared on 21 March. It took a similar line and published such resolutions even more frequently. No other leader of the revolution was receiving comparable attention from newspaper editors at this time. Kerensky's only rival was Yekaterina Breshko-Breshkovskaya, the legendary 'grandmother of the Russian Revolution' and living symbol of the party. Large numbers of Socialist Revolutionary supporters sent her greetings.

The resolution of the 2 March conference of the Petrograd Socialist Revolutionaries was printed in the very first issues of *Delo naroda* and *Zemlya i volya*.[253] This document expressed great approval of Kerensky's actions during the revolution and of his joining the Provisional Government. The regional party committee was similarly appreciative.[254] Prominent Socialist Revolutionaries who were in Petrograd at the time of the revolution publicly endorsed his action in the belief that it would enable him to keep an eye on the 'bourgeois' ministers. Publication of the resolutions of such authoritative gatherings doubtless influenced party members in other cities. At all events, the same issue of *Delo naroda* printed resolutions by other party groups, conferences and committees greeting Kerensky and endorsing the decisions of the Petrograd organizations.[255]

Even before these publications, leading Socialist Revolutionaries were expressing support for Kerensky. Not later than 5 March a group of political exiles sent him a telegram (with a copy addressed also to Nikolai Chkheidze, chairman of the Executive Committee of the Petrograd Soviet): 'We congratulate you, comrades, as spokesmen for the interests of all of toiling Russia. We believe your participation in the government will safeguard the interests of labour.' The first signatory was Osip Minor, who later became editor of the Moscow newspaper of the Socialist Revolutionaries and chairman of the Moscow City Duma. Another group of exiles congratulated the new minister of justice and urged him to take firm action. Among the signatories was Naum Bykhovsky, who was elected shortly afterwards to the party's Central Committee. A group of Socialist Revolutionaries in exile in Yakutsk greeted the minister as 'a representative of the labouring masses of the Russian population in the Provisional Government'. No later than 5 March, congratulations to the 'first champion of the revolution to become a minister' were received from the Saratov Committee of Socialist Revolutionaries.[256]

The almost simultaneous appearance of such sentiments in different parts of the country, before the publication of what might have been seen as examples of appropriate greetings in party newspapers, shows something close to political unanimity among party activists in their attitude to Kerensky and his joining the Provisional Government.

Similar resolutions continued to be published in the Socialist Revolutionary press for some time.[257] There was a variety of reasons given for supporting Kerensky's entry into the government, which in some cases was welcomed very enthusiastically. A meeting of party members in Tiflis saw the deed as 'an act of great wisdom'.[258] Sometimes support for the government was even conditional upon Kerensky's remaining in it: 'We accept the Provisional Revolutionary Government only as long as it includes a representative of the democratic forces and does not deviate from the programme worked out jointly with the Soviet of Workers' and Soldiers' Deputies,' read the resolution of a rally of workers from the Izhorsky Factory and of soldiers, published in the Socialist Revolutionary *Zemlya i volya*.[259]

In the collective letters and resolutions published in March and April in the pages of the main party newspaper, *Delo naroda*, Kerensky is not as a rule described as a leader. He is depicted as a 'defender of the interests of the people and its freedom, a guardian of human and citizens' rights', a 'staunch and tireless champion and defender of the interests of all the democratic forces of the revolution', a 'steadfast champion of freedom', the 'socialist minister', the 'citizen minister', the 'only staunch defender of the people's rights in the Provisional Government' and the 'comrade minister'. Similar characterizations appear in the resolutions published in *Zemlya i volya*: 'the representative of the democratic forces', 'a staunch champion of ideals', 'a steadfast and energetic champion of the ideals of working people', 'the representative and spokesman of the interests of the broad working sections of the population'. For those drafting resolutions, Kerensky was the personification of revolutionary ideals. They greeted 'in his person' 'the total triumph of democratic ideals and the establishment in Great Russia of a new system based on justice, freedom, equality and fraternity.'[260]

Such writings confirmed Kerensky's revolutionary reputation and his exceptional position in the government, but he was not regarded as the recognized leader of the Socialist Revolutionaries, and he remained merely a party comrade. In articles in the main party newspapers he was described in a more restrained manner than in the resolutions they published. This pointed to a certain difference between the party elite and local activists in how they felt about the Leader. The rhetoric glorifying the Leader was less in evidence in analytical writing than in the resolutions of party supporters. Even in the articles, however, Kerensky was sometimes hailed enthusiastically. For example, we find him described as a 'concentration of the live currents of the revolution'.[261]

As time passed, different socialist revolutionary newspapers began to adopt different attitudes towards Kerensky. This reflected conflicts between groupings within the party. *Delo naroda* tried to convey the opinion of the entire party, publishing items reflecting different political persuasions, although the editorial staff mostly favoured the centrists (albeit significant differences arose among them too). *Zemlya i volya*, the mouthpiece of the Petrograd Regional Committee, increasingly expressed opinion on the left of the party, although it continued printing resolutions supporting Kerensky.[262] This reflected the situation in the Socialist Revolutionaries' Petrograd organization, where the left and centre-left were stronger, as was evident in the resolutions of the Second Petrograd Regional Conference in early April. The conference voted that it was not permissible for party members to join the Provisional Government. This anti-Kerensky resolution was drafted by Nikolai Rusanov.[263] Simultaneously, Abram Gots, the conference chairman, sent greetings on behalf of the conference to the minister of justice, describing him as 'our comrade, and a steadfast, tireless champion and defender of the interests of all the democratic forces of the revolution'.[264] This prominent Socialist Revolutionary, who was subsequently to be highly critical of Kerensky, publicly affirmed his revolutionary reputation despite the negative attitude of this party forum towards the government.

This move by Gots was not able to prevent new clashes. The conference's decisions provoked protest from the right wing of the party.[265] Alexander Gukovsky and Pitirim Sorokin resigned from the editorial board of *Delo naroda*, and on 29 April the 'right-wing' Socialist Revolutionaries in Petrograd began publishing *Volya naroda* [the Will of the People], a newspaper which strongly supported Kerensky. The likelihood is that it was financed by people close to the minister.[266] *Volya naroda* supposedly did not represent any party organization and described itself as 'a literary-political daily newspaper edited by members of the Socialist Revolutionary Party'. In reality it was the main newspaper of the 'Right' Socialist Revolutionaries. The newspaper's staff included experienced journalists and renowned veterans of the revolutionary movement, which instantly enhanced its standing, and the first name among the editors was that of Breshko-Breshkovskaya.[267]

If the Right Socialist Revolutionaries had supported Russia's war effort even before the revolution, the Left SRs and many centrists were against the war.[268] After the February Days, some opponents of the war became 'revolutionary defencists', but there were differences of opinion even there, and there was frequent squabbling within the faction. Left SRs opposed cooperation with 'bourgeois' political bodies, while Right SRs welcomed the establishment of the coalition. Over time the Left SRs significantly increased their hold on some of the party's organizations, but neither the left nor the right were seeking at this time to split the party. The leaders, representing various nuances of centrist opinion, sought to preserve unity and to maintain room for diverse opinions within the party, performing a balancing act between the factions and elaborating compromise solutions. Supporters of *Volya naroda* were less adept than the Left SRs at mobilizing 'the masses', but there were many venerable long-standing party members in the ranks of the Right, and this was an important political asset. Many young party members liked to style themselves the 'grandsons' of Breshko-Breshkovskaya and supported Kerensky. The diversity of opinion within the party also began to show itself in judgements about Kerensky's actions, and these found their way into the main party newspapers. The Socialist Revolutionaries grouped around *Volya naroda* were closest to Kerensky, and their opponents even called the newspaper *Volya Kerenskogo*, 'the Will of Kerensky'.

In late April, criticism of Kerensky appeared in *Delo naroda* for the first time. Many of the party's leaders were unhappy that the minister of justice, along with other members of the Provisional Government, had approved the 'Milyukov Note', which precipitated the April Crisis. Even so, they were in no hurry to criticize Kerensky publicly. The first critical message was Rusanov's article, already mentioned, about Kerensky's speech on the subject of rebellious slaves. The article was reflecting dissatisfaction with Kerensky among some of the party's leaders, which was also evident in the fact that *Delo naroda* published his speech with cuts. *Zemlya i volya* even ignored this important speech completely. Other party members took quite a different approach. In *Volya naroda*, as we have mentioned, the speech was used to propagandize the image of Kerensky as a tribune of the people without fear or favour. Already splits were appearing among the Socialist Revolutionaries in respect of Kerensky and his speeches.

Rusanov's article set off a 'battle for Kerensky' between the Cadets' *Rech'* and the Socialist Revolutionary centrists. The Constitutional Democrats' newspaper, which favoured putting rebellious slaves in their place, reported that attitudes to Kerensky's speech delineated the main battle line in current politics. They took it upon themselves to defend Kerensky against members of his own party, the Left SRs and others to the left of centre in the party. The journalists of *Rech'* were seeking thereby to strengthen the position of the Right SRs, who on many issues were close to the Cadets. Unsurprisingly, *Delo naroda* and *Zemlya i volya* took issue with what was being written in *Rech'*, whereupon the newspaper responded that *Rech'* was 'being used as a whipping boy by Socialist Revolutionaries who are in fact at odds with A. F. Kerensky.' The line of *Volya naroda* was contrasted with that of the principal Socialist Revolutionary newspapers and was awarded the Constitutional Democrats's seal of approval.[269] The

Cadets returned to the issue after the end of the government crisis.[270] They were keen to recall the differences between the leaders of the party with the greatest popular support and the best-known minister. It is a fair bet that the battle for Kerensky between the Socialist Revolutionary leaders, the Right SRs and prominent Constitutional Democrats served only to boost his popularity. Everyone wanted Kerensky on their side. Kerensky himself, however, was in no hurry to define his position too precisely, being more interested in retaining the broadest possible support base.

A number of factors were influential in determining the attitude of different groupings of Socialist Revolutionaries towards Kerensky. The aim of instilling a 'discipline of duty' among the troops, together with preparations for the offensive, exacerbated differences among the Socialist Revolutionaries and affected attitudes towards the minister of war. Kerensky's popularity was an important political asset which the Socialist Revolutionaries did their best to exploit, for example, during local government elections. Often people voted for 'Kerensky's party', delivering electoral success for the SRs.

Ultimately the policy of the Socialist Revolutionaries was influenced by the return to Russia in April of Victor Chernov, the party's foremost theorist. Chernov's position can best be described as centre-left, and his warning to party activists in early May was widely reported: 'Either the revolutionary movement will eat the war, or the war will eat the revolution.'[271] At the same time, Chernov did his best to prevent splits in the party, which required considerable political manoeuvring.

Chernov joined the Coalition Provisional Government as minister of agriculture. The Socialist Revolutionaries, and many peasants, enthusiastically welcomed the appointment of the 'minister of the peasantry' and anticipated he would embark on a programme of radical agrarian reform. Their expectations proved overoptimistic. Chernov was fettered by agreements between the coalition partners, as well as by objective circumstances. Even the measures he did manage to introduce, compounded by his position on the war, soon made him a favourite butt for criticism in the conservative and liberal press. Eventually the Right SRs and, most notably, *Volya naroda* joined in the criticism of him.

In order to defend Chernov against these attacks, the Socialist Revolutionaries needed to develop a rhetoric for glorifying their leader, and this could not but influence the way they described Kerensky. In some instances, activists now greeted two leaders at once, and sometimes their resolutions were published in the party press. On 5 May the Assembly of Socialist Revolutionaries of the Alexander Nevsky District resolved 'to congratulate our dear party comrades V. M. Chernov and A. F. Kerensky, as well as all other socialists who, in view of the extremely serious situation facing our motherland, have joined the Provisional Revolutionary Government, which, relying on the democratic forces of the working people – the soviets of peasants', workers' and soldiers' deputies – will be a mighty revolutionary force.'[272]

In some cases, Kerensky and Chernov were both referred to in the same resolution as being the leader of the party. A meeting of the Socialist Revolutionaries of Zlatoust sent a telegram to the minister of agriculture informing him that it 'unanimously welcomed' in his person 'the participation of our comrade leaders in the coalition ministry'. There is no doubt that Kerensky was here being included as an additional 'leader', although Chernov was seen as the main representative of the socialist ministers. At the same time, the regional congress of Socialist Revolutionaries in Saratov congratulated the 'comrade citizens Kerensky and Chernov, who, as responsible leaders of their party, have taken upon themselves the exalted duty of saving their motherland in these difficult times of foreign threats and the danger of anarchy at home.'[273] The telegram was addressed to Kerensky, with a copy sent to Chernov, which implied a different hierarchy of leaders. For most party activists, however, the main leader was Chernov. The Bobruisk organizational meeting of Socialist Revolutionaries described him as 'the ideological Leader', and the party organization in Grozny greeted him as its 'ideological Leader and teacher'. A general meeting of the Petropavlovsk party sent 'comradely' greetings to its 'Leader, the pride of our party'.[274]

In several cases Chernov was addressed in the same words as Kerensky had been, and we meet the image of the 'helmsman' mentioned above. The Björneborg Party Committee congratulated the new minister of agriculture with the words, 'Dear Leader, the banner of "Land and Freedom" has been raised on the rudder [*sic*] of the ship of state. We will clear the way with all our might, and with your hands the rudder with the banner of Land and Freedom will steer the ship to its destination.' Chernov was also called the 'venerable, tested champion of the freedom and happiness of working people', 'the first people's minister', 'the tested fighter' and 'the true friend of the people'.[275]

Against that, some words are applied to Chernov which we have not found in addresses to Kerensky: 'ideological Leader', 'spiritual Leader', 'teacher'.[276] His authority as an intellectual leader was an important component in the developing of Chernov's image. The Kutaisi regional conference of Socialist Revolutionaries sent cordial greetings to 'our tried and tested theoretician and Leader'. This was the first resolution of welcome to Chernov which was published in the main party newspaper. In other resolutions of the time he is called 'dear teacher and friend'.[277]

Chernov's coming to the forefront in politics caused the word 'Leader' to occur more frequently among the Socialist Revolutionaries. It also made more noticeable the involvement of the Socialist Revolutionaries in the construction of the Kerensky cult. Some found it possible to include the minister of war on an equal footing among the venerated old luminaries of the party. The Right Socialist Revolutionaries, who opposed Chernov and supported Kerensky, created a cult of the 'Leader of the revolutionary army' in opposition to the building up of the minister of agriculture, whom they viewed as an adversary.

The trend in publication of resolutions in the main newspaper of the Socialist Revolutionary Party suggests that the party's attitude towards Kerensky was becoming an issue. In May, *Delo naroda* published at least nine resolutions lauding Chernov. Over the same period publication of resolutions supporting Kerensky declined. We have found only three such resolutions, even though, in newspapers of the liberals, the right-wing socialists, and even the conservatives, many more were published.

Some of the expressions of support for the minister of war which did find their way into *Delo naroda* would hardly have gladdened the heart of Kerensky. The participants of a general meeting of delegates of the soldiers, officials and officers of 127 Petrograd Freight Unloading Battalion declared that the meeting 'warmly congratulates A. F. Kerensky on his appointment as the new minister of war and expresses its confidence that the appointment of a socialist to a post so important and difficult at the present time will bring closer a solution and end to the war. Long live the unity of the army and the new comrade minister!'[278] That was clearly only conditional support: the troops were welcoming the new minister on the grounds that he would be bringing peace nearer.

Nevertheless, the support of other Socialist Revolutionaries for Kerensky was enthusiastic, and the image of him as Leader of the revolution was further developed. That concept of the skilled helmsman confidently steering the ship of revolution appealed to the SRs in the main base of the Baltic Fleet.[279] One article published in a local party newspaper bore the title 'Support Kerensky!'[280] If some Socialist Revolutionary organizations were hailing Chernov as the great helmsman, others preferred to entrust that mission to the minister of war.

Resolutions and articles of this kind, published in the provincial Socialist Revolutionary press, hardly appeared in *Delo naroda*. An exception was a resolution of soldiers and officers of a reserve motor-pontoon battalion, who declared that, because a socialist and 'sincere defender of the interests of the people' has been appointed minister of war, the troops can now trust all their officers, who are subordinate to the 'beloved Leader of the people'.[281] So it was that the expression 'beloved Leader of the people', indicative of Kerensky's special status, was printed in the main party newspaper – something that was probably not welcomed by all the party's activists. Even this resolution, however, was not expressing full support for continuing the war. Nor was there unanimity in the party in respect of 'iron discipline' in the army or preparations for the offensive. Indeed, not a few Socialist Revolutionaries were committed to opposing these measures, and even more made their support conditional on undertakings which Kerensky and his supporters regarded as unacceptable.

One further circumstance influenced the Socialist Revolutionaries' attitude to Kerensky. His actions could give an ambiguous impression about his attitude towards the party and its leaders. On some occasions he positioned himself as representing the young people in the party whose place was respectfully to await the advice of their more experienced leaders. This was demonstrated in his attitude towards Breshko-Breshkovskaya, whose unwavering support of her 'beloved grandson' was an important political asset. His constant exploitation of her authority was a cause of considerable irritation to some other party leaders. There was no way, however, that they could openly criticize her. The Socialist Revolutionaries were hostages of their own political tradition of glorifying the heroes, prophets and martyrs of the party's past. Criticizing the grandmother of the Russian Revolution, whose authority dated far back in history, would risk undermining the party's influence.

On other occasions, Kerensky presented himself as a veteran of the revolutionary movement who had courageously battled the tsarist regime for decades. We can be fairly sure that party members with considerably longer records of resistance must have viewed his self-certification at best ironically, and more probably very critically. Be that as it may, in some resolutions the youthful minister was presented as a doughty hero, deserving of veneration alongside the most revered figures of the revolutionary past. The organizers of meetings which took place at different times and in different places, quite independently of each other, placed his name next to those of the most renowned figures of the revolutionary movement, and analogous resolutions were printed in the party press. The eminent Socialist Revolutionaries sitting on editorial boards of the party newspapers presumably raised no objection to Kerensky's being awarded such a high symbolic status, although that attitude can hardly have been shared universally.

Sometimes, as we have seen, Kerensky adopted the position of a politician who was above party politics, a Leader of the whole people. In the first months after the February Days, remaining above all the parties conferred considerable political benefits. The citizens of Russia who had just awakened to political involvement believed that the downfall of the monarchy and the 'defeat of the forces of darkness' necessarily meant the end of all internal strife. The metaphor of 'one family' extended to include the entire population. Rivalry between parties was perceived as a sign of self-interest. His non-partisan position helped Kerensky create and re-create a political coalition of moderate socialists and liberals, but it weakened his ties with the Socialist Revolutionary Party, which led to the negative consequences he later wrote about to Maklakov.[282]

This situation affected the mood of delegates to the Third Congress of the Socialist Revolutionary Party, which opened in Moscow on 25 May. Many delegates witnessed Kerensky's triumphal entry into the ancient capital the following day, and some heard the minister's speech at the Bolshoy Theatre. At about eleven o'clock that evening the presiding chairman had already declared the session of the congress closed when cries were heard, 'Comrades, don't leave, Kerensky has arrived.' The popular politician was given the floor and, to loud and prolonged applause, ascended the podium. Kerensky presented himself to this audience as a young member of the party respectful of its veterans.

> As a weary traveller drinks from a life-giving spring, so do I, after my exertions elsewhere, plunge into the comradely environment of like-minded party members and drink here of the tonic of invigorating ideals, energy and enthusiasm. Comrades! When in the darkest years of reaction it was not only impossible to dream of a congress of our party, when our best teachers and comrades were either sentenced to hard labour, or died, or were in emigration, we, the young, fumbling in the darkness, bore as best we could the spark of our party's faith, our party's life. Many condescendingly looked down on us as the last relics of a utopian party about to disappear for good from the face of the earth because of our lack of scientific foundations. But we believed that it was precisely in our foundations that our strength and the seeds of our future victory lay. And now we see the fruits our labours. We have delivered this congress. We submit everything we have done to the only body competent to judge it, this All-Russia Congress. Let our resurgent party, having as of old in its ranks all our teachers and leaders and great champions of the past, and us, their students and rank-and-file workers, pronounce whether what we did in the past was right.[283]

The orator demonstrated his respect for the elders through his choice of language. The most frequently recurring words in the speech are 'we' (used thirty-two times), 'the party' (used sixteen times) and 'I' (used fourteen times). Kerensky admitted in the speech that, acting as a minister, it was difficult for him to conduct himself 'as a clear and unambiguous member of the party' because he had joined the government 'as a representative of all the democratic forces', but he identified with his party comrades. In other speeches to activists at various levels, at congresses and conferences, Kerensky tended to make frequent use of the pronoun 'we' in order to identify with his audience. Addressing less sophisticated listeners, the minister used the pronoun 'I' more often. In a speech to the soldier's section of the Petrograd Soviet, in the course of forty-nine sentences he used 'I' thirty-nine times. The minister's manner of speaking at rallies was thus quite different from the way he addressed congresses.[284]

Nevertheless, the substance of Kerensky's speech at the Socialist Revolutionary Congress was more of a 'rally' speech, and different in tone from the way earlier speeches had been delivered. The impression one has is that this style, which had worked well for Kerensky when he was addressing a less sophisticated and fundamentally receptive audience, was much less well received by elder statesmen who had been building up the party for many years. That day the minister of war had spoken in very diverse forums in Moscow and scored many rhetorical successes. His speech to the Socialist Revolutionaries was not one of them. Nikolai Rusanov recalled the session as follows.

> In general the racket had been terrible, and in the end those attending agreed to refrain from clapping because it was greatly interfering with

due attention being given to the speeches. I just happened to be the chairman on this ill-starred, or, rather, highly comical, day. Before we had managed to vote on the proposal, with crashing and banging the broad doors of the room were flung open wide and Kerensky appeared, trailing clouds of glory, in his quasi-military oufit, accompanied by a whole gaggle of his rapturous supporters. Thunderous applause interrupted the report of a comrade who, clearly failing to understand the historic import of the moment, continued expounding the details of a plan for a new publishing enterprise in the provinces. The clapping continued, despite some angry calls for it to desist. But then everything quietened down and the Leader of the people appeared on the podium. 'Comrades, as a wanderer in the wilderness seeks a spring with fresh water to slake his thirst, so too do I seek the company of my comrades, to tell them what issues are and should be occupying the government at this time, and to harken to wise advice from the lips of the party.' Improbably loud applause interrupted the speaker, and I did not know what to do. The truth of the matter is that I was absolutely furious. Was this really the way grown-up people should behave at a congress??? Containing my indignation, I said as calmly as I could, 'Comrades, we have just voted for a resolution prohibiting, at least temporarily, all applause and other indications of agreement or disagreement which interfere with listening to the speeches. But what are we doing now? I am sure that we are profoundly offending the democratic feelings of our dear comrade Kerensky himself, who of course is aware that he is not some special God-given individual and is pained – as I can feel – by the violation at this moment of our party discipline.'

A roar of indignation from the Kerenskyites interrupted my words, which struck the supporters of our valiant prime minister as the height of disrespectful sarcasm. 'And who might you be? How dare you be so insolent? Have you forgotten that there stands before you on the podium the man who embodies the whole spirit of Russia and all its hopes of victory? We do not need such a chairman, away with you!'

At this, however, almost all the members of the presidium and a substantial proportion of those at the meeting took my side. 'Bravo, Rusanov, we are not idolaters. We respect Kerensky wholeheartedly, but we do not bow down before him.' The gathering was clearly split, with each behaving rather unceremoniously towards the other. I mean, of course, on a verbal level, because it didn't come to fisticuffs. Kerensky and his friends decided at this critical juncture to leave our meeting.[285]

There is no record of this incident in the congress minutes, but Rusanov quotes part of Kerensky's speech fairly accurately and may be giving a truthful account of his own feelings. It is worth remembering that

Rusanov was the first prominent member of the party to criticize the minister publicly in connection with his speech about rebellious slaves. In both instances Rusanov's hostility to Kerensky's political style is palpable, although in his memoirs that attitude is even more pronounced, which may have been due to subsequent events. Nevertheless, the memoirs do convey the atmosphere of adulation surrounding Kerensky and the reaction against his style by some of the Socialist Revolutionary leaders.[286] Rusanov told the congress delegates who loudly welcomed Kerensky, 'Do not create idols!'[287]

The following day Kerensky came to the congress to answer questions.[288] Delegates were curious to hear what he understood by 'revolutionary defencism' and how accurate reports of his speeches were in the 'bourgeois press'. Finally, he was asked directly if he was representing the party in the government. Kerensky responded that his presence at the congress could speak for itself. Although this contradicted his previous statement, it was greeted with applause. Overall the minister said nothing at the congress that he had not already said in speeches to the broader public. This cannot have gone down well with the deputies, the elite of the party, who would have wanted to feel they were involved in national politics. The speech was interrupted by applause, and the verbatim record notes exclamations of 'Bravo!', followed by a standing ovation when Kerensky again rejected accusations of ambitions to become a Bonaparte. It is likely that Kerensky's male and female admirers about whom Rusanov writes were taken more by Kerensky's performance than by the substance of his speech, which contained nothing new and was neither profound in its analysis nor precise in what it said.

In conclusion, Kerensky stated that certain questions were 'technical' and asked to be excused for not answering them. This did not deter all the delegates, because questions were shouted out from the floor. Some of these Kerensky clearly did not want to respond to. One deputy wanted greater clarity on how Kerensky related to the party. Another asked about Kerensky's currently most pressing issue: active military operations. 'Do you consider it possible for us to attack at this time, when our allies have not abandoned their acquisitive tendencies?' The question went unanswered. The transcript records 'applause and noise' when Kerensky left the hall.[289] Attitudes towards his performance left the delegates divided into opposing groups.

On 1 June elections to the party's Central Committee were held. Kerensky, the country's most popular politician, was absent from the meeting and received only 134 votes in favour, with 136 against.[290] The voting was already taking place when a left SR, Pavel Dekonsky, exposed shortly afterwards as an agent of the tsarist secret police, violated the procedure. He spoke against Kerensky's candidacy on the grounds that the minister had just issued an order increasing the severity of punishments for deserters and troops who refused to carry out orders in action. This announcement caused a heated argument, as a result of which the order was read out, but no discussion was allowed. Dekonsky's intervention may well have influenced the outcome of the vote.[291]

The election result left the party leaders facing the problem of how to find an explanation acceptable to different tendencies. The chairman read out several statements in which groups and individuals gave assurances that, in not voting for Kerensky, they had been guided not by political but by practical objections: he was too burdened with work in the government to be able to participate in the everyday concerns of the Central Committee. This was not very convincing, because Chernov, who was also a member of the government, and Breshko-Breshkovskaya, whose physical condition would prevent her from devoting a great deal of time to 'everyday concerns', were elected.

The newspapers reported that the result of the vote came as a complete surprise to most of the delegates. Delegates from the front were worried because their influence in the army was dependent on the authority of the minister of war: the spell of Kerensky's name enhanced the standing of the Socialist Revolutionaries. Individuals who had joined the Socialist Revolutionaries since March quite often signed up to join 'Kerensky's party', and some officers, and even generals, joined the party of the minister of war. Some delegates were concerned that the result of the vote would give support to the Bolsheviks who were criticizing Kerensky. The next day groups of delegates got together to consider how to neutralize the incident. At a closed meeting of the congress the right-wing demanded a new vote, but the left and many in the centre declared that 'the will of the congress' in respect of Kerensky's candidacy had been expressed clearly.[292]

The result of the vote remained unchanged, but the controversy continued even after the end of the congress. The party leaders were keen to put the conflict behind them, but the Right Socialist Revolutionaries would not let it go. Breshko-Breshkovskaya publicly expressed her outrage that the congress had failed to put its trust in 'the most worthy of the worthy citizens of our Russia' and resigned from the Central Committee. In response the Central Committee reiterated its claim after the result was announced: 'It was obvious to the congress participants' that Comrade Kerensky, 'fully occupied by his work' in the government, could not 'dedicate his strength also to the Central Committee of the party'. The Central Committee expressed its 'profound respect' for Grandmother, but considered that her statement was undermining the authority of the congress and the Central Committee.[293]

The attitude towards Kerensky signalled a split in the party on a number of issues, most notably the offensive, and provoked further disagreements. *Volya naroda* continued to support the minister, but *Delo naroda*, the party's main newspaper, vacillated in an attempt to maintain a balance of opinions. In June it published only four resolutions in support of Kerensky. There was, for example, a resolution of a student battalion whose members confirmed their 'unconditional subordination to Minister Kerensky' and expressed their readiness to embark on 'active combat in defence of the Russian Revolution' whenever necessary.[294] The newspaper also published, however, the resolution of a meeting of the 6th Reserve Engineers Battalion condemning a militarist demonstration.[295] Given that those participating in the demonstration had been expressing their admiration of Kerensky, the minister of war's supporters cannot have been best pleased. There is no consistent editorial line evident from the board of *Delo naroda* in relation to Kerensky.

At the same time, many organizations of the Socialist Revolutionary Party continued to avail themselves of Kerensky's popularity. There was frequent invocation of his authority, for instance, during local government elections, mainly in Moscow and Petrograd. Contemporaries speculated that the electoral success of the Socialist Revolutionaries, unexpected even by the party's leaders, was largely a result of this factor. 'People in Moscow voted Socialist Revolutionary because of Kerensky,' noted a prominent representative of the Cadet party in her diary on 29 June.[296] The reminiscences of Kerensky and Gots quoted at the beginning of this chapter do not reflect the dynamic of conflicts in the Socialist Revolutionary Party entirely accurately.

Kerensky writes about his personal conflict with the 'dogmatic' Chernov, who lacked a creative approach to politics, but this overlooks the complicated situation in the party, which really was not at the bid and call of a single leader. The Socialist Revolutionaries consisted of a complex and fluid coalition of groups which no single leader could control, and Kerensky's isolation in the party cannot therefore be ascribed only to Chernov's conduct.

Gots's assertion that the leaders of the Socialist Revolutionary Party always regarded Kerensky as a 'chance member of the party, not organically integrated with its main nucleus of leaders', and 'a fellow traveller', also requires further examination. Some elders of the party certainly did see him as an upstart and outsider. It hardly seems likely that political calculation and rational motives alone can explain the fact that the Socialist Revolutionaries declined to elect the most popular politician in Russia to their Central Committee. This was also a rejection of an alien political culture which Kerensky represented. His gestures, which perfectly fitted the genre of the concert rally, and the behaviour of his 'groupies', were repugnant to them.

Although the party leaders might well have seen Kerensky as a fellow traveller, the party newspapers and influential party members, including Gots, for several months deliberately formed a completely different view in their readers. The top leaders of the Socialist Revolutionary Party publicly confirmed his standing as a prominent party member. The support of Breshko-Breshkovskaya and of other elders was particularly important. Their authority as champions of freedom, an authority created by the party over many years, was of great value to Kerensky.

The modern researcher Konstantin Morozov notes that, while Chernov was the senior figure for the Socialist Revolutionary leaders, the broad masses and many of the 'March' Socialist Revolutionaries, who joined the party immediately after the downfall of the monarchy, regarded Kerensky as the Leader.[297] This rivalry between the leaders can only have created tension, although the conflict was at first concealed from the bulk of party members. Yet even this statement needs to be qualified, because some of the party elders sided with the right wing, cooperating with *Volya naroda*, while not a few March Socialist Revolutionaries came to form the backbone of the left faction.

In the moulding of Kerensky's image, a decades-old revolutionary tradition of describing the Leader was put to use. A party which doggedly fought for the ideals of democratic socialism nevertheless contributed to forming a cult of the 'Leader of the people' – a cult which was to become an important element of the political culture of the Russian Revolution and, indirectly, of Soviet political culture. Initially the foremost members of the party put their authority behind confirming Kerensky's status as a champion of freedom. The actual word *vozhd'* [Leader] was little used among Socialist Revolutionaries in relation to Kerensky. The situation changed radically in May, when certain party members began to extol Chernov as the *vozhd'*, which resulted in the term then being applied to Kerensky. Some members of the party were happy to consider as *vozhd'* both Chernov and Kerensky simultaneously, while others contrasted them, considering only one or the other to be the real Leader.

After becoming minister of the army and navy, Kerensky significantly strengthened his position. He undertook to prepare the army for action, and this required the imposition of discipline in the armed forces and the creation of a broad political coalition to support the offensive. These tasks determined the direction and rhythm of his political actions: each action which would enjoy the support of the moderate socialists was balanced by simultaneous actions which would be supported by the right – the liberals and conservatives. Thus, the publication of the Declaration of Soldiers' Rights was counterbalanced by the order for the offensive, while the order to disband unruly regiments was balanced by the dismissal of General Alexeyev from the post of supreme commander-in-chief and the demotion of General Romeyko-Gurko. Kerensky's proposal to impose the 'iron discipline of duty' was a compromise which gained limited political support. The minister's allies on the right saw this as utopian, while it simultaneously caused dissension among the moderate socialists: the Mensheviks and Socialist Revolutionaries were under pressure from many in the armed forces who saw it as the first step towards reimposing prerevolutionary discipline. In this situation, holding the coalition together required the constant attention of its organizers. It was a formidable task, and Kerensky brought considerable energy and ingenuity to it. This was manifested in his orders, in his appointments, in propaganda stunts, and in a readjustment of his presentational tactics.

It was not only the substance of the orders aimed at building iron discipline that required the cooperation of the troop committees, commanders and government commissars; their style too needed to be seen as legitimate by those who were to carry out the orders, since otherwise they would simply be ignored (which is what often happened). Kerensky and his team developed a special rhetoric in which the influence of revolutionary political culture was predominant, but the imperial patriotic, military tradition was also detectable.

The minister entrusted part of his administrative duties to his aides in the army and navy departments, rightly taking the view that his priority was to generate support for his policies. Having played a major role in creating the coalition government, Kerensky went on to concentrate his attention not on negotiating with the party leaders in the coalition but on propaganda preparations for the offensive. That was why he undertook a succession of trips to the front, where his speeches to delegates of congresses and directly to the troops in units of the army gained extensive press coverage. Kerensky skilfully created news stories to ensure that his trips, exciting the interest of people at the front and in the rear, generated maximal interest.

Resolving complex political problems called for skilful exploitation of his existing authority. Great play was made of his reputation as a champion of freedom, and it was utilized to legitimate unpopular actions he had to take as minister. Kerensky himself, supportive propaganda, and those drafting resolutions of greetings made reference to this source of legitimacy. At the same time, the style of his 'theatre of revolution', of which he had made so much use in March and April, continued to contribute to the minister's popularity. Soldiers were eager to see the most famous rally orator of all, and Kerensky's speeches at the Odessa Opera House and the Bolshoy Theatre in Moscow were vivid demonstrations of his oratorical talent. At a time when even very sober politicians believed his most important task was to kindle enthusiasm, the style was much appreciated. The hugging and kissing and tossing of flowers seemed wholly appropriate even to many hard-bitten soldiers.

Kerensky continued to develop his image as a 'democratic minister' and a 'citizen-minister', using the appropriate rhetorical devices and gestures. Photographs reproduced by manufacturers of postcards, known not only in Russia but in other countries, show the minister of war shaking hands with members of the military committees and ordinary soldiers. The image of the 'democratic minister' became more military: Kerensky adopted an English-style military jacket and peaked cap, and a more steely tone was to be heard in his orders and speeches. The image of 'the hero of the revolution' also underwent changes: the minister was now shown demonstrating courage at the front and inspiring the troops. The authority of war heroes awarding the minister a military order served to consolidate the revised image. The 'Leader of the revolutionary army' image devised by Kerensky, his supporters and his temporary allies also appealed to a significant section of society, and it was in May that the minister began increasingly to be called the *vozhd'*, combining the imperial tradition of celebrating 'great military leaders' and the tradition of venerating leaders in the socialist parties.

May was also a time when negative images of Kerensky were developed intensively. Even earlier, when he was minister of justice, his actions were criticized, mainly by people who considered his attitude towards the leaders of the old regime to be too lenient. There was no serious political backing behind these complaints, and so no stable negative images resulted. On balance, public opinion viewed his work at the ministry of justice in a positive light.

Having become minister of war, however, Kerensky inevitably came under more fire because the political disagreements concerning transformation of the armed services during a period of revolution were more grave. Condemnation of Kerensky from the grassroots, by some of the soldiers and sailors, preceded the appearance of criticism from the main protagonists in the political process. In early May publications supportive of Kerensky were reporting with surprise and indignation that claims were being heard in the street that the minister had 'sold out to the bourgeoisie'. Such remarks were rejected by others participating in the discussions, but before long he was also being criticized by more organized political forces.

Kerensky's bitter remarks about politicians in Finland contributed to a negative attitude towards him in Finnish society. This, however, had little impact on how he was viewed in Russia. Although Lenin, Trotsky and some other left-wing socialists did later condemn the more imperial remarks he made, the topic was not really taken up by the political parties.

His call to establish iron discipline in the army and the adoption of the Declaration of Soldiers' Rights were a different matter. Liberal and conservative forces, although displeased by the declaration and the dismissal of Generals Alexeyev and Romeyko-Gurko, held back their criticism in view of preparations for the offensive and also appreciated the disbanding of ill-disciplined regiments.

At the same time, Kerensky could already detect the discontent of ordinary soldiers during his trip to Helsingfors. So did his opponents. The Bolsheviks, building on this mood, launched an attack on the minister of war. Certain Mensheviks and Socialist Revolutionaries joined in. Among the Socialist Revolutionaries, mixed attitudes towards Kerensky were also indicative of deep dissension within the party. The failure to elect him to the Central Committee was a major sensation and further aggravated the disagreements.

Initially the Bolsheviks criticized particular orders issued by Kerensky, but then moved on to overall political criticism, accompanied by disparagement of his political style. Left-wing socialists began to see signs of an impending Bonapartist dictatorship not only in Kerensky's political actions but also in the militarization of his image, and the popular theatrical style of his speeches was singled out for ridicule. On occasions the left were openly writing about things that more right-wing circles were talking about in private. People of different persuasions became increasingly ironic about the ecstatic speech-making and all that hugging and kissing.

Nevertheless, both Kerensky's style and his policies continued to enjoy considerable public support. The ways in which he demonstrated revolutionary and patriotic enthusiasm were seen as perfectly acceptable. Furthermore, criticism of the minister by the 'Leninists' caused all his supporters to rally round, reinforcing a diverse coalition of those in favour of the 'Leader of the revolutionary army'. The need to get on with preparing the ground for the offensive called for glorification – sincere or pragmatic – of its main protagonist. This resulted in the emergence of new forms of celebration of the Leader.

IV

The 'Kerensky Offensive'

On 20 May, Zinaida Gippius noted in her diary, 'Kerensky is the right man in the right place, as the clever English put it. Or the right man at the right moment? But what if it is only for a moment?'[1] That sentiment was echoed in his diary on 8 July by the former tsar, who wrote, 'This man is positively in the right place at the present moment. The more power he has, the better it will be.'[2] As we see, Nicholas II, unlike Gippius, had no doubts and came down categorically in favour of what the minister of war was doing. Other contemporaries shared that opinion.[3] Kerensky gained that reputation by the part he played in organizing military operations.

On 18 June 1917, the troops of the Southwestern Front launched an offensive, preceded by a mighty artillery bombardment.[4] Never before had the Russian command had at its disposal so much artillery and so many shells. 'In the same places where a year ago the breakthrough of 1916 had run into the sand, a renewed operation commenced, grandiose in size and in the numbers of heavy artillery pieces deployed,' writes a military historian.[5] The attack was initially successful, the troops breaking through enemy defences, advancing, capturing prisoners and spoils of war. The enemy, however, brought in reserves, and in the course of heavy fighting some positions changed hands several times.[6]

The offensive was supposed to be supported by troops on the Western and Northern fronts, but they managed to start the operation only in early July, when the offensive on the Southwestern Front had already stalled. Moreover, they failed to carry out the tasks assigned to them. There were occasions when the soldiers took the first line of the enemy positions but then refused to press the attack further. Even so, these attacks sometimes put the enemy in a precarious position.

On the Romanian Front, Russian and Romanian formations attacked the enemy more convincingly but were unable to follow through because, by this time, the troops of the adjacent Southwestern Front were already retreating.

The German Command, having had plenty of notice of the forthcoming operations of their adversary, made preparations in advance to repel the attack and redeployed several battle-hardened divisions from France.

There was a powerful, well-planned counter-attack. Some ill-disciplined regiments on the Southwestern Front, which had already suffered losses during the offensive, buckled. More reliable units began to retreat, fearing encirclement. Retreat sometimes turned into flight. Civilians suffered from the indiscipline of Russian soldiers. Only the use of harsh measures, including blocking detachments, made it possible to halt the enemy on a new line of defence, which ran partly along the state border. Some units of the Russian army counter-attacked, hindering the enemy's advance, which was hampered by, among other things, its attenuated lines of communication.

The losses of the armies of the Southwestern Front totalled more than 12,000 killed; more than 90,000 wounded, concussed or gassed; and more than 50,000 missing (up to 42,000 of whom were in enemy captivity. Many soldiers deserted). More than 13,000 Russian soldiers were captured in Romania. Against that, the opponents of Russia paid a high price for their advance. Their losses on the Eastern Front in July–August totalled 16,000 killed, up to 77,000 wounded, and up to 52,000 missing. The total combat damage to the troops of the adversaries of Russia (killed, wounded or missing) numbered 143,566 human beings.[7]

The question of blame for the failure of the offensive was immediately a hot topic. The arguments of the time were subsequently re-created by memoirists and historians. Some socialists lazily blamed everything on the generals of the old regime. The scapegoat for political forces ranging from moderate socialists to conservatives was – the Bolsheviks, who in early July attempted to overthrow the government in Petrograd. Their actions were described as a betrayal of the army as it was advancing. Soon the net of accusations was cast wider, and the Declaration of Soldiers' Rights was being blamed. Liberals and conservatives demanded it should be abolished, and thereby tacitly shifted part of the responsibility for the offensive's failure on to army organizations, the minister of war, Alexander Kerensky, and his transformation of the armed forces. Accusations against the minister began to be heard openly.

The main cause of the defeat of the Russian army was the most obvious: the decline in discipline made controlling the troops more difficult, and sometimes completely impossible. An anecdote of the time has an element of truth in it. German officers had supposedly been amazed as they observed Russian soldiers attacking. After each dash forward they would lie down and raise their hands, then continue the attack. The soldiers were supposedly voting each time on whether or not to continue the advance.[8] It is unlikely that this actually occurred, but the soldiers' committees, and sometimes general meetings of the soldiers, would first discuss the offensive and then take a vote on whether to take part in the operation. Sometimes such discussions took place during the battle. In the operations of a war of that time the actions of the various kinds of troops were agreed in advance and timetabled to the minute. The offensive of Russia's 'democratic army', punctiliously debating combat orders, was doomed to fail.

The question which needs to be asked is not why the offensive failed, but how the politicians and high-ranking military officials could have decided to conduct a large-scale operation of such complexity using troops in such a state in the first place.

A young officer in the Pavlovsky Guards Regiment stationed on the Southwestern Front wrote to his family in early June: 'I feel negatively about the whole idea of an offensive. I do not believe we can win with the army as it is. If the offensive fails, the government and all the entire Command will be done for. They are playing a dangerous game. In my opinion, the offensive is a frivolous escapade, and if it fails it will destroy Kerensky. Well, we'll just have to wait and see. Miracles do happen.'[9] It is a safe bet that professional soldiers, much senior to the young guardsman in rank and experience, were also hoping for a miracle. General Denikin, who was involved in preparations for the offensive, recalled the situation as follows:

> . . . in a state of passivity, with no impulsion or motivation to engage in combat, the Russian army would undoubtedly very soon have gone completely rotten, whereas an offensive combined with success could raise morale and lead to a healthier mood, if not by generating an outburst of patriotism, then by the intoxicating, enthralling sense of victory. That feeling could crush all the international dogmas sown by the enemy in the receptive soil of the socialist parties' defeatist sentiments. Victory would bring peace abroad and some possibility of peace at home. Defeat would open a bottomless abyss before the state. The risk was unavoidable, and justified by the aim of saving the Motherland.[10]

Denikin's testimony is confirmed by other sources: generals and officers, conservative and liberal politicians, made no secret of the fact that they were hoping the offensive would restore the health of the army and the country.

The military historian General Nikolai Golovin takes a negative view of Denikin's admissions:

> This excerpt typifies very well the primitive thinking we mentioned with which the High Command approached the process of the revolution . . . we see from what General Denikin wrote that the entire strategy for salvaging the Russian army centred on achieving a final victory and peace. In 1917, though, the war was still at the stage where only a strategy of attrition could succeed, and where devastating Napoleonic strikes to instantly decide the outcome were completely unrealizable.

Golovin pronounces a harsh verdict on military leaders who set unattainable goals. 'An offensive on the Russian front in June was completely pointless within the overall Allied strategy, and for Russia itself was an extremely dangerous escapade.'[11]

In 1917 the military professionals laid the blame for failure of the offensive on Kerensky. The commander of one of the army corps wrote in his diary on 7 November: 'If Kerensky had had enough intelligence and courage in June to tell the Allies unambiguously that we were in no state to attack, he would still be presiding in Petrograd and the Bolsheviks would not be the masters of Russia.'[12] The fact is that the top-ranking commanders did not seek to prevent the ill-starred operation, although their military experience meant they could foresee all its possible consequences: there had been instances even before the revolution of entire units refusing to carry out battle orders – indeed, mutinies.[13] It should have been possible to see that the 'democratized' army, subjected to mass fraternization with the enemy, would not show the requisite fortitude in the offensive. (In 1917 many units of even the more disciplined French army, which had not experienced the consequences of a revolution and where there was unity of command, refused to carry out orders and presented their own demands to the Command and government.)

How were troops who had to vote to approve battle orders persuaded to attack? A French officer who was in Russia at the time put it this way: 'So, the Russian soldier must condemn himself to death. If he does that it will be a unique act of heroism.'[14] What were the circumstances under which many soldiers did condemn themselves to death? What motivated them to perform that 'unique act' of self-immolation? How was it possible that front-line soldiers who had been fraternizing with the enemy for several weeks could resume fighting? How did it come about that soldiers who had the power 'legally' to avoid participating in the fighting, initially demonstrated discipline, courage and cohesion? Until the very last moment many commanders were uncertain whether Russian soldiers would go into battle.[15] In fact, however, not only did they attack the enemy, they sometimes showed much greater aggression and spirit than either the Russian command or the enemy were expecting. The offensive was seen by the enemy as a serious threat, despite the German and Austrian generals being fully briefed on the details of the imminent operation, thanks to the efforts of their intelligence officers and the untoward frankness of Russian soldiers engaged in fraternization.[16]

To answer these questions we need to look closely at the propaganda to which front-line soldiers were subjected. Propaganda played an unprecedented role on all fronts in the First World War, but, even so, its importance in the June Offensive was exceptional.

In preparing the offensive, the military press, military committees and the commissars of the Provisional Government were highly influential, and sometimes commanders managed to cooperate well with them. Finally, Kerensky's speeches were crucial. He joined in the meetings of committees, made speeches at rallies, and earned himself the nickname of 'commender-in-chief'. The timing of attacks was on several occasions postponed because generals wanted him to address the units due to attack. The commander-in-chief of the armies of the Southwestern Front appealed to Kerensky on 6 June: 'All those in command roles and the soldiers, with myself at the forefront, respectfully urge you to visit the troops of the assault armies for spiritual engagement with us before a general battle which may be destined to play an exceptional role in the fate of our renewed Motherland.'[17]

The enemy carefully registered where the minister of war would be speaking, something announced openly in the Russian press. A military historian writes:

> A new element of training in morale was introduced in the army in the form of Kerensky's revolutionary raptures . . . The front where attacks were planned turned into a front of ceaseless rallies in the presence of Minister of War Kerensky. These locations were diligently and accurately marked on the reconnaissance maps of the German General Staff. To allow Kerensky to visit all the assault corps, the offensive on the Southwestern Front was set back four days.[18]

The 'democratic minister of war' inspiring his soldiers was for a time a sensation in Europe. The downside was that everyone knew about the imminent offensive. The Russian generals were aware of the risk entailed in prior announcement of Kerensky's speeches but considered it a risk worth taking in order to raise the morale of the troops.[19]

1 'Commender-in-chief': rhetorical preparations for the offensive

Kerensky signed the order to commence preparations for the offensive on 12 May and that same day addressed a congress of delegates from the Southwestern Front. On 13 and 14 May the minister of war visited troops at the front, then went on to Odessa, Sevastopol and Kiev. Political support from the elected bodies of the Romanian Front, the Black Sea Fleet, and the soviets and committees of Kiev and other Ukrainian organizations was important for the offensive. On 20 May, Kerensky arrived in Mogilyov, where he had a meeting with Supreme Commander-in-Chief General Alexeyev. After a stopover in Petrograd, the minister left for the Northern Front (23–5 May), followed by a trip to Moscow. On 28 May, Kerensky again visited General Headquarters in Mogilyov, where he was met by the new supreme commander-in-chief, General Brusilov. After that, the minister returned to Petrograd.

At the front, Kerensky held meetings with generals and military committees and spoke at congresses and plenary sessions of Soviets. Delegates of combat units needed to be able to tell their electorates about meetings with the minister. Finally, he spoke directly to the troops. These were often regiments destined to play an important part in the offensive, and sometimes commanders specifically asked Kerensky to try to influence ill-disciplined units. The usual format was that unit commanders spoke first, then members of the committees, after which it was the turn of Kerensky, whose speeches were awaited with great anticipation by those assembled. News about the most important speeches was quickly transmitted to the editorial offices of the main newspapers, and some of the speeches were printed as separate leaflets and pamphlets.

In the rear Kerensky devoted most of his time to preparing the offensive: he chaired meetings, gave instructions on the drafting of orders and made appointments. A high priority was gaining political support for the offensive: negotiation with the leaders of the main parties and speeches at important forums, primarily at the All-Russia Congress of Soviets of Workers' and Soldiers' Deputies, which opened on 3 June. In Petrograd, the minister was obliged to stay longer: a demonstration the Bolsheviks were preparing for 10 June, which looked as if it might escalate into an assault on the government, required his presence in the capital. Finally, on the night of 14 June, Kerensky left Petrograd, supposedly for Kazan, to inspect the rear military districts.[20] In fact, however, the minister was heading for the Southwestern Front.

On 16 June thousands of guns on the Southwestern Front opened fire at enemy positions and were answered by enemy artillery. To the sound of incessant volleys, Kerensky addressed the regiments.

There are different opinions as to the effectiveness of Kerensky's speeches. Newspapers which supported the offensive tended to rate their impact highly, but such testimony needs to be treated with caution, because they could hardly write otherwise. As we have seen, though, we find references in private documents to the enthusiasm with which the soldiers welcomed him. There were, however, occasions when the minister suffered a reverse, of which the most famous was at a rally of the Pavlovsky and Grenadier Guards Regiments. The Bolshevik organization in the Grenadier Regiment, which began publishing its own *Pravda Grenaderskaya* [Grenadiers' Truth] in June, had several hundred members. For its radicalism it was known as the army's Kronshtadt. It was effectively under the command of Captain Ignatiy Dzevaltovsky-Gintoft, who had combat awards and became a Bolshevik after the fall of the monarchy. Dzevaltovsky told Kerensky they already knew from the newspapers what he said in his speeches and he was wasting his time trying to talk the soldiers round. He handed his exalted guest a resolution of no confidence in the government and demanded that Kerensky should resign as minister of war.[21] Dzevaltovsky wrote about the rally to the newspaper of the Bolsheviks' Military Organization.[22] In letters the Grenadiers and Pavlovtsy congratulated themselves on how they had 'cut' the minister.

> But we guardsmen, thanks to our organization, told Minister of War Kerensky straight to his face when he came to us on 16 June that we would not be doing his offensive and we did not recognize him

> as minister. And he says, what d'you mean you don't trust me, the socialist minister? And we said, no we don't trust you, and if you're such a socialist how come you don't know now we are all citizens, and why are you issuing orders about an officer has the right to shoot his subordinate for non-execution of orders and that if a subordinate doesn't execute the orders of his officer then his wife or his mother loses [the right] to get rations. . . . When the minister of war came we whistled at him.[23]

The Grenadier Regiment became a focus for soldiers refusing to obey orders. When the offensive was launched, the mutinous regiment was surrounded by a composite detachment, which included artillery and armoured cars. After receiving an ultimatum, the grenadiers surrendered their weapons; Dzevaltovsky and other activists were arrested and put on trial.

There were other military units which challenged the Command, and there were not always radical socialists behind that. On the prosperous Romanian Front, regiments of the 163rd Division formed an alliance with the local peasants, who then, aided by Russian soldiers, looted landowners' property and 'redistributed' their land. A 'Nigul Republic', over which the authorities had no control, appeared. The leader of the uprising was Lieutenant I. Filippov, who at that time was not yet a Bolshevik. He declared that he was contributing by his actions to the establishment in Holy Russia of freedom, equality and fraternity. The division received an order to redeploy, but the rebels resolved to stay in the villages they controlled until peace was concluded. They too were surrounded and disarmed, and Filippov and other leaders of the uprising were arrested.[24]

These cases stand out because of their significant scale, but there were plenty of other situations where discipline was restored only by force or the threat of force. Cavalry, artillery and armoured units were brought in for operations of this kind. The Russian army's offensive was at times preceded by little civil wars between its various regiments. The use of 'reliable' troops was possible only if sanctioned by the governnment's commissars and the troop committees, and those, in forming improvised punitive detachments, were reliant on the authority of the minister of war. News of these conflicts could deter potential mutineers, but the situation at the front remained unpredictable. 'There were some divisions ready to rebel, some regiments obeying orders in a purely formal sense. Some officers were completely indecisive, while others openly sabotaged preparations for military operations,' Kerensky himself recalled.[25]

There were times when the active preparations for the offensive caused the popularity of the minister of war to decline. The commander of one army corps reported on 7 June, 'I have to report that the 169th Division is not a viable combat unit. . . . During a visit by the corps commander to one of the regiments, he was informed that if Kerensky called for an offensive he should not be trusted either.'[26]

Regiments which welcomed the minister enthusiastically sometimes refused subsequently to go on the offensive.[27] This was no secret. On 16 June, the day the artillery bombardment began, Vladimir Purishkevich informed members of the State Duma, 'When Kerensky is here, among the regiments, among the commanders, among the soldiers, when he delivers his inspired speeches, those vermin, of whom there are a few in every regiment, those dark, dirty forces, at the moment when Kerensky is speaking – and I have been in all those places after Kerensky – these dark forces are silent while the minister is present, but when he leaves they resume their propaganda.' A Muscovite, deriving his information from the press, also wrote that the effect of the minister's speeches was short-term: 'At the moment Kerensky descends on them, under the impact of his ardent speeches, patriotic feeling of a sort ignites in the soldiers, but as soon as he rushes off somewhere else the soldiers yell, "Down with the war!"'[28] In other cases, while the commanders noted the 'splendid' effect of Kerensky's speeches, they admitted that it reached only the delegates who had actually been present at the rally.[29]

There is, nevertheless, evidence that the minister of war's meetings with the troops did have a positive impact. The 7th Army, for example, reported, 'The visit from the minister of war made a favourable impression.' One corps commander, quoted approvingly by Denikin, noted when the offensive had already begun that 'the working on the soldiers by the committees, commanders and Minister of War Kerensky did eventually move them to take that first, most difficult step.'[30] No doubt the generals exaggerated the effectiveness of the minister's speeches from a desire to please their superiors, but there certainly were instances when regiments deemed too far gone to be made combat-ready not only gave Kerensky an enthusiastic welcome but, as described in official reports, also showed fortitude during the offensive. Needless to say, one has to take propaganda communiqués lauding Kerensky with a pinch of salt, but we see even in personal documents that some of the front-line officers who were initially pessimistic about the prospects of the offensive admitted they had been overly apprehensive: army units which had seemed unreliable did, in fact, attack. A doctor of one army corps on the Southwestern Front wrote in his diary on 14 May:

> A couple of days ago Kerensky came to the front to inspect the army, in which the more credulous members of the public eagerly expect him to instil iron discipline, with application of 'the full severity of the law', in our demoralized troops. Alas, there is no sign of that so far!
>
> . . . At last the minister arrived, having talked to the soldiers about the rotten tsarist regime and about the delights of the freedoms gained. He went on in the most exquisitely polite manner to invite the assembled gang of thugs not to abandon their positions without permission, emphasizing that nobody would dream of forcing them to stay in the trenches against their will, but hoping that they would all

> be good boys and not do a bunk. 'You won't do that, will you? Will you? Will you?' With this enquiry he pointedly concluded his admonition to the rabble we have instead of soldiers. Patting them on the head, he explained that an officer was just the same as a soldier, only he had to work twice as hard and was twice, if not more, responsible than they were, bless them! It is not too difficult to foresee how all these fine speeches from the 'government' will be refracted in the thick skulls of these grey masses and how effective they will be in combating their lethal inclination just to stick their bayonets in the ground and their irresistible urge to head for the woods. In the meantime we can all see the results of our government's Tolstoyan policy of non-resistance to evil.[31]

On 10 June there is another entry in the diary.

> No one feels any joy or hope in respect of the forthcoming operation . . . All the new detachments of troops arriving are in the same state of demoralization as the units of our corps. . . . I view this offensive as our final funeral procession! In a few days Kerensky is coming. We are making a great noise about the attack, yelling, telling everyone, and as usual there will be no element of surprise for the Germans! They will administer an antidote to us from which we will not recover.[32]

And yet, contrary to these forebodings, the soldiers of this formation attacked the enemy with great tenacity, despite suffering heavy losses. 'The losses in our corps on the 18th killed and wounded is more than half our total strength! Kerensky has recognized our corps generously, promoting one soldier to officer rank and instructing us to issue ten St George crosses and ten St George medals to each company.'[33]

Someone else who, if only temporarily, overcame his pessimism was Mikhail Shik, a soldier in an engineering regiment. On the eve of the offensive, 16 June, he wrote of his dissatisfaction with the minister of war. 'Kerensky's orders unsettle the soldiers and cause discontent. They are used now to feeling that they are the masters and want no superiors telling them what to do.' Shik, however, was enthused by the outcome of the first day of the operation and now rated the minister a real hero. 'Kerensky, God grant him health, is in our midst. I saw him. According to the official telephoned dispatch he was at the artillery observation posts, but according to the soldiers he went into the attack with them and emerged unscathed.'[34]

Critical judgements of the 'new discipline' were justified, but at times contemporaries underestimated the fighting spirit of units they had believed to be completely undisciplined. The government's commissars, the committees and the minister of war himself all played a role in sustaining morale.

Kerensky's speeches had an impact even on soldiers he had not directly addressed. Newspapers, pamphlets and leaflets broadcast his speeches to a very wide audience. Telegraph agencies rapidly transmitted their content, and journalists of influential newspapers covered the trips of the popular politician. Members of committees, officers and commissars found the arguments they needed in Kerensky's speeches, referred to his authority, quoted excerpts from his speeches, and copied his techniques of oratory and presentation. Trotsky later wrote sarcastically about 'the divisional and regimental Kerenskys'.[35] And, indeed, the 'commender-in-chief' had a whole corps of energetic commenders of various ranks on whom he could rely in conducting an unprecedented propaganda campaign. Army commanders too were sometimes referred to as army commenders.[36]

A special role in this campaigning was played by representatives of the 'committee class'. In the armies of the Southwestern Front alone there were, by the summer, no fewer than 63,000 members of military committees. By the end of August, despite a campaign against the committees instituted by General Kornilov, there were at least 76,000.[37]

To many officers and generals, the committee members were mere idlers evading their military duty, or even poisonous demagogues demoralizing the army. Through them, however, the propaganda efforts of the minister of war gained an influential support network which the soldiers heeded, so he had every reason to praise them. Conversely, the committee members appreciated the assistance he provided them. Ivan Lordkipanidze, a Socialist Revolutionary and an influential member of the committee of the 6th Army of the Romanian Front who personally suppressed the Nigul Republic, stated at a meeting of the All-Russia Congress of Workers' and Soldiers' Deputies, 'It is easy to criticize Kerensky and his orders, but every front-line soldier can and will confirm that under his leadership we have achieved more in one week than was done in the previous months, because with his name, which everybody trusts, it is much easier for us, the unremarked workers, to do our job.'[38]

Supporters of Kerensky attached considerable importance not only to what he said in his speeches but also to the environment in which the speeches were delivered. His trip to the front was presented as a heroic act, and the resolution, already mentioned, to give him a military award reinforced that reputation. This kind of coverage of Kerensky's visits gave added weight to his speeches. He often spoke of loyalty to the 'democratic Allies', Britain, France and the United States. If the Russian army continued to fraternize with the enemy, even if it simply refrained from offensive operations, there would be nothing to stop Germany from moving troops to the west. The victory of the world's democracies would be put at risk, German militarism would prevail, and Russia on its own would be unable to defend democratic ideals. The ruling circles of Germany were presented as allies of Russian reaction, and the offensive was represented as defending the revolution and the world's democracies.

Sometimes the need for the offensive was said to be that a revolutionary country must demonstrate its power, not only to its opponents but also to its allies. Before the February Days many moderate socialists had condemned the 'imperialist' war, in solidarity with the ideals of the Zimmerwald International Socialist Conference. After February, they recognized the need to defend 'the most democratic country in the world', although their ideology continued to have a Zimmerwaldist tinge. Revolutionary defencists denounced imperialism, making no exception for Russia's allies. Against the thirst for conquests of the belligerent powers they pitched the concept of a general 'democratic peace' without annexations and idemnities, for which it was the duty of socialists of all countries to fight. These goals were proclaimed by the Petrograd Soviet, but the moderate socialists were opposed by those who advocated prosecuting the war to a victorious conclusion – i.e., achieving Russia's original war aims, which included the annexation of parts of Turkey, Austria-Hungary and Germany. The question of war aims was the cause of the April Crisis, and rejection of annexations and idemnities became the official foreign policy of the Coalition Government. Britain and France were in no hurry to endorse the ideal of a 'democratic peace' proposed by Russia.

This circumstance too was turned to advantage by Kerensky. It was only by demonstrating its military might that Russia would be able to impose on all a just peace which would save civilization. 'Today all the force of the Provisional Government's influence in Europe is directed to the one goal of bringing an early end to the global slaughter. For words to be powerful they need to be backed by power.' The chairman of the Soviet of Workers' and Soldiers' Deputies of Volmar in Latvia expressed confidence that Kerensky would 'make every effort for the rebirth of the power of the army, and to induce the Allied governments to submit to the will of their peoples and follow the path already taken by Russian revolutionary democracy.'[39] The ideology of 'revolutionary defencism' was used in Kerensky's order for the offensive. Russia's proposals should be backed by the power of the revolutionary army. 'Let all peoples know that it is not from weakness that we speak of peace. Let all take note that freedom has magnified our power.'[40]

This argument was well received by activist soldiers. Thus, a joint meeting of the regimental, company and divisional committees of the 19th Division declared in a resolution on 1 July, 'We captured 26 guns, took 2,000 prisoners, fought and advanced 20 miles, but that is not what we cherish, not what we are proud of. We are proud to have shown power, to have shown that Russia can not only meekly ask for its lawful and just desires to be fulfilled but can demand that, because it is strong.'[41]

The Socialist Revolutionaries's *Delo naroda* also claimed the offensive would carry a lot of weight with the Allies. 'The Russian army went on the offensive, went into battle under the red flag and emerged victorious.' The slogans which inspired the soldiers were 'Peace to all the world!', 'A peace without annexations and idemnities!', 'Freedom to every people!' 'Will this battle cry resonate with the armies of our Allies?' the author of the article wondered. 'Do their governments know that there are no other slogans that can now inspire our army?'[42]

The offensive was represented to opponents, to the Allies and, most importantly, to Russia's soldiers as the fastest way to bring the war to a conclusion on the terms of a democratic peace. It was 'an offensive for peace', 'an offensive for the liberation of all peoples'. This slogan also had a practical dimension to it: there was a palpable reluctance on the part of the soldiers to spend another winter in the trenches, and the propagandists had taken note. The Ministry of War's newspaper wrote: 'What must a Russian soldier do in order to put an end to this terrible war soon, in 2–3 months? Russian troops must go on the offensive on all fronts.' Speaking to a variety of audiences in May, Breshko-Breshkovskaya used the same arguments. 'So how do we end this war? Here's how: we must attack. While Britain and France are attacking, we too need to go on the attack. By sitting in the trenches and dozing while our allies attack, we are only dragging out the war.'[43]

The belief that an offensive would bring peace closer was particularly important for the soldiers. The military censors, analysing correspondence from May to June, concluded: 'The attitude of all officers at the front towards the Provisional Government is entirely benevolent. Willingness to support it is expressed. There is a particularly favourable attitude towards Minister of War Kerensky.' Other ranks at the front were also continuing to trust the minister of war. 'The attitude to the Provisional Government in letters from soldiers in the active army is entirely benevolent. There is complete satisfaction with the new ministers, especially Kerensky.' On the other hand, the censors warned that most of soldiers insisted that 'it is essential to conclude a peace at any cost.'[44] This final assessment can hardly have cheered Kerensky. The soldiers' support for him was conditional: their attitude towards him would be 'entirely favourable' for just as long as they believed he was bringing peace closer. It was an attitude which could not last long, but in May–June it provided a basis for propaganda in favour of an offensive.

Another circumstance which cannot be ignored is that in Russia, since the overthrow of the monarchy, there was a perceptible ambition to export the revolution, to 'liberate other peoples', and during the preparations for the offensive this attitude became more prominent. A commentator in *Svobodnaya Rossiya*, a newspaper which staunchly supported Kerensky, wrote: 'If we have gained our freedom through the war, then so must other peoples.'[45]

This mood was reflected in calls for the destruction of German imperialism (and from the February Days onwards there had been rumours that a revolution was breaking out in Germany). Russia's soldiers were seen as allies of Karl Liebknecht and other German internationalists. German socialists were said to be awaiting the Russian offensive, which would strengthen their own position. Kerensky periodically referred in his speeches to Liebknecht, who was greatly respected by many Russian socialists. One newspaper correspondent even quoted a German prisoner of war, a Social Democrat, who was said to have stated, 'Well, fine. Let the Russians go on the offensive. That will be all to the good. They can advance in freedom to Berlin and unfurl the red flag there together with us.'[46]

Those who drafted a leaflet issued on behalf of the 1st Caucasian Mortar Artillery Division were also counting on an uprising in the enemy camp. 'It is not to peace at the front with armed German soldiers that the Provisional Government is calling us, not to peace with the unseeing guns of Wilhelm, but to peace with the revolutionary German people.'[47] Again, in the resolution of the rally of the 29th Siberian Rifle Regiment, advocacy of the offensive was combined with the notion of revolutionary solidarity. The meeting saw its first priority 'not as ending the war with a separate peace, but by the revolutionary struggle of the peoples themselves. It is essential to defend our country, not excluding offensives. An offensive will help to open the eyes of the German people.'[48]

Some revolutionary defencists believed that the flag of the revolution would fly in Berlin. One orator at a congress of soldiers' deputies in Riga declared, 'We shall advance, smash Wilhelm's troops and fight until that moment when the people of Germany hoist the red flag over the Reichstag.'[49]

Continuing the war was seen as a fulfilment not only of patriotic but also of international duty. Some soldiers promised they would go into battle not only to defend their homeland and the revolution but because they would also be fighting for 'the triumph of truth throughout the world' and for the Third International.[50]

The French minister of armament, Albert Thomas, who visited the Russian front, called for exporting the revolution. 'The Russian army of freedom will, I firmly believe, together with us carry on its bayonets the banner of freedom to the last stronghold of tsarism. It will bring freedom to the whole world, and for that our descendants will call it, as once the French army was called, the Army of Liberty of the World. (Tumultuous ovation) I believe that the hour is near when Russian red banners will be seen in Wallachia and the valleys of Hungary.' These words were met with further tumultuous applause.[51]

Kerensky's authority was another argument in favour of an offensive, and a guarantee that the objectives of the operation were worth fighting for. Ilia Bunakov (Fundaminsky), a prominent Socialist Revolutionary, told the peasant congress:

> At the head of our army stands our comrade A. F. Kerensky, who will not allow a single drop of the people's blood to be shed needlessly. When he gives the order for the offensive, we must respond with all our enthusiasm and all our will to his call to attack. We shall send our deputies from this place to the front with the red banners of Land and Freedom to bless our army before the offensive. Let the army know it is fighting and dying for Russia's freedom, for peace throughout the world and for the coming socialist brotherhood of all peoples.

The delegates reacted rapturously to this call, and the army representative offered to distribute the text of the speech 'in millions of copies'. The congress unanimously resolved to print the speeches of both Bunakov and Kerensky.[52]

The newspapers printed resolutions of general meetings and committees of the troop units, expressing their readiness to go into the attack the moment they were ordered to do so by 'our Leader', 'the beloved revolutionary minister'. They were printed, for example, by the newspaper of the soldier's section of the Petrograd Soviet.[53] These publications reflected the position of many committee members and provided a model for the drafting of similar resolutions.

Immediately after his appointment as minister of war, not even waiting for a formal announcement, Kerensky had said Russia's refusal to attack had already enabled Germany to halt a major French offensive. By seeking to bring peace closer, Russia had set it back and given support not to the democratic elements of the population in Germany but to the militarists.[54] This statement already contains the arguments used in favour of the offensive: solidarity with the Allies, support for the 'democratic forces' in Germany and a desire to bring peace closer. In his order for the offensive Kerensky emphasized: 'It is impossible to drive out the enemy while standing still. You will carry on the ends of your bayonets peace, lawfulness, truth and justice.' In Odessa, he demanded the troops should attack 'for peace for the whole world'.[55]

Even some of the Bolsheviks found it impossible to ignore the arguments of those supporting the offensive, and the party members were disunited on this crucial issue.[56] Some Bolsheviks wanted to avoid being accused of betraying their front-line comrades. Leaders of the party's Military Organization described the discussions that ensued at the All-Russia Conference of Military Organizations: 'The issue of the offensive provoked a stormy debate which it proved far from easy to resolve. We could not restrict ourselves simply to refusing to attack.'[57]

There were times when the Bolsheviks could not ignore the soldiers' faith in Kerensky. A military doctor and member of the army corps committee, Efraim Sklyansky, Trotsky's future deputy as chairman of the Revolutionary Military Soviet, in the presence of Kerensky, declared, 'The soldiers trust the minister of war and will follow him wherever he orders them.'[58]

At the same time, politicians who were reluctant to abandon territorial annexations also fell back on the authority of Kerensky. Kondrat Bardizh, the leader of the Kuban Cossacks, a deputy in the State Duma and leading figure in the Constitutional Democratic Party, declared at the All-Russia Cossack Congress: 'We do not know whether we need the straits or not, but we do know that we need to attack. We have been told that by the man we all love and whom we will follow – Minister of War Kerensky. When we are victorious, let them decide at a congress whether or not we need the straits.'[59]

The liberals and conservatives, when campaigning in favour of the offensive, referred to the minister of war and did all they could to boost his authority, because that was in their interests. The minister of war himself, speaking to different audiences, used various different arguments. What he said in his speech to the Cossack Congress and what he said in his speeches at the Congress of Socialist Revolutionaries or the All-Russia Congress of Soviets was significantly different. Nevertheless, Kerensky most often spoke in terms which would appeal to moderate socialists. He could take it for granted that he would have the support of the liberals and conservatives for preparing an offensive, but he needed to fight for the consent of soldiers who were under socialist influence. Even so, some greetings he received from supporters of the offensive included demands he was hardly going to be able to support. For example, an assembly of the 150th Infantry Regiment on 29 June adopted a resolution which included the following points:

> 4) The regiment will unquestioningly perform and execute the orders of the People's Minister Comrade Kerensky and those he authorizes.
> 5) The regiment will, at the first call of Comrade Kerensky, who is carrying out the people's will, be prepared to advance immediately to wherever he or the leaders he appoints shall order.
> 6) The regiment is prepared at the first call to rush into the attack . . .

At the same time, however, the regiment requested that 'all bourgeoisie' should immediately be denied exemption and conscripted into the army, and that 'all capital acquired from super-profits' should be confiscated.[60] These radical anti-bourgeois demands were not in accord with Kerensky's aim of holding together a coalition. The various supporters of the offensive expected the minister of war to implement mutually exclusive political projects.

An important part of the propaganda campaign in favour of military action was played by revolutionary symbols. The authority of sacred symbols of the new Russia, respected by very diverse political tendencies, was used to reinforce the minister's appeals. The army was prepared for the attack to the strains of *The Marseillaise* and the fluttering of red flags. Holding a red banner, Kerensky told the soldiers: 'It is your duty to advance under these banners, spattered with the blood of Russia's finest warriors, in the battle for the happiness of the working masses, to bear them victoriously against those who deny liberty, equality and fraternity.'[61]

In a poem written by a soldier taking part in the offensive we find echoes of Kerensky's speeches, in which he summoned the army to join the 'feast of battle', and of themes of the *Internationale*.

> Fix bayonets, follow me!
> Fear not, comrades,

This bloody feast.
None shall stop
Our mighty power.
Let us die, comrades,
For this just cause.
For peace, for everyone's freedom.
We fear not the deadly battle.
Beneath our crimson banner,
Forward together, friends,
Whatever the enemy sends.
No one now is pressing
Directing us from afar
Not even a mother's blessing,
Only one mighty 'Hurrah!'[62]

Other organizers of the offensive used revolutionary symbolism, revolutionary rhetoric and the authority of the minister of war to inspire the soldiers. In his study of the war, General Andrey Zayonchkovsky noted that the officers commanding the 8th Army 'managed to instil an attacking spirit in their units and skilfully organized their first victory. They led them victoriously to the limit possible for an isolated offensive unsupported by its neighbours.' That was not something the commanders of the 7th and 11th Armies, whom Zayonchkovsky considered untalented, managed to do.[63] Meanwhile, the commander of the 8th Army, General Lavr Kornilov, turned to the methods of revolutionary motivation to instil the requisite attacking spirit. With a red flag in his hands he welcomed Kerensky, whose authority was important for the commander, who was striving to strengthen the morale of his regiments. 'With red banners in our hands, the army asks you to trust us. If the army's troops performed feats of heroism before, dying without knowing what for, now, when we are fighting for the happiness of the Russian people, the army will advance under these red flags of the Revolution and fulfil its duty.' Kornilov's order to the troops of the 8th Army was no less imbued with revolutionary rhetoric.

> Bring with you freedom to all the nations, happiness and justice to all who toil. Behind, you have the boundless expanse of Mother Russia and the blessing of all her people and their newborn freedom. Ahead is the great power of a free people, the glory of an army of the people, the strengthening of a new social system. You, the people's army of great, free Russia, you, the foremost champions of the people's revolution, will cover in the glory of new victories of a mighty people and a great country your old banners, sanctified by the blood and valorous deeds of your brothers who forged ahead with them, even under the rule of tyranny.

Participants at a meeting in honour of V. I. Semevsky, professor of history, at the offices of *Golos minuvshego* [Voice of the Past]. Standing, third from the right, A. F. Kerensky; seated, third from the left, historian S. A. Vengerov; St Petersburg, 1914. Photo by K. Bulla, Tsentral'nyi gosudarstvennyi arkhiv kinofotofonodokumentov St Peterburga (TsGAKFFD SPb.) © Central State Archive of Documentary Films, Photographs and Sound Recordings (St Petersburg).

Provisional Executive Committee of the Fourth State Duma, Petrograd, March 1917. Seated, from left to right: V. N. L'vov, V. A. Rzhevsky, S. I. Shidlovsky, M. V. Rodzyanko; standing, left to right: V. V. Shul'gin, I. I. Dmitryakov, B. A. Engelgardt, A. F. Kerensky, M. A. Karaulov. Photo by K. Bulla, TsGAKFFD SPb. © Central State Archive of Documentary Films, Photographs and Sound Recordings (St Petersburg).

Portrait of A. F. Kerensky, minister of justice in the Provisional Government. Photo by K. Bulla, TsGAKFFD SPb. © Central State Archive of Documentary Films, Photographs and Sound Recordings (St Petersburg).

Kerensky with adjutants in the Ministry of Justice. Photo by K. Bulla, TsGAKFFD SPb. © Central State Archive of Documentary Films, Photographs and Sound Recordings (St Petersburg).

Kerensky visits a naval base. © State Museum of Russian Political History, St Petersburg (GMPIR).

Kerensky addresses soldiers of the reserve battalion of a guards regiment, Petrograd, May 1917. © State Museum of Russian Political History, St Petersburg (GMPIR).

Kerensky gives a speech at the statue of poet Johan Runeberg in Helsingfors. *Uusi Suometar* (Helsinki), no. 87, 30 March 1917. Collection of the National Library of Finland, Slavonic Library © Helsinki University Library.

Cover of *Zhizn' i sud* [Life and Law] (Petrograd), nos 10–11, 1917. © Russian National Library/Periodicals Collection.

Cover of *Geroi dnia* [Heroes of the Day], no. 1, 1917. © Russian National Library/Periodicals Collection.

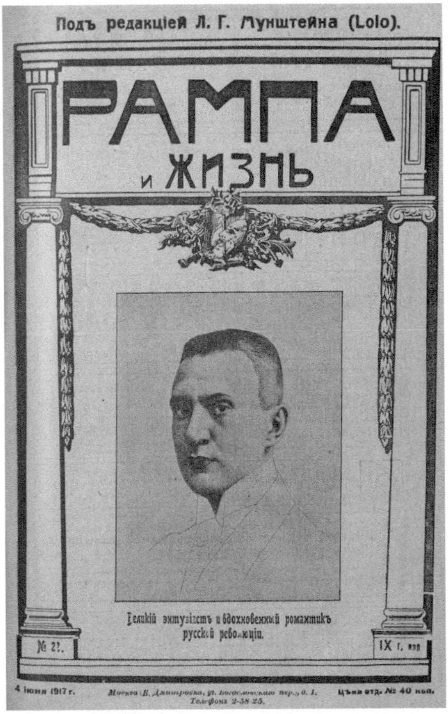

Cover of *Rampa i zhizn'* [Footlights and Life] (Moscow), no. 22, 1917. © Russian National Library.

"'Time is not only money.' 'Would you by any chance have a clock with a thirty-hour dial? In these times we can't get by in my ministry on twenty-four: it's just not enough.'" Cartoonist N. Radlov, *Novy satirikon* [New Satiricon], no. 17, 1917, p. 13. © Russian National Library.

Chairman Minister G. E. L'vov, Supreme Commander-in-Chief M. V. Alexeyev, Minister of the Army and Navy A. F. Kerensky, and commanders of fronts, Petrograd, May 1917. Photo by Ya.V. Shteynberg, TsGAKFFD SPb. © Central State Archive of Documentary Films, Photographs and Sound Recordings (St Petersburg).

Minister of War Kerensky and accompanying officers inspect the guard of honour of a reserve battalion, Petrograd, May 1917. Photo by K. Bulla, TsGAKFFD SPb. © Central State Archive of Documentary Films, Photographs and Sound Recordings (St Petersburg).

Minister of War Kerensky and accompanying officers en route to inspect a parade of the reserve battalion of a guards regiment, Petrograd, May 1917 .Photo by K. Bulla, TsGAKFFD SPb. © Central State Archive of Documentary Films, Photographs and Sound Recordings (St Petersburg).

Kerensky receives a report from the commander of the First Machine Gun Regiment, Petrograd, 1917. TsGAKFFD SPb © Central State Archive of Documentary Films, Photographs and Sound Recordings (St Petersburg).

'The safest form of attack is a stab in the back!' Cartoon in *Soldatskoe slovo* [The Soldier's Word] (Petrograd), 27 May 1917. © Russian National Library/ Periodicals Collection.

Minister of the Army and Navy A. F. Kerensky (in motor car) takes the salute at a parade, Tsarskoye Selo, 6 June 1917. Photo by K. Bulla, TsGAKFFD SPb. © Central State Archive of Documentary Films, Photographs and Sound Recordings (St Petersburg).

Minister of War Kerensky, in a motor car, inspects units of the garrison, Tsarskoye Selo, 6 June 1917. Photo by K. Bulla, TsGAKFFD SPb. © Central State Archive of Documentary Films, Photographs and Sound Recordings (St Petersburg).

'A. Kerensky and A. Brusilov'. Cover of *Le Miroir* (Paris), no. 189, 8 July 1917.

Minister of War and the Navy A. F. Kerensky visits the Northern Front, May 1917. He uses his left hand for handshakes.
© Federal Treasury Institution "Russian State Historical Archive" (RGIA), St. Petersburg, 2020 (F. 1623. Op. 1. D. 613. L. 55).

A group of workers and staff of the Baltic Shipbuilding and Machinery Factory with Kerensky, Petrograd, 1917. Photo by K. Bulla, TsGAKFFD SPb. © Central State Archive of Documentary Films, Photographs and Sound Recordings (St Petersburg).

'We shall die for freedom and the revolution! We shall advance to secure peace for the peoples!' (speech by A.F. Kerensky to the troops on 18 June). Cover of *Niva* [The Cornfield] (Petrograd), no. 27 1917. © Russian National Library/Periodicals Collection.

Maria Bochkareva in front of the batallion, 21 June 1917. Photo by K. Bulla, TsGAKFFD SPb. © Central State Archive of Documentary Films, Photographs and Sound Recordings (St Petersburg).

Demonstration celebrating the advance of the Russian army, with Georgiy Plekhanov, June 1917.

Экстра Выпускъ. Цѣна 10 к.

ВОЗЗВАНІЕ

А. Ф. КЕРЕНСКАГО къ гражданамъ Россіи

Во имя свободы и чести Россіи, во имя скорого и прочнаго мира русская армія на фронтѣ готова выполнить свой долгъ передъ страной.

Въ эту минуту великихъ жертвъ и страданій я призываю всѣхъ къ сознанію отвѣтственности передъ революціонной арміей, ибо только усиліями всѣхъ отъ мала до велика можетъ быть облегчена боевая страда ея.

Передъ нами величайшія задачи переустройства жизни на новыхъ началахъ свободы, равенства и братства, но задачи эти могутъ быть выполнены лишь въ томъ случаѣ, если борьбой на фронтѣ будетъ обезпечено существованіе свободной Россіи.

Пусть армія знаетъ, что она не покинута, что за ней дружно, непоколебимой стѣной стоитъ весь народъ.

Военный и морской министръ

КЕРЕНСКІЙ.

ВСѢХЪ МОЖНО ЗАБЫТЬ ВСЯКУЮ РОЛЬ МОЖНО СТУШЕВАТЬ

КЕРЕНСКАГО РОССІЯ НЕ ЗАБУДЕТЪ

Мы знаемъ что истиннымъ центромъ движенія, что тѣмъ человѣкомъ, который поднялъ знамя революціи въ Г. Думѣ которой взялъ на себя страшное бремя представителя демократіи въ кабинетѣ былъ Керенскій, для насъ Керенскій не министръ, не народный трибунъ, онъ пересталъ быть даже просто человѣческимъ существомъ.

КЕРЕНСКІЙ ЭТО СИМВОЛЪ ДЕМОКРАТІИ

ТЕПЕРЬ АВТОРЪ ПОСВЯЩАЕТЪ

Товарищу герою русской революціи А. Ф. Керенскому

Свобода! свобода! свобода! ты-радость, ты-разумъ, ты-свѣтъ, ты высшее счастье народа тебѣ лучезарный привѣтъ! Оковы прочь! Долой неволю злую! Весь край-одна великая семья. Я на колѣняхъ твой прахъ цѣлую о родина свободная моя!..

Съ требованіемъ обращаться: Москва, Грузинскій валъ д. 16 кв. 21. Герасиму Михайлову. Перепечатка воспрещена закономъ.

Kerensky's appeal to the citizens of Russia. Leaflet, June 1917.
© State Museum of Russian Political History, St Petersburg (GMPIR).

Kerensky at the funeral of Cossacks, July 1917.

'The Revolution destroyed this prison.' Postcard, 1917.

Although his order mentions as military symbols of battle not red flags but the glorious regimental banners, here too the talk is of the global revolutionary mission of the Russian army. It is telling that Kornilov's supporters characterized him not only as an outstanding hero of the Russian army but also as a revolutionary commander.[64] That was important for bolstering his authority as the commanding officer, but also for 'instilling an attacking spirit'.

At the same time, the need to make specific preparations for the offensive caused many troops to change their attitude towards the minister of war. Some, indeed, refused to support a person initiating the resumption of active military operations. Opposition to Kerensky's orders did not always indicate that his authority was failing. Sometimes soldiers simply refused to believe a people's politician could have put his signature to a document they saw as contrary to their interests. On the eve of the offensive, a report was received from the 184th Infantry Division to the effect that 'All orders of the minister of war and resolutions of the Soviet of Workers' and Soldiers' Deputies are believed to be forged and put out by the bourgeoises.'[65] It is difficult to gauge whether these troops were being disingenuous, but at least they were not openly criticizing Kerensky.

In their instruction to delegates sent to Petrograd, the soldiers of the 157th Reserve Infantry Regiment of the Kamyshlov garrison expressed their 'full confidence' in the minister but demanded leave to work in the fields in the middle of the offensive, in direct contradiction of Kerensky's own orders.[66] Counteracting the minister's orders was being disguised as a fairly perfunctory expression of confidence.

In addition, in some instances the participants in conflicts sought to make use of the war minister's authority to their own ends, referring to his orders, either real or imagined but, most importantly, suited to their political purposes. Thus, on the night of 28 June, by decree of the Penza Soviet of Soldiers' Deputies, the commander of a reserve regiment was arrested after signing a regimental order for officials of the Soviet not already at the front to be sent there. In the morning, the officer was freed by armed soldiers who had already been at the front. A great rally was held, which resolved that the deputies should resign their positions and go to the front. The Soviet claimed its immunity, referring to an order of the minister of war.[67] Kerensky would hardly have approved the officer's arrest, but this was not the only case when he was cited as defending actions he had heard nothing about.

According to Semyon Frank, Pyotr Struve considered the offensive criminally insane. This may have influenced Struve's attitude towards those of his friends who were given to lionizing Kerensky. They were motivated by the belief that only the minister's popularity could stem the flood of Bolshevism, and so they joined in the 'loud, totally immoderate and tasteless glorification of the "Leader and saviour of Russia"'. Struve is said to have advised them: 'Support Kerensky, but do not advertise him.'[68] It is unlikely that such advice – if indeed it was given – could have been followed, because supporting the planned offensive inevitably entailed eulogizing the man organizing and inspiring it. Many liberals and conservatives sincerely believed the offensive was the last chance for Russia to recover. They tried to ensure it would succeed, and that involved boosting Kerensky's authority and making pragmatic use of it. They were also committed to combating the opponents of the offensive, particularly the Bolsheviks, and had accordingly to defend and extol the virtues of the minister of war. The coalition of supporters of the offensive was a mixed bag. Conservatives and liberals hoped that, if it was successful, they could return to discussing the possibility of territorial gains, while moderate socialists dreamed of a revolutionary transformation of the world on 'democratic' principles, which required the rejection of annexations and indemnities. These latter were arguments to which Kerensky himself frequently resorted. This difference of approach to the objectives of the offensive required different arguments when seeking to persuade the soldiers to attack and a different approach to eulogizing the minister of war.

Kerensky was trying to establish and maintain a broad coalition of supporters of the offensive. This sort of united front of the 'live forces of the country' was both a means and an end for him, and he tried to use differentiated propaganda arguments and representational tactics. The configuration of political forces and the mood of the soldiers were such that Kerensky most often resorted to the arguments of the moderate socialists. At the same time, however, Russia was regarded as the centre of world revolution, and Russian soldiers were seen as the main players in revolutionary transformation of the world.

The combining of the traditions of Russian patriotism and elements of revolutionary political culture occurred in the middle of an acute ideological battle around preparations for the offensive. It was a battle in which revolutionary arguments, including support for world revolution, were deployed by both supporters and opponents of the offensive. A new political language was elaborated in which ideas of militant Russian patriotism intertwined with ideas of world revolution. This language was used and developed in the course of debate by opposing political forces, and that somehow bestowed legitimacy on it.

In the course of the conflicts around preparing the offensive, several images of Kerensky were further developed. Irrespective of the degree of sincerity in their attitude to the minister, differing supporters of the offensive constantly referred back to his authority, further boosting his influence. For those opposed to the offensive, Kerensky came to personify the political enemy. Attitudes towards him became an indicator, defining the lines of political division. This became very apparent at the time of the June and July crises.

2 'Kerensky' and 'Lenin'

The writer Ilya Ehrenburg, on his return from emigration in the summer of 1917, after crossing the border listened to his fellow travellers arguing. What cropped up most often was the names of Lenin and Kerensky, who were constantly being contrasted. This heated discussion required those taking part to make a clear choice and to name who was 'their' Leader. One of the disputants, a soldier, asked Ehrenburg bluntly, 'Whose side are you on? Lenin or Kerensky?' Ehrenburg expressed support for the minister of war, and the soldier immediately deduced his social and property-owning status. 'Right, you'll be a bourgeois . . . Got yer own house have you, or factory?'[69]

The two leaders were seen as personifying alternative policies, as we know from other sources. Just occasionally, though, the role of the hated 'bourgeois' was bestowed on the Bolshevik. One soldier wrote from the front on 13 June, 'We had a little meeting in our team today, and were talking about Lenin and Kerensky. The soldiers were mostly for Lenin, but the officers say Lenin is one of the most utter bourgeoises.'[70]

The history of how this opposition of the two politicians was built is important for understanding the tactics behind how the authority of both men was constructed and, accordingly, merits consideration in this volume. We should examine the representation of Lenin to the extent that it was associated with the representations of other leaders, primarily Kerensky.

Already in April the two leaders were being compared and contrasted. A naval officer serving in Revel noted in his diary that the sailors welcomed Kerensky on 9 April 'with tremendous enthusiasm', but by 14 April he was recording a change in their mood. 'One regrettable circumstance has, to my great surprise, become evident, and that is a decline in the popularity of Kerensky and an acknowledgement of the utility of the activities of the Bolshevik Lenin.'[71] At that time such sentiments were still a rarity. Many sailors in the Baltic Fleet supported Kerensky and opposed Lenin. By May discussions of this sort had become more frequent, with Kerensky's supporters often furiously denouncing the Leninists, while Bolshevik supporters claimed that the minister represented the interests of the bourgeoisie. Until the publication of the Declaration of Soldiers' Rights, however, the Bolsheviks generally refrained from attacking Kerensky personally, although at times he gave them grounds for criticism. There were several reasons for this restraint.

After Lenin's return to Russia and publication of his *April Theses*, the Bolshevik Party and, more specifically, its leader became the target of propagandistic attacks from the liberal and conservative press. Criticism of *Pravda*, already evident in March, began from this time to take on a different quality and intensity.

By the middle of April, the expression 'Leninists' had become a widespread propaganda stereotype to denote extreme, militant, mindless and anti-patriotic radicalism. The terms 'Leninists' and 'Leninish' were applied to a wide variety of phenomena, some of which were quite unrelated to the Bolsheviks. Opponents of radical change in the Russian Orthodox Church, for example, sometimes called their opponents 'ecclesiastical Leninists'. A more frequently used expression was 'ecclesiastical Bolshevism'.[72]

That anti-Lenin sentiment was widespread is also indicated by its having penetrated even the Bolshevik Party. If the leaders of the Russian Bureau of the Central Committee, the editors of *Pravda* and the Petersburg Committee were not initially prepared to accept the ideas in Lenin's *April Theses*, some newer Bolsheviks who had joined the party after the events of February may have been influenced directly by anti-Lenin propaganda. In the spring a young sailor at a meeting asked the speaker, an 'old Bolshevik': 'Is it true that Comrade Lenin is a spy?' Neither the memoirist (who was to become a member of the Kremlin commandant's staff) nor other young party members seem to have found anything odd about the question. 'After some hesitation, I joined the Bolshevik Party. My hesitation was quite considerable: why would anyone join a party whose leader was a spy?'[73]

The term 'Leninists' could mean different things, and the writers and orators who used it could be pursuing very diverse goals. Some Socialist Revolutionaries and Mensheviks hoped the moderate leaders, people prepared to compromise with the revolutionary defencists, would prevail among the Bolsheviks and that Lenin and his Leninists would be isolated.[74]

At the same time, the label could be applied to moderate socialists who opposed the Bolsheviks. Georgiy Plekhanov's supporters, who found some prominent Menshevik and Socialist Revolutionary leaders unduly radical, called them 'quasi-Leninists', a term which caught on.[75] As for the Left Socialist Revolutionaries, they became 'SR Leninists'.[76] Another well-known Marxist, Alexander Potresov, whose pronouncements were readily quoted by the major newspapers, wrote about the relationship between the ideology of Lenin and the moderate socialists. 'Lenin's fanatical ideology is merely a concentrated, and perhaps hyperplasic, expression of ideas and emotions, some of which are on the loose in the brains of a significant proportion of the democratic forces and find a home in the basic class instinct before it has developed into class consciousness disciplined by experience.'[77]

The strictures of Potresov, Plekhanov and the Plekhanovites were readily passed on by the conservative and liberal press.[78] It was part of their tactics. They prematurely congratulated themselves on a supposedly successful propaganda attack on the Leninists and tried to repeat it on the Mensheviks and Socialist Revolutionaries. Alexander Izgoev (Aron Lande) wrote in the Constitutional Democrats' newspaper about the 'Leninness' [*leninstvo*] of the moderate socialists. 'In "Lenin" the Russian people has personified everything it does not like in the aspirations of the extreme revolutionaries. *Izvestiya* [The News] of the Soviet of Workers and Soldiers' Deputies, who are currently engaged in defending Lenin, probably feel rightly that the popular anger at Lenin is targeted not only at this dunce but also at more intelligent gentlemen conducting the same criminal policy, only more dextrously and tactfully.'[79] Another prominent Cadet wrote about 'this pernicious poison of "Leninness" which also infects the more moderate socialist parties.'[80] This expansive interpretation of Leninness caused concern among those writing for the socialist newspapers.

Readers responded to criticism of the Leninists in the press. It was quoted in letters and diaries, which indicates what an important and emotional topic it was for contemporaries.[81]

Some military units passed resolutions demanding condemnation and the arrest of Lenin, and that he should be expelled from Russia. The mood of the soldiers in the Petrograd garrison was especially dangerous for the Bolsheviks. Representatives of the Reserve Battalions of the 1st Guards Infantry Division went out of their way to emphasize in their resolution of 12 April: 'None of us share the opinions of Mr Lenin and we consider his appeals a shameful betrayal of the motherland. The more people put their faith in what he says, the more bloodshed there will be at the front.'[82] On 14 April, officers and soldiers of the Petrograd quartermaster's supplies store 'expressed a resolution of protest at the doctrine of Lenin'. The resolution ended resoundingly, 'Long live the Revolution! Long live the Internationale! Down with Leninism!' It was signed by Pavel Lazimir, the chairman of the soldiers' committee of the store.[83] Lazimir later joined the Left Socialist Revolutionaries and, in the autumn, became chairman of the Military Revolutionary Committee of the Petrograd Soviet (by which time it must be assumed that his views on Lenin and Leninism had changed substantially). On 18 April a joint meeting of the soldiers and officers of the 3rd Company of the 1st Machine-Gun Regiment resolved: 'We are not going to extend our hand to Wilhelm and his clique, which is exactly what Comrade Lenin and his followers are urging us to do.'[84] Even in this unit, renowned for its radicalism, anti-Leninist views had traction.

Condemnation of the Leninists is also found in resolutions sent to the editors of *Izvestiya*. At the end of May a member of the staff described them.

> A large number of resolutions condemn the Leninists' tactics, sometimes in very harsh language, sometimes more mildly. Thus, a resolution of the 45th Artillery Brigade expresses 'mistrust and censure of newspapers, such as *Okopnaya pravda* [Truth of the Trenches], and orators such as Lenin and Co., who sow confusion and disorganization in our ranks. We urge our comrade soldiers not to drink this poison, which is so harmful to our fighting strength.' Committees of the Reserve Caucasian Guards Regiment, marching battalions of the entire Guards Cavalry and the Muraviov garrison address the same

> issue with considerably more restraint. 'On the matter of Lenin's propaganda, without denying his sincere desire to serve the interests of the democratic masses, we consider, nevertheless, that calls for the overthrow of the Provisional Government are premature, that calls for ending the war without achieving any aims are unwise in national terms; calls for communist arrangements are premature and can lead only to civil war.'[85]

As we see, even a number of troop committees which deferred to the Petrograd Soviet, even in late May, were condemning Lenin and the Leninists, although there was considerable variation in how the Bolsheviks and their leader were assessed. Harsh condemnation sometimes came from top-tier committees. Thus, the committee of the 4th Army (Romanian Front) stated bluntly that 'the propaganda and activities of Lenin and his associates are criminal and clearly damaging both for freedoms so recently won and for the combat-readiness of the army.'[86]

Condemnation of Lenin in a variety of propagandistic writings, resolutions and personal documents differed greatly in style and content, in the accusations made, in the forms of censure and in the means of punishment proposed. In some cases there was concern over the errors of 'Comrade Lenin', who, although misguided, was nevertheless seen as deserving of respect. In others, the Bolshevik leader was branded a criminal and a traitor who should be arrested and deported. By the time of the April Crisis there was a broad anti-Lenin coalition, not without internal disagreements, but, despite these differences, the situation for the Leninists at times looked fraught. Unfavourable attitudes towards them affected even some of the Petrograd workers, but considerably more threatening was the reaction of the soldiers of the Petrograd garrison. There were demonstrations with demands that Lenin should be sent to Germany, and reports that soldiers wanted to smash up the offices of *Pravda*.[87]

In the provinces, Leninophobia could assume bizarre forms. In late April there were panicky rumours in Crimea that Lenin was about to arrive on the peninsula. Some of the townsfolk turned up at the station to get a sight of the celebrity from the capital, and the local Soviets passed resolutions banning the Bolshevik leader. A joint meeting of delegates of the fleet and the Sevastopol Fortress decided, 'after a passionate debate', to take measures to prevent Lenin from gaining access to the Black Sea ports. Guards checked identity documents at the railway stations; hotels were searched.[88]

Crimea's example was followed elsewhere. Troops in units deployed in Minsk petitioned 'that Lenin should not be allowed to stay in major military areas, and particularly not in the active army.' They protested 'against the arrival of Lenin and company in Minsk'.[89]

The Bolsheviks embarked on a campaign of counter-propaganda. They defended the Leader and printed appropriate articles in the party and Soviet press. They attempted to get their resolutions adopted at rallies and meetings. In mid-April the crew of a training ship *Pamiat' Azova* [Memory of Azov] resolved that, 'having discussed Lenin's theses, [it] associated itself entirely with their provisions based on scientific socialism . . . and welcomed Comrade Lenin as the foremost champion of the Russian revolutionary proletariat.'[90] The need to defend their party leader required bolstering his reputation as a 'champion of freedom', a technique, as we have seen, used not just in respect of the Bolshevik leader.

Those campaigning against the propaganda attack included not only Bolsheviks but also a number of other socialists. A resolution adopted on 20 April by the Soviet of the 4th Narva Subdistrict (Petrograd) was printed in the Socialist Revolutionaries' newspaper. It read: 'We, people of different tendencies, protest against the hounding by the bourgeois press of Comrade Lenin and his supporters and demand that the bourgeois press immediately desist.'[91] It would seem that the Left Socialist Revolutionaries, who by this time had increased their influence in the Petrograd party organization, considered it necessary at the height of the April Crisis to stand up to the bourgeois press. A number of soviets condemned the 'unfair persecution' of Comrade Lenin and his followers.

The battle against the Leninists, developing into criticism of the moderate socialists, was related to another line of propaganda. Articles criticizing the industrial workers were now also appearing in liberal and conservative newspapers. After the February Days, many workers achieved the right to work only an eight-hour day and also received substantial cash payments. The 'bourgeois' press began writing about the unpatriotic selfishness of proletarians interested only in their own comfort while soldiers on the front line were sitting in cold, damp trenches for days in constant mortal danger. The simultaneous appearance of articles of this kind resulted not only from the concerns of entrepreneurs but also from current political tactics. Pitting the soldiers against the workers might weaken the support base of the soviets. That was a distinct possibility, given that the mood of the soldiers, even of the Petrograd garrison, was far from clear, and some front-line units had adopted resolutions critical of the workers. Hostility towards the workers is reflected in soldiers' private correspondence.[92]

All this caused consternation to both the leaders of the Petrograd Soviet and to the Petrograd workers. At industrial enterprises, resolutions were passed condemning the bourgeois press, and conservative and liberal newspapers were boycotted. Workers' organizations and workers of particular enterprises tried to improve relations with the soldiers, inviting delegations from the front line to plants and factories, showing their visitors that defence production had not been halted. A campaign was launched to collect Easter and May Day presents for the army in the field, and specially chosen delegates took the gifts to the front. These efforts enabled the soviets to remain in good standing with the soldiers. The anti-soviet and anti-worker newspaper campaigns, however, seriously weakened the effect of the anti-Bolshevik, anti-Lenin campaign. Many workers no longer trusted the newspapers when they were attacking Lenin, because the same publications had been criticizing them. This contributed to the workers and, to some extent, the soldiers developing a degree of immunity in respect of subsequent anti-Lenin campaigns.[93]

At this time Kerensky took no part in the anti-Lenin propaganda campaign. This can be seen as part of his usual tactics: he did his best not to increase the number of those opposing him if at all possible. Before February, he had sought to establish a bloc of enemies of the autocracy, including people who supported and people who opposed the war. Then, after the overthrow of the monarchy, he attempted to build a broad political coalition of the 'live forces of the country' under the slogan of defending the gains of the revolution from German imperialism. That was broad enough to include both revolutionary defencists and supporters of war to a victorious conclusion. As long as any hope remained that the Bolsheviks might support revolutionary defencism and refrain from attacking Kerensky, he did not attack them.

On the other side, as we have seen, Lenin and other Bolsheviks, finding themselves in difficulties, also were not looking to extend the front of committed political enemies, so did not openly criticize Kerensky. For the Bolsheviks, those who personified the political enemy on the eve of the April Crisis were Guchkov and Milyukov. The tensions between Kerensky and Milyukov were no secret, and the Bolsheviks criticized him only indirectly. A further consideration was that Kerensky's prestige was high among many left-wing socialists, especially in the provinces. Some, indeed, hoped to see a broad socialist front stretching from Kerensky to Lenin (see chapter II, § 6).[94]

The attacks on Lenin and the Leninists came to a head during the April Crisis. The May Day holiday (on 18 April by the old-style calendar) was described in some newspapers as a political defeat for the Bolsheviks. Those writing for the Cadet newspaper pointed out that, although the Leninists were certainly active on the day, their speeches flopped. They had few receptive listeners at the holiday rallies.[95] A journalist writing in one of the less high-brow newspapers was more categorical: 'They tried to be ever so serious, the puffed-up Leninists, to show how ever so right they are, but good-natured people just laughed at them. . . . The Workers' Holiday taught Lenin a big lesson. This was the day people saw right through the mysterious émigré, and the fearsome Leader was turned into the hapless Pierrot. By evening the Leninists had completely given up on their venomous speechifying.'[96]

News of the publication of the Milyukov Note changed everything. Some people at the time saw the April Crisis as a conflict between Kerensky and Milyukov. Nikolai Ustryalov wrote in his diary on 20 April: 'If the government departs, a cabinet may be formed, ideally under Kerensky . . . Or Milyukov may win, Kerensky may leave, and the government will lose the support of the "soviets of deputies". Or the government may survive just as it is, but lose the support of the soviets anyway.'[97] Ustryalov, later to write about the need for a 'change of landmarks', saw it as perfectly likely that both Milyukov and Kerensky would survive in the government, but in that case the position of the latter, now without the support of the Soviet, would be significantly weakened.

For the Bolsheviks and some of the left-wing socialists it was the foreign minister who personified 'the bourgeoisie', and they used the slogan of fighting against Milyukov and the 'Milyukovites' to mobilize support. Lenin in fact objected to the tactic of personifying the image of the enemy, believing that demanding Milyukov's resignation would obscure the class nature of the crisis. 'The demonstrations began as *soldiers'* demonstrations, under the contradictory, misguided and ineffectual slogan: "Down with *Milyukov*" (as though a change of persons or groups could change the *substance* of policy!).'[98] Lenin did not, however, object when he himself was viewed as a personification of the political movement opposing Milyukov. The Bolshevik leader evidently found that this type of criticism objectively strengthened his own position.

During the crisis the Constitutional Democrats and their allies brought their supporters out on to the streets under slogans in defence of Milyukov and attacking Lenin and 'Leninness'. They carried placards reading 'Send Lenin and company back to Germany', 'Down with Lenin!', 'Arrest Lenin!' and 'Lenin is ruining Russia!'. The Cadet newspaper emphasized that these slogans were supported by the soldiers and sailors, which gave additional weight to the demands. A reporter for *Novaya zhizn'* gave this description of the speeches of Milyukov's supporters: 'The name of Lenin was literally never off the lips of the people crowding Nevsky Prospect. . . . Everyone was talking only about Lenin, blaming only him, and stridently demanding his immediate arrest. They simply believe that Lenin has declared war on the Provisional Government and that the citizens and the army have come out in defence of the government and against Lenin.'[99] Milyukov's supporters made no mention of his note, which had precipitated the crisis.

The April Crisis was described as a struggle between the supporters and opponents of Lenin also by a Cadet journalist, who later played a major role in the eulogizing of Kerensky.

> In fact, the crowd was divided into two unequal halves – against Lenin (the vast majority) – and for Lenin (an insignificant, but angry, minority). . . . On the twenty-first, however, a very ordinary man gave a speech, and the situation changed in an instant. The debate about imperialism and internationalism was displaced and instead there was an uprising of the common man against Lenin, an uprising supported by the soldiers and therefore verging on an armed clash. . . . because the name of Lenin stood in reality for anarchy, and battling Lenin was to battle for the authority of the state.[100]

This supporter of the Cadet leader makes no mention of the Milyukov Note, because it was politically expedient to present the Cadets as the vanguard of the struggle against the nefarious leader of the Bolsheviks and consolidate a united anti-Leninist front.

Lenin himself observed with some satisfaction that his name was central in the conflict: 'The bourgeoisie takes over Nevsky – "Milyukovsky" in the words of one newspaper – Prospekt and the adjacent quarters of wealthy Petrograd, the capital of capitalists and officials. Officers come out to demonstrate, students, the "middle classes", for the Provisional Government. One slogan often to be seen inscribed on their banners is "Down with Lenin!"'[101]

Milyukov's supporters were shouting their condemnation of Lenin in the streets and calling anyone who criticized the Milyukov Note a Leninist. Sometimes this provoked protest, with workers responding, 'We are not Leninists, we are workers from the Lessner Factory.' For Milyukov's supporters, however, the political position of anyone demonstrating against them was a sign that they belonged to 'Leninness'. 'No, you are Leninists, not workers!' The outraged demonstrators retorted, 'We are not Leninists. Down with bourgeois harassment!' Some workers, rejecting the label of Leninism, tried to turn the spat into a joke. 'I'm not from Lenin's lot, I'm from Smolensk.' Eventually, however, the workers lost patience and really did start supporting the Bolshevik leader: 'Long live Comrade Lenin!' They then began to head towards the city centre, defiantly chanting, 'Long live Lenin!'[102] The newspaper of the Ministry of War even reported that some were shouting 'Power to Lenin, the Leader of socialism!', 'Power to our Leader, Lenin'.[103]

It is difficult to reconstruct the mood of the demonstrators, but it seems that the urge to confront political opponents goaded many critics of the Milyukov Note into adopting the label of 'Leninists' which was being imposed on them by the adversary. Some did so with considerable reluctance. It is interesting that the episode with the Lessner factory workers refusing to call themselves Leninists was reported in *Pravda*. At that time even several on the editorial board of *Pravda* would not have accepted that all of its readers would be happy to be called Leninists.

The April Crisis ended in defeat for Milyukov. His proposals for a confrontation between the Provisional Government and the Soviet were rejected. Milyukov lost the post of foreign minister and refused to join a new coalition government. At this point, players in the political process found themselves hostages to their own rhetoric: as the crisis had been presented as a standoff between Milyukovites and Leninists, the manifest defeat of Milyukov could be seen as a victory for Lenin. The April Crisis substantially strengthened Lenin's position in the country in general and in his own party in particular. Publication of the Milyukov Note confirmed predictions that had been made by the Bolshevik leader, and many opponents of Milyukov either overcame their hostility to Lenin or even declared themselves 'Leninists'. The Bolsheviks' April conference demonstrated convincingly that Lenin's opponents in the party had no serious support.

Moreover, as the situation had developed, the Bolsheviks had no option but to support their leader because the continuing attacks on him endangered the whole party. More and more resolutions appeared in support of him in the Bolshevik press. The workers of the Moscow Telephone Factory hailed him as an 'orthodox champion', the railway officials called themselves 'followers of Lenin', and the Sokolniki Bolshevik Club hailed him as their 'ideological Leader who has always held high the banner of the Internationale.'[104] We do not know the circumstances in which these resolutions were adopted and cannot be sure they accurately reflected the views of those in whose names they were promulgated. They do, however, give an idea of what forms of leader glorification were considered acceptable by party activists and desirable by the editors of the main Bolshevik newspaper. The necessity of defending their leader obliged even those who initially had reservations about him to glorify Lenin as a 'Leader'. Directly by his supporters, and indirectly by his opponents, the Bolshevik leader was represented as a politician on the national stage, comparable in stature with a popular statesman such as Kerensky. And opposed to him.

Other leaders of the Bolsheviks did their best, with varying degrees of commitment, to defend Lenin. Grigoriy Zinoviev was the most active. Several resolutions condemning persecution of the party's leaders by the 'bourgeois press' incorporated greetings not only to Lenin but also to Zinoviev. After Zinoviev's speech on 16 April in the hall of the Marine Corps, the following resolution was passed: 'We find that it was the duty of honest champions which prompted Comrades Lenin, Zinoviev and others in the interests of the cause and of freedom, for want of a different route, to make use of passage through Germany.'[105] The workers of the Izhorsky Factory's shell casing and brass workshop declared, 'Lenin and Zinoviev are true champions of freedom and defenders of the working class.' Members of the League of Youth called them 'true and steadfast fighters for overthrowing the yoke of capital'.[106] For Zinoviev, it was a step up to be bracketed with Lenin as one of the 'proletarian' leaders whose defence was being proclaimed an important task for class-conscious workers.

At the same time, certainly military leaders substantially overstated the influence of Lenin and the 'Leninists', ascribing virtually any breach of discipline by soldiers as due to their activities. (We need to treat the applied political science of generals no less circumspectly than the memories of the old Bolsheviks. They both 'Leninized' the conflicts of the time in their own interests.) The commander of the 43rd Army Corps told an officer of the French military mission that, after the disorder caused by the revolution, there had been a significant improvement, but that Lenin's return to Russia had caused a very serious relapse for a time.[107]

Disorder in any regiment was attributed to 'a handful of Leninists'.[108] Some generals reported that a 'handful of Leninists', or even just one, had corrupted a whole regiment, while others complained that five marching companies that had arrived from Petrograd consisted entirely of

Leninists.[109] Judgements of this kind really did contribute to Lenin being perceived as a figure of great power. His actual political assets were exaggerated, which only raised his status.

On the other hand, in early May contemporaries registered dissatisfaction with Kerensky 'in the streets'. The situation changed in mid-May after publication of the Declaration of Soldiers' Rights and preparations for a military offensive. The Bolsheviks and left-wing socialists began to criticize Kerensky, encouraged by a change of mood among the troops.

Now those who opposed the Bolsheviks sought to appear as defenders of Kerensky from attacks by the Leninists. Vladimir D. Nabokov, for example, characterized the 'preaching' of Lenin's supporters as 'political futurism'. 'Their programme is a kind of futuristic "easy as mooing."' Nabokov described the new themes in Bolshevik propaganda: 'However, they are restricting themselves to mooing, and in recent days there has even been some butting going on, expressed, incidentally, in disapproval of Kerensky, this activist with great willpower, enthusiasm and energy, sizzling in the fire of political life and devoting all his strength to restoring and inspiring the army.'[110] If up until then supporters of the Cadets had commonly referred to a Lenin–Milyukov antithesis, now the antithesis was between the Leader of the Bolsheviks and the popular minister of war.

For Bolshevik supporters it was now increasingly Kerensky who personified the enemies of the revolution. One opponent of the Leninists discovered this the hard way when he decided to make his views clear on 11 June on one of the avenues in the Vyborg district. He heard someone in a crowd talking about Kerensky having sold out to the bourgeoisie and spoke out in defence of a man who, in his opinion, had devoted his life to serving the people. Those opposed to the minister of war declared the speaker himself to be a *burzhui*. He was beaten up and taken to the guardhouse of the Reserve Battalion of the Moscow Regiment (which may in fact have saved him from more serious unpleasantness).[111] The episode demonstrates the level of the passions then prevailing in working-class districts of Petrograd and in the barracks of certain regiments.

There were other instances where mentioning the name of the minister of war could cause a storm of indignation. The standoff between the politicians is reflected in different sources. The 538th Infantry Regiment (135th Division) even declared it would like to see Lenin appointed minister of war.[112]

Some soldiers preferred Lenin to Kerensky in other situations. After the failure of the June Offensive, soldiers of the 17th Siberian Division wrote to Lenin, 'Our unanimous comrade Lenin [*sic*], we most graciously petition you to resort to our aid and not put us into the hands of the bourgeoises, so as which drank our blood in the past and now they want to drink it again. We ask you, comrade Bolsheviks, to beat the bourgeoises who shout: war till victory. . . . Pass on to Minister of War Kerensky he would do better not come to us if he wants to be alive.'[113]

The juxtaposition of Lenin and Kerensky in the same resolution is uncommon, but their images were not infrequently used in mutually antagonistic processes of political mobilization. If the April Crisis was described by some as machinations by the Leninists but by others as a campaign against Milyukov, then in May the images of Lenin and Kerensky were being used by some as tools for political radicalization, for 'deepening the revolution', while for others they were important propaganda tools in preparing the offensive at the front. If Kerensky came to personify the offensive, Lenin personified the fight against it. It has to be said that not all Bolsheviks were happy at becoming 'Leninists' and not all supporters of Kerensky were sincere. The logic of political confrontation both obliged them to eulogize 'their' Leader and denigrate the other and dictated the tactics behind this personalization.

Both Kerensky and Lenin benefited in different ways from the confrontation. A broad and not entirely compatible coalition of opponents of Leninness rallied round the minister of war, united by the need to confront a common danger. For representatives of a whole range of political viewpoints, Lenin had come to personify all that was evil in the revolution.

This antithesis was, nevertheless, more advantageous to the Leader of the Bolsheviks. Subsequently, Lenin himself wrote, in his work 'Left-Wing Communism: An Infantile Disorder': 'When the Russian Cadets and Kerensky began furiously to hound the Bolsheviks – especially since April 1917, and more particularly in June and July 1917 – they overdid things. Millions of copies of bourgeois papers, clamouring in every key against the Bolsheviks, helped the masses to make an appraisal of Bolshevism; apart from the newspapers, all public life was full of discussions about Bolshevism, as a result of the bourgeoisie's "zeal".'[114] Lenin might have added that, politically, he personally was the principal beneficiary, substantially strengthening his influence in the party. In Russia as a whole, the juxtaposition with Kerensky, an influential minister and the most popular politician in the country, brought Lenin's name to the attention of the entire nation. Opinions of the Bolshevik leader differed greatly, but the scale of the opportunities open to him in the light of so much publicity increased vastly. The main antagonist, which is how many perceived Lenin, benefited from his conflict with the protagonist. The Bolshevik leader saw himself promoted to the status of a politician at the national level.

Widespread use of the words 'Leninism' and 'Lenin', to which wildly different meanings could be attached, did in some situations contribute to the spread of a fashion for Leninism. The Kerensky–Lenin antithesis led to a situation where any dissatisfaction with the actions of the minister of war redounded to the benefit of the Leninists.

The events of May and June substantially affected the forming of the cults of the leaders. Both the Bolsheviks and supporters of Kerensky sought new arguments, new words and new images to glorify their own Leader and discredit the Leader of their opponents. Authors of studies on the Lenin cult underestimate the impact of this confrontation.[115] The celebrity did not automatically confer authority on Lenin but was a prerequisite for it to be acquired.

Supporters of both Kerensky and Lenin were apt to use similar expressions. Both might be described as a 'steadfast champion' and a 'champion of ideas', and the reputation of a revolutionary 'champion of freedom' set the seal on the authority of both of them. This use of the same expressions by opposed teams tended to legitimate the revolutionary political discourse, of which the leader cult was an important part.

3 The June Crisis and the June Offensive

The poet Leonid Kannegiser has gone down in history as the man who, on 30 August 1918, assassinated Moisey Uritsky, head of the Petrograd Extraordinary Commission for Combating Counter-Revolution (the Cheka). On 27 June 1917, Kannegiser, then a cadet gunner, wrote a eulogy of Kerensky, the victorious Leader inspiring the soldiers to fight.

In sunlight, with bayonets gleaming –
foot-soldiers. Beyond, in the deep –
Don Cossacks. In front of the legions –
Kerensky upon a white steed.
His weary eyelids are lifted.
He's making a speech. No one stirs.
O voice! To remember for ages:
Russia. Liberty. War.
Then hearts become fire and iron,
the spirit – an oak green with life,
and the *Marseillaise* eagle comes flying,
ascending from silvery pipes.
To battle! – we'll beat back the devils,
and through the dark pall of the sky,
Archangels will gaze down,
jealous to see us rejoice as we die.
And if, staggering, aching,
I fall upon you, mother earth,
to lie in a field, forsaken,
with a bullet hole near my heart,
on the verge of the blessed gateway,
in my jubilant dying dream,
I'll recall it – Russia, Liberty,
Kerensky upon a white steed.[116]

The poem reflects the enthusiasm that engulfed a considerable section of society in late June. Kannegiser wrote it in Pavlovsk, which Kerensky visited on 6 June. A battery of horse artillery, a hundred men of the

Cossack Guards Regiment and a heavy artillery division were drawn up on the parade ground. There was a mounted exercise involving firing the gun batteries. The Cossacks spread out in attack formation and charged. The minister expressed his confidence that the army, having overcome the old regime, would similarly dispatch the enemies of the revolution in good order. His words were followed by a cry of 'Hurrah!' from the troops and the strains of *The Marseillaise*.[117]

The commander of the troops of the Petrograd Military District, General Pyotr Polovtsov, later claimed he had persuaded the minister that he had to inspect the cavalry ranks on horseback because his car might frighten the horses. Although horse riding was medically contraindicated for Kerensky, he consented, and a white horse was brought for him. The cavalry general, whom he later dismissed, describes with malicious glee the inspection of the troops by the minister of war. 'He heaved himself into the saddle and, taking the curb rein on one side and the snaffle rein on the other, rode along the front with one groom on foot at the horse's head periodically giving it direction, and another running behind, probably for the purpose of picking Kerensky up if he fell off. The sour looks on the faces of the Cossacks of the Reserve Joint Guards Hundred left me in no doubt about the impression produced by the inspection.'[118] Polovtsov may in retrospect have deliberately been painting the scene in more garish colours, although there is no reason to suppose Kerensky would have been a good rider. Rumours spread that he had been inspecting the troops on the horse formerly used by the tsar, and this may have contributed to the spread of negative images. If for Kannegiser the horseman reviewing the parade epitomized the Leader of the revolutionary army, other contemporaries interpreted the image as that of 'a dictator-in-waiting', 'a counter-revolutionary', of 'Alexander IV'.[119] The image of the Leader on horseback may have reinforced intimations of Kerensky as Napoleon.

Irrespective of what actually happened in Pavlovsk, that image of the Leader on a white horse did not go away. There were rumours that Kerensky had ridden into Moscow on a white horse, and they even found their way into the files of the British War Office.[120] In November there were reports that the minister rode into Tsarskoye Selo on a white horse.[121]

In some iterations, 'Kerensky on a white horse' denoted a strong politician (revolutionary or counter-revolutionary). In others it denoted a tragicomic pretender claiming to be the Leader for no good reason. He mounts another man's horse, cannot control his steed, or, indeed, anything else, and cannot therefore be a real Leader. The image of the victorious Leader could easily morph into the image of a future dictator, the Napoleon of the Russian Revolution. That this negative interpretation was fairly widespread we gather from what Kerensky's defenders were saying about his enemies: that they avidly clutched at the minister's every imperious gesture 'in order, in their snide, subversive language, to spread innuendo about Kerensky the Dictator, Kerensky the Bonaparte, who was planning to ride a white horse in triumph the length and breadth of a Russia he had subjugated.'[122] His review of the troops in Pavlovsk could be interpreted as a domineering gesture of that kind but could also, as we have seen, arouse rapturous enthusiasm.

Cadet Kannegiser had a very different memory of the minister of war inspecting that parade of the troops from that of the cavalry general. In fact, of course, the poem could have been written without any input at all from the event. The poet's imagination could have spontaneously created that image of the conqueror, the great Leader on his white horse. Other supporters of Kerensky had amazing visions of the inspirer and organizer of victory, and these, for all their exaggeration, had claims to reflect reality. They were generated by the febrile atmosphere as preparations were made for the offensive.

In early June the political situation worsened dramatically. Kerensky, his political allies, the generals and members of military committees were cooperating to prepare an offensive, and at this very moment the Bolsheviks planned a violent coup against the government in Petrograd. Various images of Kerensky played a prominent role in the political mobilization of both supporters and opponents of the offensive.

The Bolsheviks were collaborating with groups of anarchists, internationalist Marxists, Left Socialist Revolutionaries and Socialist Revolutionary Maximalists, who had their own tactics for disrupting the functioning of the Provisional Government. Inside these various groups, and even among the Bolsheviks, there was no agreement on the best tactics in the struggle for power. Various members of the Bolshevik Central Committee proposed plans, but the Bolshevik Petersburg Committee and the Bolshevik Military Organization put forward their own ideas. At grassroots level the situation was evidently even more confused. Thus, in the highly radical 1st Machine-Gun Regiment there were rival Bolshevik groups, and the operations of the anarchists only further complicated the situation. In the provinces and at the front, where, for a long time, there had been joint Social Democratic organizations uniting Bolsheviks and Mensheviks of different strains, the tactics of the left could be very different from what was going on in Petrograd, and political conflict had its own quirks.[123]

Local soviets and committees defied the Provisional Government and its representatives: the best-known conflict was between the government and the Kronshtadt Soviet. The government's problems were not always caused only by Bolsheviks and anarchists. In the provinces some Socialist Revolutionary organizations struck out with their own agrarian policy, which was not necessarily compatible with that of the 'minister of the peasantry', Victor Chernov. Images of Kerensky, however, do not seem to have played any significant role in mobilizing the peasants' movement.

One factor which was of major importance was radicalization of the workers' movement. Plans to 'unload' the capital by evacuating industrial enterprises deep into the interior stirred up the populace on the outskirts of the city. A reflection of these changing sentiments came on the night of 1 June when, for the first time, the workers' section of the Petrograd Soviet adopted a Bolshevik resolution.[124] Images of Kerensky had little impact on this process either. There were other methods for mobilizing the workers politically.

The minister of war, however, inevitably found himself at the centre of another conflict. The Ukrainian national movement now put forward new demands, and the provinces over which the Central Rada in Kiev was claiming jurisdiction were areas to the rear of the Southwestern Front, which was where the offensive was first to be launched. For added leverage, the Rada convened a Second Ukrainian Military Congress in Kiev. Kerensky banned it, stating that the issue of national troops which the Ukrainian activists had raised was being submitted for immediate discussion to the government.[125] This ban caused alarm among delegates to the All-Ukrainian Peasant Congress, which was being held at that time. 'What has induced Kerensky to violate the right to freedom of assembly? Kerensky is saying it is because of the military situation, but the Polish Military Congress is currently taking place, the All-Russia Congress of Workers' and Soldiers' Deputies is opening, and these are also taking people away from the front.' The Central Rada absolved itself of all responsibility for 'possible consequences' and sent a protest to the minister about 'this first case of violation of the law on freedom of assembly'.[126] Kerensky's decision was used to galvanize the Ukrainian movement. Demonstrations and rallies of Rada supporters condemned the order. A military congress was held anyway and, in defiance of the ban, some 2,000 delegates arrived in Kiev. The congress decreed that orders of the Ukrainian Military Committee were binding on all Ukrainians.[127] The delegates declared the ban on the congress to have been illegal and demanded that its own decisions should be implemented. A corresponding decree was sent to all fronts, districts and garrisons and to the minister of war himself.[128] This was the first, very serious, instance of a succession of outright challenges to his authority. The order banning the Ukrainian Military Congress provoked protests even from some of Kerensky's supporters. Articles appeared in Socialist Revolutionary newspapers. The author of one open letter chided 'dear Alexander Fyodorovich':

> We were surprised to learn that you had not found it possible to allow the convening of a second Ukrainian military congress, which could actually be of great assistance to you in speeding up the organizing of a Ukrainian army. What is the meaning of this? Is it a step backwards? Be bold as you always have been, our foremost champion of freedom, and have no hesitation in leading forward to its conclusion reformation of the old army.[129]

If some of Kerensky's supporters mildly reproached him, his political opponents exploited the Ukrainian issue to mount an outright propaganda attack. Lenin accused the minister of violating democracy and called on the Socialist Revolutionary Party to make its position clear. 'Does it approve of the ban imposed on the Ukrainian congress by its honorary member Citizen Kerensky?'[130] Lenin attempted to use the Ukrainian issue to provoke dissension within the Socialist Revolutionary Party. Not all socialists supported Lenin's accusations, but even among them criticism of the minister was growing. On 31 May the bureau of the Executive Committee of the Petrograd Soviet resolved to hear Kerensky's explanation of why he had banned the congress.[131]

Even right-wing circles, which one might have expected to be in favour of keeping the Russian Empire in one piece, used Kerensky's congress ban to denounce the hated 'radical'. The Petrograd far-right newspaper *Groza* [The Storm] had miraculously survived the fall of the monarchy. Before the revolution it had been published by the Society for the Study of the Jewish Tribe, and it retained its militant slogan 'Russia for the Russians'. It remained unwaveringly anti-Semitic and monarchist, retaining its allegiance to Nicholas II and lambasting politicians, generals and even some members of the Romanov family for betraying him. The newspaper did so from a position of opposition to the war, and this affected its attitude towards Kerensky. In April it contrasted his supposed position of accepting only a war of self-defence to the unpatriotic 'landowners, bankers and merchants' who were supposedly insisting on prosecuting the war 'at the behest of the Allies'. After Kerensky was appointed minister of war, the newspaper started to criticize him, anticipating the Bolsheviks in this respect. *Groza* was particularly outspoken in its opposition to preparations for the offensive.

> The French threatened not to allow Russia to defer paying interest on its loans if it further delayed the offensive by Russian troops against the Germans. At the request of the socialist ministers, the French agreed to deferral until 1 June, by which time barrister Kerensky, as minister of the army and navy, was expected to use his rhetorical skills to persuade the soldiers to sacrifice their lives for the convenience of the Allies.

The image of a talkative and ambitious lawyer, irresponsibly taking on something far beyond his competence, was subsequently used by not a few of Kerensky's opponents. *Groza* also hinted that the minister seemed particularly to favour Jews. 'The Little Russians and Jews asked to hold military congresses to bring their troops up to strength. War Minister Kerensky allowed the Jews to, but refused the Little Russians.'[132]

The journalists at *Groza*, who avoided even using the term 'Ukrainians', and the internationalist Lenin found themselves cast in the role of the legal defence for the Ukrainian national movement, not because of any liking for the Central Rada but because they did not want to miss any opportunity to criticize Kerensky. Even so, the minister's opponents made relatively little use of the issue of the ban on the Ukrainian Military Congress.

For Petrograd it remained a peripheral matter, because in the capital there were other grounds for causing political trouble. Indeed the leaders of the Central Rada themselves did not seem particularly motivated to defy Kerensky. The crowds in Kiev welcomed him warmly during his visits to the city. It may also be that some of the Ukrainian movement's leaders continued to be grateful to Kerensky for having defended their interests in the State Duma in the past.[133] For the time being, the leaders of the Central Rada were in no hurry to worsen their relations with such an influential politician, and they contented themselves with attacking other politicians they saw as personifying Russian imperialism. Kerensky, for his part, valued his reputation as a friend of the Ukrainian people and also sought to reach a compromise.

A major cause of the developing June Crisis was preparation for the offensive. If many soldiers at the front flatly refused to engage in combat operations, troops in the rear did all they could to avoid being sent to the front. Popular opposition to Kerensky's policy provided an opportunity to articulate that mood and turn it to political advantage. There was also indignation over the cancellation of leave of absence. On 3 June an order was issued requiring soldiers over forty years of age, who had earlier been released to go back to work in the fields, to return to their units.[134]

The dissatisfaction with some of Kerensky's orders among groups of soldiers laid a foundation for political radicalization and favoured the propaganda of the Bolsheviks and others opposed to the offensive. These continued to attack the Declaration of Soldiers' Rights and to criticize both the orders disbanding mutinous regiments at the front and other unpopular actions. This propaganda provoked a ferment among the soldiers and made it possible to represent their grumbles as legitimate and politically meaningful.

At a meeting of the Reserve Battalion Committee of the Petrograd Regiment, stationed in the city, it was observed that, 'In many companies, soldiers feel hostile towards Kerensky and liken his actions to those of the recently deposed Tsar Nicholas II.'[135] It was not everywhere that the minister of war was being compared to the last emperor, but his popularity did fall even in regiments where, at the beginning of May, he had been warmly welcomed.

Meanwhile the government newspaper, targeted at the general public, saw Kerensky's personal authority as a vital resource for holding the country together. 'We must consider it great good fortune that there is in Russia a person everybody trusts, on whom everyone can rely, starting from those at the very bottom of the crowds in the street right up to the top echelons of educated society.'[136]

Shortly before this, on 4 June, at the First All-Russia Congress of Soviets, Lenin had staked the Bolsheviks' claim to power. Irakliy Tsereteli, the Menshevik leader, declared in his speech, 'At the present moment there is no political party in Russia which could say, "Give power to us. Go away. We will replace you." There is no such party in Russia.' From his seat, Lenin objected, 'Yes, there is!'[137] The journalist of the government newspaper was stating at the height of the June Crisis that Russia had an irreplaceable leader who enjoyed the full and absolute confidence of the country. 'There is . . . such a person!' he wrote of the minister of war. A day later this same newspaper demanded, 'Only have faith, comrades, have faith in our leader Kerensky, in whom all of Russia has faith and in whom the universe rejoices.'[138] The polarization of political forces was evident in the fact that, for some, the minister of war was the embodiment of hope that the country could be saved, while, for others, he was the personification of evil.

Dissatisfaction with Kerensky was exploited by the Bolsheviks and their allies in preparing a demonstration timed for 10 June. The intention was that a mass demonstration under the slogan of 'All power to the Soviets!' would provoke a new government crisis and force the leaders of the First All-Russia Congress of Soviets, which had opened on 3 June, to take power. Although the main body of delegates consisted of moderate socialists who supported the coalition with the Provisional Government, the Bolsheviks speculated that the logic of how the crisis would develop, together with the pressure of revolutionary crowds in the streets, would force the congress to change its position.

The organizers of the demonstration did their best to keep details of the preparations secret, but an impending political demonstration of this magnitude could not be kept under wraps for long. The leaders of the congress took a decision to cancel all demonstrations, and groups of delegates were sent to the factories and regiments to persuade the soldiers and workers to support the decision of the congress.[139]

The minister of war also took part in this exercise of political containment. He wisely did not go to visit the garrison regiments expressing dissatisfaction with his orders, because that could have had an unpredictable outcome. Instead, Kerensky went to the Obukhovsky Steel Plant, where support for the Socialist Revolutionaries was strong. (At the time the SR organization there had some 500 members, against only 50 who were Bolsheviks.)[140] As was to be expected, the visit was an easy propaganda victory for the minister. The chairman of the factory's executive committee addressed a speech to Kerensky which was entirely amenable to defencist propaganda and suitable as an advertisement for the head of the navy department, to whom the factory was subordinate. Welcoming their distinguished guest, the representative of an industrial enterprise renowned for its participation in the protest movement praised the Leader in the best traditions of revolutionary hagiography.

> It is with a sense of profound satisfaction that we welcome you, dear champion, who courageously took up the great, sacred standard of the Russian Revolution. You stood sentinel, firm and resolute in the days of the murky twilight of Russian servitude, a guiding beacon on the glorious path of revolutionary democracy, and were a bright

> light in the darkest days of reaction. You were a bright light, a banner for all who suffered and strove towards the great light and glorious existence we had dreamed of for hundreds of years and thanks to which we have merged with that great fusion of the liberated family of humanity. So stand firm, glorious champion, on that great democratic foundation which is becoming stronger and stronger.[141]

Supporters of Kerensky who visited other factories and regiments could not expect anything like that welcome. They often found enraged workers and soldiers who had harsh criticism for the envoys of the Congress of Soviets.[142]

The decision of the congress wrong-footed the Bolsheviks. It was difficult to demand the transfer of all power to the soviets if their representative body was refusing to support it. Some of the moderate socialist leaders, indeed, were prepared to sanction the use of armed force against those making such demands. After heated discussion, the Bolshevik leaders cancelled the demonstration. This provoked protests from many party members, as well as indignation among workers and soldiers who had supported the Bolsheviks and could not wait to take to the streets. Some radically inclined workers and soldiers began shifting their loyalties from the Bolsheviks to the anarchists.

Meanwhile, the Menshevik and Socialist Revolutionary leaders decided to hold a demonstration on 18 June. That was approved by the congress which, moreover, declared a free choice of the slogans the protesters could carry. In an attempt to vent some of the steam of the soviets' supporters, the moderate socialists intended to control the preparation and conducting of the demonstration, to curtail the influence of the Bolsheviks, and to expand their own power base of political support. Furthermore, at just this moment right-wing radicals raised their heads, and demands were heard for a military dictatorship to be established.[143] The demonstration, it was hoped, would counter that tendency too.

Although the decision to hold a demonstration did reduce tension in Petrograd, its moderate socialist initiators soon realized they had been overhasty. Contrary to their expectations, the demonstration on 18 June proved a triumph for the Bolsheviks and their allies. The Constitutional Democrats refused to take part in it. Groups of supporters of the Provisional Government who came on to the streets faced abuse, which sometimes turned ugly. Many demonstrators were carrying flags and banners condemning both the offensive and the Provisional Government's policies and demanding the transfer of power to the soviets. The political victory of the left in Petrograd was evident not only in their having more flags and placards. The moderate socialists did not dare to display slogans openly supporting the Provisional Government. The Mensheviks and Socialist Revolutionaries rightly believed such appeals would meet with little support. Their concerns were borne out, although some demonstrators did demand continuation of the war and praised Kerensky.

One placard, carried by guardsmen of the Reserve Battalion of the Preobrazhensky Regiment, was inscribed 'Faith in Comrade Kerensky'. The 3rd Rifle Regiment carried the slogan 'Faith in Kerensky!', and demonstrating war disabled declared 'Long live Kerensky!' The most fervent support for the minister came from the staff of a military hospital: 'Long live our Leader, Comrade Kerensky!'[144] These calls to support the government were drowned in a flood of anti-government sentiment.

The outcome of the 18 June demonstration confirmed a change of attitude among the workers and soldiers of the capital, and that presented new opportunities for the Bolsheviks and anarchists to attack the government. The impact of this manifestation of the power of those opposing the government was dampened by news that the offensive on the Southwestern Front had begun.

The effect of reports of the Russian troops' initial successes was dramatic. The developing political crisis was halted, if only for a time. Even radical workers and soldiers felt unable to press home the attack on the government at a time when the army was fighting in bloody battles. The Left Socialist Revolutionaries stated that, in the present situation, they would do nothing that might provide grounds for accusing them of disorganizing the revolutionary troops. In the provinces, demonstrations that were to have been anti-government even assumed a defencist character in the light of news from the front. The offensive was supported by the First All-Russia Congress of Soviets, the Petrograd Soviet, and many other soviets and committees.[145]

This could not but affect the mood of the workers and, above all, of the soldiers. There were widespread hopes that the troops' success would prove a turning point in the war and lead to achieving the longed-for peace.[146] The news of victories created favourable conditions for political mobilizing of Kerensky's supporters, as even the Bolsheviks admitted. 'We do not deny the fact that the movement to support the offensive has engulfed the broad masses of the soldiers, who have believed the socialist minister's promise of a swift peace,' wrote the newspaper of the Bolsheviks' Military Organization.[147]

Jubilant crowds of supporters of the offensive poured on to the streets of Petrograd. The demonstrations continued until late at night on 19 June. One of the first groups of demonstrators was led by a famous commander, General Nikolai Ruzsky. The procession emerged from Staff Headquarters and marched to Mariinsky Palace, the seat of the Provisional Government. Soldiers bearing red flags to which portraits of the minister of war were attached walked in front. Thousands-strong crowds gathered the whole length of Nevsky Prospect, and especially in the square in front of Kazan Cathedral, which in the tradition of the city was a special place for demonstrations of political protest. The correspondents of several newspapers particularly noted that the cries of 'War to a victorious conclusion!' and 'Long live Kerensky!' echoed round a square 'soaked with the blood of the champions of freedom'. Leaflets glorifying the offensive were thrown from cars. The demonstrators carried portraits of Kerensky that were decorated with flowers, banners with slogans extolling the army, and placards congratulating the minister of war. 'The hero of the day is, of course, Kerensky, portraits of whom, as the inspiration of the army, were everywhere among the demonstrators,' reported *Malen'kaya gazeta*.[148]

If some supporters of the offensive were carrying the red flags now traditional after the revolution, others bore the white, blue and red national flag. It would have been difficult in the past to imagine such unity. In the spring, supporters of the national flag might have been declared counter-revolutionary. On 19 June, however, the symbols of empire and revolution coexisted peacefully, united by the image of the 'organizer of the offensive'. People with widely divergent views attached the Leader's portrait to their flags. Sometimes the minister's image was raised on flags during the demonstration, which led to a standing ovation in honour of Kerensky.[149] This was in itself a symbolic expression of the unity among supporters of the offensive and of the success of the broad coalition Kerensky had created. 'The national tricolour was seen side by side with the red flag: what a sight!' a French officer wrote enthusiastically. A portrait of Kerensky attached to the Russian flag – an American officer too found that a striking combination.[150]

The participation of famous figures in these demonstrations was particularly significant both for support of the offensive and for enhancing the reputation of its inspirer. Georgiy Plekhanov marched with the Yedinstvo [Unity] group, and a photographer captured the Father of Russian Marxism beside Kazan Cathedral. In front of Plekhanov, demonstrators are holding a portrait of Kerensky, and in the corner of the photo you can see part of a flag and part of the portrait. It could appear that the portrait of Kerensky is being held by Plekhanov himself, who was speaking in favour of the offensive. Reporters liked to focus on those carrying the banners and other distinctive demonstrators. The attention of the street crowd was particularly attracted by two elderly officers who were respectfully carrying a large portrait of Kerensky.[151]

The demonstrations continued over the following days. The crowd on Nevsky Prospect demonstrated with Kerensky's portrait and the hymn 'Save, Lord, Thy people' was sung. The assault company of the Vladimir Cadet School marched through the city on its way to the front under a banner reading 'Long live Kerensky and the regiments of 18 June'.[152]

On 21 June a ceremonial review of volunteer battalions was held in Petrograd, at which their banners were consecrated. The Women's Battalion participated. On the square in front of Mariinsky Palace were drawn up Cossack regiments, students of military colleges, and the crew of the 2nd Baltic Fleet with their band. After the ceremony, these troop units, cheered by crowds of citizens, marched down Nevsky Prospect, a sea of red flags visible in the distance, surrounded by Cossack lances. The minister of war was symbolically present at this ceremony. Placards were raised inscribed 'Long Live the Provisional Government, Kerensky and our Valiant Allies!', 'Long Live Kerensky', 'Let us Obey Our Leader Kerensky'. There were portraits of the minister of war.[153]

Such a demonstration of power could not but unsettle those who had demonstrated against the offensive on 18 June. A meeting of the 6th Reserve Sapper Battalion passed a resolution calling those who had participated in what they called the 'armed demonstration' on 21 June 'traitors to the cause of the people's freedom', because they had demonstrated despite a decision of the Petrograd Soviet.[154] There is no mention of Kerensky in the sappers' resolution, but the fact that the demonstrators on 18 June had been bearing his portrait did not make the demonstration legitimate in their eyes. Publication of the resolution in the principal Socialist Revolutionary newspaper suggests that they too had suspicions about the nature of the demonstration.

Demonstrations in honour of the offensive were also held in the provinces. In Kiev the red-and-black flag of the assault battalions of death was borne aloft with a portrait of Kerensky flaunted beneath it. The minister's image was greeted with a wholehearted 'Hurrah!' The Union of Knights of St George of the Kiev Military District and volunteers of the revolutionary assault battalion passed a special resolution addressed to Kerensky: the Union 'on the occasion of this demonstration by all the forces of democracy lowers before you its revolutionary banners and awaits your order, as the beloved Leader of the revolution, to die for the happiness of the motherland and the peace of all mankind.'[155]

There would be demonstrations of patriotism when there was news of successes at the front, when sending off marching companies, or on the return of wounded soldiers from the army in the field. In Kharkov, a hospital train was ceremonially greeted at the station by troops of the garrison and townspeople. The wounded men sent greetings to the minister: 'Long live the Provisional Government and heroic Kerensky'; 'Kerensky will not needlessly shed a single drop of blood.'[156]

Different forces exploited the political asset of news of successes in the offensive in different ways. Kerensky, in his calls to action, emphasized the revolutionary nature of the attacking army. He went out of his way to acknowledge the contribution to the offensive made by members of the military committees and proposed awarding red battle honours to the revolutionary regiments that most distinguished themselves.[157]

Liberal and conservative newspapers, meanwhile, used news of the offensive to attempt to strengthen traditional discipline, constantly extolling the heroism of officers. There were toasts in honour of Supreme Commander-in-Chief General Alexey Brusilov. The Petrograd *Malen'kaya gazeta*, which was now becoming one of the main rallying centres of the right, urged its readers: 'Help Brusilov, the Russian eagle! Help Kerensky, the heart of Russia!'[158] That order of priority was typical of only a few newspapers. *Malen'kaya gazeta* was currently leading a campaign in favour of establishing 'firm government' and probably saw the popular general as a candidate for the role of military dictator. For a broad front of supporters of the offensive, Kerensky remained the focus of unity.

Kerensky was sent many letters and telegrams expressing support. A resolution adopted on 19 June by a general meeting of officials, engineers and workers of Kreutzburg railway station read:

> The first joyful news of the devastating offensive of the Russian army has strengthened our confidence and filled us with hope that only in this way will we bring the war to an early end and ensure shortly after that the triumph of the ideal of the brotherhood of nations and perpetual, inviolable peace throughout the world. After a nightmarish hitch, let this first blow unite all revolutionary Russia. Let us be done with strife and discord! Down with the traitors and hypocrites! . . . Long live the soul of the healthy revolutionary impulse, Minister of War Comrade Kerensky.

Those at the meeting sent the minister 641 rubles, 26 kopeks, collected for the families of heroes of the 'regiments of 18 June', fallen in battle or wounded. The donors expressed confidence that 'our initiative has probably been anticipated by other citizens throughout Russia.'[159] And indeed there were collections of money and patriotic auctions in aid of the heroes of the offensive and their families, in which portraits of the minister of war featured prominently. The tobacco factory owners of Petrograd donated more than 5 million cigarettes to him for distribution to the 'regiments of 18 June'. Business representatives made known their satisfaction at the actions of the minister of war. 'Kerensky, the organizer and inspirer of the offensive, has done something for Russia that no finance minister could have done,' one financier told the correspondent of *Birzhevye Vedomosti*.[160]

Kerensky's authority was also strengthened by messages from well-known politicians and from organizations claiming influence with the public. On behalf of the Provisional Committee of the State Duma, Mikhail Rodzyanko assured Kerensky, 'The State Duma will always remember that it was you who, with your fervent speech and personal example, put fire in the hearts of the soldiers and awakened in them a sense of their duty to defend the freedom gained by the revolution.'[161] The inspirer of the offensive was congratulated by the Fifth Congress of the Trud group, the Jewish Group, and the Petrograd Soviet of Officers' Deputies.[162] Kerensky was hailed by the ministers of the Allied governments and the world's leading periodicals, and these praises were reprinted in the Russian press.

Groups intent on seeing a military dictatorship established also deemed it appropriate to support the minister at this time. The Military League, one of the rallying centres of right-wing forces, issued a leaflet, *ALL HAIL the Troops of 18 June and Their Inspirer Citizen Alexander KERENSKY!*[163] In fact these panegyrics from the right-wing and conservative press were not always helpful to Kerensky's propaganda efforts. Their long-standing reputation did nothing to strengthen the minister's authority: '*Novoye vremya* is emptying the filth of its admiration all over Kerensky,' wrote Alexander Blok in his diary on 19 June.[164]

Both in official announcements and in the reports of war correspondents there were descriptions of Kerensky's involvement in organizing the offensive and in maintaining the troops' morale, and the news filled many with hope. One former lady of the court, still loyal to the imperial family, damned the revolutionary changes and the revolutionaries but made an exception for the minister of war: 'Our troops are continuing to attack. Kerensky is there among them, trying to maintain their fighting spirit. We see him now on foot, sometimes on horseback, sometimes in a car, sometimes an aeroplane. His energy is quite astounding. He is the only person in this frightful government with a good head and strong will.'[165]

At times, however, exaggeration in the newspapers was so excessive that even readers in the rear noticed them. There were sceptical comments, sometimes combined with a sense of foreboding. Kerensky's propaganda failures were also reported. A Moscow civil servant wrote about the soldiers' behaviour.

> They insult Kerensky, the generals and officers. ... How must Kerensky be feeling now, our people's hero, our answer to Napoleon or Joan of Arc? No wonder he is constantly rushing to the front, by car, by aeroplane, even on foot. He flies under artillery bombardment, close to the military action. He shouts out his fiery speeches, squabbles with those stirring up mischief in the souls of the troops, threatens, stamps his feet, kisses the heroes and himself bandages their wounds. Death is very close by, but not only does he not fear it, he perhaps even longs for it. And, if this is so, then the Leader of the revolution himself has despaired of the reasonableness of the 'liberated slave', the characterless Russian nonentity. Perhaps he is himself ashamed of having believed in us Russians, of having had faith in our goodheartedness and spirituality, and sees now that our people are blackhearted and as uncouth as savages.[166]

At this same time, admirers of the minister of war were painting the image of a resolute hero and able architect of victory. Not later than 23 June, rumours began to circulate in Petrograd that the minister himself had led the troops into the attack. They were being spread also by an officer working as a military journalist, which gave them a cachet of professional knowledgeability.[167]

The newspapers reprinted a letter from a soldier which gives an idea of the rumours circulating at the front and in the rear.

> Our hero, Comrade Kerensky, and Comrade Brusilov were in two separate dugouts. When they came out, they took rifles and said,

> 'Comrades, we are going to defend freedom.' Then our soldiers took them in their arms and carried them back to the dugouts where they had been before that, and the regiments went as one into the attack. I was told that by a soldier in our regiment of steel who had been wounded. The tears flowed from my eyes.

It was rumoured that the minister had led the troops into battle with a red banner in his hands.

> Is that really true? We can expect that kind of heroism from someone as fiery as Kerensky, who has risked his life in the past in the cause of Russia's freedom. The ardent leader of Free Russia, at the head of his troops, defending the life and honour of a great nation with the red banner of freedom in his hands! What a wonderful, unforgettable picture! What an answer to the evil slander with which blackhearted traitors in the camp of Lenin and his friends are trying to sully the radiant reputation of the Leader of Russia's army!

In the days that followed, Kerensky's taking part in the battles was generally accepted as an established fact. 'And, as we know, when the offensive began, Kerensky, Kerensky himself, led the wavering battalions of soldiers into the attack with the red banner of freedom in his hands.'[168]

The minister of war did visit the front line and put his life at risk, but he did not literally lead his regiments into battle. The basis for the rumours was in Kerensky's speeches, where he declared his wish to share the fate of the soldiers attacking the enemy. 'Say the word, and I will go wherever you instruct me to. Only those who are with us are on the side of freedom.' The press also reported that the minister always appeared where there was real danger. 'The soldier expects that Kerensky, when necessary, is prepared to do anything, to sacrifice his own life. The army fears that. It fears for Russia, which at this time has such need of Kerenskys.'[169] Reports of that kind provided the context for the spread of rumours of the minister's personal participation in the fighting.

Panicky rumours circulating in the army and in the rear also testify to Kerensky's popularity. One front-line soldier wrote home on 24 June, 'Here are some examples to give you an idea of the soldiers' rumours: "Kerensky has been wounded in his left hand." "No, a bullet has gone straight through his stomach." "Kerensky has flown to Germany in an aeroplane." (That is an example of a deliberately false Bolshevik rumour, of which there are quite a few.)'[170] Wounded soldiers arriving at the dressing stations asked whether Kerensky was alive. Variations on the rumour of his having been wounded circulated in provincial cities. It was even said he had been killed. That rumour was causing consternation in the rear, in Yekaterinodar, even before the start of the offensive. The Ministry of War officially denied such rumours, which testifies to how prevalent they were.[171]

By 27 June, rumours of Kerensky's death had reached Odessa. That day our student at the Conservatory jotted in her diary, 'Kerensky has performed miracles and inspired the soldiers. He has been constantly in the firing line and, endangering his life, has been flying above enemy positions in an aeroplane. There were persistent rumours recently that he had been killed, and later that he has supposedly resigned.'[172]

Another of Kerensky's admirers, a young aristocrat who lived on her estate in Ukraine, noted in her diary on the same day: 'A welcome exception is Minister of the Army and Navy Kerensky, who himself led the soldiers in the offensive on 18 June. Now, though, it is rumoured he has been either wounded or assassinated by a treacherous shot in the back.'[173] In his supporters' imagination, the only way their romantic hero could be killed was by a perfidious attack by some traitor from behind. In other rumours, Kerensky had been the victim of a 'Bolshevik' act of terrorism. No doubt press reports of death threats to the minister from soldiers contributed to this. Rumours about Kerensky's death while inspiring the revolutionary troops during the offensive show his heroic image at its most dramatic.

Even during the patriotic demonstrations fêting the troops, even before reports of victories were being doubted, there were violent clashes between supporters and opponents of the government, manifesting different attitudes towards Kerensky. The Bolsheviks were concerned that the overheated situation might lead to a spontaneous, premature political explosion outside the party's control and called on their supporters to show restraint. Further conflict was, however, inevitable.

The left-wing socialists reacted negatively to the patriotic demonstrations. Some were outraged by what was being celebrated – the offensive – while others were angry about the form they took. The presence of national flags was seen by the left as signalling a danger of counter-revolution, while the abundance of portraits of Kerensky was thought to be a manifestation of a monarchist political culture. 'Demonstrations on the main thoroughfares. Portraits of Kerensky, strewn with flowers. Just like the tsar. Only the crown missing,' Martin Latsis, a prominent Bolshevik, noted in his diary.[174] The Bolshevik newspaper in Kronshtadt also remarked on portraits of the minister. 'The dread spectre of civil war is concealed from the bourgeoisie by portraits of Kerensky. What raptures, what adulation, what roses! And all this in honour of? The little hero of a last romance in the twilight of his days.'[175] The last straw for left-wing socialists was that those taking part in the demonstrations were the 'well-dressed' bourgeois public 'entrenched in the rear'.[176]

Political conflict was sometimes accompanied by violent clashes with those holding different views. The Bolshevik group in the Central Executive Committee even passed a resolution deploring violence on the streets of the capital. 'In recent days there have been armed demonstrations of plainly counter-revolutionary groups who have arrested [*sic*] and beaten up soldiers, sailors and workers who disagree with the demonstrators. These groups march with the portrait of Minister Kerensky and hide behind the name of the Provisional Government.'[177] Those behind the resolution accused their opponents of political mimicry, of 'hiding behind' the reputation of the government and, evidently, using the portrait of the popular minister to camouflage the real aims of those organizing the demonstrations. Notably, the resolution, while calling for defensive action against the danger of counter-revolution, contains no criticism of Kerensky personally. Those who drafted it clearly considered it impolitic to represent him as the main personification of the political enemy.

At the same time, supporters of the offensive were not immune from attack. An attempt by Kerensky's supporters to distribute leaflets in the workers' district led to violence. In another incident a car drove into the Vyborg district, its passengers handing out posters reading 'Forward for Kerensky'. Soldiers of the Moscow Regiment arrested them, tore up their posters, and presented the car to the even more radical Machine-Gun Regiment.[178]

In Peterhof, cadets from the school of ensigns organized a patriotic demonstration under the slogan of 'Long live Brusilov and Kerensky'. They were attacked by soldiers of a reserve regiment, who brutally beat them with rifle butts and crippled one of their number. The soldiers were particularly incensed by the fact that the protesters were carrying a portrait of Kerensky.[179] It was the minister of war rather than the commander-in-chief who was the hate figure for opponents of the offensive.

Undoubtedly such conflicts arose in part because of Bolshevik propaganda, although even within the party there were different nuances in how the current situation was interpreted. There were divergent reactions also to demonstrations in support of the offensive. Some activists, considering this the wrong moment for confrontation, called for restraint. Others were all for harsh opposition of 'the bourgeois public'. There were differences too among the moderate socialists. As a result of the efforts of the Menshevik Internationalists, the order for the offensive was condemned by the Committee of Petrograd Organizations of Mensheviks, in which representation of the left was strong. Under the influence of the Bolsheviks and others opposed to the offensive, analogous resolutions were passed by meetings of workers and soldiers.[180]

The growing crisis was accompanied by increasingly heated debate around Kerensky. Thus, the soldiers of the 1st Reserve Infantry Regiment, which had so warmly welcomed him in early May, 'cursed Minister Kerensky for the offensive he had undertaken, calling him a traitor who had betrayed his homeland, and a thief as a former lawyer, and proposed taking measures against him because otherwise he would be a dictator.'[181]

This kind of attitude was not confined to the soldiers of the Petrograd garrison. The chairman of the Soviet of Military Deputies of Tver declared, 'The offensive launched on 18 June should be considered an act of counter-revolution by the Provisional Government.' He also called Kerensky an anarchist.[182]

We cannot on the basis of isolated examples (although there are more of them) judge how prevalent such sentiments were. It seems clear, however, that they were becoming a factor of major political importance. It was not for nothing that Kerensky's supporters viewed criticism of the minister of war with growing alarm and tried to have resolutions passed that were favourable to the 'organizer of victories'. Thus, the battalion committee of the Reserve Battalion of the Guard of the 3rd Infantry Regiment resolved that 'The victorious offensive of the Russian army which has begun, demonstrating the power and strength of the revolutionary spirit of the masses of soldiers, has been achieved through the labours of the inspirer and creator of the new army, Comrade Kerensky. He has done something that until now we considered both incredible and impossible. Confidence, glory and honour to the people's Leader.' An assembly of the committees of the Reserve Battalion of the Izmailovsky Guards Regiment formulated the unit's position as follows: 'We have complete faith in the orders of Minister of War Kerensky, who also has the confidence of our newspaper. . . . Full confidence in the Soviet of Workers' and Soldiers' Deputies and Minister of War A. F. Kerensky.' It is telling that such resolutions should have been printed in the newspaper of the Constitutional Democrats.[183] This was just the kind of reaction from the soldiers that the leaders of the Cadets wanted to see at this time. They regarded the image of 'the people's Leader' as a useful political tool. Comparison of these resolutions, which were printed side by side, enables us to highlight nuances in the attitudes of those who formed the coalition of support for Kerensky. In the first resolution he is described as a unique leader who has created the new army: in the second he is definitely being supported, but that support is linked to support for the Soviet. It is also telling that the editors of *Rech'* felt they needed to jump on the bandwagon of the cult of the unique Leader, although most of the Cadet leaders had little time for Kerensky.

Meanwhile, it was the minister of war who became, not only for left-wing socialists but also for some pacifists, the embodiment of the war they so hated. On 27 June the artist Konstantin Somov made an entry in his diary characterizing the mood of his friends – Alexander Benois, artist, art historian and art critic, and Stepan Yaremich, artist and art historian. 'Breakfast at Shura's. Myself, then Yaremich. Both of them foaming at the mouth over the war. Cursing Kerensky and everybody else.'[184]

At the same time, the new situation that had arisen with the offensive enhanced the political status of the minister of war. A resolution of the 4th Cossack Don Regiment, published in the main Menshevik newspaper, reads: 'In A. F. Kerensky we have as our Leader a tried and trusted champion of the people's cause. We warmly congratulate our Leader, the great champion of the people, builder of great Russia on new, democratic principles, inspirer and assembler of the army, Minister Kerensky, and send him a resounding Cossack "Hurrah!"'[185] As we see, the Cossacks called Kerensky not only their Leader but also the 'builder of great Russia on new, democratic principles', thereby acknowledging his exceptional role and primacy over the other leaders of the February Revolution, of the soviets, and of other members of the Provisional Government. It is interesting that the Mensheviks, who were observing the politicization of the Cossacks with some apprehension, suspecting their sympathies lay with the conservatives, did nevertheless publish the resolution. Evidently, the democratic rhetoric framing the respectful attitude towards the 'Leader' made the resolution politically acceptable to them.

Nikolai Krylenko also spoke about the strengthening of Kerensky's special status at the Bolshevik All-Russia Conference of Military Organizations, noting that, in the present situation, 'the revolution is endowing just one person, Kerensky, with the fullness of power.'[186]

This was openly remarked on in several Bolshevik newspapers. *Pravda Grenaderskaya*, distributed on the Southwestern Front, referred to the initial composition of the Provisional Government as 'the government of Guchkov and Milyukov' and to the later coalition government as 'the government of the capitalist, Kerensky'.[187] It is noteworthy that it was not Prime Minister Prince Georgiy Lvov who was seen by the radical soldiers on the front line as personifying the hated government, but the minister of war.

Kerensky again and again found himself the focus of heated discussion at all sorts of meetings and in city streets. 'People are talking on Znamenskaya Square about the offensive, about Kerensky, arguing passionately, not holding back from offensive gestures and profanity,' reported the Mensheviks' *Rabochaya gazeta*.[188] Sometimes these disputations could include threats to Kerensky. The internationalist newspaper *Novaya zhizn'* printed two letters from the army in the field which horrified many contemporaries. Importantly, both letters were reprinted in several other newspapers. One was sent in the name of a Siberian company of fusiliers and demanded the release of Lieutenant Flavian Khaustov, an editor of the *Okopnaya pravda* newspaper. (At that time the newspaper was under predominantly Bolshevik influence. Khaustov himself was a Maximalist Socialist Revolutionary.) The riflemen threatened the minister of war directly.

> In the event of non-compliance with our resolution, we will be in Petrograd, a team of three persons from our company, we will take decisive measures with you, Mr Kerensky, by armed force, and you will be killed like a former dog that was not yet gorged itself full of blood. You are a traitor of our freedom, you want to be the ruler of Russia, but no, you cannot be because your head has not been hewed from the right end. Down with you, Kerensky, publisher of iron discipline, you want to put everything back like it was before. Leave your post before it is too late because for us three people death for freedom in battle will be fine. Down with you, Kerensky! Down with you! Long live the peasants' and soldiers' deputies! Down with the whole Provisional Government which consists of damned bourgeoises! Down with you, go before it is too late. Down with the lousy

> bastard! Down with him! Down with him! Down with the disbander of regiments, Kerensky.

The second letter was addressed to Kerensky and Supreme Commander-in-Chief General Brusilov. 'You asked us to attack the Germans. No, we are not going to attack the Germans but soon we will attack the Russian bourgeoises, we will bayonet them all and at the same time bayonet Gen. Brusilov, we will bayonet Kerensky. You are going to die, Kerensky and Brusilov!'

The newspaper of the Socialist Revolutionaries, which also published these letters, complained that these 'savage threats', reflecting the 'low cultural level of the masses', were provoked by the Bolsheviks' radical slogans.[189] The editors of other newspapers, supposing that the letters would horrify their readers, also published them in order to discredit Lenin and his followers.[190]

The Bolshevik correspondent, however, without expressing open approval of those who had written the letters, argued that the policy of the offensive which was being pursued by Kerensky was the cause of such vengefulness among soldiers on the front line. 'There are no better agitators against your policy, gentlemen, than you yourselves. Who needs "Leninists" when the very stones cry out against you?'[191] It should be noted that, in the discussion of the letters, nobody cast doubt on the genuineness of such threats to the minister. Nobody raised the possibility that they might have been forgeries. The commentators, whatever their viewpoint, might have been appalled by the ferocity of the letters, but they all found it entirely credible that some soldiers at the front really did hate the man behind the offensive so much that they would threaten to murder him.

It is no surprise that people of differing views later reminisced about Kerensky particularly as he was at the time of the July Crisis. Historians disagree about the events of 3–4 July in Petrograd. Some see them as a failed putsch organized by the Bolsheviks, while others emphasize the spontaneity of a movement which the Bolsheviks were forced to join in order not to be left behind by their supporters. It is hardly plausible to claim that all the demonstrators' actions were spontaneous, although there clearly were some groups which took their own initiatives.[192] At the same time it makes no sense to talk about a fully coordinated direction of the movement. We have seen that there were significant differences between various factions within the Bolshevik Party. Moreover, anarchists and activists quite unattached to the party were actively involved in the events.

Negative images of Kerensky played a significant part in the political mobilization of opponents of the Provisional Government on the eve of the July Crisis, when news began to spread in the capital of the failure of the offensive on the Southwestern Front. The day before the events, on 1 July, a large rally had been held at the Reserve Battalion of the Grenadier Guards Regiment. Delegates fresh from the front spoke, relating that Dzevaltovsky and other grenadiers had been arrested. A resolution was adopted expressing 'complete lack of confidence in the Provisional Government, Minister Kerensky and the parties that support him.'[193] On 2 July a rally of soldiers of the 1st Machine-Gun Regiment also protested 'against the policy of unrestrained violence of the Provisional Government and Minister of War Kerensky towards revolutionary troops, resurrecting the old methods of Nicholas the Bloody.'[194]

Meanwhile the Bolsheviks were attacking Kerensky at meetings of the Petrograd Soviet and at rallies.[195] Slogans directed against the minister of war were also carried during demonstrations. Two non-commissioned officers of the Reserve Battalion of the Moscow Guards Regiment paraded a placard reading 'Down with Kerensky, and with him the offensive'. Shortly afterwards they disappeared, and the remaining demonstrators in the column destroyed the placard at the request of one of the officers.[196]

It was reported that some soldiers took to the streets of Petrograd during the July Days with the slogan 'The first bullet is for Kerensky!'[197] Some radical groups of soldiers tried to arrest the minister of war as he was leaving for the front, but missed his train. Kerensky was already on his way. Certain newspaper reports linked the two incidents, claiming that 'On 4 July the machine-gunners rushed to the Warsaw Railway Station to intercept the minister of war with a flag reading "The first bullet is for Kerensky!"'[198]

At rallies in the streets the Bolsheviks continued to decry Kerensky, although sometimes the Socialist Revolutionaries managed to make speeches in defence of their party comrade.[199] At times, a kind of 'street Bolshevism' converged with 'street anti-Semitism'. In the centre of Petrograd, one worker was arrested and taken to the police station for whipping up a crowd against Kerensky. He had been claiming as a well-known fact that the minister of war was a Christianized Jew.[200] Opponents of the Bolsheviks, printing the report, were keen to tar the Leninists as allies of the anti-Semites and paid special, probably exaggerated, attention to the episode. It is nevertheless the case, as we have seen, that at times *Pravda* and the Black Hundred *Groza* attacked Kerensky at the same time and on the same issue, although their rhetoric was very different.[201]

Criticism of Kerensky, bringing together anti-Semitic, anti-bourgeois attitudes and general hostility to those at the rear, is found in a letter from a front-line soldier sent in early July to the government commissar of the 7th Army. 'The traitors are not the soldiers but, on the contrary, we soldiers and officers in the trenches, we consider you, the people at the rear, that is the commissars, the bourgeoises and Kerensky, because he comes from the bourgeoises and probably, as you can see from his surname, is of the Jewish religion . . . what we're going to do is quit the trenches and go to Petrograd and strangle buggers like you, and the first bullet is specially for Kerensky.'[202] Unlike many soldiers' letters of that time there is no railing against the officers. The writer speaks on behalf of all those at the front and wants Kerensky dead, the minister of war who personifies all the shrill, belligerent loud-mouths and the miscellaneous other representatives of the rear.

In other cities, highly emotional discussion of Kerensky was an important part of the July Crisis. In Moscow, the newspapers reported, one speaker even called on his listeners to murder the minister of war and was nearly torn to pieces by the crowd for his pains.[203] If for some Kerensky remained the irreplaceable Leader and saviour, others now believed that only by physically removing the minister of war could the motherland be saved.

In the second half of June, the popularity of Kerensky, inspirer and participant in the offensive, had peaked. This was evident not only in the fact that his image was at the centre of patriotic demonstrations but also in a particular emotional tension behind the eulogizing of the minister of war, as well as in new forms of glorifying him. By the end of June it was already clear to the Command, and to Kerensky himself, that the troops were not obeying orders to carry out combat operations. In the rear many people continued to believe the operation was going according to plan, did their best to support the army, and/or attempted to use the offensive as political capital.

In parallel, the opponents of the offensive, above all the Bolsheviks, intensified their attacks on Kerensky. If some saw him as the Leader on a white horse saving the nation, others saw that as an omen of impending counter-revolution. Both sides were effectively promoting a similar image of the victorious leader, but at this stage that image of the minister, his words, and the rhetoric of those eulogizing him provoked bitter conflict, not infrequently accompanied by violence. Harsh condemnation of the politician morphed into a brutish demand for him to be 'liquidated'.

The furious attacks on Kerensky only intensified the determination of supporters of the offensive to elevate the person who personified it, and the image of the minister of war became a vitally important tool for mobilizing patriotic forces. The figure of Kerensky on a white horse was one of the images of a victorious leader of the revolutionary army, and rumours of his wounding, or even death, raised his reputation as a hero to a new level. The Leader of the revolutionary army became a living symbol of revolutionary Russia.

4 A popular 'brand' and symbol of the revolution

The Petrograd newspapers reported a juicy scandal which played out on 11 July right in the centre of Petrograd, on Nevsky Prospect, near the Nevsky Farce Theatre. In this theatre, located in the premises of the Yeliseyev trading building, there was a new play, *The Minister's Dream*. The announcement read: 'Première Today! New play! Sensation! Sensation! The Minister's Dream (Offensive of 18 June 1917). New spectacular scenery.'[204]

A journalist remarked that the theatre's sensational new play was a straightforward rip-off of the popularity of A. F. Kerensky, the inspirer of the offensive. The Nevsky Farce had a reputation for rip-offs based on topical heroes, and news of the army's victories had galvanized the authors into devising this new production, which looked set to make money. A newspaper report gives us an idea of what the play was about.

> The popular minister is depicted in three scenes. In the first he appears in a tent at the front where, together with a sentry, he is wakeful before the renowned offensive. The minister falls asleep and has a nightmare: Russian soldiers are fraternizing with the Germans. Treachery promptly approaches in the form of a flirtatious, ingratiating woman by the name of Provocation. The Minister awakens from his nightmare and calls for an offensive. The thunder of artillery fire is heard, betokening the offensive of the regiments of 18 June.[205]

The cause of the disturbance was in fact not the production itself but the way it was advertised, which caused great offence to passers-by. 'The money-grubbing administration of the theatre decided it was not enough only to depict A. F. Kerensky on stage, and displayed a portrait of the people's leader in an advertising showcase, in the very spot formerly adorned by posters for *The Harlot Mitrodora* and *Girl with a Little Mouse*.' According to the reporter, the public on Nevsky Prospect were very much on edge after all the events of recent days.[206] People offended by the poster might have witnessed the demonstration on 18 June, the celebrations on 19 June and, finally, the July Days. Many of these had taken place right in front of the building in which the Nevsky Farce was housed. Some of these people had defended the Leader from the attacks of supporters of the Bolsheviks and anarchists and were not prepared to put up with this insult from the promoters of a farce. Seeing the portrait of their favourite politician in such an insalubrious setting, passers-by demanded its removal. A large crowd gathered and the tension heightened. Their sense of indignation demanded an immediate outlet and they took the law into their own hands. The showcase was broken and the ill-fated poster torn to pieces. However, the crowd did not stop at that but forced the closing of the box office and made the cashier leave. They demanded that the play in which Kerensky was 'depicted' should be removed from the repertoire and threatened that otherwise irate citizens would come to the show and smash the theatre up. The evening performance did, in fact, go off without further trouble, but with almost no audience.[207]

The sympathies of the newspaper reporters seem to have been with the public, despite their having damaged a showcase with impunity, caused a breach of the peace and infringed the right to freedom of expression. The reporters condemned the theatre's directors for their cynical exploitation of the image of a newsworthy politician, but neither the disturbance nor the newspaper reports prevented the directors from continuing to run the farce, advertisements for which appeared periodically in the very newspapers which had reported the incident.[208]

There were other occasions when the ire of journalists was raised by 'farce marauders', theatrical wheeler-dealers out to make money by linking the public's interest in high politics with its liking for undemanding entertainment. 'When speculators in farce set their greasy paws on the sacred Russian Revolution, vulgarizing it in the most unbelievable manner, it is time to protest.'[209]

As this shows, some people saw the entire field of revolutionary politics as being such an elevated, sacred realm that they would not countenance the use of revolutionary imagery in works of undemanding entertainment. It is, however, noteworthy that the outburst of violence among the crowd on Nevsky Prospect was caused by a performance which they felt insulted their Leader, even though he was being depicted as a hero in the sketch which was being offered. The creators of the production and the indignant crowd evidently had a difference of opinion over the extent to which the events of the 'sacred Russian Revolution' should be seen as sacrosanct.

In many of the conflicts of 1917 we see either a battle between the supporters and opponents of Kerensky or a struggle 'for Kerensky', a desire to claim this influential politician for oneself, to have him on your side, to make use of his authority. Underlying the incident outside the Nevsky Farce was a disagreement over acceptable uses to which the image of the Leader could be put. If some people thought it was fine to make a profit out of reproducing images of the minister which people wanted to buy, even to include them in the genre of undemanding entertainment, others thought that impudent exploitation of the Leader's popularity was an insult to Kerensky, brought his authority into disrepute, and caused appreciable damage to his policies. Such 'frivolous' mass production of the Leader's image was seen as detracting from his charisma, and his supporters protested.

For historians, the reasons behind the politicization of the repertoire of a vaudeville theatre are of interest. No less interesting are the motives of those outraged by such commercialization of their idol. The politicization of leisure provided a business opportunity for those offering a revolution-related product to the audiences of such theatres, which at least confirms the demand for imagery of Kerensky. Indiscriminate cashing in by overly opportunistic entrepreneurs could, however, encounter resistance from members of the public for whom their beloved leader was sacrosanct. Kerensky's marketability was evidence of his popularity, but the revulsion of the public on Nevsky Prospect, and their practical instant theatre censorship, testify to his sacralization, which called for propriety in the ways he was celebrated and deemed some of them taboo.

The devotees of the minister of war were not incensed by the mere dramatization of him, or even by the initiative to make money out of him. They had, after all, bought tickets to hear the renowned orator perform in the principal theatres of Russia at a time when his opponents were already accusing their idol of histrionics. They were offended by the translation of their leader to a low genre. The high tragedy of the revolution, in which their chosen one was the lead actor, should not be turned into a skit, debasing the image of the great revolutionary Leader. They furiously defended the border between the sacred and the profane. This somewhat disputed symbolic frontier, poorly marked but nonetheless sacred for that, was important for defending certain crucial political values. It defined the principles on which a new political culture was to be formed.

The appearance and elaboration of Kerensky's images is best understood within a context of mass consumption of revolutionary symbolism in 1917. During the February Days, enterprising street vendors were already selling red bows, and demonstrators happily bought them. In the ensuing days and weeks, the demand for 'revolutionalia' led to the appearance of all manner of goods and services which the citizens of the new Russia, rapidly becoming more politically aware, were keen to snap up.[210] They were prepared to spend time and money to be part of revolutionary politics. They bought tickets to concert rallies and cinematographic showings in which newsreels and films exposed the evils of the old regime and celebrated the champions of freedom. They bought songbooks with the words of revolutionary anthems and gramophone records on which the anthems were performed by famous orchestras and singers. They sent their relatives postcards with portraits of revolutionary leaders to mark family celebrations and public holidays and proudly wore badges with revolutionary symbols. They feverishly bought up any pamphlet that mentioned revolution. This rapidly expanding market would never have developed without the involvement of political parties and public bodies, for which it was an important part both of their campaigning and of their financial revenues. Nor, however, would it have developed without the frenetic activity of entrepreneurs whose aim was to make money and who satisfied, and sometimes created, demand on the part of the revolutionary consumer. The logic of market dynamics could actually play against the prospects for capitalist development in Russia. No sooner did they detect that 'anti-bourgeois' sentiment was taking root in certain social strata than highly adaptable businessmen set about publishing pamphlets and postcards criticizing capitalism, denouncing the bourgeoisie, and extolling socialism.[211]

The popular figure of Kerensky was bound to be exploited. Hundreds of thousands of people wanted to see and hear him, to know more about him, to read his speeches, to identify with him. Here was a demand in urgent need of being satisfied. Political parties fell over each other to offer different images of Kerensky in accordance with their partisan aims, and entrepreneurs offered whichever images of the Leader particular segments of the market demanded.

The market was an indicator of how prominent a particular politician was and not infrequently contributed to moving their popularity up a notch. The announcement that Kerensky would be participating in a concert rally was the best way to ensure a large audience, thanks in no small measure to the minister's rhetorical gifts and image as an artist-politician. The famous concert rally at the Moscow Bolshoy Theatre was remarkable for its scale, but public interest was drummed up by news of the minister's earlier oratorical triumphs in similar performances.

Portraits of Kerensky were much in demand. In spring 1917, Prince Vladimir Drutskoy-Sokolinsky, who until the fall of the monarchy had been governor of Minsk, visited the Petrograd apartment of Nikolai Opochinin, who had been a district marshal of the nobility in Smolensk province and a deputy of the State Duma. Opochinin's daughters were fervent admirers of Kerensky, and this was reflected in the way the apartment was decorated. 'In the dining room I was struck by the numerous portraits of Kerensky on the walls. His insolent, clean-shaven, degenerate-looking physiognomy peered at one from every direction,' recalled the prince in his memoirs.[212] It is evident from these that the prince was an out-and-out monarchist, so one ought not to expect objectivity in his judgement of Kerensky or, indeed, a balanced appreciation of the minister's admirers. However, he is not alone in some of the views expressed in his memoirs.

The correspondence of people close to Dmitry Merezhkovsky and Zinaida Gippius gives insight into a particular instance of the use of political portraits in 1917. The 37-year-old sister of Zinaida, the sculptor Natalia Gippius, wrote on 14 May to Dmitry Filosofov, expressing her symbolic solidarity with the politicians defeated during the April Crisis. 'I love Rodzyanko, Shulgin and Milyukov with such tender love. I have them all hanging on my wall. Milyukov and Guchkov hang under the icon shelf, in a national frame. Guchkov has a rosette in the national colours; Milyukov has the flags of the Allies. I hung them there after they were driven out, in defiance. I have also framed Shulgin with a national ribbon with a bow. So there!'[213] The June Offensive, however, saw her extend the group of politicians to whom she accorded her particular support: she added Kerensky to her personal pantheon of statesmen of the new Russia. The forty-year-old painter Tatiana Gippius, long an admirer of the minister of war, wrote with some satisfaction on 30 June, 'Kerensky has been awarded a place of honour by Nata, along with Guchkov and Milyukov. He hangs there, covered in ribbons in the national colours, under a candle in honour of the war.'[214]

The behaviour of Natalia Gippius, who was deeply religious, reflects her specific religious and political orientation, manifested in her canonization of statesmen. Her actions may, however, tell us something about a political shift in the views of people with liberal and conservative beliefs, who came to admire Kerensky because of his identification with the offensive. She created a domestic gallery of leaders symbolizing her ideal patriotic united front: Shulgin, Guchkov, Milyukov and Kerensky. She was evidently unconcerned that in the circumstances of June 1917 any such coalition was out of the question, but she was not the only person who longed for a patriotic united front extending from Shulgin to Kerensky. It is also telling that she decorated Kerensky's portrait with ribbons of white, blue and red, clearly perceiving the minister of war not as revolutionary but as a national leader. Portraits of Kerensky, decorating the rooms of citizens, both male and female, of the new Russia, were a sign that private space was becoming politicized.

The intrusion of politics into private space is further evident from the considerable availability of postcards depicting Kerensky. In the modern catalogue of a large private collection we find six postcards showing all the members of the initial Provisional Government, including, of course, Kerensky. There are also nine series where each postcard is dedicated to one of the ministers.[215] There are notably no series in the catalogue devoted to members of the Coalition Government created in May or the cabinets which replaced it. Evidently by this time interest in the portraits of most ministers was fading. The exception is Kerensky, who continued to be favoured with the attention of postcard manufacturers and, presumably, of their customers. The catalogue includes twelve postcards in which he is depicted, and that does not take into account the others which were part of the series already mentioned. No other minister of the Provisional Government, no other figure active during the February Days, received as much attention from postcard manufacturers. Moreover, no fewer than seven postcards of Kerensky were issued after he became minister of the army and navy. It can safely be assumed that demand for images of him at this time only increased. Some postcards are fairly rough-and-ready affairs, often based on photographs by local photographers. This too demonstrates a continuing demand.

The publishing house of Maria Snopkova, who was associated with the Socialist Revolutionary Party, in June issued a series of letter cards titled *A Gallery of Portraits of Revolutionaries*. It depicted Stepan Balmashev, Yekaterina Breshko-Breshkovskaya, Grigoriy Gershuni, Ivan Kalyaev, Alexander Kerensky, Nikolai Mikhailovsky, Yegor Sozonov and Vera Figner.[216] The minister of war was the only one of the 1917 leaders to be included in the pantheon of veterans of the liberation movement, heroes and thinkers considered important for Narodniks and Revolutionary Socialists to remember. The absence of Victor Chernov, a highly prominent leader of the Socialist Revolutionaries, is striking.

Postcards and small portraits of Kerensky indicate that the Leader's images were in demand and had found their way into people's private lives. Large portraits played their part in a number of political contexts. After Kerensky's appointment as minister of the army and navy his portraits were especially in demand there, and the propagandists of the ministry did their best to meet the demand. Kerensky's portrait had symbolic significance among the troops. When he visited Riga, he was greeted by ranks of soldiers and sailors. Some units had his portrait on their right flank.[217] The troops may have regarded their non-regulation action only as a gesture of hospitality, but placing the portrait on the right flank, where the banner should be, during a ceremonial greeting of the minister of war made it clear that the portrait was being accorded a particular, symbolic role. The Command did not object and may even have been pleased to see such veneration of the head of their ministry.

Portraits of the minister of war took on particular significance during the demonstrations welcoming the June Offensive. Their sudden appearance on the streets in such abundance in itself testifies to how widespread and available they were. If Kerensky's devotees were attaching symbolic meaning to the portraits, opponents of the offensive expressed outrage at the deference shown to these 'new icons'. For them the portrait of the minister of war symbolized only their political opponent, and to seek to incorporate his portrait into the system of revolutionary symbols struck them as nothing short of sacrilege and a step towards reviving the traditions of tsarist political culture.

As mentioned, in May and June, portraits of the 'best of citizens' were offered as lots in various patriotic auctions in a number of cities. In that respect, the Bolshoy Theatre auction was unusual only for the large sum bid. Here too we find images of the Leader functioning as symbols of the revolution, of Russia, and of the offensive.

Grigoriy Belykh, in an autobiographical story, describes a group of Petrograd children during the revolutionary period imitating the adults. Politicizing their games, they decide to organize a political club. They make a dugout in the courtyard and promptly put a portrait of Kerensky on the wall.[218] This was evidently what, in the children's opinion in 1917, a real club should look like. Indeed, portraits of the minister of war, alongside the portraits of earlier champions of freedom, did adorn the walls of some soldiers' clubs which opened that summer. We note that the children playing in a courtyard on the outskirts of Petrograd had no difficulty in acquiring a portrait of Kerensky, which also indicates how available such images were. Better-off members of the public had portraits of the Leader painted for them. In early July, 190 rubles was raised at a meeting of the Petrograd Committee of Commerce to commission a portrait of Kerensky which, shortly afterwards, was hung in the committee room.[219]

Further testimony to the prevalence of portraits of the minister and the strength of feeling they inspired is provided by incidents when they were defaced. Shortly after the attempted coup by General Lavr Kornilov, on the night of 3 September, a group of officers and volunteers who had gathered in the Freedom Coffee Shop in Oryol was engaged in an overly casual conversation about the current situation. At the suggestion of one of their number, the companions ostentatiously ripped down the portrait of Kerensky, outraging the other patrons. There was a major row. The militia arrived with a patrol of the Horse-Drawn Artillery Battalion, and the six would-be demonstrators were arrested.[220] In this tale everything has significance: the name of the fashionable coffee house, the topic of the diners' heated discussion, focused on Kerensky, the act of small-scale iconoclasm, and the portrait itself on the wall, which again confirms the ubiquitousness of depictions of the minister. Especially interesting, however, is the extreme reaction of the public, a reaction which confirms the incident's ritual significance.

A tsarist legal attitude was being projected on to the new era. Tsarist legislation had prescribed quite severe punishments for insulting members of the imperial family or depictions of them.[221]

A need for a similar sacralization of the representatives of the highest authority and their images was firmly rooted in the political consciousness of the new citizens who supported the minister-democrat, and this is evidence of the covert influence of the tsarist political tradition. The old, repressive legal statutes had been repealed, but a need for them was still felt. The public, outraged by the conduct of the directors of the Nevsky Farce Theatre, censored the repertoire by taking the law into their own hands and thus reviving the censorship functions of the Ministry of the Imperial Court, which, until the revolution, had managed the publication of works of art and consumer goods that referred to or depicted representatives of the supreme power and members of their families.[222] The conduct of people demanding that the authorities should intervene where the leaders of the revolution or depictions of them were subjected to derogatory treatment demonstrated that the attitudes protecting the sanctity of political symbols, which before the overthrow of the monarchy had included members of the imperial family, were still alive and well.[223]

Sculptural portraits of Kerensky were also sought after. A plaster bust preserved in the State Central Museum of Contemporary History of Russia in Moscow (formerly the Museum of the Revolution) has the title *A. F. Kerensky, the Sublime Poetry of the Revolution.* The sublime and poetic nature of the political Leader is depicted by two wings sprouting from the minister's temples, making it appear that his head may be about to take flight. The work truly demonstrates the sacralization of his image and reminds one of the traditional Russian depiction of a cherub.

Sculptured busts of 'the people's minister', which were in considerable demand, were presented to anyone acquiring at least 25,000 rubles' worth of Freedom Loan bonds. The reward was evidently prized, because there were not always enough busts to go round and some generous lenders were left feeling cheated.[224] Here Kerensky was personifying the patriotic mobilization of revolutionary Russia, and his image symbolized the new society.

We can be sure that the proud bond purchasers will have exhibited their bust of the Leader, thus demonstrating their patriotism. As we have mentioned, Marina Tsvetaeva recalled that a bust of the minister of war graced the Prague Dining Rooms in Moscow, which she frequented. (After the Bolshevik seizure of power it was replaced by a bust of Trotsky.) That was not the only artefact with Kerensky's likeness which she recalled: 'I still have a souvenir, a little turquoise-coloured cardboard book with gilded pages. You open it wide and there is a broken mirror on the left, and on the right – Kerensky! Kerensky, gazing day and night into the shattered fragments of his hopes. I received this relic from Nadya's nanny, in exchange for a real mirror, in one piece, without The Dictator.'[225] Whoever manufactured the mirror was evidently confident that the Kerensky brand would have a favourable effect on sales. How many women, gazing into these mirrors, saw side by side with themselves a popular politician whom some of his contemporaries considered a 'dictator'?

After the revolution there was great demand for badges and tokens. The proceeds from sales of these were donated to patriotic charities. Sometimes they depicted popular commanders, such as General Brusilov, or people who symbolized the national aspirations of the peoples of the empire, for example, Taras Shevchenko. Sometimes they depicted red flags and other symbols of the revolution. Most common, however, were badges and tokens dedicated to Kerensky. They imitated similar badges and tokens with images of Nicholas II. One badge in honour of the revolutionary minister is highly typical. Its description in the catalogue reads, on the obverse, 'a depiction of A. F. Kerensky in leafwork, facing right' and, on the reverse side, the inscription 'Glorious – Wise – True and beloved Leader of the people 1917'. Some tokens with Kerensky's image became a model for the badges of the Soviet era, which, from as early as 1918, featured the portrait of Vladimir Lenin. They were created in the same workshops, to the same patterns.[226]

In the feverish spread of the cult of the revolutionary leader there were even rumours that new medals would be struck with the image of Kerensky. Some even imagined the badges were state awards: 'But now medals have appeared with someone in Roman profile impressed on them which are worn next to the St George's Cross,' wrote one aristocratic lady to her relatives on 20 June.[227] From the context of the letter it is clear she is referring to Kerensky. Rumours in those circles tended to overstate the influence of royal tradition, such as the profile of the tsar as a state symbol, on the formation of the cult of the revolutionary leader. They did in some measure anticipate the odd partial symbolic restoration implemented by Stalin in the 1940s, when the profile of a still living Leader appeared on USSR medals.

Not only depictions but even the words of the minister became objects of veneration and instruments of sacralization. Thus things Kerensky had said, picked out in flowers, adorned the graves of victims of the revolution.[228]

The very name of the Leader became politically emblematic. In May someone had the idea of creating a special Friend of Humanity A. F. Kerensky Foundation. That was a proposal submitted to the Petrograd Soviet. The cadets of the Alexander Military College asked that the graduation year of 1917 should be known as the Kerensky Cohort. It was with difficulty that the minister dissuaded them. Simultaneously, however, the revolutionary Leader's enthusiastic fellow countrymen were naming a new unit of volunteers in Simbirsk in his honour, recruiting members of the Kerensky Legion.[229]

Streets too were renamed in honour of the minister. In early June a group of soldiers in the active army appealed to the mayor of Kiev to change the 'tsarist' names of city streets. First and foremost they wanted Stolypin Street renamed Kerensky Street.[230]

Kerensky was not the only hero of the February Days whose name featured in toponymic changes, but renamings in his honour were many. His name was mentioned in plans to rename streets in several cities. At an early stage of the revolution he had an entire district named after him. In April a telegram arrived in the Ministry of Justice from Tomsk province, addressing the minister as 'Citizen Kerensky'. It indicated that the Sergievo-Mikhailovsky Volost People's Assembly had resolved unanimously to abolish the name of the volost, 'given in honour of the grand duke from the hateful house of Romanov'. The minister was informed that

> The assembly resolved to give itself the name of you, the best citizen of free Russia. May the memory of you, the tireless champion of freedom for the humiliated and insulted, for the land and freedom, be held sacred from now on, not only by the citizens of Kerensky Volost but also by every citizen of the free Russian democratic republic. Our fervent thanks to you for all you have done. May Citizen Kerensky flourish for many years to come!

It seems unlikely that the entire population of the volost actively supported this resolution – rather, that it reflected the view of a group of local activists. For them the name of the great revolutionary had become a symbol of the new way of life. Kerensky's reaction is interesting: he wrote on the telegram, 'Thank them.' The official reply, sent on 13 April on behalf of the minister to the Kerensky Volost Assembly reads, 'Thank you for your greeting and the honour you have given me.'[231] Neither the minister nor his staff were embarrassed by such forms of glorification.

If the renaming of streets and administrative districts testified to the political allegiance of local authorities, the choice of personal names indicated major politicization of personal life. A boy born in Kiev in June 1917 was given the name Alexander in honour of Alexander Kerensky.[232] The name was common, of course, so few people would necessarily have guessed later on that the parents had been motivated by admiration for the minister of war at the time. Those who in 1917 decided to change their surname to Kerensky were in a different situation.[233] They clearly believed the glory of their idol was going to last for a long time.

In June 1917 Kerensky was not only the most popular politician of the February Revolution, he was the personification of the revolution itself, its symbol. That is how he was represented in pamphlets glorifying the Leader of the revolution. 'The noble symbol of the noble February Revolution'; 'The name of Kerensky stands for so much. Kerensky is a symbol of truth, a guarantee of success. Kerensky is a lighthouse, a beacon to which the swimmers reach out their arms, swimmers who have given their all and now, from his fire, from his words and clarion calls obtain an influx of more and more strength for the hard struggle.'[234]

Frequent likening of Kerensky to the sun also points to the unique role of the Leader who has become symbolic of the revolution. 'The sun of Russia's Freedom', he was called in newspapers which supported him. When he arrived in Smolensk, those welcoming him carried placards reading 'Long live Kerensky, Russia's sun!' Nobody found anything surprising about another slogan, 'Long live Kerensky, the sun of freedom!' The correspondent Vasiliy Kiriakov, who was close to Kerensky, wrote: 'His name has become synonymous with the beauty, purity and clarity of our smiling revolution. A. F. Kerensky has become the darling and the hope, the "red sun" of the Russian people.' This image was taken up by Kerensky's 1917 biographers.[235]

The image of the 'sun of the Russian Revolution' came into use soon after the overthrow of the monarchy. Already in March a letter was published from a group of working women in Tver, which was partially quoted above.

> The name of Kerensky has long become dear and loved in every nook of our country. In the darkest days of the recent past we cherished the echoes of Kerensky's words and thoughts. Now that name and A. F. Kerensky in person have become the Sun of Russia, the Conscience of Free Citizens.
>
> We grandmothers, mothers, sisters and daughters, 'cumbered Marthas', beg you, brothers, you who are close to him, guard his life, guard his time, make sure he gets at least a minimum of sleep and proper food, so that the strength of of New Russia's Sun is not overtaxed. We bow low to the Conscience and Heart of the free citizens of Russia, A. F. Kerensky.[236]

Kerensky, the democratic minister, was also called 'the symbol of democracy'. 'For us Kerensky is not a minister, not a tribune of the people; he has ceased to be even just a human being. Kerensky is the symbol of the revolution,' wrote admirers of the people's minister who considered themselves adherents of democracy. Such is the text of a leaflet published in 1917.[237]

That writing stands out for its categorical tone, but other sources also testify that, for many, Kerensky did indeed symbolize the revolution and the new revolutionary social system. 'Russia's freedom speaks to us with your lips,' the minister of war was told by the committee and commander of the 3rd Naval Regiment of the Baltic Naval Division. A resolution adopted by a general assembly of the workers of the S.A. Trainin Factory read: 'We hope that the revolutionary government created by A. F. Kerensky, the symbol of democracy, will be steered by the captain saving our sinking ship and that Russia, with the support of all the live forces of the country, will embark on its radiant voyage to the future.'[238] Kerensky's status as a symbol of the revolution was recognized by other politicians and taken into account when deciding policy. Nikolai Nekrasov, the minister of communications in the first Provisional Government, declared early in March, 'Citizens, for us Kerensky is, let me say, not a minister, not even a tribune of the people, he may even cease to be a human being – he is a symbol of democracy.'[239] (His words may have been used by those who compiled the leaflet quoted above.) Another minister, Mikhail Skobelev, a prominent Menshevik, said at an important meeting of the leading institutions of the soviets on the night of 25 July, 'The name Kerensky is a symbol of the revolution, and the work he is doing gains him the support of all the forces in Russia.' This statement was greeted with prolonged applause.[240]

Both Nekrasov and Skobelev were collaborating closely with Kerensky and belonged to the top echelon of political Freemasonry. The political friends of the Leader of the revolution consciously created this political symbolism of the new Russia, with Kerensky at its heart.

Kerensky's status as a political symbol was recognized also by people who were gradually becoming disillusioned with his policies. On the eve of the Kornilov Affair a group of Petrograd intellectuals, which included Merezhkovsky, Gippius, Filosofov and Yevgeny Lyatsky, strongly advised Kerensky either to take power and rule himself or hand over executive power to more capable politicians such as Boris Savinkov. The proposal was that Kerensky should become a non-partisan president, a 'much-needed symbol'.[241] For the present study, what is important is that critics of Kerensky's policies considered he was nevertheless the lead candidate for the role of an indispensable symbol (which implied recognition of his uniqueness), and that they felt the need for such a symbol even if executive power were to lie elsewhere.

Kerensky's status was recognized by other critics of his policies. Literally at the same time, on 20 August, Zakhariy Frenkel observed at a meeting of the Central Committee of the Constitutional Democratic Party: 'If, seen at too close quarters, Kerensky seems a nonentity, outside the confines of a narrow circle he is regarded as a symbol of state power, and that needs to be taken into account, without giving excessive weight to personal impressions.'[242] Members of the political elite who had seen Kerensky 'at close quarters' believed they knew his true worth and no longer harboured any illusions about what he was and was not capable of. By this time, however, the revolutionary minister's reputation had become a free-standing factor of immense importance, and it would be short-sighted to overlook this personified symbol of the state when devising a new political course. The political forces supporting the offensive found themselves hostages to the very images of Kerensky they themselves had created in May–June, and that obliged them to temper their subsequent criticism of the head of the Provisional Government.

In the summer of 1917, one of the main Russian journals published *A. F. Kerensky*, a poem by Lidiya Lesnaya, in which the minister is represented as a Leader, a hero, a wise legislator and a genius creating a new world.

And in red smoke the icon lamps are sparkling
With light so pure, imperishable, bright.
You, eagle-eyed, have lit them in the darkness
You, wreathed in inspiration, in the light.
We mortals here in earthly flames were burning,
You brought Prometheus' fire in place of fear.
The pastoral of the past is past returning.
We'll shed no tear.
On broken balconies and floors,
With ghosts of books no longer so concerned,
We are learning now to love those other laws
Which, as your spirit in the heavens soars,
In other worlds your wisdom has discerned.
Our genius and hero! Russia's Leader!
A champion, to life and peace forever true,
Go forth in dauntless boyishness to where you're needed.
We are with you![243]

Similar images – the Leader, the genius, the wise helmsman – can be found in the poem which an ordinary soldier dedicated to Kerensky:

In times of strife, in times of glory,
Amid the storms and darkling sky,
Your genius wrote Russia's story
And held the flag of freedom high
Freedom's ship you next were steering,
Boldly to redemption's port.
We see the new life now appearing
That long the revolution sought.
The storm will still, the sea be silent,
All will be tranquil in the bay.
To him, who suffering salved and sorrow,
The people will their debt repay.[244]

The scandal about the play *The Minister's Dream* at the Nevsky Farce Theatre is portentous in several respects. Important images and rhetorical devices which shaped Kerensky's charisma were created and became widespread in the course of conflicts which accompanied the propaganda build-up to the June Offensive. Even after that operation failed, many people continued to see the minister of war as the Leader of a victorious revolutionary army.

In the eyes of many who opposed the offensive, however – and they came from across the political spectrum – Kerensky's actions deprived him of the status of Leader of the revolution. Nevertheless, any attempt to delegitimize (and desacralize) him prompted his supporters to produce new images and writings glorifying him.

The news of defeats on the Southwestern Front naturally restricted further elaboration and use of the image of a victorious Leader but did not completely rule out making use of it. Kerensky was described by some of his supporters as the conqueror of the real 'enemy within' who had deprived Russian soldiers of their deserved victory. The political defeat of the Bolsheviks and their allies in the July Days was portrayed as revenge for the military victories of an alliance headed by Germany. Images of Kerensky as a hero and the unique Leader and saviour of Russia, which had been developed after the revolution, and particularly in May and June when he became minister of war and was preparing the offensive, were entirely applicable in the new circumstances. The culminating phase in the creation of the cult of the Leader was reached in the last weeks of June, when, during the June Crisis, interrupted by the offensive, there were mass patriotic demonstrations with the figure of Kerensky firmly centre stage.

It was at this time that two cultural traditions came together which had received a new impetus after the February Days. The traditional glorification of the Leader of the army, the great, supreme leader, which had been an important element in the Russian patriotic tradition, was impacted by revolutionary political culture. Simultaneously, the tradition of glorifying authoritative champions of freedom, revolutionary leaders and leaders of political parties underwent a degree of militarization and was used by revolutionary defencists to prepare the ground for the offensive. To a lesser degree the monarchist tradition exerted a covert, but still palpable, influence on the development of the leader cult. It would certainly seem to be present in comparison of Kerensky to the sun. Images and rhetorical techniques appeared which were to be pressed into service later in Soviet political culture. The figure of Kerensky was at the point of intersection of these cultural and political processes, and the creative minister himself made a considerable contribution to establishing a proto-Soviet political culture. An important part of his contribution was the cult of the Leader. Creators of the cults of Lenin, of Trotsky and, later, of Stalin, and of cults of Soviet leaders further down the scale, actively availed themselves of ideas tested and widely applied by supporters of Kerensky.

Alongside the red flag and *The Workers' Marseillaise* and other revolutionary songs, Kerensky for a time himself became an important political symbol of the new Russia. The popularity of the minister, promoted by a number of political forces and commercial interests, was a prerequisite for sacralizing him. In turn, the sacralization of Kerensky, variously interpreted, began to affect how he was eulogized and, indeed, to see certain forms of glorification as no longer appropriate. The status of a genius, a symbol, a sun-god did not allow for even a hint of detraction from the image of the Leader. The Great Leader was certainly not a figure suitable for recycling as light entertainment. This censorship, exercised on the initiative of citizens of the new Russia and reminiscent of the practices of tsarism, was a resounding proclamation of the arrival of a fully fledged Cult of Kerensky.

Conclusion

In May 1917 an article was published in *Novaya zhizn'*, the Petrograd newspaper of the internationalists. It examined the attitude of the different parties to their leaders.[1] A well-known philosopher, writer, economist and natural scientist, the physician Alexander Bogdanov knew the political culture of the socialist movement at first hand: from 1905 to 1909, together with Lenin, he was one of the leaders of the Bolsheviks. Bogdanov noted that a 'dictatorship of the Leaders' played a major role in various Russian political parties. It represented spiritual power exercised on the basis of voluntary faith. The author's hypothesis was that, if what came to power was a party whose organization was based on the authority of its Leader, the principles underlying the way it acted would affect the emerging social and state system of the country.

> Every organization, when it succeeds in acquiring decisive influence in public life and the social system, inevitably, regardless of the formal provisions of its programme, will strive to impose *its own* form of organization on society, because that is what is immediately to hand and familiar. Every social collective restructures, as far as it is able, the entire social environment in its own image and likeness. If that is of an authoritarian type, based on domination and subordination, even if only mental, then an authoritarian tendency in the structuring of society follows fatally from that, no matter how democratic, communistic or whatever its programme may be.

Bogdanov warned that, given such leader-centric principles of party organization, even the most progressive ideology would present no obstacle to the establishment of an authoritarian regime. 'We know from history such forms as Caesarism, based on democracy, communism with supreme power of the prophets or priests . . .' He looked back to the experience of the past. 'Anyone who studies the history of the Great French Revolution will, of course, have been amazed how quickly and easily republicans, Jacobins, turned into loyal Bonapartists.' Bogdanov believed it was mistaken to suppose this trend could be put down purely to renegacy, to self-serving opportunism on the part of former revolutionaries who adapted adroitly to changing conditions. More significant was the fact that the French politicians 'had gone through a school of submission and devotion to their leaders, the political heroes of the far left, during the rise of the revolutionary cause.' For Russian democracy, 'not politically firm and culturally weak', that authoritarian risk was a particular threat. Bogdanov examined authoritarianism on the example of the Bolsheviks, being particularly knowledgeable about the history of that party, and considering the trends in its development entirely typical. Indeed, not only did Bogdanov not consider authoritarianism a feature which had from the outset been exclusive to the party. 'Hostility towards authorities was even a distinguishing feature of Bolshevism. The word "leader" was usually used ironically.' Initially, according to Bogdanov, the word 'Leninists' was used only by their opponents, as a derogatory characterization of their tendency in social democracy. With the growth of Lenin's authority, however, the Bolsheviks themselves began applying it to themselves. (As we have seen, even in 1917 not all Bolsheviks were prepared to acknowledge that they were 'Leninists'.)

Authoritarianism, Bogdanov believed, developed in other parties and was evident in the glorification of their leaders. He particularly mentioned the cult of Georgiy Plekhanov, created by supporters of the 'Father of Russian Marxism'. He emphasized the inclination of the Narodniks to create cults of their leaders and saw it as rooted in the traditions of peasants who had undergone 'authoritarian education for centuries'. Bogdanov barely mentioned the 'bourgeois' parties but had no doubt that there was authoritarianism in their parties too.

The overthrow of the monarchy had not eradicated authoritarian attitudes. 'What has been overthrown politically continues to live culturally.' He formulated an urgent task: 'A majority of our socialists in name and by manifesto have yet to become even democrats in their thinking. . . . A cultural revolution is essential.'

To summarize, the overthrow of an authoritarian political system was effected by various forces which proclaimed their commitment to the democratic ideal but remained bearers of an authoritarian, 'leaderist' political culture. This created the conditions for regeneration, on a new ideological basis, of an authoritarian political system centred on a cult of the Leader of the party and the state.

Bogdanov's views seem prophetic. At least, many writers described (and are still describing) Russia's subsequent history as an adaptation of political ideology to the deep structures of the traditional political culture. In fact, though, they are most often writing about the direct, albeit covert, influence of a patriarchal, authoritarian, monarchist tradition.[2] Bogdanov, however, was pointing out the authoritarian political culture of Russia's political parties, including all the left-wing parties.

The article in *Novaya zhizn'* evoked a response from *Delo naroda*, the Socialist Revolutionaries' principal newspaper. Its author did not, of course, accept that the Narodniks were predisposed to authoritarianism but considered the question about leaders not only topical but urgent. The Socialist Revolutionary author used his discussion of Bogdanov's ideas to berate his political opponents, noting the ease with which 'we form parties centred on particular individuals – a party of Leninists, a party of Plekhanovites.' He shared Bogdanov's concerns and approvingly quoted his conclusion – that 'what has been overthrown politically continues to live culturally.'[3] The author did not doubt the need for a cultural revolution to democratize the socialists' political style.

Bogdanov did not mention Kerensky by name, but it is highly likely that, working on this article in May 1917, the philosopher had in mind the cult of the 'Leader of the revolutionary army' which was being developed at that time. It is entirely likely that the correspondent of *Delo naroda* was not enthused by the forms glorification that his fellow party member was taking. Certainly by this time some Socialist Revolutionaries were having doubts about the Kerensky cult.

In this study I have given examples of the representation of Lenin and Chernov, seeking to demonstrate that glorification of their leaders by the Bolsheviks and Socialist Revolutionaries was often a reaction to the actions on the part of their opponents. Similar tactics were adopted by other political forces. For example, on 27 March 1917, at the Seventh Congress of the Constitutional Democratic Party, the philosopher Prince Yevgeny Trubetskoy eulogized Pavel Milyukov as follows.

> When we see the enemy at the door, when we see anarchy at the door, that is when we come together. In a single national thought, in a single national feeling we unite around those national Leaders who express that thought. That, gentlemen, is the reason, that is the explanation for the applause that dear Pavel Nikolaevich has just heard.
>
> Gentlemen, everyone in their locality has been closely watching the steps taken by this valiant Leader of the party of freedom for the people. We have been unable to detect in them a single error.

Prince Trubetskoy directly indicated that it was the actions of the political enemy, which he described as aggressive, that obliged the Cadets to unite around their 'Leader' and glorify him. For the left-wing socialists, 'Milyukov of the Dardanelles' was the personification of Russian imperialism, and the Cadets came out strongly in his defence. In his speech Trubetskoy several times called Milyukov 'the Leader' and standard-bearer. His welcome to the party's Leader was greeted with 'tumultuous applause' (which turned into a 'prolonged ovation').[4]

In party forums, representatives of the Cadets' student organizations referred to Milyukov as 'our old, experienced champion, our Leader'. They swore allegiance to the party's banner and Leader, 'who holds this banner and will carry it forwards in defiance of all dangers and obstacles'. The speeches ended with exclamations of 'Long live our

Central Committee, long live our Leader, our glory and our banner: Pavel Nikolaevich Milyukov.' The congress delegates applauded.[5]

It is not only the way the Leader was greeted that is interesting but also how that was written up in the Cadet press. One reporter describes Milyukov's arrival at the congress: 'All the members of the congress, and the numerous members of the public in the gallery, rise and give the Leader of the party a rousing ovation. All the members of the presidium and the speaker join in the applause.'[6] Milyukov held a special position among the leaders of the Cadets, but the party could hardly be called 'leader-centric' – although, as we have seen, the eulogizing of its Leader by prominent representatives certainly occurred. Different Cadets had different ideas about the tactic of glorifying the Leader, and probably had varied attitudes towards Milyukov himself, but the style of such eulogizing was not objected to, and we have seen how the party press described support for the Leader.[7]

Bogdanov's remarks about the leader-centrism of Georgiy Plekhanov's supporters is borne out by other sources in 1917. The Yedinstvo group, which united Social Democrats of extreme defencist views, was numerically small, so the authority of the Father of Russian Marxism was a particularly important asset. His supporters called Plekhanov their 'wise Leader', 'the beloved Leader of Russian Social Democracy', 'the Great Leader and champion of the class interests of the proletarian world'.[8] They also called him the 'teacher of Russian Social Democracy' and their 'dear teacher'.[9]

The tradition of glorifying party leaders affected the development of political language in 1917. A radically anti-monarchist revolution put a taboo on the rhetoric and symbolism of the monarchy, although these resurfaced in covert and sometimes unconscious forms, as we have seen. After a time, educated contemporaries stopped tittering about simple people who aspired to 'a democratic republic with a good tsar'. The search for new ways of representing political leaders become more urgent, and the turn to glorification and strengthening of the authority of party leaders, about which Bogdanov had written, became more evident.

After the overthrow of the monarchy, another tradition developed. The word *vozhd'* [Leader with a capital 'L'] was often applied in the political language of pre-revolutionary Russia to top military leaders and commanders of various ranks. The tsar, who was in command of the armed forces, was called the 'Sovereign Leader', and during the First World War the supreme commander-in-chief, Grand Duke Nikolai Nikolaevich, was called the 'Supreme Leader'. The cult of the supreme commander-in-chief was supposed to maintain and strengthen the cult of the tsar but, in fact, began to rival it. The rising political status of the 'Supreme Leader' was one of the reasons for the grand duke's dismissal in August 1915, when Nicholas II himself became supreme commander-in-chief. The rivalry between the Sovereign Leader and the Supreme Leader, which threatened the regime, was eliminated.[10]

Other military commanders, commanders-in-chief of fronts, commanders of armies, were also called *vozhd'*. The term was rarely applied to military administrators, no matter how high their rank. Before the revolution, as far as can be judged, the minister of war, for example, did not merit the title.

In this sense, the word *vozhd'* continued to be used after the overthrow of the monarchy, but now there were additional demands made of military leaders and new criteria for evaluating their status. *Novaya zhizn'*, for example, questioned the right of General Alexeyev to be the real 'Leader of the Russian revolutionary army', because his conservative political statements appeared to debar him from such a style.[11] Accordingly, several military leaders adopted elements of revolutionary political culture to demonstrate their loyalty to the new regime. Their 'democraticness' strengthened their claim to be a *vozhd'*. The image of the great military Leader itself became politicized. When, after the overthrow of the monarchy, General Lavr Kornilov was appointed to the important post of commander of the Petrograd Military District, although only the general of a military district in the rear rather than of front-line troops, the press began to call him the *vozhd'* of the people's army.[12] Such an appellation would have been impossible before the downfall of the tsar. As evidence of the general's closeness to the people, and indeed of his democratic credentials, his humble origins were cited, his democratic way of behaving, his ability to speak with the soldiers in simple language. When Kornilov became a pretender to the role of a national, 'people's' *vozhd'*, he was being considered primarily in political terms, and the military component of his claim retreated to the background. 'General Kornilov cannot be dismissed because he is the real Leader of the people,' declared the Soviet of the Union of Cossack Troops in early August 1917.[13] The implication was that those whom the 'real' Leader of the people opposed lacked the qualifications for the job. If authoritarianism in the political culture of socialist parties was sometimes masked by anti-authoritarian ideology, the tradition of glorifying military leaders, although politicized and 'democratized' after the February Revolution, was authoritarian from start to finish.

These sources of authority, alongside the cult of champions of freedom, which became a highly important factor in revolutionary political culture, were used in creating the representation of leaders at the national level. Mikhail Rodzyanko, initially perceived by many as the main instigator of the coup, was described as the 'first citizen of Russia' and sometimes called the *vozhd'*. However, images of Kerensky very soon eclipsed those of Rodzyanko and other contenders for the role of the Leader of the coup. It was the charismatic 'revolutionary minister' and not, for example, Prince Georgiy Lvov, the head of the Provisional Government, who came to personify the February Revolution.

The image of the 'Leader of Democracy', created after the February Days, received new impetus in May. When Kerensky became minister of war, he was proclaimed the 'Leader of the revolutionary army'. In

June, with the beginning of the offensive, rhetorical techniques, symbols and rituals were devised to articulate the cult of the irreplaceable Leader and saviour who now symbolized revolutionary Russia. Other claimants, leaders of political parties and military leaders, sometimes also had the title conferred upon them in various publications of the period, and sometimes laid claim to the status themselves, but none of them were perceived as Leaders of all the people and, for the present, could not rival Kerensky. It was only after General Kornilov became supreme commander-in-chief that he and his supporters were able to challenge Kerensky's status as the irreplaceable Leader.

This is not to say that the Kerensky cult in 1917 is comparable as a socio-political institution with the later cults of Lenin, Trotsky and, particularly, Stalin. Nevertheless, the main cultural forms of glorifying the Leader of the People and exploiting his authority were developed in March–June 1917 and later pressed into service when creating other revolutionary cults, including cults of the Soviet, and even of the White Russian, leaders.

Several traditions were brought together when constructing the Kerensky cult. The reputation of a 'champion of freedom' was extremely important in legitimizing many political leaders, and Kerensky was no exception. His career, however, particularly attracted the attention of publishers and readers. No other politician could boast such a quantity of biographical pamphlets. His reputation as a tribune of the people who had fought the old regime, the halo of his prophetic status in predicting the collapse of the autocracy, served to confirm his status as the *vozhd'*. The truth of the matter is that the biographies of many politicians of the revolutionary era employed similar techniques, and sometimes the exact same turns of speech, developed over generations by participants in the liberation movement. Kerensky and other leaders of the revolutionary era were described as champions of freedom, and the politically usable parts of their life stories were slotted into the sacred history of the liberation movement, a history which became the basis of the politics of memory of revolutionary Russia.

Kerensky's entry into the Provisional Government as minister of justice necessitated a search for new ways of representing state power. The images of a 'minister of the people's truth' and a 'democratic minister' called for a new rhetoric, new 'democratic' gestures and rituals. Kerensky rejected images proposed to him that were blatantly reminiscent of the old regime (although that did not prevent critics later comparing the actions of the revolutionary minister to those of the last tsar).

The special atmosphere of the 'festival of revolution', a seemingly universal euphoria at the overthrow of the autocracy, produced a singular political style vividly demonstrated in Kerensky's public speeches. Here elements of the political traditions of the revolutionary underground intertwined with the public politics of the era of the State Duma and the artistic, Nietzsche-tinged culture of the Silver Age. In later years many memoirists, writers and historians deemed this combination eclectic, unnatural and vulgar. Indeed, the whole wave of revolutionary ecstasy in March 1917, manifested in emotional aestheticization of politics, gave rise later to much critical irony. In the circumstances of the time, however, that massive outburst of excitement was a huge political asset, and Kerensky's 'histrionic' speeches and the image he projected were wholly in harmony with the jubilant mood and political culture of his audiences and enabled him to provoke, mould, strengthen, direct and exploit that enthusiasm to his own ends.

Much of what Kerensky did was determined by the configuration of the major political forces. He was not backed by any politically powerful body, and even in his 'own' Socialist Revolutionary Party did not enjoy universal or unconditional support. The fate of the revolutionary minister thus depended on the durability of the coalition of moderate socialists and liberals, which, in the language of the time, reflecting the cultural hegemony of socialists, was styled an arrangement between 'democratic forces' and 'the bourgeoisie'. That alliance, also described as an alliance of 'all the live forces' of the country, was not only consonant with the most fundamental convictions of Kerensky, who wanted to prevent a civil war while continuing to participate in the world war. It also corresponded to his tactical political interests. Kerensky himself had no prospect of being a national Leader outside a coalition in which he was the central figure. Accordingly, he sought constantly to create, maintain and re-create that coalition. This affected how he was represented and how the image of the Leader developed.

Kerensky, simultaneously a member of the Provisional Government and deputy chairman of the Executive Committee of the Petrograd Soviet, occupied a place in politics which helped him to accomplish the task of creating and re-creating an 'arrangement' between the so-called bourgeoisie and democratic forces in the unstable situation of dual power. His position as a minister on the right flank of the moderate socialists who was prepared to cooperate with liberal politicians also facilitated this. Finally, the experience of bringing together diverse forces of the opposition, which Kerensky had acquired during the world war and the February Days, was also very important. This advantageous political positioning did not of itself guarantee success in building a coalition. It was a task which required constant energetic efforts, new initiatives, and swift responses to dangerous and unexpected challenges. It also called for adaptability in representation of the Leader, which needed constantly to change in the light of urgent issues affecting the maintaining and restoring of the coalition. His position as the conciliator of all Russia's live forces was to some extent reflected in the representations of 'Kerensky' and how they were perceived, but it was not the dominant theme in the system of images of the Leader of the people. Nevertheless, the political tactics, of which representation as a popular minister was part, were always determined by that overriding political objective. The unique political position of the revolutionary minister brought about his reputation as the irreplaceable Leader, which was important for accumulating charisma.

The task of furthering political unity was made more difficult by Kerensky's lack of powerful and committed supporters among the main leaders of the political parties, although at certain stages he found important allies. Of particular importance was the assistance of Irakliy Tsereteli, an authoritative Menshevik leader who ensured the support of Kerensky by many influential moderate socialists. Already in March, however, Kerensky sometimes completely ignored the leaders of the Petrograd Soviet while simultaneously openly challenging Milyukov, the leader of the Constitutional Democrats. He was able to do so because his influence beyond the circle of the new political elite, his authority with the masses who were rapidly becoming politicized, was exceptionally great. For the 'March Socialist Revolutionaries' and new recruits in other political parties, including even some new members of the Bolshevik Party, he was the most famous and influential, popular and outstanding Leader of the February Days. Kerensky's influence over non-party delegates of sundry soviets and committees was even greater, and he appealed to them on more than one occasion over the heads of their party leaders. This, of course, did nothing for his relations with the moderate socialist leaders.

These circumstances need to be taken into account when assessing the role of Freemasonry in furthering Kerensky's career. The influence of that shadowy organization certainly cannot be overlooked and requires further study, but the power of the revolutionary minister within the political elite derived primarily not from behind-the-scenes collusion but from his authority on the streets, manifest from the February Days onwards. Neither the leaders of the 'bourgeoisie' nor the leaders of the 'democratic forces' could afford to ignore the asset represented by this popular politician, although both had a growing list of resentments against the darling of the revolution. At the time, however, they chose not to make them public.

Kerensky's authority came under severe strain during the April Crisis. The circumstances surrounding the publication of Milyukov's Note could have left the revolutionary minister politically isolated. Both moderate socialists and liberals suspected him of double-dealing. In that situation, he executed an important manoeuvre, delivering what proved to be one of his best-known, and most unexpected, speeches. Using the image of 'rebellious slaves', he was able to tap into and mould a sense of anxiety which was growing in society. Kerensky thereby significantly increased his authority, although, again, the speech did not improve relations with the leaders of the moderate socialists. A way out of the crisis was found, with the active participation of the minister and on conditions especially advantageous to him. The speech strengthened his status as Leader. He made use of the widespread sense of anxiety to create a new wave of enthusiasm and established his status as the exemplary citizen, the Great Citizen, marshal and inspirer of free citizens as opposed to rebellious slaves.

The creation of the first Coalition Provisional Government in May substantially increased Kerensky's influence. He not only moved to the important post of minister of the army and navy but further increased his popularity. The difficult, and indeed ultimately unrealizable, task of creating a 'discipline of duty' in the armed forces, based on the civic consciousness of a citizen-soldier, required a compromise between the generals and increasingly influential members of the military committees. This, in turn, made it essential to adjust the representation of the head of the army and navy departments.

Falling back on the already established and popular images of the 'champion of freedom' and the 'democratic minister', Kerensky militarized his appearance, his style and his speeches, creating an image of the 'Leader of the revolutionary army'. This became an important component of the propaganda campaign for the June Offensive, and a variety of supporters of the offensive contributed to developing and disseminating the new image.

On the other hand, preparations for active hostilities at the front contributed also to a mobilization of opponents of the minister of war: the Bolsheviks, some of the left socialists, and the anarchists. Negative images of Kerensky were important tools here. For many soldiers, the minister of war came to personify the offensive they so hated. For the first time he came under sustained propaganda attacks. To articulate negative sentiment, his opponents created a gallery of negative images, attacking both the minister's policies and his political style.

It was, however, these propaganda attacks which helped to consolidate a broad and heterogeneous coalition in favour of the offensive. It had the support of the generals, the business elite, the liberals and a substantial section of the moderate socialists. In varying degrees and in a variety of ways, they sought to strengthen the authority of the minister of war, who served for them as the embodiment of the planned military operation. Members of this coalition might have their own grudges against Kerensky, but they postponed criticizing him, recognizing that eulogizing the minister of war was good for the propaganda campaign in favour of the offensive. New, positive images of the Leader were devised and propagated. Some had a mixed reception. Comparisons with Napoleon, for example, were resented by some but welcomed by others, in whom they roused hope that order would be restored in the country.

The coalition supporting the offensive was unstable. The moderate socialists, who predominated in the leading councils of the Mensheviks and Socialist Revolutionaries, were often opposed to the conservatives, liberals and right-wing socialists. This was particularly visible in the disputations between *Rech'* and *Delo naroda*, the principal newspapers of the Constitutional Democrats and the Socialist Revolutionaries. Various parties in these debates tried to claim Kerensky as their ally, referred to his authority, offered their own interpretations of his image as Leader, and criticized the same tactic in their opponents. Kerensky himself declined to be pinned down. He was in no hurry to commit to any position, and it was not unknown for him to express different opinions to different audiences.

This led to his being celebrated by both the left and the right, with the result that his gallery of positive images became all the more diverse.

Even during the preparation of the offensive, friendly propaganda presented Kerensky not only as the inspiration behind the offensive but also as a 'hero of the offensive'. His image as a 'hero' and as 'the hero of the revolution' had been used to describe him in March and was now revived with a new, patriotic colouration. Against a background of enthusiastic propaganda bulletins, rumours were born to the effect that, holding aloft a red banner, Kerensky was leading the regiments of the revolutionary army into battle under fire from the enemy.

The image of 'hero' was exceptionally important in forming Kerensky's charisma. He had already figured as a prophet, a revolutionary ascetic, a unique and irreplaceable politician, the last hope of the country, a Leader and saviour. The celebration of the first victories of the Russian army in the June Offensive signalled, however, that there was a fully fledged cult of the Great Leader. Kerensky was now portrayed as the symbol of revolutionary Russia. The cultural forms required to describe the charisma of the revolutionary Leader were duly found. This leader cult became a major political asset and proved itself during the July Crisis when the Bolsheviks and their allies mounted a challenge to the power of the Provisional Government.

In different phases, different forces involved themselves in developing and disseminating Kerensky's images. Researchers into leader cults ponder the question of who, primarily, creates them. Often they theorize that they were created principally 'from above', by political, business and cultural elites who, using heavyweight political resources, mainly of the state bureaucracy, inculcate the cults in the masses. Sometimes an alternative view is expressed, even in respect of the ossified, 'frozen' cults of the Soviet era. 'The cult of Stalin grew from the grassroots of society and was supported from above,' writes Alexander Zinoviev, a meticulous contemporary and impassioned researcher of communism.[14] We can hardly agree with that proposition: the cult of Stalin was created by the mighty bureaucratic machine of the Russian party and state, which specialized in propaganda and the mobilization of the populace. Any attempt to oppose it was crushed by the secret police. That included unauthorized individual initiatives to glorify the Leader undertaken by sincere Stalinists. Such simplistic, one-dimensional spatial metaphors as 'above' and 'below', which are used only too often in the scholarly literature, are simply not up to the task of describing a phenomenon as complex as a leader cult. They are wildly inappropriate when describing the era of the revolution and the Civil War when the cults were only in the process of evolving. The Kerensky cult was primarily the product of political conflicts on different levels and of different kinds, including conflicts at micro level. The parties involved in these conflicts were seeking to enhance their own authority, to which end they participated in campaigns to legitimize or delegitimize the Leader of the revolution, adopting or rejecting, proliferating, developing and inventing a variety of images of him.

The revolutionary minister personally created images of himself. The particular political and emotional atmosphere of the initial stage of the revolution suited the way he was presented and his oratorical style. His notorious 'political impressionism' played a part, but the 'minister of revolutionary theatricality' not only operated as an actor with a talent for improvisation and a producer of dramatic scenes, he was also a skilled and calculating impresario. Kerensky ably exploited the leading periodicals of Petrograd and Moscow. He adroitly created news stories of interest to newspaper readers and made time to hobnob with influential journalists, editors and publishers. A succession of publishing projects glorifying the Leader of the People was launched with Kerensky's assistance.

Only small groups of moderate socialists and democrats supported the revolutionary minister steadfastly and unreservedly. Those closest to him were the Trudoviks, the People's Socialists, some of the defencist Mensheviks, and especially the Right Socialist Revolutionaries grouped around *Volya naroda*. (The influence of the last group on the party was not great, but it was very important that some veterans of the revolutionary movement supported Kerensky, most notably Yekaterina Breshko-Breshkovskaya.) These groups received financial support with the aid of Kerensky and his team, which allowed them to conduct their propaganda on a respectable scale. As already noted, most of the biographies glorifying the Leader in 1917 were published by Narodniks, primarily the Right Socialist Revolutionaries. The Narodnik approach to eulogizing heroes, martyrs and leaders was reflected in them.

At the same time, some of Kerensky's political allies, while approving his policies, were cool towards his personality cult. One such was Georgiy Plekhanov. His newspaper *Yedinstvo* represented the views of defencist Marxists for whom even the Menshevik party was too far to the left. *Yedinstvo* supported the coalition with the 'bourgeoisie' and the offensive of the Russian army, but Plekhanov's supporters found Kerensky's political style unacceptable and they never described him as a Leader. Nevertheless, *Yedinstvo*, and Plekhanov personally, took an active part in demonstrations celebrating the beginning of the June Offensive, thus indirectly glorifying its instigator. The Father of Russian Marxism was himself seen as both their teacher and their *vozhd'* and effectively facilitated construction of the Kerensky cult, whether he considered him a *vozhd'* or not.

Some of Kerensky's opponents on the right became tactical allies for the time being. In their own interests they pragmatically made use of images of the revolutionary Leader, helping to strengthen the minister's authority and affirmation of his cult. This can be said of a number of liberal and conservative politicians and influential periodicals. It applies also to many army and naval officers, admirals and generals. In some cases they genuinely supported his actions, particularly the preparations for the offensive. In other cases they were simply seeking to consolidate their own power by referring to the authority of a popular and influential politician. Generals Mikhail Alexeyev, Alexey Brusilov and Dmitry Shcherbachyov, and other military leaders, for a time publicly extolled Kerensky, seeking to strengthen discipline in the army with references to his authority and, in the process, to strengthen their own position. In this respect Admiral Alexander Kolchak and General Lavr Kornilov were no exception. The future leaders of the White Russian cause also contributed their might to creating the cult of the revolutionary Leader, availing themselves of the minister's authority and aspects of the revolutionary tradition to achieve their goals. Among the prominent entrepreneurs who provided financial support to Kerensky was Alexey Putilov, who made statements publicly supporting Kerensky and helped to consolidate his authority.

Kerensky based his reputation as Leader of the revolutionary army on the support of heroes of the Russian army. Enthusiastic greetings to him from veterans at the front and knights of the St George's Cross symbolized the confidence the army needed to have in its minister. This tactic for strengthening personal authority had been used before the revolution and was employed by other political leaders. The presentation by soldiers of their military awards to the minister of war in May 1917 was unprecedented. It represented authoritative endorsement of his status as a Leader and a hero and was an essential contribution to his charisma.

Well-known writers, directors, scholars and artists also did their bit to build up the Kerensky cult. Some did so through public statements; others eulogized the Leader with their works. Fyodor Batyushkov, Vladimir Bogoraz-Tan, Arkadiy Bukhov, Dmitry Filosofov, Zinaida Gippius, Mark Krinitsky (Mikhail Samygin), Alexander Kuprin, Sergey Kusevitsky, Lidiya Lesnaya (Lidiya Shperling), Dmitry Merezhkovsky, Vasiliy Nemirovich-Danchenko, Vladimir Nemirovich-Danchenko, Pyotr Olenin-Volgar, Alexander Roslavlev, Mikhail Rundaltsov, Boris Savinkov, Konstantin Stanislavsky, Nikolai Tikhonov, Marina Tsvetaeva and Semyon Vengerov found new words and images for describing the Leader. The authority of the politician was confirmed by the authority of celebrities. They contributed with varying degrees of talent and varying degrees of conviction, and their offerings met with varying degrees of public appreciation. In eulogizing Kerensky, these figureheads of Russian culture had equally varying motivations. Some sincerely supported his policies. Others were crazy about this fashionable politician. Others again tried ardently to support 'their' representative in the world of big politics. Kerensky had long-standing ties of friendship and kinship with different groups and circles of the radical and liberal intelligentsia. Finally, there could be a material incentive: Kerensky was selling well at this time. A politicized society was prepared to pay up for images of the idol and writing dedicated to him. Badges, postcards, portraits and busts of the Leader sold like hotcakes. In some instances there was also a straightforward commission from a propaganda publication whose editors wanted the endorsement of a famous author in order to attract readers.

Comparing what was written by respected authors and ordinary people caught up in the events does not always find any great difference between a 'high' culture of the intelligentsia and a 'low' culture of the masses. Not infrequently both were bearers of the same authoritarian political culture. Often neither representatives of the educated upper classes nor semi-literate representatives of the grassroots could see any possibility of further political progress in Russia without a strengthening of the power of a unique, redemptive Leader, and all thought it made sense to participate in exalting him, although they did so using different words and images. Semi-literate soldiers at the front and sophisticates of the Silver Age phrased their political enthusiasms differently, while remaining firmly in the sphere of influence of the authoritarian 'leader-centric' political culture Bogdanov had described.

Much of what was said about Kerensky, and many of his images, came about not after long contemplation in the stillness of people's studies but as the instant reaction of active participants at various levels to a rapidly changing political environment. In May and June 1917, images of Kerensky were brought into play in conflicts, mostly in the course of the political battle over the June Offensive. In some cases the disagreement was between people who were for or against Kerensky; in others it could be that all parties to the dispute attempted to use his authority to bolster their case, attributing to him words or actions which proved their point. Some of these were wholly implausible, but this too is an indicator of the immense prestige enjoyed by the minister of war.

Increasingly, for Bolsheviks, left-wing socialists, anarchists, pacifists and opponents of the offensive of no particular party, Kerensky came to personify the enemy. The miscellaneous propaganda attacks on him by these groups obliged both his staunch supporters and his more opportunistic allies to come to his defence, setting their various gripes to one side for a time. These impassioned conflicts too gave birth to new images and words, and thus even Kerensky's political opponents indirectly contributed to the emergence of the leader cult.

Of particular importance for the creation of the cult was the political standoff in the armed forces. Representations of Kerensky, his images and gestures, and conflicts over the minister of war in connection with preparing and implementing the June Offensive contributed to improving the political literacy and solidarity of members of the military committees at various levels, whose authority Kerensky was keen to enhance. The appearance of the Kerensky cult and the formation of a numerous 'committee class' which played a huge role in the destiny of Russia were inextricably linked. They created a fundamentally new political situation. Although members of the military committees held differing views, and a great many of them did not belong to any party, they were on the whole inclined to defencism and were more moderate than representatives of the soviets. Initially, at least, the tone in the military committees was set by Right Mensheviks and Socialist Revolutionaries. Kerensky's authority there was high, and his rhetoric and how he was represented influenced the political style of the committee members. These, by copying the Leader of the revolutionary army, by quoting and celebrating him, made a substantial contribution to the evolution of his cult. In political terms, his utopian project of creating an army of citizen soldiers was not without its successes. The 'democratized' armed forces proved completely ill-adapted to waging a modern war but could crush any internal enemy of the new regime. Kerensky acquired a powerful political asset in the form of a network of influential organizations. With his authority as the Leader of the people, and with the support of the military committees, he was able to fend off the left-wing attacks on the Provisional Government during the July Crisis and the threat of the Kornilov Affair in August.

In creating the Kerensky cult, Kerensky himself, his staff, supporters and allies drew on a number of sources. Many components of the cult of the Leader were developed long before 1917 in the political culture of the revolutionary underground, and in 1917 they were pressed into service to endorse the authority of leaders of different political parties. The cult of 'champions of freedom', which was extended to include contemporary political leaders, became an important source of legitimation during the revolution. It is highly germane that the rhetoric and symbolism of the revolutionary underground were often called upon by opposed political forces. This in itself confirms their special, sacred role as a source of legitimation. Different parties fought over this resource and thereby confirmed its potency.

The Kerensky cult incorporated important elements from other traditions. Although revolutionary symbolism and rhetoric dominated in the creation of the new political culture, we can identify lessons learned from the patriotic mobilization at the outbreak of the First World War and, in a covert form, from the patriotic traditions of the monarchy, primarily of the tsarist army, subordinate as it was to its 'Sovereign Leader', and led by those other Leaders of the army, the commanders-in-chief. This amalgamation of the revolutionary and military traditions was particularly important when it came to resolving urgent political problems, and most notably in preparing the offensive.

All this cultural creativity in the spring and summer of 1917 was important for the following period. Many of the cultural forms of glorification of the 'Leader of the people' devised during this period were taken over, reworked and elaborated by the Bolsheviks. The Soviet political language was preceded by a proto-Soviet language, and the Bolshevik language was originally a particular dialect of revolutionary language (which later facilitated the task of 'speaking Bolshevik').[15] This revolutionary language, in the elaboration of which Kerensky, his staff and supporters participated in a major way, was very widespread in 1917. It was sometimes used by the future leaders of the White movement, which enhanced their status and made them known to the country. That affected their subsequent destinies and how they were seen.

According to some researchers, the leader cult is unthinkable without the support of developed state institutions controlled by the creators of the cult. Jan Plamper writes: 'Modern personality cults emerged only in closed societies. Closed societies have a highly circumscribed public space, making media-transmitted criticism of a leader cult or the introduction of a rival cult nearly impossible. In most closed societies the state exercises a high degree of violence, and the political personality cult is usually crucial in defining the relationship between ruler and ruled.'[16]

Such an approach makes it possible to understand the functioning of a developed leader cult: the images of Mussolini and Hitler, Lenin and Stalin, images which lived in the mass consciousness, are indeed unthinkable without the apparatus of mass propaganda and mass organized influencing. They were supported also by an apparatus of terror. However, this kind of interpretation omits the matter of the genesis of the cultural forms necessary for the emergence of a leader cult: important images and texts, which were subsequently distributed by a powerful party and state machine, were created under conditions of an intensely competitive political struggle. That was case with the cults of Lenin, Hitler and Mussolini, while the cult of Stalin drew on the already considerably developed cults of Lenin and Trotsky. In this respect, the multidimensional processes of cultural and political creativity which occurred in 1917 had a considerable impact on Soviet – and post-Soviet – political culture.

It is important to note that, in 1917, the leader cult as a form of personification of state power does not arouse particular criticism. (Alexander Bogdanov's article criticizing the authoritarian tendencies of several socialist parties which were creating cults of their leaders is more the exception than the rule.) Some opponents of Kerensky criticized his policies, others his political style. Sometimes he was considered a failed candidate for the position of Leader of the people, and sometimes he was called a false Leader. What was never questioned, however, was the actual need for a strong political Leader. What was doubted was the legitimacy of a candidate's claims to the role of Leader, not the principle of legitimation through glorification of the Leader. In 1917 one commentator suggested that the questions perplexing the citizens of Russia were: 'Whom should we to listen to? Whom can we call the real Leader? Whom should we follow?' The need was to distinguish the true Leader from miscellaneous other would-be Leaders, from demagogues who had no business claiming that status.[17] The actual need for a Leader was never questioned. The political choice facing Russia was formulated in terms of choosing the true Leader of the people.

The bearers of authoritarian political culture in 1917 were people with widely differing views. They included many supporters of Kerensky and many of his opponents.

Notes

Introduction

1 George Buchanan, *My Mission to Russia and Other Diplomatic Memories* (London: Cassell, 1923), vol. 2, pp. 86, 114. See also pp. 111, 128, 216–17 (https://archive.org/details/mymissiontorussi02buch/page/n7).
2 Louis de Robien, *The Diary of a Diplomat in Russia, 1917–1918* (London: Michael Joseph, 1969), p. 24; *War, Revolution and Peace in Russia: The Passages of Frank Golder, 1914–1927*, ed. Bertrand M. Patenaude and Terence Emmons (Stanford, CA: Hoover Institution, 1992), p. 46.
3 The military censorship's documentation is preserved in several different archives: *Rossiiskii gosudarstvennyi voenno-istoricheskii arkhiv* (*RGVIA*, the Russian State Archive of Military History), *fond* 2003, *opis'* 1, *delo* 1494, *list* 14; *Otdel rukopisei Rossiiskoi natsional'noi biblioteki* (*OR RNB*, the Manuscript Department of the Russian National Library, *fond* 152, *opis'* 1, *delo* 98, *list* 34; and *Rossiiskii gosudarstvennyi arkhiv Voenno-Morskogo Flota* (*RGA VMF*, the Russian State Archive of the Navy), *fond* 418, *opis'* 1, *delo* 5666, *list* 4.
4 See D. P. Os'kin, *Zapiski praporshchika* (Moscow: Federatsiia, 1931), pp. 110–11; Basil Gourko, *War and Revolution in Russia, 1914–1917* (New York: Macmillan, 1919), pp. 326–7; 'Iz ofitserskikh pisem s fronta v 1917 g.', publication by L. Andreev, *Krasnyi arkhiv*, vol. 1–22 (50–51) (1932), pp. 194–210. The letter was written by I. D. Grimm.
5 For different ways in which the term 'democracy' and some others were understood, see Boris Kolonitskii, '"Democracy" in the Political Consciousness of the February Revolution', *Slavic Review*, 57/1 (1998): 95–106.
6 Max Weber, 'Politics as Vocation', in *Max Weber: Essays in Sociology*, trans. H. H. Gerth and C. Wright Mills (New York: Oxford University Press, 1946), p. 78 (https://ia802705.us.archive.org/12/items/frommaxweberessa00webe/frommaxweberessa00webe.pdf).
7 Ibid., pp. 78–9.
8 On the concept of 'revolution', see Neithard Bulst, Jörg Fisch, Reinhart Koselleck and Christian Meier, 'Revolution, Rebellion, Aufruhr, Bürgerkrieg', in *Geschichtliche Grundbegriffe: Historisches Lexikon zur politisch-sozialen Sprache in Deutschland*, 8 vols (Stuttgart: Klett-Cotta, 1972–97), vol. 5, pp. 653–788.

9 Iurii Tokarev, *Narodnoe pravotvorchestvo nakanune Velikoi Oktiabr'skoi sotsialisticheskoi revoliutsii* (Leningrad: Nauka, 1965).
10 Nina Tumarkin, *Lenin Lives! The Lenin Cult in Soviet Russia* (Cambridge, MA: Harvard University Press, 1983); Benno Ennker, *Die Anfänge des Leninkults in der Sowjetunion* (Cologne: Böhlau, 1997); Olga Velikanova, *Making of an Idol: On Uses of Lenin* (Göttingen: Muster-Schmidt, 1996).
11 Jan Plamper, *The Stalin Cult: A Study in the Alchemy of Power* (New Haven, CT: Yale University Press, 2012).
12 Vasilii Maklakov, *Iz vospominanii* (New York: Chekhov, 1954).
13 *Petrogradskii voenno-revoliutsionnyi komitet: Dokumenty i materialy*, ed. Dmitrii Chugaev et al. (Moscow: Nauka, 1967), vol. 3, pp. 194, 616.
14 A brief list of Kerensky's books: *Delo Kornilova* (Moscow: Zadruga, 1918); *Gatchina (Iz vospominanii)* (Moscow: Knigopechatnik, 1922); *Izdaleka: Sbornik statei (1920–1921 g.)* (Paris: Povolotskii, 1922); *The Catastrophe: Kerensky's Own Story of the Russian Revolution* (New York: Appleton, 1927); *La Révolution russe (1917)* (Paris: Payot, 1928); *The Crucifixion of Liberty* (London: Barker, 1934); *Russia and History's Turning Point* (New York: Duell, Sloan & Pearce, 1965).
15 Vitalii Startsev, *Krakh Kerenshchiny* (Leningrad: Nauka, 1982). Startsev wrote other publications about Kerenskii: 'Begstvo Kerenskogo', *Voprosy istorii*, no. 11 (1966): 204–6; 'Kerenskii: Sharzh i lichnost'', *Dialog*, no. 16 (1990); *Russkoe politicheskoe masonstvo nachala XX v.* (St Petersburg: Tret'ia Rossiia, 1996); *Tainy russkikh masonov* (St Petersburg: D.A.R.K., 2004). This last book is a supplemented edition of *Russkoe politicheskoe masonstvo*.
16 Gennadiy Sobolev, *Revoliutsionnoe soznanie rabochikh i soldat Petrograda v 1917 g. Period dvoevlastiia* (Leningrad: Nauka, 1973). Sobolev also compiled a collection of primary materials on Kerensky's political career titled *Aleksandr Kerenskii: liubov' i nenavist' revoliutsii: dnevniki, stat'i, ocherki, vospominaniia sovremennikov* (Cheboksary: Chuvashskii universitet, 1993).
17 Richard Abraham, *Alexander Kerensky: The First Love of the Revolution* (London: Sidgwick & Jackson, 1987).
18 Genrikh Ioffe, *Semnadtsatyi god: Lenin, Kerenskii, Kornilov* (Moscow: Nauka, 1995).
19 Mikhail Basmanov, Grigorii Gerasimenko and Krill Gusev, *Aleksandr Fedorovich Kerenskii* (Saratovskaia gosudarsvennaia ekonomicheskaia akademiia, 1996); Vladimir Fediuk, *Kerenskii* (Moscow: Molodaia gvardiia, 2009); Stanislav Tiutiukin, *Aleksandr Kerenskii: Stranitsy politicheskoi biografii (1905–1917 gg.)* (Moscow: ROSSPEN, 2012). Andrei Nikolaev published an article about a 1917 interview in which Kerenskii described the February Revolution: Andrei Nikolaev, 'A. F. Kerenskii o Fevral'skoi revoliutsii', *Klio*, no. 3 (2004): 108–16. The latest publication of this primary source is in Semion Lyandres, ed., *The Fall of Tsarism: Untold Stories of the February 1917 Revolution* (Oxford: Oxford University Press, 2013). Aleksandr Rabinovich, 'A. F. Kerenskii i V.I. Lenin kak politicheskie lidery perioda krizisa', in *Politicheskaia istoriia Rossii XX veka. K 80-letiiu professora Vitaliia Ivanovicha Startseva: Sbornik nauchnykh trudov* (St Petersburg: Rossiiskii Gosudarstvennyi Universitet imeni A. I. Gertsena, 2011), pp. 209–16.
20 Andrei Golikov, 'Fenomen Kerenskogo', *Otechestvennaia istoriia*, no. 5 (1992), pp. 60–73. See also letters of the young Kerensky, discovered in the archives and prepared for pubication by Golikov: '". . . Budushchii artist Imperatorskikh

teatrov": Pis'ma Aleksandra Kerenskogo roditeliam', *Istochnik: Dokumenty russkoi istorii* [Supplement to *Rodina*, vol. 3 (1994), pp. 4–22].

21 Sobolev, *Revoliutsionnoe soznanie rabochikh i soldat Petrograda.*

22 Richard S. Wortman, *Scenarios of Power: Myth and Ceremony in Russian Monarchy*, 2 vols (Princeton, NJ: Princeton University Press, 1995).

23 Boris Kolonitskii, *'Tragicheskaia erotika': Obrazy imperatorskoi sem'i v gody Pervoi mirovoi voiny* (Moscow: Novoe literaturnoe obozrenie, 2010).

24 There is frequent mention of rumours in Valentin Diakin's authoritative, and in many respects unrivalled, study of the political elite during the First World War. See Valentin Diakin, *Russkaia burzhuaziia i tsarizm v gody Pervoi mirovoi voiny (1914–1915)* (Leningrad: Nauka, 1967), pp. 99, 112, 115, 116 and elsewhere. Diakin points out many instances where rumour affected the political situation.

25 At sessions of the Provisional Government Chernov would write articles for the party newspaper, despite being implored by his ally, the Menshevik Irakliy Tsereteli, to take part in the discussion of important matters. Oliver Radkey, the historian of the Socialist Revolutionaries, observes that, instead of drafting laws, the party's leader was writing newspaper articles. Oliver Radkey, *The Agrarian Foes of Bolshevism: Promise and Default of the Russian Socialist Revolutionaries, February to October, 1917* (New York: Columbia University Press, 1958), pp. 332, 333–4. This was the style of political leadership with which Chernov was familiar.

26 In her important publication, Olga Porshneva does not take this sufficiently into account when studying these letters as a source for reconstructing the thinking of the humbler members of society. See Ol'ga Porshneva, *Mentalitet i sotsial'noe povedenie rabochikh, krest'ian i soldat Rossii v period Pervoi mirovoi voiny (1914– mart 1918 g.)* (Ekaterinburg: Ural'skii gosudarstvennyi universitet imeni A. M. Gor'kogo, 2000).

27 Fediuk, *Kerenskii*, p. 144.

28 On surveys of the press created by various departments, see Irina Zhdanova, '"Vek propagandy": Upravlenie informatsiei v usloviiakh voiny i revoliutsii v Rossii v marte–oktiabre 1917 g.', *Otechestvennaia istoriia*, no. 3 (2008): 129–36. Kerenskii carefully studied such surveys. See ibid., p. 135.

29 On the basis of documentation in the Hoover Institute of Stanford University, Kerensky published, jointly with Robert Browder, *The Russian Provisional Government, 1917: Documents*, 3 vols, ed. Robert P. Browder and Alexander F. Kerensky (Stanford, CA: Stanford University Press, 1961).

30 Portraits of Kerensky were printed most frequently in the periodical press. Thus, in 1917 his portrait appeared in no fewer than thirty-two magazines, and twelve printed it in two or more issues. This compares with portraits of Milyukov, printed that year in seventeen magazines, Breshko-Breshkovskaya in sixteen, Guchkov in fifteen, Rodzianko in thirteen, Chernov in twelve, Plekhanov in eight and Lenin in six. See *Russkie portrety, 1917–1918 gg.*, ed. Matvei Fleer (Petrograd: [Gosudarstvennoe izdatel'stvo], 1921; repr. Moscow: Izdatel'stvo V.Iu. Sekachev, 2010). Fleer did not manage to encompass all the periodicals of the time, but he did take in the main illustrated magazines.

31 I have examined aspects of Kerensky's political biography during the whole of 1917 in a number of publications: Boris Kolonitskii, 'A. F. Kerenskii i Merezhkovskie', *Literaturnoe obozrenie*, no. 3 (1991): 98–106; 'Kerensky', in

Critical Companion to the Russian Revolution, ed. Edward Acton, Vladimir Cherniaev and William Rosenberg (London: Hodder Arnold, 1997), pp. 138–49; 'Kul't A. F. Kerenskogo: Obrazy revoliutsionnoi vlasti', *Soviet and Post-Soviet Review*, 24/1–2 (1997): 43–66; 'Britanskie missii i A. F. Kerenskii (mart–oktiabr' 1917 goda)', in *Rossiia v XIX–XX vv.: Sbornik statei k 70-letiiu R. S. Ganelina*, ed. Aleksandr Fursenko (St Petersburg: Dmitrii Bulanin, 1998), pp. 67–76; 'Kul't A. F. Kerenskogo: Obrazy revoliutsionnoi vlasti', *Otechestvennaia istoriia*, no. 4 (1999): 105–8; '"We" and "I": Alexander Kerensky in His Speeches', in *Autobiographical Practices in Russia*, ed. Jochen Hellbeck and Klaus Heller (Göttingen: [Vandenhoek & Ruprecht Unipress], 2004), pp. 179–96; 'Aleksandr Fedorovich Kerenskii kak "zhertva evreev" i "evrei"', in *Jews and Slavs*, vol. 17: *The Russian Word in the Land of Israel, the Jewish Word in Russia* (Jerusalem, 2006), pp. 241–53; 'A. F. Kerenskii kak "pervyi grazhdanin"', in *Fakty i znaki: Issledovaniia po semiotike istorii*, ed. Boris Uspenskii and Fedor Uspenskii, *vyp.* 2, Moscow, 2010, pp. 134–49; 'Feminizatsiia obraza A. F. Kerenskogo i politicheskaia izoliatsiia Vremennogo pravitel'stva osen'iu 1917 goda', in *Mezhvuzovskaia nauchnaia konferentsiia 'Russkaia revoliutsiia 1917 goda: Problemy istorii i istoriografii': Sbornik dokladov* (St Petersburg: Gosudarstvennyi elektrotekhnicheskii universitet, 2013), pp. 93–103; 'Russian Leaders of the Great War and Revolutionary Era in Representations and Rumors', in *Russian Culture in War and Revolution, 1914–22*, ed. Murray Frame, Boris Kolonitskii, Steven G. Marks and Melissa K. Stockdale (Bloomington, IN: Slavica, 2014), book 1, pp. 27–54; etc.

Chapter I Revolutionary Biography and Political Authority

1 *Edinstvo*, 14 May 1917.
2 Irina Zhdanova, '"Vek propagandy": Upravlenie informatsiei v usloviiakh voiny i revoliutsii v Rossii v marte–oktiabre 1917 g.', *Otechestvennaia istoriia*, no. 3 (2008): 129–36, here p. 130.
3 Aleksandr Kerenskii, *Rechi A. F. Kerenskogo o revoliutsii, s ocherkom V. V. Kir'iakova 'Kerenskii kak orator'* (Petrograd: Kopeika, 1917), p. 50.
4 V. B. Zhilinskii, 'Organizatsiia i zhizn' okhrannogo otdeleniia vo vremena tsarskoi vlasti', *Golos minuvshego*, nos. 9/10 (1917): 255.
5 O. L-v, 'A. C. [*sic*] Kerenskii pod nabliudeniem okhranki', *Novaia zhizn'*, 20 April 1917. The author of this publication may have been O. L. Leonidov, who is mentioned in the text. See also 'Tsarskaia okhranka ob A. F. Kerenskom', *Petrogradskaia gazeta*, 27 June 1917.
6 A file of documentation relating to Kerensky was found in Saratov (he was elected to the State Duma as a representative of Saratov province). *Zhivoe slovo*, 12 March 1917.
7 Here and hereafter the figures for print runs are taken from *Knizhnaia letopis'* for 1917.
8 *Aleksandr Fedorovich Kerenskii (Po materialam Departamenta politsii)* (Petrograd: Tsentral'nyi komitet Trudovoi gruppy, 1917), p. 3.
9 *Rechi A. F. Kerenskogo* (Kiev: Blago naroda, 1917), pp. iii–iv.
10 Anon, *Syn Velikoi Russkoi Revoliutsii Aleksandr Fedorovich Kerenskii: Ego zhizn', politicheskaia deiatel'nost' i rechi* (Petrograd: Petrogradskii listok, 1917).

11 Vasilii Kir'iakov, *Zapiski deputata 2-i Gosudarstvennoi Dumy* (St Petersburg: Vernyi put', [1907]).
12 Rafail Ganelin, *Rossiia i SShA, 1914–1917: Ocherki istorii russko-amerikanskikh otnoshenii* (Leningrad: Nauka, 1969), p. 371.
13 Vasilii Kir'iakov, 'A. F. Kerenskii', *Niva*, no. 19 (1917): 287–8; no. 20 (1917): 294–7.
14 Kir'iakov, *Niva*, no. 20, p. 294.
15 Ibid., p. 287; V–i V. [Vasilii Vasil'evich Kir'iakov], *A. F. Kerenskii* (Petrograd, 1917), p. 3.
16 Ibid., p. 36.
17 Ibid., p. 35.
18 Ibid., p. 16.
19 Vasilii Kir'iakov, *Dedushka i babushka russkoi revoliutsii: N. V. Chaikovskii i E. K. Breshko-Breshkovskaia* (Petrograd: Novaia Rossiia, 1917).
20 Oleg Leonidov, *Vozhd' svobody A. F. Kerenskii* (Moscow: Koshnitsa, 1917). Leonidov continued to publish popular biographies of political and military figures in the Soviet period. See [Oleg Leonidov], *Kliment Efremovich Voroshilov: Zhizn' i boevaia rabota*, ed. Sergei Orlovskii (Moscow: Gosudarstvennoe voennoe izdatel'stvo, 1925); *M. V. Frunze: Biografiia* (Moscow: Ogonek, 1925); *S. M. Budennyi, vozhd' krasnoi konnitsy: Materialy dlia biografii S. M. Budennogo i istorii I Konnoi armii* (Leningrad: Gubkompom, 1925); etc. Leonidov also wrote screenplays on themes from the history of the revolution, for example, *Moskva v Oktiabre (Bor'ba i pobeda)* (1927). Other screenplays were *Deti kapitana Granta* (1936) and *Ostrov sokrovishch* [Treasure Island] (1937).
21 Oleg Leonidov, *Vozhd' svobody A. F. Kerenskii*, 2nd, supplemented edition (Moscow: Koshnitsa, 1917), pp. 5–6, 17.
22 Ibid., pp. 31, 32.
23 Ibid., pp. 4–5.
24 Ibid., pp. 8, 16, 31.
25 Ibid., pp. 3, 24, 25, 26.
26 E. V[ladimirovi]–ch, *A. F. Kerenskii narodnyi ministr* (Odessa: Vlast' naroda, 1917).
27 Ibid., p. 3.
28 The only other studies to appear were of Breshko-Breshkovskaya, Brusilov and Kropotkin. See *Russkie portrety, 1917–1918 gg.*, ed. Mikhail Fleer (Petersburg: GIZ, 1921), pp. 6, 7, 25.
29 Tan (Vladimir Bogoraz), 'A. F. Kerenskii: Liubov' russkoi revoliutsii', *Geroi dnia: Biograficheskie etiudy. Obshchestvenno-politicheskii ezhenedel'nik* (Petrograd), no. 1 (1917), pp. 2–4.
30 Ibid., pp. 2, 4.
31 Ibid., p. 2.
32 Ibid., pp. 3, 4.
33 The July Crisis, or 'July Days' of 3–5 July, after the failure of the June Offensive against Austria and Germany and the resignation from the Provisional Government of the Constitutional Democrats, was a period of left extremist demonstrations demanding disbandment of the Provisional Government and the transfer of all power to the soviets of workers' and soldiers' deputies. When the attempted coup failed, the Bolshevik leaders, Lenin and Zinoviev, went into hiding. [*Trans.*]

34 V. Vysotskii, *Aleksandr Kerenskii* (Moscow: Tipografiia tovarishchestva Riabushinskikh, 1917), p. 21.
35 Ibid., pp. 9–10, 31.
36 Ibid., pp. 7, 11, 18, 19, 20.
37 Ibid., pp. 19–20.
38 *Partiia sotsialistov-revoliutsionerov: Dokumenty i materialy*, 3 vols, ed. Nikolai Erofeev (Moscow: ROSSPEN, 2000), vol. 3, part 1: 'February–October 1917', pp. 331, 333, 724.
39 Lidiia Armand, *Kerenskii* (Petrograd: [Kopeika], 1917), p. 4.
40 Ibid., pp. 3, 15.
41 Ibid., pp. 8, 13, 14.
42 Ibid., p. 8.
43 Vasilii Kir'iakov, 'A. F. Kerenskii', *Niva*, no. 19 (1917), p. 287; V–i V., *A. F. Kerenskii*, p. 4.
44 Kir'iakov, *Niva*, no. 19 (1917), p. 287.
45 E. V–ch, *A. F. Kerenskii narodnyi ministr*, p. 4.
46 V–i V., *A. F. Kerenskii*, p. 4. Kerensky himself subsequently wrote about these childhood impressions in *The Kerensky Memoirs: Russia and History's Turning Point* (London: Cassell, 1966), p. 4. 'N. Lenin' was the pseudonym of Vladimir Ul'ianov.
47 Anon, *Syn Velikoi Russkoi Revoliutsii*, p. 3.
48 Tan, 'A. F. Kerenskii', p. 2; E. V–ch, *A. F. Kerenskii narodnyi ministr*, pp. 4–5.
49 F. M. Kerensky's autobiographies are preserved in several archives: Rossiiskii gosudarstvennyi istoricheskii arkhiv [*RGIA*, the Russian State Historical Archive], *fond* 733, *opis'* 225, *delo* 203, *listy* 19–22 *ob.*; and *Rukopisnyi otdel Instituta russkoi literatury* [the Manuscript Department of the Institute of Russian Literature], *fond* 274, *opis'* 1, *delo* 398, *list* 145.
50 Photographs of Kerensky as a child with his mother were published in a number of booklets and magazines: *Solntse Rossii*, no. 368 (10) (1917), p. 3; E. V–ch, *A. F. Kerenskii narodnyi ministr*, p. 4.
51 Foreign diplomats believed she was Jewish. See George Buchanan, *My Mission to Russia and Other Diplomatic Memories* (London: Cassell, 1923), vol. 2, p. 64.
52 On how anti-Semites viewed Kerenskii, see Kolonitskii, 'Aleksandr Fedorovich Kerenskii kak "zhertva evreev" i "evrei"', in *Jews and Slavs*, vol. 17: *The Russian Word in the Land of Israel, the Jewish Word in Russia* (Jerusalem, 2006), pp. 241–53.
53 *Solntse Rossii*, no. 368 (10) (1917), p. 4; E. V–ch, *A. F. Kerenskii narodnyi ministr*, p. 9.
54 Tan, 'A. F. Kerenskii', p. 2.
55 *Narodnaia gazeta*, 15 July 1917.
56 Kir'iakov, 'A. F. Kerenskii', *Niva*, no. 19 (1917), p. 288.
57 Kerensky, *The Kerensky Memoirs*, p. 17.
58 E. V–ch, *A. F. Kerenskii narodnyi ministr*, p. 5.
59 Tan, 'A. F. Kerenskii', p. 2; Kir'iakov, 'A. F. Kerenskii', *Niva*, no. 19 (1917), p. 288.
60 *Solntse Rossii*, no. 368 (10) (1917), p. 4. In 1917 the boys were aged twelve and nine.
61 Kir'iakov, 'A. F. Kerenskii', *Niva*, no. 19 (1917), p. 288. Another writer also

claimed that Kerenskii became an SR while still a student. See E. V–ch, *A. F. Kerenskii narodnyi ministr*, p. 5.

62 *Aleksandr Fedorovich Kerenskii (Po materialam Departamenta politsii)*, p. 5; Kerensky, *The Kerensky Memoirs*, pp. 47–50.

63 E. V–ch, *A. F. Kerenskii narodnyi ministr*, p. 5.

64 *Edinstvo*, 6 May 1917.

65 *Aleksandr Fedorovich Kerenskii (Po materialam Departamenta politsii)*, pp. 5–6; Kerensky, *The Kerensky Memoirs*, pp. 71–2; Kerensky, *The Crucifixion of Liberty* (London: Barker, 1934), pp. 114–19; Richard Abraham, *Alexander Kerensky: The First Love of the Revolution* (London: Sidgwick & Jackson, 1987), pp. 21–35.

66 E. V–ch, *A. F. Kerenskii narodnyi ministr*, p. 5.

67 'Novyi voennyi i morskoi ministr', *Russkii invalid*, 5 May 1917.

68 Leonidov, *Vozhd' svobody A. F. Kerenskii*, p. 8.

69 E. V–ch, *A. F. Kerenskii narodnyi ministr*, p. 6.

70 Kerenskii, *Rechi A. F. Kerenskogo o revoliutsii, s ocherkom V. V. Kir'iakova 'Kerenskii kak orator'*, p. 7.

71 Abraham, *Alexander Kerensky*, pp. 39–40; Kerensky, *The Crucifixion of Liberty*, p. 121; Kerensky, *The Kerensky Memoirs*, pp. 74–5.

72 E. V–ch, *A. F. Kerenskii narodnyi ministr*, p. 7. See also Kir'iakov, 'A. F. Kerenskii', *Niva*, no. 19 (1917), p. 289.

73 Tan, 'A. F. Kerenskii', p. 2.

74 Anon, *Syn Velikoi Russkoi Revoliutsii*, pp. 3, 9.

75 Vasilii Maklakov, *Iz vospominanii* (New York: Chekhov, 1954), p. 266. Jörg Baberowski suggests that all political defence lawyers used court hearings to make political speeches, Maklakov included. See Baberowski, *Autokratie und Justiz: Zum Verhältnis von Rechtsstaatlichkeit und Rückständigkeit im ausgehenden Zarenreich 1864–1914* (Frankfurt am Main: Klostermann, 1996), pp. 577–8.

76 Leonidov, *Vozhd' svobody A. F. Kerenskii*, pp. 10–11. Kerenskii's Odessan biographer wrote about him in similar terms. See E. V–ch, *A. F. Kerenskii narodnyi ministr*, p. 7.

77 Kerensky, *The Kerensky Memoirs*, pp. 76–80.

78 Leonidov, *Vozhd' svobody A. F. Kerenskii*, pp. 11–12.

79 E. V–ch, *A. F. Kerenskii narodnyi ministr*, pp. 7–8.

80 Armand, *Kerenskii*, p. 3.

81 *Gosudarstvennyi arkhiv Rossiikoi Federatsii* [*GARF*, the State Archive of the Russian Federation], *fond* 1807, *opis'* 1, *delo* 242, *listy* 42–3; *delo* 244, *listy* 4–5.

82 *Shestoi s"ezd RSDRP (bol'shevikov), avgust 1917 goda: Protokoly* (Moscow: Gospolitizdat, 1958), p. 30.

83 Armand, *Kerenskii*, pp. 3–4.

84 Leonidov, *Vozhd' svobody A. F. Kerenskii*, p. 14.

85 For this purpose, Kerenskii had to 'acquire' a small house in the town. The transaction was fictitious, although Kir'iakov insists that the election was 'strictly within the law'. Kerenskii described himself in the application form as a 'property owner of the town of Vol'sk' and was then elected as a representative of Saratov province at the provincial electoral assembly. See Abraham, *Alexander Kerensky*, pp. 56–7; Kir'iakov, 'A. F. Kerenskii', *Niva*, no. 19 (1917), p. 289; *RGIA*, *fond* 1278, *opis'* 9, *delo* 341, *list* 1. The most thorough study of Kerenskii's activities in the Duma is Stanislav

Tiutiukin, *Aleksandr Kerenskii: Stranitsy politicheskoi biografii (1905–1917 gg.)* (Moscow: ROSSPEN, 2012), pp. 38–106.
86 Kir'iakov, 'A. F. Kerenskii', *Niva*, no. 19 (1917), p. 289; E. V–ch, *A. F. Kerenskii narodnyi ministr*, p. 8.
87 Anon, *Syn Velikoi Russkoi Revoliutsii*, p. 3.
88 Armand, *Kerenskii*, p. 5; *Aleksandr Fedorovich Kerenskii (Po materialam Departamenta politsii)*, p. 3.
89 E. V–ch, *A. F. Kerenskii narodnyi ministr*, pp. 8–9, 10. 'That is how it was, and that is how it will be!' was the utterance of Interior Minister Aleksandr Makarov in respect of the Lena goldfields massacre. It caused widespread public outrage.
90 Anon, *Syn Velikoi Russkoi Revoliutsii*, p. 9.
91 Armand, *Kerenskii*, pp. 4–5.
92 'Doneseniia L. K. Kumanina iz ministerskogo pavil'ona Gosudarstvennoi Dumy, dekabr' 1911–fevral' 1917 goda', *Voprosy istorii*, no. 1 (2000), pp. 12–13; no. 3 (2000), p. 4.
93 Rashel' Khin-Gol'dovskaia, 'Iz dnevnikov 1913–1917', *Minuvshee: Istoricheskii al'manakh* (St Petersburg), *vyp*. 21 (1997), p. 576.
94 Armand, *Kerenskii*, p. 4.
95 *Aleksandr Fedorovich Kerenskii (Po materialam Departamenta politsii)*, pp. 38, 39.
96 Nikolai Tagantsev, 'Iz moikh vospominanii (Detstvo. Iunost')', in *1917 god v sud'bakh Rossii i mira: Fevral'skaia revoliutsiia (Ot novykh istochnikov k novomu osmysleniiu)* (Moscow: Institut rossiiskoi istorii Rossiiskoi akademii nauk, *IRI RAN*, 1997), p. 246.
97 Leonidov, *Vozhd' svobody A. F. Kerenskii*, p. 5.
98 Kerenskii was a delegate representing the Vol'sk Association of Ledger Clerks. He proposed himself for membership and confirmed in writing his willingness to pay the membership fee. See Gosudarstvennyi arkhiv Saratovskoi oblasti, *fond* 53, *opis'* 1 (1913), *delo* 3, *list* 202–202 *ob*.
99 *Pravye partii: Dokumenty i materialy*, ed. Iu. I. Kir'ianov, vol. 2: *(1911–1917)* (Moscow: ROSSPEN, 1998), pp. 349–50.
100 *Aleksandr Fedorovich Kerenskii (Po materialam Departamenta politsii)*, p. 9; Kerensky, *The Crucifixion of Liberty*, p. 163; Abraham, *Alexander Kerensky*, pp. 52, 64.
101 *Aleksandr Fedorovich Kerenskii (Po materialam Departamenta politsii)*, p. 11; Kerensky, *The Crucifixion of Liberty*, pp 173–4.
102 In memoirs and the research literature this organization is often described as Masonic, and Kerenskii himself described it as such. Kerensky, *The Kerensky Memoirs*, pp. 88–91. The Great Orient of the Peoples of Russia did not, however, resemble the majority of Masonic lodges: there were virtually no mystical rituals, and little time was devoted to discussing problems of moral philosophy. The association was an elite, non-partisan society striving to overthrow the system of monarchy.
103 Nathan Smith, 'Political Freemasonry in Russia, 1906–1918: A Discussion of the Sources', *Russian Review*, 44/2 (1985), p. 158.
104 'Zapis' besedy s A.Ia. Gal'pernom, 1928 g.', in Boris Nikolaevskii, *Russkie masony i revoliutsiia* (Moscow: Terra, 1990), p. 74.
105 *Russkii invalid*, 24 May 1917.
106 *RGIA*, *fond* 1278, *opis'* 5, *delo* 442, *listy* 4–99 *ob*.

107 Abraham, *Alexander Kerensky*, pp. 68–9, 72.
108 'Kerenskii o kanune Fevralia', *Vozrozhdenie*, 22 April 1932. Kerenskii even later claimed the left-wing parties had not wanted a revolution during the war and that the insurgency had been provoked by the autocracy. This is at variance with reality. In offering this interpretation, conspiracy-based and with the benefit of hindsight, he was evidently seeking to present himself as having been a moderate politician.
109 *Gazeta-kopeika*, 27 July 1914.
110 *Pervyi Vserossiiskii s"ezd Sovetov*, ed. Veniamin Rakhmetov (Moscow and Leningrad: Gosizdat, 1930), vol. 1, p. 80.
111 When the renowned 'hunter of agents provocateurs' Vladimir Burtsev, a convinced defencist, was arrested in 1914, he chose not to avail himself of Kerensky's legal services, considering him an opponent of the war. This reputation became firmly attached and he found himself a hostage to it. See Vladimir Burtsev, 'Vospominaniia', *Novyi zhurnal* [New York], no. 69 (1962), pp. 181–2.
112 Abraham, *Alexander Kerensky*, pp. 76–9; Michael Melancon, *The Socialist Revolutionaries and the Russian Anti-War Movement, 1914–1917* (Columbus: Ohio State University Press, 1990), pp. 46, 62–6, 101–3, 106, 202, 224, 236; Vladimir Stankevich, *Vospominaniia, 1914–1919 gg.* (Leningrad: Priboi, 1926), p. 13.
113 Melancon, *The Socialist Revolutionaries*, p. 221.
114 Aleksei Badaev, *Bol'sheviki v Gosudarstvennoi dume: Bol'shevistskaia fraktsiia IV Gosudarstvennoi dumy i revoliutsionnoe dvizhenie v Peterburge. Vospominaniia* (Moscow and Leningrad: Gosudarstvennoe izdatel'stvo, 1930), pp. 384, 405; 131; Grigorii Aronson, *Rossiia v epokhu revoliutsii: Istoricheskie etiudy i memuary* (New York: [self-published], 1966), pp. 19–20; Abraham, *Alexander Kerensky*, pp. 83–5; Tiutiukin, *Aleksandr Kerenskii*, pp. 74–6.
115 *Pravye partii: Dokumenty i materialy*, vol. 2, p. 473.
116 *Golos soldata*, 6 May 1917; *Edinstvo*, 6 May 1917.
117 'Tsarskaia okhranka ob A. F. Kerenskom', *Petrogradskaia gazeta*, 27 June 1917; *Aleksandr Fedorovich Kerenskii (Po materialam Departamenta politsii)*, pp. 11–25; E. V–ch, *A. F. Kerenskii narodnyi ministr*, pp. 13–14; Vladimir Zenzinov, 'Fevral'skie dni', *Novyi zhurnal* [New York], vol. 34 (1953), p. 190; Abraham, *Alexander Kerensky*, pp. 81–3, 90–1, 94, 100, 404; Melancon, *The Socialist Revolutionaries*, pp. 62–6, 84–5, 89, 101–6, 303–4. The report by the director of the police department was published: see 'A. F. Kerenskii v bor'be za Uchreditel'noe sobranie v 1915 g.', *Golos minuvshego*, nos. 10–12 (1918), p. 236.
118 Melancon, *The Socialist Revolutionaries*, pp. 106, 303–4.
119 Vladimir Lenin (Ul'ianov), *Polnoe sobranie sochinenii*, 55 vols (Moscow: Izdatel'stvo politicheskoi literatury, 1967–81), vol. 49 (1970), pp. 148–9.
120 Ivan Stepanov, 'O Moskovskom soveshchanii', *Spartak*, no. 6 (1917), pp. 11, 12. The Bol'shevik Ivan Skvortsov-Stepanov is mentioned in research as having been a Freemason. See Vitalii Startsev, *Tainy russkikh masonov* (St Petersburg: D.A.R.K., 2004), pp. 119–21.
121 Mark Vishniak, *Dan' proshlomu* (New York: Chekhov, 1954), p. 240.
122 See Kornelii Shatsillo, '"Delo" polkovnika Miasoedova', *Voprosy istorii*, no. 4 (1967), pp. 103–16; William C. Fuller, Jr, *The Foe Within: Fantasies of*

Treason and the End of Imperial Russia (Ithaca, NY: Cornell University Press, 2006).

123 *RGIA*, *fond* 1405, *opis'* 539, *delo* 773, *listy* 2–2 *ob*. The real author of the letter was a feature writer, Dmitrii Filosofov. See his 'Dnevnik (1917–1918)', *Zvezda*, no. 1 (1992), pp. 189–205; no. 2, pp. 188–204; no. 3, pp. 147–66.

124 *RGIA*, *fond* 1405, *opis'* 539, *delo* 773, *listy* 1–1 *ob*.; Valerii Karrik, 'Voina i revoliutsiia: Zapiski, 1914–1917 gg.', *Golos minuvshego*, nos 4–6 (1918), pp. 14–15.

125 *RGIA*, *fond* 1405, *opis'* 530, *delo* 1127, *listy* 3–3 *ob*. The letter was used in a leaflet issued by the Petersburg Committee of Bolsheviks. See Aleksandr Shliapnikov, *Kanun semnadtsatogo goda: Semnadtsatyi god*, 3 vols (Moscow: Politizdat, 1992), vol. 1, p. 168. See also: *Revoliutsionnoe dvizhenie v armii i na flote v gody Pervoi mirovoi voiny (1914 – fevral' 1917): Sb. dokumentov*, ed. Arkadii Sidorov (Moscow: Nauka, 1966), p. 183.

126 *Aleksandr Fedorovich Kerenskii (Po materialam Departamenta politsii)*, pp. 14–16; Abraham, *Alexander Kerensky*, pp. 86–7.

127 See Boris Kolonitskii, *'Tragicheskaia erotika': Obrazy imperatorskoi sem'i v gody Pervoi mirovoi voiny* (Moscow: Novoe literaturnoe obozrenie, 2010).

128 *Gosudarstvennaia duma. Chetvertyi sozyv. Stenograficheskie otchety. Sessiia chetvertaia* (Petrograd: Gosudarstvennaia tipografiia, 1915–16), p. 110.

129 Leonidov, *Vozhd' svobody A. F. Kerenskii*, p. 15.

130 On this expedition, see 'Turkestan i Gosudarstvennaia duma Rossiiskoi imperii: Dokumenty TSGA Respubliki Uzbekistan, 1915–1916 gg.', publication by Tat'iana Kotiukova, *Istoricheskii arkhiv*, no. 3 (2003), pp. 126–36. On Kerensky's speech to the Duma about the results of his expedition, see '"Takoe upravlenie gosudarstvom – nedopustimo": Doklad A. F. Kerenskogo na zakrytom zasedanii Gosudarstvennoi dumy, dekabr' 1916 g.', publication by Dinara Amanzholova, *Istoricheskii arkhiv*, no. 2 (1997), pp. 4–22. See also: *Vosstanie 1916 goda v Turkestane: Dokumental'nye svidetel'stva obshchei tragedii (Sb. dokumentov i materialov)*, ed. Tat'iana Kotiukova (Moscow: Mardzhani, 2016).

131 *Narodnaia niva* (Helsingfors), 6 (19) May 1917.

132 Leonidov, *Vozhd' svobody A. F. Kerenskii*, p. 16.

133 *GARF*, *fond* 1807, *opis'* 1, *delo* 391. Letters and telegrams from various correspondents to A. F. Kerenskii expressing sympathy in connection with his illness.

134 Ibid., *listy* 7, 9, 13, 14, 17, 20, 21, 23, 26a, 29–29 *ob*., etc.

135 Among the officers was Captain Mikhail Murav'ev, who later became an organizer of shock battalions and subsequently commanded Soviet detachments which in autumn 1917 fought Kerenskii's troops. On one occasion Kerensky's friend Count Pavel Tolstoi came to see him, on behalf of Grand Duke Mikhail Aleksandrovich, to ask how the workers might react to the coronation of the emperor's brother. See Sergei Mel'gunov, *Na putiakh k dvortsovomu perevorotu (Zagovory pered revoliutsiei 1917 goda)* (Paris: Rodnik, 1931), pp. 197, 208–9; Alexander F. Kerensky, *The Catastrophe: Kerensky's own Story of the Russian Revolution* (New York: Appleton, 1927), pp. 101–2; Kerensky, *The Kerensky Memoirs*, pp. 147, 149–51; Abraham, *Alexander Kerensky*, pp. 89, 99–100, 117–19.

136 Letter from Vasilii Maklakov to Aleksandr Kerenskii, 3 June 1951, Hoover Institution on War, Revolution and Peace Archives, A. F. Kerensky Papers,

box 1. Vladimir Stankevich met Kerenskii in January 1917 at a meeting of an 'intimate circle', which might mean a Masonic lodge, although Stankevich is not usually written of as being a Freemason. The question of a court coup was being discussed there. See Vladimir Stankevich, *Vospominaniia, 1914–1919 gg.* (Leningrad: Priboi, 1926), p. 30; Stankevich, *Piat' nenuzhnykh let: Vospominaniia odnogo iz vinovnikov voiny (1914–1919)*, Hoover Institution on War, Revolution and Peace Archives, B. I. Nikolaevsky Collection, box 122, sheet 39.

137 Abraham, *Alexander Kerensky*, pp. 123–4.

138 Lenin (Ul'ianov), Vladimir Il"ich, *Polnoe sobranie sochinenii*, 5th edn (Moscow: Politizdat, 1960–81), vol. 30 (1969), pp. 243, 341.

139 'Privetstvie sotsialistov-revoliutsionerov A. F. Kerenskomu', *Novoe vremia*, 5 March 1917.

140 Kir'iakov, 'A. F. Kerenskii', *Niva*, no. 20 (1917), p. 296; E. V–ch, *A. F. Kerenskii narodnyi ministr*, p. 11.

141 Aleksandr Kerenskii, *Prorocheskie slova A. F. Kerenskogo, proiznesennye 19 iiulia 1915 goda v Gosudarstvennoi dume* (Petrograd: Broshiura, 1917).

142 Kerenskii, *Rechi A. F. Kerenskogo o revoliutsii*, p. 3.

143 Ibid., pp. 13–48; Kerensky, *The Catastrophe*, p. 104; Melancon, *The Socialist Revolutionaries*, p. 217; Vladimir Obolenskii, *Moia zhizn': Moi sovremenniki* (Paris: YMCA Press, 1988), p. 511.The government did indeed try to bring Kerenskii to trial, for which it required the full text of his speech. The Duma chairman, however, had had it excised from the official record. Rodzianko came to the deputy's defence, and the Duma resolved that the version approved for printing by the Duma chairman should be considered the verbatim account and that the version typed up from shorthand notes should be considered only raw material for compiling the record. Accordingly, the typed-up notes of the shorthand typist could not be handed over on demand to a government ministry. Only the judiciary had authority to require such information. See Kerensky, *The Kerensky Memoirs*, p. 187; 'Doneseniia L. K. Kumanina iz Ministerskogo pavil'ona Gosudarstvennoi Dumy, dekabr' 1911–fevral' 1917 goda', *Voprosy istorii*, no. 6 (2000), p. 21.

144 Kir'iakov, 'A. F. Kerenskii', *Niva*, no. 20 (1917), p. 296.

145 'Perepiska pravykh i drugie materialy ob ikh deiatel'nosti v 1914–1917 godakh', *Voprosy istorii*, no. 10 (1996), p. 122.

146 'K istorii poslednikh dnei tsarskogo rezhima (1916–1917 gg.)', publication by Petr Sadikov, *Krasnyi arkhiv*, vol. 1 (14) (1926), p. 246; Abraham, *Alexander Kerensky*, p. 123.

147 Boris Sokoloff, *The White Nights: Pages from a Russian Doctor's Notebook* (London: Holborn, 1956), pp. 7–8.

148 *Aleksandr Fedorovich Kerenskii (Po materialam Departamenta politsii)*, p. 20; Nikolai Sukhanov, *Zapiski o revoliutsii* (Berlin: Grzhebin, 1922), *kn.* 1, pp. 63, 69.

149 Zenzinov, 'Fevral'skie dni', *Novyi zhurnal* [New York], *kn.* 34 (1953), pp. 196–8.

150 Kerensky, *The Kerensky Memoirs*, p. 189.

151 M. Merzon, 'A. F. Kerenskii v Moskve', *Nizhegorodskii listok*, 1 June 1917.

152 Sergei Mel'gunov, *Martovskie dni 1917 goda* (Paris: Veche, 1961), p. 20; Zenzinov, 'Fevral'skie dni', p. 210; Aleksandr Kerenskii, '"Fevral'skaia revoliutsiia": Protokol oprosa', *Orion: Literaturno-khudozhestvennyi ezheme-*

siachnik [Tiflis], no. 2 (1919), pp. 61–2; Il'ia Iurenev (Konstantin Krotovskii), '"Mezhraionka" (1911–1917 gg.)', *Proletarskaia revoliutsiia*, no. 2 (25) (1924), pp. 136–8; Kerensky, *The Catastrophe*, pp. 6–7. Meetings between legal and illegal political figures had been held earlier, in late January and early February, in the apartments of Nikolai Sokolov, Aleksandr Gal'pern and Kerenskii, who were the principal organizers of these meetings. Boris Nikolaevskii writes about the 'Sokolov–Kerenskii–Gal'pern group'. Boris Nikolaevskii, 'Iz istorii Fevral'skoi revoliutsii', *Novoe russkoe slovo*, 5 May 1957.

153 Vladimir Obolenskii, a Constitutional Democrat and Freemason close to Kerenskii, recalled that the latter had also underestimated the scale of the movement and expected the unrest to be suppressed. Obolenskii, *Moia zhizn'*, p. 510.

154 Kerensky, *The Kerensky Memoirs*, p. 189.

155 Basil Gourko, *War and Revolution in Russia, 1914–1917* (New York: Macmillan, 1919), pp. 331–2.

156 On 26 February, Kerenskii learned of the mutiny of the 4th Company of the Pavlovsky Guards Regiment, and even reported to the deputies of the Duma that the entire regiment had mutinied. Vladimir Cherniaev, 'Vosstanie Pavlovskogo polka 26 fevralia 1917 g.', *Rabochii klass Rossii, ego soiuzniki i politicheskie protivniki v 1917 godu: Sbornik nauchnykh trudov*, ed. Oleg Znamenskii (Leningrad: Nauka, 1989), p. 163. This was incorrect. The company's mutiny was isolated, and many soldiers were arrested by troops loyal to the government. News of the Pavlovsky mutiny influenced soldiers of other regiments, but on the night of 26 February Kerenskii could not have known that.

157 Kerensky, *The Catastrophe*, pp. 1–2; Stankevich, *Vospominaniia* (Leningrad: Priboi, 1926), p. 36.

158 Kerensky, *The Kerensky Memoirs*, p. 195.

159 181 Kerensky, *The Catastrophe*, pp. 7–8, 10–11; Kerensky, *The Kerensky Memoirs*, pp. 195–6.

160 Kerensky, *The Kerensky Memoirs*, pp. 195–6; *Fevral'skaia revoliutsiia 1917 goda: Sb. dokumentov i materialov*, ed. Ol'ga Shashkova (Moscow: Rossiiskii gosudarstvennyi gumanitarnyi universitet, RGGU, 1996), p. 72; Andrei Nikolaev, *Gosudarstvennaia duma v Fevral'skoi revoliutsii: Ocherki istorii* (Riazan': Notre Dame University, 2002), pp. 24–5; Andrei Nikolaev, *Revoliutsiia i vlast': IV Gosudarstvennaia duma 27 fevralia–3 marta 1917 goda* (St Petersburg: Rossiiskii gosudarstvennyi pedagogicheskii universitet imeni A. I. Gertsena, RGPU im. Gertsena, 2005), pp. 120–37.

161 E. V–ch, *A. F. Kerenskii narodnyi ministr*, p. 15.

162 Vasilii Vodovozov, 'Ob"iasnenie po povodu moego pis'ma k A. F. Kerenskomu', *Den'* [Petrograd], 8 March 1917.

163 Mel'gunov, *Martovskie dni 1917 goda*, p. 26; Semion Lyandres, 'On the Problem of "Indecisiveness" among the Duma Leaders during the February Revolution: The Imperial Decree of Prorogation and Decision to Convene the Private Meeting of February 27, 1917', *Soviet and Post-Soviet Review*, 24/1–2 (1997), pp. 115–28; 'Chastnoe soveshchanie chlenov Gosudarstvennoi Dumy 27 fevralia 1917 [goda]', publication by Semion Lyandres, *Berliner Jahrbuch für osteuropäische Geschichte: 1997* (Berlin: Humboldt University, 1998), pp. 305–24.

164 Nikolaev, *Gosudarstvennaia duma v Fevral'skoi revoliutsii*, pp. 47–9; Nikolaev, *Revoliutsiia i vlast'*, pp. 176–9.
165 Zenzinov, 'Fevral'skie dni', p. 210; Mel'gunov, *Martovskie dni 1917 goda*, p. 27; *The Russian Provisional Government, 1917: Documents*, 3 vols, ed. Robert P. Browder and Alexander F. Kerensky (Stanford, CA: Stanford University Press, 1961), vol. 1, pp. 45–7; Aleksandr Spiridovich, *Velikaia voina i Fevral'skaia revoliutsiia, 1914–1917 gg.*, 3 vols (New York: Vseslavianskoe izdatel'stvo, 1960–62), vol. 3, p. 126; Eduard Burdzhalov, *Vtoraia russkaia revoliutsiia: Vosstanie v Petrograde* (Moscow: Nauka, 1967), p. 228.
166 Nikolaev, *Gosudarstvennaia duma v Fevral'skoi revoliutsii*, pp. 48–51; Nikolaev, *Revoliutsiia i vlast'*, pp. 181–4.
167 Kerensky, *The Catastrophe*, pp. 14–15; Kerensky, *The Kerensky Memoirs*, pp. 196–7; Aleksandr Poliakov, 'Komnata no. 10', *Novoe russkoe slovo*, 23 March 1947; Mel'gunov, *Martovskie dni 1917 goda*, pp. 29–30.
168 Aleksei Ksiunin, 'Kak proizoshla revoliutsiia', *Novoe vremia*, 5 March 1917.
169 Anon, *Syn Velikoi Russkoi Revoliutsii*, p. 4.
170 Vodovozov, 'Ob"iasnenie po povodu moego pis'ma k A. F. Kerenskomu'.
171 *Petrogradskii Sovet rabochikh i soldatskikh deputatov v 1917 godu: Protokoly, stenogrammy i otchety, rezoliutsii, postanovleniia obshchikh sobranii, sobraniia sektsii, zasedaniia Ispolnitel'nogo komiteta i fraktsii, 27 fevralia–25 oktiabria 1917 goda*, 5 vols, ed. Bella Gal'perina and Vitalii Startsev, vol. 1 (St Petersburg: Zvezda, 1993), p. 589.
172 Ivanchikov, 'Ministr Kerenskii', *Nizhegorodskii listok*, 29 April 1917.
173 E. V–ch, *A. F. Kerenskii narodnyi ministr*, p. 15.
174 *Volia naroda*, 4 May 1917.
175 The April Crisis arose out of disagreement over war aims between the Provisional Government and the Petrograd Soviet and led to the establishment of a coalition Provisional Government which included six socialist ministers nominated by the Soviet. [Trans.]
176 *Soldatskaia pravda*, 11 May 1917.
177 Anon, *Syn Velikoi Russkoi Revoliutsii*, p. 4.
178 Kerensky, *The Catastrophe*, pp. 15–16; Mel'gunov, *Martovskie dni 1917 goda*, p. 116; Kerensky, *The Kerensky Memoirs*, p. 197.
179 Kerensky, *The Kerensky Memoirs*, p. 200; *The Russian Provisional Government, 1917: Documents*, vol. 1, pp. 65–6; Nikolaev, *Revoliutsiia i vlast'*, pp. 190–201.
180 As a consequence of a printers' strike a number of publications had ceased to appear, and *Izvestiia Petrogradskogo Soveta rabochikh deputatov* was published only from 28 February.
181 It is possible that Mstislavskii, a notable memoirist who took part in the revolution, is describing a conversation with Kerenskii after the arrest of Shcheglovitov, although he refers to the former head of the government, Boris Shtiurmer. 'Kerenskii burst out laughing and, like a naughty boy, slapped his pocket, delved into it and pulled out an enormous old-fashioned door key. "That's where I'm keeping Shtiurmer! You should have seen their ugly mugs when I locked him up . . . Rodzyanko nearly had a fit! He was all set to greet him as one of the family!"' Sergei Mstislavskii, *Piat' dnei: Nachalo i konets Fevral'skoi revoliutsii* (Berlin: Grzhebin, 1922), p. 24.
182 *Partiia sotsialistov-revoliutsionerov: Dokumenty i materialy*, p. 25; Zenzinov, 'Fevral'skie dni', p. 213.

183 Merzon, 'A. F. Kerenskii v Moskve'.
184 Kerenskii personally wrote out an authorization on the headed notepaper of the chairman of the State Duma: 'The Provisonal Committee delegates to member of the State Duma Kerenskii management of the ministerial pavilion where particularly important individuals are under arrest.' Rodzyanko signed the authorization. See Burdzhalov, *Vtoraia russkaia revoliutsiia*, p. 264.
185 Kerensky, *The Catastrophe*, p. 29.
186 'Aleksandr Fedorovich Kerenskii (Shtrikhi k politicheskomu portretu)', Gennadiy Sobolev, *Aleksandr Kerenskii: Liubov' i nenavist' revoliutsii: dnevniki, stat'i, ocherki, vospominaniia sovremennikov* (Cheboksary: Chuvashskii universitet, 1993), p. 19.
187 Vladimir Stankevich, *Vospominaniia (1914–1919)* (Berlin: Ladyzhnikov, 1920), p. 75; Sukhanov, *Zapiski o revoliutsii*, *kn.* 1, p. 63; Vasilii Shul'gin, *Dni. 1920: Zapiski* (Moscow: Sovremennik, 1989), pp. 179, 180, 185; Mel'gunov, *Martovskie dni 1917 goda*, pp. 116–17.
188 Ol'ga Kerenskaia, [Fragmentary reminiscences], House of Lords Record Office [London], Historical Collection, no. 206: The Stow Hill Papers, DS 2/2, Box 8, p. 4; Poliakov, 'Komnata no. 10'; Mel'gunov, *Martovskie dni 1917 goda*, p. 51; Kerensky, *The Catastrophe*, pp. 59, 76.
189 *Narodnyi tribun*, 14 October 1917.
190 *Den'* [Petrograd], 9 March 1917.
191 *Rossiiskii gosudarstvennyi arkhiv sotsial'no-politicheskoi istorii* [*RGASPI*, Russian State Archive of Socio-Political History], *fond* 662, *opis'* 1, *delo* 58, *list* 98.
192 *Novoe vremia*, 5 March 1917.
193 *GARF*, *fond* 1807, *opis'* 1, *delo* 361, *list* 66.
194 *RGIA*, *fond* 1278, *opis'* 5, *delo* 1324, *list* 62; *fond* 1405, *opis'* 538, *delo* 177, *list* 51; *GARF*, *fond* 1807, *opis'* 1, *delo* 363, *list* 1.
195 *GARF*, *fond* 1807, *opis'* 1, *delo* 359, *list* 151; *delo* 361, *list* 17, 19; *delo* 363, *list* 13.
196 The Duma received some 20,000 such telegrams and letters. Nikolaev, *Revoliutsiia i vlast'*, p. 573.
197 Ekaterina Gavroeva, 'Pis'ma vo vlast': Rabochie i M. V. Rodzianko (Mart 1917 g.)', *Revoliutsiia 1917 goda v Rossii: Novye podkhody i vzgliady: Sbornik nauchnykh statei*, ed. Andrei Nikolaev (St Petersburg: Tsentral'nyi gosudarstvennyi istoricheskii arkhiv Sankt-Peterburga [*TsGIA SPb*, the Central State Archive of History, St Petersburg], 2015), pp. 76–82; Gavroeva, 'Pis'ma vo vlast': Soldaty i M. V. Rodzianko (Mart 1917 g.)', *Peterburgskie voenno-istoricheskie chteniia: Sbornik statei*, ed. Andrei Nikolaev (St Petersburg: RGPU im Gertsena, 2015), pp. 112–17.
198 *RGIA*, *fond* 1278, *opis'* 5, *delo* 1324, *list* 87.
199 Gavroeva, 'Pis'ma vo vlast': Soldaty', p. 117.
200 *GARF*, *fond* 1807, *opis'* 1, *delo* 354, *listy* 19–22.
201 *Russkii invalid*, 8 March 1917; *GARF*, *fond* 1807, *opis'* 1, *delo* 359, *list* 7.
202 *Delo naroda*, 7 July 1917.
203 Nadezhda Krupskaia, 'Stranichka iz istorii Rossiiskoi sotsial-demokraticheskoi partii', *Soldatskaia pravda*, 13 May 1917. Quoted from Krupskaia, *Izbrannye proizvedeniia* (Moscow: Izdatel'stvo politicheskoi literatury, 1988), pp. 44–8; *Sotsial-demokrat* [Moscow], 26 May, 9 June 1917.
204 *Saratovskii Sovet rabochikh deputatov (1917–1918): Sbornik dokumentov*

(Moscow and Leningrad: Gosudarstvennoe sotsial'no-ekonomicheskoe izdatel'stvo, 1931), p. 162.

205 *RGIA*, *fond* 1405, *opis'* 538, *delo* 177, *list* 52. The text was sent no later than 22 March.

206 *GARF*, *fond* 1779, *opis'* 1, *delo* 293, *list* 293; *Russkoe slovo*, 21 May 1917.

207 *GARF*, *fond* 1778, *opis'* 1, *delo* 362, *list* 221.

208 *RGIA*, *fond* 1412, *opis'* 16, *delo* 537, *list* 2.

209 Hoover Institution on War, Revolution and Peace Archives, B. I. Nicolaevsky Collection, box 149, file 3, F. [Navotnyi], [Propaganda], p. 88.

210 *GARF*, *fond* 1807, *opis'* 1, *delo* 354, *listy* 95–6.

211 'Vserossiiskii s"ezd uchitelei', *Delo naroda*, 9 April 1917.

212 For further detail, see Kolonitskii, *Simvoly vlasti i bor'ba za vlast': K izucheniiu politicheskoi kul'tury Rossiiskoi revoliutsii 1917 goda* (St Petersburg: Dmitrii Bulanin, 2001; 2nd edn, St Petersburg: Liki Rossii, 2012).

213 *Velikaia russkaia revoliutsiia v ocherkakh i kartinakh* (Moscow: N. V. Vasil'ev, 1917), *vyp.* 4: '80-e gody. Bortsy za svobodu. Letopis' revoliutsii'; *Bortsy za svobodu (Biografii revoliutsionerov, kaznivshikh Aleksandra II)* (Moscow: D. M. Kumanov, 1917); *Bortsy za svobodu: [Sbornik]* (Petrograd: Severnoe izdatel'stvo, 1917); Mikhail Gernet, *Bortsy za svobodu v Shlissel'burgskoi kreposti* (Moscow: Nachalo, 1917).

214 Bertliev, *Borets za svobodu i chest' naroda: Pamiati Egora Sazonova* (Moscow: [Zemlia i volia?], 1917); Viacheslav Pirogov, *Smert' Egora Sazonova* (Petrograd: Partiia sotsialistov-revoliutsionerov, 1917).

215 Kirik Levin, *Pervyi borets za svobodu russkogo naroda: Zhizn' i deiatel'nost' A. N. Radishcheva* (Moscow: Knigoizdatel'stvo E. D. Miagkogo 'Kolokol', 1906); Evgenii Shveder, *Pervyi russkii borets za svobodu Aleksandr Nikolaevich Radishchev: Biograficheskii ocherk* (Moscow: Pechatnik, 1917).

216 A pamphlet in the series 'Pervye bortsy za svobodu' was *Dekabrist Mikhail Sergeevich Lunin: Ocherk ego biografii, ego zaveshchanie, pis'ma iz ssylki i politicheskie stat'i* (Petrograd: Khudozhestvennaia pechatnia, 1917).

217 *Sine-fono*, nos. 11–12 (1917), pp. 26–7, 35, 97; *Priboi* [Helsingfors], 6 August 1917; *Velikii Kinemo: Katalog sokhranivshikhsia igrovykh fil'mov Rossii, 1908–1919*, ed. Veronika Ivanova et al. (Moscow: Novoe literaturnoe obozrenie, 2002), pp. 364, 370.

218 Even the delegates of the All-Russia Congress of Cossacks paid respect to the memory of Lieutenant Schmidt by standing and singing the funeral anthem *Memory Eternal*. See 'Kazachii s"ezd', *Novoe vremia*, 8 June 1917. Among the delegates were some who would later be active in the White cause. On the politics of memory in Sevastopol, see Kolonitskii, 'Pamiat' o Pervoi rossiiskoi revoliutsii v 1917 godu (Sluchai Sevastopolia i Gel'singforsa)', *Cahiers du Monde Russe*, no. 3 (48) (2007), pp. 519–37.

219 *S"ezdy i konferentsii Konstitutsionno-demokraticheskoi partii: 1905–1920 gg.*, 3 vols (Moscow: ROSSPEN, 2000), vol. 3, *kn.* 1, '1915–1917 gg.', pp. 362, 365.

220 Abraham, *Alexander Kerensky*, p. 50.

221 Tan, 'A. F. Kerenskii', p. 3.

222 Kolonitskii, *Simvoly vlasti*, pp. 222–3.

223 *Krasnyi arkhiv*, vol. 5 (24) (1927), p. 209.

224 Aleksandr Kerenskii, 'O pamiatnike zhertvam revoliutsii (pis'mo v redaktsiiu "Dela naroda")', *Delo naroda*, 8 April 1917. His contemporaries took great note of this initiative, and the letter was included in publications of his

speeches. See, for example, Kerenskii, *Rechi A. F. Kerenskogo o revoliutsii*, pp. 59–60.

225 Dmitrii Merezhkovskii, 'Perventsy svobody', *Niva*, no. 16 (1917), pp. 230–3; no. 17, pp. 245–9; Merezhkovskii, *Perventsy svobody: Istoriia vosstaniia 14-go dekabria 1825 g.* (Petrograd: Narodnaia vlast', 1917). On the meeting, see Zinaida Gippius, *Siniaia kniga: Peterburgskii dnevnik, 1914–1918* (Belgrade: Radenkovich, 1929), p. 118. For evidence of Gippius's authorship, see an early version of her 'diary': Gippius, *Sovremennaia zapis'*, *OR RNB*, *fond* 481, *opis'* 1, *delo* 3, *list* 148.

226 'Zapisnye knizhki polkovnika G. A. Ivanishina', publication by A. D. Margolis, N. K. Gerasimova and N. S. Tikhonova, *Minuvshee: Istoricheskii al'manakh*, (Moscow and St Petersburg), vol. 17 (1994), p. 540; *Izvestiia Revel'skogo soveta rabochikh i voinskikh deputatov*, 15 April 1917.

227 *Russkii invalid*, 9 May 1917.

228 *Russkii invalid*, 10 May 1917. The congress organizers themselves paid obeisance to the revolutionary tradition. The delegates visited the Field of Mars and knelt at the graves of the champions of freedom.

229 *Krymskii vestnik* [Sevastopol'], 18 May 1917; *Russkii invalid*, 19 May 1917; *Prikazy i rechi pervogo russkogo Voennogo i Morskogo Ministra-Sotsialista A. F. Kerenskogo* ([No location]: Shtab osoboi armii, 1917), pp. 32–3; A. F. Kerenskii, *Ob armii i voine* (Petrograd: Narodnaia volia, 1917), p. 12. There is also an Odessa publication of this title with different pagination.

230 Kir'iakov, *Dedushka i babushka russkoi revoliutsii*, p. 3.

231 See *Babushka i vnuki* (Petrograd: Narodnaia vlast', 1917).

232 *Partiia sotsialistov-revoliutsionerov: Dokumenty i materialy*, pp. 238–9.

233 *Volia naroda*, 6 May 1917.

234 'Pomoshch' politicheskim', *Novoe vremia*, 25 March 1917.

235 E. Breshko-Breshkovskaia, *Babushka russkoi revoliutsii*, pp. 17, 42, Hoover Institution on War, Revolution and Peace Archives, B. I. Nicolaevsky Collection, box 87, folder 1.

236 E. Breshkovskaia, '1917-i god', *Novyi zhurnal* [New York], vol. 38 (1954), p. 197; Abraham, *Alexander Kerensky*, p. 244.

237 *Revel'skoe slovo*, 15 April 1917.

238 Katerina Breshkovskaia, *Hidden Springs of the Russian Revolution* (Stanford, CA: Stanford University Press, 1931), p. 347. A photograph of Breshko-Breshkovskaia has survived in Vladimir Zenzinov's archive, with an inscription which gives us a clear impression of the attitude of the grandmother of the Russian Revolution towards her political grandson. 'To Alexander Kerensky. You see, I have kept you, whom I fervently love. So that my eye can see how my dear grandson is getting along in life and invariably doing good work. How often I hear him sigh, both because his work is so hard and when he thinks of the suffering his people must bear. May my dear one sense that I share his thinking and gaze far ahead into the future. And that to you, my friend, I bequeath my last sigh, a sigh of the hope and love which always inspired me. Your Gran, Kate Breshkovskaia.' The inscription is dated 21 February 1921, and has a note added at the end: 'Always with you, always on your side.' See Columbia University Library, Bakhmetieff Archive, Zenzinov Papers, box 3. Breshko-Breshkovskaia called Kerensky's children her grandchildren (communicated to the author by Kerensky's grandson, Stephen Kerensky).

239 Breshko-Breshkovskaia, *Babushka russkoi revoliutsii*, p. 45.
240 *Volia naroda*, 8 June 1917.
241 *Volia naroda*, 5 September 1917.

Chapter II 'Revolutionary Minister'

1 *Delo naroda*, 10 May 1917. Quoted from *Partiia sotsialistov-revoliutsionerov: Dokumenty i materialy*, 3 vols, ed. Nikolai Erofeev (Moscow: ROSSPEN, 2000), vol. 3, part 1, p. 107.
2 Lev Trotskii, *Sochineniia* (Moscow-Leningrad: Gosizdat, 1924–7), vol. 3: *1917*, part 1: 'Ot Fevralia do Oktiabria', p. 227.
3 *GARF*, *fond* 1807, *opis' 1*, *delo* 359, *list* 35.
4 'Dobryi genii russkoi revoliutsii', *Petrogradskaia gazeta*, 19 March 1917.
5 Anon, *Syn Velikoi Russkoi Revoliutsii Aleksandr Fedorovich Kerenskii: Ego zhizn', politicheskaia deiatel'nost' i rechi* (Petrograd: Petrogradskii listok, 1917), p. 9.
6 In the final version of his memoirs, Kerenskii himself claimed that all the talk about 'dual power' had been a myth concocted by both left- and right-wing opponents of the Provisional Government, which, he asserted, had been fully and genuinely in power. See Kerensky, *The Kerensky Memoirs: Russia and History's Turning Point* (London: Cassell, 1966), p. 239. Elsewhere in the memoirs he paints a different picture: 'In March or April it would not have been possible to move the former Tsar without endless consultations with the Soviets. But on August 14, Nicholas II and his family left for Tobolsk upon my personal order and with the consent of the Provisional Government' (ibid., p. 336). Here Kerenskii admits that the Provisional Government was not, in fact, fully in control.
7 *Delo naroda*, 15 March 1917. Quoted from *Partiia sotsialistov-revoliutsionerov: Dokumenty i materialy*, vol. 3, part 1, p. 27.
8 Review of events in Petrograd, 8–16 March (compiled from reports by the naval attaché in Petrograd), p. 13. See National Archives (Washington, DC), RG 54, WA 6, box 716, folder 4, p. 13.The diplomat was evidently struggling with the finer nuances of Russian politics, and even said Kerenskii was a Social Democrat.
9 'Delegatsiia ot Chernomorskogo flota u Vremennogo pravitel'stva', *Delo naroda*, 16 March 1917.
10 'Rech' Kerenskogo v Narodnom Dome', *Narodnaia niva* [Helsingfors], 11 May 1917.
11 See Dmitrii Filosofov, 'Dnevnik (17 ianvaria–30 marta 1917 g.)', *Zvezda*, no. 3 (1992), p. 147; Zinaida Gippius, *Siniaia kniga: Peterburgskii dnevnik, 1914–1918* (Belgrade: Radenkovich, 1929), pp. 119–20, 129–30.
12 Kerensky, *The Crucifixion of Liberty* (London: Barker, 1934), p. 267.
13 *Delo naroda*, 6 April 1917. Quoted from *Partiia sotsialistov-revoliutsionerov: Dokumenty i materialy*, vol. 3, part 1, p. 57.
14 Kerensky, *The Catastrophe: Kerensky's Own Story of the Russian Revolution* (New York: Appleton, 1927), p. 32.
15 Kerensky, *The Crucifixion of Liberty*, pp. 248–9.
16 Konstantin Bal'mont made this slogan the refrain of a poem. See Bal'mont, 'Edinenie', *Russkoe slovo*, 7 March 1917.

17 *Petrogradskii Sovet rabochikh i soldatskikh deputatov v 1917 godu: Protokoly, stenogrammy i otchety, rezoliutsii, postanovleniia obshchikh sobranii, sobraniia sektsii, zasedaniia Ispolnitel'nogo komiteta i fraktsii, 27 fevralia–25 oktiabria 1917 goda*, 5 vols, ed. Bella Gal'perina and Vitalii Startsev, vol. 1 (St Petersburg: Zvezda, 1993), p. 604; *Rechi A. F. Kerenskogo* (Kiev: Blago naroda, 1917), p. 18.

18 Pavel Miliukov, *Rossiia na perelome (Bol'shevistskii period russkoi revoliutsii)* (Paris: O. Zeluk, 1927), vol. 1: *Proiskhozhdenie i ukreplenie bol'shevistskoi diktatury*, p. 71.

19 *Petrogradskii Sovet rabochikh i soldatskikh deputatov v 1917 godu*, vol. 3 (2002), pp. 136, 143.

20 Richard Abraham, *Alexander Kerensky: The First Love of the Revolution* (London: Sidgwick & Jackson, 1987), insert between pp. 272 and 273.

21 Irakli Tsereteli, *Vospominaniia o Fevral'skoi revoliutsii* (Paris: Mouton, 1963), vol. 1, pp. 123–4; vol. 2, pp. 35, 388.

22 Oleg Leonidov, *Vozhd' svobody A. F. Kerenskii* (Moscow: Koshnitsa, 1917), p. 17.

23 *Delo naroda*, 17 September 1917; *Volia naroda*, 19 September 1917.

24 Viktor Chernov, *Pered burei: Vospominaniia* (New York: Chekhov, 1953), p. 338.

25 Fedor Stepun, *Byvshee i nesbyvsheesia* (New York: Chekhov, 1956), vol. 2, pp. 143–4.

26 *Petrogradskii Sovet rabochikh i soldatskikh deputatov v 1917 godu*, vol. 3, pp. 72, 80.

27 Miliukov, *Rossiia na perelome*, vol. 1, pp. 84–5; Lenin (Ul'ianov), Vladimir Il"ich, *Polnoe sobranie sochinenii*, 5th edn (Moscow: Politizdat, 1960–81), vol. 34, pp. 48–9; Kerensky, *The Catastrophe*, p. 281.

28 Lev Trotskii, *Istoriia russkoi revoliutsii* (Berlin: Granit, 1931–3), vol. 1, pp. 398–9; Miliukov, *Rossiia na perelome*, vol. 1, p. 86. See 'He sat between all the stools and did not see the abyss opening up beneath him': Pavel Dybenko, *Miatezhniki (Iz vospominanii o revoliutsii)* (Moscow: Krasnaia nov', Glavpolitprosvet, 1923), p. 62.

29 Pero, 'Sluchainye zametki', *Nizhegorodskii listok*, 1 June 1917; Igor' Arkhipov, 'Kornilovskii miatezh' kak fenomen politicheskoi psikhologii, *Novyi chasovoi*, no. 2 (1994), p. 26.

30 Lenin, *Polnoe sobranie sochinenii*, vol. 39, pp. 174–6.

31 George Buchanan, *My Mission to Russia and Other Diplomatic Memories* (London: Cassell, 1923), vol. 2, p. 215.

32 *Kollektsiia pochtovykh kartochek sovetskogo perioda s 1917 po 1945 g. iz sobranii M. A. Voronina: Katalog* (St Petersburg: Welcome, 2009), vol. 1, pp. 152–6. This series sold very successfully and is found in several collections.

33 *Rechi A. F. Kerenskogo*, p. 29.

34 Kolonitskii, *Simvoly vlasti i bor'ba za vlast'* (St Petersburg: Liki Rossii, 2012), pp. 32–7.

35 Sergei Mel'gunov, *Martovskie dni 1917 goda* (Paris: Veche, 1961), pp. 12, 107–8, 110; Iosif Gessen, 'V dvukh vekakh', *Arkhiv russkoi revoliutsii* [Berlin], vol. 22 (1937), p. 366; Kerensky, *The Catastrophe*, p. 51. There were rumours in Moscow on 28 February that Kerenskii was to be appointed minister of the interior. Aleksei Oreshnikov, *Dnevnik, 1915–1933*, 2 vols, ed. Petr Gaidukov et al. (Moscow: Nauka, 2010–11), vol. 1: *1915–1924*, p. 108. In the absence of

reliable information, the rumour mill included Kerenskii in the government, which also testifies to the authority he already had.

36 See the newspaper report in *Novoe vremia*, 5 March 1917.

37 It is interesting to note that Miliukov's words were quoted in 1917 by some of Kerenskii's biographers. See Anon, *Syn Velikoi Russkoi Revoliutsii*, p. 6.

38 *S"ezdy i konferentsii Konstitutsionno-demokraticheskoi partii: 1905–1920 gg.*, 3 vols (Moscow: ROSSPEN, 2000), vol. 3, *kn.* 1, p. 466.

39 *Russkoe slovo*, 3 March 1917; Aleksandr Kerenskii, *Rechi A. F. Kerenskogo o revoliutsii, s ocherkom V. V. Kir'iakova 'Kerenskii kak orator'* (Petrograd: Kopeika, 1917), p. 51.

40 *Russkoe slovo*, 3 March 1917; Kerenskii, *Rechi A. F. Kerenskogo o revoliutsii*, pp. 51, 55.

41 Anon, *Syn Velikoi Russkoi Revoliutsii*, pp. 6–7.

42 See Aleksandr Benua (Alexandre Benois), *Moi dnevnik: 1916–1917–1918* (Moscow: Russkii put', 2003), pp. 148–50.

43 Dmitrii Filosofov, 'Dnevnik', *Zvezda*, no. 2 (1992), p. 199; Sergei Zavadskii, 'Na velikom izlome (Otchet grazhdanina o perezhitom v 1916–1917 gg.)', *Arkhiv russkoi revoliutsii* [Berlin], vol. 8 (1923), pp. 15–16.

44 Ronald Suny, *The Baku Commune, 1917–1918: Class and Nationality in the Russian Revolution* (Princeton, NJ: Princeton University Press, 1972), p. 70.

45 Vasilii Kravkov, *Velikaia voina bez retushi: Zapiski korpusnogo vracha* (Moscow: Veche, 2014), p. 298.

46 Edward Heald, *Witness to Revolution: Letters from Russia (1916–1919)*, ed. James Gidney (Kent, OH: Kent State University Press, 1972), p. 63.

47 'A. F. Kerenskii v Tsarskom sele', *Rabochaia gazeta*, 28 March 1917.

48 See Aron Avrekh, 'Chrezvychainaia Sledstvennaia Komissiia Vremennogo pravitel'stva: Zamysel i ispolnenie', *Istoricheskie zapiski*, vol. 118 (1990), pp. 72–101.

49 *GARF*, *fond* 539, *opis'* 1, *delo* 1300, *list* 8 *ob.* (newspaper clipping).

50 Leonidov, *Vozhd' svobody*, p. 28.

51 Ol'ga Ol'neva, '"Ptentsy Kerenskogo": Revoliutsiia i ugolovnaia prestupnost', *Voprosy otechestvennoi i zarubezhnoi istorii: Materialy konferentsii 'Chteniia Ushinskogo'* (Yaroslavl: Iaroslavskii gosudarstvennyi pedagogicheskii universitet, 2002), pp. 45–7.

52 'Kak nakhodiatsia liudi?', *Malen'kaia gazeta*, 7 March 1917.

53 Maurice Paléologue, *An Ambassador's Memoirs*, vol. 3: *August 19, 1916–May 27, 1917*, trans. F. A. Holt (London: Hutchinson, 1925), entry for Saturday 17 March 1917 [Old Style] (http://net.lib.byu.edu/estu/wwi/memoir/FrAmbRus/pal3-09.htm).

54 Mikhail Suganov, 'Ko vstreche s Kerenskim', *Malen'kaia gazeta*, 2 April 1917.

55 A. Borisov, 'Vezdesushchii (Vpechatleniia delegata na sobranii S.R. i S.D. v Petrograde)', *Respublika* [Odessa], no. 5 (1917), p. 9.

56 *Novyi Satirikon*, no. 17 (1917), p. 13.

57 *Saratovskii Sovet rabochikh deputatov (1917–1918): Sbornik dokumentov* (Moscow and Leningrad: Gosudarstvennoe sotsial'no-ekonomicheskoe izdatel'stvo, 1931), p. 56.

58 *GARF*, *fond* 1807, *opis'* 1, *delo* 359, *list* 119 (Pozdravlenie ot Komiteta obshchestvennoi bezopasnosti Porokhovskogo zavoda pri stantsii Rubezhnoi).

59 Ibid., *delo* 361, *list* 41 (Pozdravlenie ot prisiazhnoi advokatury Kishineva).
60 Ibid., *list* 47 (Pozdravlenie ot pravleniia Obshchestva gruzin, Stavropol').
61 Ibid., *delo* 359, *list* 108.
62 Ibid., *delo* 361, *list* 33.
63 Ibid., *fond* 124, *opis'* 68, *delo* 13, *list* 2.
64 Ibid., *fond* 1807, *opis'* 1, *delo* 354, *listy* 26–7, 114, 121.
65 Ibid., *listy* 15, 78; *delo* 361, *list* 34; *delo* 363, *list* 13.
66 Anon, *Syn Velikoi Russkoi Revoliutsii*, pp. 12–13.
67 *RGA VMF*, *fond* 1340, *opis'* 1, *delo* 236, *list* 15.
68 *GARF*, *fond* 1807, *opis'* 1, *delo* 354, *listy* 37, 124.
69 Ibid., *listy* 17, 112, 121; *fond* 124, *opis'* 68, *delo* 9, *list* 109; *Skorbnyi put' Romanovykh, 1917–1918 gg.: Sb. dokumentov i materialov* (Moscow: ROSSPEN, 2001), p. 71.
70 Georgii Kniazev, 'Iz zapisnoi knizhki russkogo intelligenta za vremia voiny i revoliutsii 1915–1922 gg.', *Russkoe proshloe*, no. 2 (1991), p. 127.
71 *Izvestiia Gel'singforsskogo soveta*, 21 March 1917; *Russkii invalid*, 22 March 1917.
72 *Petrogradskii Sovet rabochikh i soldatskikh deputatov v 1917 godu*, vol. 1, p. 588.
73 See messages from the Kislovodsk Civil Executive Committee and the Executive Committee of the Saratov Soviet of Workers' Deputies to the minister of justice, and Kerensky's replies, *RGIA*, *fond* 1405, *opis'* 538, *delo* 177, *list* 65; *Saratovskii Sovet rabochikh deputatov (1917–1918)*, pp. 40, 75; *RGIA*, *fond* 1405, *opis'* 538, *delo* 177, *list* 29.
74 *Rabochaia gazeta*, 25 March 1917; *Novoe vremia*, 25 March 1917.
75 *Delo naroda*, 28 March 1917; *Izvestiia Gel'singforsskogo Soveta deputatov armii, flota i rabochikh Sveaborgskogo porta*, 29 March 1917.
76 See Boris Kolonitskii, *'Tragicheskaia erotika': Obrazy imperatorskoi sem'i v gody Pervoi mirovoi voiny* (Moscow: Novoe literaturnoe obozrenie, 2010).
77 'Petrograd, 21 marta', *Zemlia i volia* [Petrograd], 21 March 1917.
78 *RGASPI*, *fond* 662, *opis'* 1, *delo* 34, *list* 5; quoted from Vladimir Buldakov and Tat'iana Leont'eva, *Voina, porodivshaia revoliutsiiu: Rossiia, 1914–1917 gg.* (Moscow: Novyi khronograph, 2015), p. 534.
79 *S"ezdy i konferentsii konstitutsionno-demokraticheskoi partii*, vol. 3, part 1, p. 479.
80 Elizaveta Naryshkina, *Moi vospominaniia: Pod vlast'iu trekh tsarei* (Moscow: Novoe literaturnoe obozrenie, 2014), pp. 423–6. On the positive reaction on the part of Grand Dukes Sergei Mikhailovich and Nikolai Mikhailovich to Kerenskii's actions in March, see Mel'gunov, *Martovskie dni 1917 goda*, p. 278; '"Moment, kogda nel'zia dopustit' oploshnostei": Pis'ma velikogo kniazia Nikolaia Mikhailovicha vdovstvuiushchei imperatritse Marii Fedorovne', publication by Dilara Ismail-Zade, *Istochnik*, no. 4 (35) (1998), p. 24.
81 *Novoe vremia*, 14 April 1917; *Russkaia volia*, 15 April 1917.
82 *GARF*, *fond* 1807, *opis'* 1, *delo* 361, *list* 30.
83 Ibid., *delo* 354, *listy* 125, 137.
84 Kerensky, *The Catastrophe*, p. 133.
85 *Sotsial-demokrat* [Moscow], 30 April 1917.
86 Kravkov, *Velikaia voina bez retushi*, p. 297.
87 *GARF*, *fond* 539, *opis'* 1, *delo* 1300, *list* 8 *ob.* (newspaper clipping).
88 *Novaia zhizn'*, 2 May 1917.

89 Rashel' Khin-Gol'dovskaia, 'Iz dnevnikov 1913–1917', *Minuvshee: Istoricheskii al'manakh* (St Petersburg), *vyp*. 21, p. 577.
90 Katerina Breshkovskaia, *Hidden Springs of the Russian Revolution* (Stanford, CA: Stanford University Press, 1931), p. 354.
91 M. Merzon, 'A. F. Kerenskii v Moskve', *Nizhegorodskii listok*, 1 June 1917.
92 Some officers, however, tried to avoid this unwelcome innovation and campaigned against handshaking on the grounds of hygiene or cited hot weather. Every room in the headquarters of the 11th Army had a notice on the door: 'Handshaking is abolished in hot weather.' See Alfred Knox, *With the Russian Army* (London: Hutchinson, 1921), vol. 2, p. 634.
93 Ivanchikov, 'Ministr Kerenskii', *Nizhegorodskii listok*, 29 April 1917.
94 A. F. Kerenskii, *Izdaleka: Sbornik statei (1920–1921 g.)* (Paris: Povolotskii, 1922), p. 218; Gennadiy Sobolev, *Aleksandr Kerenskii: Liubov' i nenavist' revoliutsii: dnevniki, stat'i, ocherki, vospominaniia sovremennikov* (Cheboksary: Chuvashskii universitet, 1993), p. 22; Sobolev, *Revoliutsionnoe soznanie rabochikh i soldat Petrograda v 1917 g. Period dvoevlastiia* (Leningrad: Nauka, 1973), p. 162; Andrei Golikov, 'Fenomen Kerenskogo', *Otechestvennaia istoriia*, no. 5 (1992), pp. 64–5.
95 Kerenskii's asceticism was selective. He used the tsar's motor car, a fact which can be interpreted in different ways: was it a simple manifestation of personal vanity, or was the minister trying to emphasize his special, higher status over the other ministers?
96 Miliukov, *Rossiia na perelome*, vol. 1, p. 82.
97 Kerenskii, 'O kniaze' [G. E. L'vov], *Dni*, 12 March 1925. Quoted from Igor' Kir'ianov, 'Pidzhak v rossiiskoi politike: Pervaia primerka', *Tavricheskie chteniia, 2013, Aktual'nye problemy parlamentarizma: istoriia i sovremennost'*, ed. Andrei Nikolaev (St Petersburg: ElekSis, 2014), part 1, pp. 89–90.
98 Andrei Mikhailov, 'Pskovskie kadety v politicheskikh sobytiiakh nachala XX veka', *Pskov*, no. 3 (1995), p. 115.
99 Igor' Kir'ianov, 'Dress-kod dlia rossiiskikh parlamentariev nachala XX v.', *Vestnik RUDN*, series 'Istoriia Rossii', no. 2 (2009), pp. 24–30; Kir'ianov, 'Pidzhak v rossiiskoi politike', pp. 86–91.
100 Vladimir D. Nabokov, *Vremennoe pravitel'stvo* (Berlin: Arkhiv russkoi revoliutsii, 1921), vol. 1; repr. (Moscow: Terra, Politizdat, 1991), vols. 1–2, p. 16.
101 Benua, *Moi dnevnik*, p. 15.
102 *Pervoe pravitel'stvo svobodnoi Rossii i vystavka voiny* [catalogue] (Petrograd: Obshchestvo popecheniia o bespriutnykh detiakh, [1917]), p. 5.
103 Buchanan, *My Mission to Russia*, vol. 2, p. 118; Ol'ga Dobrovol'skaia, 'Iz vospominanii o pervykh dniakh revoliutsii', *Russkaia letopis'*, *kn.* 3 (1922), p. 188; *Den'* [Petrograd], 16 March 1917; *Petrogradskaia gazeta*, 19 March 1917; Louis de Robien, *The Diary of a Diplomat in Russia, 1917–1918* (London: Michael Joseph, 1969), pp. 35–6; Nikolai Karabchevskii, *Chto glaza moi videli* (Berlin: D'iakova, 1921), vol. 2: *Revoliutsiia i Rossiia*, p. 120.
104 Gippius, *Siniaia kniga*, p. 119; Filosofov, 'Dnevnik', *Zvezda*, no. 3 (1992), p. 147.
105 Ivanchikov, 'Ministr Kerenskii'.
106 P. F. Arzub'ev (Petr Guber), *A. F. Kerenskii na fronte* (Petrograd: Kopeika, 1917), p. 2.
107 This photograph was used to illustrate Kir'iakov's biographical sketch. See Vasilii Kir'iakov, 'A. F. Kerenskii', *Niva*, no. 19 (1917), p. 289.

108 *Rampa i zhizn'*, no. 22, 4 June 1917, p. 1 (cover).
109 For greater detail, see Kolonitskii, 'Feminizatsiia obraza A. F. Kerenskogo i politicheskaia izoliatsiia Vremennogo pravitel'stva osen'iu 1917 goda', in *Mezhvuzovskaia nauchnaia konferentsiia 'Russkaia revoliutsiia 1917 goda: Problemy istorii i istoriografii': Sbornik dokladov* (St Petersburg: Gosudarstvennyi elektrotekhnicheskii universitet, 2013), pp. 93–103.
110 Vladimir Lenin, 'K s"ezdu Sovetov', *Polnoe sobranie sochinenii*, vol. 32, p. 447.
111 Alisa Koonen, *Stranitsy zhizni* (Moscow: Iskusstvo, 1985), p. 233. Alisa Koonen's memory has evidently failed her. Most probably she heard Kerenskii's speech in the Bolshoy Theatre in Moscow on 26 May.
112 *GARF*, *fond* 1807, *opis'* 1, *delo* 244, *listy* 343–4 *ob*.
113 The Kornilov Affair of 10–13 September 1917 was an unsuccessful attempt at a *coup d'état* by General Lavr Kornilov, supreme commander-in-chief of the Russian army. He aimed to overthrow the Provisional Government and establish a military dictatorship instead. [Trans.]
114 Andrei Golikov, '"... Budushchii artist Imperatorskikh teatrov": Pis'ma Aleksandra Kerenskogo roditeliam', *Istochnik: Dokumenty russkoi istorii* [Supplement to *Rodina*, vol. 3 (1994): 4–22], pp. 16–18.
115 Eduard Pantserzhanskii, 'Ot Fevralia k Oktiabriu', *Sever*, no. 7 (1987), p. 78.
116 A. Turov, 'Poet revoliutsii (Kerenskii)', *Svobodnaia Rossiia*, 12 June 1917.
117 It is no surprise to find, in research on the cult-like admiration of opera singers, that Kerenskii gets a paragraph to himself. Anna Fishzon finds similarities. See Fishzon, *Fandom, Authenticity and Opera: Mad Acts and Letter Scenes in Fin-de-Siècle Russia* (Basingstoke: Palgrave Macmillan, 2013), pp. 188–93.
118 *Birzhevye vedomosti* (evening edn), 21 April 1917.
119 'Spekuliatsiia na Kerenskom', *Narodnaia niva* [Helsingfors], 7 June 1917.
120 Heald, *Witness to Revolution*, p. 73.
121 *Russkaia volia*, 2 May 1917. On Kerenskii's speech at the teachers' congress, see Nikolai Smirnov, *Na perelome: Rossiiskoe uchitel'stvo nakanune i v dni revoliutsii 1917 goda* (St Petersburg: Nauka, 1994), pp. 177–9.
122 Dobrovol'skaia, 'Iz vospominanii o pervykh dniakh revoliutsii', p. 189.
123 Leonidov, *Vozhd' svobody*, p. 29.
124 As a representative of the Provisional Government, Kerenskii was already receiving honours and medals when he was minister of justice. On 30 March he received awards collected by the garrison soldiers in Berdichev. See *Delo naroda*, 31 March 1917. After he was appointed minister of war and the navy, this became more frequent.
125 *Volia naroda*, 18 May 1917; *Prikazy i rechi pervogo russkogo Voennogo i Morskogo Ministra-Sotsialista A. F. Kerenskogo* ([No location]: Shtab osoboi armii, 1917), p. 25.
126 N. Rakhmanov, 'Demokraticheskoe soveshchanie: Pod pervym vpechatleniem', *Delo naroda*, 15 September 1917.
127 Dietrich Geyer, *The Russian Revolution: Historical Problems and Perspectives*, trans. Bruce Little (Leamington Spa: Berg, 1987), p. 73; Nikolai Sukhanov, *Zapiski o revoliutsii* (Berlin: Grzhebin, 1922), vol. 1, p. 70.
128 Sergei Mstislavskii (Maslovskii), *Piat' dnei* (2nd edn, Berlin, Petersburg and Moscow: Grzhebin, 1922), pp. 61–2.

129 Arzub'ev, *A. F. Kerenskii na fronte*, p. 4.
130 Mikhail Narokov, *Biografiia moego pokoleniia: Teatral'nye memuary* (Moscow: VTO, 1956), pp. 184–5.
131 Ibid.
132 Vasilii Nemirovich-Danchenko, 'Kerenskii (Profil')', *Russkoe slovo*, 30 May 1917.
133 Ibid.
134 Narokov, *Biografiia moego pokoleniia*, pp. 184–5.
135 *Volia naroda*, 11 May 1917.
136 Lev Trotskii, 'Itogi i perspektivy', *Proletarii*, 15 August 1917; Viktor Chernov, *Rozhdenie revoliutsionnoi Rossii (Fevral'skaia revoliutsiia)* (Paris, Prague and New York: Iubileinyi komitet po izdaniiu trudov V. M. Chernova, 1934), p. 332.
137 On the 'Eastertide' perception of the revolution, see Kolonitskii, *Simvoly vlasti i bor'ba za vlast'*. On the 'ecclesiastical revolution', see Pavel Rogoznyi, *Tserkovnaia revoliutsiia 1917 goda (Vysshee dukhovenstvo Rossiiskoi tserkvi v bor'be za vlast' v eparkhiiakh posle Fevral'skoi revoliutsii)* (St Petersburg: Liki Rossii, 2008).
138 Valerian Murav'ev, 'Rim chetvertyi', *Russkaia svoboda* [Petrograd], no. 2 (1917), p. 11.
139 *Russkoe slovo*, 11 May 1917.
140 Andrei Snesarev, *Dnevnik: 1916–1917* (Moscow: Kuchkovo pole, 2014), pp. 439, 441.
141 *Novoe vremia*, 25 March 1917.
142 Zavadskii, 'Na velikom izlome', p. 33.
143 Nikita Okunev, *Dnevnik moskvicha, 1917–1924*, 2 vols (Moscow: Voenizdat, 1997), vol. 1, pp. 38–9. The diarist recorded the minister's kisses subsequently. Ibid., pp. 42, 44.
144 Kolonitskii, *'Tragicheskaia erotika'*.
145 Vladimir Fridkin, 'Tonik: Natan Eidel'man v zastol'e', *Znamia*, no. 11 (2009), p. 45.
146 Borisov, 'Vezdesushchii (Vpechatleniia delegata na sobranii S.R. i S.D. v Petrograde)', p. 9.
147 *Petrogradskii Sovet rabochikh i soldatskikh deputatov v 1917 godu*, vol. 1, pp. 574–6, 585–91.
148 *Russkoe slovo*, 7 May 1917.
149 *Edinstvo*, 7 May 1917; *Russkoe slovo*, 9 May 1917; *Russkii invalid*, 9 May 1917; *Narodnaia niva* [Helsingfors], 11 May 1917.
150 Viktor Shklovskii, *Revoliutsiia i front* (Petrograd: 23-ia Gosudarstvennaia tipografiia, 1921), p. 15.
151 Pavel Kupriianovskii, *Neizvestnyi Furmanov* (Ivanovo: Ivanovskii gosudarstvennyi universitet, 1996), p. 61.
152 Mikhail Zoshchenko, 'Besslavnyi konets', *Literaturnyi sovremennik*, no. 1 (1938), pp. 224–5; *Zoshchenko, Rasskazy, 1937–1938* (Leningrad: Sovetski pisatel', 1938), p. 179.
153 Marietta Chudakova, *Literatura sovetskogo proshlogo* (Moscow: Iazyki russkoi kul'tury, 2001), pp. 82, 84.
154 Petr Krasnov, *Na vnutrennem fronte* (Berlin: Arkhiv russkoi revoliutsii, 1922), vol. 1; repr. (Moscow: Terra, Politizdat, 1991), vol. 1, p. 150.
155 Alexandre Benois described Kerenskii's appearance as follows: 'Naturally

haggard, today Kerenskii seemed to me to have a deathly pallor.' Benua, *Moi dnevnik*, p. 149.
156 Merzon, 'A. F. Kerenskii v Moskve'.
157 Arzub'ev, *A. F. Kerenskii na fronte*, p. 3.
158 *Zhivoe slovo*, 9 March 1917; *Den'*, 9 March 1917.
159 Mark Vishniak, *Dan' proshlomu* (New York: Chekhov, 1954), p. 230.
160 *Novaia zhizn'*, 30 April 1917; Shklovskii, *Revoliutsiia i front*, p. 15.
161 *Izvestiia Gel'singforsskogo Soveta deputatov armii, flota i rabochikh Sveaborgskogo porta*, 19 and 21 March 1917.
162 Vasilii Vodovozov, 'Ob"iasnenie po povodu moego pis'ma k A. F. Kerenskomu', *Den'* [Petrograd], 8 March 1917.
163 *Vserossiiskoe soveshchaniie Sovetov rabochikh i soldatskikh deputatov (29 marta–3 aprelia 1917 goda): Stenograficheskii otchet* (Moscow and Leningrad: Gosizdat, 1927), p. 146.
164 Several resolutions referred to the minister's 'strong will'. See *Russkii invalid*, 8 June 1917 (Resolution of the Revel naval committee).
165 Leonidov, *Vozhd' svobody*, pp. 3, 4.
166 V–i V. [Vasilii Vasil'evich Kir'iakov], *A. F. Kerenskii* (Petrograd, 1917), p. 49.
167 Leonidov, *Vozhd' svobody*, p. 27.
168 Borisov, 'Vezdesushchii (Vpechatleniia delegata na sobranii S.R. i S.D. v Petrograde)', p. 9.
169 E. V[ladimirovi]–ch, *A. F. Kerenskii narodnyi ministr* (Odessa: Vlast' naroda, 1917), pp. 31–2.
170 *Vestnik Tverskogo gubernskogo Ispolnitel'nogo komiteta*, 16 March 1917.
171 *Delo naroda*, 6 April 1917.
172 *Volia naroda*, 7 May 1917.
173 Ivanchikov, 'Ministr Kerenskii'.
174 Kerenskii was likened to a healer releasing the units of the armed forces from their political ailments. One of the minister's supporters wrote after his visit to the main base of the Baltic Fleet, 'With his speeches Comrade Kerensky healed our wounds and infused our ailing hearts with healing balm.' See *Narodnaia niva* [Helsingfors, 18 (31) May 1917.
175 Pero, 'Sluchainyie zametki', *Nizhegorodskii listok*, 1 June 1917.
176 *Svobodnaia tserkov'* [Petrograd], 28 July 1917.
177 *Rabochaia gazeta*, 7 March 1917; *Zhivoe slovo*, 5 and 11 March 1917.
178 *GARF*, *fond* 1807, *opis'* 1, *delo* 359, *listy* 95–6; *delo* 361, *list* 13.
179 Khronika, *Zemlia i volia* [Petrograd], 29 April 1917.
180 An. Borisov, 'Izo dnia v den"', *Svobodnaia Rossiia* (evening edn), 8 May 1917.
181 Boris Filatovich (Boris Baratov), 'Beregite Kerenskogo!', *Svobodnaia Rossiia* (evening edn), 8 May 1917.
182 *Russkoe slovo*, 28 May 1917.
183 *Russkii invalid*, 14 June 1917.
184 The Russian offensive of 18–22 June, undertaken because of pressure from the Western Allies and, for a variety of reasons, from certain Russian military and political circles, attacked Austro-Hungarian troops but, after the initial success of elite units, had to be abandoned because of indiscipline and mutiny among the Russian infantry.
185 *Kievlianin*, 10 June 1917; *Rech'*, 14 June 1917.
186 *Volya naroda*, 17 May 1917.

187 See Philippe Roger, 'L'homme de sang: l'invention sémiotique de Marat', *La Mort de Marat*, ed. Jean-Claude Bonnet (Paris: Flammarion, 1986).
188 *Russkoe slovo*, 8 March 1917. Quoted from Sobolev, *Aleksandr Kerenskii: Liubov' i nenavist' revoliutsii*, p. 24.
189 *GARF*, *fond* 1807, *opis'* 1, *delo* 354, *listy* 95–6.
190 *Peterburgskii komitet RSDRP(b) v 1917 godu: Protokoly i materialy zasedanii* (St Petersburg: Bel'veder, 2003), p. 53.
191 Lenin, 'Telegram to the Bolsheviks Leaving for Russia', *Collected Works* (Moscow: Progress, 1964), vol. 23, p. 292 (www.marxists.org/archive/lenin/works/1917/mar/06.htm).
192 *Peterburgskii komitet RSDRP(b) v 1917 godu*, pp. 104, 106.
193 Lenin, 'Letters from Afar: The First Stage of the First Revolution', *Collected Works*, vol. 24, pp. 297–309 (www.marxists.org/archive/lenin/works/1917/lfafar/first.htm#v23pp64h-297).
194 Lenin, 'Letters from Afar: The New Government and the Proletariat', ibid., pp. 309–20 (www.marxists.org/archive/lenin/works/1917/lfafar/second.htm#v23pp64h-309).
195 Karl Marx and Friedrich Engels, 'Introduction to the Leaflet of L. A. Blanqui's Toast Sent to the Refugee Committee in London' [1851], *Marx and Engels Collected Works*, vol. 10 (London: Lawrence & Wishart, 1978), p. 537.
196 Karl Marx, 'The Eighteenth Brumaire of Louis Bonaparte [1852]', trans. Saul Padover (www.marxists.org/archive/marx/works/1852/18th-brumaire/).
197 Lenin, 'To our Comrades in War-Prisoner Camps', *Collected Works*, vol. 23, pp. 343–9 (www.marxists.org/archive/lenin/works/1917/mar/15.htm).
198 Lenin, 'The Revolution in Russia and the Tasks of the Workers of All Countries', ibid., vol. 23, pp. 350–4 (www.marxists.org/archive/lenin/works/1917/mar/12b.htm).
199 Lenin, 'The Tasks of the Russian Social-Democratic Labour Party in the Russian Revolution', ibid., vol. 23, pp. 355–61 (www.marxists.org/archive/lenin/works/1917/mar/16.htm).
200 Lenin, 'Blancism', ibid., vol. 24, pp. 34–7 (www.marxists.org/archive/lenin/works/1917/apr/08.htm).
201 Ibid.
202 Lenin also writes about this in 'I. G. Tsereteli and the Class Struggle', ibid., vol 24, pp. 326–9 (www.marxists.org/archive/lenin/works/1917/apr/29k.htm).
203 Lenin, 'The Class Character of the Revolution that Has Taken Place', ibid., p. 57 (www.marxists.org/archive/lenin/works/1917/tasks/ch01.htm#v24zz99h-057-GUESS).
204 Lenin, 'Concluding Remarks in the Debate Concerning the Report on the Present Situation April 14 (27)', ibid., vol. 24, pp. 148–51 (www.marxists.org/archive/lenin/works/1917/petcconf/14b.htm#v24zz99h-148-GUESS).
205 Lenin, 'Against the Riot-Mongers', ibid., vol. 24, pp. 127–30 (www.marxists.org/archive/lenin/works/1917/apr/14b.htm).
206 *Kronshtadtskii Sovet v 1917 godu: Protokoly i postanovleniia* (St Petersburg: Bulanin, 2017), vol. 1: *Mart – iiun' 1917 goda*, p. 61.
207 *Pravda*, 25 April 1917.
208 Nikolai Efimov, 'Sergei Mironovich Kirov', *Voprosy istorii*, nos. 11–12 (1995), p. 52. The author quotes *Terek*, 6 and 7 May 1917.
209 In March–April, unified organizations existed in fifty-four provincial capitals. See Khanan Astrakhan, *Bol'sheviki i ikh politicheskie protivniki v 1917*

godu: Iz istorii politicheskikh partii v Rossii mezhdu dvumia revoliutsiiami (Leningrad: Lenizdat, 1973), pp. 112–20.

210 Matvei Muranov telegraphed Kerenskii on 5 March from Turukhansk region: 'Request you provide material support return of exiles. Leaving very shortly. Greetings, good wishes for success' (*GARF*, *fond* 1807, *opis'* 1, *delo* 354, *list* 111). Muranov was evidently anticipating aid from Kerenskii for other exiles returning with him to European Russia. These included Lev Kamenev and Iosif Stalin.

211 See Al G–ko, 'Prodannye brat'ia', *Sotsial-demokrat* [Moscow], 17 May 1917.

212 *Soldatskaia pravda*, 18 April 1917.

213 Alexander Rabinowitch, *Prelude to Revolution: The Petrograd Bolsheviks and the July 1917 Uprising* (Bloomington: Indiana University Press, 1991); Rabinowitch, *The Bolsheviks Come to Power: The Revolution of 1917 in Petrograd* (New York: W. W. Norton, 1976).

214 Astrakhan, *Bol'sheviki i ikh politicheskie protivniki v 1917 godu*.

215 'Znaite: armii net . . .', publication by Veronika Lin'kova, *Rodina*, no. 8 (2014), p. 98.

216 Konstantin Dushenko, *Tsitaty iz russkoi istorii: Spravochnik* (Moscow: Eksmo, 2005), p. 124.

217 Kerensky, *The Kerensky Memoirs*. He makes a passing reference to the speech in an early version of his memoirs: Alexandre Kerenski, *La Révolution russe (1917)* (Paris: Payot, 1928), pp. 188–9.

218 Aleksandr Solzhenitsyn paid close attention to this speech. See Solzhenitsyn, *Krasnoe koleso: Povestvovan'e v otmerennykh srokakh* (Paris: YMCA, 1985–91), *Uzel* IV: *Aprel' semnadtsatogo* (1991), pp. 232–41. It is noteworthy that Solzhenitsyn had his characters mention this speech by Kerenskii, thereby demonstrating how well known it was.

219 *Rech'*, 20 April 1917.

220 Buchanan, *My Mission to Russia*, vol. 2, p. 119. (https://archive.org/details/mymissiontorussi02buch/page/118).

221 Paléologue, *An Ambassador's Memoirs*, vol. 3, ch. 12, 2 May (19 April) 1917 (http://net.lib.byu.edu/estu/wwi/memoir/FrAmbRus/pal3-12.htm).

222 On the April Crisis, see the chapter by Iurii Tokarev in a monograph written by a team of contributors: *Oktiabr'skoe vooruzhennoe vosstanie: Semnadtsatyi god v Petrograde*, ed. Anton Fraiman (Leningrad: Nauka, 1967), *kn*. 1: 'Na putiakh k sotsialisticheskoi revoliutsii: Dvoevlastie', pp. 217–50.

223 *Birzhevye vedomosti* (morning edn), 22 April 1917. The public were even told that Kerenskii was in bed. *Delo naroda*, 21 April 1917.

224 A similar sentiment was evident, for example, in the resolution of the committee of the Reserve Battalion of the Eger Guards regiment. See *Bol'shevizatsiia Petrogradskogo garnizona: Sb. materialov i dokumentov*, ed. Arvid Drezen (Leningrad: Leningradskoe oblastnoe izdatel'stvo, 1932), p. 79; Sobolev, *Revoliutsionnoe soznanie rabochikh i soldat Petrograda*, p. 226. At the beginning of May activists queried why the minister had signed the Provisional Government's note. *Volna* [Helsingfors], 14 May 1917; *Soldatskaia pravda*, 20 May 1917.

225 *Malen'kaia gazeta*, 22 April 1917; *Russkii invalid*, 23 April 1917.

226 *Novaia zhizn'*, 20 and 21 April 1917.

227 Ibid., 29 April 1917; *Delo naroda*, 29 April 1917; *Russkoe slovo*, 29 April 1917; *Malen'kaia gazeta*, 29 April 1917.

228 He informed Albert Thomas, a French minister who was in Petrograd, that there was such a plan. See Abraham, *Alexander Kerensky*, p. 181.
229 Aleksei Kuropatkin, 'Iz dnevnika A. N. Kuropatkina', *Krasnyi arkhiv*, vol. 1 (20) (1927), p. 65, entry of 29 April 1917.
230 Pavel Miliukov, *Istoriia vtoroi russkoi revoliutsii* (Moscow: ROSSPEN, 2001), p. 91.
231 There were twenty-three votes against a coalition and twenty-two in favour, with a number of abstentions. See *Petrogradskii Sovet rabochikh i soldatskikh deputatov v 1917 godu*, vol. 2 (1995), pp. 416, 418.
232 *Russkii invalid*, 28 April 1917; *Russkoe slovo*, 28 and 29 April 1917.
233 *Delo naroda*, 28 April 1917; *Russkoe slovo*, 28 April 1917.
234 *Russkoe slovo*, 28 and 29 April 1917.
235 *Russkii invalid*, 29 April 1917; *Russkoe slovo*, 28 and 29 April 1917; *Rech'*, 28 April 1917.
236 'Otechestvo na kraiu gibeli', *Den'* [Petrograd], 29 April 1917.
237 *Novaia zhizn'*, 3 May 1917.
238 One of the lower-grade newspapers claimed Kerenskii had said, 'Guchkov is the first rat deserting a sinking ship.' 'Kerenskii ob ukhode Guchkova', *Malen'kaia gazeta*, 3 May 1917. This claim by a paper which was critical of Guchkov seems untrustworthy, but it may have been based on rumour which exaggerated the reaction of ministers to their cabinet colleague's departure.
239 *Novaia zhizn'*, 26–29 April 1917.
240 Kerenski, *La Révolution russe*, pp. 186–7. Guchkov admitted that Kerenskii had wanted to keep him in the government and work for him as an aide to the minister of war, enabling the latter to concentrate on 'technical issues'. See *Aleksandr Ivanovich Guchkov rasskazyvaet . . . Vospominaniia predsedatelia Gosudarstvennoi dumy i voennogo ministra Vremennogo pravitel'stva*, ed. Vladimir Polikarpov (Moscow: Voprosy istorii, 1993), p. 109.
241 Kerensky's appointment shortly afterwards as minister of war was accepted by the political elite and public opinion as entirely to be expected. See Abraham, *Alexander Kerensky*, p. 188. Kerenskii had also conducted negotiations with influential young officers of the General Staff, which played an important part in the creation of the coalition government and his appointment as minister of war. See Semion Lyandres, ed., *The Fall of Tsarism: Untold Stories of the February 1917 Revolution* (Oxford: Oxford University Press, 2013), pp. 126–7 (testimony of Lev Tugan-Baranovskii).
242 *Stenograficheskii otchet delegatov fronta: Zasedanie 29 April* (Petrograd, 1917), p. 22.
243 *Russkoe slovo*, 30 April 1917. The *Russkoe slovo* report contains a mistake which distorts the meaning of the final sentence. In the transcript it makes better sense.

> At the present time the situation of the Russian state is complicated and extraordinarily difficult. The difficulty is not only that we have at present a painful period of history, a transition from the old regime to something new, a transition from despotism straight to the freest of democratic republics. This transition, this transformation of a servile state to a free state, cannot of course proceed as tidily as in the old days the troops paraded on the Field of Mars. This is not a parade but a very difficult and agonizing task, an organic process which comes with a whole succession of deviations, confusions and misunderstandings, and it is a soil from which very

often seeds germinate and flourish, seeds sown sometimes intentionally, sometimes unintentionally, of faintheartedness, mistrust, seeds which turn the country into a whole succession of atomized organizations, atomized human beings. (*Stenograficheskii otchet delegatov fronta*, p. 23)

244 *Russkoe slovo*, 30 April 1917.
245 Ibid.
246 Ibid.
247 Ibid.
248 Ibid.
249 Ibid.
250 Ibid.
251 Ibid.
252 Tsereteli, *Vospominaniia o Fevral'skoi revoliutsii*, vol. 1, p. 124.
253 *Russkoe slovo*, 30 April 1917.
254 Nikolai Rusanov, 'Russkaia revoliutsiia i posledniaia rech' Kerenskogo', *Delo naroda*, 2 May 1917.
255 Quoted from Aleksandr Iablonovskii, 'Na skvoznom vetru', *Russkoe slovo*, 4 May 1917. The title of the article alludes to Leo Tolstoy's remark about Leonid Andreev: 'He tries to frighten people, but I am not scared.'
256 *Volia naroda*, 30 April, 2 May 1917.
257 *Russkoe slovo*, 30 April 1917.
258 *Utro Rossii* [Moscow], 4 May 1917.
259 Vladimir Nevskii, 'Bessilie vlasti', *Soldatskaia pravda*, 3 May 1917; M. Mil'shtein, 'Tragiki', ibid., 9 May 1917.
260 This newspaper of the Military Organization of the RSDRP wrote more harshly about Kerenskii at this time than did *Pravda*, the main party newspaper.
261 *Russkii invalid*, 2 May 1917.
262 *Russkaia volia*, 2 May 1917.
263 *Russkoe slovo*, 4 May 1917.
264 'Pechat' i zhizn': Rydaniia grazhdanina Svatikova', *Delo naroda*, 5 May 1917.
265 *Rech'*, 6 May 1917.
266 *Russkaia volia*, 30 April 1917. Quoted from Leonid Andreev, *Pered zadachami vremeni: Politicheskie stat'i 1917–1919 godov*, ed. Richard Davies (Benson, VT: Chalidze, 1985), pp. 69–88.
267 *Russkaia volia*, 3 and 4 May 1917. The article was published as a brochure as Leonid Andreev, *Gibel' (Stat'ia)* (Petrograd: Knizhnyi postavshchik, 1917); also Andreev, *Gibel' (Chto zhdet Rossiiu)* (Moscow: Volia, 1917).
268 Mikhail Levidov, 'Malen'kii fel'eton', *Novaia zhizn'*, 3 May 1917; Sergei Mstislavskii, 'Geroi tyla', ibid.; *Delo naroda*, 4 May 1917.
269 T. Ardov (i.e., Vladimir Tardov), 'Perelom', *Utro Rossii* [Moscow], 2 May 1917.
270 Abraham, *Alexander Kerensky*, pp. 187–90.
271 Boris Filatovich, 'Beregite Kerenskogo!'.
272 *Russkoe slovo*, 6 May 1917. See also *Burzhuaziia i pomeshchiki v 1917 godu: Chastnye soveshchaniia chlenov Gosudarstvennoi dumy*, ed. Arvid Drezen (Moscow and Leningrad: Partiinoe izdatel'stvo, 1932), pp. 16–17.
273 Aleksandr Solzhenitsyn supposed that Maklakov had cut Kerenskii down to size for 'claiming the credit for someone else's words'. See Solzhenitsyn, *Krasnoe koleso*, *Uzel* IV, p. 463. It is possible that the image of 'rebellious

slaves' had been suggested to Kerenskii by none other than Maklakov shortly before he gave the speech, which was what Maklakov himself surmised, and that opinion is shared by his biographer. See Oleg Budnitskii, 'Netipichnyi Maklakov', *Otechestvennaia istoriia*, nos. 2–3 (1999), p. 76; Budnitskii, 'Maklakov', *Rossiiskie liberaly: Sbornik statei* (Moscow: ROSSPEN, 2001), p. 524; Budnitskii, 'Posly nesushchestvuiushchei strany', in *'Sovershenno lichno i doveritel'no!' B. A. Bakhmet'ev–V. A. Maklakov: Perepiska, 1919–1951*, 3 vols (ROSSPEN/Hoover Institute/Russian Academy of Sciences, 2001), vol. 1: *Avgust 1919–sentiabr' 1921*, p. 96. It seems more plausible to suppose that Kerenskii was referring back to a speech by Fedor Rodichev, which Maklakov had related to him with his own commentary. See Kolonitskii, '"Vzbuntovavshiesia raby" i "velikii grazhdanin": rech' A. F. Kerenskogo 29 aprelia 1917 i ee politicheskoe znachenie', *Journal of Modern Russian History and Historiography*, no. 7 (2014).

274 *Russkoe slovo* [Moscow], 3 May 1917.

275 *OR RNB, fond* 481, *opis'* 1, *delo* 60, *list* 9 *ob.*

276 Nikolai Breshko-Breshkovskii, 'Vzbuntovavshiisia rab!..', *Svobodnaia Rossiia* (evening edition), 8 May 1917; Ivan Lukash, 'Grazhdane i raby', *Trud i volia* (Petrograd), 29 July 1917; Arkadii Averchenko, 'Vzbuntovavshiesia raby', *Novyi Satirikon*, no. 21 (June), 1917, p. 7.

277 *OR RNB, fond* 152, *opis'* 3, *delo* 98, *list* 47, 'Obzor perepiski za mai–iiun' 1917 g.'

278 *RGA VMF, fond* R-29, *opis'* 1, *delo* 153, *listy* 234–47; *fond* 479, *opis'* 2, *delo* 1328, *list* 173.

279 *Russkoe slovo*, 13 May 1917.

280 Kerenskii, *Ob armii i voine*, p. 13 and *passim*.

281 V. Ropshin (i.e., Boris Savinkov), 'V deistvuiushchei armii', quoted from *Russkii invalid*, 28 June 1917; *Russkaia volia*, 11 July 1917, quoted from Andreev, *Pered zadachami vremeni*, p. 103

282 Kniazev, 'Iz zapisnoi knizhki russkogo intelligenta', p. 164; Okunev, *Dnevnik moskvicha, 1917–1924*, vol. 1, p. 57; see also pp. 51–2.

283 *Soldatskaia mysl'*, 4 May 1917; *Russkii invalid*, 10 May 1917. The expression 'velikii grazhdanin' as applied to Kerenskii crops up in other sources too. See *Razlozhenie armii v 1917 godu* (Moscow and Leningrad: Gosudarstvennoe sotsial'no-ekonomicheskoe izdatel'stvo, 1925), pp. 70–1.

284 Vol'noopredeliaiushchiisia Khil'kevich, 'A. F. Kerenskii', *Soldatskoe slovo*, 6 May 1917.

285 Ziva Galili, *The Menshevik Leaders in the Russian Revolution: Social Realities and Political Strategies* (Princeton, NJ: Princeton University Press, 1989), p. 173.

Chapter III 'Leader of the Revolutionary Army'

1 *Novaia zhizn'*, 2 May 1917.

2 *Edinstvo*, 2 May 1917.

3 *Russkoe slovo*, 3 May 1917.

4 *Novaia zhizn'*, 2 and 30 May 1917.

5 *Russkoe slovo*, 3 May 1917.

6 *Russkaia volia*, 2 May 1917.

7 *Russkii invalid*, 5 May 1917.
8 *Iskry* [Moscow], no. 18 (1917), p. 138.
9 *Russkoe slovo*, 10 May 1917.
10 *Golos soldata*, 13 May 1917.
11 Soldat Shel'menko, 'Pis'ma k matushke', *Soldatskoe slovo*, 7 May 1917.
12 K. Posadskii, 'Na vol'nom mitinge (Partiia narodnoi svobody)', *Krymskii vestnik* [Sevastopol'], 7 May 1917.
13 *Narodnaia niva* [Helsingfors], 9 May 1917. We surmise that the resolution was drafted by members of the ship's committee.
14 *Soldatskoe slovo*, 9 May 1917.
15 *Russkoe slovo*, 10 May 1917.
16 *Soldatskoe slovo*, 9 May 1917.
17 *Svobodnaia Rossiia*, 8 May 1917.
18 *Russkii invalid*, 5 May 1917; *Edinstvo*, 5 May 1917; *Russkaia volia*, 5 May 1917.
19 *Edinstvo*, 6 May 1917.
20 Valerii Zhuravlev, *Bez very, tsaria i otechestva: Rossiiskaia periodicheskaia pechat' i armiia v marte–oktiabre 1917 goda* (St Petersburg: Ministerstvo obrazovania RF, SPbGU Ministerstva vnutrennikh del RF, 1999), p. 109.
21 Feliks Rostkovskii, *Dnevnik dlia zapisyvaniia: 1917-i: revoliutsiia glazami otstavnogo generala* (Moscow: ROSSPEN, 2001), p. 191; Nikita Okunev, *Dnevnik moskvicha, 1917–1924*, 2 vols (Moscow: Voenizdat, 1997), vol. 1, p. 40. See also Aleksei Oreshnikov, *Dnevnik, 1915–1933*, 2 vols, ed. Petr Gaidukov et al. (Moscow: Nauka, 2010–11), vol. 1, p. 116.
22 Vasilii Kravkov, *Velikaia voina bez retushi: Zapiski korpusnogo vracha* (Moscow: Veche, 2014), pp. 323–4.
23 *Utro Rossii* [Moscow], 9 May 1917.
24 Ibid.
25 *Russkii invalid*, 9 May 1917; Aleksandr Kerenskii, *Golos 1-go narodnogo ministra k krest'ianam i rabochim o zemle i vole* (Petrograd: Gramotnost', 1917), p. 10.
26 Aleksei Kuropatkin, 'Iz dnevnika A. N. Kuropatkina', *Krasnyi arkhiv*, vol. 1 (20) (1927), pp. 69–70; Andrei Snesarev, *Pis'ma s fronta, 1914–1917* (Moscow: Kuchkovo pole, Berkut, 2012), p. 648.
27 *Russkii invalid*, 9 May 1917.
28 A. F. Kerensky, *The Kerensky Memoirs: Russia and History's Turning Point* (London: Cassell, 1966), pp. 272–3.
29 *Delo naroda*, 9 May 1917.
30 *Soldatskoe slovo*, 9 May 1917; *Rabochaia gazeta*, 9 May 1917; *Soldatskaia mysl'*, 9 May 1917; *Delo naroda*, 9 May 1917.
31 *Delo naroda*, 7 May 1917.
32 *Russkoe slovo*, 7 May 1917. See also *Rechi A. F. Kerenskogo* (Kiev: Blago naroda, 1917), p. 12; Kerenskii, *Golos 1-go narodnogo ministra k krest'ianam i rabochim*, pp. 5–8.
33 *Soldatskoe slovo*, 7 May 1917.
34 *Golos soldata*, 6 May 1917; *Malen'kaia gazeta*, 6 May 1917.
35 *Volia naroda*, 7 May 1917.
36 *Edinstvo*, 6 and 7 May 1917; *Svobodnaia Rossiia* (evening edn), 8 May 1917.
37 *Russkii invalid*, 9 May 1917.

38 B. V., 'Chto uspel sdelat' Kerenskii za 3 chasa', *Narodnaia niva* [Helsingfors], 11 May 1917.
39 *Golos soldata*, 9 May 1917. Kerenskii was also mentioned as 'Leader of the army' in a number of resolutions adopted in May. See *Volia naroda*, 19 and 25 May 1917.
40 *Russkii invalid*, 9 May 1917.
41 *Russkoe slovo*, 9 May 1917; *Russkii invalid*, 10 May 1917.
42 Ibid., 11 May.
43 'Iz zapisnoi knizhki arkhivista: Zapiski A. I. Koz'mina (1917 g.)', publication by Vladimir Maksakov, *Krasnyi arkhiv*, vol. 5 (60) (1933), p. 145.
44 *Soldatskoe slovo*, 9 May 1917; *Narodnaia niva* [Helsingfors], 10 May 1917.
45 *Russkoe slovo*, 11 May 1917.
46 Konstantin Tarasov, *Voennaia organizatsiia bol'shevikov i bor'ba za vlast' v Petrogradskom garnizone v 1917 g.: Dissertatsiia na soiskanie uchenoi stepeni kandidata istoricheskikh nauk* (St Petersburg: SPbII RAN, 2014), pp. 95, 326–7.
47 *Edinstvo*, 10 May 1917.
48 Viktor Petrash, *Moriaki Baltiiskogo flota v bor'be za pobedu Oktiabria* (Moscow and Leningrad: Nauka, 1966), p. 88.
49 Aleksei Kuropatkin, 'Dnevnik, 1917 god', *Istoricheskii arkhiv*, no. 1 (1992), p. 72.
50 *Edinstvo*, 12 May 1917.
51 *Volia naroda*, 6 and 12 May, 10 June 1917.
52 *Periodicheskaia pechat' Rossii v 1917 godu: Bibliograficheskii ukazatel'* (Leningrad: Gosudarstvennaia publichnaia biblioteka im. M. E. Saltykova-Shchedrina, 1987), vol. 2: *N–Ia*, pp. 156–7. The newspaper of the *Otriadnyi komitet russkikh voisk vo Frantsii* [Brigade Committee of Russian Troops in France], which was published in Paris from 1917 to 1920, had the title *Russkii soldat-grazhdanin vo Frantsii'* [the Russian Citizen Soldier in France].
53 Aleksandr Astashov, *Russkii front v 1914–nachale 1917 goda: Voennyi opyt i sovremennost'* (Moscow: Novyi khronograf, 2014), pp. 6–7, 39, 597. While linking the transformations of the war period to the participation of front-line soldiers in the revolution, the author makes no mention of the contemporaneous political campaigns of 1917.
54 *Golos soldata*, 7 May 1917.
55 Translated from a translation into Russian by E. Iu. Dubrovskaia.
56 Vladimir Cherniaev, 'Rossiiskoe dvoevlastie i protsess samoopredeleniia Finliandii', in *Anatomiia revoliutsii, 1917 god v Rossii: Massy, partii, vlast'*, ed. Cherniaev (St Petersburg: Glagol", 1994), p. 310. Cherniaev calls the situation which developed in Finland 'triple power'. In more recent research, the term 'double radicalization' is used. See Elena Dubrovskaia, 'The Russian Military in Finland and the Russian Revolution', *Russia's Home Front in War and Revolution, 1914–1922*, ed. Aaron Retish, Sarah Badcock and Liudmila Novikova (Bloomington, IN: Slavica, 2015), Book 1: *Russia's Revolution in Regional Perspective*, pp. 247–66.
57 Richard Abraham, *Alexander Kerensky: The First Love of the Revolution* (London: Sidgwick & Jackson, 1987), p. 101.
58 The Provisional Government confirmed the Finnish Senate under the leadership of Oskari Tokoi. The Senate was the executive branch but not a fully fledged government, only the representative of the Provisional Government,

from whom it derived its legitimacy. See Eino Ketola, 'Russkaia revoliutsiia i nezavisimost' Finliandii', in *Anatomiia revoliutsii, 1917 god v Rossii*, p. 294.

59 *Delo naroda*, 17, 18 and 19 March 1917.

60 *Obzory finliandskoi periodicheskoi pechati*, nos. 1073, 1077, Riksarkivet, Helsinki, VeSa. 342:4. 3168.

61 *Delo naroda*, 1 April 1917; Abraham, *Alexander Kerensky*, p. 166.

62 A Finnish postcard published after the overthrow of the monarchy depicts figures symbolizing the peoples of Finland and Russia: a male and female Finnish worker and a Russian soldier and peasant are walking towards each other. The Finnish man holds the flag of the Grand Duchy, a golden lion on a red background, while the soldier holds the new symbol of revolutionary Russia, a red flag with the inscription 'Liberty, Equality, Fraternity'. Above these figures is a portrait of Kerenskii. See *Kollektsiia pochtovykh kartochek sovetskogo perioda s 1917 po 1945 g. iz sobranii M. A. Voronina: Katalog* (St Petersburg: Welcome, 2009), vol. 2, p. 70.

63 *Obzor finliandskoi periodicheskoi pechati*, no. 1146, 19 August (1 September), '*Kansan Aeni*', 28 August, Riksarkivet, Helsinki, VeSa. 342:4. 3168.

64 Abraham, *Alexander Kerensky*, pp. 165–6.

65 Ketola, 'Russkaia revoliutsiia i nezavisimost' Finliandii', p. 294; Cherniaev, 'Rossiiskoe dvoevlastie i protsess samoopredeleniia Finliandii', p. 311.

66 *Narodnaia niva* [Helsingfors], 10 May 1917.

67 *Volna* [Helsingfors], 24 May 1917.

68 Elena Dubrovskaia, *Gel'singforsskii Sovet deputatov armii, flota i rabochikh (mart–aprel' 1917 g.)* (Petrozavodsk: KNTs RAN, 1992), p. 92.

69 Denis Bazhanov, *Shchit Petrograda (Sluzhebnye budni baltiiskikh drednoutov v 1914–1917 gg.)* (St Petersburg: RGPU im. A. I. Gertsena, 2007), pp. 115–16; *Russkii invalid*, 11 May 1917.

70 *Volna* [Helsingfors], 14 May 1917.

71 *Izvestiia Gel'singforsskogo Soveta deputatov armii, flota i rabochikh Sveaborgskogo porta*, 14 May 1917.

72 *Prikazy i rechi pervogo russkogo Voennogo i Morskogo Ministra-Sotsialista* ([No location]: Shtab osoboi armii, 1917), pp. 18–20; A. F. Kerenskii, *Ob armii i voine* (Petrograd: Narodnaia volia, 1917), pp. 3–4; Kerenskii, *Ob armii i voine* (Odessa), pp. 3–7.

73 Dubrovskaia, *Gel'singforsskii Sovet deputatov armii, flota i rabochikh*, p. 92.

74 *Volna* [Helsingfors], 11 May 1917.

75 *Narodnaia niva* [Helsingfors], 10 May 1917.

76 'Prebyvanie A. F. Kerenskogo v Gel'singforse', *Rech'*, 11 May 1917.

77 *Narodnaia niva* [Helsingfors], 11 May 1917.

78 *Obzory finliandskoi periodicheskoi pechati*, nos. 1073, 1077, Riksarkivet, Helsinki, VeSa, 342:4, 3168.

79 *Izvestiia Gel'singforsskogo Soveta deputatov armii, flota i rabochikh*, 16 May 1917.

80 Quoted from Zhuravlev, *Bez very, tsaria i otechestva*, p. 110.

81 Kerensky, *The Kerensky Memoirs*, p. 276.

82 *Narodnaia niva* [Helsingfors], 17 May 1917.

83 *Izvestiia Gel'singforsskogo Soveta deputatov armii, flota i rabochikh*, 7 May 1917.

84 Vladimir Zalezhskii, 'Gel'singfors vesnoi i letom 1917 goda', *Proletarskaia revoliutsiia*, no. 5 (17) (1923), p. 139.

85 *Izvestiia Gel'singforsskogo Soveta deputatov armii, flota i rabochikh*, 16 May 1917.
86 *Volna* [Helsingfors], 14 May 1917.
87 *Izvestiia Gel'singforsskogo Soveta deputatov armii, flota i rabochikh*, 16 May 1917.
88 *Volna* [Helsingfors], 19 May, 1 June 1917.
89 Sergei Volynskii, 'Kak mozhno "i nevinnost' sobliusti, i kapital priobresti" ', ibid., 21 May 1917.
90 S. Chekhlov, 'Pis'mo v redaktsiiu', *Narodnaia niva* [Helsingfors], 18 May 1917.
91 *Izvestiia Gel'singforsskogo Soveta deputatov armii, flota i rabochikh*, 13 May 1917. See *Narodnaia niva* [Helsingfors], 18 (31) May 1917.
92 Petrash, *Moriaki Baltiiskogo flota v bor'be za pobedu Oktiabria*, p. 127; Bazhanov, *Shchit Petrograda*, pp. 118–20.
93 Cherniaev, 'Rossiiskoe dvoevlastie i protsess samoopredeleniia Finliandii', p. 314.
94 *Russkii invalid*, 11 May 1917.
95 *Rech'*, 11 May 1917.
96 *Russkii invalid*, 12 May 1917; *Delo naroda*, 12 May 1917.
97 *Russkii invalid*, 14 May 1917.
98 Stanislav Tiutiukin, *Aleksandr Kerenskii: Stranitsy politicheskoi biografii (1905–1917 gg.)* (Moscow: ROSSPEN, 2012), pp. 170–71.
99 *Prikazy i rechi pervogo russkogo Voennogo i Morskogo Ministra-Sotsialista*, p. 23.
100 *Russkii invalid*, 14 May 1917.
101 Viktor Miller, *Soldatskie komitety russkoi armii v 1917 g. (Vozniknovenie i nachal'nyi period deiatel'nosti)* (Moscow: Nauka, 1974), p. 12.
102 On the drafting of the declaration, see Gennadii Sobolev, 'Deklaratsiia prav soldata (mart–mai 1917 g.)', *Vspomogatel'nye istoricheskie distsipliny* (Leningrad: Nauka), vol. 8 (1976), pp. 20–36; Berta Gal'perina, 'Fevral'skaia revoliutsiia i prava soldat', *Voprosy istorii*, no. 10 (2000), pp. 66–9.
103 Allan Wildman, *The End of the Russian Imperial Army* (Princeton, NJ: Princeton University Press) vol. 2 (1987): *The Road to Soviet Power and Peace*, p. 42.
104 V. Petrov (V. V. Adamovich), 'Kerenskii – dusha prikaza No. 1 (Chernye stranitsy iz istorii Russkoi revoliutsii)', *Novaia Rus'*, 6 October 1917.
105 Vera Alekseeva-Borel', *Sorok let v riadakh russkoi imperatorskoi armii: General M. V. Alekseev* (St Petersburg: Bel'veder, 2000), p. 513.
106 Wildman, *The End of the Russian Imperial Army*, vol. 2, pp. 22–3.
107 *Prikazy i rechi pervogo russkogo Voennogo i Morskogo Ministra-Sotsialista*, pp. 5–6.
108 Vladimir Fediuk, *Kerenskii* (Moscow: Molodaia gvardiia, 2009), pp. 158–9.
109 Quoted from Gennadii Sobolev, *Petrogradskii garnizon v bor'be za pobedu Oktiabria* (Leningrad: Nauka, 1985), pp. 137–8.
110 *Russkii invalid*, 26 May 1917.
111 G. P., 'Deklaratsiia prav soldata', *Rech'*, 11 May 1917.
112 *Izvestiia Petrogradskogo Soveta rabochikh i soldatskikh deputatov*, 31 May 1917.
113 Mikhail Frenkin, *Russkaia armiia i revoliutsiia, 1917–1918* (Munich: Logos, 1978), pp. 354–5.

114 *Soldatskaia pravda*, 12 May 1917.

115 Reports of Trotsky's speech in the press were inconsistent, but his criticism of Kerenskii was in all of them. Lev Trotskii, *Sochineniia* (Moscow-Leningrad: Gosizdat, 1924–7), vol. 3: *1917*, part 1: 'Ot Fevralia do Oktiabria', pp. 50–51; *Petrogradskii Sovet rabochikh i soldatskikh deputatov v 1917 godu: Protokoly, stenogrammy i otchety, rezoliutsii, postanovleniia obshchikh sobranii, sobraniia sektsii, zasedaniia Ispolnitel'nogo komiteta i fraktsii, 27 fevralia–25 oktiabria 1917 goda*, 5 vols, ed. Bella Gal'perina and Vitalii Startsev, vol. 3, pp. 59, 62, 66, 69, 72–3, 76, 79–80, 155.

116 *Revoliutsionnoe dvizhenie v russkoi armii: Sbornik dokumentov (27 fevralia–24 oktiabria 1917 goda)*, ed. Luka Gaponenko and E. P. Voronin (Moscow: Nauka, 1968), p. 290.

117 Petrash, *Moriaki Baltiiskogo flota v bor'be za pobedu Oktiabria*, p. 139; *RGA VMF, fond* R-402, *opis'* 2, *delo* 406, *listy* 137, 155.

118 Natsional'nyi arkhiv Respubliki Belarus', *fond* 35-p (Ispolkom Zapadnogo fronta), *opis'* 1, *delo* 16, *listy* 3, 4, 5 *ob.*

119 Tarasov, *Voennaia organizatsiia bol'shevikov*, p. 100.

120 *Pravda*, 16 and 18 May 1917; *Soldatskaia pravda*, 17 May 1917. Kerenskii mistakenly attributed this article to Lenin. See Kerensky, *The Kerensky Memoirs*, p. 273, n7.

121 Quoted from Tarasov, *Voennaia organizatsiia bol'shevikov*, pp. 101–3.

122 Vladimir Utgof (pseudonym Petr Deriuzhinskii), 'Deklaratsiia prav soldata', *Delo naroda*, 21 May 1917.

123 'Po povodu "Deklaratsii prav soldata"', *Izvestiia Petrogradskogo Sovieta rabochikh i soldatskikh deputatov*, 26 May 1917; see also 'Ot redaktsii', ibid., 30 May 1917.

124 *Revoliutsionnoe dvizhenie v Rossii v mae–iiune 1917 g.: Iiun'skaia demonstratsiia (Dokumenty i materialy)* (Moscow: Akademiia nauk SSSR, 1959), p. 484.

125 *Sotsial-demokrat* [Moscow], 24 and 26 May 1917.

126 *Volna* [Helsingfors], 24 May 1917.

127 *Baltiiskie moriaki v podgotovke i provedenii Velikoi Oktiabr'skoi sotsialisticheskoi revoliutsii* (Moscow and Leningrad: Akademiia nauk SSSR, 1957), p. 36; *Pravda*, 20 May 1917; *Bol'shevizatsiia Petrogradskogo garnizona: Sb. materialov i dokumentov*, ed. Arvid Drezen (Leningrad: Leningradskoe oblastnoe izdatel'stvo, 1932), p. 98.

128 Gennadiy Sobolev, *Revoliutsionnoe soznanie rabochikh i soldat Petrograda v 1917 g. Period dvoevlastiia* (Leningrad: Nauka, 1973), p. 248.

129 *Bol'shevizatsiia Petrogradskogo garnizona*, p. 97. The resolution was published in *Soldatskaia pravda*, 25 May 1917.

130 See *Pravda*, 8 June 1917.

131 *Volna* [Helsingfors], 28 May 1917.

132 *Revoliutsionnoe dvizhenie v Rossii v mae–iiune 1917 g.*, p. 353. Resolution of a meeting of the soldiers of Khar'kov Garrison.

133 *Pravda*, 18 June 1917. The June Crisis saw demonstrations against the Coalition Provisional Government's policies in continuing the war. A number of enterprises in Petrograd went on strike on 8 June, and on 10 June the Bolsheviks planned a demonstration. This was cancelled by the moderate socialist leaders of the First Congress of Soviets, who proposed their own demonstration for 18 June. To their dismay, this proved predominantly

pro-Bolshevik, but the protests were abruptly curtailed by the announcement that the June Offensive against enemy forces had begun. [Trans.]

134 *Revoliutsionnoe dvizhenie v Rossii v mae–iiune 1917 g.*, pp. 494, 496.

135 Quoted from Samuil Rabinovich, *Bor'ba za armiiu v 1917 g.* (Moscow and Leningrad: Gosizdat: Otdel voennoi literatury, 1930), p. 75.

136 On 'front-line Bolshevism', see Wildman, *The End of the Russian Imperial Army*, vol. 2. On the diversity of the Bolsheviks in Petrograd, see Alexander Rabinowitch, *Prelude to Revolution: The Petrograd Bolsheviks and the July 1917 Uprising* (Bloomington: Indiana University Press, 1991); Rabinowitch, *The Bolsheviks Come to Power: The Revolution of 1917 in Petrograd* (New York: W. W. Norton, 1976). Bolshevism was also a very mixed bag in the provinces. Even some delegates at a Menshevik congress described themselves as Bolsheviks: 'Bolshevik adherent', 'Bolshevik Unifier', 'Bolshevik Internationalist'. See Khanan Astrakhan, *Bol'sheviki i ikh politicheskie protivniki v 1917 godu: Iz istorii politicheskikh partii v Rossii mezhdu dvumia revoliutsiiami* (Leningrad: Lenizdat, 1973), p. 299. It is no wonder that attitudes to Kerenskii and his orders varied greatly among the Bolsheviks.

137 *Okopnaia pravda*, 2 July 1917.

138 *Narodnaia niva* [Helsingfors], 24 May, 14 June 1917.

139 Grigorii Zinov'ev, 'Eshche o deklaratsii prav soldata', *Pravda*, 24 May 1917.

140 *Russkaia volia*, 21 May 1917.

141 Sobolev, *Revoliutsionnoe soznanie rabochikh i soldat Petrograda*, pp. 254–5.

142 *Prikazy i rechi pervogo russkogo Voennogo i Morskogo Ministra-Sotsialista*, p. 22; *A. F. Kerenskii ob armii i voine* (Petrograd: Narodnaia volia, 1917), pp. 8–13; Kerenskii, *Golos 1-go narodnogo ministra k krest'ianam i rabochim*, pp. 11–12. The publishing house 'Demokraticheskaia Rossiia', associated with the entourage of General Lavr Kornilov, printed this speech as a leaflet: *Rech' A. F. Kerenskogo na frontovom s"ezde v Kamenets-Podol'ske* (Petrograd: Demokraticheskaia Rossiia, 1917). On this publishing house, see Kolonitskii, 'Izdatel'stvo "Demokraticheskaia Rossiia", inostrannye missii i okruzhenie L. G. Kornilova', *Rossiia v 1917 godu: Novye podkhody i vzgliady: sbornik nauchnykh trudov* (St Petersburg: Tret'ia Rossiia, 1994), *vyp*. 2, pp. 28–31.

143 *Russkii invalid*, 27 May 1917.

144 'The new minister of war, Citizen Kerenskii, has stated that he intends to restore "iron discipline" in the army.' K. Stalin [Iosif Stalin], 'Vchera i segodnia (Krizis revoliutsii)', *Soldatskaia pravda*, 13 June 1917. Quoted from I. V. Stalin, *Sobranie sochinenii* (Moscow: Gosudarstvennoe izdatel'stvo politicheskoi literatury, 1953), vol. 3, p. 81.

145 Alexei Brusilov, *Moi vospominaniia* (Moscow: ROSSPEN, 2001), pp. 208–9.

146 *Russkoe slovo*, 17 May 1917.

147 Andrei Snesarev, *Dnevnik: 1916–1917* (Moscow: Kuchkovo pole, 2014), pp. 434–5.

148 Special Diplomatic Mission of the USA to Russia, Library of Congress, Manuscript Division, E. Root Papers, box 192, p. 20.

149 In a skit, Kerenskii is represented as Aleksandr Fedorovich Khlestakov – a 'young man in a quasi-military field jacket' ('molodoi chelovek v zemgusarskom frenche'). Vatrantsev (Viktor Kaisarov), *Russkaia revoliutsiia, ili Velikii Khlestakov* (Harbin, [no publisher identified], 1919), p. 5.

150 Kerenskii took great care of how he dressed even in very difficult circumstances. Recalling his appearance among the Cossacks during the fighting

for Tsarskoe Selo in October 1917, he does not omit to mention that he was wearing his 'semi-military outfit to which the population and troops have become so accustomed.' . . . I saluted, as always a little casually and with a slight smile.' A. F. Kerenskii, *Izdaleka: Sbornik statei (1920–1921 g.)* (Paris: Povolotskii, 1922), p. 204.

151 Snesarev, *Dnevnik: 1916–1917*, pp. 443–4, 446.
152 Ibid., pp. 446, 454.
153 Kravkov, *Velikaia voina bez retushi*, p. 331.
154 *Russkii invalid*, 20 May 1917.
155 *Pis'ma s voiny, 1914–1917*, ed. Aleksandr Astashov and Paul Simmons (Moscow: Novyi khronograf, 2015), p. 746.
156 *Tsarskaia armiia v period mirovoi voiny i Fevral'skoi revoliutsii*, ed. Aleksandr Maksimov (Kazan': Tatizdat, 1932), p. 141.
157 Florence Farmborough, *Nurse at the Russian Front: A Diary, 1914–18* (London: Book Club Associates, 1974), p. 270.
158 Okunev, *Dnevnik moskvicha, 1917–1924*, vol. 1, pp. 41, 42, 44.
159 Rostkovskii, *Dnevnik dlia zapisyvaniia*, pp. 200, 201.
160 Kuropatkin, *Iz dnevnika A. N. Kuropatkina*, pp. 72–4, 77; Kuropatkin, 'Dnevnik, 1917 god', *Istoricheskii arkhiv*, no. 1, 1992, p. 161.
161 Aleksandr Popov, 'Diplomatiia Vremennogo pravitel'stva v bor'be s revoliutsiei', *Krasnyi arkhiv*, vol. 1 (20) (1927), pp. 17, 19.
162 *Delo naroda*, 12 and 18 May 1917.
163 Snesarev, *Dnevnik: 1916–1917*, pp. 439, 441, 451.
164 For further detail, see Kolonitskii, *Simvoly vlasti i bor'ba za vlast'* (St Petersburg: Liki Rossii, 2012), pp. 144–7.
165 *Izvestiia Petrogradskogo Soveta rabochikh i soldatskikh deputatov*, 25 May 1917. On the same day, another Petrograd newspaper published an address from the soldiers of the Engineers' Company of 18th Infantry Division, who sent their awards and medals to 'our Leader'. *Volia naroda*, 25 May 1917.
166 *Russkoe slovo*, 20 May 1917. Fedor Stepun recalled that officers and soldiers would throw their medals into the minister's car. Stepun, *Byvshee i nesbyvsheesia* (St Petersburg: Aleteiia, 1994), p. 364.
167 *Russkii invalid*, 21 May 1917.
168 *Zhivoe slovo*, 14 June 1917.
169 *GARF*, *fond* 1807, *opis'* 1, *delo* 354, *list* 89.
170 Ibid., *listy* 93, 97; *delo* 359, *listy* 6, 123, 126; *Utro Rossii* [Moscow], 9 May 1917.
171 *Russkii invalid*, 1 June 1917.
172 Ibid., 14 June 1917.
173 Elena Lakier, 'Otryvki iz dnevnika – 1917–1918', in *'Preterpevshii do kontsa spasen budet': Zhenskie ispovedal'nye teksty o revoliutsii i grazhdanskoi voine v Rossii*, ed. Ol'ga Demidova (St Petersburg: Evropeiskii universitet, 2013), pp. 136, 141.
174 Ibid., pp. 141–2.
175 See, for example, 'Pechat' i zhizn': Ruki proch'!', *Delo naroda*, 19 May 1917.
176 Kerensky, *The Kerensky Memoirs*, p. 278.
177 Frenkin, *Russkaia armiia i revoliutsiia, 1917–1918*, p. 100; Wildman, *The End of the Russian Imperial Army*, vol. 2, pp. 28, 31–2, 37, 69, 77.
178 *Krasnoarmeets* [Moscow], nos. 28–30 (1920), p. 58. This theme was exploited also in soviet satirical texts of the civil war period. For example,

In the palace once he worked,
All so arty-farty.
Posturing he never shirked,
Like some Bonaparte.

See Krasnoe zhalo, 'Krasnyi Oktiabr': Istoriia o tom, kak narod burzhuev razvenchal', *Vooruzhennyi narod*, 10 November 1918.

179 'Zabyvshi i klassy i partii, / idet na dezhurnuiu rech', / Glaza u nego bonarpart'I / i tsveta zashchitnogo french.' Vladimir Maiakovskii, *Polnoe sobranie sochinenii*, 13 vols, ed. Vasilii Katanian (Moscow: Gosudarstvennoe izdatel'stvo khudozhestvennoi literatury, 1955–61), vol. 8: *1927* (1958), pp. 240–1.

180 '*Oktiabr'* (Postanovochnyi stsenarii)', Sergei Eizenshtein, *Izbrannye proizvedeniia*, 6 vols, ed. S. I. Iutkevich et al. (Moscow: Iskusstvo, 1964–71), vol. 6 (1971), p. 72.

181 Petr Krasnov, *Na vnutrennem fronte* (Berlin: Arkhiv russkoi revoliutsii, 1922), vol. 1; repr. (Moscow: Terra, Politizdat, 1991), p. 150.

182 Boris Gerua, *Vospominaniia o moei zhizni* (Paris: Tanais, 1969–70), vol. 2, p. 189. Grishka Otrep'ev was, according to Boris Godunov, a runaway monk falsely claiming to be Prince Dmitry, the youngest son of Ivan the Terrible, whom Godunov apparently had assassinated in 1591. His exploits are seen as having ushered in the Time of Troubles in Russia, and his name is used to epitomize treachery. [Trans.]

183 Quoted from Gennadiy Sobolev, *Aleksandr Kerenskii: Liubov' i nenavist' revoliutsii: dnevniki, stat'i, ocherki, vospominaniia sovremennikov* (Cheboksary: Chuvashskii universitet, 1993), p. 39.

184 Those producing comic images of a Napoleonic Kerenskii in the Soviet period could not fail to recall Sergei Eizenshtein's discussion of 'Bonapartism' and criticism in respect of Kerenskii. In autumn 1917, for example, he produced a series of 'venomous drawings' directed against Kerenskii and offered them to *Birzhevye vedomosti*. See Eizenshtein, *Izbrannye proizvedeniia*, vol. 1, p. 278.

185 Dmitrii Shliapentokh has studied contemporary comparisons of Kerenskii with other historical figures, primarily with Napoleon and other leaders of the French Revolution. Shliapentokh's sources are mainly contemporary accounts in the English-language press. See Shlapentokh, *The Counter-Revolution in Revolution: Images of Thermidor and Napoleon at the Time of the Russian Revolution and Civil War* (Basingstoke: Palgrave Macmillan, 1999). See particularly pp. 37–47.

186 Snesarev, *Dnevnik: 1916–1917*, p. 349.

187 P. Arzub'ev (Petr Guber), 'On', *Rech'*, 3 May 1917.

188 *Edinstvo*, 4 May 1917.

189 Arzub'ev was one of the reporters who subsequently accompanied Kerenskii on his visit to the front. See Arzub'ev, *A. F. Kerenskii na fronte*.

190 *Vserossiiskii tserkovno-obshchestvennyi vestnik*, 26 May 1917.

191 *Volia naroda*, 29 June, 4 July 1917; *Rech'*, 20 May 1917. Nobody in Russia seems to have compared Kerenskii to Peter the Great. The *New York Times*, however, in July 1917 claimed that, in terms of his energy, the revolutionary minister was Peter's equal, and in wisdom he was twice the man. Quoted from Shlapentokh, *The Counter-Revolution in Revolution*, p. 43.

192 Sukhanov, *Zapiski o revoliutsii*, *kn*. 4, p. 68; Irakli Tsereteli, *Vospominaniia o Fevral'skoi revoliutsii* (Paris: Mouton, 1963), vol. 2, p. 35.

193 *Iuzhnaia mysl'*, 16 May 1917; *Prikazy i rechi pervogo russkogo Voennogo i Morskogo Ministra-Sotsialista*, p. 40; Abraham, *Alexander Kerensky*, pp. 151, 163, 173. On the other hand, in a number of publications of his speeches a fragment is included in which Kerenskii contrasted the Russian and French revolutions: 'You recall the French Revolution. It was merciless towards everyone who obstructed it from the right and the left. We do not want to duplicate its bloody horrors and have abolished the death penalty. We have been seeking to ensure that great ideas are not sullied by violence and bloodshed.' 'A. F. Kerenskii na frontovom s"ezde', *Novoe vremia*, 18 May 1917.

194 *Novaia zhizn'*, 19 May 1917. The reference is to Konstantin Mikhailov, 'Kristallizatsiia vlasti', *Novoe vremia*, 18 May 1917.

195 The lawyer Nikolai Murav'ev, who headed the Extraordinary Investigative Commission established by the Provisional Government to investigate crimes committed by officials of the old regime, repeated to colleagues Kerenskii's remark that 'We need to be a tiny bit like Marat.' Fedor Rodichev, *Vospominaniia i ocherki o russkom liberalizme* (Newtonville, MA: Oriental Research Partners, 1983), p. 126. Other contemporaries recall that, before the revolution, Kerenskii admired Mirabeau more than Robespierre and Danton. Quoted from Oliver Radkey, *The Agrarian Foes of Bolshevism: Promise and Default of the Russian Socialist Revolutionaries, February to October, 1917* (New York: Columbia University Press, 1958), p. 147.

196 N. Rakhmanov, 'Orel i pigalitsy', *Delo naroda*, 6 September 1917. The writer is evidently alluding to Nikolai Nekrasov's lines 'That heart will never learn to love . . . which has of hating merely wearied.' From the poem 'Zamolkni, Muza mesti i pechali!'.

197 The Kornilov Affair refers to an attempt by General Lavr Kornilov, the Provisional Government's supreme commander-in-chief, to seize control of Petrograd and establish a right-wing military dictatorship. Kerensky was obliged to rely on the far left to suppress the coup attempt. [Trans.]

198 *Volia naroda*, 15 June 1917; *Svobodnaia Rossiia*, 12 June 1917.

199 'Na kraiu gibeli', *Rech'*, 9 May 1917.

200 Lenin, 'Ishchut Napoleona', *Pravda*, 10 May 1917. Quoted from Lenin (Ul'ianov), Vladimir Il"ich, *Polnoe sobranie sochinenii*, 5th edn (Moscow: Politizdat, 1960–81), vol. 32, p. 61.

201 'Pechat' i zhizn'', *Delo naroda*, 11 May 1917.

202 Oleg Leonidov, *Vozhd' svobody A. F. Kerenskii* (Moscow: Koshnitsa, 1917), pp. 20–21.

203 'Rech' Verkhovnogo glavnokomanduiushchego', *Rech'*, 10 May 1917.

204 'Travlia A. F. Kerenskogo', *Utro Rossii* [Moscow], 24 May 1917.

205 *Petrogradskii Sovet rabochikh i soldatskikh deputatov v 1917 godu*, vol. 3, pp. 67, 72, 76.

206 *Delo naroda*, 20 September 1917.

207 P. Tanas [Lev Trotskii], 'Bonapartiata', *Rabochii put'*, 7 September 1917; Trotskii, *Sochineniia*, vol. 3, p. 230.

208 *Petrogradskii Sovet rabochikh i soldatskikh deputatov v 1917 godu*, vol. 3, pp. 59, 72–3.

209 *Volia naroda*, 24 May 1917.

210 E. V[ladimirovi]–ch, *A. F. Kerenskii narodnyi ministr* (Odessa: Vlast' naroda, 1917), p. 32.

211 Mikhailov, 'Kristallizatsiia vlasti'.

212 'Krasnoe sukno rasstilaiut', *Novaia zhizn'*, 19 May 1917.
213 *Golos soldata*, 27 May 1917.
214 Leonidov, *Vozhd' svobody*, pp. 5–6.
215 Marina Tsvetaeva, *Sobranie sochinenii*, 7 vols, ed. A. Saakiants and L. Mnukhina (Moscow: Ellis Lak, 1994–5), vol. 4 (1994), p. 521.
216 Tsvetaeva, *Sobranie sochinenii*, vol. 1 (1994), pp. 350–1, 606; Simon Karlinsky, *Marina Cvetaeva: Her Life and Art* (Berkeley: University of California Press, 1966), p. 41.
217 Nikolai Filatov, 'Soldatskie pis'ma 1917 goda', *Pamiat': Istoricheskii sbornik* (Paris: YMCA Press, 1981), *vyp.* 4, p. 346.
218 Kravkov, *Velikaia voina bez retushi*, p. 351, entry for 30 July 1917.
219 *Petrogradskii Sovet rabochikh i soldatskikh deputatov v 1917 godu*, vol. 3, p. 112.
220 A picture of how the session went can be gained from the minutes and newspaper reports. See ibid., pp. 135–8, 140–5, 147–8, 149–56, 159–62, 164–7.
221 Letter to Anna Lunacharskaia of 23 May 1917. See *1917: Chastnye svidetel'stva o revoliutsii v pis'makh Lunacharskogo i Martova*, ed. N. S. Antonova and Gennadii Bordiugov (Moscow: Rossiiskii universitet druzhby narodov, 2005), pp. 196–7.
222 *Russkoe slovo*, 29 April 1917; Abraham, *Alexander Kerensky*, p. 148.
223 Pavel Miliukov, *Istoriia vtoroi russkoi revoliutsii* (Moscow: ROSSPEN, 2001), p. 105.
224 *Svobodnaia Rossiia* (evening edn), 12 June 1917.
225 Nikolai Berdiaev, *Sobranie sochinenii*, ed. Nikita Struve, 4 vols (3rd edn, Paris: YMCA Press, 1989–90), vol. 1, p. 263.
226 Andrei Belyi, *Revoliutsiia i kul'tura* (Moscow: Leman & Sakharov, 1917), p. 18.
227 Ibid., p. 17.
228 Cf. 'Symbols do not "talk" in Nietzsche: they only "nod", you simpleton,' he exclaims. 'Who wants to be told anything by them?' Also 'That leaves Nietzsche himself. . . . But he does not talk, he only nods wordlessly to us.' Belyi, *Arabeski* (Moscow: Musaget, 1911), p. 78.
229 Vl. Savskii, 'Kerenskii – revoliutsioner', *Svobodnaia Rossiia* (evening edn), 12 June 1917.
230 *Russkoe slovo*, 20 May 1917; *Soldat-grazhdanin* [Moscow], 30 May 1917.
231 *Utro Rossii* [Moscow], 27 May 1917.
232 A. Tamarin [i.e., Aleksei Okulov], 'Tolpa i ministr', ibid.
233 *Soldat-grazhdanin*, 27 May 1917; *Russkoe slovo*, 27 May 1917.
234 R. H. Bruce Lockhart, *Memoirs of a British Agent* (London: Putnam, 1932), pp. 179–80.
235 'Na mitinge v Bol'shom teatre', *Utro Rossii* [Moscow], 27 May 1917.
236 *Soldat-grazhdanin* [Moscow], 30 May 1917.
237 Belyi, *Revoliutsiia i kul'tura*, pp. 18–19.
238 *Svobodnaia Rossiia*, 12 June 1917. Kuprin was the paper's editor. The whole issue was devoted to Kerenskii. Encomia were published by, among others, the writers Boris Mirskii [Mirkin-Getsevich], Mark Krinitskii and Arkadii Bukhov; the lawyer Nikolai Karabchevskii; and the scholars Fedor Batiushkov and Semen Vengerov. Some of these efforts anticipate the encomia lauding the 'Leader of the people' by leading lights on the cultural

scene in the Soviet period, and indeed Nikolai Vasil'ev's article is actually titled 'Leader of the People'.

239 Tamarin, 'Tolpa i ministr', *Utro Rossii* [Moscow], 27 May 1917.

240 *Nizhegorodskii listok*, 1 June 1917.

241 *Utro Rossii* [Moscow], 27 May 1917.

242 *Pravda*, 27 June 1917.

243 *Soldatskaia pravda*, 18 April 1917.

244 K. Golenko, 'Rozy i krov'', *Sotsial-demokrat* [Moscow], 27 May 1917; *Kievlianin*, 3 July 1917. See also *Rechi A. F. Kerenskogo* (Kiev), p. vi.

245 Nikolai Valentinov, *Nasledniki Lenina*, ed. Yuri Felshtinsky (Moscow: Terra, 1991), p. 187. Valentinov's testimony is confirmed by other sources. On the feminization of Kerenskii's image in connection with the recoding of his reputation for theatricality and creative originality, see Kolonitskii, 'Feminizatsiia obraza A. F. Kerenskogo i politicheskaia izoliatsiia Vremennogo pravitel'stva osen'iu 1917 goda', in *Mezhvuzovskaia nauchnaia konferentsiia 'Russkaia revoliutsiia 1917 goda: Problemy istorii i istoriografii': Sbornik dokladov* (St Petersburg: Gosudarstvennyi elektrotekhnicheskii universitet, 2013).

246 *1917: Chastnye svidetel'stva o revoliutsii*, p. 201.

247 Ieronim Iasinskii published poems in *Birzhevye vedomosti* which were pastiches of *Thus Spake Zarathustra*. He later recalled: 'I published my poems there, mainly transpositions of Nietzsche's philosophical aphorisms, endowing his superman with the attributes of a Bolshevik.' Quoted from Maria Koreneva, 'Vlastitel' dum', *F. Nitsshe* [Friedrich Nietzsche], *Stikhotvoreniia, Filosofskaia proza*, ed. Koreneva (St Petersburg: Khudozhestvennaia literatura, 1993), pp. 5–20.

248 Simonetta Falasca-Zamponi, 'The "Culture" of Personality: Mussolini and the Cinematic Imagination', in *Personality Cults in Stalinism = Personenkulte im Stalinismus*, ed. Klaus Heller and Jan Plamper (Göttingen: V & R Unipress, 2004), pp. 87–8, 92–3.

249 Kerenskii is referring to his 'Nezadacha russkogo liberalizma', *Sovremennye zapiski* [Paris], *kn*. 63 (1937), pp. 383–90. This is a review of Vasilii Maklakov's *Vlast' i obshchestvennost' na zakate staroi Rossii: Vospominaniia sovremennika*, 4 vols (Paris: Illiustrirovannaia Rossia, 1936). Vadim Rudnev, a prominent Socialist Revolutionary, was one of the journal's leading figures. In his review, Kerenskii emphasized Maklakov's 'exceptional political intuition' and hinted that his observations might profitably be applied to other parties. Evidently the friction between leaders who were theoreticians remote from reality, on the one hand, and pragmatic leaders resolving urgent problems, on the other, was a preoccupation of Kerensky's at various times as he grappled with issues in the history of the revolution.

250 Hoover Institution Archives, Vasilii Maklakov Papers, box 8, file 20, pp. 1–2.

251 Konstantin Morozov, 'Rukovodstvo partii s.-r. vsegda rassmatrivalo Kerenskogo . . . kak v izvestnoi mere poputchika', *Rossiiskaia istoriia*, no. 4 (2013), p. 32.

252 Abram Gots was arrested in 1937 and sentenced in 1939 to twenty-five years' imprisonment. He died in Siberia, apparently in 1940. [Trans.]

253 In 1917, Socialist Revolutionary newspapers bearing the same title of *Zemlia i volia*, but with divergent political tendencies, were being published in different cities. Reference in the text hereafter is to the Petrograd publication.

254 *GARF*, *fond* 1807, *opis'* 1, *delo* 354, *list* 91. Published in *Delo naroda*, 15 March 1917; *Zemlia i volia* [Petrograd], 21 March 1917.
255 *Delo naroda*, 15 March 1917.
256 *GARF*, *fond* 1807, *opis'* 1, *delo* 354, *listy* 104, 107, 112; *delo* 358, *list* 33.
257 *Zemlia i volia*, 22, 28, 30 March, 1, 5 April 1917; *Delo naroda*, 13 April 1917.
258 *Delo naroda*, 18 March 1917.
259 *Zemlia i volia*, 30 March 1917.
260 *Zemlia i volia*, 18 March 1917 (Resolution of the Factory Commission of the Independent Russia Society).
261 Vladimir Zenzinov, 'Predstavitel'stvo revoliutsionnoi demokratii v pravitel'stve', *Delo naroda*, 12 April 1917.
262 From 5 April until 6 May Kerenskii is indicated as 'participating in the newspaper'.
263 Nikolai Erofeev, Evgenii Chapkevich and Nikolai Rusanov, *Politicheskie partii Rossii: Konets XIX–nachalo XX veka: Entsiklopediia* (Moscow: ROSSPEN, 1996), p. 526.
264 *Delo naroda*, 7 April 1917.
265 Andrei Argunov et al., 'Pis'mo v redaktsiiu', *Zemlia i volia*, 22 April 1917.
266 On the financing of *Volia naroda* by foreign missions in the autumn of 1917, see Rafail Ganelin, *Rossiia i SShA, 1914–1917* (Leningrad: Nauka, 1969), pp. 359–88 and *passim*.
267 It seems unlikely that Breshko-Brezhkovskaia's schedule of visits and state of health would really have enabled her to carry out the duties of being an editor, although she may have influenced the overall direction of the newspaper.
268 Stanislav Tiutiukin, *Voina, mir, revoliutsiia: Ideinaia bor'ba v rabochem dvizhenii Rossii, 1914–1917 gg.* (Moscow: Mysl', 1972), pp. 67–71, 192–3 and *passim*; Michael Melancon, *The Socialist Revolutionaries and the Russian Anti-War Movement* (Columbus: Ohio State University Press, 1990), pp. 28–9 and *passim*.
269 'Pechat'', *Rech'*, 4 May 1917.
270 'Petrograd', ibid., 11 May 1917; 'Pechat'', ibid., 12 May 1917.
271 'Soedinennoe zasedanie organizatsii partii sotsialistov-revoliutsionerov', *Zemlia i volia*, 5 May 1917. On Viktor Chernov, see Kirill Gusev, *V. M. Chernov: Shtrikhi k politicheskomu portretu (Pobedy i porazheniia V. Chernova)* (Moscow: ROSSPEN, 1999); Hannu Immonen, *Mechty o novoi Rossii: Viktor Chernov (1873–1952)* (St Petersburg: Evropeiskii universitet v Sankt-Peterburge, 2015); Anatolii Avrus, Anna Goloseeva and Aleksandr Novikov, *Viktor Chernov: Sud'ba russkogo sotsialista* (Moscow: Kliuch-C, 2015).
272 *Zemlia i volia*, 10 May 1917.
273 *RGASPI*, *fond* 274, *opis'* 1, *delo* 6, *listy* 22, 56.
274 Ibid., *listy* 4, 17, 50, 66, 67.
275 Ibid., *listy* 2, 5, 9, 28, 33, 54.
276 Ibid., *listy* 4, 6, 7, 29, 53.
277 *Delo naroda*, 30 April, 9 May 1917.
278 *Delo naroda*, 7 May 1917.
279 On Gunner E. Shubmatin's poem, see note 000 below.
280 Ibid., 17 May.
281 *Delo naroda*, 27 May 1917.
282 The debating of Kerenskii's party allegiance continued subsequently. *Volia naroda* in August defended the head of the Provisional Government from

criticism by the Socialist Revolutionary Party's main party newspaper: 'People whose intellectual horizon is limited by the pillars of factional politics measure Comrade Kerenskii's speech by their party yardstick and discover he is "manoeuvring between the left and right". These people have not noticed that the chairman minister has risen above party interests and views issues from the standpoint of what is in the national interest, which seeks not to divide but to unite.' This article in turn provoked new critical comment in *Delo naroda*, which demanded greater clarity from a member of the Socialist Revolutionary Party. *Delo naroda*, 16 August 1917.

283 *Partiia sotsialistov-revoliutsionerov: Dokumenty i materialy*, 3 vols, ed. Nikolai Erofeev (Moscow: ROSSPEN, 2000), vol. 1, p. 238.

284 See Kolonitskii, '"We" and "I": Alexander Kerensky in His Speeches', in *Autobiographical Practices in Russia*, ed. Jochen Hellbeck and Klaus Heller (Göttingen: [Vandenhoek & Ruprecht Unipress], 2004).

285 We are quoting Nikolai Rusanov from a document in *OR RNB*. At the time of writing, Rusanov's memoirs are being prepared for publication by Aleksei Gnoevykh. I am grateful to him for drawing my attention to this source, and to Elizaveta Zhdankova for copying the text for me.

286 In his memoirs Rusanov makes use of another device for detracting from the image of the romantic hero of the revolution.

> A couple of hours later I went round to my relative's apartment and found him in an exceptionally jolly mood. 'Kolia, my friend, have you heard about our latest episode with Kerenskii's lady admirers? An hour ago two rich merchants' wives, passionate worshippers of the great Aleksandr Fedorovich and friends of my wife, arrived out of breath, and asked her in a stricken whisper, "Katya, sweetie, can we use your toilet to change our pantaloons. We cheered Kerenskii so wildly on Red Square that we've wet our pants."'

The reaction of the overexcited 'merchants' wives' is highly reminiscent of Andrei Belyi's rapturous enthusiasm as related in Berdiaev's memoirs. In hindsight, memoirists are highly sarcastic of those who succumbed to Kerenskii's political style.

287 Abraham, *Alexander Kerensky*, p. 208.

288 *Partiia sotsialistov-revoliutsionerov: Dokumenty i materialy*, vol. 1, pp. 254–64.

289 Ibid.

290 A few weeks previously, in the election for the Executive Committee of the All-Russia Soviet of Peasants' Deputies, Chernov scored the highest number of votes – 810. Kerenskii was immediately behind him with 804.

291 The result of the vote soured relations between Kerenskii and Chernov, as was evident over the following months. Some historians have surmised that the vote might have been rigged by Chernov, but in fact he defended Kerenskii against attacks from the left at the congress. See Immonen, *Mechty o novoi Rossii*, p. 186. We might add that the ill-feeling over the vote was not in Chernov's interests: he was trying to hold the party together.

292 Maria Ancharova, 'Vserossiiskii s"ezd partii sotsialistov-revoliutsionerov', *Rech'*, 6 June 1917; 'Raznye izvestiia', ibid.

293 *Volia naroda*, 21 June 1917; *Delo naroda*, 22 June 1917; *Zemlia i volia*, 23 June 1917.

294 *Delo naroda*, 14 June 1917.

295 Ibid., 25 June 1917.
296 Ariadna Tyrkova-Vil'iams, *Nasledie Ariadny Vladimirovny Tyrkovoi: Dnevniki: Pis'ma*, ed. Natal'ia Kanishcheva (Moscow: ROSSPEN, 2012), p. 183.
297 Morozov, 'Rukovodstvo partii s.-r. vsegda rassmatrivalo Kerenskogo . . . kak v izvestnoi mere poputchika', p. 32.

Chapter IV The 'Kerensky Offensive'

1 Zinaida Gippius, *Siniaia kniga: Peterburgskii dnevnik, 1914–1918* (Belgrade: Radenkovich, 1929), p. 140.
2 'Dnevnik Nikolaia Romanova', *Krasnyi arkhiv*, vol. 2 (21) (1927), p. 91.
3 Miliukov characterized the situation of the socialists in summer 1917 as follows: 'Even if Kerenskii was not a real person in a real place, it was essential that he should at least appear to be.' Pavel Miliukov, *Rossiia na perelome (Bol'shevistskii period russkoi revoliutsii)* (Paris: O. Zeluk, 1927), vol. 1: *Proiskhozhdenie i ukreplenie bol'shevistskoi diktatury*, p. 82.
4 On the offensive, see *Strategicheskii ocherk voiny 1914–1918 gg.*, ed. Andrei Zaionchkovskii (Moscow: Gosudarstvennoe voennoe izdatel'stvo, 1924), part 7: *Kampaniia 1917 goda*; Aleksandr Kavtaradze, 'Iiun'skoe nastuplenie russkoi armii v 1917 godu', *Voenno-istoricheskii zhurnal*, no. 5 (1967), pp. 111–17; Ivan Rostunov, *Russkii front Pervoi mirovoi voiny* (Moscow: Nauka, 1976); Aleksandr Zhilin, *Poslednee nastuplenie: Iiun' 1917 goda* (Moscow: Nauka, 1983); Allan Wildman, *The End of the Russian Imperial Army* (Princeton, NJ: Princeton University Press) vol. 2 (1987): *The Road to Soviet Power and Peace*; Sergei Nelipovich, '". . . Front sploshnykh mitingov": Obobshchennye arkhivnye dannye ob iiun'skom nastuplenii 1917 goda voisk Iugo-Zapadnogo fronta', *Voenno-istoricheskii zhurnal*, no. 2 (1999), pp. 34–47; Sergei Nelipovich, 'Iiun'skoe (Letnee) nastuplenie 1917', *Rossiia v Pervoi mirovoi voine, 1914–1918: Entsiklopediia*, 3 vols, ed. Andrei Sorokin (Moscow: ROSSPEN, 2014), vol. 1: *A–I*, pp. 813–18; *Vooruzhennye sily Rossii v Pervoi mirovoi voine (1914–1917)*, ed. Viacheslav Shatsillo, 2 vols (Moscow: Megapolis, 2014), pp. 321–31; Oleg Airapetov, *Uchastie Rossiiskoi imperii v Pervoi mirovoi voine (1914–1917), 1917 god: Raspad* (Moscow: Kuchkovo pole, 2015).
5 *Strategicheskii ocherk voiny 1914–1918 gg.*, part 7, p. 69.
6 In some sectors a situation which threatened the enemy forces developed, and German and Austro-German troops fought heavy defensive battles. The Russian Command appears not even to have been aware that the enemy forces were in a critical situation (as is evident from post-war Austrian publications). See Anton Kersnovskii, *Istoriia russkoi armii*, 4 vols (Moscow: Golos, 1994), vol. 4: *1915–1917 gg.*, p. 285.
7 Nelipovich, 'Iiun'skoe (Letnee) nastuplenie 1917', pp. 813–18.
8 Fedor Rodichev, *Vospominaniia i ocherki o russkom liberalizme* (Newtonville, MA: Oriental Research Partners, 1983), p. 120.
9 'Iz ofitserskikh pisem s fronta v 1917 g.', published by L. Andreev, *Krasnyi arkhiv*, vol. 1–22 (50–51) (1932), pp. 208–9. Kerenskii recalled that not a few officers of different ranks were sceptical about the offensive. Kerensky, *The Kerensky Memoirs: Russia and History's Turning Point* (London: Cassell, 1966), p. 276. There were, however, no protests from high-ranking officers against preparations for it.

10 Anton Denikin, *Ocherki Russkoi Smuty*, 5 vols (Paris and Berlin: Povolotskii, Slovo, 1921; repr. 1991), vol. 1, part 1: 'Krushenie vlasti i armii (Fevral'–sentiabr' 1917)', p. 178.

11 Nikolai Golovin, *Voennye usiliia Rossii v mirovoi voine* (Paris: Ob"edinennye izdateli, 1939; repr. Moscow: Zhukovskii, 2001), p. 358.

12 Aleksei Budberg, 'Dnevnik barona Alekseia Budberga, 1917 god', *Arkhiv russkoi revoliutsii* [Berlin] vol. 12 (1923), p. 245. Later General Golovin came to a similar view of Kerenskii's position: 'Kerenskii had not the civic courage to tell the Allies openly that the Russian people did not wish to continue the war, and at the same time he was afraid of quarrelling with left-wing revolutionary circles.' Golovin, *Voennye usiliia Rossii v mirovoi voine*, p. 370.

13 This topic received a great deal of attention from Soviet scholars, no doubt because of the ideological framework of the time. There are, however, important observations on discipline and soldiers in the active army mutinying (even in guards units) by a modern scholar who introduces valuable sources into the literature. See Aleksandr Astashov, *Russkii front v 1914–nachale 1917 goda: Voennyi opyt i sovremennost'* (Moscow: Novyi khronograf, 2014), pp. 677–713. Even before the revolution, officers could find themselves obliged to persuade their men to attack, straightforward orders being insufficient. They were not always successful: on occasions soldiers would express their preparedness to defend already occupied positions but refuse to attack the enemy. Unsurprisingly, after the February events, such incidents greatly increased in frequency.

14 Pierre Pascal, *Mon journal de Russie: À la Mission militaire française 1916–1918* (Lausanne: L'Âge d'homme, 1975), p. 127.

15 Alexandre Kerenski, *La Révolution russe (1917)* (Paris: Payot, 1928), p. 220.

16 'Of the 220 infantry divisions stationed at the front line, 165 fraternized, and of these 38 promised the Germans they would not attack.' Kersnovskii, *Istoriia russkoi armii*, vol. 4, p. 270. According to German reports, German and Austrian propagandists and spies established direct contact with service personnel of 107 Russian divisions (out of the 214 stationed at the front). See Mikhail Frenkin, *Russkaia armiia i revoliutsiia, 1917–1918* (Munich: Logos, 1978), p. 173.

17 Nelipovich, '". . . Front sploshnykh mitingov"', p. 37. The changing of time for the offensive also had the positive result that the enemy was misled regarding when the operation would begin. See Kavtaradze, 'Iiun'skoe nastuplenie russkoi armii v 1917 godu', p. 115.

18 *Strategicheskii ocherk voiny 1914–1918 gg.*, part 7, p. 66.

19 A number of generals deliberately invited Kerenskii to give speeches in order, if things went wrong, to be able to evade responsibility themselves. See Kersnovskii, *Istoriia russkoi armii*, vol. 4, p. 283.

20 *Delo naroda*, 14 June 1917.

21 *Revoliutsionnoe dvizhenie v russkoi armii: Sbornik dokumentov (27 fevralia–24 oktiabria 1917 goda)*, ed. Luka Gaponenko and E. P. Voronin (Moscow: Nauka, 1968), p. 241.

22 *Soldatskaia pravda*, 29 June 1917.

23 *Revoliutsionnoe dvizhenie v Rossii v mae–iiune 1917 g.: Iiun'skaia demonstratsiia (Dokumenty i materialy)* (Moscow: Akademiia nauk SSSR, 1959), pp. 365–6.

24 *Pervyi Vserossiiskii s"ezd Sovetov*, ed. Veniamin Rakhmetov (Moscow and

Leningrad: Gosizdat, 1930), vol. 1, pp. 414–15; Frenkin, *Russkaia armiia i revoliutsiia, 1917–1918*, pp. 110–12.

25 Kerenski, *La Révolution russe*, p. 220.

26 Zhilin, *Poslednee nastuplenie: Iiun' 1917 goda*, pp. 39–40.

27 See Vera Alekseeva-Borel', *Sorok let v riadakh russkoi imperatorskoi armii: General M. V. Alekseev* (St Petersburg: Bel'veder, 2000), p. 537; Denikin, *Ocherki Russkoi Smuty*, vol. 1, *vyp.* 1, p. 429. Kerenskii acknowledged that, when commanders, commissars and committees were unable to grasp the psychological importance of what he had said, the effect was generally short-lived. Kerensky, *The Kerensky Memoirs*, p. 278.

28 *Burzhuaziia i pomeshchiki v 1917 godu: Chastnye soveshchaniia chlenov Gosudarstvennoi dumy*, ed. Arvid Drezen (Moscow and Leningrad: Partiinoe izdatel'stvo, 1932), p. 124; Nikita Okunev, *Dnevnik moskvicha, 1917–1924*, 2 vols (Moscow: Voenizdat, 1997), vol. 1, p. 52.

29 Wildman, *The End of the Russian Imperial Army*, vol. 2, pp. 30–31. The reference is to the 159th Division of the 7th Army.

30 *Razlozhenie armii v 1917 godu* (Moscow and Leningrad: Gosudarstvennoe sotsial'no-ekonomicheskoe izdatel'stvo, 1925), p. 91; Denikin, *Ocherki Russkoi Smuty*, vol. 1, part 1, pp. 433–4. Kerenskii's speeches could be understood in completely unpredictable ways. There were rumours that he had promised to allow any soldiers wounded during the offensive to go back home immediately. See Konstantin Oberuchev, *Vospominaniia*, 2 parts (New York: Gruppa pochitatelei Pamiati K. M. Oberucheva, 1930), p. 210.

31 Vasilii Kravkov, *Velikaia voina bez retushi: Zapiski korpusnogo vracha* (Moscow: Veche, 2014), p. 326.

32 Ibid., p. 335.

33 Ibid., p. 338.

34 *Nepridumannye sud'by na fone ushedshego veka: Pis'ma M[ikhaila] V[ladimirovicha] Shika (sviashchennika Mikhaila) i N[atal'i] D[mitrievny] Shakhovskoi (Shakhovskoi-Shik)*, 2 vols (Moscow: Preobrazhenie, 2015), vol. 1: *1911–1926*, pp. 219, 221.

35 Lev Trotskii, *Istoriia russkoi revoliutsii* (Berlin: Granit, 1931–3), vol. 1, p. 411.

36 'Verkhovnyi komissar M. M. Filonenko ob armii', *Den'*, 1 August 1917.

37 Mikhail Frenkin, *Revoliutsionnoe dvizhenie na Rumynskom fronte, 1917 g.–1918 g.: Soldaty 8-i armii Rumynskogo fronta v bor'be za mir i vlast' Sovetov* (Moscow: Nauka, 1965), p. 124; Frenkin, *Russkaia armiia i revoliutsiia, 1917–1918*, pp. 102–3. For comparison, 57,000 men were members of the committees of the Western Front by the end of the summer, which is similar to the number of men in an army corps. See Kavtaradze, notes to Denikin, *Ocherki Russkoi Smuty*, vol. 1, *vyp.* 1, p. 506.

38 *Delo naroda*, 13 June 1917. In the minuted record, this part of Lordkipanidze's speech is given more fully. See *Pervyi Vserossiiskii s"ezd Sovetov*, vol. 1, p. 417.

39 *Russkii invalid*, 18 and 25 May 1917.

40 Ibid., 20 June 1917.

41 *RGASPI, fond* 662, *opis'* 1, *delo* 60, *list* 64.

42 *Delo naroda*, 20 June 1917.

43 *RGASPI, fond* 274, *opis'* 4, *delo* 215, *list* 9.

44 46 *OR RNB, fond* 152, *opis'* 3, *delo* 98, *list* 48 *ob.* Letters from soldiers at the front were different from those of soldiers in the reserve units in the rear.

Military censors noted that in the rear they came across negative judgements of the government. The example given is: 'The new ministers, including Kerenskii, are not real socialists. They are in the service of the bourgeoisie' (ibid., *list* 49). Garrisons in the rear were subjected to more influence from radical socialists and, moreover, were drawn into all manner of political, social and ethnic conflicts. Clashes over being sent to the front precipitated major confrontation within units, and this was reflected also in attitudes towards Kerenskii.

45 *Svobodnaia Rossiia* (evening edn), 8 May 1917.

46 *Russkaia volia*, 3 May 1917.

47 *RGASPI, fond* 662, *opis'* 1, *delo* 58, *list* 48.

48 *Izvestiia Petrogradskogo Soveta rabochikh i soldatskikh deputatov*, 31 May 1917.

49 *Edinstvo*, 14 May 1917. The efforts of Russian soldiers to export revolution to Germany forced German propagandists to react. A leaflet addressed to Russian front-line soldiers read: 'Finally, you are inviting us to change our form of government, we ask you finally to stop meddling in our internal affairs. The German people is united with its sovereign and his government! We all want peace! Stop therefore with your attacks on our sovereign, they will in any case get you nowhere!' *RGASPI, fond* 662, *opis'* 1, *delo* 58, *list* 46. The fact of the existence of such a leaflet testifies to the scale of the attempts by Russian soldiers to 'revolutionize' enemy soldiers.

50 Wildman, *The End of the Russian Imperial Army*, vol. 2, p. 32.

51 'Rech' Toma predstaviteliam russkoi armii v Iassakh', *Novoe vremia*, 19 May 1917.

52 'Krest'ianskii s"ezd', *Rech'*, 11 May 1917.

53 *Golos soldata*, 1, 2 and 6 June 1917.

54 *Russkii invalid*, 5 May 1917.

55 *Prikazy i rechi pervogo russkogo Voennogo i Morskogo Ministra-Sotsialista* ([No location]: Shtab osoboi armii, 1917), pp. 5–6; *Russkii invalid*, 16 and 18 May 1917.

56 Wildman, *The End of the Russian Imperial Army*, vol. 2, p. 28.

57 B. Elov, 'Petrogradskaia organizatsiia RSDRP(b) nakanune iiul'skikh sobytii', in *3-go – 5-go iiulia 1917 g.: Po neizdannym materialam sudebnogo sledstviia arkhiva Pet. K-ta R. K. P.* (Petrograd: Petrogubkom RKP, 1922), p. 58.

58 *Edinstvo*, 26 May 1917.

59 *Russkii invalid*, 14 June 1917.

60 *RGASPI, fond* 662, *opis'* 1, *delo* 58, *listy* 66–66 *ob.*

61 *Russkii invalid*, 21 and 30 June 1917.

62 *RGASPI, fond* 702, *opis'* 1, *delo* 70, *listy* 16–16 *ob.* The author was Private Goriachev, 9th Company, 172nd Lida Regiment.

63 *Strategicheskii ocherk voiny 1914–1918 gg.*, part 7, p. 73.

64 *Russkii invalid*, 27, 28 and 30 June 1917. At a meeting at General Headquarters on 16 July, General Denikin spoke out against senior ranks who 'zealously wave red flags and, by a habit passed down from the time of the Mongol Horde, crawl on their bellies before the new gods of the revolution in exactly the same way they crawled before the tsars' (Denikin, *Ocherki Russkoi Smuty*, vol. 1, *vyp.* 1, p. 438). The butt of his criticism was probably General Brusilov. However, the same could have been said of Kornilov's actions. In later years

monarchists reminded him of the 'enormous red ribbon' with which the general adorned himself. Konstantin Kologrivov, 'Arest Gosudaryni imperatritsy Aleksandry Fedorovny i avgusteishikh detei ikh velichestv', *Russkaia letopis'*, *kn.* 3 (1922), p. 194.

65 *Revoliutsionnoe dvizhenie v russkoi armii*, p. 139.

66 Frenkin, *Russkaia armiia i revoliutsiia, 1917–1918*, p. 339.

67 *Delo naroda*, 1 July 1917.

68 Semen Frank, *Biografiia P. B. Struve* (New York: Chekhov, 1956), pp. 117–18.

69 *Birzhevye vedomosti*, 21 July 1917. Quoted from Il'ia Erenburg, *Lik voiny: Vospominaniia s fronta, 1919, 1922–1924: Gazetnye korrespondentsii i stat'i, 1915–1917* (St Petersburg: Evropeiskii universitet v Sankt-Peterburge, 2014), p. 286.

70 Quoted from Trotskii, *Istoriia russkoi revoliutsii*, vol. 1, p. 469. Exploitation of 'anti-bourgois' rhetoric by opposing forces was an important discursive frame of reference which influenced the development of conflicts at the time of the revolution. For further detail, see Kolonitskii, 'Antibourgeois Propaganda and Anti-"Burzhui" Consciousness in 1917', *Russian Review*, vol. 53 (1994), pp. 183–96.

71 Baron Nikolai Apollonovich Tipol't, 'Dnevnik', *RGA VMF*, *fond* 315, *opis'* 1, *delo* 1312, *listy* 122 *ob.*, 124–124 *ob.*

72 See Pavel Rogoznyi, 'Genezis termina "Tserkovnyi bol'shevizm": K izucheniiu bor'by za vlast' v Rossiiskoi pravoslavnoi tserkvi (aprel' 1917–mart 1918 g.)', *Politicheskaia istoriia Rossii pervoi chetverti XX veka: Pamiati professora Vitaliia Ivanovicha Startseva* (St Petersburg: D.A.R.K., 2006), pp. 329–40.

73 Georgii Korolev, *Proshlye dni, Lenin i krasnyi flot* (Leningrad: Morved, 1924), pp. 41–2.

74 The device of opposing the notion of Bolsheviks to Leninists was periodically used by the liberal press. 'Even the Bolsheviks are rejecting Lenin', *Rech'*, 21 April 1917. See also 'Bol'sheviki protiv "leninstva"', *Svobodnaia Rossiia* (evening edn), 8 May 1917. Sometimes journalists and those drafting resolutions criticized 'the Bolsheviks and the Leninists', making it clear that they did not see the terms as synonymous.

75 Nikolai Iordanskii, 'Neosnovatel'nye pritiazaniia', *Edinstvo*, 12 May 1917; Georgii Plekhanov, 'Dve nedeli na razmyshlenie', ibid., 7 July 1917; Grigorii Aleksinskii, 'Chto nuzhno seichas Rossii?', ibid., 8 July 1917.

76 Valerian Rafailov-Chernyshov, 'Po stopam lenintsev', ibid., 30 May 1917.

77 *Russkoe slovo*, 29 April 1917.

78 On occasions, accusations of 'Leninist leanings' could be directed at some of the liberals. One conservative commentator, for example, described Nikolai Nekrasov, the minister of communications, as a Constitutional Democrat with 'Leninist tendencies'. Ippolit Gofshtetter, 'Demagogiia vlasti', *Novoe vremia*, 9 June 1917.

79 Aleksandr Izgoev, 'Narodnyi prazdnik', *Rech'*, 20 April 1917.

80 'Mitingi partii narodnoi svobody', *Rech'*, 26 May 1917.

81 See, for example, Kravkov, *Velikaia voina bez retushi*, p. 315.

82 *Rech'*, 20 April 1917; Konstantin Tarasov, *Voennaia organizatsiia bol'shevikov i bor'ba za vlast' v Petrogradskom garnizone v 1917 g.: Dissertatsiia na soiskanie uchenoi stepeni kandidata istoricheskikh nauk* (St Petersburg: SPbII RAN, 2014), p. 54.

83 *RGASPI*, *fond* 662, *opis'* 1, *delo* 58, *list* 23.
84 Ibid., *list* 28.
85 *Izvestiia Petrogradskogo Soveta rabochikh i soldatskikh deputatov*, 25 May 1917.
86 Ibid., 28 May 1917; *Russkii invalid*, 25 May 1917.
87 Kolonitskii, 'Rezoliutsii rabochikh i soldat o burzhuaznoi pechati (mart–aprel' 1917 g.)', *Vspomogatel'nye istoricheskie distsipliny* (Leningrad: Nauka), vol. 19 (1987), pp. 227–37.
88 *Russkoe slovo*, 2 and 6 May 1917; Maksim Bunegin, *Revoliutsiia i grazhdanskaia voina v Krymu (1917–1920 gg.)* (Simferopol': Krymgosizdat, 1927), p. 34; Anatolii Zarubin and Viacheslav Zarubin, *Bez pobeditelei: Iz istorii Grazhdanskoi voiny v Krymu* (Simferopol': Tavriia, 1997), pp. 27–8. The 'anti-Leninism' of influential Crimean organizations and the manifest weakness of the local Bolsheviks were no hindrance to the radicalization of the troops. In Crimea a conflict developed between Admiral Kolchak and elected organizations in the Black Sea Fleet, and the admiral resigned from his post as commander of the fleet. This is an important but by no means unique example of radicalization without Bolshevization. The success of anti-Leninist propaganda sometimes proved no obstacle to radicalization. The propagandists of the Ministry of War nevertheless linked the conflict to Leninist activity. See 'Sevastopol'skie sobytiia i admiral Kolchak', *Russkii invalid*, 10 June 1917. This incorrect interpretation of the incident subsequently suited both communist and anti-communist historians.
89 *Russkii invalid*, 16 June 1917.
90 Quoted from Viktor Petrash, *Moriaki Baltiiskogo flota v bor'be za pobedu Oktiabria* (Moscow and Leningrad: Nauka, 1966), p. 63.
91 *Zemlia i volia* [Petrograd], 22 April 1917.
92 Testimony to this is to be found in the surveys of troops' correspondence compiled by the military censorship. *RGVIA*, *fond* 2003, *opis'* 1, *delo* 1496, *listy* 16, 59, 60, 61.
93 Kolonitskii, 'Rezoliutsii rabochikh i soldat o burzhuaznoi pechati (mart–aprel' 1917 g.)'.
94 People with right-wing views also viewed Lenin and Kerenskii as allies. 'Kerenskii and Lenin are now in reality like Mazepa and Charles XII of Sweden.' Boris Nikol'skii, *Dnevnik, 1896–1918*, ed. Denis Shilov and Iurii Kuz'min (St Petersburg: Bulanin, 2015), vol. 2: *1904–1918*, p. 312. This judgement dates from late August, but we may surmise that extreme monarchists in spring 1917 also saw little difference between the two.
95 'Prazdnovanie 1 maia', *Rech'*, 20 April 1917; 'Shestviia i mitingi', ibid.
96 V. Petrov, 'Krasnyi prazdnik truda', *Malen'kaia gazeta*, 20 April 1917.
97 Nikolai Ustrialov, *Byloe – revoliutsiia 1917 g. (1890-e–1919 g.): Vospominaniia i dnevnikovye zapisi* (Moscow: Ankil, 2000), pp. 136–7.
98 Lenin, 'Uroki krizisa', *Pravda*, 23 April 1917. Quoted from Lenin, 'Lessons of the Crisis', trans. Bernard Isaacs, *Collected Works*, vol. 24 (1964), pp. 213–16 (www.marxists.org/archive/lenin/works/1917/apr/22b.htm).
99 'Demonstratsii i mitingi', *Rech'*, 21 April 1917; 'Manifestatsii', ibid., 22 April 1917; *Russkii invalid*, 22 and 23 April 1917; St. Gorev, 'Leninskie "vagonshchiki" izbili beznogikh invalidov', *Malen'kaia gazeta*, 28 April 1917; 'Demonstratsiia gruzovikov', *Novaia zhizn'*, 22 April 1917; 'Trebovanie aresta Lenina', ibid.

100 Petr Arzub'ev, 'Bunt protiv Lenina (Iz ulichnykh nabliudenii 21 Aprelia)', *Rech'*, 23 April 1917.
101 Lenin, 'Lessons of the Crisis'.
102 'Aprel'skie dni 1917 goda v Petrograde', publication by P. Stulov, *Krasnyi arkhiv*, vol. 2 (33) (1929), pp. 39, 46, 54, 56, 73; *Pravda*, 28 May, 20 June 1917.
103 *Russkii invalid*, 23 and 26 April 1917.
104 *Pravda*, 5, 12, 13, 15, 16 May 1917.
105 Konstantin Shelavin, 'Iiul'skoe delo', in *3-go – 5-go iiulia 1917 g.*, p. 24.
106 *Pravda*, 11 and 16 May 1917. Lenin and Zinov'ev, having gone into hiding after the July Days, were again bracketed together in pro-Bolshevik resolutions. Thus on 3 October a meeting of soldiers of the Kyshtym garrison greeted the 'Leaders of the proletariat', Lenin, Zinov'ev and the Bolshevik Central Committee. *Rabochii put'*, 18 October 1917.
107 Pascal, *Mon journal de Russie*, p. 120.
108 Kravkov, *Velikaia voina bez retushi*, p. 320.
109 Wildman, *The End of the Russian Imperial Army*, vol. 2, pp. 39, 47, 52–3.
110 'Mitingi partii narodnoi svobody', *Rech'*, 26 May 1917.
111 The following day the battalion committee apologized to the opponent of the Leninists and set him free. See V. Aliev, 'Za chto menia skhvatili po-romanovski', *RGASPI, fond* 662, *opis'* 1, *delo* 37, *listy* 27–27 *ob*.
112 Wildman, *The End of the Russian Imperial Army*, vol. 2, pp. 46–7.
113 *Revoliutsionnoe dvizhenie v russkoi armii*, pp. 224–5.
114 Lenin, '"Left-Wing Communism: an Infantile Disorder', trans. Julius Katzer, *Collected Works*, vol. 31 (1964), pp. 117–18 (www.marxists.org/archive/lenin/works/1920/lwc/ch10.htm).
115 Nina Tumarkin, *Lenin Lives! The Lenin Cult in Soviet Russia* (Cambridge, MA: Harvard University Press, 1983); Benno Ennker, *Die Anfänge des Leninkults in der Sowjetunion* (Cologne: Böhlau, 1997).
116 Leonid Kannegiesser, 'On Review', trans. James Manteith, *Cardinal Points*, vol. 7 (New York: StoSvet, 2017), pp. 145–6. See also *Leonid Kannegiser: Stat'i Georgiia Adamovicha, Marka Aldanova i Georgiia Ivanova: Iz posmertnykh stikhov Leonida Kannegisera* (Paris, 1928), pp. 80–81. Sergei Esenin knew Kannegiser and later included a similar representation of Kerenskii in his portrait of Russia after the February Revolution: 'Svoboda vzmetnulas' neistovo, I v rozovo-smradnom ogne, Togda nad stranoiu kalifstvoval, Kerenskii na belom kone' [Freedom fluttered frantically, in roseate fumes in the lead, Caliph of all the Russias, Kerenskii rode a white steed] (Esenin, *Sochineniia*, 3 vols (Moscow: Pravda, 1970), vol. 2, p. 191). Kerenskii is depicted as a hapless pretender to the role of 'caliph' of Russia, both head of state and religious-political leader.
117 *Russkii invalid*, 9 June 1917.
118 Petr Polovtsov, *Dni zatmeniia* (Moscow: Gosudarstvennaia publichnaia istoricheskaia biblioteka, 1999), pp. 102–3.
119 The poet Boris Sadovskii later recalled: 'When Kerenskii reviewed the troops in Pavlovsk he demanded that he should be mounted on the tsar's horse. The trainer gave him a white horse, but not the tsar's mount. Kerenskii looked pathetic in the saddle. The yokels welcomed him with bread and salt, kissed his feet and in their ardent zeal all but pulled him out of the saddle.' Boris Sadovskii, 'Zametki: Dnevnik (1931–1934)', publication by I. Andreeva, *Znamia*, no. 7 (1992), p. 179. General Polovtsov, however, states that

Kerenskii was indeed given the horse ridden by Nicholas II. Polovtsov, *Dni zatmeniia*, p. 102.

120 National Archives of the United Kingdom, War Office, 158/964: Russia, Political Parties, Ministers, Statesmen, 1917–1918, p. 6.

121 John Reed, *Ten Days That Shook the World*, chapter VIII, 'Counter-Revolution' (www.marxists.org/archive/reed/1919/10days/10days/ch8.htm).

122 Leonidov, *Vozhd' svobody A. F. Kerenskii* (Moscow: Koshnitsa, 1917), p. 5.

123 Oleg Znamenskii, *Iiul'skii krizis 1917 goda* (Moscow and Leningrad: Nauka, 1964), pp. 123–208.

124 *Piterskie rabochie i Velikii Oktiabr'*, ed. Oleg Znamenskii et al. (Leningrad: Nauka, 1987, p. 173.

125 Possibly Kerenskii's decision was influenced by rumours that the Ukrainian soldiers who had assembled in Kiev might undertake an assault on the local authorities after the fashion of the April Crisis in Petrograd. See Vladimir Buldakov, *Khaos i etnos: Etnicheskie konflikty v Rossii, 1917–1918 gg.: Usloviia vozniknoveniia, khronika, kommentarii, analiz* (Moscow: Novyi khronograf, 2010), p. 249.

126 *1917 god na Kievshchine: Khronika sobytii* (Kiev: Gosudarstvennoe izdatel'stvo Ukrainy, 1928), pp. 96, 97, 103. The news of the holding of a Congress of Polish Soldiers in Petrograd no doubt particularly riled the leaders of the Ukrainian movement.

127 *Delo naroda*, 9 June 1917.

128 Dmitrii Bondarenko, *Vzaimootnosheniia Vremennogo pravitel'stva i Ukrainskoi Tsentral'noi Rady* (Odessa: Odesskii iuridicheskii institut, 2004), p. 78.

129 Ukrainets – staryi did A. I. Skalovskii, 'Otkrytoe pis'mo voenno-morskomu ministru', *Narodnaia niva* [Helsingfors], 7 June 1917.

130 Lenin, 'Ne demokratichno, grazhdanin Kerenskii', *Pravda*, 2 June 1917. Quoted from Lenin (Ul'ianov), Vladimir Il"ich, *Polnoe sobranie sochinenii*, 5th edn (Moscow: Politizdat, 1960–81), vol. 32, pp. 253–4.

131 *Petrogradskii Sovet rabochikh i soldatskikh deputatov v 1917 godu: Protokoly, stenogrammy i otchety, rezoliutsii, postanovleniia obshchikh sobranii, sobraniia sektsii, zasedaniia Ispolnitel'nogo komiteta i fraktsii, 27 fevralia–25 oktiabria 1917 goda*, 5 vols, ed. Bella Gal'perina and Vitalii Startsev, vol. 3, p. 254.

132 *Groza*, 2 April, 7 May, 9 July 1917.

133 After the February Days, Ukrainian activists in Kiev welcome Kerenskii as the person who had 'from the tribune of the State Duma proclaimed the slogan of autonomy for Ukraine.' Vladislav Verstiuk, Viktor Gorobets' and Oleksii Tolochko, *Ukraïns'ki proekti v Rosiis'kii imperiï* (Kiev: Naukova Dumka, 2004), p. 421. The Ukrainian Committee of Odessa on 5 March sent Kerenskii the following message:

> We greet in your person a splendid champion for the freedom of Russia and its peoples. The Ukrainian people, deprived of democratic representation in the State Duma, always found in you an ardent defender during a dark period when it was denied its rights to national existence and development. You have thereby linked your splendid name with the history and bright future of the Ukrainian people in unity with all peoples. (*RGIA*, *fond* 1278, *opis'* 5, *delo* 1324, *list* 62)

134 *Vestnik Vremennogo pravitel'stva*, 6 June 1917. These soldiers aged over forty tried to protest, and a considerable number gathered in Petrogad. On 5 June

they held a meeting on Palace Square before marching to the residence of the minister of war to inform him of their unwillingness to interrupt their leave. See *Novoe vremia*, 6 June 1917.

135 Gennadiy Sobolev, *Revoliutsionnoe soznanie rabochikh i soldat Petrograda v 1917 g. Period dvoevlastiia* (Leningrad: Nauka, 1973), pp. 254–5.

136 *Sel'skii vestnik*, 7 June 1917.

137 *Pervyi Vserossiiskii s"ezd Sovetov*, vol. 1, p. 65.

138 *Sel'skii vestnik*, 9 June 1917.

139 *Oktiabr'skoe vooruzhennoe vosstanie: Semnadtsatyi god v Petrograde*, ed. Anton Fraiman (Leningrad: Nauka, 1967), *kn.* 1: 'Na putiakh k sotsialisticheskoi revoliutsii: Dvoevlastie', p. 296; *Piterskie rabochie i Velikii Oktiabr'*, p. 209.

140 Khanan Astrakhan, *Bol'sheviki i ikh politicheskie protivniki v 1917 godu: Iz istorii politicheskikh partii v Rossii mezhdu dvumia revoliutsiiami* (Leningrad: Lenizdat, 1973), p. 234.

141 *Russkii invalid*, 14 June 1917.

142 *Piterskie rabochie i Velikii Oktiabr'*, p. 209.

143 Vladimir Cherniaev, 'Iz istorii Iiun'skogo krizisa 1917 g. v Rossii', *Gosudarstvennye uchrezhdeniia i klassovye otnosheniia v otechestvennoi istorii*, part 1 (Moscow and Leningrad: Institut istorii, 1980), p. 87.

144 *Bol'shevizatsiia Petrogradskogo garnizona: Sb. materialov i dokumentov*, ed. Arvid Drezen (Leningrad: Leningradskoe oblastnoe izdatel'stvo, 1932), p. 120; *Revoliutsionnoe dvizhenie v Rossii v mae–iiune 1917 g.*, p. 530, 531, 532; Pavel Kornakov, '1917 god v otrazhenii veksillologicheskikh istochnikov (po materialam Petrograda i deistvuiushchei armii)' (Leningrad: unpublished thesis, 1989), p. 155.

145 Znamenskii, *Iiul'skii krizis 1917 goda*, p. 14; Vladimir Cherniaev, 'Iiun'skii politicheskii krizis 1917 g. v Rossii' (Leningrad, thesis synopsis [*avtoreferat*], 1986), p. 20.

146 *Oktiabr'skoe vooruzhennoe vosstanie: Semnadtsatyi god v Petrograde*, *kn.* 1, pp. 306–8.

147 *Soldatskaia pravda*, 29 June 1917.

148 Znamenskii, *Iiul'skii krizis 1917 goda*, p. 15; *Birzhevye vedomosti* (evening edn), 19 June 1917; *Malen'kaia gazeta*, 20 June 1917.

149 Kornakov, '1917 god v otrazhenii veksillologicheskikh istochnikov', pp. 172–5; Kolonitskii, *Simvoly vlasti i bor'ba za vlast'* (St Petersburg: Liki Rossii, 2012), p. 103.

150 Pascal, *Mon journal de Russie*, p. 142; J. Butler Wright, *Witness to Revolution: The Russian Revolution Diary and Letters of J. Butler Wright*, ed. William Allison (Westport, CT: Praeger, 2002), p. 96.

151 *Russkii invalid*, 21 June 1917.

152 Znamenskii, *Iiul'skii krizis 1917 goda*, p. 15; *Volna* [Helsingfors], 22 June 1917.

153 *Russkii invalid*, 22 June 1917; *Birzhevye vedomosti (vechernii vypusk)*, 21 June 1917; *Krymskii vestnik* [Sevastopol'], 14 June 1917.

154 *Delo naroda*, 25 June 1917.

155 *Kievlianin*, 20 June 1917.

156 *Russkii invalid*, 27 June 1917.

157 Prince Georgii L'vov, the head of the Provisional Government, supported the proposal of his minister of war, but the subsequent defeats prevented its

implementation. The practice of awarding revolutionary red banners was later implemented by the Bolsheviks. The image of an army advancing under red banners was exploited not only by socialists. See, for example, P. Sh-shin, 'Pobedy krasnykh znamen', *Petrogradskaia gazeta*, 2 July 1917.

158 *Malen'kaia gazeta*, 10 June 1917.

159 *RGASPI*, *fond* 662, *opis'* 1, *delo* 34, *listy* 22–3.

160 *Russkii invalid*, 21 June 1917; *Birzhevye vedomosti* (evening edn), 21 June 1917. In Ekaterinoslavl, patriotic auctions were held in several cafés on 'Den' invalida' [Disabled Troops' Day]. A portrait of Kerenskii made 390 rubles. In another café a nurse sold kisses, bringing the organizers 150 rubles. Petr Stolpianskii, 'Den' invalidov v provintsii', *Russkii invalid*, 28 June 1917.

161 *Krymskii vestnik* [Sevastopol'], 23 June 1917.

162 *Delo naroda*, 23 June 1917; *Russkii invalid*, 23 June 1917; *Rech'*, 29 June 1917.

163 *Svet i teni Velikoi voiny: Pervaia mirovaia v dokumentakh epokhi*, ed. Aleksandr Repnikov, Elena Rudaia and Andrei Ivanov (Moscow: ROSSPEN, 2014), p. 312.

164 Aleksandr Blok, *Sobranie sochinenii*, 8 vols (Moscow and Leningrad: Gosudarstvennoe izdatel'stvo khudozhestvennoi literatury, 1960–63), vol. 7 (1963), p. 266.

165 Elizaveta Naryshkina, *Moi vospominaniia: Pod vlast'iu trekh tsarei* (Moscow: Novoe literaturnoe obozrenie, 2014), p. 437.

166 Okunev, *Dnevnik moskvicha, 1917–1924*, vol. 1, pp. 51–2.

167 Pascal, *Mon journal de Russie*, pp. 150, 152.

168 *Trud i volia* [Petrograd), 22 and 24 June, 4 July 1917.

169 Ibid., 22 and 24 June 1917.

170 *Nepridumannye sud'by na fone ushedshego veka*, vol. 1, p. 224.

171 *Novaia zhizn'* [Ekaterinodar], 17 June 1917; *Russkii invalid*, 24 June 1917.

172 Elena Lakier, 'Otryvki iz dnevnika – 1917–1918', in *'Preterpevshii do kontsa spasen budet': Zhenskie ispovedal'nye teksty o revoliutsii i grazhdanskoi voine v Rossii*, ed. Ol'ga Demidova (St Petersburg: Evropeiskii universitet, 2013), p. 143.

173 Ekaterina Sain-Vitgenshtein, *Dnevnik (1914–1918)* (Paris: YMCA Press, 1986), p. 85.

174 Martin Latsis, 'Iiul'skie dni v Petrograde (Iz dnevnika agitatora)', *Proletarskaia revoliutsiia*, no. 5 (17) (1923), p. 111.

175 A. G., 'Pod trekhtsvetnym flagom', *Golos pravdy* [Kronshtadt], 24 June 1917.

176 This topic was raised in the left Socialist Revolutionary press: Vladimir Trutovskii, 'Burzhui v okopy!', *Zemlia i volia*, 20 June 1917.

177 *Golos pravdy* [Kronshtadt], 24 June 1917; *Volna* [Helsingfors], 25 June 1917.

178 Latsis, 'Iiul'skie dni v Petrograde', p. 111.

179 'Vserossiiskii s"ezd Sovetov rabochikh i soldatskikh deputatov: Doklad sledstvennoi komissii', *Zemlia i volia*, 24 June 1917.

180 Znamenskii, *Iiul'skii krizis 1917 goda*, pp. 14, 24, 25.

181 *Bol'shevizatsiia Petrogradskogo garnizona*, p. 167. The reference to Kerenskii as a 'barrister' reminds us of the description of him in the pages of *Groza* as 'the lawyer Kerenskii'.

182 'Protokol'nye stranitsy bor'by Kerenskogo s bol'shevikami (Tver')', *Proletarskaia revoliutsiia*, no. 5 (17) (1923), p. 310.

183 'V armii', *Rech'*, 22 June 1917.

184 *Konstantin Andreevich Somov: Pis'ma. Dnevniki. Suzhdeniia sovremennikov* (Moscow: Iskusstvo, 1979), p. 178.
185 *Rabochaia gazeta*, 20 June 1917.
186 *Voiskovye komitety deistvuiushchei armii (Mart 1917 g.–mart 1918 g.)*, ed. Sergei Bazanov (Moscow: Nauka, 1982), p. 199.
187 Chernov had grounds for his assertion that such propaganda contributed to growing resentment among the soldiers being directed at the minister of war. 'We can hardly be surprised that, among the ignorant masses following in the wake of the Bolsheviks we hear shouts of "Death to Kerenskii!"' Viktor Chernov, 'Tezisy s illiustratsiei', *Delo naroda*, 28 June 1917.
188 *Rabochaia gazeta*, 24 June 1917.
189 *Delo naroda*, 30 June 1917.
190 *Edinstvo*, 27 June 1917; *Den'*, 28 June 1917; *Zhivoe slovo*, 27 June 1917.
191 S. Shtilin, 'V nastupaiushchei armii', *Volna* [Helsingfors], 29 June 1917.
192 This shows in the attempts by separate groups to seize and control not the infrastructure centres of government institutions but the largely 'symbolic space' of Nevskii Prospekt. It seemed to Maksim Gor'kii and several other contemporaries that these acts were completely irrational. Those involved in skirmishes on Nevskii Prospekt may, however, have had the experience of the February Days and April Crisis in mind. On the significance of Nevskii Prospekt for the spontaneous self-organization of various political groups, see Kolonitskii, 'Politicheskaia topografiia Petrograda i revoliutsiia 1917 goda (Nevskii prospekt)', *Istoricheskie zapiski*, vol. 6 (124) (1923), pp. 327–41.
193 *Bol'shevizatsiia Petrogradskogo garnizona*, p. 134; Znamenskii, *Iiul'skii krizis 1917 goda*, p. 45.
194 *Piterskie rabochie i Velikii Oktiabr'*, p. 230.
195 *Delo naroda*, 4 July 1917; *Piterskie rabochie i Velikii Oktiabr'*, p. 232.
196 *Bol'shevizatsiia Petrogradskogo garnizona*, pp. 151, 154.
197 *Revoliutsionnoe dvizhenie v Rossii v iiule 1917 g.: Iiul'skii krizis: Dokumenty i materialy*, ed. Luka Gaponenko et al. (Moscow: Akademiia nauk SSSR, 1958), p. 247. Other front-line soldiers wished agonizing torture on the minister of war. Thus a soldier in the active army wrote to the Petrograd Soviet, 'When is Kerenskii going to have his tongue cut out? Although there is free speech, that is essential, because there are not enough sons and mothers for all the regiments Kerenskii is disbanding and executing.' *Soldatskie pis'ma 1917 goda*, ed. Olga Chaadaeva (Moscow and Leningrad: Gosudarstvennoe izdatel'stvo, 1927), pp. 93–4.
198 'Iz dnei vosstaniia bol'shevikov (Nekotorye porazitel'nye podrobnosti)', *Petrogradskaia gazeta*, 12 July 1917.
199 *Rech'*, 14 July 1917; *Delo naroda*, 4 July 1917; *Bol'shevizatsiia Petrogradskogo garnizona*, p. 179.
200 *Edinstvo*, 7 July 1917.
201 Later on, Bolshevik and anti-Semitic criticism of Kerenskii had points of overlap. See Kolonitskii, 'Aleksandr Fedorovich Kerenskii kak "zhertva evreev" i "evrei"', in *Jews and Slavs*, vol. 17: *The Russian Word in the Land of Israel, the Jewish Word in Russia* (Jerusalem, 2006).
202 *Revoliutsionnoe dvizhenie v russkoi armii*, p. 205.
203 *Delo naroda*, 8 July 1917.
204 *Petrogradskaia gazeta*, 8 and 12 July 1917.

205 'Spekuliatsiia A. F. Kerenskim', *Birzhevye vedomosti* (evening edn), 13 July 1917.
206 'Nel'zia oskverniat' imia Kerenskogo: Negodovanie naseleniia protiv "farsovykh" del'tsov', *Petrogradskaia gazeta*, 12 July 1917.
207 *Birzhevye vedomosti* (evening edn), 13 July 1917; *Petrogradskaia gazeta*, 7 and 12 July 1917.
208 *Petrogradskaia gazeta*, 13 July 1917.
209 'Troitskii fars – "Burzhui i bol'shevik" ', *Birzhevye vedomosti* (evening edn), 13 July 1917.
210 Kolonitskii, *Simvoly vlasti i bor'ba za vlast'* (St Petersburg: Dmitrii Bulanin, 2001), pp. 318–25.
211 Kolonitskii, 'Antibourgeois Propaganda and Anti-"Burzhui" Consciousness in 1917'.
212 Vladimir Drutskoi-Sokolinskii, *Na sluzhbe Otechestvu: Zapiski russkogo gubernatora* (Moscow: Russkii put', 2010), p. 246.
213 *OR RNB*, *fond* 481, *opis'* 1, *delo* 218, *list* 30 *ob.*
214 T. N. Gippius to Z. N. Gippius, D. S. Merezhkovskii and D. V. Filosofov, ibid., *delo* 217, *list* 11 *ob.*
215 *Kollektsiia pochtovykh kartochek sovetskogo perioda s 1917 po 1945 g. iz sobranii M. A. Voronina: Katalog* (St Petersburg: Welcome, 2009), vol. 1, pp. 150–63.
216 *Delo naroda*, 29 June 1917.
217 *Russkii invalid*, 2 June 1917.
218 Grigorii Belykh, *Dom veselykh nishchikh* (Leningrad: Priboi, 1930), p. 172.
219 *Petrogradskaia gazeta*, 13 July 1917.
220 *Russkoe slovo*, 5 September 1917.
221 See Nikolai Tagantsev, *Ulozhenie o nakazaniiakh ugolovnykh i ispravitel'nykh 1885 g.*, 18-e izdanie, peresmotrennoe i dopolnennoe (Petrograd, 1916), p. 338.
222 On censorship by the court, see Sergei Grigor'ev, *Pridvornaia tsenzura i obraz verkhovnoi vlasti, 1831–1917* (St Petersburg: Aleteiia, 2007).
223 On insults to members of the royal family, see Boris Kolonitskii, *'Tragicheskaia erotika': Obrazy imperatorskoi sem'i v gody Pervoi mirovoi voiny* (Moscow: Novoe literaturnoe obozrenie, 2010).
224 *Birzhevoi kur'er*, 28 July 1917; E. Iu. Smirnova, 'Iazyk revoliutsii v finansovykh periodicheskikh izdaniiakh', typescript, p. 5. I am grateful to Ms Smirnova for communicating this information.
225 Marina Tsvetaeva, 'Zemnye primety', in Tsvetaeva, *Sobranie sochinenii*, 7 vols, ed. A. Saakiants and L. Mnukhina (Moscow: Ellis Lak, 1994–5), vol. 1, p. 606.
226 Sergei Rafal'skii, *Chto bylo i chego ne bylo* (London: Overseas Publications Interchange, 1984), p. 59; *Russkaia armiia, 1917–1920: Obmundirovanie, znaki razlichiia. Nagrady i nagrudnye znaki*, ed. Oleg Kharitonov and V. V. Gorshkov (St Petersburg: Karavella, 1991), pp. 47–8; V. D. Krivtsov, *Avers No. 2: Sovetskie znaki i zhetony (Katalog dlia kollektsionera)* (Moscow: Avers, 1996), pp. 172–3.
227 *RGIA*, *fond* 1623, *opis'* 1, *delo* 613, *list* 37 *ob.*
228 *Blagorodnaia zhertva Fevral'skoi revoliutsii 1917 goda student Petrogradskogo universiteta Vladimir Ivanovich Khlebtsevich* (Syzran', 1918), p. 28.
229 *Izvestiia Petrogradskogo Soveta*, 24 May 1917; *Petrogradskaia gazeta*, 13

July 1917; Richard Abraham, *Alexander Kerensky: The First Love of the Revolution* (London: Sidgwick & Jackson, 1987), p. 202.
230 *Kievlianin*, 3 June 1917.
231 *RGIA, fond* 1405, *opis'* 538, *delo* 177, *listy* 49–51.
232 I am grateful to Marina Vitukhnovskaia for informing me of this.
233 Andrew Verner, 'What's in a Name? Of Dog-Killers, Jews and Rasputin', *Slavic Review*, 53/4 (1994), p. 1070.
234 V–i V., *A. F. Kerenskii*, p. 3; Leonidov, *Vozhd' svobody*, p. 4.
235 *Prikazy i rechi pervogo russkogo Voennogo i Morskogo Ministra-Sotsialista*, p. 29; Aleksandr Kerenskii, *Rechi A. F. Kerenskogo o revoliutsii, s ocherkom V. V. Kir'iakova 'Kerenskii kak orator'* (Petrograd: Kopeika, 1917), p. 13; Lidiia Armand, *Kerenskii* (Petrograd: [Kopeika], 1917), p. 11; Abraham, *Alexander Kerensky*, p. 200.
236 *Vestnik Tverskogo gubernskogo Ispolnitel'nogo komiteta*, 16 March 1917.
237 *Gosudarstvennyi muzei politicheskoi istorii Rossii* (Sankt-Peterburg), *fond* 2, no. 10964. See also Aleksei Kulegin and Valentin Bobrov, 'Istoriia bez kupiur', *Sovetskie muzei*, no. 3 (1990), pp. 5–6.
238 *Russkii invalid*, 24 June 1917; *Zemlia i volia*, 28 July 1917; *RGASPI, fond* 662, *opis'* 1, *delo* 34, *list* 51.
239 *Birzhevye vedomosti* (evening edn), 10 March 1917.
240 *Delo naroda*, 26 July 1917.
241 Gippius, *Siniaia kniga*, p. 171; *OR RNB, fond* 481, *opis'* 1, *delo* 3, *list* 201.
242 *Revoliutsionnoe dvizhenie v avguste 1917 g. Razgrom kornilovskogo miatezha*, ed. Dmitrii Chugaev et al. (Moscow: Akademiia nauk SSSR, 1959), p. 375.
243 Lidiia Lesnaia (i.e., Lidiia Shperling), 'A. F. Kerenskomu', *Solntse Rossii*, no. 373 (1917), p. 15. The Russian text is: No v krasnykh dymakh iskriatsia lampady / Neumiraiushchei, netlennoi chistoty. / Vozzheg ikh ty, geroi, orlinym vzglyadom, / Ty, vdokhnoveniem venchannyi, – ty! / Zemnye, my v ogniakh zemli sgorali, / Ty – prometeev nam ogon' prines, / I my nad tikhoi byl'iu pastorali / Ne l'em naprasnykh slez. / I na oblomkakh kamennykh balkonov, / Minuia teni pyl'nykh knig, / My uchimsya liubit' tvoi zakony, / Kotorye, – skvoz' topoli i kleny, – / V mirakh inykh tvoi mudryi dukh postig. / Geroi i vozhd'! Rossii svetlyi genii! / Za zhizn' i mir idi na smertnyi boi, / Idi, velikii, radostnyi, vesennii, – / My – s toboi!
244 E. Shubmatin, *artillerist*, 'Vozhdiu Revoliutsii (Posviashchaetsia Kerenskomu)', *Narodnaia niva* [Helsingfors], 19 July 1917. The Russian text is: V godinu bed, v godinu slavy, / Sredi i bur', i nepogod / Tvoi iasnyi genii zlatoglavyi / Khranil nezyblemost' svobod. / Ty po volnam korabl' svobody / Na reid spasen'ia smelo vel / I stroil novoi zhizni svody – / Revolyutsionnyy oreol. / Utikhnet shtorm, zamolknet more, / Povsiudu budet tish' da glad'. . . / Tomu, kto snial s stradal'tsev gore, / Narod sumeet dolg vozdat'.

Conclusion

1 Aleksandr Bogdanov, 'Chto zhe my svergli?', *Novaia zhizn'*, 17 May 1917.
2 Modern scholars, for example, emphasize the influence of political tradition: revolution in an empire built on archaic principles could not be a mere change of political regime, because in the system of power and subordination too much was dependent on emotions towards the sacrosanct figure of the tsar.

Vladimir Buldakov and Tat'iana Leont'eva, *Voina, porodivshaia revoliutsiiu: Rossiia, 1914–1917 gg.* (Moscow: Novyi khronograph, 2015), p. 465.
3 'Pechat' i zhizn': Kul'turnaia revoliutsiia', *Delo naroda*, 18 May 1917.
4 *S"ezdy i konferentsii Konstitutsionno-demokraticheskoi partii: 1905–1920 gg.*, 3 vols (Moscow: ROSSPEN, 2000), vol. 3, part 1, p. 460.
5 Ibid., p. 650.
6 Ibid., pp. 672, 683.
7 In the ranks of the Cadets, Miliukov was not the only person seen as the Leader. In different forums other senior figures in the part were described as 'the Leader'. For instance, at a session of a food congress in May, one of the delegates greeted the minister Andrey Shingarev with the words, 'Hurrah for our splendid Leader, our true hero in the struggle for freedom of the Russia state'. This exclamation was 'taken up by the participants in the congress and elicited tumultuous and protracted applause.' See 'Prodovol'stvennyi s"ezd', *Rech'*, 9 May 1917.
8 *Edinstvo*, 5 and 28 May 1917.
9 Ibid., 3 and 5 May 1917.
10 See Boris Kolonitskii, *'Tragicheskaia erotika': Obrazy imperatorskoi sem'i v gody Pervoi mirovoi voiny* (Moscow: Novoe literaturnoe obozrenie, 2010).
11 S–", 'General Alekseev', *Novaia zhizn'*, 12 May 1917.
12 'Vozhd' narodnoi armii', *Russkii invalid*, 14 March 1917.
13 *Delo naroda*, 11 August 1917.
14 Aleksandr Zinov'ev, *Russkaia sud'ba, ispoved' otshchepentsa* (Moscow: Vagrius, 2005), p. 354.
15 Here I am using Stephen Kotkin's image in his *Magnetic Mountain: Stalinism as a Civilization* (Berkeley: University of California Press, 1995), pp. 198–237.
16 Jan Plamper, *The Stalin Cult: A Study in the Alchemy of Power* (New Haven, CT: Yale University Press, 2012), p. xvii.
17 Nikolai Abramovich, *Komu zhe verit'? (Vozhdi i demagogi)* (Moscow: Koshnitsa, 1917), pp. 11, 32.

Index